Benchmark Papers
in Acoustics

Series Editor: R. Bruce Lindsay
Brown University

PUBLISHED VOLUMES

UNDERWATER SOUND / *Vernon M. Albers*
ACOUSTICS: Historical and Philosophical Development / *R. Bruce Lindsay*
SPEECH SYNTHESIS / *James L. Flanagan and L. R. Rabiner*
PHYSICAL ACOUSTICS / *R. Bruce Lindsay*
MUSICAL ACOUSTICS, PART I: Violin Family Components / *Carleen M. Hutchins*
MUSICAL ACOUSTICS, PART II: Violin Family Functions / *Carleen M. Hutchins*
ULTRASONIC BIOPHYSICS / *Floyd Dunn and William D. O'Brien*
VIBRATION: Beams, Plates, and Shells / *Arturs Kalnins and Clive L. Dym*
MUSICAL ACOUSTICS: Piano and Wind Instruments / *Earle L. Kent*
ARCHITECTURAL ACOUSTICS / *Thomas D. Northwood*
SPEECH INTELLIGIBILITY AND SPEAKER RECOGNITION / *Mones E. Hawley*

Benchmark Papers
in Acoustics / 11
A BENCHMARK® Books Series

SPEECH INTELLIGIBILITY
AND SPEAKER
RECOGNITION

Edited by
MONES E. HAWLEY

Dowden, Hutchinson & Ross, Inc.
Stroudsburg, Pennsylvania

Copyright © 1977 by **Dowden, Hutchinson & Ross, Inc.**
Benchmark Papers in Acoustics, Volume 11
Library of Congress Catalog Card Number: 77–24049
ISBN: 0–87933–299–9

79   78   77   1   2   3   4   5
Manufactured in the United States of America.

LIBRARY OF CONGRESS CATALOGING IN PUBLICATION DATA

Main entry under title:
Speech intelligibility and speaker recognition.
   (Benchmark papers in acoustics; 11)
   Includes indexes.
   1. Speech, Intelligibility of. 2. Telecommunication. 3. Speech processing
systems. 4. Architectural acoustics. 5. Audiology. I. Hawley, Mones E.
TK7882.S65S67   620.2   77–24049
ISBN 0–87933–299–9

Exclusive Distributor: **Halsted Press**
A Division of John Wiley & Sons, Inc.
ISBN: 0–470–99303–0

SERIES EDITOR'S FOREWORD

The "Benchmark Papers in Acoustics" constitute a series of volumes that make available to the reader in carefully organized form important papers in all branches of acoustics. The literature of acoustics is vast in extent and much of it, particularly the earlier part, is inaccessible to the average acoustical scientist and engineer. These volumes aim to provide a practical introduction to this literature, since each volume offers an expert's selection of the seminal papers in a given branch of the subject, that is, those papers that have significantly influenced the development of that branch in a certain direction and introduced concepts and methods that possess basic utility in modern acoustics as a whole. Each volume provides a convenient and economical summary of results as well as a foundation for further study for both the person familiar with the field and the person who wishes to become acquainted with it.

Each volume has been organized and edited by an authority in the area to which it pertains. In each volume there is provided an editorial introduction summarizing the technical significance of the field being covered. Each article is accompanied by editorial commentary, with necessary explanatory notes, and an adequate index is provided for ready reference. Articles in languages other than English are either translated or abstracted in English. It is the hope of the publisher and editor that these volumes will constitute a working library of the most important technical literature in acoustics of value to students and research workers.

The present volume, *Speech Intelligibility and Speaker Recognition*, has been edited by Mones E. Hawley of Washington, D.C., a Fellow of the Acoustical Society of America. In its carefully chosen 40 articles it covers the chief features of the intelligibility of perceived speech together with the important area of speaker recognition. Emphasis is placed on the three principal periods in the development of the subject from its origin around 1900 to the present time. The first period extended from the beginning to the middle of World War II and was principally marked by the early attempts to improve speech recognition in telephone conversations. The second period, from the middle of World War II to the early 1960s, dealt primarily with the more sophisticated work of the sensory psychologists, who used more elaborate equipment, like the tape recorder. The third period, from the early 1960s to the present, has seen the introduction of the digital computer in special studies. The final six papers are of particular interest in their emphasis on the possibility of the use of speech and speech spectrograms for speaker recognition and indentification. These articles also point out the difficulties inherent in this possible use. The editor's commentaries provide a thorough critical evaluation of all included papers, and the unusually extensive bibliographical references make the volume particularly valuable for all workers in the field.

R. BRUCE LINDSAY

PREFACE

My interest in speech intelligibility first became vital about two miles above Anzio, Italy, on 16 February 1944, when my airplane was destroyed because of misunderstandings on the interphone. The other members of my crew were killed. During the next year and a quarter that I was a barracks guest of the Luftwaffe, I decided to make my career in acoustics, and six years later, partly through chance, I was the systems engineer responsible for intelligibility testing of the U.S. Air Force's first high intelligibility interphone. These were the beginnings of a continuing fondness for all branches of acoustics and for communications, written and spoken, which is now more than thirty years old and which led to my editing this book.

Acoustics is fun. It can be skimmed over, dabbled in, or plunged into with enjoyment, and always one will meet delightful fellows. Reading the works of early acoustical scientists is pleasant and instructive, but one might best begin the study of speech intelligibility by watching the 1938 version of the film *Pygmalion*. Prof. Higgins's laboratory, with its aeolian flames, acoustical gramophones, spinning mirrors, and smoked glass plates may not be accurate, but it is indicative of the techniques and instruments used by early scientists in the field. Although their techniques seem terribly crude today, their thinking does not. They established the fundamentals of descriptive linguistics, the taxonomy of phonetics, and the quantities by which speech is usually measured today. Rayleigh, Sabine, Miller, and Paget obtained their results by keen intelligence, rigorous logic, and hard work. The modern investigator who is planning an experiment or who is puzzled by some early results may be tempted mindlessly to toss in another amplifier channel, to install another tape recorder, or to make another computer run. He would do better to try to think about his problem as Helmholtz might have, reducing it to one of finding the way that the scientific method most economically might be applied rigorously to test his hypothesis. Then in writing his report, let the modern researcher emulate William James; for then, as now, the best scientists often were the best writers. In fairness, the pioneer had one advantage the modern scientists validly may envy. As recently as 1940 one could obtain talkers and listeners for twenty-five cents an hour with no indemnification or tax forms.

If one wishes to make original contributions to the field or if he wants to apply the results of others' investigations constructively and honestly, he must read widely and deeply. I remember a meeting at which, after an eminent psychologist had finished presenting a paper describing his new and powerful instrument for speech research, a member of the audience rose and announced that the same device had been described in a respectable German engineering journal several years earlier. One scientist wrote, "Phonemic analysis is described, with various emphases, in the writings of. . . . Any nonlinguist who is tempted to seriously discuss or investigate linguistic phenomena has two choices: to resist that temptation or to read those writings. If he does neither, he becomes an object of merriment for the judicious, and he is very likely to waste a lot of his time and other people's money."*

The Acoustical Society of America is the best vehicle for a tour of all aspects of the subject of speech intelligibility. It is everything a scientific society ought to be: the dominant authority in its field, the publisher of the best journal, moderately progressive, encouragingly eclectic, friendly in welcoming newcomers, and heavily involved in one's special interest. (A count shows that of the thirty-nine presidents the Society has had, eleven are authors of papers that have been chosen for reproduction in this volume.) I urge anyone who is interested in contributing to speech intelligibility or in its applications to join and to participate actively in the Society.

In editing this book I have been fortunate in being able to supplement my own library with the resources of the fine libraries of the University of California at Los Angeles and of the superb libraries in the Washington, D.C. area, where I have used the Library of Congress, the National Library of Medicine, and the libraries of the National Institutes of Health, National Bureau of Standards, Federal Communications Commission, Department of the Interior, Volta Bureau, American University, Catholic University of America, Georgetown University, Gallaudet College, and the Washington Medical Center, to all of which I express my appreciation. Most of all I wish to thank my mentors in acoustics, some of whom have since died: Benjamin Olney, Frank Slaymaker, Willard

* Twaddell (1952), p. 608n, full citation given in Part IX.

Meeker, A. H. Kettler, M. L. Graham, J. C. R. Licklider, Karl Kryter, V. O. Knudsen, Gordon Peterson, and Pierre Chavasse, who was impeded by my faltering French when I was one of the first members of the Groupement des Acoustitiens de Langue Française. I also wish to express gratitude to James L. Flanagan, Ira Hirsh, Arthur House, Karl Kryter, and John Webster, who have reviewed this manuscript constructively and attentively.

December 1976   MONES E. HAWLEY

CONTENTS

Contents

PART III: THE STATISTICS OF SPEECH AND THE PREDICTION OF SPEECH INTELLIGIBILITY

PART IV: METHODS OF MEASURING SPEECH INTELLIGIBILITY

Contents

text P356

PART IX: APPLICATIONS TO SPEECH SYNTHESIS AND ANALYSIS

PART X: SPEECH QUALITY AND SPEAKER RECOGNITION

CONTENTS BY AUTHOR

Contents by Author

SPEECH INTELLIGIBILITY AND SPEAKER RECOGNITION

INTRODUCTION

PURPOSE

When one visits a vantage point from which he can obtain a panoramic view of distant heights, he frequently finds himself aided by a profile map which identifies the principal features in each direction and their distances. This volume is intended to offer such assistance to the reader who is looking over speech intelligibility for the first time or who is familiar with one part of the field and wishes a broader outlook. In each direction of the subject some peaks of accomplishment are reproduced and their position in the continuity of the field is explained. Sources of available information on each topic are given in extensive bibliographies totaling about a thousand items.

SCOPE

This volume is concerned primarily with evaluation of the basic characteristic of speech communication systems from the production of normal speech to its reception by normal ears. It includes the identity, attributes, language, speech characteristics, environment, and equipment of the talker; all the communications media and equipment; and the equipment, environment, listening characteristics, language, and attributes of the listener and his method of responding to the stimulus. Listeners whose hearing is impaired are treated in a section on speech audiometry, where diagnostic and prognostic applications and the fitting of hearing aids are considered. The intelligibility of talkers whose speech is impaired is excluded from the scope by limitations of space and the editor's capability. Most of the literature on the effect of delayed sidetone (feedback by which the talker hears his speech) on the talker's performance is omitted, but the use of this

1

effect to detect malingering in audiological examination is included. The emphasis is on the evaluation of a communication system as defined above, but there are sections devoted to investigations of the factors that affect the intelligibility of such systems and to the prediction of the results of the evaluations from a knowledge of these factors.

Intelligibility as used in this volume means the recognizability of a speech stimulus (a basic speech sound, word, sentence, etc.) and the response to it by repeating it, writing it down, choosing it from alternatives offered, or stating that the listener recognized it. There are some tests that require comprehension of stimuli that have meaning, and they are referred to in this book. Intelligibility tests are frequently called articulation tests, discrimination tests, recognition tests, and other things. In a description of his first telephone, Alexander Graham Bell wrote, "Indeed as a general rule, the articulation was unintelligible except when familiar sentences were employed. ... The elementary sounds of the English language were uttered successsively into one of the telephones and its effects noted at the other. Consonantal sounds, with the exception of L and M, were unrecognizable. Vowel sounds in most cases were distinct."[1] He thus established a precedent (in telephony a precedent quickly becomes a tradition) for testing the intelligibility of articulation by means of isolated speech sounds. Speech therapists quite properly use *articulation* to mean the ability to form and to utter speech sounds, and K. S. Wood[2] used the term articulation index to describe the progress of a group of children with functional articulation defects. In this volume the term Articulation Index (AI) refers to the method of calculating a measure of the intelligibility of a system from acoustical and electrical measurements of its characteristics. Lehiste and Peterson[3] sensibly and constructively discuss the terms articulation and intelligibility and their alternatives, and Owens and Schubert[4] go further and suggest that the term speech discrimination should be used when the objective is to observe or to assess some property of impaired ears, and speech intelligibility should be used when the objective is to observe or to assess some property of a system connecting unimpaired talkers and unimpaired listeners. The editor of this volume has not used the term speech discrimination, and he has used the terms talker and speaker interchangeably.

Readers are assumed to have or to be acquiring a working knowledge of acoustical concepts and terminology. The editor has tried to avoid terms with highly specialized meanings for experts. No reader is expected to understand completely the meaning of *all* the terms allophone, cepstrum, verification, orthotelephonic gain,

2

and sensorineural hearing loss, for example, so none of them is used. One term, logatom, although widely used in the field is not listed in dictionaries of English. It means a pronounceable speech unit, but is it is used unevenly in the literature cited here mostly to mean nonsense syllables. No attempt has been made to reconcile the terminologies of the authors whose papers are reproduced.

As the reader will note from an examination of the table of contents, the book is divided into ten parts. The first one treats all aspects of speech intelligibility in its early period. The next three parts describe the principles and the techniques of the field. Parts V through IX deal with its applications, and the last part treats topics allied to speech intelligibility and of which it is a part, quality and recognizability. Each part contains a commentary written by the editor, an extensive bibliography, and the reproduced material.

About three-quarters of the pages in this volume are reproductions of previously published papers which have been selected for their initial importance, enduring merit, and suitability for this format. Although the authors come from various countries, all the papers are in English. Informed readers may be disappointed that their favorite papers are not included. The criteria for selection excluded many worthy papers; review papers, long monographs, and highly detailed papers on one aspect of the field had to be left out to obtain balance within the limitations of space. Another volume in this series of Benchmark Papers in Acoustics, *Speech Synthesis*, edited by J. L. Flanagan and L. R. Rabiner, complements a part of the subject of this book and reproduces some papers that might have been used here. Readers of the present volume are encouraged to read Flanagan and Rabiner, for theirs is an excellent work.

HISTORY

Although the problems of measuring and improving the intelligibility of speech are as old as speech communication itself, no scientific investigations were undertaken until the telephone was developed. Ancient theaters used reflectors and resonators to improve audibility, but there seems to have been no improvement specifically for speech. Medieval buildings had reflectors and daises, but little attempt was made to suppress echos or to measure their effects on intelligibility until the nineteenth century. Spoken word testing for deafness began in the sixteenth century or earlier, but there were no scientific tests of hearing loss for speech until the twentieth century. By then progressive otologists had turned to pure tone audiometry. All things considered, it is correct to think of speech intelligibility as almost entirely a twentieth century science. Then, the field seems to break rather conveniently into three periods, each with a dominant academic discipline, each with a new device that made major advances possible, two cases with a single laboratory leading the way. The first period is that of the physicists, the vacuum tube amplifier, and the telephone laboratories; the second is that of the psychologists, the tape recorder, and the university laboratories; and the third is that of the stored program digital computer and its engineers.

The first period extends from before World War I until the middle of World War II. Part I describes the earliest work on telephone intelligibility. World War I created new problems. Two early patents for noise-cancelling, or pressure gradient, microphones specifically cite airplane noise as the origin of the requirement. "The need for a telephone system which will clearly and distinctly transmit speech from an observer to a pilot, or vice versa, in a aeroplane is especially crying and since the beginning of the present war inventors and research workers everywhere have been striving to produce such an apparatus."[5] "The invention was suggested by the necessity of telephoning in or from airplanes where the noise of the engines interferes seriously with the operation of ordinary telephone transmitters. . . ."[6] Soon the vacuum tube amplifier and its associated electrical components allowed investigators for the first time to control and to measure accurately and easily the levels at which signals and noise are received, transmitted, and presented to listeners over a wide variety of transducers. Before that, voices could be made to sound louder to the listener only by speaking more loudly. This changes the spectrum, timing, and pronunciation of the speech and the distribution of the sound field around the head of the talker. Now, losses due to transmission or filtering could be compensated for, spectra could be shaped, and noise could be introduced in controlled amounts at various points in the experiments. The whole field of signal-to-noise and bandwidth experiments was open to investigation. The investigators, who usually had been trained in physics departments, were learning and doing things that today are more likely to be taught in psychology or engineering departments. The laboratories of the telephone organizations were dominant, and the most conspicuous and important establishment was the Bell Telephone Laboratories (Bell Labs) in the United States. Its specific research contributions are described in Part I, but the field of speech intelligibility and acoustics in general owes a far greater

4

debt to Bell Labs than is generally mentioned. Not only was a great deal of pioneer research on speech and hearing done there, but it was very important in the organization and the growth of the Acoustical Society of America and in the recognition of acoustics as a discipline that extends across the boundaries of several departments of universities. Although the early investigators seem not to have been much concerned that they were working in an interdisciplinary field, their research programs, their literature citations, and their publication policies make it clear that they were aware of the fact. Bell Labs had an enormous effect on the Acoustical Society because of the high standard it set for presented and published paprs. The Acoustical Society was the first professional society in which your editor was active, and he was amazed when he later attended meetings of other societies and found that the well-prepared, well-delivered paper with clear, legible, illustrations on an important piece of original investigation, which was the rule for the Acoustical Society, was the exception in those other groups. In the very earliest days some of the papers in the *Bell System Technical Journal* were distributed as parts of the *Journal of the Acoustical Society of America(JASA)*. The high degree of scholarship, editorial skill, and significance of the content of the older publication clearly influenced the younger one and helped to make it the world's foremost publication on acoustics. *JASA* has published nearly as many papers on speech intelligibility as all the other publications combined, and the influence of Bell Labs has indeed been profound.

The second period in the field extends from the middle of World War II to the early 1960s. Although during that war all nations had the same problems of communication in noise in ships' engine rooms, armored vehicles, and aircraft (where high altitudes and oxygen masks introduced additional problems), the United States was the only nation that placed a high priority on the problems and had sufficient scientific resources to allow considerable concentration of work on them by several laboratories and training stations. As a result, at the end of that war there was a reserve of research and development achievements and of manpower trained in this branch of acoustics. Scientists in other countries had to become familiar with U.S. literature before they could make significant contributions themselves. Many of the papers in the European literature from 1946 to 1950 are recapitulations of U.S. reports and results for foreign readers. Two laboratories established at Harvard University in 1940 did much of the World War II research and development in speech intelligibility. The Electro-Acoustic Laboratory directed by L. L. Beranek was concerned primarily with transducers and electronic equipment; the Psycho-Acoustic Laboratory directed by S. S. Stevens was concerned primarily with talkers and listeners. Both were concerned with systems and worked together closely. A third laboratory was established in 1945 to specialize in shipboard systems. All three laboratories were assigned to the acoustics section of the physics division of the Office of Scientific Research and Development. The section chief was Harvey Fletcher. This combination of leadership, organization, and extremely well-qualified staff resulted in a very successful program.[7] The other laboratories were disbanded at the end of the war, but the Psycho-Acoustic Laboratory continued and increased in importance both for the work performed there and for the researchers who were trained there. The number of significant contributions by psychologists who worked there is truly astonishing. Fully half of the notable papers on speech intelligibility that were published between 1945 and 1955 have as senior author a scientist who worked at Harvard's Psycho-Acoustic Laboratory.

The most important item of new equipment was the tape recorder, a device as well suited to encourage research in experimental psychology as the amplifier had been in physics. The device made possible for the first time the easy and accurate reproduction of noise and speech stimuli, precisely the same every time, or with changes in sequence, duration, intensity, phase, frequency, interruption, or other modification, all precisely controlled. Disc recordings had permitted some of this control, but discs are not as durable as tapes and do not permit as many variations in technique. Tape recordings also could be made under difficult field conditions for later reproduction, analysis, and experimentation. Tape loops permitted exact repetition of the same stimulus again and again, and re-recording techniques could produce almost any mixture of stimulus and interference the experimenter wanted. Playing tape recordings of word lists through clinical audiometers made speech audiometry a reliable technique for the normal otologist and encouraged the development of audiometry as a separate skill.

Beginning in the late 1950s the digital computer became an important tool in speech intelligibility research first as a controller, analyzer, and synthesizer of speech itself and then as a controller of experiments and as an analyzer of the results. The physicists, engineers, and psychologists learned to use the machines for their purposes, but the chief contributions during the third period, which began a little more than a decade ago, have come from the investigators who are sufficiently familiar with computers to be

6

able to identify themselves as computer engineers. No laboratory or even any nation now dominates the field. Significant work has been reported regularly from Japan, the USSR, Germany, the United Kingdom, and the United States.

It seems to the editor that research and development on the intelligibility of speech will continue at a low level. Architectural acoustics will continue largely to ignore it, speech audiometry will become automated in the presentation of material, in the collection and analysis of responses, and in the presentation of the results for interpretation. The same trend will continue in evaluations of communication systems and equipment, particularly in the evaluation of speech synthesizers and analyzers, which increasingly will replace humans as the talkers and listeners in cases where there is no important interaction between the individuals and their environment or their equipment.

LITERATURE

There is no generally available book* devoted to or specializing in the subject of speech intelligibility; it has been the subject of only one major symposium.† However, there are books on speech audiometry, on communication systems, on acoustical measurements, and on the effects of noise on man. They are cited in the bibliographies in the parts of this volume. Readers who wish to investigate the literature in related fields should start with the *Journal of the Acoustical Society of America (JASA)*. It is by far the oldest acoustical journal and has published far more than any other (more than 3000 pages per year now on all topics of acoustics). Members and contributors are from all over the world. The scholarship and the refereeing of papers are very good, each paper has an informative abstract, and all papers and letters are indexed and cross indexed for ease in locating the appropriate literature. *JASA* also publishes annotated lists of U.S. patents on acoustical devices and the abstracts of all papers accepted for presentation at the semiannual meetings. (There were 619 such papers for the meeting in November 1976.) These abstracts are also indexed in each volume of the journal. *JASA* publishes lists of citations of contemporary papers on acoustics in other journals, of govern-

---

*Pokrovskiy (citation in Part IV) in Russian is out of print; the English translation is available from the U.S. Department of Commerce, National Technical Information Service.

†Liège, 1973 (citation in Part V).

ment contract reports, of reports from independent laboratories, and of other books and serials. These, too, are indexed in the same system as *JASA*. Readers using the indexes are cautioned that as activities in the field of acoustics have changed over the years, the indexing arrangements have been modified. *JASA* issues a cumulative index every five years.

Acustica was first published in 1951 to present high quality papers, in French, English, and German with abstracts in all three languages, on a wide variety of topics of interest to Europeans. (*Revue d'Acoustique*, begun in 1932, and *Akustische Zeitschrift*, in 1936, had not survived the war, but a new *Revue d'Acoustique* began publication in 1968.) *Akusticheskii Zhurnal* began publishing papers in Russian in 1955, and the American Institute of Physics has published translations of all the papers in English under the title *Soviet Physics—Acoustics*. The *Journal of the Acoustical Society of Japan* (since 1945) publishes in English and in Japanese with English abstracts. The papers in Japanese now usually have English coordinates and legends on exhibits. The British Acoustical Society (since 1968, now the Institute of Acoustics) had a more modest publication program; most of its papers have been on acoustical engineering and have appeared in *Sound and Vibration*.

Of these journals only *JASA* regularly publishes both on hearing and on speech communication engineering. *Audiology* (from 1962, first called *International Audiology*) and the *Journal of Auditory Research* (since 1960) are the most productive of the nonmedical journals for topics in speech audiometry and related areas. *Laryngoscope* (St. Louis, since 1896), *Acta Oto-Laryngology* (Stockholm, since 1918), *Archives of Otolaryngology* (Chicago, since 1925) and *Annals of Otology, Rhinology, and Laryngology* (St. Louis, since 1897) are the medical journals that carry the largest number of papers on speech audiometry, but journals of otology all over the world carry papers on this and related fields, and readers are advised to use *Index Medicus* and *Exerpta Medica*. In the fields of psychological acoustics, other than *JASA*, the largest repositories are in the *Journal of Speech and Hearing Disorders* (started as the *Journal of Speech Disorders* in 1936) and in its companion, the *Journal of Speech and Hearing Research* (since 1958). *Speech Monographs* (since 1934) and *Language and Speech* (since 1960) have excellent papers on a wide range of topics. The rest of the literature in English is found in a great variety of journals of psychology and human engineering.

Acoustical engineering and speech communication engineering papers are published by *JASA*, the *Bell System Technical Journal*, the *Journal of the Institution of Electrical Engineers* (U.K.), the

Post Office Engineering Journal (U.K.), the *Journal of the Audio Engineering Society* (U.S.), and the publication of the acoustics and audio group of the Institute of Electrical and Electronic Engineers (U.S.). This last publication began as a serial of short papers and then in 1953 gave sequential volume numbers to publications under various names: *IRE Transactions on Audio* **AU-1** to **AU-10**; *IEEE Transactions on Audio*, **AU-11** to **AU-13**; *IEEE Transactions on Audio and Electroacoustics*, **AU-14** to **AU-21**; and *IEEE Transactions on Acoustics, Speech, and Signal Processing*, **ASSP-22** to date.

BIBLIOGRAPHIES

There are sizeable bibliographies for each part of this volume, although there are some overlaps from one part to another, for some books and papers treat topics included in more than one part. To save space the citations are not duplicated. The references cited in the commentary for each part are to the surname of the first listed author and date of the proper citation in the bibliography for that part. If there are two such citations, the figure two in parentheses, (2), appears after the date. In preparing these bibliographies the editor has examined all the papers related to the subjects of this volume that were published from the date of first publication to 1975 in all of the following journals: *Acustica, Akustische Zeitschrift, Bell System Technical Journal, IRE Transactions on Audio et seq., International Audiology et seq., JASA, Journal of the Acoustical Society of Japan* (except volumes 1–7), *Journal of Auditory Research, Journal of Speech and Hearing Disorders, Journal of Speech and Hearing Research, Language and Speech, Revue d'Acoustique* (old and new), *Sound et seq., Sound and Vibration*, and *Soviet Physics—Acoustics*. He also listed and searched for all the applicable papers cited in the References to Contemporary Papers on Acoustics section of *JASA* and almost all the references cited in the papers he examined. He also used several bibliographies on related fields and topics.

The bibliographies for the various parts consist of about half of the books and journal articles that the editor examined and found pertinent to the subjects of this volume. Titles of papers in English, French, German, Spanish, Portugese, and Italian are cited as printed. Titles of papers in other languages are given in English and the original language is named. Almost no citations of theses, abstracts, government contract reports, patents, or laboratory progress reports are given. Limitations of space prevented their inclusion, and it was assumed that most work of high quality eventually is published in a reputable journal with a refereeing procedure. The editor has collected over three thousand citations, which are available to readers by arrangement.

REFERENCES

1. Bell, A. G., "Researches in Telephony," *Proc. Am. Acad. Arts Sci.* **12**:1–10 (1876), p. 8.
2. Wood, K. S., "Parental Maladjustments and Functional Articulatory Defects in Children," *J. Speech Hear. Dis.* **11**:255–275 (1946).
3. Lehiste, I., and G. E. Peterson, "Linguistic Considerations in the Study of Speech Intelligibility," *J. Acoust. Soc. Am.* **31**: 280–287 (1959).
4. Owens, E. and E. D. Schubert, "The Development of Constant Items for Speech Discrimination Testing," *J. Speech Hear. Res.* **11**:656–667 (1968).
5. Pridham, E. S., and P. L. Jensen, U.S. Patent 1,430,356, Sept. 26, 1922, applied for Aug. 17, 1917.
6. Meissner, B. F., U.S. Patent 1,507,081, Sept. 2, 1924, applied for Mar. 12, 1919.
7. Miller, G. A., and F. M. Wiener, *Transmission and Reception of Sounds under Combat Conditions*, (New York: Columbia Univ. Press, (1948).

Part I

ORIGINS

Editor's Comments
on Papers 1 Through 5

This part is concerned with the first of the three periods described in the Introduction—from 1900 to World War II. The number of books and papers on speech intelligibility is not large, but their importance is great because they established a very firm base for the work in later periods. Most of the research was done in the physics departments of universities and in laboratories of telephone companies, especially in the Bell Telephone Laboratories. The emphasis was on learning the physical properties of the speech waveform: its energy, frequency distribution, duration, transition characteristics, phase effects, and statistical distribution among speakers, all quantities that could be defined and measured reliably with the instruments of the time. One can only speculate how the field of speech intelligibility would be different today if the sciences of neurology, linguistics, perceptual psychology, phonetics, or computers had been sufficiently advanced and instrumented so that they might have led the field before 1940.

However, physics and electrical engineering did lead it. In Hungary Georg von Békésy, as a physicist working for the national telephone system's laboratory, began to investigate how much better the ear is than the telephone system was then (Stevens, 1961).* The investigation led him to a series of outstanding achievements in research on hearing, to a Nobel prize in medicine, and to recognition as the foremost acoustical scientist of the century. According to Gabor (1947, refer to Part VII) intelligibility testing was being done at the Post Office laboratories in Great Britain as early as 1905, but there were no publications.

In the United States, first Irving B. Crandall and then Harvey Fletcher led a group of outstanding scientists and engineers at Bell Telephone Laboratories (Bell Labs) who discovered many of the phenomena and rules of behavior on which later research was based. For example, Figure 9 in one of John Steinberg's papers (1934) clearly foreshadows the speech spectrogram. Homer Dudley (1939[2]) developed the first important speech synthesizer, A. H. Inglis (1938) introduced the concept of orthotelephonic gain, C. F. Sacia (1925) defined, measured, and discussed various speech power factors, and Dunn and White (1940) established the basis for the calculation of the Articulation Index and for the measurement of the performance of most radio communication systems for speech.

Three of the Bell Labs papers are reproduced here. Paper 1 by Campbell is the earliest of the important papers describing Bell Labs' intense concern with the recognition of the individual sounds of speech. It was assumed that there were only thirty to fifty of these and that speech could be made up from them as one sets a line of type. Paper 2 by Crandall is a long abstract of a paper in which the vowels and consonants are treated separately because of the differences in their spectral energy distributions. Paper 3 by Fletcher and Steinberg, of which only a short part is reproduced because of space limitations, is the first major paper on intelligibility testing. (Although the authors use the term articulation testing in the title, on page 807 they say it is better applied to the determination of speaking abilities.) The reader is urged to find and to peruse the whole paper, for it is a classic and the most important paper in its field in this period. Fletcher's book (1929) contained a wealth of new data and presented previously published data in a carefully organized form. It quickly became the most cited work on psychological acoustics throughout the world for the next quarter of a century.

Paper 4 by Collard of International Telephone and Telegraph in England is a part of the most original paper of a series (1929, 1933, 1934) in which he laid the basis for using physical measure-

* References are included in the bibliography at the end of the commentary for each section.

13

ments to predict intelligibility, a subject which is treated more fully in Part III. He developed notions of linearly additive bands of frequencies for intelligibility calculations, of the probability that the speech signal will exceed some threshold or noise level in each band, and of the recognition process as a selection from available alternatives with various probabilities. His work is too seldom cited in the North American literature.

In Los Angeles, Vern O. Knudsen, with no sizeable laboratory to support him, used speech intelligibility tests to make significant advances in architectural acoustics (1929, 1938), in audiology (1935, Jones and Knudsen, 1935), and in hearing aid selection (1935). Paper 5 by him is a very early study of the factors interfering with the intelligibility of speech. The next section of this book is devoted entirely to such studies, but most of them were done at least twenty-five years after this paper appeared. Knudsen's text (1932) also became a classic and for a long while it contained the only description of speech intelligibility measurements actually carried on in auditoria.

The Bell Labs also contributed importantly to audiology, for, in cooperation with The Corporation of the American Federation of Organizations of the Hard of Hearing, they developed a speech audiometer later marketed as the Western Electric 4A (and then as the 4C). It was used for rapid mass screening. Most of the historical material on speech audiometry is in Part VI.

A recent survey article (Anonymous, 1968) names Soviet acoustical scientists who worked on the intelligibility of speech over communications systems in noise in 1937–1938, and there are bibliographies of the literature primarily in French and German for this early period in *Revue d'Acoustique* and *Akustische Beihefte*.

BIBLIOGRAPHY

Anonymous, "Soviet Acoustics during the Last Fifty Years," *Sov. Phys.— Acoust.* **13**:415–454 (1968).

Black, J. W., "The Effect of the Consonant on the Vowel," *J. Acoust. Soc. Am.* **10**:203–205 (1939).

Black, J. W., "The Effect of the Consonant on the Vowel," *J. Accoust. Soc. Am.* **10**:203–205 (1939).

Collard, J., "A Theoretical Study of the Articulation and Intelligibility of a Telephone Circuit," *Elec. Commun.* **7**:168–186 (1929).

Collard, J., "The Accurate Measurement of Articulation," *Post Office Elec. Eng. J.* **23**:25–35 (1930).

Collard, J., "An Automatic Device for Recording, Correcting and Analysing Articulation Results," *Elec. Commun.* **10**:140–146 (1932).

Collard, J., "A New Criterion of Circuit Performance," *Elec. Commun.* **11**:226–233 (1933).

Collard, J., "The Practical Application of the New Unit of Circuit Performance," *Elec.. Commun.* **12**:270–275 (1934).

Crandall, I. B., "The Sounds of Speech," *Bell Syst. Tech. J.* **4**:586–625 (1925).

Crandall, I. B., "Dynamical Study of the Vowel Sounds. Part II," *Bell Syst. Tech. J.* **6**:100–116 (1927).

Crandall, I. B., and D. MacKenzie, "Analysis of the Energy Distribution in Speech," *Phys. Rev.* **19**, Ser. 2:221–232 (1922).

Crandall, I. B., and C. F. Sacia, "A Dynamical Study of the Vowel Sounds," *Bell Syst. Tech. J.* **3**:232–237 (1924).

Dewey, Godfrey, *Relative Frequency of English Speech Sounds*, Harvard Univ. Press, Cambridge, Mass. (1923).

Dudley, H., "Automatic Synthesis of Speech," *Acad. Sci., Proc.* **25**:377–383 (1939).

Dudley, H., "Remaking Speech," *J. Acoust. Soc. Am.* **11**:169–179 (1939).

Dudley, H., "The Carrier Nature of Speech," *Bell Syst. Tech. J.* **19**:495–515 (1940).

Dunn, H. K., and D. W. Farnsworth, "Exploration of Pressure Field around the Human Head During Speech," *J. Acoust. Soc. Am.* **10**:184–199 (1939).

Dunn, H. K., and S. D. White, "Statistical Measurements on Conversational Speech," *J. Acoust. Soc. Am.* **11**:278–288 (1940).

Fletcher, H., "The Nature of Speech and Its Interpretation," *J. Franklin Inst.* **193**:729–747 (1922).

Fletcher, H., "Useful Numerical Constants of Speech and Hearing," *Bell Syst. Tech. J.* **4**:375–386 (1925).

Fletcher, H., *Speech and Hearing*, D. Van Nostrand, New York (1929).

Fletcher, H., "Loudness, Masking and Their Relation to the Hearing Process and the Problem of Noise Measurement," *J. Acoust. Soc. Am.* **9**:275–293 (1938).

Fletcher, H., "Auditory Patterns," *Rev. Mod. Phys.* **12**:47–61 (1940).

Fletcher, H., and W. A. Munson, "Relation between Loudness and Masking," *J. Acoust. Soc. Am.* **9**:1–10 (1937).

Fletcher, H., and J. C. Steinberg, "The Dependence of the Loudness of a Complex Sound upon the Energy in the Various Frequency Regions of the Sound," *Phys. Rev.* **24**, Ser. 2:306–317 (1924).

Frankfurther, W., and Rudolf Thiele, "Experimentelle Untersuchungen zur Bezoldschen Sprache," *Beitr. zur Akust. u. Musikwiss.* **7**:134–160 (1913). Also in *Z. f. Sinnephysiol.* **47**:192–218 (1913).

French, N. R., and W. Koenig, Jr., "The Frequency of Occurence of Speech Sounds in Spoken English," *J. Acoust. Soc. Am.* **1**:110–120 (1929).

Gemelli, A., and G. Pastori, "L'Analisi Elettroacustica del Linguaggio," **7**, Ser. 6:*Societ. edit. "Vita e pensiero,"* Milan (1934).

Inglis, A. H., "Transmission Features of the New Telephone Sets," *Bell Syst. Tech. J.* **17**:358–380 (1938).

Jones, I. H., and V. O. Knudsen, "Diagnosis of Hearing Impairments," *Laryngoscope* **45**:24–47 (1935).

Kellogg, E. W.. Reversed Speech," *J. Acoust. Soc. Am* **10**:324–326 (1939).

Knudsen, V. O., "The Hearing of Speech in Auditoriums," *J. Acoust. Soc. Am.* **1**:56–82 (1929).

Knudsen, V. O., *Architectural Acoustics*, Wiley, New York (1932).

Knudsen, V. O., "Some Cultural Applications of Modern Acoustics," *J. Acoust. Soc. Am.* **9**:175–184 (1938).

Knudsen, V. O., and I. H. Jones, "Artifical Aids to Hearing," *Laryngoscope* **45**:48–69 (1935).

Knudsen, V. O., and I. H. Jones, "Basic Principles Underlying Tests of Hearing," *Laryngoscope* **45**:1–23 (1935).

Köhler, W., "Akustische Untersuchungen I" and "Akustische Untersuchungen II," *Beitr. zur Akust. u. Musikwiss.* **4**:134–182 (1909) and **6**:1–82 (1911).

Lifshitz, S., "Acoustics of Large Auditoriums, " *J. Acoust. Soc. Am* **4**:112–121 (1932).

Marro, M., "On the Persistence of the Sensation of Speech," *Philos. Mag.* **22**:847–854 (1936).

Martin, W. H., "Rating the Transmission Performance of Telephone Circuits," *Bell Syst. Tech. J.* **10**:116–131 (1931).

Mayer, H. F., "Verständlichkeit-messungen an Telephonie-Übertragungssystem," *Elektr. Nachrichtentech.* **4**:184–188 (1927).

Obata, J., and T. Tesima, "Physico-Phonetical Studies of the Chinese Language," *Proc. Imp. Acad.* **9**:510–512 (1933) and **10**:322–325 (1934).

Olson, H. F., *Elements of Acoustical Engineering*, D. Van Nostrand, New York (1940).

Paget, Sir Richard, "Production of Artificial Vowel Sounds," *Proc. R. Soc.* **A102**:752 (1923).

Paget, Sir Richard, *Human Speech,* Harcourt-Brace, New York (1930).

Pocock, L. C., "Faithful Reproduction in Radio Telephony," *Inst. Elec. Engrs. J.* **62**:791-807. disc. 807-815 (1924).

Pocock, L. C., "Transmission Testing of Subscribers' Apparatus," *Elec. Commun.* **10**:82–93 (1931).

Pocock. L. Č., "The Calculation of Articulation for Effective Rating of Telephone Circuits," *Elec. Commun.* **18**:120–132 (1939).

Rocard, Y., "Sur un effet physiologique concernant l'écoute dans le bruit," *Rev. Acoust.* **7**:37–38 (1938).

Sacia, C. F., "Speech Power and Energy," *Bell Syst. Tech. J.* **4**:627–641 (1925).

Sacia, C. F., and C. J. Beck, "Power of the Fundamental Speech Sounds," *Bell Syst. Tech. J.* **5**:393–403 (1926).

Sivian, L. J., "Speech Power and Its Measurement," *Bell Syst. Tech. J.* **8**:646–661 (1929).

Steinberg, J. C., "Effects of Distortion upon the Recognition of Speech Sounds," *J. Acoust. Soc. Am.* **1**:121–137 (1929).

Steinberg, J. C., "Application of Sound Measuring Instruments to the Study of Phonetic Problems," *J. Acoust. Soc. Am.* **6**:16–24 (1934).

Stevens, S. S., "Georg von Békésy, " *J. Acoust. Soc. Am.* **33**:1150 (1961).

Steven, S. S., and Davis, H., *Hearing*, Wiley, New York (1939).

Strecker, F., "Verständlichkeit und Lautstärke bei Frequenz- und Amplituden begrenzung," *Z. tech. Phys.* **17**:568–572 (1936).

Tierbach, D., and H. Jacoby, Über die Verteilung der Sprechspannung bei der Übertragung zahlreicher trägerfrequenter Gespräche, *Z. tech. Phys.* **17**:553–557 (1936).

Trendelenburg, F., "Objektive Klangaufzeichnung mittels des Kondensatormikrophons," *Wiss. Ver. a.d. Siemens-Konzern* **3**:43–66 (1924) and **4**:1–13 (1925).

Trendelenburg, F., *Klänge und Geräusche*, J. Springer, Berlin (1935).

von Braunmühl, H. J., "Über die Intensitätsverhältnisse von natürlichen Klangbildern mit besonderer Berücksichtigung der Rundfunksendung," *Z. tech. Phys.* **14**:507–512 (1933).

von Braunmühl, H. .J., and W. Weber, *Einfuhrung in die angewandte Akustik*, S. Hirzel, Leipzig (1936).

Vysotski, B. F., and S. I. Tetelbaum, "On Improving the Articulation of Loudspeakers in an Auditorium with a Noisy Background," *Izv. Elektroprom. Slab. Toka* no. 1, 17–21 (1938). in Russian.

Watson, F. R., "Bibliography of Acoustics of Buildings," *J. Acoust. Soc. Am* **3**:14–43 (1931).

Watson, N. A., and V. O. Knudsen, "Selective Amplification in Hearing Aids," *J. Acoust. Soc. Am.* **11**:406–419 (1940).

1

Reprinted from *Philos. Mag.* **19**, ser. 6:152–159 (1910)

TELEPHONIC INTELLIGIBILITY

George A. Campbell

IN the August 1908 number (vol. xvi. p. 242) of the 'Philosophical Magazine' a paper by Lord Rayleigh contains some notes upon the acousticon, in the course of which he says:—

"The reproduction of speech, given at about one foot away from the microphone, was better than anything I had ever heard before. The first impression was that all the consonantal sounds were completely rendered, but this turned out to be an illusion. In listening to the numerals, given in order, the observer would feel confident that he heard the *f* in *five* and the *s* in *six*. But if the initial sound was prolonged —*fff ive*, *s s s ix*, the observer could not tell until he heard the sequel which it was going to be. Further, if the sounds were given as *s s ive*, *f f ix*, they were heard normally as five and six. It was plain that there was no difference in the rendering of *f* and *s*. I am informed that this is a well-known difficulty in ordinary telephoning, and that in spelling a name containing *f* or *s* it is usual to say '*f* for Friday' or '*s* for Saturday.' But the articulation of the acousticon is so superior that it was surprising to find the failure complete. The characterization of *sh* was not much better, though after a little practice I could distinguish it from *s* or *f*, but probably only by a greater loudness.

"These failures might have been ascribed to my rather defective hearing, but other observers with normal hearing did no better."

This statement of telephonic intelligibility is typical of the impression made by the general use of the telephone. Most of us feel that we understand almost everything transmitted by the telephone or next to nothing, according as we are listening to a familiar voice talking upon some well-known subject, or as we are obliged to listen to disconnected syllables spoken possibly in a strange tone of voice. This is obviously a case for the statistical analysis of results.

Some time ago the American Telephone and Telegraph

Company began an investigation of the distortion introduced
by the telephone instruments and transmission network.
The work has not advanced sufficiently to warrant general
statements as to the telephonic intelligibility of the 5000
phonetic syllables employed in the English language, but
what has been done seems to show the order of intelligibility
of the consonantal sounds with some definiteness.

For the tests which will be described the following twenty
syllables, each ending in long *i* and preceded by one of the
simple consonant sounds, were used :—

bi	as in bee	ni	as in knee
chi	Chi(le)	pi	pea
di	de(pot), dee	ri	re(bus), rei
fi	fee	si	see
gi	Gi(zeh)	shi	she
hi	he	ti	tea
ji	gee	thi	the(ory)
ki	key	vi	ve(nus), vee
li	lee	yi	ye
mi	me	zi	ze(bra), zee.

The list contains seventeen words and three syllables which
occur in compound words. According to the scientific
alphabet used in the Standard Dictionary, there are but
twenty-four elementary English consonant sounds. All of
these consonant sounds are included except *dh, ng, w,* and
zh; *dh* is somewhat like *th*, and was similarly recorded in an
earlier series of tests; *w* was recorded correctly in 99 per
cent. of the cases in a set of twelve thousand records; *ng*
and *zh* are not of frequent occurrence, and do not seem to be
used as syllables with merely long *i* following.

Ten lists of one hundred syllables each were prepared,
every one of which contained the twenty consonants five
times in a perfectly haphazard manner. All of the ten lists
were spoken over the telephone connexion and a record made
of the consonant heard. The tests were then continued, the
experimentors changing places. All records were made in a
quiet room and over quiet lines. Before this series of tests
was begun the observers had made at least fifteen thousand
records, and had become perfectly familiar with the method
of test. The syllables were never repeated for any one given
record, and the observer always made a record however
uncertain he might feel as to its correctness. While the
sequence of the lists and of the syllables was perfectly haphazard, the observer knew that each syllable occurred the
same number of times in each list of one hundred syllables.
This may have led in some cases of uncertainty to recording
a syllable merely for the reason that it did not seem to have

received its proper share of records. It does not seem probable that this influenced the results to any considerable extent. As far as such an effect occurred it would correspond in a general way to the condition obtaining in the practical use of the telephone, where the subject matter and the preceding syllables give some clue as to the syllable which may be expected.

The telephonic network included regular common battery subscribers' sets at each end, common battery transformers and cord circuits at the central offices, and a line of about one hundred miles of loaded No. 16 or No. 14 B. and S. gauge cable, with the addition of from three to sixteen miles of non-loaded No. 19 B. and S. gauge cable. The series of tests over this connexion included twelve thousand records.

For comparison, tests were also made with direct transmission through the air, the same observers facing each other with no intervening obstruction but not looking at each other. The observers were fifteen feet apart in a quiet room. This series contained two thousand records.

Table I. shows the distribution of all records. Where there are two figures in a square the upper refers to the test made through the air. The syllables have been arranged in such an order as to bring those which are most frequently mistaken for each other as near together as possible. This brings the surds or voiceless consonants, *f, s, h, sh, ch, k, t,* and *p* together. The remaining consonants are all voice consonants with the exception of *th.* The occurrence of *th* among the voice consonants may be accounted for by the fact that *th* is liable to confusion with the voice consonant *dh* as in *thee,* and it is possible that in these tests the distinction between the two was not properly made. In an earlier series of tests which included *dh* in place of *th* the same mistakes were made as in the present series with *th,* that is, *dh* was confused with *v* on one side and *z* on the other. In the table the voiceless explosives *k, t,* and *p* come together, also the voice explosives *g, d,* and *b,* and the nasals *m* and *n.*

A blank square indicates that no record was made by either observer corresponding to that case. The table shows 156 such squares, and therefore of the possible incorrect cases only 59 per cent. occurred. A zero indicates that not over one-half of one per cent. of the total records for that syllable fell within that square. Had the distribution of records been entirely haphazard the average number in each square would have been 5 per cent. The table actually shows only 34 squares with 5 per cent. or more incorrect records, therefore only 9 per cent. of the incorrect cases occurred with a frequency equal to or greater than the probability corresponding to a perfectly haphazard distribution of records.

20

The consonants may be divided into three groups, as indicated by the heavier lines in the table, which are sufficiently distinct so that no consonant in one group is mistaken for any consonant in the other groups as frequently as 5 per cent. of the time.

The totals in the last column of Table I. show that the records were not evenly divided among the twenty syllables. Thus *knee* was recorded only 27 per cent. as many times as it was called, while *tea* was recorded nearly twice as often as called. The scattering of the records increases somewhat with the total number of records, but not proportionately.

In general each consonant was much more frequently mistaken for some one consonant than for any other. Table II. gives the correct records and the leading mistakes for transmission through the air, and in Table III. the same records are given for telephonic transmission. The last columns of these tables show that 96 per cent. of the records were correct for transmission through the air, and 59 per cent. correct for telephonic transmission. The leading mistake made for air transmission occurred in 3 per cent. of the cases (total correct and incorrect records), while for telephonic transmission the leading mistake amounted to 26 per cent. of the cases. The mistakes made through the air were also made over the telephone, but additional mistakes also occurred, and often these are the more frequent ones. The most common mistake made over the telephone was in recording *me* when *knee* was called. This occurred in 67 per cent. of the cases when *knee* was called. *Knee* is thus naturally the syllable least often recorded correctly, occurring in only 24 per cent. of the cases. *Lee* was recorded correctly in 98 per cent. of the cases, a record excelling the average for direct transmission through the air.

The records tabulated in the above tables were all made by Mr. W. L. Richards and Mr. E. C. Molina. They differed considerably in the distribution of records, but presumably the averages are about normal as far as the personal element goes. With the best possible articulation the intelligibility would undoubtedly be considerably higher.

Our tests indicate that the greater part of the distortion occurs in the subscriber's set, and that a short length of line may actually improve intelligibility as compared with zero line. As the length of line reaches the commercial limit the intelligibility gradually falls off. The tests indicate, as would be expected, that changes in the telephone apparatus and the line affect the different syllables quite differently.

It will be seen that the syllables *fee* and *see* are confused with each other in telephonic transmission. They were interchanged in 27 per cent. of the cases, and recorded correctly in 58 per cent. of the cases, which makes *f* and *s* an average pair of consonants, as the twenty consonants were recorded correctly in 59 per cent. of the cases, and the leading mistake was made in 26 per cent. of the cases. Even as the records stand, it will be seen that *f* and *s* are correctly recorded twice as frequently as they are interchanged with each other. While these results are not directly applicable to the acousticon, which is the instrument referred to by Lord Rayleigh, the difference should be in favour of the acousticon, for our tests were made with commercial instruments over long commercial lines.

As the conditions of our tests differed from those of Lord Rayleigh in almost every particular, further tests, summarized in Table IV., have been made which bring the conditions more nearly into agreement. The number of syllables in each list was here reduced to two, and the six distinct series of tests included Lord Rayleigh's test syllables five and sive; fix and six, and also fee and see; ohm and own; am and an; me and knee. Each list contained one hundred syllables, and was varied each time it was called. The lists were called over the telephone by six persons, here designated as E, F, G, H, I, J; of these I and J were young women. Four telephone receivers were arranged in series, parallel at the receiving station, and four persons A, B, C, D, listened simultaneously and made independent records. This method materially reduced the time and labour of making this set of 14,400 records, and it also enables us to compare directly the records of different observers with any one person calling or of any one observer with different persons calling. Observer E listened directly to H, I, and J, and these records are added to the table. The ten persons who assisted in these tests were familiar with the use of the telephone, but they had had little or no practice in syllabic tests. The telephone connexion from the talking to the listening station was made through the private branch exchange of the office, and therefore the length of line included was almost negligible.

It will be seen that the records made by E for direct receiving through the air were in general nearly perfect, but that for " ohm " and " own " they were in some cases poorer than the telephonic records. Comparison of the original records for each calling of the lists shows that the distribution of mistakes was, on the whole, purely accidental, and could not be traced to definite irregularities in the pronunciation of the lists.

For Lord Rayleigh's syllables fix and six, five and sive, about 85 per cent. of the records were correct ; haphazard records would have averaged but 50 per cent. correct. In one case, F calling and D recording, a perfect record was made for the " five-sive " list.

While it is obvious that the telephone seriously distorts speech-waves, nevertheless even those consonants which most nearly resemble each other are not distorted sufficiently to be indistinguishable.

TABLE I.
Distribution of Telephonic Records in Percentages
(Air Records above).

CALLED

	f	s	h	sh	ch	k	t	p	j	g	d	b	y	v	th	z	m	n	l	r	Total.
f	97/48	20	1	5	1			1	0			1		0	0		0				77
s	34	100/69	28	10/17	2/3	0		2	1			2		3	1	1		0	0		160
h	0	0	99/45	8	2	0		1	1	0				0	0						58
sh	0	4	1	88/33	1				0												39
ch	1	5	9	2/35	97/41			0	5	1/0	0		0	0	0					0	96
k	1	0	1	0	45	100/45	4	1	3	7					1						108
t	6		2	0	5	49	98/70	45	4	11	2	1	0	0	1/1	0	0	0			197
p	2/3		1	0	1	5	1/25	100/45	0	0	3	4	0	0					0	0	87
j	0		2		1/1	0		0	87/61	12/10	0		1	0	0	2					77
g			2		0	0			13/17	87/47	1/0				0	1	0				67
d	1	0	1			0	0	4	1	23	97/91	40	1	2	3	0		0			169
b	1/1		1/1				1/0	1	0	1	2/3	99/46	4/1	1/1	0	1	1		0		58
y		0	3					2	0			1	98/76	0	0/0	1		1		0	84
v	2	1	1			0	1	1	0	0	1/3	1/9	90/41	8/24	7	0	0	0	0		91
th	0			1		1			0		1	1/2	6/32	88/41	15	0					93
z	1	1	2	0	0		0	0	1	0		1	4	19	25	100/72		0			127
m		0	1	0	0				0			2		0			100/90	5/67	1		162
n	0													0			3	94/24	1/0		27
l	1	0	0	0	0	0			1	0	0	0	3	1	2		5	1/6	99/98	7	125
r	0					0	0	0	1	0			1	0		0	0		1	100/92	96

RECORDED

TABLE II. — Air Records.

CALLED

	f	s	h	sh	ch	k	t	p	j	g	d	b	y	v	th	z	m	n	l	r	Av.
Correct	97	100	99	88	97	100	98	100	87	87	97	99	98	90	88	100	100	94	99	100	96
1st incorrect ...	p 2		b 1	s 10	s 2		b 1		g 13	j 12	b 2	v 1	v 1	th 6	v 8			m 5	n 1		3
All others	1	0	0	2	1	0	1	0	0	1	1	0	1	4	4	0	0	1	0	0	1

TABLE III.—Telephonic Records.

CALLED

		f	s	h	sh	ch	k	t	p	j	g	d	b	y	v	th	z	m	n	l	r	Av.
Correct Records ...		48	69	45	33	41	45	70	45	61	47	91	46	76	41	41	72	90	24	98	92	59
Incorrect Records.	1st ...	s 34	f 20	s 28	ch 35	k 45	t 49	p 25	t 45	g 17	d 23	b 3	d 40	v 9	th 32	z 25	th 15	l 5	m 67	m 1	l 7	26
	2nd ...	t 6	ch 5	ch 9	s 17	t 5	p 5	k 4	d 4	ch 5	t 11	p 3	p 4	z 4	z 19	v 24	v 7	n 3	l 6	r 1	0	7
	3rd ...	p 3	sh 4	y 3	h 8	s 3	0	th 1	s 2	t 4	j 10	t 2	v 3	l 3	d 2	d 3	j 2	b 1	b 1	0	0	3
	All others	9	2	15	7	6	1	0	4	13	9	1	7	8	6	7	4	1	2	0	1	5

TABLE IV.

		Me.						Knee.					
		A	B	C	D	Av.	E	A	B	C	D	Av.	E
	E	66	86	96	96	86		38	68	72	84	65	
	F	80	92	70	68	77		80	88	92	68	82	
	G	78	90	92	56	79		88	98	96	82	91	
	H	94	96	82	90	90	100	86	98	96	92	93	100
	I	52	54	54	78	59	94	50	84	76	74	71	100
	J	60	88	72	84	76	90	46	72	74	64	64	98
						78						78	

		Am.						An.					
		A	B	C	D	Av.	E	A	B	C	D	Av.	E
	E	84	64	86	52	71		70	78	62	90	75	
	F	64	76	84	78	75		64	52	50	64	57	
	G	76	74	66	54	67		92	88	94	66	85	
	H	90	94	88	82	88	98	90	98	98	92	94	94
	I	68	62	72	74	69	96	96	94	96	96	95	84
	J	80	80	64	76	75	92	90	84	84	86	86	68
						74						82	

TABLE IV. (*continued*).

	Ohm.						Own.					
	A	B	C	D	Av.	E	A	B	C	D	Av.	E
E	82	88	66	94	82		68	66	88	54	69	
F	84	86	72	86	82		90	90	92	94	91	
G	96	88	86	90	90		74	82	98	94	87	
H	94	80	82	96	88	76	96	90	94	86	91	80
I	76	82	64	76	74	72	96	88	98	88	92	82
J	80	80	68	90	79	90	94	90	92	96	93	54
					82						87	

	Fee.						See.					
	A	B	C	D	Av.	E	A	B	C	D	Av.	E
E	70	94	98	44	76		74	96	74	98	85	
F	54	90	80	40	66		74	62	96	92	81	
G	90	90	94	76	87		76	96	96	90	89	
H	68	62	76	60	66	100	82	84	90	66	80	98
I	66	70	84	70	72	100	66	44	62	66	59	100
J	66	78	88	86	79	100	68	64	60	74	66	100
					74						77	

	Fix.						Six.					
	A	B	C	D	Av.	E	A	B	C	D	Av.	E
E	92	100	92	58	86		92	84	92	78	86	
F	88	96	96	72	88		76	84	94	90	86	
G	94	96	94	78	90		86	88	98	78	87	
H	86	70	64	58	69	100	80	80	80	68	77	100
I	76	66	78	78	74	100	88	80	86	70	81	100
J	88	86	96	90	90	100	80	60	74	84	74	96
					83						82	

	Five.						Sive.					
	A	B	C	D	Av.	E	A	B	C	D	Av.	E
E	90	100	100	94	96		86	92	92	92	90	
F	100	98	100	100	99		88	100	96	100	96	
G	94	96	96	78	91		82	98	92	100	93	
H	99	100	68	78	85	100	72	80	90	96	84	98
I	60	74	90	70	73	100	64	70	82	82	74	100
J	96	86	100	94	94	100	70	60	70	96	74	98
					90						85	

2

Reprinted from *Phys. Rev.* **10**, ser. 2:74–76 (1917)

THE COMPOSITION OF SPEECH.[1]

BY I. B. CRANDALL.

THIS paper deals with the composition of average speech from sounds of different frequencies, speech being considered as a continuous flow of distributed energy, analogous to total radiation from an optical source. This idea of speech is a convenient approximation, useful in the study of speech reproduction by mechanical means.

Two properties characterize perfect speech reproduction: (1) The accurate transfer of the language used, and (2) the preservation of the tone-quality of the original speech. For expressing the ideal property of literal accuracy in transfer various terms have been used, such as, "clearness," "intelligibility," "articulation," and so on. The term "articulation" will be chosen to describe this property of literal reproduction.

In reference to the other idea, namely, the preservation of the tone-quality of speech, the term "naturalness" will be used. The idea of naturalness includes the preservation of the human or artistic quality of speech.

Consider first the relative importance of the different speech frequencies from the standpoint of articulation. Before we can determine this factor, we must have a method of measuring articulation; this involves the choice of a number of representative sounds, and the adoption of a testing routine which will give the per cent. of such sounds accurately transferred by the reproducing apparatus.[2] For a first attempt a list of the representative consonant sounds in the English language has been taken, for experience has shown that it is possible to identify most words in a given context without taking notice of the vowels. The routine of articulation testing is rather tedious and need not be gone into, as we are only interested in the result—

[1] Abstract of a paper presented at the Washington meeting of the Physical Society, April 20–21, 1917.

[2] The method used is a development of that originally proposed by Dr. G. A. Campbell in his article on "Telephonic Intelligibility," Phil. Mag., 19, 1910, p. 152.

the per cent. of consonant sounds accurately transferred by any given apparatus.

It is possible to measure the relative importance of different speech frequencies if we make a series of articulation tests using apparatus which completely suppresses certain frequencies, while at the same time the remaining frequencies are perfectly reproduced. It suffices to state here that electromechanical reproducing systems are available which have exactly these characteristics.

Denoting the *importance to articulation* of any frequency p by the function $D(p)$, we may consider the articulation χ of a system which reproduces all frequencies equally to be

$$\chi_{max.} = \int_0^\infty D(p)dp = 1.00.$$

By measuring χ when different, limited ranges of frequencies are reproduced, it is possible to find $D(p)$. This method has been worked out in detail by the writer and has yielded a good determination of the relative importance $D(p)$ of the different frequencies which compose the consonant sounds.

Coming now to the question of naturalness, the tone-quality of speech is clearly defined if the relative amounts of energy associated with the different frequencies are known: for this purpose we make use of another function of frequency $S(p)$ which indicates the *energy distribution* in speech. The composition of one unit of speech energy from energy of different frequencies may be expressed by

$$\int_0^\infty S(p)dp = 1.00.$$

Measurements of the relative intensities of different sounds are readily carried out, and it is possible to determine the function $S(p)$ in a number of ways. One way would be to use apparatus similar to that used for the determination of $D(p)$ in which certain frequencies were absolutely suppressed. Instead of measuring articulation, we should measure the loss in loudness or energy corresponding to a given suppression, from which data $S(p)$ could be easily found. Another way would be to experiment with systems which reproduce all frequencies, but which overemphasize certain ranges of frequency. Some rough experiments of this kind have been made from which preliminary values of the function $S(p)$ have been obtained.

The interesting thing, in the energy distribution in speech, is that the vowels are the determining factors of this distribution, whereas the consonants are the determining factors in the matter of importance to articulation. The importance of the consonant frequencies in speech is thus utterly out of proportion to the amount of energy associated with them.

On account of the fact that the energy in speech resides almost wholly in the vowel sounds, it is possible to obtain the curve $S(p)$ synthetically if the energy distributions in the different vowel sounds are known. Making use of

Professor Miller's well-known results for energy distribution in the vowel sounds and weighting each vowel for frequency of occurrence, I have constructed such a synthetic curve; the agreement between the synthetic curve and the experimental values obtained from speech as a whole is practically complete. More accurate data for the energy distribution will be offered in a subsequent paper.

Because of the small amount of energy in the consonant sounds, they are difficult to investigate; but experiments are in progress from which we hope to obtain an interpretation of what has been called the *importance* of a given consonant frequency. It is also hoped to give a complete treatment of the reproduction of speech, based on the idea of the composition of speech given in the present paper.

3

ARTICULATION TESTING METHODS

H. Fletcher and J. C. Steinberg

[*Editor's Note*: In the original, material precedes this excerpt.]

It is frequently necessary to test very poor systems where the standard lists giving an articulation of a few per cent, are not satisfactory. The vowel consonant lists are somewhat more satisfactory under these circumstances. Lists of sentences have also been found to be very useful for such purposes. The sentences were of the interrogative or imperative form containing a simple idea. They were designed to test the observer's acuteness of perception rather than his intelligence. Tests were made with these sentences and the standard lists on various circuits, involving carbon transmitter circuits and various filter systems. The data are shown in Fig. 11. The

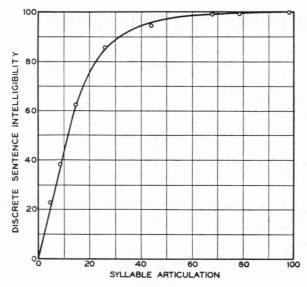

Fig. 11—Discrete sentence intelligibility vs. articulation

sentences were considered to be understood if the observer either recorded the sentence correctly or recorded an intelligent answer. As stated earlier, the percentage correctly observed is called the discrete sentence intelligibility.

It will be seen that for changes in distortion, the changes in the discrete sentence intelligibility will be small for systems having syllable articulations greater than 30 per cent, but very large for systems having syllable articulations below 20 per cent. It is for systems in this latter class that these test sentences are useful. A case in point is the measurement of the degree of secrecy obtained in sound proofing telephone booths, or in dealing with cross-talk. The sentences have also been found to be useful in making quick qualitative tests of the goodness of an audiphone set for a particular case of deafness.

Because of their general usefulness for these purposes, the complete lists of sentences are given in the appendix. Due to memory effects a set of sentences can be used with the same personnel only a very few times. The psychological factors are also more prominent with sentences than with simple syllable.

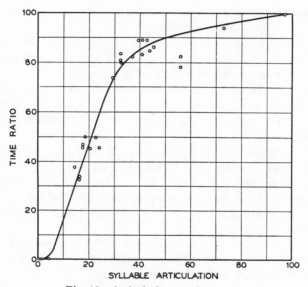

Fig. 12—Articulation vs. time ratio

Sentence lists of the above type have also been used to obtain a notion of how the time taken to transmit an idea correctly over a system depends upon the articulation. To do this, the observer was instructed to reply orally to the question. If the reply indicated that the observer failed to understand, the speaker repeated the question. Both speaker and observer tried to carry out the test in a normal conversational manner. The observer could ask the speaker to repeat, reword or spell out difficult parts of the sentence.

The tests were made on a variety of systems of known syllable articulation. The results that were obtained are shown in Fig. 12. The ordinates of the curve give the ratio of the time required to transmit correctly one of these test sentences over an ideal system to the time required over the system under test.   With the crew used in making these tests, and with an ideal transmission system, it required an average time of 5.2 seconds after the speaker started to pronounce the sentence before the observers grasped the idea.   It will be seen from the curve that for systems having approximately 20 per cent articulation, the time required is twice as great.   Fig. 11 shows that one out of every four of the sentences is mistaken for this value of articulation.   If it is assumed that an observer asks that only sentences which he fails to understand be repeated, it can be shown that this time ratio is equal to the discrete sentence intelligibility.[11]

It is evident from Figs. 11 and 12, that the observed time ratio is appreciably less than the discrete sentence intelligibility.   This difference may be taken to indicate that an observer not only asks that sentences which he fails to understand be repeated, but also that sentences about which he is uncertain be repeated.   In other words, the time element reflects both factors, the understandability and the uncertainty.

As has been previously mentioned, tests have been made with various types of English word lists.   Because of the manner in which the words were selected, and also due to uncertain psychological factors entering into the tests when such words are used repeatedly, it is difficult to compare the results so obtained with syllable articulation results.

However, it was found that if a definite rule were followed in selecting words from a newspaper, consistent results could be obtained with lists containing 500 or more words per list.   The method of selection was to take the first word from every third line of a newspaper column.   In this selection all proper names and the following six most frequent words of English were excluded, the, of, and, to a, in. When a word was hyphenated from the previous line, the whole word was used.   Each of eight callers called a list of 66 words to four observers in the manner of an ordinary standard articulation test.   Tests were made with the carbon transmitter circuit and the six circuits indicated in Fig. 3.   The data were analyzed to give the discrete word intelligibilities for the one, two, three, four, and five-syllable words occurring in the lists, as well as for the lists as a whole. The lists on the average contained 46.3 per cent one-syllable, 29 per cent two-syllable, 16.8 per cent three-syllable, 6.4 per cent four-

---

[11] "A Theoretical Study of Articulation and Intelligibility of a Telephone Circuit," John Collard, *Electrical Communication*, 7, page 168, January, 1929.

syllable, and 1.5 per cent five-syllable words, and an average number of two syllables per word. The discrete word intelligibility vs. syllable articulation as obtained with the standard lists is shown in Fig. 13. The dashed curves indicate the relations for the various types of words, and the solid curve for the word lists as a whole. The data for two syllable words practically coincided with the solid curve. Owing to the small amount of data, the curves for the four- and five-syllable words are less reliable than those for the other types. Curves of the above type, both for words and sentences, depend very

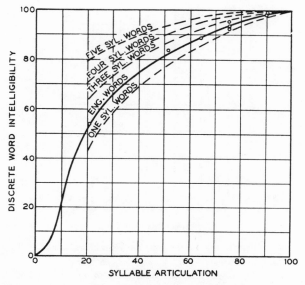

Fig. 13—Discrete word intelligibility vs. syllable articulation

much upon the way the speech material is selected. If, for example, only "different" words had been included in the word lists, appreciably smaller values of discrete word intelligibility would have been obtained.

Tests have also been made with lists made up of the following numbers, 1, 2, 3, 4, 5, 6, 8. These numbers were combined at random into groups of three and called in the manner of an ordinary articulation syllable. The distinguishing characteristic of each of the above numbers is a vowel sound, so that, they are interpreted primarily from recognizing the vowel. Such lists, therefore, do not give a very good picture of the speech capabilities of a system which distorts speech. They are, however, very useful in measuring the deafness of an observer, for the reason that the number articulation decreases very rapidly as the sounds approach the threshold of hearing. As may be seen from Fig. 14, the number articulation passes from practically 100 per cent to 0 per cent in the short range of 10 or 15 db. It is evident that such lists give a critical measure of the point at which

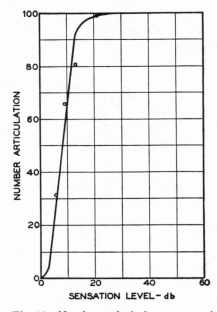

Fig. 14—Number articulation vs. sensation level

an observer fails to hear the sounds. Lists of this type have been used extensively in testing the hearing of school children.

[*Editor's Note*: Material has been omitted at this point.]

CALCULATION OF THE ARTICULATION OF A TELEPHONE CIRCUIT FROM THE CIRCUIT CONSTANTS

J. Collard

[*Editor's Note*: In the original, material precedes this excerpt.]

Development of Formulae

This section gives a detailed description of the fundamental theory and the development of the

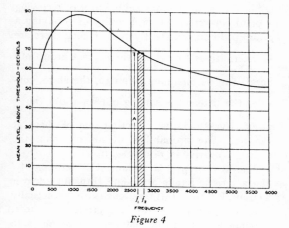

Figure 4

formulae from which the articulation is calculated. To some extent it repeats what has already been said in the previous section.

From the point of view of this study it is unnecessary to consider in great detail the different theories that have been put forward to explain the production of speech sounds. These theories have been described and discussed in various publications to which reference is given in the Bibliography. In particular, the book *Speech and Hearing* recently written by Dr. Harvey Fletcher gives a very complete discussion of the subject.

All that is necessary to know here is that a speech sound consists of a large number of components distributed throughout the audible frequency range. Due to the effect of certain resonant cavities of the mouth and throat, some of these components are considerably greater in amplitude than the others, and it is by noting at what frequencies these prominent components occur that the brain is able to distinguish one sound from another. Owing to the fact that the resonance of the mouth and throat give rather flat resonant curves, the prominent components occur in little groups of frequencies rather than as single isolated frequencies. This fact is clearly brought out by the frequency spectra given by Fletcher ([13]) and other authors for the different sounds.

Since it is by the position in the frequency range of these little groups or bands of frequencies that one sound is distinguished from another, they are called the characteristic bands of the sounds. Some sounds have only one characteristic band while others have as many as five.

The actual frequency components present in a given sound differ for different speakers, and even for one speaker they may differ from moment to moment. They always occur, however, in approximately the same frequency region or band. In order to make this clear, Figure 2 has been prepared. This shows two frequency spectra for an imaginary two band sound. In one case the fundamental cord tone of the speaker is assumed to be 200 periods per second. In this case the frequency components occur at intervals of 200 periods. In the second case the fundamental is assumed to be 100 periods per second, and in this case the components occur at intervals of 100 periods. In the second case, therefore, there are twice as many components as in the first case, but, owing to the fact that the prominent components still occur in the same frequency bands, the listener is able to recognise the two spectra as representing the same speech sound.

The next step in the development of the theory of articulation is to consider what happens when a conversation is taking place over a telephone circuit. As each sound is spoken at the transmitting end of the circuit, the various frequency components are transformed into electrical energy, are transmitted to the receiving end of the circuit with varying attenuation, and are finally reproduced at the listener's ear in a more or less distorted condition.

When the attenuation of the telephone circuit varies with frequency, the different characteristic bands arrive at the listener's ear with such distortion that he often mistakes one for another. A further factor tending to make it difficult for the listener to distinguish one sound from another is the presence of additional frequency components due either to noise in the telephone circuit or in the room, or to asymmetric distortion in the circuit.

Assume that, when an articulation test is carried out over a telephone circuit, the probability that the listener will receive a characteristic band correctly is, on the average, b. This means that, if it were possible to transmit the characteristic bands of speech one by one over the circuit, a fraction b of the bands would be correctly received. On the average, therefore, ceah band can be mistaken for $\frac{1}{b}$ other bands.

Now suppose that by some means it were possible to form at random groups of l characteristic bands from the total number of possible bands. These groups would not necessarily be actual sounds although some of them, of course, might happen to be. Suppose, also, that it were possible to produce these groups and to transmit them over a telephone circuit to the listener who has some means of recording what he thinks he has received.

Since b is the average probability of receiving a band correctly, the probability of receiving a group of l bands correctly is b^l. Hence there are $\frac{1}{b^l}$ alternatives for which the correct group of l bands can be mistaken. We can, therefore, consider the listener as setting out mentally the $\frac{1}{b^l}$ alternatives and just selecting one of them at random. The probability of his choosing the right alternative is, of course, b^l.

The next step is to assume that groups of l characteristic bands are being transmitted over a circuit but that, this time, each group is actually a sound and not a random group as before. Assume also that the listener knows he is to receive actual sounds and not random groupings. Then, as before, there will be $\frac{1}{b^l}$ alternatives from which the listener has to select one. This time, however, if he carries out his mental review of the $\frac{1}{b^l}$ possible alternatives, he will notice that some of them are not actual sounds. He thus rejects all these alternatives and is, therefore, left with a certain fraction of the $\frac{1}{b^l}$ alternatives which are actual sounds.

Of the total $\frac{1}{b^l}$ alternatives, one is the correct one and is, therefore, necessarily an actual speech sound. There are thus $\frac{1}{b^l} - 1$ alternatives which may or may not be actual sounds. The proportion of these alternatives which are actual sounds depends, of course, on the number of the total possible combinations which are used as sounds. Let this proportion be c_l for sounds having l characteristic bands.

Then $c_l\left(\frac{1}{b^l} - 1\right)$ of the $\frac{1}{b^l} - 1$ alternatives will be actual sounds. The listener is, therefore, left with the $c_l\left(\frac{1}{b^l} - 1\right)$ alternatives, plus the correct one, from which he has to make his choice. The probability that he will choose the correct one is, therefore,

$$\frac{1}{1 + c_l\left(\frac{1}{b^l} - 1\right)}$$

But the probability of his choosing the correct alternative is the sound articulation d_l, for sounds of l characteristic bands.

Hence

$$d_l = \frac{1}{1 + c_l\left(\frac{1}{b^l} - 1\right)}$$

From this it follows that the average ideal sound articulation for all sounds is given by the expression

$$d_i = \sum \frac{k_l}{1 + c_l\left(\frac{1}{b^l} - 1\right)}$$

where k_l is the proportion of sounds in speech having l characteristic bands and b is the average band articulation.

This expression thus gives the average ideal sound articulation for a given circuit in terms of

the average band articulation. The problem, therefore, resolves itself into the determination of the band articulation for the given circuit.

A statement was made in the previous section to the effect that, if b_{12} was the band articulation obtained over a circuit so arranged as to pass only frequencies in the range f_1 to f_2, and if b_{34} was the corresponding value for the range f_3 to f_4, then, if b_{1234} was the band articulation when both frequency ranges were passed together, these quantities were connected by the equation

$$b_{12} + b_{34} = b_{1234}$$

No conclusive theoretical proof of this relation has so far been discovered but, as the result of numerous tests, it has been found that this relation does hold in practice, except in certain limited cases which do not usually occur. These cases are mentioned in the section *Determination of Constants.*

In general, therefore, we can take the expression

$$b = \Sigma \, \Delta \, b$$

where Δ b is the band articulation for a small frequency region, and b is the total band articulation.

The factors that determine whether a given frequency region is transmitted from the speaker to the listener are:

(a) The amount of energy in this region produced by the speaker's voice.

(b) The attenuation of the circuit and apparatus transmitting the speech from the speaker's mouth to the listener's ear.

(c) The sensitivity of the listener's ear in the frequency range.

It should be noted that the effects of asymmetric distortion and noise are not considered here; they will be dealt with later.

If we determine the average relative amounts of energy present in the voice at different frequencies and express them as so many decibels above or below some given reference value, and then determine the average sensitivity of the are at different frequencies, also expressed in decibels above or below the same reference value, the difference between these two curves will give the average amount, in decibels, at different frequencies that the energy in the voice is above the minimum amount required to produce an audible sensation. In other words, this average speech level-threshold curve indicates the average amount by which a component of speech at a frequency f_1 must be attenuated before it becomes inaudible. This curve is shown in Figure 4.

If we assume for a moment that for all voices all the components in speech at a given frequency have the same level above threshold and that all ears have the same threshold value, then obviously, if we attenuate a given frequency by an amount greater than that given by the average speech level-threshold curve, that component will be inaudible, and will contribute nothing to the articulation. In order, therefore, to determine the articulation obtainable over a circuit having different amounts of attenuation at different frequencies, all we have to do is to determine what frequencies are attenuated so as to be below threshold, and what frequencies remain above threshold. Then we add up the value of Δ b for the frequency ranges above threshold, and so determine the total value of b for all frequency regions above threshold. Finally, we determine the corresponding value of the ideal sound articulation d_i, by means of the expression

$$d_i = \sum \frac{k_l}{1 + c_l \left(\frac{1}{b^l} - 1\right)}$$

It should be noted that in speaking here of the attenuation of a circuit, what is meant is the air-to-air attenuation of the circuit, so that this value includes not only the attenuation of the telephone circuit itself, but also of the transmitter and receiver.

Actually the method of determining the articulation for a circuit is not so simple as that described above. This is due to the following reasons:

(a) The ear threshold curves for individual listeners differ considerably from the average curve.

(b) The components, at a given frequency, for individual sounds differ from the average value at that frequency for all sounds.

(c) The loudness with which a speaker talks varies from speaker to speaker, and even in the case of a given speaker the loudness will vary from time to time.

The result of all these effects can best be under-

stood by considering a circuit arranged to pass only those frequency components within a range f_1 to f_2. Assume that a number of different speakers are taking it in turn to talk over the circuit, and that a number of listeners are taking it in turn to listen. Then assume that the attenuation of the circuit in the range f_1 to f_2 is gradually increased from zero to a very large value.

At first when the attenuation is small the components between f_1 and f_2 of the different sounds

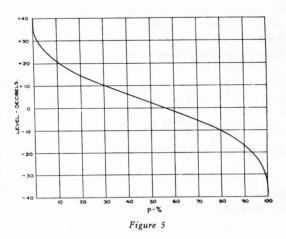

Figure 5

will be heard by all listeners and for all speakers. As the attenuation is increased those sounds which have only small components in the range f_1 to f_2 will fail to be heard, and even some of the louder components will fail to get through if they happen to be spoken by someone who speaks in a quiet voice, or if they happen to be received by someone who is rather deaf.

As the attenuation is increased, more and more of the components will fail to get through until finally the attenuation will be so great that no sounds at all will get through, even with the loudest speaker and the listener with the most acute hearing.

If we were to carry out an experiment of this nature, and were to determine for each level the percentage number of components that get through, we could plot a curve showing the number of components as a function of the level.

Such a curve is shown in Figure 5, the level in this case being expressed as so many decibels above or below the mean level above threshold.

The procedure in determining the articulation for a given circuit is then as follows: Divide the frequency range up into a number of small intervals, say, 100 periods. Consider the curve given in Figure 6, where Curve No. 1 is the average speech level-threshold curve given in Figure 4. Curve No. 2 is the air-to-air attenuation curve of the given circuit.

Consider one of the 100 period frequency bands f_1 to f_2. The ordinate A gives the average level of speech above threshold in this range f_1 to f_2. Ordinate C is the overall attenuation in this range introduced by the telephone circuit. Hence $B = A - C$ is the average level above threshold at which the speech arrives at the listener's ear.

Now, from the curve given in Figure 5, we can determine what proportion p of the components in speech between f_1 and f_2 are above threshold when the mean level in that range is B decibels above threshold. Since, for the interval f_1 to f_2, only p of the speech components are above threshold and b_{12} is the value of band articulation for the interval f_1 to f_2 when all components in the interval are above threshold, the probability of receiving a characteristic band correctly in the present case is pb_{12}.

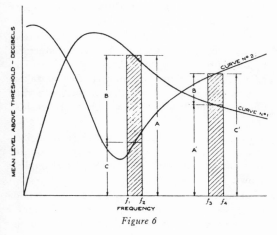

Figure 6

Hence the total band articulation is given by the expression

$$b = \Sigma \, p \, b$$

Having obtained the value of b in this way

the corresponding value of d^i is obtained from the expression

$$d^i = \sum \frac{k_l}{1 + c_l \left(\frac{1}{b^i} - 1 \right)}$$

So far only the effect of attenuation on the articulation of the circuit has been considered.

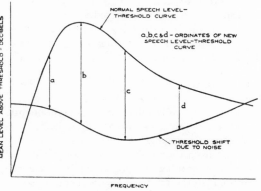

Figure 7

A second factor materially affecting the articulation is the presence of noise in the circuit due to crosstalk from some other circuit, induction from neighbouring power systems, bad contacts in some part of the circuit, or to some other cause.

Wegel and Lane ([2]) have shown that if a single frequency is introduced into the ear the effect is to raise the threshold for other frequencies in the neighbourhood. In other words, the amount of the second frequency which is required to give an audible sensation is greater when the first frequency is present than it is when the second frequency is introduced into the ear alone. The effect of a single frequency component on the ear is to set the basilar membrane into vibration. The amplitude of the vibration of the membrane is greater at one point and falls off on either side of this maximum point. This point of maximum amplitude of vibration varies according to the frequency which is causing the vibration.

Since the effect of introducing frequency components into the ear is to shift the threshold value by different amounts at different frequencies, the effect of noise on articulation can be taken into account by determining the amount of threshold shift produced by the noise. This modified threshold curve is then used to determine the speech level-threshold curve instead of the normal threshold curve used in Figure 4. In other words, a threshold shift of, say, 50 decibels at a given frequency is equivalent to increasing the attenuation of the circuit at that frequency by 50 decibels.

The threshold shift produced by a given complex tone can either be measured by an exploring tone, or, if the frequency spectrum of the noise is known, an approximate idea of the masking at various frequencies can be obtained in the following way:

The resultant masking of a complex tone is due, of course, to the combined effect of the masking by the individual frequency components. The threshold shift at different frequencies due to a given frequency at a given level can be obtained from the masking curves of Wegel and Lane. The problem is, therefore, how are the threshold shifts at a given frequency due to several different frequency components to be combined to give the resultant threshold shift.

Figure 8 represents what happens when an exploring frequency f_2 is used to determine the amount

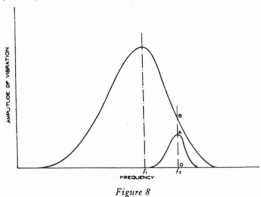

Figure 8

of masking at f_2 due to the frequency f_1. The level of the exploring frequency f_2 is increased until it is just audible in the presence of f_1. The height OB represents the amplitude of vibration of the basilar membrane at the point O due to the masking frequency f_1. The point O is the point of maximum amplitude of vibration of the membrane for the frequency f_2. Since the basilar membrane is already in movement at the point

O due to the presence of f_1, the introduction of the frequency f_2 has the effect of increasing the amplitude of vibration at the point O. If the level of f_2 is increased until f_2 is just audible in the presence of f_1, then OA is the amplitude of vibration due to f_2 which, when added to the existing amplitude of vibration OB, produces an increase in vibration which is just perceptible. Wegel and Lane state that the value of OA is approximately equal to OB. This means that the amplitude of vibration of the basilar membrane at a frequency f_2 due to a frequency f_1 is equal to the amplitude of vibration produced by an exploring frequency f_2 at such a level that it is just perceptible in the presence of f_1. The amplitude of vibration of the basilar membrane V in terms of the threshold amplitude, is, therefore, determined from the expression 20 $\log_{10}$ $V = S_t$, where S_t is the threshold shift given by the masking curves.

Having determined V for the different frequencies present in the masking tone, the resultant value V^1 is found by summing as the square root of the sum of the squares.

The corresponding value of resultant threshold shift S_t^1 is then determined from the expression 20 $\log_{10}$ $V^1 = S_t^1$. This procedure is repeated for any given point along the basilar membrane and so the resultant threshold shift frequency curve is obtained.

The effect of noise, then, is to raise the threshold by different amounts at different frequencies and so produce a new threshold curve. This effect can, therefore, be allowed for by taking this new threshold curve, instead of the normal one, when constructing the speech level-threshold curve.

In other words, the threshold shift in decibels at each frequency is added to the corresponding air-to-air attenuation in decibels. An example is shown in Figure 7.

In addition to the effect of ordinary distortion and noise on articulation, there is a third factor whose effect is rather in the nature of a combination of the first two. This third factor is asymmetric distortion which occurs when some part of the circuit departs from a linear characteristic. Some of the common causes of asymmetric distortion are overloading of iron cored coils and vacuum tubes, carbon microphones and overloading taking place in the ear.

Very little has been published on the question of asymmetric distortion and, owing to lack of time, not much work has been done on this subject in connection with the present study. The method of taking into account the effect on articulation of asymmetric distortion is therefore not very fully developed. So far as it has gone, however, it has given reasonable results, so a short description has been given here as a matter of interest.

The question of asymmetric distortion and its effect on articulation is a very important one, since all commercial telephone circuits are subject to a certain amount of such distortion. Further work on this subject is therefore being planned. In general, it can be said that the effect of asymmetric distortion is to produce in the circuit or ear all the harmonic series of any frequency originally present. As the amplitude of the original frequency increases, the amplitude of the harmonics due to asymmetric distortion increases very rapidly until the latter may become as large as the original frequency.

The effect of asymmetric distortion is similar to that of noise; that is to say, the harmonics cause masking of the speech components. There is the essential difference, however, that the effect varies with the volume of speech and depends on the particular sound being spoken. The masking curves published by Wegel and Lane[2] show that the masking effect of a given frequency on frequencies below it is small compared with the effect of the frequency on frequencies above it. This effect is due to the asymmetric distortion taking place in the ear.

Except at very large volumes, the amplitude of one frequency must be considerably greater than that of the second before the first will cause any appreciable masking of the second. We should expect, therefore, that it would only be in the case of those sounds that have a high level low frequency component and a low level high frequency component that the effect of asymmetric distortion would be noticeable. From an inspection of Fletcher's curves[13] of articulation against level for individual sounds, together with the list of frequencies and levels for the characteristic bands given in this paper, it will

be seen that this is the case. Sounds having only one characteristic band do not, therefore, show signs of the overloading of the ear, nor do sounds in which the different bands have about the same level.

From a knowledge of the relation between input and output voltage at different levels for any piece of apparatus causing asymmetric distortion, it is possible to calculate by simple mathematical formulae the magnitude of the different harmonics caused by asymmetric distortion when a given voltage is applied to the apparatus. These formulae are too well known to require to be given here. Once the magnitude of the harmonics is known, the masking effect when these harmonics are introduced into the ear is determined in the same way as for noise.

The effect of asymmetric distortion has only been considered, so far as this study has gone at present, in connection with the overloading effect taking place in the ear itself. In this case the method has given good results, but as to whether it would give equally good results for other types of asymmetric distortion has not yet been tried owing to the lack of the necessary data.

The method employed in connection with the overloading of the ear was as follows: Since the maximum level of speech above threshold occurs at about 1200 periods and is about 88 decibels, as shown in Figure 4, the effect of asymmetric distortion was considered as though it were due only to a 1200 period component. For any particular sound this will not give correct results, but on the average it does give results which agree with practical measurements. The level at which this 1200 period component arrives at the ear for any given circuit is 88 decibels minus any attenuation at that frequency produced by the circuit. The masking of other frequencies produced by this 1200 period tone is determined from the curves of Wegel and Lane, and the effect on articulation is determined in the same way as that described for noise. It should be noted, however, that the effect of asymmetric distortion only occurs in the case of about 10 of the 36 sounds, so that a resultant value of b is obtained by taking 10 times the value of b calculated with asymmetric distortion and 26 times the value without asymmetric distortion, adding the two together and dividing by 36. It will be obvious that there are a number of approximations and assumptions used in this method, but it would appear that they are permissible since they give results in good agreement with measured values. A further study of this part of the subject is being undertaken.

Determination of Constants

The formulae developed in the previous section for the calculation of the sound articulation were:

$$d_i = \sum \frac{k_l}{1 + c_l \left(\frac{1}{b^l} - 1\right)}$$

$$b = \Sigma \, p \, \Delta \, b$$

The following constants have, therefore, to be determined: p, Δb, l, c_l, and k_l.

In his book *Speech and Hearing*, Fletcher gives curves which show the variation of articulation for the different sounds when the cut-off frequency of his high quality circuit is changed. Two curves are given for each sound, one curve corresponding to the case when all frequencies from the given frequency to infinity are passed, and the other curve corresponding to the case when all frequencies from zero up to the given frequency are passed.

The high quality circuit was constructed so as to pass all speech components in the pass range without distortion, and to suppress entirely all components outside the pass range.

It will be seen that each pair of curves cross, or would cross if carried far enough, at a certain frequency. This crossing frequency is different for different sounds. The articulation corresponding to this crossing frequency is the value obtained either by passing all components from the crossing frequency to infinity, or by passing all components from zero to the crossing frequency. It follows that the value of β of the band articulation for all components from zero to the crossing frequency will be the same as the value of β for all components from the crossing frequency to infinity.

But the probability of receiving a band correctly when all frequencies are passed is unity in the ideal case. Hence, the value of β for either of the regions, zero to the crossing frequency, or crossing frequency to infinity, must be 0.5 since $\beta = \Sigma \, \Delta \, \beta$.

If d_i^1 is the articulation corresponding to the crossing frequency, then we can write the expression

$$d_i^1 = \frac{1}{1 + c_l \, (2^l - 1)}$$

This expression contains two unknowns, c_l and l. It would, of course, be possible to evaluate these two unknowns if we knew some other corresponding values of d and β. A second pair of values could be obtained, for instance, by dividing up the frequency range zero to the crossing frequency in such a way that the articulation for the range zero to the new frequency was the same as that for the range from the new frequency to the crossing frequency. We should then know that the value of β for either of these sub-ranges would be 0.25.

Since, however, no information of this nature is available, it is necessary to determine both l and c_l from the one relation; and fortunately this can be done.

It is found that c_l does not vary greatly for different values of l. It follows, therefore, from the expression

$$d_i^1 = \frac{1}{1 + c_l \, (2^l - 1)}$$

that the greater the value of l the smaller will be the value of d_i^1. Those sounds having the largest values of d_i^1 will, therefore, be one band sounds; the next largest will be two bands sounds, and so on. From an examination of various published oscillograms, and analyses of speech sounds, it is possible to determine fairly definitely how many bands there are in some of the sounds, and this information, together with the values of d_i^1 enables us to determine values of l for all the sounds. It is possible that in some instances errors may have occurred; but, owing to lack of sufficient data, it is impossible at the moment to determine the values in any more exact manner. It is probable, however, that the effect on the final result will be small due to any errors that may have occurred in this way. As soon as further data are available, these values can be checked.

Having obtained a value for l in this way, the value of c_l for each sound can be determined directly from the expression

$$d_i^1 = \frac{1}{1 + c_l\,(2^l - 1)}$$

The value of k_l, the fraction of the total number of sounds which has l bands, follows at once from the evaluation of l for the different sounds.

Finally, having determined the values of k_l, c_l, and l, the relation between d_i^1 and b can be evaluated from the expression

$$d_i = \sum \frac{k_l}{1 + c_l\left(\dfrac{1}{b^l} - 1\right)}$$

A curve for this expression has been worked out and is given in Figure 1.

In order to determine the value of Δb, which is the average probability of receiving a characteristic band correctly when a small frequency region f_1 to f_2 only is passed to the listener, use is made of the curve given in Figure 136 of *Speech and Hearing*. This curve gives the average syllable articulation for the high quality circuit for different cut-off frequencies. As was pointed out in a previous paper, [12] and as Fletcher himself points out, [13] the relation between sound and syllable articulation for his lists is given by the expression

$$s = 0.2\ d^2 + 0.8\ d^3$$

Hence, by using this expression and the curve between d_i and b just obtained, it is possible to obtain from Fletcher's syllable articulation against cut-off curves, corresponding curves of b against cut off.

Now, since $b = \Sigma\ \Delta b$, we can obtain the value of Δb for any frequency region f_1 to f_2 by determining values of b corresponding to f_1 and f_2 from either the low pass or high pass curves, and subtracting one from the other. If the theory developed here is correct, the corresponding values of Δb, determined from the two curves, high pass and low pass, should be the same. Actually this is the case for frequencies from O

up to 2500 periods. Above 2500 periods the frequency regions contribute less to articulation when frequencies from O to 1500 periods are present than they do when these latter frequen-

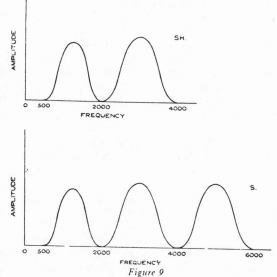

Figure 9

cies are absent. This is due to the frequency spectra of the sounds such as S and Z. Figure 9 illustrates the frequency spectra for S and SH. It will be clear from this that the ear is in the habit of associating the SH sound with two bands; one from 500 to 2000, and one from 2000 to 4000. The sound S is associated with three bands, the first two being approximately the same as for SH, while the third is from 4000 to 6000.

When frequencies from O to 2000 only are passed, the two sounds have very nearly the same spectra, but neither is the one usually presented to the ear. The listener, therefore, will not know whether a given sound is S or SH, but each will seem equally likely to him. He is thus likely to guess the sound as S 50% of the time, and as SH the other 50%.

When the range 2000 to 4000 is passed as well as the range O to 2000, the state of affairs is very different. Now the listener is receiving the whole spectrum for SH so that the articulation for this becomes 100%. When S is called, however, the listener receives very nearly the same spectrum as he is in the habit of associating with SH. Hence, for quite a large number of times he will mistake S for SH, so that the articulation of S will fall.

Finally, when the range 4000 to 6000 is passed as well as the other two, the listener receives the full spectrum for both S and SH.

When the region O to 2000 is absent, and only the region 2000 to 4000 is passed, the spectra for S and SH are the same, but neither are what the listener is used to receiving. The effect of the region 2000 to 4000 is now approximately the same for both sounds.

Hence, the value of the region 2000 to 4000, from the point of view of articulation, will depend for certain sounds on whether the region 500 to 2000 is present or not. If the latter is present, then the region 2000 to 4000, instead of helping articulation, actually hinders it. A similar state of affairs exists for certain other pairs of sounds.

Since for all practical circuits the region 500 to 2000 is present, it is the values of Δ b determined from the low pass curve that we should take. A curve giving values of Δ b for frequency bands of 100 periods is given in Figure 10, for

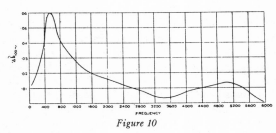

Figure 10

this case. For certain exceptional cases where the region 500 to 2000 is wholly or partially suppressed, it is necessary to take different values for Δ b in the region 2000 to 4000, but, since this so seldom occurs, it has not been necessary to go into the question more fully at the present time.

There only remains to be determined the value of p. If the speech components in a certain range f_1 to f_2 are passed from the speaker to the listener without distortion, but with a certain uniform attenuation, then, if a very large number of speakers take it in turn to talk to a very large

number of listeners, p is the fraction of the total number of conversations in which the region f_1 to f_2 reaches the listener at such a level to be above threshold. It is, therefore, the average probability that the region f_1 to f_2 will reach the listener above threshold, when the given loss is introduced in the region. Its value can, therefore, be obtained by determining for the given range f_1 to f_2 the probability that a speaker will have a mean speech level a given amount above or below the average of all speakers, the probability that a speech sound will have a level a given amount above or below the average for all sounds, and the probability that a listener's threshold will be a given amount above or below the average for all listeners, and then combining the three probability frequency curves.

Values for the variation from speaker to speaker were obtained from a curve published by Fletcher[5]. Values of the variation from sound to sound were obtained from the figures published by Sacia and Beck[9], on the assumption that the variations for the different frequency regions are the same as the variations of peak power. The variations of threshold from listener to listener were actually measured, since no data appeared to have been published.

The combined result of these three curves is given in Figure 5.

Apart from the constants which have now been evaluated, there still remains to be determined the speech level-threshold curve shown in Figure 4. This curve gives at each frequency the average level of speech components above threshold for initial speech intensity. It should be noted that we are only concerned here with those frequency components of the sounds which actually serve to distinguish one sound from another. The average level of these components for any frequency region is not necessarily the same as the average energy level for the same regions, because a sound may have quite a large amount of energy in some frequency region without this region contributing in any way to the articulation. It is not sufficient, therefore, to use the average energy spectrum for speech for determining the speech level-threshold curve, and it is necessary to arrive at the desired result by a rather roundabout method.

If the mean frequency and mean level above threshold could be obtained for each of the characteristic bands of speech, the speech level-threshold could be obtained by plotting points on frequency-level axes and drawing a mean curve through the points. This has been done, and the resulting curve is given in Figure 4. The method of obtaining the mean frequency and level for each characteristic band is by means of two sets of curves published by Fletcher[13]. The first, from which the mean frequency is obtained, is the set of curves giving articulation against cut-off frequency for the different sounds when transmitted over the high quality circuit.

From the relation

$$d_l = \frac{1}{1 + c_l \left[\frac{1}{\beta^l} - 1\right]}$$

a series of curves can be constructed from the articulation cut-off curves of Fletcher, giving β against cut-off frequency. For each sound there will be two curves corresponding to the high pass and low pass circuits.

If a one band sound is taken and the characteristic band is divided into two parts by a frequency f so that the value of β for each part is equal, i.e., $\beta = 0.5$, then the frequency f can be considered as the mean frequency of the band. Hence for one band sounds the mean frequency is taken as that frequency corresponding to a value of β of 0.5 on the curves just constructed.

For a two band sound the mean frequency of the first band is that frequency corresponding to a value of β of 0.25 on the low pass curve or 0.75 on the high pass curve. Similarly, the mean frequency of the second band corresponds to a value of β of 0.75 on the low pass curve or 0.25 on the high pass curve.

In a similar way the mean frequencies for a three band sound correspond to values of β of 0.166, 0.5 and 0.883, and so on for other numbers of bands.

The second set of curves, from which the mean levels of the different bands are determined, is the set giving the articulation against intensity level for each sound. As before, these curves are transformed into a corresponding set of curves giving β against intensity level.

For a one band sound the mean level is that corresponding to a value of β of 0.5.

For a two band sound, if the levels of the two bands are such that when the intensity level has been dropped so as to cut one band out entirely the whole of the other still remains above threshold, the mean levels correspond to values of β of 0.25 and 0.75, respectively.

If the two bands overlap as regards level, the above rules do not apply, and a different method must be used. It has been found that for one band sounds the shape of the curve of β against intensity level is approximately the same whatever the mean frequency of the band. In fact, this curve is merely the same curve as that previously given in Figure 5, since one curve gives the probability that a band will be received

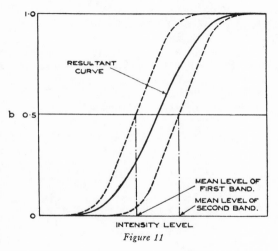

Figure 11

above threshold while the other gives the proportion of cases in which the components in a given frequency range will reach the listener at a level above threshold.

For a two band sound the curve of β against intensity level will be obtained by combining two of the curves for one band sounds, the two curves being placed so that the value of β of 0.5 in each case occurs at the mean level for the band. An example is shown in Figure 11. By trial and error it is possible to find for each of the two band sounds, the position of the two component curves such that the resultant curve fits the particular curve of β against level for the sound. The levels of the two bands of the sound are the same as the levels corresponding to the two component curves.

For sounds having a greater number of bands the same principle can be applied but with greater difficulty, of course.

In this way the mean frequency and mean level can be determined for each band in a sound, but, since the frequencies and levels are determined separately, there is no means of telling which particular level belongs to a particular frequency in the case of a multi-band sound. This difficulty was overcome partly by reference to oscillograms of the various sounds, and partly by the use of a curve giving the mean level of speech energy above threshold. This curve was obtained by combining the mean threshold curve and energy frequency spectrum of average speech given by Fletcher in his book, *Speech and Hearing*. This curve so obtained is not necessarily exactly the same as the curve giving the mean level above threshold of the characteristic bands of speech. It is, however, a sufficiently close approximation to it to enable us to allot the different levels to the different frequencies in this case.

LIST OF SOUNDS AND KEY WORDS

SOUND	KEY WORD	SOUND	KEY WORD
$\bar{\text{E}}$	ME	H	HE
E	GET	J	JUST
AH	PART	K	KICK
$\bar{\text{I}}$	MY	L	LET
I	IN	M	ME
$\bar{\text{A}}$	PAY	N	NO
A	AT	P	UP
$\bar{\text{O}}$	NO	R	RED
$\overline{\text{OO}}$	TOO	S	SO
OO	GOOD	T	IT
U	MUCH	V	GIVE
OW	HOW	W	WIN
AW	LAW	Y	YES
ER	HER	Z	PRIZE
B	BY	CH	WHICH
D	DO	SH	SHE
F	IF	TH	THAT
G	GET	EG	RING

In order to reduce the time required to calculate the articulation for a given circuit, values of p $\dot{\Delta}$ b have been worked out for each 100-period frequency region from O to 6000 periods

and for different values of overall attenuation. These values have been tabulated and a small section of the whole table is given below. This section is given merely to indicate the way in which the table is drawn up. The values in it are based only on the approximate determination of the constants, so that it was considered desirable not to give the complete table until the more exact evaluation of the constants has been completed.

The way in which the values of this table were obtained can be seen from Figure 6. Consider the frequency region f_1 to f_2 and let it be required to determine the value of p $\dot{\Delta}$ b for this region for an overall attenuation of C decibels. The average level above threshold A of speech components in the region f_1 to f_2 is known from the speech level-threshold curve, curve No. 1, Figure 6. Hence the value $B = A - C$ is obtained. From the curve of Figure 5 we know that if the speech components are B decibels below the mean curve, the value of p has a certain value. From the curve of Figure 10 we also know the value of $\dot{\Delta}$ b for the region f_1 to f_2. The value of p is multiplied by the value of $\dot{\Delta}$ b and the value is inserted in the table at the point corresponding to the frequency region f_1 to f_2 and the attenuation C.

Comparison of Calculated and Measured Results

In order to show with what accuracy the articulation can be calculated by the method described in this paper, a number of examples are given for which the articulation has been calculated and for which actual measured results are available. In judging these results, it should be remembered that the constants used in the calculated values of articulation are only approximate, so that when the final evaluation of these constants is made the agreement between measured and calculated results should be even better than it is now.

The examples which have been worked out here have been taken from Fletcher's book, *Speech and Hearing*, and the values he gives are the values of syllable articulation actually measured by his testing crews. The values of ideal sound articulation calculated by the method described

MEAN FREQUENCY AND LEVEL OF ARTICULATION BANDS

Sound.	No. of Bands.	Freq.	Level.	Freq.	Level.	Freq.	Level.	Freq.	Level.	Freq.	Level.
Ē	1	1575	90								
L	1	1000	80								
NG	1	1725	82								
Y	1	2125	84								
Ī	1	1425	87								
R	2	1250	85	2000	85						
I	2	600	92	2000	87						
Ā	2	500	93	1900	98						
D	2	1375	76	3125	71						
CW	2	900	98	1375	93						
O̅O̅	2	650	85	1900	85						
SH	2	1720	86	2700	86						
U̅	2	700	81	1225	101						
W	22	825	81	1125	86						
J	2	1050	82	2900	82						
A	2	875	93	2100	83						
H	2	1100	80	1575	50						
N	2	1000	85	3200	65						
AW	2	875	86	1375	106						
CH	2	1575	92	3250	62						
M	2	775	72	2000	67						
B	2	500	79	2375	59						
K	2	1375	78	3125	58						
G	2	1360	82	2625	62						
V	2	750	66	3000	46						
AH	2	790	92	2050	92						
T	2	1875	78	4500	68						
Z	2	1250	70	4250	45						
ER	3	750	98	1625	98	2400	93				
P	3	1075	85	1925	65	2750	50				
E	3	650	85	1000	85	1750	85				
F	3	1000	96	2250	66	4200	56				
U	3	625	84	1250	104	2125	78				
S	3	1350	60	2700	60	5500	60				
OO	4	250	69	800	105	1700	95	3000	79		
TH	5	200	20	625	110	1875	100	3800	70	6600	40

VALUES OF p Δ b.

FREQUENCY	OVERALL ATTENUATION (DECIBELS)							
	52–54	54–56	56–58	58–60	60–62	62–64	64–66	66–68
1200–1300	0206	0259	0258	0257	0255	0252	0249	0245
1300–1400	0240	0239	0238	0236	0234	0231	0228	0222
1400–1500	0220	0219	0218	0217	0215	0212	0209	0204
1500–1600	0199	0199	0198	0196	0194	0191	0188	0184
1600–1700	0189	0188	0187	0185	0183	0180	0176	0172
1700–1800	0178	0177	0175	0173	0171	0167	0164	0160
1800–1900	0168	0167	0165	0162	0160	0156	0153	0149
1900–2000	0157	0155	0153	0151	0147	0144	0140	0136
2000–2100	0150	0148	0146	0143	0140	0135	0131	0126
2100–2200	0140	0137	0134	0131	0128	0125	0121	0115
2200–2300	0129	0126	0123	0120	0116	0113	0107	0102
2300–2400	0118	0115	0113	0110	0104	0102	0098	0092
2400–2500	0107	0105	0102	0099	0097	0092	0088	0082
2500–2600	0096	0094	0090	0088	0084	0080	0075	0069
2600–2700	0090	0088	0085	0082	0078	0073	0068	0063
2700–2800	0079	0076	0074	0070	0066	0061	0057	0052

in this paper have, therefore, been converted to the corresponding ideal syllable articulation for comparison with Fletcher's results. The calculated values of syllable articulation will, of course, always be a little higher than the measured values because the calculated values are the ideal values and the measured are not. In most of Fletcher's results the measured values are very near the ideal values because his testing crews were so highly trained as to approximate very nearly to the ideal crew. In some cases sufficient information was available to enable the constant Z of Fletcher's crew to be determined; in these cases the actual measured results have been corrected to the corresponding ideal syllable articulation, using the method given in the appendix.

The cases worked out are as follows:

(1) The articulation for the high quality circuit at different intensity levels. The results are given in Figure 12. The measured curve is

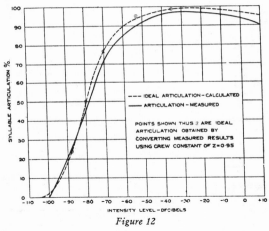

Figure 12

Fletcher's mean curve and the points are values of ideal syllable articulation obtained by correcting one set of his measured values using a crew constant of $Z = .95$. The crew constant of 0.95 was obtained by noting the value of articulation obtained by the crew at an intensity level of 75 decibels, since the value of b for this level is 0.5.

The measured curve, as would be expected, is a little lower than the calculated, but the corrected points lie very well on the calculated curve.

(2) The high quality circuit with a resonant circuit tuned to 1100 periods per second and a damping of 450 bels per second.

The calculated value of ideal syllable articula-

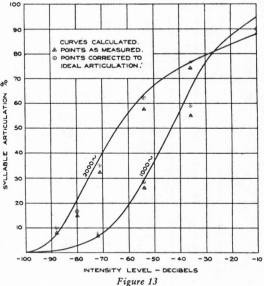

Figure 13

tion was 94% and the measured value was 92%.

(3) The same as above but with the resonant circuit having a damping of 35 bels per second.

The calculated value of ideal syllable articulation was 83.5% and the measured value was 80%.

(4) The high quality circuit with added 1000 period and 2000 period noise. The results are given in Figure 13.

The upper points were obtained by correcting the measured results with a crew constant of $Z = 0.95$. The lower points are the actual measured values.

The corrected figures are in good agreement with the calculated curves.

On the whole the measured and calculated results are in good agreement; where the actual crew constant could be obtained the agreement is still closer.

In the case of the upper parts of the curves given in Figures 12 and 13, and in the case of the values given for cases (2) and (3) the allowance for overloading had to be made. It appears to give reasonable results.

Conclusions

As pointed out at the beginning of this paper, the evaluation of the constants is approximate only, since it was carried out with the aid of such data as had been published, and was done in order to determine, before going more fully into the subject, whether the theory was capable of giving results in agreement with practice. This point should be kept in mind when considering the results since it explains differences which occur in some instances between calculated and measured results. In spite of the approximate values of the constants, the agreement between the calculated articulation and the measured values is, in most cases, quite good and within the limits of experimental error. There are, admittedly, still many points which require further investigation, and it is hoped in the course of the next year to devote time to the study of these points in addition to a more accurate evaluation of the constants.

In conclusion, it can be said that, except for minor modifications, the theory can be taken as representing the actual conditions with sufficient accuracy to enable it to be applied to the calculation of articulation in practical cases. Further, the tabular form in which the results have been presented makes it possible to calculate the articulation for a given circuit in a very short space of time. The use of the Ideal Sound Articulation as a criterion of the quality of speech obtainable over a circuit deserves some mention. This quantity is independent of errors due to the testing crew and is, therefore, a true measure of the characteristics of the circuit.

This fact, together with the easy method described here for converting the articulation as measured by a given crew to the corresponding ideal sound articulation, makes the Ideal Sound Articulation particularly useful as a measure of the performance of a telephone circuit. An added advantage is the fact that syllable articulation, word articulation, intelligibility and time efficiency can all be calculated from the Ideal Sound Articulation.

Before concluding this paper, the author would like to express his appreciation of the many papers written by members of the Bell Laboratories of America, to which constant reference has been made throughout this work. It is no exaggeration to say that without the results published in these papers, this preliminary demonstration of the accuracy of the theory could not have been made at the present time. In addition, thanks are due to those members of the staff of the Development and Research Laboratories of the International Telephone and Telegraph Corporation who have helped in the work and the preparation of this paper.

LIST OF SYMBOLS

b = Average band articulation for all sounds.
β = The band articulation for a given sound.
Δb = The value of b for a small frequency range f_1 to f_2.
l = Number of characteristic bands in a sound.
c_l = Constant depending on the total number of groups of l characteristic bands and the number of sounds having l characteristic bands.
k_l = Proportion of sounds in speech having l characteristic bands.
d_l = Sound articulation for sounds with l characteristic bands.
d_i = Average Ideal Sound Articulation.
d_i^1 = Value of d_i at frequency where high pass and low pass articulation-frequency curves cross.
d = Average sound articulation obtained by a given testing crew.
P = Proportion of speech components in a given range which are above threshold for a given level of speech.
Z = Crew Constant.
= Average probability that a given crew will receive a characteristic band correctly over a circuit for which $b = 1$.

BIBLIOGRAPHY

Where reference numbers occur in the text they refer to the correspondingly numbered work in this bibliography.
1. Physical Measurements of Audition and their Bearing on the Theory of Hearing. H. Fletcher. Bell System Technical Journal. October 1923.
2. Auditory Masking and Dynamics of the Inner Ear. R. L. Wegel and C. E. Lane. Physical Review. February 1924.
3. A Dynamical Study of the Vowel Sounds. I. B. Crandall and C. F. Sacia. Bell System Technical Journal. April 1924.
4. Dependence of Loudness of a complex Sound upon the Energy. H. Fletcher and J. C. Steinberg. Bell System Technical Journal. September 1924.
5. Useful Numerical Constants of Speech and Hearing. H. Fletcher. Bell System Technical Journal. July 1925.

6. The Loudness of Speech and its Physical Stimulus. J. C. Steinberg. Physical Review. October 1925.
7. Speech Power and Energy. C. F. Sacia. Bell System Technical Journal. October 1925.
8. The Sounds of Speech. I. B. Crandall. Bell System Technical Journal. October 1925.
9. The Power of Fundamental Speech Sounds. C. F. Sacia and C. J. Beck. Bell System Technical Journal. July 1926.
10. Dynamical Study of the Vowel Sounds. II. I. B. Crandall. Bell System Technical Journal. January 1927.
11. A Direct Comparison of the Loudness of Pure Tones. B. A. Kingsbury. Physical Review. April 1927.
12. A Theoretical Study of the Articulation and Intelligibility of a Telephone Circuit. John Collard. Electrical Communication. January 1929.
13. Speech and Hearing. H. Fletcher. Published by D. Van Nostrand Co., Inc.

[*Editor's Note*: The appendix on the calibration of articulation testing crew has been omitted.]

5

Reprinted from pp. 133–137 of *Phys. Rev.* **25**, ser. 2:133–138 (1925)

INTERFERING EFFECT OF TONES AND NOISE UPON SPEECH RECEPTION

By Vern O. Knudsen

Abstract

The interfering effect upon speech of tones and noise was measured by determining the percentage of vowel, consonant and word articulations correctly heard by an observer who listened in the presence of a tone or noise to meaningless monosyllables spoken at a distance of 2 meters. The interfering tones varied in pitch by octaves from C_2 (128 d.v.) to C_7 (4096 d.v.) and in loudness from slightly above minimal audibility to near the painful limit. The interfering effect increases with increasing loudness of tone or noise at an accelerated rate; for tones with a loudness less than the loudness of the speech, the effect is almost independent of the pitch, but as the interfering tone becomes louder, the tones of lower pitch produce a relatively greater and greater interference. These results are consistent with the auditory masking data of Fletcher, Wegel and Lane. A noise produces twice the interfering effect of a tone of the same loudness. These results indicate that for good hearing in an auditorium the speech energy should be from 1000 to 10,000 times the energy of any interfering noises, and that sound-absorbent materials for the reduction of noises in auditoriums should absorb equally tones of all pitches below C_7. Some experiments with rather deaf persons will be reported elsewhere.

THE work described in this paper is part of a larger program, the object of which is to determine quantitatively the influence of the various factors which affect the quality of speech in an auditorium. The specific object of the present problem, as the title suggests, is to determine (1) the relative interfering effect upon speech of tones of different pitch and loudness, and (2) the interfering effect upon speech of typical noises of different loudness.

Telephone engineers have done considerable work upon the interfering effect of noise upon speech transmitted over various types of telephone circuits. Up to the present, however, there has been very little published upon the subject. The work of the writer differs from the work done by telephone engineers in that the writer's tests are conducted in a typical small auditorium, and the observer listens directly to the voice of the speaker rather than to the speaker's voice transmitted over a telephone circuit.

The tests were all conducted in a room having a volume of 15,000 cubic feet and a period of reverberation of 1.3 seconds. The interfering tone or noise was conducted to the observer's ears by means of a pair of telephone receivers which were adjusted so that each receiver was at a fixed distance of 2 cm from the ear to which it was attached. The speaker, or "caller," spoke with a natural, easy, conversational voice, at a distance of two meters from the observer. The energy of the speech reaching the observer was slightly less than 10^5 times the minimal audible speech energy. Preliminary comparisons of the loudness of the speech with the loudness of tones of which the energy could be accurately determined, indicated that the loudness of the speech was approximately 47 logarithmic units.[1] This loudness of speech is comparable with the loudness of speech in an average auditorium.

The measurements were made by the usual method of articulation tests commonly used in testing the transmission efficiency of a telephone circuit. The "caller" called out meaningless consonant-vowel, vowel-consonant and consonant-vowel-consonant monosyllables, and the observer recorded what he heard, or thought he heard. By comparing the observer's lists with the lists called, the number and nature of the errors can be determined. The results of such tests are expressed as the percentage vowel articulation, the percentage consonant articulation, and the percentage "word" articulation.

The total number of speech-sounds called in making these tests was 29,000. These speech-sounds or "words" were called in groups of three, at the rate of one speech-sound each .85 of a second. Tests were made with interfering tones of C_2 (128 d.v.), C_3 (256 d.v.), C_4 (512 d.v.), C_5 (1024 d.v.), C_6 (2048 d.v.), and C_7 (4096 d.v.). Tests were also made with a typical noise as the interfering source. The interfering tones and the noises were maintained at various loudness levels, ordinarily at 20, 40, 60 and either 70 or 80 log-units. After many tests had been completed it was obvious that it was superfluous to take measurements below 40 log-units. 400 speech-sounds were called for each condition tested. Half were called by the writer, and the other half by an assistant. The observer and caller changed positions four times during the tests of each interfering condition. The tests with the same interfering source also were distributed over at least four different periods of observation. This would tend to make all of the results more nearly comparable. An indication of the uniformity of the speech and hearing of the two observers is the fact that the average percentage word articulation of one observer,

---

[1] This unit of loudness, proposed by telephone engineers, is very convenient. The loudness of the tone, expressed in this unit, is ten times the logarithm to the base ten of the ratio of the energy of the tone to the energy of a barely audible tone of the same pitch. For example, a tone whose energy is one million times the energy of a barely audible tone of the same pitch, is 60 log-units.

for the entire series, differed only two percent from the average of the other observer.

Results of the tests are shown in a series of curves, Figs. 1 to 3. Fig. 1 shows the results of the tests with tones as the interfering source. The percentage articulations for vowels, consonants and words are plotted as

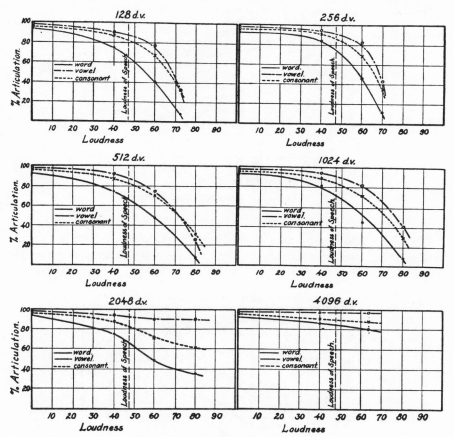

Fig. 1.   Interfering effect of tones.

a function of the loudness. Fig. 2 shows the results obtained with a noise consisting of a series of clicks in the telephone receivers, produced by interrupting a current flowing through an inductance in series with the telephone receivers. Curve (1) expresses the word articulation when the frequency of the clicks was 14 per second; curve (2) the word articulation when the frequency of interruption of the clicks was 20 per second. Fig. 3 indicates how the percentage articulations for vowels, consonants and words varied with the pitch of the interfering tone, at two different loudness levels, viz., 47 log-units, the loudness of the speech, and 70 log-units.

The conclusions which may be drawn from the data are as follows.

1.   The interfering effect of tones of which the loudness is less than the loudness of the speech, is almost independent of the pitch of the tones. However, for very high tones, above C_6 (2048 d.v.) the interfering effect seems to decrease as the pitch rises, so that tones above C_7 (4096

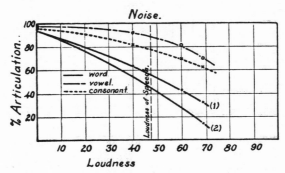

Fig. 2.   Interfering effect of noise.

d.v.) should have practically no interfering effect.   A tone of any pitch below C_6, equal in loudness to the speech loudness, reduces the word articulation to about seventy percent.   This may be seen from an inspection of Fig. 3.

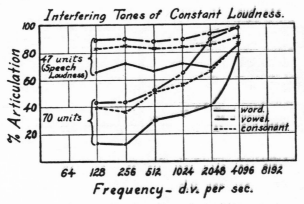

Fig. 3.   Variation of interfering effect with frequency.

2.   The interfering effect of tones whose loudness is greater than the loudness of the speech depends very much upon the pitch of the tones, decreasing markedly as the frequency increases.   For example, at 70 log-units, the vowel, consonant and word articulations for C_3 (256 d.v.) are 43 percent, 36 percent and 13 percent, and for C_7 (4096 d.v.) are 98

percent, 85 percent and 78 percent, respectively. This conclusion is consistent with the data of Fletcher, Wegel and Lane on the auditory masking of one tone upon another. As the interfering tones become louder, the non-linear response of the ear's mechanism introduces many combinational or "subjective" tones, all of which are higher in pitch than the fundamental. Hence, as tones of low pitch become louder, they introduce many combinational tones which will lie within the important speech range. On the other hand, the tones of high pitch will introduce combinational tones of which most will be above the important speech range; therefore, when the loudness of these tones is increased, the interfering effect does not increase nearly as rapidly as it does with an increasing loudness of low tones. These results are clearly indicated in Fig. 3. It is to be noted therefore that the interfering effect of the low frequency components of noises, provided the noises are loud, is greater than the interfering effect of the high frequency components.

3. The interfering effect of tones and noises, generally, is felt more in relation to consonants than to the vowels. However, low pitched interfering tones reduce the consonant articulation only slightly more than they do the vowel articulation, whereas high pitched tones reduce the consonant articulation very much more than they do the vowel articulation.

4. A noise produces a greater interfering effect than a tone of any pitch. Thus a typical noise, of loudness equal to the loudness of the speech, reduces the word articulation to about fifty percent, whereas any tone below C_6 (2048 d.v.) of the same loudness, reduces the word articulation to only about seventy percent.

5. From an inspection of Fig. 2 it will be seen that even a little noise reduces the word articulation appreciably. Roughly, it may be concluded that the speech must be at least 30 or 40 log-units louder than the noise if the noise is not to produce a harmful effect. Expressed in energy, the energy of the speech should be from 1000 to 10,000 times the energy of the interfering noises. This indicates the necessity for extreme reduction of noises in any auditorium.

6. A practical conclusion indicated by these data is that sound-absorbent materials for the reduction of noises in architectural interiors should absorb equally, tones of all pitch below C_7 (4096 d.v.). This, of course, is also desirable from the standpoint of having no distortion of speech or music.

[*Editor's Note*: Material has been omitted at this point.]

Part II

FACTORS AFFECTING SPEECH INTELLIGIBILITY

Editor's Comments
on Papers 6 Through 11

This section is concerned with the influences on speech intelligibility of various conditions that occur naturally or which can be introduced artificially to degrade it. The purpose of the studies considered here was usually one or more of the following: (1) to investigate the deleterious effects of a factor commonly encountered in communications, architecture, or audiology (e.g., noise in telephone lines, reverberation in rooms, high frequency hearing loss in the elderly), (2) to determine the loss in intelligibility performance associated with a change in equipment design (e.g., clippers in radio transmitters, compressors in hearing aids), (3) to obtain a better understanding of the speaking-listening system in man (e.g., delayed sidetone or dichotic listening). None of the investigators could improve on the intelligibility of unimpaired subjects talking at normal levels close together without electrical or mechanical aids in a quiet, non-reverberant space. The studies start with speech from unimpaired talkers (talkers with impairments are outside the scope of this volume) and end with listeners who usually have unimpaired hearing. In between almost anything can happen. Table 1 is an organized list of almost all of the disturbances reported in the papers cited in the bibliography. There are too many papers to classify them individually according to the factors in the table; usually the title adequately reveals the paper's scope. A few effects are not listed in the table. An interesting one is in the papers by Warren (1961, 1968) concerning the "verbal transformations" which occur when a single word or phrase is repeated so often that the listeners change their responses to a rhyme or a phonetic distortion of the stimulus. The editor's favorite distortion of them all is that of the combination of speaking as fast as possible while eating a submarine sandwich (Harris 1960). The consumption of part of the experimental equipment is guaranteed to prevent accurate replication!

Among the papers reproduced in this section, Paper 6 is one of the earliest journal articles from the Psycho-Acoustics Laboratory at Harvard University, where so much valuable, fundamental work was done during and after World War II. It exemplifies the high level of attention to experimental detail and insight into the results which made reports from this laboratory so helpful to other investigators. Paper 7 by Licklider and Pollack is a landmark in speech communications research because of its findings that the intelligibility of speech in quiet surroundings can be retained at a high percentage even if the wave form is distorted into a set of rectangular pulses. Such a distortion can double the rms speech power without increasing the power capacity of a transmitter. The process of infinite clipping also reduces the speech wave form to a sequence of binary states well suited to generation and processing by a digital computer; much of the later speech syntheses and analyses are based on the findings reported in this paper. Paper 8 is more important for the effect it had on understanding how the human hearing system works than for its influence on communications engineering, although some bandwidth compression systems have been based on this paper. The paper is particularly valuable for its treatment of both speech and noise and their interaction.

In Paper 9 Rosenzweig and Postman convincingly show that a listener's choice of response to a speech stimulus is related to the number of available alternatives which he has and their relative familiarity to him. It implies a weighted sorting process and has been used extensively in interpreting the results of other experiments. Paper 10 by Kimura is a landmark in the popular field of

Table 1. Factors Affecting Speech Intelligibility Treated in the Bibliography for Part II

Interference
    continuous white, pink, speech spectrum, aircraft, machinery noise
    impulsive, interrupted, fading, modulated noise
    sine waves, square waves, sawtooth waves
    competing messages, backwards speech
Speech processing
    high-pass, low-pass, band-pass, specially shaped filtering
    compression, expansion in time with or without frequency shift
    shifts, transposition, or inversion of frequencies
    compression, limiting in dynamic range
    center or peak clipping
    intermodulation or harmonic distortion
    interruption with different duty cycle, switching rate, gaps empty or filled
        with noise, same words, other words
Speech characteristics
    pitch, rate of speaking, vocal effort, inflection, regional or national accent,
        language, age, sex of speaker
Listener characteristics
    intelligence, motivation, vocabulary size, hearing impairments, speech
        impairments, native language, age and sex of listener
Speaking conditions
    reverberation time, sidetone with or without delay and level change
    in noise, high or low air pressure, helium, confining equipment
Listening conditions
    free field or on earphones
    in noise or competing messages from same or different azimuth
    reverberation time
    listening level, forward or backward masking
    monaural or binaural presentation, speech at same or different phase at
        two ears, noise at same or different phase
    signal simultaneous or delayed at two ears, with and without noise
    signal switched between ears at various rates, with and without noise
    different signals at two ears (dichotic listening)
    in noise, high or low air pressure, underwater, confining equipment
Combinations of all of the above

---

hemispheric specialization and has led to many investigations of the situations in which one ear identifies stimuli more accurately than the other and of the functions of the brain which are responsible for the effect. Paper 11 is the report of such an investigation in which another discovery, the "lag effect" is reported.

There is some unavoidable overlap between the studies surveyed in this part and those in later parts. Readers who are interested in speech intelligibility as a tool for testing communications equipment, for investigating hearing, and for research in speech perception and linguistics should look at the bibliographies of parts VII, VI, and VIII, respectively, in addition to the bibliography for this part, in which the following papers are particularly recommended to the reader: Agrawal (1975), Atkinson (1954), Black (1964), Bocca (1951), Cherry (1953), Dirks (1970), Dukes (1955), Egan (1946, 1957), Foulke (1969), Hirsh (1953, 1954, 1971), Horii (1971), House (1962), Kozlenko (1974), Lane (1971), Licklider (1946, 1948,

1950, 1957), Miller (1947), Nordlund (1963), Oekin (1963), Pickett (1956, 1958), Pollack (1948, 1954), Powers (1973), Shankweiler (1967), Speaks (1972, 1974), Webster (1962, 1964, 1965), and Williams (1971).

BIBLIOGRAPHY

Acton, W. I., "Speech Intelligibility in a Background Noise and Noise-Induced Hearing Loss," *Ergonomics* **13**:546–556 (1970).

Agrawal, A., and W. C. Lin, "Effects of Voiced Speech Parameters on the Intelligibility of PB Words," *J. Acoust. Soc. Am* **57**:217–222 (1975).

Ahmend, R., and R. Fatechand, "Effect of Sample Duration on the Articulation of Sounds in Normal and Clipped Speech," *J. Acoust. Soc. Am.* **31**:1022–1029 (1959).

Ainsworth, W. A., "Relative Intelligibility of Different Transforms of Clipped Speech," *J. Acoust. Soc. Am.* **41**:1272–1276 (1967).

Anonymous, "Issue Bibliography on Speech Compression," *J. Commun.* **18**:293–297 (1968).

Ansberry, M. "The Effect upon the Ability to Discriminate between Speech Sounds by the Elimination of Frequencies above 4000 Cycles," *Q. J. Speech* **24**:381–389 (1938).

Atkinson, C. J., "Some Effects on Intelligibility as the Sidetone Level and the Amount of Sidetone Delay Are Changed," *Proc. Iowa Acad. Sci.* **61**:334–340 (1954).

Bandet, L., "Propos sur le problème de l'intelligibilité de la parole," *Rev. de l'ouïe* **47**:71–75 (1972).

Barrasch, G., "Der Einfluss von Dynamik-Kompression und -Expansion auf die Sprachverständlichkeit," *Hochfrequenztech. u. Elektroakust.* **70**:187–195 (1961).

Beasley, D. S., B. S. Forman, and W. F. Rintelmann, "Perception of Time-Compressed CNC Monosyllables by Normal Listeners," *J. Aud. Res.* **12**:71–75 (1972).

Beasley, D. S., S. Schwimmer, and W. F., Rintelmann, "Intelligibility of Time-Compressed CNC Monosyllables," *J. Speech Hear. Res.* **15**:340–350 (1972).

Bennett, D. N., and V. W. Beyers, "Increased Intelligibility in the Hypacusic by Slow-Play Frequency Transposition," *J. Aud. Res.* **7**:107–118 (1967).

Black, J. W., "Accompaniments of Word Intelligibility," *J. Speech Hear. Disord.* **17**:409–418 (1952).

Black, J .W., "The Reception of Repeated and Overlapping Speech Patterns," *J. Acoust. Soc. Am.* **27**:494–496 (1955).

Black, J. W., "Equally Contributing Frequency Bands in Intelligibility," *J. Speech Hear. Res.* **2**:81–83 (1959).

Black, J. W., "Predicting the Intelligibility of Words," *Folia Phoniatr.* **12**:260–272 (1960).

Black, J. W., and J. G. Agnello, "The Prediction of the Effects of Combined Deterrents to Intelligibility," *J. Aud. Res.* **4**:277–284 (1964).

Black, J. W., and M. H. Hast, "Speech Reception with Altering Signal," *J. Speech Hear. Res.* **5**:70–75 (1962).

Black, J. W., and G. C. Tolhurst, "The Relative Intelligibility of Language Groups," *Q. J. Speech* **41**:57–60 (1955).

Black, J. W., and G. C. Tolhurst, "Intelligibility as Related to the Path of Airborne Side-Tone," *J. Speech Hear. Disord.* **21**:173–178 (1956).

Bladier, B., and F. Santon, "Sur la déformation de la parole dans les conditions de réverbération," *C.R. Acad. Sci. Paris* **B266**:367–369 (1968).

Blesser, B., "Speech Perception under Conditions of Spectral Transformation: I. Phonetic Characterisitcs," *J. Speech Hear. Res.* **15**:5–41 (1972).

Bocca, E., "Factors Influencing Binaural Integration of Periodically Switched Messages," *Acta Oto-Laryng.* **53**:142–144 (1961).

Bocca, E., and A. Pellegrini, "Studies on the Perception of the Distorted Voice," *Acta Oto-Laryng.* **39**:473–484 (1951).

Brandt, J. F., and H. Hollien, "Underwater Speech Reception Thresholds and Discrimination," *J. Aud. Res.* **8**:71–80 (1968).

Breakey M. R., and H. Davis, "Comparisons of Thresholds for Speech: ' Word in Sentence Test; Receiver vs. Field, and Monaural vs. Binaural Listening," *Laryngoscope* **59**:236–250 (1949).

Broadbent, D. E., *Perception and Communication*, Pergamon, London (1958).

Broadbent, D. E., and M. Gregory, "Accuracy of Recognition for Speech Presented to the Right and Left Ears," *Q. J. Exp. Psychol.* **16**:359–360 (1964).

Bruce, D. J., "Effects of Context upon Intelligibility of Heard Speech," in *Information Theory, Third London Symposium*, C. Cherry, ed., Butterworths, London (1956), pp. 245–252.

Bryden, M. P., "Ear Preference in Auditory Perception." *J. Exp. Psychol.* **65**:103–105 (1965).

Busch, A. C., and D. Eldredge, "The Effect of Differing Noise Spectra on the Consistency of Identification of Consonants," *Lang. and Speech* **10**:194–202 (1967).

Butyrskii, L. S., and B. I. Petlenko, "Structural Variations of Speech Produced in a Helium-Oxygen Medium," *Sov. Phys.—Acoust.* **19**:419–424 (1974).

Bykoff, S., "Soviet Work on the Theory of Intelligibility of Speech," *Bull. Acad. Sci.,USSR Phys. Ser.* **13**:728–732 (1949). in Russian.

Calearo, C., G. Teatini, and G. Pestalozza, "Speech Intelligibility in the Presence of Interrupted Noise," *J. Aud. Res.* **2**:179–186 (1962).

Caraway, B. .J., and R. Carhart, "Influence of Compressor Action on Speech Intelligibility," *J. Acoust. Soc. Am.* **41**:1424–1433 (1967).

Carhart, R., T. W. Tillman, and E. S. Greetis, "Perceptual Masking in Multiple Sound Background," *J. Acoust. Soc. Am.* **45**:694–703 (1969).

Carhart, R., T. W. Tillman, and K. R. Johnson, "Binaural Masking of Speech by Periodically Modulated Noise," *J. Acoust. Soc. Am.* **39**:1037–1050 (1966).

Carter, N. L., and K. D. Kryter, "Masking of Pure Tones and Speech," *J. Aud. Res.* **2**:66–98 (1962).

Ceypek, T., and J. Kuzniarz, "The Significance of Octave Frequency Bands for the Understanding of the Polish Language," *Otolaryngol. Pol.* **24**:429–433 (1970). in Polish, abs. in English.

Cherry, E. C., "Some Experiments on the Recognition of Speech, with One and Two Ears," *J. Acoust. Soc. Am.* **25**:975–979 (1953).

Cherry, E. C., and W. K. Taylor, "Some Further Experiments upon the Recognition of Speech, with One and Two Ears," *J. Acoust. Soc. Am.* **26**:554–559 (1954).

Chuang, C. K., S. Hiki, T. Sone, and T. Nimura, "Acoustical Features of the Four Tones in Monosyllabic Utterances of Standard Chinese," *J. Acoust. Soc. Japan* **31**:369–380 (1975). in Japanese, abs. and figs. in English.

Cohen, A., and S. K. Madden, "Intelligibility of "Double Talk"," *J. Aud. Res.* **2**:145–158 (1962).

Cole, R. A., "Listening for Mispronunciations: A Measure of What We Hear During Speech," *Percept. Psychophysiol.* **13**:153–156 (1973).

Cooper, J. C., Jr., and B. P. Cutts, "Speech Discrimination in Noise," *J. Speech Hear. Res.* **14**:332–337 (1971).

Corliss, E. L. R., E. D. Burnett, M. T. Kobal, and M. A. Bassin, "The Relative Importance of Frequency Distortion and Changes in Time Constants in the Intelligibility of Speech," *IEEE Trans. Audio Electroacoust.* **AU-16**:36–39 (1968).

Costermans, J., "L'intelligibilité du langage dans diverses bandes de bruit blanc," *J. Psychol. Norm. Pathol.* **2**:157–172 (1964).

Curry, F. F. W., "A Comparison of Left-Handed and Right-Handed Subjects on Verbal and Nonverbal Dichotic Listening Tasks," *Cortex* **3**:343–352 (1967).

Davis, H., "S. Smith Stevens 1906–1973," *J. Acoust. Soc. Am.* **53**:1190–1192 (1973).

Decroix, G., and J. Dehaussy, "Prothèse auditive en stéréophonie et intelligibilité," *J. fr. Oto-Rhino-Laryngol.* **11**:1035–1058 (1962). An English translation appeared as "Binaural Hearing and Intelligibility," *J. Aud. Res.* **4**:115–134 (1964).

Dirks, D. D., "Perception of Dichotic and Monaural Verbal Material and Cerebral Dominance for Speech," *Acta Oto-Laryngol.* **58**:73–80 (1963).

Dirks, D. D., and D. R. Bower, "Masking Effects of Speech Competing Messages," *J. Speech Hear. Res.* **12**:229–245 (1969).

Dirks, D. D., and D. R. Bower, "Effect of Forward and Backward Masking on Speech Intelligibility," *J. Acoust. Soc. Am.* **47**:1003–1008 (1970).

Dirks, D. D., and R. H. Wilson, "The Effect of Spatially Separated Sound Sources on Speech Intelligibility," *J. Speech Hear. Res.* **12**:5–38 (1969).

Dirks, D. D., R. H. Wilson, and D. R. Bower, "Effects of Pulsed Masking on Selected Speech Materials," *J. Acoust. Soc. Am.* **46**:898–906 (1969).

Dreher, J. J., and J. J. O'Neill, "Effects of Ambient Noise on Speaker Intelligibility for Words and Phrases," *J. Acoust. Soc. Am.* **29**:1320–1323 (1957).

Dukes, J. M. C., "The Effect of Severe Amplitude Limitation on Certain Types of Random Signals: A Clue to the Intelligibility of Infinitely Clipped Speech," *J. Inst. Electr. Eng.* **102C**:88–97 (1955).

Egan, J. P., "The Effect of Noise in One Ear upon the Loudness of Speech in the Other Ear," *J. Acoust. Soc. Am.* **20**:58–62 (1948).

Egan. J. P. "Monitoring Task in Speech Communication," *J. Acoust Soc. Am.* **29**:482–489 (1957).

Egan, J. P., E. C. Carterrette, and E. J. Thwing, "Some Factors Affecting Multichannel Listening," *J. Acoust. Soc. Am.* **26**:774–782 (1954).

Egan, J. P., and F. M. Wiener, "On the Intelligibility of Bands of Speech in Noise," *J. Acoust. Soc. Am.* **18**:435–441 (1946).

Ellis, L., A. J. Derbyshire, and M. E. Joseph, "Perception of Electronically Gated Speech," *Lang. and Speech* **14**:229–240 (1971).

Epstein, A., T. G. Giolas, and E. Owens, "Familiarity and Intelligibility of Monosyllabic Word Lists," *J. Speech Hear. Res.* **11**:435–438 (1968).

Ewing, G. D., and N. W. Huddy, Jr., "RF Clipping and Filtering to Improve the Intelligibility of Speech in Noise," *IEEE Trans. Audio Electroacoust.* **AU-14**:184–186 (1966).

Fairbanks, G., W. Everitt, and R. Jaeger, "Methods for Time or Frequency Compression-Expansion of Speech," *IRE Trans. Audio* **AU-2**:7–12 (1954).

Fairbanks, G., N. Guttman, and M. S. Miron, "Effects of Time Compression upon the Comprehension of Connected Speech," *J. Speech Hear. Disord.* **22**:10–19 (1957).

Fairbanks, G., and F. Kodman, "Word Intelligibility as a Function of Time Compression," *J. Acoust. Soc. Am.* **29**:636–644 (1957).

Fairbanks, C., and M. S. Miron, "Effects of Vocal Effort upon the Consonant-Vowel Ratio within the Syllable, *J. Acoust. Soc. Am.* **29**:621–626 (1957).

Feldmann, H., "Die Bedeutung des binauralen Hörens für die sprachliche Verständigung unter Lärmeinwirkung," *Acta Oto-Laryngol.* **59**:133–139 (1965).

Flanagan, J. L. "Effect of Delay Distortion upon the Intelligibility and Quality of Speech," *J. Acoust. Soc. Am.* **23**:303–307 (1951).

Foulke, E., and T. G. Sticht, "Review of Research on the Intelligibility and Comprehension of Accelerated Speech," *Psychol. Bull.* **72**:50–62 (1969).

Franklin, B., "The Effect of Consonant Discrimination of Combining a Low-Frequency Passband in One Ear and a High-Frequency Passband in the Other Ear," *J. Aud. Res.* **9**:365–378 (1969).

Friedman, H. L., and R. L. Johnson, "Compressed Speech: Correlates of Listening Ability," *J. Commun.* **18**:207–218 (1968).

Garstecki, D. C., and A. Mulac, "Effects of Test Material and Competing Message on Speech Discrimination," *J. Aud. Res.* **14**:171–178 (1974).

Garvey, W. D., "The Intelligibility of Abbreviated Speech Patterns," *Q. J. Speech* **39**:296–306 (1953).

Garvey, W. D., "The Intelligibility of Speeded Speech," *J. Exp. Psychol.* **45**:102–108 (1953).

Gay, T., "Effects of Filtering and Vowel Environment on Consonant Perception," *J. Acoust. Soc. Am.* **48**:993–998 (1970).

Gerber, S. E., "Phase and Speech Discrimination in Noise: An Expectation and First Look," *Int. Audiol.* **6**:397–400 (1967).

Gerber, S. E., "Dichotic and Diotic Presentation of Speeded Speech," *J. Commun.* **18**:272–282 (1968).

Gerber, S. E., and P. Goldman, "Ear Preference for Dichotically Presented Verbal Stimuli as a Function of Report Strategies," *J. Acoust. Soc. Am.* **49**:1163–1168 (1971).

Gilbert, H. R., and J. H. Saxman, "The Use of Learning Rate, Recall and Listener Confidence Ratings to Assess Effects of Acoustically Distorted Speech Stimuli," *Lang. and Speech* **17**:337–346 (1974).

Gjaevenes, K., and T. Schoel, "Masking of Speech by "White" and "Pink" Wide-Band Noise," *J. Aud. Res.* **7**:31–34 (1967).

Gray, S. F., and R. C. Berry, "Intelligibility of Speech in Noise with Varying Amounts of Interaural Time Delay," *J. Aud. Res.* **14**:203–207 (1974).

Hahn, R., and G. Demichels, "L'audition de messages concomitants chez les sujets avec prothèse auditive," *Int. Audiol.* **6**:307–310 (1967).

Halle, M., *For Roman Jakobson*, Mouton, The Hague (1956).

Harris, J. D., "Combinations of Distortion in Speech," *Arch. Otolaryngol.* **72**:227–232 (1960).

Hecker, M. H. L., K. N. Stevens, G. von Bismark, and C. E. Williams, "Manifestation of Task-Induced Stress on the Acoustic Speech Signal," *J. Acoust. Soc. Am.* **44**:993–1001 (1968).

Hecker, M. H. L., K. N. Stevens, and C. E. Williams, "Measurement of Reaction Time in Intelligibility Tests," (L) *J. Acoust. Soc. Am.* **39**:1188–1189 (1966).

Hirsh, I. J., "The Relation between Localization and Intelligibility," *J. Acoust. Soc. Am.* **22**:196–200 (1950).

Hirsh, I. J., Masking of Speech and Auditory Localization," *Audiol.* **10**:110–114 (1971).

Hirsh, I. J., and W. D. Bowman, "Masking of Speech by Bands of Noise," *J. Acoust. Soc. Am.* **25**:1175–1180 (1953).

Hirsh, I. J., E. G. Reynolds, and M. Joseph, "Intelligibility of Different Speech Materials," *J. Acoust. Soc. Am.* **26**:530–538 (1954).

Hogan, D. D., and T. D. Hanley, "Some Effects of Listener Accuracy of Competing Messages Varied Systematically in Number, Rate, and Level," *J. Acoust. Soc. Am.* **35**:293–295 (1963).

Holloway, C. M., "Added Noise Enhances Intelligibility after Removal of Weakly Voiced Components," *Nature* **226**(5241):178–179 (1970).

Holloway, C. M., "Some Effects of Noise on a Speech Communication Task," *Sound* **6**:27–31 (1972).

Hopkinson, N. T., "Combined Effects of Interruption and Interaural Alternation on Speech Intelligibility," *Lang. and Speech* **10**:234–243 (1967).

Horii, Y., A. S. House, and G. W. Hughes, "A Masking Noise with Speech-Envelope Characteristics for Studying Intelligibility," *J. Acoust. Soc. Am.* **49**:1849–1856 (1971).

House, A. S., K. N. Stevens, T. T. Sandel, and J. B. Arnold, "On the Learning of Speechlike Vocabularies," *J. Verbal Learn. Verbal Behav.* **1**:133–143 (1962).

Huggins, A. W. F., "Distortion of the Temporal Pattern of Speech: Interruption and Alternation," *J. Acoust. Soc. Am.* **36**:1055–1064 (1964).

Katz, S. J., and R. C. Berry, "Recognition of Speech Modulated Noise," *J. Aud. Res.* **11**:120–123 (1971).

Keith, R. W., and H. P. Talis, "The Effects of White Noise on PB Scores of Normal and Hearing-Impaired Listeners," *Audiology* **11**:177–186 (1972).

Kelly, J. C., and M. D. Steer, "Intelligibility Testing in Three Conditions Involving Masking Noise," *J. Speech Hear. Disord.* **14**:369–372 (1949).

65

Kimura, D., "Some Effects of Temporal-Lobe Damage on Auditory Perception," *Can. J. Psychol* **15**:156–165 (1961).

Kimura, D., and S. Folb, "Neural Processing of Backward-Speech Sounds," *Science* **161**:395–396 (1968).

Klumpp, R. G., and J. C. Webster, "Intelligibility of Time Compressed Speech," *J. Acoust. Soc. Am.* **33**:265–267 (1961).

Klumpp, R. G., and J. C. Webster, "Physical Measurements on Equally Speech-Interfering Navy Noises," *J. Acoust. Soc. Am.* **35**: 1328–1338 (1963).

Kozlenko, N. I., and R. N. Ryzhkova, "Articulation Characteristics of Extremally Coded Speech," *Sov. Phys.—Acoust.* **19**:238–240 (1973).

Kozlenko, N. I., and R. N. Ryzhkova, "Articulation Characteristics of Extremally Encoded Speech with Two-Band Filtering '" *Sov. Phys.—Acoust.* **20**:29–31 (1974).

Kruel, E. J., "Speech Intelligibility for Interaural Alternated Speech with and without Intervening Noise for Words and Nonsense," *Lang. and Speech* **14**:99–107 (1971).

Kryter, K. D., "Effects of High Altitude on Speech Intelligibility," *J. Appl. Psychol.* **32**:503–520 (1948).

Kryter, K. D., "The Effects of Noise on Man," *J. Speech Hear. Disord. Mono. Suppl. 1* (1950).

Kryter, K. D., *The Effects of Noise on Man*, Academic Press, New York (1970).

Kurtović, H., "The Influence of Reflected Sound upon Speech Intelligibility," *Acustica* **33**:32–39 (1975).

Kuźniarz, J., "Masking of Speech by Continuous Noise," *Otolaryngol. Pol.* **21**:401–407 (1967). in Pol, abs. in English, English translation appears in *Pol. Med. J.* **7**:1001–1008 (1968).

Kuźniarz, J., "Importance of Higher Frequencies of the Speech Spectrum for Its Comprehension in Noise," *Otolaryngol. Pol.* **22**:427–435 (1968). in Polish, abstract in English.

Kuźniarz, J., "Masking of Speech by Means of Impulse Noise," *Otolaryngol. Pol.* **22**:421–425 (1968). in Polish, abstract in English.

Lane, H., "Foreign Accent and Speech Distortion, *J. Acoust. Soc. Am.* **35**:451–453 (1963).

Lane, H., and B. Tranel, "The Lombard Sign and the Role of Hearing in Speech," *J. Speech Hear. Res.* **14**:677–709 (1971).

Lehmann, R., "Contribution à l'étude du masquage de la parole," H34 in *Proc. 4th Int. Cong. Acoust.* Copenhagen (1962).

Lehmann, R., "L'influence de mode de présentation des stimuli dans le masquage de la parole par un bruit blanc," *C.R. Acad. Sci. Paris* **255**:2832–2834 (1962).

Lehmann, R., "Quelques données relatives à l'intelligibilité du langage dans le silence," *J. fr. Oto-Rhino-Laryngol.* **11**: 877–888 (1962).

Lehmann, R., "L'influence de la fréquence d'interruption des signaux sur l'intelligibilité du langage parlé," *C.R. Acad. Sci. Paris* **261**:5653–5656 (1965).

Levitt, H., and L. Rabiner, "Binaural Release from Masking for Speech and Gain in Intelligibility," *J. Acoust. Soc. Am.* **42**:601–608 (1967).

Licklider, J. C. R., "Effects of Amplitude Distortion upon the Intelligibility of Speech," *J. Acoust. Soc. Am.* **18**:429–434 (1946).

Licklider, J. C. R., "The Influence of Interaural Phase Relations upon the Masking of Speech by White Noise," *J. Acoust. Soc. Am.* **20**:150–159 (1948).

Licklider, J. C. R., "The Intelligibility of Amplitude-Dichotomized, Time Quantized Speech Waves," *J. Acoust. Soc. Am.* **22**:820– 823 (1950).

Licklider, J. C. R., D. Binda, and I. Pollack, "The Intelligibility of Rectangular Speech-Waves," *Am. J. Psychol.* **61**:1–20 (1948).

Licklider, J. C. R., and N. Guttman, "Masking of Speech by Line-Spectrum Interference," *J. Acoust. Soc. Am.* **29**:287–296 (1957).

Licklider, J. C. R., and G. A. Miller, "The Perception of Speech," in *Handbook of Experimental Psychology*, S. S. Stevens, ed. Wiley, New York (1951).

Lowe, S. S., J. K. Cullen, Jr., C. I. Berlin, C. L. Thompson, and M. E. Willett, "Perception of Simultaneous Dichotic and Monotic Monosyllables," *J. Speech Hear. Res.* **13**:812–822 (1970).

MacKeith, N. W., and R. R. A. Coles, "Binaural Advantages in Hearing of Speech, "*J. Laryngol. Otol.* **85**:213–232 (1971).

Mantel, J., "Untersuchungen zur Verständlichkeit amplitudenbegrenzten und im Frequenzband reduzierter Sprache," *Frequenz* **26**:70–77 (March 1972).

Martin, D. W., R. L. Murphy, and A. Meyer, "Articulation Reduction by Combined Distortions of Speech Waves," *J. Acoust. Soc. Am.* **28**:597–601 (1956).

Maspétiol, R., A. Robert, and D. Semette, "La valeur d'intelligibilité des différent frequences," *Ann. otolar.* (Paris) **73**:812–824 (1956).

Matsuda, R., "Tonal Differential Limen of the Speech Transmission System Containing Single Dip in Frequency-Response," in *Rep. of 6th Int. Cong. Acoust.*, Y. Kohasi, ed., Maruzen, Tokyo (1968), pp. A109–A112.

Miller, G. A., "The Masking of Speech, " *Psychol. Bull.* **44**:105–129 (1947).

Miller, G. A., "Speech and Language," in *Handbook of Experimental Psychology*, S. S. Stevens, ed., Wiley, New York (1951).

Miller, J. D., "The Effects of Noise on People, " *J. Acoust. Soc. Am.* **56**:729–764 (1974).

Moncur, J. P. and D. Dirks, "Binaural and Monaural Speech Intelligibility in Reverberation," *J. Speech Hear. Res.* **10**:186–195 (1967).

Moray, N., "The Effect of the Relative Intensities of Dichotic Messages in Speech Shadowing," *Lang. and Speech* **1**:110–113 (1958).

Morrow, C. T., "Speech in Deep Submergence Atmospheres," *J. Acoust. Soc. Am.* **50**:715–728 (1971).

Moser, H. M., J. J. Dreher, and S. Adler, "Comparison of Hyponasality, Hypernasality, and Normal Voice Quality on the Intelligibility of Two-Digit Numbers," *J. Acoust. Soc. Am.* **27**:872–874 (1955).

Myasnikov, L. L., E. N. Miasnikova, and M. Y. Pekel'nyi, "Infrasonic Cues for the Automatic Recognition of Speech Sounds," *Sov. Phys.— Acoust.* **14**:522–524 (1969).

Nábělek, A. K., and J. M. Pickett, "Reception of Consonants in a Classroom As Affected by Monaural and Binaural Listening, Noise, Reverberation, and Hearing Aids," *J. Acoust. Soc. Am.* **56**:628–639 (1974).

Nachchon, I., and A. Carmon, "Stimulus Familiarity and Ear Superiority in Dichotic Listening," *J. Acoust. Soc. Am.* **57**:223–227 (1975).

Nakatsui, M., and J. Suzuki, "Perceptual Nature of Helium Speech," *J. Acoust. Soc. Japan* **30**:477–485 (1974). in Japanese, English abstract and figures.

Neely, K. K., and S. E. Farshaw, "Speaking and Listening through the Head: 1. The Intelligibility of Speech Recorded in Quiet at Different Positions on the Head and Throat," *J. Aud. Res.* **5**:151–157 (1965).

Nixon, C. W., "Influence of Selected Vibrations upon Speech. I. Range of 10 cps to 50 cps.," *J. Aud. Res.* **2**:247–266 (1962).

Nordlund, B., and B. Fritzell, "The Influence of Azimuth on Speech Signals," *Acta Oto-Laryngol.* **56**:632–642 (1963).

Nowicki, J., "Understandability of the Polish Language Depending on the Frequency Band," *Otolaryngol. Pol.* **26**:7–14 (1972). in Polish, English abstract.

Oekin, F. W., "Untersuchungen über das Sprach- und Sprachlautverständnis bei Frequenztransponierung," *Phonetica* **10**:92–109 (1963).

Ohta, F., N. Yanagihara, and I. Hosoda, "Intelligibility of Interrupted Japanese Vowels," *Stud. Phonol.* **4**:56–69 (1966).

Orr, D. B., and H. L. Friedman, "Effect of Massed Practice on the Comprehension of Time-Compressed Speech," *J. Educ. Psychol.* **59**:6–11 (Feb. 1968).

Oyer, H. J., H. M. Moser, and S. M. Wolfe, "Relationship of Phonetic Structure to the Intelligibility of Words Simultaneously Recorded at Ear and Lips," *J. Speech Hear. Res.* **3**:44–51 (1960).

Peterson, G. E., E. Siversten, and D. L. Subrahmanyam, "Intelligibility of Diphasic Speech," *J. Acoust. Soc. Am.* **28**:404–411 (1956).

Pickett, J. M., "Effects of Vocal Force on the Intelligibility of Speech Sounds," *J. Acoust. Soc. Am.* **28**:902–905 (1956).

Pickett, J. M., "Limits of Direct Speech Communication in Noise," *J. Acoust. Soc. Am.* **30**:278–281 (1958).

Pickett, J. M., and I. Pollack, "Intelligibility of Excerpts from Fluent Speech: Effects of Rate of Utterance and Duration of Excerpt," *Lang. and Speech* **6**:151–164 (1963).

Plomp, R., "Binaural and Monaural Speech Intelligibility of Connected Discourse in Reverberation as a Function of Azimuth of a Single Competing Source (Speech or Noise)," *Acustica* **34**:200–211 (1976).

Pollack, I., "Effects of High Pass and Low Pass Filtering on the Intelligibility of Speech in Noise," *J. Acoust. Soc. Am.* **20**:259–266 (1948).

Pollack, I., "On the Effects of Frequency and Amplitude Distortion on the Intelligibility of Speech in Noise," *J. Acoust. Soc. Am.* **24**:538–540 (1952).

Pollack, I., "The Masking of Speech by Repeated Bursts of Noise," *J. Acoust. Soc. Am.* **26**:1053–1055 (1954).

Pollack, I., "Speech Intelligibility at High Noise Levels: Effect of Short Term Exposure," *J. Acoust. Soc. Am.* **30**:282–285 (1958).

Pollack, I., "Message Reception and Message Repetition," *J. Acoust. Soc. Am.* **31**:1509–1515 (1959).

Pollack, I., "Reaction Times to Unknown Word Sets in Noise," *Lang. and Speech* **6**:189–195 (1963).

Pollack, I., and L. Decker, "Consonant Confusions and the Constant Ratio Rule," *Lang. and Speech* **3**:1–6 (1960).

Pollack, I., and J. M. Pickett, "Effect of Noise and Filtering on Speech Intelligibility at High Levels," *J. Acoust. Soc. Am.* **29**:1328–1329 (1957).

Pollack, I., and J. M. Pickett, "Interaural Effects upon Speech Intelligibility at High Noise Levels," *J. Acoust. Soc. Am.* **30**:293–296 (1958).

Pollack, I., and J. M. Pickett, "Masking of Speech by Noise at High Sound Levels," *J. Acoust. Soc. Am.* **30**:127–130 (1958).

Pollack, I., and J. M. Pickett, "Stereophonic Listening and Speech Intelligibility against Noise Babble," *J. Acoust. Soc. Am.* **30**:131–133 (1958).

Pollack, I., and J. M. Pickett, "Intelligibility of Peak-Clipped Speech at High Noise Levels," *J. Acoust. Soc. Am.* **31**:14–16 (1959).

Pollack, I., H. Rubenstein, and L. Decker, "Intelligibility of Known and Unknown Message Sets," *J. Acoust. Soc. Am.* **31**:273–279 (1959).

Pollack, I., H. Rubenstein, and L. Decker, "Analysis of Incorrect Responses to an Unknown Message Set," *J. Acoust. Soc. Am.* **32**:454–457 (1960).

Powers, G. L., and C. Speaks, "Intelligibility of Temporally Interrupted Speech," *J. Acoust. Soc. Am.* **54**:661–667 (1973).

Reid, R. H., "Grammatical Complexity and Comprehension of Compressed Speech," *J. Commun.* **18**:236–242 (1968).

Repp, B. H., "Dichotic Masking of Consonants by Vowels," *J. Acoust. Soc. Am.* **57**:724–735 (1975).

Riedel, P., "Über den Einfluss des Rühörpegels auf Tonhöhe und Lautstärke beim Sprechen," *Frequenz* **16**:44–49 (1962).

Rosenzweig, M. R., "Intelligibilité, visibilité et fréquence des mots," *Cah. Etud. Radio-Telev.* **12**:283–289 (1956).

Rosenzweig, M. R., and L. Postman, "Frequency of Usage and the Perception of Words," *Science* **127**:263–266 (1958).

Rubenstein, H., L. Decker, and I. Pollack, "Word Length and Intelligibility," *Lang. and Speech* **2**:175–178 (1959).

Rupf, J. A., G. W. Hughes, and A. S. House, "Effect of Interaural Switching on the Recognition of Speech Sounds," *J. Acoust. Soc. Am.* **51**:1304–1308 (1972).

Santon, F., "Mesure de coefficient de perception dans des conditions de réverbération, à l'aide d'une méthode de corrélation," *C.R. Acad. Sci. Paris* **B266**:311–313 (1968).

Sapozhkov, M. A., "Factors Determining Speech Intelligibility," *Telecommun. Radio Eng.* **25**:122–124 (1971).

Sato, T., "Some Results of the Articulation Test for Various Combinations of Bandpass Filters," *J. Acoust. Soc. Japan* **14**:159–164 (1958). in Japanese, abstract in English.

Schindler, O., G. Demichelis, and R. Piazza, "Considerazioni sull'indice d'intelligibilità verboacustica in rapporto alle dimensioni di frequenze della banda passante," *Minerva otorinolaringol.* **18**:113–122 (1968).

Schindler, O., G. Demichelis, and R. Piazza, "Intelligibilité du message vocal filtré par bandes d'intensité," *Audiol.* **12**:142–147 (1972).

Schmidt, K. O., "Eine Betrachtung über die Aufbauelemente der Sprache (Vokale und Konsononten) und ihre Anteile an der Silbenverständlichkeit," *Arch. Elektr. Übertrag.* **7**:579–584 (1953).

Schubert, E. D., "Some Preliminary Experiments on Binaural Time Delay and Intelligibility," *J. Acoust. Soc. Am.* **28**:895–901 (1956).

Schubert, E. D., and M. C. Schultz, "Some Aspects of Binaural Signal Selection," *J. Acoust. Soc. Am.* **34**:844–849 (1962).

Schultz, M. C., "Word Familiarity Influences in Speech Discrimination," *J. Speech Hear. Res.* **7**:395–400 (1964).

Scott, R. J., "Time Adjustment in Speech Synthesis," *J. Acoust. Soc. Am.* **41**:60–65 (1967).

Sen, T. K., "Masking of Crosstalk by Speech and Noise," *Bell Syst. Tech J.* **49**:561–584 (1970).

Sergeant, R. L., "Concurrent Repetition of a Continuous Flow of Words," *J. Speech Hear. Res.* **4**:373–380 (1961).

Shankweiler, D., and M. Studdert-Kennedy, "Identification of Consonants and Vowels Presented to Left and Right Ears," *Q. J. Exp. Psychol.* **19**:59–69 (1967).

Sharf, D. J., "Intelligibility of Reiterated Speech," *J. Acoust. Soc. Am.* **31**:423–427 (1959).

Singh, S., and J. W. Black, "A Study of Nonsense Syllables Spoken by Two Language Groups in Varying Conditions of Sidetone and Reading Rate," *Lang. and Speech* **8**:208–213 (1965).

Singh, S., and J. W. Black, "Study of Twenty-Six Intervocalic Consonants as Spoken and Recognized by Four Language Groups," *J. Acoust. Soc. Am.* **39**:372–387 (1966).

Smith, G. M., "The Effect of Prolonged Mild Anoxia on Speech Intelligibility," *J. Appl. Psychol.* **30**:255–264 (1946).

Smith, G. M., and C. P. Seitz, "Speech Intelligibility under Various Degrees of Anoxia," *J. Appl. Psychol.* **30**:182–191 (1946).

Speaks, C. A., J. Jerger, and S. Jerger, "Performance-Intensity Characteristics of Synthetic Sentences," *J. Speech Hear. Res.* **9**:305–312 (1966).

Speaks, C. A., and J. L. Karmen, "The Effect of Noise on Synthetic Sentence Identification," *J. Speech Hear. Res.* **10**:859–864 (1967).

Speaks, C. A., J. L. Karmen, and L. Benitez, "Effect of a Competing Message on Synthetic Sentence Identification," *J. Speech Hear. Res.* **10**:390–396 (1967).

Speaks, C., B. Parker, C. Harris, and P. Kuhl, "Intelligibility of Connected Discourse, " *J. Speech Hear. Res.* **15**:590–602 (1972).

Speaks, C., and T. T. Trooien, "Interaural Alternation and Speech Intelligibility," *J. Acoust. Soc. Am.* **56**:640–644 (1974).

Spreen, O., and A. R. Boucher, "Effects of Low Pass Filtering on Ear Asymmetry in Dichotic Listening and Some Uncontrolled Error Sources," *J. Aud. Res.* **10**:45–51 (1970).

Sticht, T. G., "Some Relationship of Mental Attitude, Reading Ability, and Listening Ability Using Normal and Time Compressed Speech," *J. Commun.* **18**:243–258 (1968).

Strong, R. A., V. G. Chant, S. E. Forshaw, and K. K. Neely, "Speaking and Listening through the Head: II. The Intelligibility of Speech Recorded in Noise," *J. Aud. Res.* **6**:385–391 (1966).

Studdert-Kennedy, M., and D. Shankweiler, "Hemispheric Specialization for Speech Perception," *J. Acoust. Soc. Am.* **48**:579–594 (1970).

Sumby, W. H., "On the Choice of Strategies in the Identification of Spoken Words Mixed with Noise," *Lang. and Speech* **5**:119–124 (1962).

Sumby, W. H., "The Control Tower Language: A Case Study of a Specialized Language-in-Action," *Lang. and Speech* **3**:61–70 (1960).

Takefuta, Y., and E. Swigart, "Intelligibility of Speech Signals Spectrally Compressed by a Sampling-Synthesizing Technique'" *IEEE Trans. Audio Electroacoust.* **AU-16**:271–274 (1968).

Tarnóczy, T., "Nouvelle méthode pour la determination du spectre de la parole," *Fol. Phoniatr.* **8**:65–70 (1956).

Thomas, I. B., "The Influence of First and Second Formants on the Intelligibility of Clipped Speech," *J. Aud. Eng. Soc.* **16**:182–185 (1968).

Thomas, I. B., and R. J. Niederjohn, "Enhancement of Speech Intelligibility at High Noise Levels by Filtering and Clipping," *J. Aud. Eng. Soc.* **16**:412–415 (1968).

Thompson, P. O., and J. C. Webster, "The Effect of Talker-Listener Angle on Word Intelligibility," *Acustica* **13**:313–323 (1963).

Thompson, P. O., and J. C. Webster, "The Effect of Talker-Listener Angle on Word Intelligibility. II. In an Open Field," *Acustica* **14**:44–49 (1964).

Thompson, P. O., J. C. Webster, and R. S. Gales, "Liveness Effects on the Intelligibility of Noise-Masked Speech," *J. Acoust. Soc. Am.* **33**:604–605 (1961).

Tiffany, W. R., and D. N. Bennett, "Intelligibility of Slow-Played Speech," *J. Speech Hear. Res.* **4**:248–258 (1961).

Tiffany, W. R., and D. N. Bennett, "Phonetic Distortions in the Serial Transmission of Short Speech Samples," *J. Speech Hear. Res.* **11**:33–48 (1968).

Tolhurst, G. C., "Effects of Duration and Articulation Changes on Intelligibility, Word Reception and Listener Preference," *J. Speech Hear. Disord.* **22**:328–334 (1957).

Tolhurst, G. C., and R. W. Peters, "Effect of Attenuating One Channel of a Dichotic Circuit upon the Word Reception of Dual Messages," *J. Acoust. Soc. Am.* **28**:602–605 (1956).

Traul, G. N., and J. W. Black, "The Effect of Context on Aural Perception of Words," *J. Speech Hear. Res.* **8**:363–369 (1965).

Velichkin, A. I., "Amplitude Clipping of Speech, " *Sov. Phys.—Acoust.* **8**:130–134 (1962).

Voor, J., and J. Miller, "The Effect of Practice upon the Comprehension of Time-Compressed Speech," *Speech Monogr.* **32**:452–454 (1965).

Warren, R. M., "Illusory Changes of Distinct Speech upon Repetition—The Verbal Transformation Effect," *Brit. J. Psychol.* **52**:249–258 (1961).

Warren, R. M., "Verbal Transformation Effect and Auditory Perceptual Mechanism," *Psychol. Bull.* **70**:261–270 (1968).

Wathen-Dunn, W., and S. B. Michaels, "Some Effects of Gas Density on Speech Production," *Ann. N.Y. Acad. Sci.* **155**:368–378 (1968).

Webster, J. C., "Generalized Speech Interference Noise Contours," *J. Speech Hear. Res.* **7**:133–140 (1964).

Webster, J. C., "Speech Communication as Limited by Ambient Noise," *J. Acoust. Soc. Am.* **37**:692–699 (1965)

Webster, J. C., and R. G. Klumpp, "Effects of Ambient Noise and Nearby Talkers on a Face-to-Face Communication Task," *J. Acoust. Soc. Am.* **34**:936–941 (1962).

Weiss, M. S., and A. S. House, "Perception of Dichotically Presented Vowels," *J. Acoust. Soc. Am.* **51**:51–58 (1973).

Weston, P. B., J. D. Miller, and I. J. Hirsh, "Release from Masking for Speech," *J. Acoust. Soc. Am.* **38**:1053–1054 (1965).

Willaims, C. E., and M. H. L. Hecker, "Relations between Intelligibility Scores for Four Test Methods and Three Types of Speech Distortion," *J. Acoust Soc. Am.* **44**:1002–1006 (1968).

Williams, C. E., K. S. Persons, and M. H. L. Hecker, "Speech Intelligibility in the Presence of Time-Varying Aircraft Noise," *J. Acoust. Soc. Am.* **50**:426–434 (1971).

Wilson, R. H., and R. Carhart, "Influence of Pulsed Masking on the Threshold for Spondees," *J. Acoust. Soc. Am.* **46**:998–1010 (1969).

Winkel, F., "Die psychoakustische Bewertung des Spektrums," *Fol. Phoniatr.* **12**:129–136 (1960).

Wise, C. , and L. P. -H. Chong, "Intelligibility of Whispering in a Tone Language," *J. Speech Hear. Disord.* **22**:335–338 (1957).

Yamamura, K., and A. Okada, "Studies on the Masking of Speech by White Noise," *Jpn. J. Hyg.* **26**:321–324 (1971). in Japanese, English abstract.

Yegnanarayana, B., and B. S. Ramakrishna, "Intelligibility of Speech under Nonexponential Decay Conditions," *J. Acoust. Soc. Am.* **58**: 853–857 (1975).

Zemlin, W. R., R. G. Daniloff, and T. H. Shriner, "The Difficulty of Listening to Time-Compressed Speech," *J. Speech Hear. Res.* **11**:875–881 (1968).

Zwicker, E., "Die elementaren Grundlagen zur Bestimmung der Information-kapazität des Gehörs," *Acustica* **6**:365–381 (1956).

6

Reprinted from *Acoust. Soc. Am. J.* **18**:418–424 (1946)

The Masking of Speech by Sine Waves, Square Waves, and Regular and Modulated Pulses*

S. S. Stevens, Joseph Miller, and Ida Truscott

Psycho-Acoustic Laboratory, Harvard University, Cambridge, Massachusetts

(Received June 1, 1946)

The ability of three standard wave forms to mask speech, by raising its threshold of perceptibility, was measured as a function of the intensity and frequency of the masking signal. Depending on the other parameters of the interfering signal, optimal masking is produced when the fundamental frequency lies in the range 100 to 500 c.p.s. Intense sine waves mask best when their frequency is about 300 c.p.s., whereas for weaker sine waves the most effective frequency is about 500 c.p.s. Square waves are less critical as to frequency and intensity; fundamental frequencies between about 80 and 400 c.p.s. mask with approximately equal effectiveness. Pulses of 10-microsecond duration are most effective at a prf of about 200 p.p.s. When the time interval between successive pulses is made irregular (random interval-modulation), their ability to mask speech is dramatically increased. The increase in masking is a function of the original prf, the rate of modulation (determined by the spectrum of the modulating voltage), and the range of modulation. By a proper adjustment of the parameters of its random interval-modulation the train of pulses can be made to sound like a band of white noise.

INTRODUCTION

IT is well known that the presence of an extraneous sound raises the threshold level at which speech is just perceptible. The number of decibels by which the threshold level is raised defines the *masking* produced by the interfering tone or noise. It was the purpose of these experiments to determine the manner in which the masking of speech is related to the parameters of three types of interfering signal: sine waves, square waves, and pulses. It was also desired to compare the masking produced by steady trains of pulses with that produced by pulses subjected to a form of modulation involving a randomization of the time intervals between successive pulses.

The procedure involved simply the measurement of the faintest levels of speech at which the meaning of connected discourse could be followed by trained listeners exerting attentive effort. The minimal level thus determined is defined as the *Threshold of Perceptibility*, and experience has shown that normal listeners agree with one

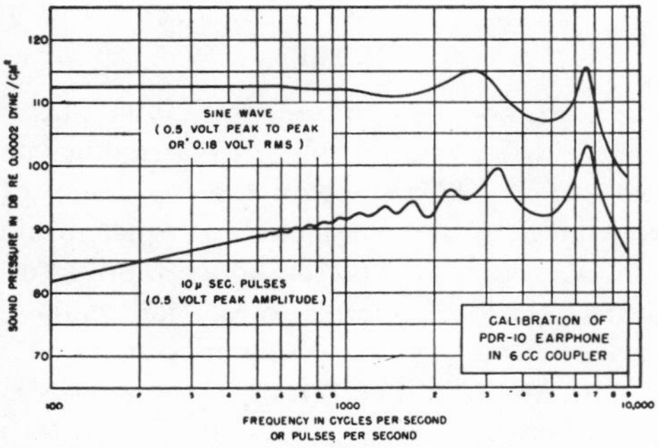

FIG. 1. Showing the sound-pressure level generated in a 6-cc coupler by a PDR-10 earphone driven by sine waves and by pulses of constant voltage amplitude. Measurements were made with a condenser microphone, Western Electric Type 640-A, and a thermocouple meter (Sensitive Resistance Instrument Company, Model A). The maxima in the pulse curve fall at submultiples of the upper cut-off frequency.

* This research, begun under an OSRD contract, is continuing under contract with the U. S. Navy, Office of Research and Inventions (Contract N5ori-76-II, Report PNR-14). Other members of the Psycho-Acoustic Laboratory who contributed to various phases of the present project were A. Dix Brown, James P. Egan, Wendell R. Garner, J. C. R. Licklider, and George A. Miller.

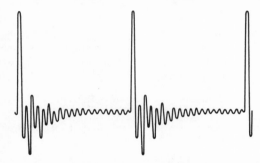

FIG. 2. Showing the wave form of the acoustic pressure produced by 10-microsecond pulses.

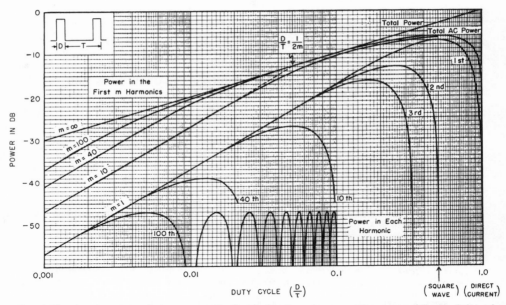

FIG. 3. Showing the power relations among the harmonics of a pulse wave. The peak amplitude of the pulses is assumed to be constant at the value corresponding to 0 db on the ordinate. The upper group of curves gives the total power in various numbers of the harmonics of the pulse. The lower group of curves shows the behavior of individual harmonics as the duty cycle is changed.

another within about 3 db when they are required to set the level of speech at this threshold by adjusting an attenuator.[1] Most of the datum points on the graphs presented below are based on the averages of five such settings by each of two listeners. The speech to which they listened was transduced from high fidelity recordings of passages from Adam Smith's *The Wealth of Nations*, chosen for its uniform level of difficulty and interest. When interfering signals were used, they were mixed electrically with the speech, and this mixture was transduced and brought to the ears of the listeners by a matched pair of PDR-10 earphones connected in series. Calibration curves for one of the earphones are shown in Fig. 1. Both sine waves and pulses were used as the calibrating signals. The curve for 10-microsecond pulses lies below that for the sine wave by an amount that is predictable on the basis of the *duty cycle* (ratio of duration to period) of the pulse.

The form of the acoustic wave generated in the 6-cc calibrating coupler and picked up by the 640-A condenser microphone is shown in Fig. 2. The basic frequency of the wiggles in this pulse wave corresponds to the cut-off frequency of the earphone (about 6600 c.p.s.).

PULSES

In a train of pulses having individual durations as short as 10 microseconds, all harmonics of the basic prf which fall within the frequency range transduced by the earphone are equal in amplitude, and as an aid to the understanding of the power relations among these harmonics the curves in Fig. 3 were prepared by Mr. A. Dix Brown. Among other things, these curves show that for each doubling of the prf the power in a single harmonic of a pulse wave, having pulses of fixed duration and amplitude, grows at the rate of 6 db. This growth continues until the duty cycle approaches a value equal to the reciprocal of the number of the harmonic. Thus the second harmonic vanishes when the pulse becomes a square wave (duty cycle = 0.5). It is also shown in Fig. 3 that, with the prf held

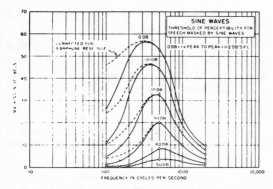

FIG. 4. Showing the amount by which various pure tones mask speech, as measured by the change in the threshold of perceptibility. The curve for 0 db corresponds to a sound-pressure level of the masking tone equal to 112 db. All measurements were made binaurally.

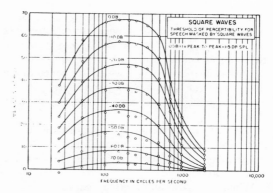

FIG. 5. The masking of speech by square waves.

constant, the power in an individual harmonic grows 6 db for each doubling of the pulse duration, again until the duty cycle approaches the critical value.

The upper curves in Fig. 3 show how the power grows when various numbers (m) of the harmonics are added together. For a constant pulse duration the total a.c. power ($m = \infty$) grows at the rate of 3 db for each doubling of the prf, until the duty cycle approaches approximately 0.1. When smaller numbers of harmonics are considered, the power grows 6 db for each doubling of the prf, until the duty cycle approaches the value $1/2m$. This value is useful in determining the position of the power curve for a group of harmonics, because it is at a value of the duty cycle equal to $1/2m$ that the straight portion of the power curve intersects the curve defining total a.c. power.

Finally, it can be determined from Fig. 3 that, when a train of pulses of constant duration and amplitude is passed through a system having a fixed upper cut-off frequency, the total power in the wave grows 3 db for each doubling of the prf. The lower curve in Fig. 1 exhibits this relation. Actually, the growth in power is of a cyclical nature, because as the prf increases the individual harmonics of the pulse are successively eliminated by the upper cut-off frequency of the system. Hence the wavy appearance of the curve in Fig. 1.

RESULTS

The masking of speech by sine waves, square waves, and pulses is shown in Figs. 4–6. In order to compare these wave forms on the basis of a common measurement the peak-to-peak voltage amplitude of the wave was used in all cases. This voltage was impressed on the two earphones connected in series, and half of the total voltage appeared across each earphone. With the aid of the calibration curves in Fig. 1 the sound-pressure level (SPL) corresponding to a given voltage may be ascertained.

The dashed portion of the curves for sine-wave masking (Fig. 4) indicates a correction for the loss of sound pressure due to leakage around the earphone cushion at low frequencies. With the small sponge-rubber cushions (MX-41/AR) this leakage amounts to about 9 db at 100 c.p.s.

It is interesting to note that for weak intensities the maximal masking is produced by sine waves in the vicinity of 500 c.p.s., whereas at high intensities the greatest masking occurs near 300 c.p.s. This effect is presumably caused by the rapid upward spread of masking as the intensity of the masking tone is increased.[2] This upward spread is presumably aided by the fact that distortion in the ear produces aural harmonics at high sound levels.

As shown in Fig. 5, square waves are more effective in masking speech than are sine waves.

[2] R. L. Wegel and C. E. Lane, "The auditory masking of one pure tone by another and its probable relation to the dynamics of the inner ear," Phys. Rev. **23**, 266–285 (1924). Cf. also R. Galambos and H. Davis, "The response of single auditory-nerve fibers to acoustic stimulation," J. Neurophysiol. **6**, 39–58 (1946).

When the two waves are equated for sound-pressure level, this difference in effectiveness amounts to about 7 db at 300 c.p.s. Owing to the richer harmonic structure of the square wave, it masks effectively over a wider frequency range than does the sine wave, particularly at the lower frequencies. The same is true of pulses, as shown in Fig. 6.

The optimal masking prf for pulses is about 200 p.p.s. and this optimum appears to be independent of intensity, as is also the case for square waves.

When the parameters of the curves in Fig. 6 are transformed, with the aid of Fig. 1, from voltage amplitude to sound-pressure level, the optimal prf for masking shifts slightly downward. Also, when compared on the basis of SPL the pulse wave is, as we should expect, the most effective of the three wave forms for masking speech. At 200 p.p.s. and 90-db SPL the pulse is about 7 db more effective than the square wave.

It should be noted, however, that at the higher frequencies 1000 and 2000 c.p.s., all three wave forms mask approximately equally when equated for SPL. At 2000 c.p.s. and above all wave forms are very ineffective maskers of speech.

The duration of the pulse used to obtain the curves of Fig. 6 was arbitrarily set at 10 microseconds. But masking curves for other durations can be derived directly from those in Fig. 6 on the basis of the assumption that masking is a function of the product of duration and amplitude. This reciprocity was tested for durations from 2.5 to 40 microseconds. (prf = 250) and found to hold precisely, i.e., in order to maintain constant masking, the amplitude of the pulse had to be reduced to one-half whenever the duration of the pulse was doubled. For much longer durations, of course, this simple relation would not hold, for the duty cycle would increase beyond the range in which the power in the 26 harmonics of the 250 p.p.s. transduced by the earphone grows 6 db for each doubling of the duty cycle. In general, the expected relations between masking and pulse duration can be predicted with fair approximation from Figs. 5 and 6 with the aid of Fig. 3, provided proper weighting is given to the masking efficiency of the various harmonics of the pulse.

PULSE-INTERVAL MODULATION

Although interference to speech communication in the form of trains of evenly spaced pulses is sometimes encountered, a more common form of interference is radio static, which involves pulses randomly distributed in time. It was of interest, therefore, to explore systematically the effect of irregularity in the spacing between the pulses in a train. This irregularity was achieved by one type of what is commonly called *pulse-time modulation*.

Since any one of several parameters of a pulse may be modulated to produce a form of pulse-time modulation, we are faced here with a minor problem of terminology. As a solution to this problem it is proposed that the term pulse-time modulation be used as the generic term for any time-variation in any of the parameters of a pulse wave in which the pulses are of constant amplitude. Then in order to distinguish further among the varieties of time modulation we may use a scheme in which the name given to a type of modulation is based on the parameter held constant during the modulation process. It is necessary to consider the parameter which is held constant rather than a parameter that is being modulated, because in general it is impossible to modulate one parameter without modulating others. Table I summarizes these considerations and suggests appropriate names.

Thus when in addition to the amplitude, the duration of the pulse is held constant while other parameters are varied the resulting effect is called *pulse-interval modulation*. This is the variety used in the following experiments.

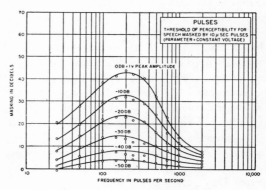

FIG. 6. The masking of speech by pulses.

MODULATING PROCEDURE

In order to modulate in an irregular fashion the intervals between pulses having constant amplitudes and durations, a commercial pulse generator (Colonial Radio, Model 700-A) whose prf is normally controlled by an externally impressed sine wave was so arranged that it could be controlled by means of an irregular wave derived from an electronic "noise" generator—a gas tube producing a random "white" noise having a continuous, flat spectrum. Actually, the noise voltage was made first to modulate the frequency of a special square-wave generator (multivibrator) which in turn controlled the pulse generator. Figure 7 shows the general arrangement of the apparatus, including the provision for mixing the recorded speech signal with the interfering pulses.

When the prf of a pulse wave is modulated by an alteration of the interval between pulses, two dimensions of the modulation must be considered—and controlled: (a) the *rate* of the modulation and (b) the *degree* or range of the modulation. In the present system these two aspects were controlled by the frequency and the amplitude of the noise voltage at the output of the variable filter which followed the noise generator (Fig. 7). The filter passed a band of frequencies whose value determined the rate of the interval modulation, i.e., how fast the prf was made to change; and the voltage of this signal determined the degree of the modulation, i.e., by how much the prf was altered by the modulation process. The degree of modulation is conveniently expressed as the percentage change relative to the initial prf of the pulse. Thus 100-percent modulation means that the prf is made to change from a value equal to twice the original prf to a value corresponding to the lowest prf the system is able to pass (in this case about 20 p.p.s.). These changes take place at a rate equal to the fre-

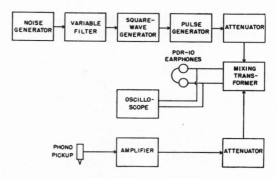

Fig. 7. Schematic arrangement of apparatus.

quency of the modulating signal. And if proper care is taken, the *average* prf of the modulated pulses can be kept identical with the original, unmodulated prf.

Since the modulating signal of interest here is a portion of a random noise spectrum, the net result of its use is a random scattering of the pulses. This scattering tends to spread the energy continuously over the spectrum, and a uniform distribution of the energy in the spectrum of the pulse wave is essentially achieved when the degree of modulation is 100 percent and the rate is that produced by a band of modulating frequencies extending from about 20 c.p.s. to a frequency corresponding to half the prf being modulated. The limitation of the modulating band to half the prf is necessary in order to keep the average prf constant at its unmodulated value. Thus for the purpose of modulating a prf of 2000 p.p.s. the optimal modulating band is that between 20 and 1000 c.p.s., and it is with this rate and degree of modulation that the greatest masking of speech is achieved. The spectrum resulting from pulses modulated in this manner is continuous and essentially uniform over a wide frequency range. To the ear this signal sounds very much like white noise itself.

The effects of different degrees of interval modulation are shown in Fig. 8. For each prf tested the modulation rate was optimal, i.e., it comprised the frequencies from 20 c.p.s. to half the original prf. The unmodulated pulses give a masking curve similar to those in Fig. 6, and the process of interval modulation clearly increases the masking effectiveness. Among the prf's tested the most dramatic increase occurs

TABLE I.

Kind of modulation	Parameter held constant (k)			
	Period T	duration d	interval i	duty-cycle d/T
Frequency				k
Duration			k	
Interval		k		
Ratio	k			

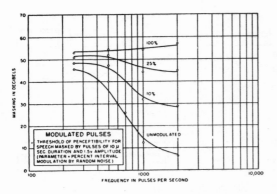

FIG. 8. The effect of random interval-modulation on the masking produced by pulses of constant amplitude. The abscissa gives the average prf of the pulses. For each prf the rate of modulation was determined by the band of frequencies between 20 c.p.s. and the value equal to half the prf. The range or degree of modulation is indicated for each curve as the maximal percentage deviation of the prf from its unmodulated value.

at 2000 p.p.s., where the change due to 100-percent random interval-modulation amounts to 50 db.

The change in the masking produced by a prf of 2000 p.p.s. as a function of rate and degree of modulation is shown in detail in Fig. 9. There we note that low rates of modulation (frequency band 20 to 125 c.p.s.) are relatively less effective than the higher rates. This is because the rate of modulation determines the *spacing* of the side bands relative to the original unmodulated frequency. With low rates of modulation, the energy tends to remain in the vicinity of the original prf (2000 p.p.s.). At higher rates of modulation the energy in the side bands tends to be scattered more widely, which means that some of the energy is displaced to the low frequency end of the spectrum, where it is more effective in masking speech. How much of the energy gets displaced in this manner depends upon the degree of modulation. Thus when the distribution of energy is wide (rate = 20 to 1000 c.p.s.) even a slight increase in the degree of modulation (say from 0 to 20 percent) throws a considerable amount of energy into the low frequency region where speech is masked effectively.

Actually this account of the matter is something of an over-simplification. If we were dealing here with pure frequency-modulation (duty cycle held constant) the precise distribution of the

side-band energy would be a function of the ratio of degree to rate of modulation, and this distribution could be predicted with the aid of Bessel functions. With interval modulation, however, the duration of the pulses is held constant, which means that the duty cycle changes as the intervals are altered. And from the curves in Fig. 3 it is obvious that, when the duty cycle varies, the energy in each of the low numbered harmonics of the pulse also changes. This change in the magnitude of the harmonics is equivalent, therefore, to an amplitude modulation, and the net result of the process of interval modulation is a hybrid case involving the modulation of both frequency and amplitude.

Furthermore, since the pulses in the modulated train all have the same polarity with respect to the time axis, they resemble a rectified signal having a varying d.c. component. This d.c. component varies in amplitude at a frequency

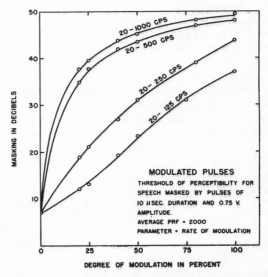

FIG. 9. Showing the masking produced by pulses (average prf = 2000) when they are subjected to various rates and degrees of interval modulation.

given by the original *rate* of modulation, and it therefore follows that in the case of pulse-interval modulation, the frequency of the modulating signal is present in the spectrum of the modulated pulse wave. On the other hand, when the amplitude or the frequency of a sine wave is modulated, the modulating signal is not represented in the resulting spectrum until the wave is passed through a rectifier or a discriminator.

The presence of the modulating frequency in the spectrum resulting from pulse-interval modulation is dramatically demonstrated when speech is used to modulate a prf of about 20,000 p.p.s. If the modulated pulses are then impressed directly on an earphone, the speech may be heard clear and undistorted.

We find, then, that when pulses of constant duration and constant peak amplitude are subjected to interval modulation the resulting spectrum contains (a) a band of energy at a frequency corresponding to that of the modulating signal, (b) side bands created by frequency modulation, and (c) side bands created by amplitude modulation. The side bands are set up on either side of the fundamental prf and on either side of each of its harmonics. The result is an exceedingly complex spectrum, even when the modulating signal is a sine wave. When the modulating signal is a continuous band of noise, the spectrum created is also continuous.

7

Copyright © 1948 by the Acoustical Society of America

Reprinted from *Acoust. Soc. Am. J.* **20**(1):42–51 (1948)

Effects of Differentiation, Integration, and Infinite Peak Clipping upon the Intelligibility of Speech*

J. C. R. LICKLIDER AND IRWIN POLLACK

Psycho-Acoustic Laboratory, Harvard University, Cambridge, Massachusetts

(Received September 29, 1947)

Previous experiments on the effects of distortion in voice communication circuits have shown that intelligibility is impaired surprisingly little by the type of amplitude distortion known as peak clipping. It has been found, in fact, that conversation is possible even over a system that introduces "infinite" peak clipping, i.e., that reduces speech to a succession of rectangular waves in which the discontinuities correspond to the crossings of the time axis in the original speech signal.

The intelligibility of the rectangular speech waves depends critically upon the frequency-response characteristics of the speech transmission circuits used in conjunction with the "infinite clipper." In the present experiments, resistance-capacitance circuits with sloping frequency-response characteristics (tilting circuits) were introduced into the system at points preceding and/or following the clipping circuit. The interactions of the nonuniform frequency characteristics of the resistance-capacitance circuits with the nonlinear amplitude characteristic of the clipping circuit were studied by means of articulation tests. That there was strong interaction is evidenced by the fact that word articulation scores of 97 and 15 percent were obtained with two systems consisting of the same components in different orders. The components were (1) a tilter with a frequency-response characteristic *rising* 6 db per octave (a "differentiating" circuit), (2) an infinite peak clipper, and (3) a tilter with a frequency-response characteristic *falling* 6 db per octave (an "integrating" circuit). When these distorters were cascaded in the sequence 1–2–3 the speech output consisted of triangularly shaped waves which sounded very much like normal speech and which were highly intelligible (97 percent). When the reverse sequence (3–2–1) was used, the speech output consisted of sharp pulses giving rise to extremely poor quality and very low intelligibility (15 percent).

Tests with single distorters and with pairs of distorters indicated that: (1) In the absence of frequency distortion, infinitely clipped speech is of poor quality but moderate intelligibility (50 to 90 percent depending on the listeners' skill and familiarity with the test words). (2) A differentiator or an integrator preceding the clipper determines the degree to which intelligibility is impaired by infinite clipping. (3) A differentiator or an integrator following the clipper (or used alone in a linear system) affects the quality but not the intelligibility of the speech transmitted by the system.

INTRODUCTION

THE waves of normal speech are so irregular and so complex that it is difficult to give even a statistical description of them. An instrument capable of transmitting or storing or reproducing them faithfully must have a dynamic range of 35 db or more, and it must be capable of preserving their highly intricate and ever-changing patterns. Regarded from one point of view, the problem of preserving the variety and complexity of speech waves presents a challenge. Regarded from another point of view, it prompts the question: to what extent can the speech waves be simplified without destroying their intelligibility?

A method of reducing speech to a simple bivariate (on-off) code was suggested by the results of experiments conducted during the war to determine the effects of overload distortion upon intelligibility. It was found in those experiments that, although it suffered in quality and timbre, speech remained at least moderately intelligible no matter how much peak clipping was introduced. In its most extreme form, peak clipping reduced speech to a series of rectangular waves.[1] These code-like waves were passed through electronic switching circuits without further impairment of intelligibility. Pulses, marking the instants at which the two-valued rectangular wave switched from one amplitude value to the other, were transmitted *via* pulse-modulated carrier, detected, and reconverted into intelligible "rectangular speech" with the aid of an Eccles-Jordan trigger circuit.

It was evident from these observations that a considerable amount of information was con-

* This research is being carried out under contract with the U. S. Navy, Office of Naval Research (Contract N5ori-76, Report PNR-44).

[1] J. C. R. Licklider, *Effects of Amplitude Distortion upon the Intelligibility of Speech*, Psycho-Acoustic Laboratory Report OSRD No. 4217, 15 November 1944, PB 19775. This report and other Psycho-Acoustic Laboratory reports are available through the Office of Technical Services, U. S. Department of Commerce, Washington, D. C.

tained in the temporal pattern of the crossings of the time axis in the original speech wave, for this temporal pattern was all that remained of the original wave after it had passed through the clipping and switching circuits. The curious feature of this result was not that the information *could be* represented by a series of elementary waves or impulses suitably spaced in time—this form of representation is the basis of frequency modulation, phase modulation, and pulse-time modulation techniques—but rather that, without resorting to the use of a modulation procedure at all, but simply by clipping off the peaks of the speech wave until it was reduced to a two-valued function of time, we should produce an intelligible temporal pattern. The pattern was not, however, *highly* intelligible. Although conversation was carried on with little difficulty in rectangular speech, articulation scores for discrete words were as low as 50 percent. The problem, if infinite clipping were to provide a usable bivariate code, was to improve intelligibility without sacrificing the simplicity of the rectangular wave form.

The way of achieving this result was suggested by experiments on design objectives for hearing aids[2] and for radio transmitters.[3]

In these experiments, it was found that the impairment of intelligibility due to severe peak clipping was reduced when a circuit with a rising frequency-response characteristic (pre-emphasis of the high frequency components of speech) was introduced ahead of the clipping circuit. Pre-emphasis of the low frequency components of speech, on the other hand, was found to increase the impairment of intelligibility caused by peak clipping.

PLAN AND PROCEDURE OF EXPERIMENT

The present experiment was planned with two related aims: (1) to study the possibility of producing highly intelligible speech patterns through

the use of frequency-selective circuits in conjunction with an infinite peak clipper, and (2) to examine the interactions between the types of frequency distortion produced by two simple resistance-capacitance circuits and the type of amplitude distortion introduced by the infinite clipper.

The resistance-capacitance circuits, which are shown in Fig. 1, were driven by low impedance sources (cathode followers) and operated into high impedance loads (grids). Since in circuit *A* the impedance to current flow is determined almost entirely by the reactance of the capacitor, the instantaneous current through the circuit (hence the instantaneous voltage across the resistor) is proportional to the rate of change of the input voltage. Thus circuit *A* acts as a "differentiator" of the wave form of the input signal. Or, to take an alternative view, the effective current through arrangement *A* (hence the effective voltage across the resistor) is proportional to the frequency of the input signal, and circuit *A* "tilts" the input spectrum upward, introducing 6 db less attenuation for each octave increase in frequency throughout the range of speech frequencies. In circuit *B*, the impedance to the flow of audio-frequency current is essentially constant since it is determined almost entirely by the resistance. The instantaneous voltage across the condenser is therefore proportional to the amount of current that has flowed into the capacitor, and thus to the time integral of the input voltage. Circuit *B* acts, therefore, as an "integrator" of the input wave form. Or, again to take an alternative view, the effective voltage across the condenser is inversely proportional to the frequency of the input signal, and circuit *B* gives the spectrum a downward tilt of 6 db per octave.

The clipping circuit consisted of five series-diode clippers of the type shown in Fig. 2*A*, isolated from each other by conventional re-

[2] H. Davis, *et al.*,' *Hearing Aids: An Experimental Study of Design Objectives* (Harvard University Press, Cambridge, 1947).
[3] K. D. Kryter and M. I. Stein, *The Advantages of Clipping the Peaks of Speech Waves Prior to Radio Communication*, Psycho-Acoustic Laboratory Report IC-83, 10 October 1944, PB 22859. N. B. Gross and J. C. R. Licklider, *Effects of Tilting and Clipping upon the Intelligibility of Speech*, Psycho-Acoustic Laboratory Report PNR-11, 15 April 1946, PB 52337. G. A. Miller and S. Mitchell, "Effects of distortion on the intelligibility of speech at high altitudes," J. Acous. Soc. Am. 19, 120–125 (1947).

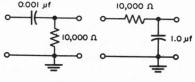

A DIFFERENTIATOR   B INTEGRATOR

FIG. 1. The differentiating circuit (*A*) and the integrating circuit (*B*) used in the articulation tests.

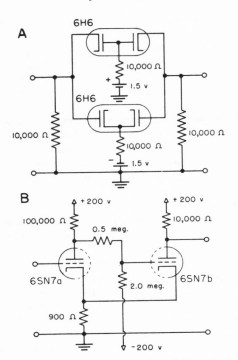

A

6H6

10,000 Ω

+ 1.5 v

6H6

10,000 Ω   10,000 Ω

10,000 Ω

− 1.5 v

B

+ 200 v   + 200 v

100,000 Ω   0.5 meg.   10,000 Ω

6SN7a   2.0 meg.   6SN7b

900 Ω

−200 v

FIG. 2. The nonlinear circuits of the infinite peak clipper used in the articulation tests. *A* is the basic clipper circuit of the peak-clipping amplifier. The amplifier included 5 of these clippers, separated by resistance-capacitance coupled amplifiers. *B* is the all-or-nothing switch (Schmidt circuit) used to remove any deviations from rectangularity which remained in the wave after the repeated clipping.

sistance-capacitance coupled amplifiers which provided a total voltage gain of over 100 db. The nearly rectangular output of the cascaded clippers was further amplified and passed through the Schmidt circuit[4] shown in Fig. 2B. This circuit, which acts as an all-or-nothing switch, served to minimize any deviations from ideal rectangularity which may have remained in the output of the clippers.

The differentiator, the integrator, and the infinite clipper were introduced, in various combinations, into an otherwise high quality system described below. Of the 16 cascade arrangements of the three circuits, taken none, one, two, or three at a time, six arrangements could be eliminated as effectively duplicating others because the operations of differentiation and integration, performed in succession, left the speech wave

[4] O. S. Puckle, *Time Bases* (John Wiley and Sons, Inc., New York, 1944), p. 57.

undistorted. The ten remaining arrangements were:

(1) No distortion	(6) Int.+Clip.
(2) Differentiation (Diff.)	(7) Clip.+Diff.
(3) Integration (Int.)	(8) Clip.+Int.
(4) Infinite clipping (Clip.)	(9) Diff.+Clip.+Int.
(5) Diff.+Clip.	(10) Int.+Clip.+Diff.

The effect of each of these operations upon sine waves and speech waves is illustrated schematically in Fig. 3. The triangular waves and trains of pulses are shown as consisting of straight line segments. Actually, since the differentiator and the integrator provided close approximations of the mathematical operations only in the range of audio frequencies, the triangular waves and pulses were made up of exponential curves with very slight curvature. Extension of the frequency ranges of the resistance-capacitance circuits would have had little or no effect upon the results of the experiment, however, since frequencies above 7500 cps were attenuated by the earphones.

In order to determine the effect upon intelligibility of each of the 10 arrangements of the three distortions, word articulation tests were conducted with the distorters introduced into an otherwise high-quality audio communication system. The word lists were Nos. 1–5 of the Psycho-Acoustic Laboratory PB lists (50 monosyllabic words per list).[5] Five scramblings of each list were recorded by a single talker on acetate disks, and these tests were played back through a system equalized within ±3 db from 100 to 7000 cps. The microphone was Western Electric Type 633-A, and the earphones were Permoflux PDR-10's in sponge-neoprene cushions (MX/41-AR). Under each of the test conditions, the sound pressure level of the speech in the listeners' ears was approximately 85 db re 0.0002 dyne/cm^2, rms.

In all, 250 articulation tests were made: 25 with each of the 10 arrangements of the distorting circuits, 10 with each of the five scramblings of each of the five word lists. The tests were so arranged that each combination of distortions was tested once in each block of 10 tests and, during the experiment, once with each of the 25 recorded lists. Except for these re-

[5] These lists are described by J. P. Egan in *Articulation Testing Methods II*, Psycho-Acoustic Laboratory Report OSRD No. 3802, 1 November 1944, PB 22848.

strictions, the tests were made in random sequence, the schedule having been set up with the aid of a table of random numbers.

EFFECTS OF THE DISTORTIONS ON INTELLIGIBILITY

The effects of the several combinations of distortion upon intelligibility are shown in Figs. 4 and 5. In Fig. 4, the successive test scores (averages for the five listeners) are presented, and smooth curves are shown to indicate the trend of the listeners' improvement with practice. In Fig. 5, the smooth curves are brought together in a single plot to facilitate intercomparison of the effects of the various permutations of differentiation, integration, and infinite peak clipping. It is evident that the ten curves fall into four groups.

The first group represents the intelligibility scores obtained with no distortion, with differentiation alone, and with integration alone. These scores all very near 100 percent, and the differences among them are statistically insignificant. (A statistical analysis of the data is described in an appendix.) This result concerning their intelligibility is in marked contrast to the observations concerning their naturalness and timbre. Because it greatly emphasizes the fricative consonants and weakens the low-pitched vowels, differentiation makes speech sound overly crisp. Integration, on the other hand, emphasizes the low-pitched vowels, weakens the consonants, and makes speech sound muffled and "boomy." The safety factor of voice communication is such, however, that neither differentiation nor integration impairs the intelligibility of speech heard in quiet.

The fourth and fifth curves, which constitute the second group in Fig. 5, were obtained (1) with infinite clipping preceded by differentiation and (2) with infinite peak clipping preceded by differentiation and followed by integration. The intelligibility scores were over 90 percent, even for unpracticed listeners. After becoming familiar with the vocabulary and with the effects of distortion, the listeners missed only about 3 words in a hundred. (Scores over 90 percent on word tests corresponds to essentially perfect reception of meaningful sentences.) Comparison of the two curves in this pair indicates that the action of the integrating circuit had essentially no

effect upon the intelligibility of the output of the infinite peak clipper. If anything, the integrator made the speech slightly more intelligible, but the effect upon intelligibility was completely negligible compared to the effect upon quality. Actually, the only feature seriously marring the quality of differentiated-clipped-integrated speech was the low frequency noise which came through with considerable volume between words. When this noise was suppressed, it was very hard to believe that the speech could possibly have been through a series of distortions which, at one stage of the process, had removed all trace of the original amplitude pattern.

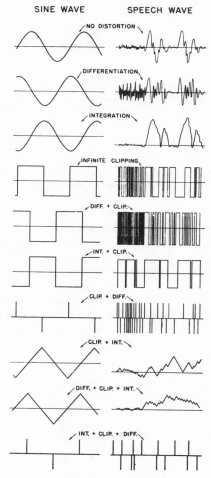

FIG. 3. Schematic illustration of the effects of the distortions upon sine waves and upon speech waves.

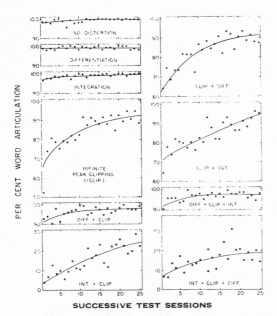

FIG. 4. Showing the articulation scores (averages for five listeners) for tests with each of the 10 arrangements of the distorting circuits.

The third group of curves in Fig. 5 includes the three curves obtained with the combinations in which infinite clipping was the initial distortion: infinite clipping alone, infinite clipping plus differentiation, and infinite clipping plus integration. Again it is evident that the process that follows clipping has but little effect on intelligibility, and again it is true that the articulation scores fail to reflect differences in quality and timbre that are quite striking to the listener. The downward tilt of the spectrum provided by the integrator makes the effect of infinite clipping sound less noticeable without in fact restoring any of the cues for recognition which were destroyed by the clipper. On the other hand, the upward tilt introduced by the differentiator made

TABLE I. Recognition of words from the test vocabulary as compared with false recognition of words not used in the tests.

Certainty of recognition	Words actually in test vocabulary	Words actually not in test vocabulary
1	786	29
2	152	44
3	87	73
4	225	1104

the clipped speech sound even worse without eliminating any important cues. It should be noted that the initial articulation scores for infinite clipping are well within the range obtained in previous experiments. The marked rise to a level of 90 percent word articulation is due presumably to the unusual diligence of the listening crew and to the fact that the vocabulary of test words was limited to 250.

The fourth and lowermost group of curves in Fig. 5 is the pair for which integration preceded infinite clipping. Obviously, predistortion of the type introduced by the integrating circuit is incompatible with severe clipping. Again, the effect of the circuit following the clipper is not great, but there does appear to have been more improvement with practice when the differentiator was not used.

Comparison of the four groups of curves indicates that, although infinite clipping is always associated with some impairment of intelligibility, the amount of impairment depends markedly upon the circuit preceding the clipper. When that circuit is a differentiator, intelligibility is impaired very little. It remains high enough, in fact, to be adequate for many communication purposes. And when an integrator is used as a third circuit following the clipper, even subjective quality is reasonably good.

The Listeners' Improvement with Practice

A striking feature of the results is the degree to which the articulation scores improved during the course of the experiment (cf. Fig. 4). Inasmuch as the same recorded word lists were used in successive tenths of the experiment, this improvement cannot be the result of increased clarity of enunciation on the part of the talker. It must be attributed to learning on the part of the listeners, who prior to the experiment had had no experience with articulation tests. The question is, what did the listeners learn? Did they learn what words were on the test lists and what words were not? Did they learn the sequences in which the words occurred in the several scramblings? Or did they acquire a general skill that enabled them to understand distorted speech, whether or not it consisted of words from the test vocabulary?

At the end of the experiment, the listeners were presented with a series of 500 words: the 250 words of the five lists used in the articulation tests and 250 words from five other PB lists to which they had never been exposed. Words from the two sources were called in random sequence. The listeners were asked to indicate for each word whether or not it had been a part of the articulation-test vocabulary. A rating of *one* represented virtual certainty that the word had been on one of the test lists used in the main experiment; a rating of *four*, that it had not been. It is clear from the ratings, which are summarized in Table I, that the listeners had learned to recognize the words of the test vocabulary with considerable accuracy, though by no means infallibly. Ability to identify a word as belonging, or as not belonging, to the test vocabulary would of course allow the listener to record words correctly on the basis of reduced cues. Familiarity with the composition of the word lists would thus operate to increase the articulation scores in much the same way as do the contextual relations of connected discourse.

After the recognition test, the five listeners were given a series of 25 supplementary articulation tests in which the recorded word lists were played back just as they were in the main experiment except that every fifth word was blanked out. The listeners were asked to write down the words they heard and to fill in the missing words from memory, guessing in case of doubt. Ten words were blanked out on each of the 25 tests. In all, 1250 attempts to recall were made. Only 26 of the 1250 responses (approximately 2 percent) were correct. It would appear, therefore, that although the listeners did learn to recognize the words on the test vocabulary, they did not learn the sequences of the words in the 25 scramblings well enough to affect the articulation scores appreciably through direct recall, as distinguished from recognition.

As a final observation on the listeners' improvement with practice, a short series of articulation tests were made with three sets of recorded word lists: (1) the words used in the main experiment in their original sequences, (2) the same words in new sequences, and (3) an entirely different set of words, also from PB lists, and very nearly equal in difficulty to the words used in the main experiment. Ten lists from each of three sets were read in random sequence. Half the tests

TABLE II. Results of supplementary articulation tests and of comparable parts of the main experiment. (Each value of percent word articulation is the average for five tests with each of five listeners.)

Lists	Infinite clipping	Infinite clipping plus differentiation
Old words, old sequence	95.4	95.8
Old words, new sequence	94.8	95.4
New words	85.8	86.3
First five tests of main experiment	71.1	72.2
Over-all average of main experiment	85.9	84.7

were conducted with infinite peak clipping, half with infinite peak clipping plus differentiation. The results are summarized in Table II. For purposes of comparison, averages for part of the main experiment are also included.

As shown in the table, the scores were only about half a percentage unit lower with new scramblings of the familiar word lists than they were with scramblings which had been heard ten times each. This confirms the finding that the listeners did not learn the sequences in which the words occurred. With new words, however, the scores were about 10 percentage units lower than they were with the familiar vocabulary. This confirms the finding that familiarity with the test vocabulary is an important factor. The table

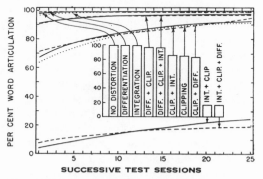

FIG. 5. Showing the effects of various combinations of differentiation, integration, and infinite peak clipping upon intelligibility. The smooth curves are replotted from Fig. 4 to facilitate intercomparison. The heights of the bars of the column diagram (inset) indicate the over-all averages for the ten arrangements of the distorting circuits.

also shows, however, that the scores with new words in the supplementary tests were almost 15 percentage units higher than the corresponding scores were at the beginning of the main experiment, at which time the word lists used in that experiment were new to the listeners. The skill developed by the listeners during the tests is thus only in part specific to the words of the test vocabulary. It is to a considerable extent a general skill, an ability to identify words correctly despite severe distortion.

Comparison of the third and fifth lines of Table II shows that the scores obtained in the supplementary tests with the new words are nearly equal to the averages for the 25 tests of the main experiment. This coincidence provides a convenient interpretation for the average scores of the main experiment. They may be regarded as approximate values of the intelligibility of unfamiliar distorted words to listeners who have had experience with severely distorted speech. For inexperienced listeners, the intelligibility of unfamiliar words is in general somewhat lower as indicated in Figs. 4 and 5.

DISCUSSION

Bivariate Code

It is evident from the results that a differentiator and a clipper may be used to reduce speech to an intelligible bivariate code, and that this code can be restored to a reasonably natural-sounding reproduction of the original speech simply by passing it through an integrating circuit. For some applications it might be convenient to replace the rectangular waves with pulses (one pulse to indicate each switch of the rectangular wave). This substitution and the inverse operation required to recover the rectangular wave from the pulses are easily handled by simple electronic circuits. However, the substitution of pulses for rectangular waves does not alter the formal characteristics of the code, which can still be thought of as always having one or the other of two amplitude values.

The practical utility of rectangular speech waves or their derivatives will of course depend to a considerable extent upon the number of square waves or pulses per second that are required to provide high intelligibility. If it should

turn out, for example, that pulse-time modulation techniques were more efficient in producing an intelligible bivariate code than are combinations of tilting and clipping, then there would be little interest in the latter as the basis of a practical procedure. But preliminary observations suggest that the efficiency of the code obtained by tilting and clipping is somewhat higher, when expressed in terms of intelligibility per pulse (or intelligibility per switch of the rectangular wave), than is the efficiency of the codes which result from the application of conventional pulse modulation procedures. When a typical sample of normal speech is subjected to differentiation and then to infinite peak clipping, about 1500 rectangular waves, and therefore 3000 switchings, are produced each second. Pulse modulation schemes, on the other hand, usually provide at least five pulses for each cycle of the highest frequency component to be transmitted, thereby requiring about 15,000 pulses per second to provide fair reproduction out to 3000 c.p.s. There is little doubt that lower repetition frequencies could be used without destroying intelligibility completely. But the presence of a strong component at the repetition frequency of the unmodulated pulses reacts against the use of the conventional methods of modulating the position, duration, or repetition frequency of pulses when the average number of pulses is as few as 3000 per second.

Root-Mean-Square Harmonic Distortion

Previous experiments have suggested that there is little or no correlation between the impairment of intelligibility due to amplitude distortion and the severity of distortion as expressed in terms of measurements with sinusoidal test signals.[6] The present results provide supplementary data on this point.

In the present experiment, the situation is unusually simple because, although there were seven arrangements of distorting circuits which introduced nonlinear distortion, they gave rise to only three different output wave forms (cf. Fig. 3). The three arrangements in which the infinite clipper was the final circuit gave rise to rectangular waves. The two arrangements in which the clipper was followed by the integrating circuit

[6] See reference 1, pp. 43–49.

produced triangular waves. The two arrangements in which the clipper was followed by the differentiating circuit gave rise to trains of pulses. All that is necessary is (1) to calculate how severely a sine wave is distorted when it is converted into a rectangular wave, a triangular wave, or a train of pulses and (2) to correlate the calculated indices of distortion with the measures of intelligibility provided by the articulation tests. This is done in Table III. The values of percentage distortion were computed from the formula

$$100\frac{(E_2{}^2+E_3{}^2+E_4{}^2+\cdots+E_n{}^2)^{\frac{1}{2}}}{(E_1{}^2+E_2{}^2+E_3{}^2+E_4{}^2+\cdots+E_n{}^2)^{\frac{1}{2}}}$$

in which E_n is the amplitude of the nth harmonic. The first 49 harmonics of the output wave were taken into account. The table shows rather conclusively that distortion measurements made with sinusoidal test signals do not get at the important factors governing intelligibility.

Intensity Distribution in Speech as a Factor Governing Intelligibility

Because it eliminates many of the characteristic features of the speech wave, infinite peak clipping provides a method of determining whether or not certain features are important for intelligibility. For example, infinite clipping reduces the envelope of the speech wave to the simplest possible form—two parallel straight lines. This is the case whether or not one of the tilting circuits is introduced ahead of the clipper, and it remains the case even if the differentiator (but not the integrator) follows the clipper. Inasmuch as essentially perfect communication is possible with at least one of the circuit arrangements that reduces the envelope to this simple form, it is evident that the so-called dynamic characteristics of speech are not of vital importance for intelligibility. It is apparently just as well to reproduce all the fundamental speech sounds (or what is left of them after infinite clipping) at the same intensity level as it is to preserve their normal intensities.

This fact poses a problem for any theory of intelligibility in which the distribution of speech intensities is regarded as a fundamental determinant of intelligibility. This is not to say that

TABLE III. Showing the lack of relation between values of percentage harmonic distortion and the articulation scores.

Output	Percentage distortion	Articulation scores		
Triangular waves	11.6	97.4		86.0
Square waves	42.7	97.9	85.9	14.8
Pulses	98.0		84.7	14.7

the intensity distribution of normal speech does not influence the intelligibility of normal speech. But the variations in intensity from moment to moment appear not to be basic cues for the recognition of words.

Noise Between Words

One of the characteristics of normal speech is that there are intervals between words or phrases during which the talker generates no signal. It often happens, of course, that these intervals are filled with noise, but under these circumstances the speech itself is heard against a background of noise, and intervals between words and phrases are relatively, if not absolutely, quiet. With an infinite peak clipper in the communication circuit, however, the intervals between words are just as full of sound as are the periods occupied by the words. Since the infinite clipper acts in such a way that the output wave switches whenever the input wave crosses the time axis, the intervals between words are full of "rectangular noise." In the articulation tests, this noise was due largely to record scratch. When records are not used, it is due either to hum from the supply lines or to fluctuation noise in the input circuits of the speech amplifier (shot noise or resistance noise).

A listener's first reaction to the noise between words is usually one of amazement that speech can be so clear in the presence of such loud noise. After a minute or two, however, the listener notices that the noise diminishes as soon as the speech appears, and thereafter he regards the noise simply as a nuisance. In the articulation tests, nothing was done to eliminate the noise, although clearly in any practical application a "squelch" circuit to silence the intervals between words would be indicated. The question did arise, however: Is intelligibility impaired by the presence of rectangular noise between the words of

TABLE IV. Mean articulation scores for each of the treatments principal experimental variables.*

A. Distortion

(1) No distortion......	99.6	(6)	I-C..........	14.8
(2) Differentiation (D).	99.5	(7)	C-D..........	84.7
(3) Integration (I)....	99.5	(8)	C-I..........	86.0
(4) Infinite clipping (C)	85.9	(9)	D-C-I........	97.4
(5) D-C..............	97.9	(10)	I-C-D........	14.7

B. Listener

B 87.0;   C 86.5;   H 85.6;   S 85.2;   K 80.0

C. Block of 10 tests

(1)	68.2	(6)	80.3	(11)	84.7	(16)	85.7	(21)	89.8
(2)	77.2	(7)	81.7	(12)	86.9	(17)	88.7	(22)	87.9
(3)	79.0	(8)	83.1	(13)	86.0	(18)	89.0	(23)	87.7
(4)	81.3	(9)	80.7	(14)	85.3	(19)	86.1	(24)	89.3
(5)	80.4	(10)	85.0	(15)	88.2	(20)	89.6	(25)	88.1

* The values in the table are actually the percentage scores that correspond to the means of the transformed scores described in the text.

rectangular speech? The problem is essentially one of the temporal spread of masking. It concerns the capacity of the listener's auditory system to establish a figure-ground relation between components of the acoustic stimulus presented in temporal alternation.

In order to assess the effect of the noise between words, it was necessary to find a suitable way of suppressing it. This was accomplished by making the noise ultrasonic. By introducing a 20,000-cycle sine wave at an intensity just sufficient to override the background noise, it is possible to eliminate all audible noise between words. This method is applicable, however, only when the speech-to-noise ratio at the input to the clipping circuit is quite high. If the intensity of the speech is not well above that of the ultrasonic tone, there is danger that a spurious effect, a "duty-cycle modulation" of ultrasonic rectangular waves, will make the rectangular speech waves more intelligible than they would be with infinite clipping per se.[7]

When the ultrasonic tone was made just intense enough to override the background noise, switching it off and on had a dramatic effect upon the apparent quality of the overall transmission, but there was little or no change in intelligibility.

[7] The high-frequency tone, passing through the infinite clipper, tends to give rise to square waves at high repetition frequency. Because speech is superimposed upon the tone, however, these waves are not square, but are modulated in on-off fraction or in duty-cycle. Normal speech thereby manages to get through the infinite clipper as a type of modulation which requires only a low-pass filter for its 'detection.'

TABLE V. Summary of the analysis of variance.

Source of variation	n	Mean square variation	F	P
Distortion (D)	9	237,442	2730	<0.01
Listener (Li)	4	3,596	41.4	<0.01
Learning (Le)	24	1,850	21.3	<0.01
Interactions and error	1211	86.9		
D × Li	36	235.6	4.45	<0.01
D × Le	216	204.7	3.87	<0.01
Li × Le	96	71.8	1.36	<0.01
Triple interaction and error	863	52.9		

This result is in line with what would be expected on the basis of extrapolation from data on the temporal spread of masking[8] and on the effect of cutting off the initial segments of words.[9] When the masked sound alternates with the masking sound, and when the two sounds are equally intense, not more than 2 or 3 milliseconds of the masked sound are rendered inaudible. Since the elimination of a 2- or 3-millisecond segment from the beginning of each syllable in a list of undistorted consonant-vowel-consonant syllables causes essentially no decrement in articulation, it is not unreasonable that the noise between the words of infinitely clipped speech should produce little or no impairment of intelligibility.

APPENDIX

Statistical Analysis of the Articulation Data

It is convenient to think of the 1250 scores made by the five listeners on the 250 articulation tests of the main experiment as forming a three-dimensional matrix in which the variables are distortion, listener, and learning. The 10 arrangements of the three distorting circuits are then regarded as 10 treatments of the variable, distortion. The five listeners are looked upon as five treatments of the variable, listener. And the 25 blocks, of 10 tests each, are thought of as 25 treatments of the variable, learning, or more precisely as 25 treatments of a temporal variable

[8] R. L. Miller, "Masking effect of periodic pulses of vibrations as a function of time and frequency," J. Acous. Soc. Am. 19, 735 (1947). Also, personal communication from G. A. Miller, May, 1947.
[9] J. C. Steinberg in Electrical Engineer's Handbook (John Wiley and Sons, New York, 1936), Chap. 9, p. 34.

that affords an opportunity for the listeners to show improvement with practice. The mean articulation percentages for the 10 distortions, for the 5 listeners, and for the 25 blocks of tests are shown in Table IV. Inasmuch as the average scores for the five different word lists fell within a range of 2.4 percentage units, there is no need to complicate the picture by taking account of the variation among word lists.

In order to obtain an indication of the potencies of the three variables just mentioned, relative to each other and to the 'error' fluctuation within the experiment, an analysis was made of the variations within the matrix of data. Actually, since the articulation scores themselves showed the heterogeneity of variance that is characteristic of percentages, a form of Fisher's arc sine transformation[10] was applied to each of the 1250 percentage scores (A) and the analysis of variance was made with the transformed scores (I),

$$I = 50 \sin^{-1}(A/50 - 1).$$

The results of this analysis are shown in Table V.

In Table V, the three principal variables and their interactions are listed as sources of variation, and for each source the number of degrees of freedom (n) and the mean square variation per degree of freedom are indicated. F is the ratio of the mean square variation associated with a particular source to the residual mean square variation, and P is the probability that there would arise as the result of the fluctuations of random sampling an F as high as, or higher than, the one actually obtained. It is evident from the table that, of the three main variables, distortion was the predominant one, and that each of the principal variables completely overshadowed the interactions and 'error' combined. Thus, although the effects of the 10 distortions were not entirely the same for all five listeners (significant $D \times Li$ interaction), and although the listeners improved with practice more with some distortions than with others (significant $D \times Le$ interaction), and although some listeners learned more than others (significant $Li \times Le$ interaction), these

[10] R. A. Fisher, "On the dominance ratio," Proc. Roy. Soc., Edinburgh **42**, 321–341 (1922). An excellent discussion of transformation to homogenize variance is contained in C. Eisenhart, M. W. Hastay, and W. A. Wallis, *Selected Techniques of Statistical Analysis* (McGraw-Hill Book Co., New York, 1947), Chap. 16.

qualifications are of minor moment relative to the large variations in intelligibility caused by the distortions themselves.

It is of some interest to consider the magnitude of the variance designated in the table as "triple interactions and error." Since triple interactions tend to be quite small in experiments of this type, the value 52.9 can be taken as an estimate of the error variance, i.e. the variance that would be obtained if a very large number of 50-word articulation tests were conducted under "constant conditions" with a system that provided, as a long-run average, 50-percent word articulation. But it is possible, on the simplifying assumption that all of the test words are of the same degree of difficulty, to compute the parametric value of the variance of the percentage scores of such a series of tests. This "true" variance is

$$\sigma^2 = 4Npq = 4(50)(1/2)(1/2) = 50$$

where N is the number of words in the test, p is the probability that a word will be heard correctly, and q is the probability that a word will be missed. The parametric value 50 agrees surprisingly well with the obtained value 52.9.

As an estimate of the inherent variability in the experiment, therefore, we have a variance of about 50 square units, or a standard deviation of a little over 7 units for a distribution of individual scores.

The units in terms of which this estimate is expressed are the units of the transformed scale. The relation between the transformed scale and the percent word articulation scale is such that 7 percentage units is an unbiased estimate of the standard deviation for articulation scores near 50 percent, but an overestimate for articulation scores near either end of the percentage scale. It is convenient, nevertheless, to take 7 units as the standard error of a single score, remembering that it tends everywhere except at the 50-percent point to be a little too high. On this basis, the standard error of the mean score for any one of the 10 arrangements of the distorting circuits is $\sigma_D = (50/125)^{\frac{1}{2}} = 0.63$ in percentage units, since the mean is based on 125 individual scores. Similarly, the standard error of an individual listener's mean is estimated by $\sigma_{Li} = (50/250)^{\frac{1}{2}} = 0.45$, and the standard error of the mean score for a set of 25 tests is estimated by $\sigma_{Block} = (50/50)^{\frac{1}{2}} = 1.00$.

8

Reprinted from *Acoust. Soc. Am. J.* **22**(2):167–173 (1950)

The Intelligibility of Interrupted Speech*

GEORGE A. MILLER AND J. C. R. LICKLIDER
Psycho-Acoustic Laboratory, Harvard University, Cambridge, Massachusetts
(Received October 22, 1949)

This paper concerns the effects of interrupting speech waves—turning them on and off intermittently or masking them with intermittent noise—upon their intelligibility. The effects were studied with various rates of interruption and with the speech left undisturbed various percentages of the time. Tests were conducted (1) with speech turned on and off in quiet, (2) with continuous speech masked by interrupted white noise, and (3) with speech and noise interrupted alternately, the speech wave being turned on as the noise wave was turned off, and vice versa.

(1) When the speech wave is turned on and off infrequently, the percentage of the message that is missed is approximately the same as the percentage of time the speech is off. When the interruptions are periodic and occur more often than 10,000 times per second, the interruptions do not interfere with the reception of the message. In the quiet it is easy to understand conversational speech so long as the interruptions occur more than 10 times per second.

(2) When continuous speech waves are masked by noise that is interrupted more than 200 times per second, intelligibility is independent of the interruption frequency and of the percentage of time the noise is on, provided the ratio of average speech power to average noise power is held constant. Interrupted masking noise impairs intelligibility least if the frequency of interruption is about 15 per second.

(3) When interrupted speech and interrupted noise alternate at frequencies below 10 alternations per second, the noise does not impair intelligibility. At higher frequencies of alternation the temporal spread of masking becomes appreciable.

The general features of these results are approximately the same whether the interruptions occur periodically or at random.

S TUDIES of frequency and amplitude distortion have made it evident that undistorted speech waves contain more information than is necessary for intelligibility. Because they do it is often possible to economize on the band width or on the peak-power capacity of a speech-transmission system. It is also possible to economize in the time domain without sacrificing performance. One of the simplest ways to save time is to turn the speech off at intervals so the system can be used for another transmission. Effects of such interruptions upon intelligibility, as determined in a series of articulation tests, are described in this paper.

INTERRUPTED SPEECH IN QUIET

The kind of interruption used in these studies is equivalent to 100-percent amplitude modulation by a train of rectangular pulses. Periodic interruptions are illustrated in Fig. 1. The undistorted speech wave at the top of Fig. 1 is multiplied by the modulating wave to produce the interrupted speech wave at the bottom of the figure. The basic variables are: (a) The number of interruptions per second, the *frequency of interruption;* (2) The proportion of the time the speech is on, the *speech-time fraction;* and (3) The degree of *regularity* of the interruptions.

The speech materials used in the articulation tests were the phonetically balanced ("PB") lists of monosyllabic words published by Egan.[1] They were recorded phonographically by two talkers and reproduced for the articulation tests by an equalized playback. A crew of five listeners (male college students with normal

hearing) was used, and each datum point is based upon the results of at least two 50-word tests, one with each talker. The electronic switch used to produce the interruptions was the one described by Miller and Taylor.[2] When it turned the signal off it in fact reduced the level approximately 80 db. With that much attenuation, no speech sounds could be heard during the interruptions. The listeners heard the speech through Permoflux dynamic receivers PDR-8. The frequency-response characteristic of the entire system (earphones terminating in a 6-cc coupler) was essentially uniform from 200 to 7000 c.p.s. This characteristic has been published by Licklider.[3]

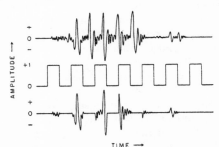

FIG. 1. Multiplying the continuous speech wave (top line) by the square wave (middle line) produces the interrupted speech wave (bottom line).

* This research was carried out under contract between Harvard University and the ONR, U. S. Navy, Project NR147-201, Report PNR-50. Reproduction for any purpose by the U. S. Government is permitted.

[1] J. P. Egan, "Articulation testing methods," Laryngoscope 58, 955–991 (1948).

[2] G. A. Miller and W. G. Taylor, "The perception of repeated bursts of noise," J. Acous. Soc. Am. 20, 171–182 (1948).

[3] J. C. R. Licklider, "The influence of interaural phase relations upon the masking of speech by white noise," J. Acous. Soc. Am. 20, 150–159 (1948); see Fig. 1, p. 152. The function labeled "electrical" is essentially the response of the system preceding the electronic switch, and the function labeled "acoustic" is the response of the entire system, including earphones.

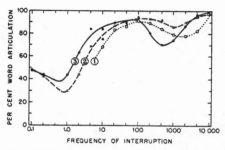

FIG. 2. Word articulation as a function of rate of interruption for a speech-time fraction of 0.5. Curve (1) was obtained with naive listeners, (2) with the same listeners after a few days practice, (3) again with the same listeners, but with a system having a more uniform frequency-response characteristic.

Regularly Spaced Interruptions

Consider first the results obtained with regularly spaced interruptions and a speech-time fraction of 0.5. The frequency of interruption was varied between 0.1 and 10,000 per second. In Fig. 2 the percentage of the words heard correctly is plotted on the ordinate, and the frequency of interruption is given on the abscissa.

The three curves of Fig. 2 were obtained under slightly different conditions. Curve 1 is based on the tests conducted at the beginning of the experiments. The listeners had never before served as subjects in articulation tests. Curve 2 was obtained after a few days practice. Note that the scores are consistently higher. At this point the frequency-response characteristic of the phonograph playback was equalized. (In the preliminary tests—curves 1 and 2—the system had a response that de-emphasized the low frequency components of the speech.) Curve 3 shows the results obtained after the response was equalized. Here the dip at 460 interruptions per second is greater, and intelligibility is less affected at the lower frequencies of interruption.

The general shapes of the three functions are approximately the same, and about what we should expect on the basis of an analysis of the experimental conditions. If the frequency of interruption is low enough, the articulation score must be equal to the product of the speech-time fraction (here 0.5) and the articulation score for uninterrupted speech (here almost 100 percent). With the speech on 5 seconds, then off 5 seconds, the listeners heard half of the words correctly. At the other extreme, if the frequency of interruption is high enough, the words must be just as intelligible as if they were not interrupted at all. The very rapid oscillations between on and off were not transduced by the earphones, but even if they had been transduced, the mechanical transmission system in the middle ear would have acted as a low pass filter to eliminate the interruptions

and restore the speech wave essentially to its original form.

Between the very low and the very high frequencies of interruption the functions pass through a minimum, a maximum, then another minimum. The first minimum occurs in the neighborhood of one interruption per second. It is reasonable to expect intelligibility to be low when the duration of the "on" period is approximately equal to the duration of one word. The entire word can be heard correctly only if the "on-time" coincides rather exactly with the occurrence of the word. The word is likely to be missed if either its initial or its final phoneme is chopped off. However, as the listeners

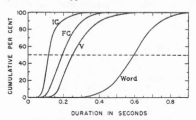

FIG. 3. Durations of speech sounds in the monosyllabic words used in the articulation tests. Initial consonants (IC) were shortest, final consonants (FC) next, and vowels (V) were longest. The average word lasted about 0.6 second.

grow more familiar with the word lists they become better able to recognize the mutilated words. In curve 3, which was obtained after the listeners had considerable experience, the minimum has almost disappeared.

The maximum between 10 and 100 interruptions per second is also attributable to the temporal characteristics of the spoken words. The average duration of a word in these tests was 0.6 second. Five interruptions per second would, on the average, give the listeners three 'looks' at each word. For the majority of the words this is enough to ensure a glimpse of every phoneme. It appears that one glimpse per phoneme is sufficient.

Since, according to this interpretation, the durations of the phonemes are important in determining the articulation scores over the range from 1 to 10 interruptions per second, an attempt was made to measure the durations. Cathode-ray oscillograms were made of the recorded words, and from them the durations of the initial consonants, the vowels, the final consonants and the entire words were measured to the nearest 0.01 second. The results are shown in Fig. 3. The durations are somewhat longer than would be obtained for conversational speech. Even with no time allowed for spaces between words, the median duration of 0.6 second corresponds to only 100 words per minute. Since conversational rates average around 130 words per minute, including pauses and polysyllabic words, it appears that the two talkers pronounced the words slowly and carefully when they made the records. If they had used normal conversational rates, the word articulation scores probably would have reached their maximum at a slightly higher rate of interruption.[4]

Intelligibility remains high until the frequency of interruption reaches 100 per second, but between 200 and 2000 per second there is a slight, though significant, deterioration. Consider the speech as a carrier modulated by a 1000-cycle square wave. Each component in the speech spectrum will have sidebands spaced at 1000-cycle intervals on either side of it, and these sidebands will constitute a noisy masking signal to interfere with intelligibility. Apparently such sidebands are not a serious consideration when the modulating frequency is less than 100 per second. When the frequency is greater than 3000 interruptions per second, on the other hand, the sidebands do not seriously overlap the range of speech frequencies, and intelligibility is high.

It is possible to account in the manner just outlined for the various inflections in the functions of Fig. 2 when the interruptions are regular and the speech-time fraction is 0.5. Does the picture change when different speech-time fractions are employed? The answer is given by the set of functions shown in Fig. 4. These functions were obtained with speech-time fractions ranging from 0.063 to 0.75 and with periodic interrup-

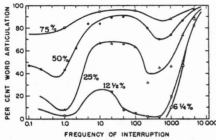

FIG. 4. Word articulation as a function of frequency of interruption, with speech-time fraction as the parameter. The interruptions were spaced regularly in time.

tions. These functions follow roughly similar courses. However, as the speech-time fraction decreases, the maxima grow lower and narrower. Fewer words get through between gaps, and interference due to modulation products becomes more serious.

[4] An incidental but related observation concerns the effect of an interrupted sidetone on a talker's normal rate of speaking. If slowly interrupted speech is fed back at a high intensity to the talker's own ears, there is a strong tendency to slow down. At 1 interruption per second, the talker tries to drawl out his words until each speech sound is heard at least once. At somewhat higher rates of interruption, he tends to synchronize his vowels with multiples of the frequency of interruption. (Our attention was called to this last point by J. M. Stroud, who suggests that our articulation scores might have been slightly higher had we used 'live' talkers and sidetone monitoring.)

Irregularly Spaced Interruptions

The data we have just examined are represented in another way in Fig. 5: the speech-time fraction is plotted against the frequency of interruption. The resulting curves are equal-articulation contours. The solid curves of Fig. 5 are based upon the data of Fig. 4 and hold for regularly spaced interruptions.

The dashed curves of Fig. 5 are for irregular interruptions. The electronic switch was arranged in such a way that it could be triggered on and off by pulses derived from two noise generators. Every time the randomly fluctuating voltage of one of the noises rose past a predetermined amplitude the switch turned on and stayed on until the other noise voltage rose past its predetermined amplitude level. By varying the two levels at which the switch would trigger it was possible to produce random interruptions at various rates and speech-time fractions. Because the triggering was random, however, it was not possible to tell exactly what the frequency and speech-time fraction were going to be until the test was completed. It was necessary to run the test and then see what had happened. The average frequency of interruption during the test was determined with the aid of an electronic counter, and the average speech-time fraction was determined from the time integral of the triggering voltage. Once these values were determined, the articulation score could be indicated at the proper point on a graph like that of Fig. 5. From these points the dashed curves of Fig. 5 were obtained.

The functions for random interruption turn out to be straighter than the functions for regular interruption. This result is to be expected because random interruption in some parts of the test to frequencies of interruption that are higher than average and in other parts to frequencies of interruption that are lower than average. Similarly, a range of speech-time fractions is involved in every test. The effect is to smooth out the variations in the curves, just as a running average smooths out fluctuations in a column of numbers.

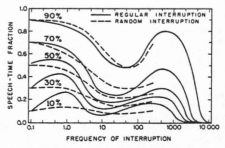

FIG. 5. Equal-articulation contours obtained with regularly spaced and with randomly spaced interruptions of speech.

These results are displayed in still a third manner in Fig. 6. The word articulation score is plotted against the speech-time fraction, with the rate of interruption as the parameter, for both regular and irregular interruption. At nearly all points the articulation score lies above the speech-time fraction.

Gradual Modulation, Periodic Inversion, and Double Talk

A few tests were conducted with regularly spaced interruptions that were gradual rather than abrupt.

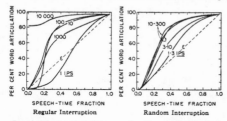

SPEECH-TIME FRACTION
Regular Interruption

SPEECH-TIME FRACTION
Random Interruption

FIG. 6. Word articulation as a function of the speech-time fraction, with frequency of interruption as the parameter, for both regularly spaced and randomly spaced interruptions.

The modulating voltage took various proportions of the time to rise from 0 to 1 and to return. The results of these tests are shown in Fig. 7, where the articulation score is plotted as a function of the percentage of the time occupied by the build-up and decay of the speech burst. These data were obtained with regular interruptions 4 and 16 times per second and, figuring the speech to be "on" whenever it is more than half-way on, with a speech-time fraction of 0.5. Changing from abrupt to gradual modulation improved both the quality and the intelligibility of the interrupted speech.

Returning to abrupt modulation, a curious effect was obtained when, instead of turning the speech wave off, we simply turned it over. At low frequencies, periodic inversion of the speech wave form did not affect intelligibility, but as the frequency of inversion is increased a number of the speech sounds acquired a W-like character. The process of reversing polarity turned itself into "the pwowess of wewersing."

In a short series of tests, we examined the listeners' ability to hear two talkers at once. In some of the tests, the talkers' voices were interwoven as the electronic switch alternated between them 10 or 100 times per second. In other tests the talkers spoke together and their speech waves were superposed without switching. And, in still other tests for purposes of comparison, the talkers spoke singly. The results are summarized in Table I. When both voices were on continuously the listeners heard correctly more than half the words spoken by each talker. The total number of words heard correctly was greater (126) than when either talker spoke alone (99). When the talkers' voices

alternated 10 times per second the listeners got 92 words correct which is the same number of words they heard when one talker spoke alone. When the voices alternated 100 times per second, the listeners got fewer words correct (75) than when either talker spoke alone (98). Alternating the two voices does not reduce the interference between them: if two talkers are going to speak to a listener at the same time, no advantage can be gained by switching back and forth between the two voices. In the series of tests with two talkers only about two-thirds of the words that were heard correctly were attributed to the talker who had uttered them.

Applications

Interruptions that do not seriously impair intelligibility are of practical utility. Time-multiplex and pulse-code systems of speech transmission take advantage of the fact that intelligibility is not impaired by regular interruptions at a high frequency. These systems sample the fluctuating amplitude of the speech wave at very frequent intervals and the sample contains all the information that is carried by the original wave. (Shannon has shown that a signal confined to band width W can be described uniquely by $2W$ samples per second.)[5]

A related but quite different application would take advantage of the maximum between 10 and 100 interruptions per second in the curve relating intelligibility to interruption rate. In 1936 Marro, who repeated the earlier work of Poirson,[6] suggested the use of two-way transmission in a single frequency channel by switching from transmit to receiver and back about 20 times per second.[7] Switching would allow the transmitters at both

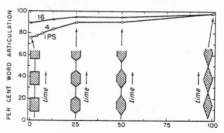

PERCENTAGE OF TIME OCCUPIED BY RISE AND FALL

FIG. 7. Effects of reducing the abruptness with which the speech is turned on and off. Gradual transition from off to on and back produces less interference than abrupt transition if speech is "half-way on" for the same fraction of the time.

[5] C. E. Shannon, "Communication in the presence of noise," Proc. Inst. Rad. Eng. 37, 10–21 (1949).

[6] E. Poirson, "Sur les déformations systematiques des courants téléphoniques. Application à un procédé de téléphonie secrète." Bull. Soc. Franc. Élect. 103, 147–161 (1920).

[7] M. Marro, "On the persistence of the sensation of speech," Phil. Mag. 22, 847–854 (1936); "Amplificateur téléphonique duplex employant un phénomène de persistance d'impressions sonores sur l'ouïe," Rev. Gén. Élect. 39, 458–461 (1936); "Two-way speech by wireless. Method of utilizing persistence of hear-

TABLE I. Articulation scores obtained with two talkers speaking alone and together.

| | Interruptions (or alternations) per second | | |
	None	10	100
Talker H alone	99.8%	89.0	97.6
Talker L alone	98.8	94.6	98.4
H and L together:			
H's words	64.5	34.3	32.8
L's words	62.1	58.0	41.9
Average	63.3	46.2	37.4

ends of the link to operate in the same frequency channel without blocking the adjacent receivers.

Recently the idea of infrasonic switching was proposed again by Montani.[8] Montani made the statement, however, that—because of the persistence of hearing—15 interruptions per second are inaudible. We agree that interruptions are inaudible, but only in the sense that little is heard during interruptions. Despite 15 gaps per second, it is easy to understand what is being said, but the talker sounds as though he has a strange defect of phonation. A very similar effect is obtained by patting the lips lightly and rapidly while speaking.

SPEECH INTERRUPTED BY NOISE

We turn now to the situation in which speech is left on continuously but is heard in the presence of interrupted masking noise. The speech is not intermittently attenuated—it is intermittently masked. The experiments already described must be duplicated to explore the same variables—noise-time fraction, frequency and regularity of interruption—but now these apply to noise rather than to speech. To these three variables we must add a fourth, the signal-to-noise ratio.

The signal-to-noise ratios to be given will refer to

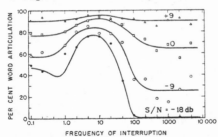

FIG. 8. The masking of continuous speech by interrupted noise. Word articulation is plotted against the frequency of interruption of the noise, with the speech-to-noise ratio in decibels as the parameter. Noise-time fraction, 0.5.

ing," Electrician 118, 5 (1937); "À propos d'un phénomène de persistance des impressions sonores sur l'ouïe: radio téléphonie duplex simultanée," Rev. Gén. Élect. 41, 527–530 (1937); "Esperienze relative alla persistenza della sensazione uditiva," Arch. Ital. Psicol. 17, 67–70 (1939); "Two-way speech by wireless," Phil. Mag. 28, 248–251 (1939); "Secrecy by inversion of syllables," Phil. Mag. 29, 205–207 (1940).

[8] A. Montani, "Infrasonic switching," Electronics 19, No. 3, 214–222 (1946).

the intervals during which the noise is on. These ratios, which will be stated in decibels, can be changed to averages for the entire cycle by expressing the silent-time fraction in decibel notation and subtracting it. Thus, if the noise is on half the time, the silent-time fraction is 0.5 or −3 db, and the signal-to-noise ratio averaged over the cycle is 3 db higher than the signal-to-noise ratio measured during a typical burst of noise.

The signal-to-noise ratios, measured during bursts of noise and in the frequency band from 100 to 7000 c.p.s., were −18, −9, 0, and +9 db. The average speech level

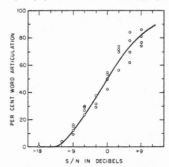

FIG. 9. Word articulation for continuous speech heard in the presence of continuous noise, plotted as a function of the signal-to-noise ratio in decibels. The average level of the speech was held constant at approximately 90 db re 0.0002 dyne/cm².

was held constant at 90 db re 0.0002 dyne/cm². The tests with interrupted noise were run during the same sessions and with the same equipment and personnel as the tests with interrupted speech that are summarized in Figs. 4, 5, and 6. Therefore the results to be discussed now can be compared directly with the results discussed in the preceding section.

Regularly Spaced Bursts of Noise

Figure 8 summarizes the results obtained with regular interruptions of the masking noise and a noise-time fraction of 0.5. At the lowest frequencies of interruption the articulation score behaves in about the same way it does when the speech is interrupted by silence. Consider first the function obtained with a signal-to-noise ratio of −18 db. When the noise is on it completely masks the speech, so 5 seconds of speech and noise alternating regularly with 5 seconds of speech alone gives an articulation score of approximately 50 percent; all the words heard at all are heard correctly. As the frequency of interruption is increased to 10 per second the articulation score rises (see lower most curve of Fig. 8 and curve 3 of Fig. 2). When there were 10 bursts of noise per second the listeners were able to get several glimpses of every word and to patch these glimpses together well enough to record three-fourths of the test words correctly.

When the slow bursts of noise do not drown out completely the speech that occurs with them, the articulation score is higher than the silent-time fraction. In a test of 100 words, for example, about 50 of the words will occur in the silent interval and will be heard correctly. The remaining 50 words are heard in the presence of noise, and the articulation score for these masked words depends upon the signal-to-noise ratio. Figure 9 presents the results obtained when speech was masked by a continuous noise. With Fig. 9 it is possible to estimate what fraction of the masked words are heard correctly. For example, with a signal-to-noise ratio of 0 db the listeners heard correctly 50 percent of the masked

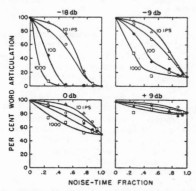

FIG. 10. Word articulation plotted against noise-time fraction, with the frequency of interruption of the noise and the signal-to-noise ratio as parameters.

words. If the noise is interrupted half the time and once every 10 seconds, the listeners should get 50 percent for the unmasked words plus half of the masked words, or a total articulation score of approximately 75 percent. This method of estimation is relatively accurate for interruption frequencies below one per second.

At the other extreme of interruption frequency, also, the masking produced by interrupted noise can be estimated from Fig. 9. When the noise is interrupted several hundred times each second it is effectively continuous insofar as aural masking is concerned. With a noise-time fraction of 0.5 the level of the noise averaged over a full on-off cycle is 3 db lower than it would have been had the noise been on all the time. Thus the articulation score obtained in the presence of a noise interrupted 1000 times a second and half the total time is the same as the one obtained in the presence of a continuous noise 3 db lower in intensity.

The range of interruption frequencies between 10 and 1000 per second remains to be discussed. This portion of the functions can be estimated with the aid of results obtained by Miller and Garner in their study of

the masking of tones by interrupted noise.[9] Their results are summarized in a single function that relates the masking efficiency of an interrupted noise (ratio of masking by interrupted to masking by continuous noise) to the duration of the silent intervals. When the silent interval is shorter than 3 or 4 milliseconds—higher than about 150 interruptions per second at a noise-time fraction of 0.5—the interrupted noise is effectively continuous. For lower frequencies the masking by interrupted noise is a proper fraction of the masking by continuous noise. Miller and Garner's results can be used to estimate the change in the masked threshold for tones, and from the new masked threshold the articulation score can be computed in the manner described by French and Steinberg.[10]

The effects of varying the noise-time fraction are summarized in Fig. 10. Four rates of interruption were used—1, 10, 100 and 1000 per second. At all noise-time fractions and all signal-to-noise ratios, 10 bursts of noise per second produced the least interference and 1000 bursts of noise per second produced the most interference. Since the signal-to-noise ratios refer to the intervals during which the noise is on, the amount of interference of course increases with increasing noise-time fraction.

Irregularly Spaced Bursts of Noise

The effects of irregular interruption of the masking noise were explored at a signal-to-noise ratio of −9 db. The method for turning the noise on and off at random was the same as that described in the preceding section for turning speech on and off at random. The results are summarized in Fig. 11, where the noise-time fraction is plotted against the frequency of interruption, with articulation score as the parameter. The solid functions represent the results obtained with regular interruptions (see Fig. 10), and the dashed functions

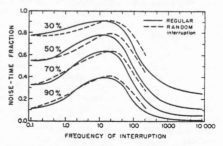

FIG. 11. Equal-articulation contours obtained with a masking noise interrupted regularly and at random. Signal-to-noise ratio, −9 db.

[9] G. A. Miller and W. R. Garner, "The masking of tones by repeated bursts of noise," J. Acous. Soc. Am. 20, 691–696 (1948), see Figs. 3 and 6, and Eq. (2).
[10] N. R. French and J. C. Steinberg, "Factors governing the intelligibility of speech sounds," J. Acous. Soc. Am. 19, 90–119 (1947).

represent the results obtained with irregular interruptions. The effect of irregularity is to smooth the functions slightly, but qualitatively the picture is quite similar for regularly and randomly interrupted masking noise.

SPEECH ALTERNATING WITH NOISE

The preceding sections have discussed the results obtained (1) when speech is interrupted by silence, and (2) when continuous speech is masked by an interrupted noise. A third class of tests explored the effects of alternating speech and noise. These tests are similar to (1), except that the silent intervals are filled with noise. They are similar to (2), except that the speech is not present when the masking noise is on. By comparing the results with (1) we obtain an estimate of how much the masking effect of a burst of noise 'spills over' into temporally adjacent intervals. If the ear recovered immediately from the masking produced by a burst of noise, no effect would be observed when noise was introduced during the silent interval. By comparing the results with (2) we obtain an estimate of how much the speech during the bursts of noise contributes to intelligibility.

Results of Articulation Tests

The articulation scores obtained when speech alternated with noise are shown in Fig. 12. The speech-time fraction was 0.50, the frequency of interruption was varied from 0.1 to 10,000 per second, and the signal-to-noise ratio was varied from −18 to +9 db. The top curve in Fig. 12 has been taken from Fig. 4 and represents the scores obtained when no noise is introduced into the intervals between successive bursts of speech. So long as the frequency of alternation is below 4.6 per second the introduction of noise during the "no-speech" intervals has practically no effect upon the articulation scores. With intervals longer than about 0.1 second the alternation between speech and noise is not different from the alternation between speech and silence. The recovery time of the auditory system is negligible (for the noise levels used) in comparison to intervals of 0.1 second or longer.

When the frequency of alternation is increased to or beyond 215 per second, the noise masks the speech with which it alternates just as effectively as if both speech and noise were on at the same time. Thus, although the decay of the masking effect is rapid enough that the intelligibility of a 100-millisecond burst of speech is not impaired by the noise preceding and following it, the decay is not instantaneous. At 215 alternations per second between speech and noise intervals of equal length, the intervals are 2.3 milliseconds long. During a speech interval of that duration the auditory system does not recover sufficiently to derive any information at all from the speech wave.

As an intermediate example we can take 100 alternations per second, which gives intervals of speech and of noise each 5 milliseconds long. In this instance a sur-

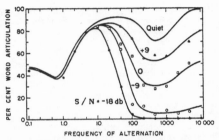

FIG. 12. Word articulation as a function of the frequency of alternation between speech and noise, with signal-to-noise ratio in decibels as the parameter.

round of noise 18 db more intense than the speech lowers the articulation score from 90 to 4 percent (see Fig. 12). From Fig. 9 we find that this shift is equivalent to that produced by a change of 24 db (12 to −12 db) in signal-to-noise ratio. Hence the "spill over" into temporally adjacent regions must be about 24 db greater with 5-millisecond intervals than with 100-millisecond intervals.

The principal difference between alternating speech and noise and masking speech with interrupted noise appears in the region from 200 to 2000 interruptions per second. In that region unintelligible components arising from the modulation of the speech by the interrupter contribute significantly to the masking. We have the dip in the quiet curve of Fig. 12 *plus* the "spill-over" masking due to the noise. Above 2000 per second the functions approach the values indicated for continuous speech and noise in Fig. 9.

The "Picket Fence" Effect

An interesting effect is observed if noise is introduced into the gaps between bursts of speech when the speech is interrupted about 10 to 15 times per second. Without the noise the talker's voice sounds hoarse and raucous. The speech is intelligible, but the interruptions are quite evident. When noise is introduced between the bursts of speech, the on and off transients are assimilated into the noise and, when the noise is somewhat more intense than the speech, the speech begins to sound continuous and uninterrupted. It is much like seeing a landscape through a picket fence—the pickets interrupt the view at regular intervals, but the landscape is perceived as continuing behind the pickets. The same effect can be obtained with pure tones. An interrupted tone will sound quite pure and continuous if the intervals between the bursts of tone are filled with a sufficiently intense white noise. When interrupted tone is made to sound continuous by 'masking the silent intervals,' the listener feels that the speech is certainly more natural and probably more intelligible. As Fig. 12 shows, however, no actual improvement in intelligibility was obtained by adding noise.

9

Reprinted from *J. Exp. Psychol.* **54**(6):412–422 (1957)

INTELLIGIBILITY AS A FUNCTION OF FREQUENCY OF USAGE[1]

MARK R. ROSENZWEIG AND LEO POSTMAN

University of California

Frequency of usage of words has been demonstrated to be the most important factor determining thresholds of *visual* recognition of individual words in tachistoscopic tests (**5**). There are some indications in the literature that frequency of usage may also be an important factor in determining intelligibility of words in *auditory* tests. The results obtained to date in audition do not seem conclusive, however, so we have attacked this question directly in two experiments, one in English[2] and the other in French.[3]

Recognition of the possible role of frequency was shown in the preparation of the PB (phonetically balanced) monosyllabic word lists by the Psycho-Acoustic Laboratory (**2**). Words of an original list were rated for familiarity, and the less familiar items were eliminated from the final list. Black (**1**) in 1952 determined intelligibility scores for more than three thousand words, and he investigated a number of correlates of intelligibility. He concluded that intelligibility scores varied with frequency of usage.[4] He

also confirmed previous findings that longer words tend both to be more intelligible and to occur less frequently in the language than do shorter words. "Thus two contrary influences, word familiarity and word complexity, appear to operate in the auditory recognition of words somewhat independently of the phonetic content" (**1**, p. 417). Black's results are limited by the fact that he excluded from his experiment words which were found in pretests to be more than 80% or less than 20% intelligible. Howes (**4**) in a preliminary study reanalyzed the results of Mason and Garrison (**8**) on the intelligibility of three-word sentences. He correlated the intelligibility scores of the sentences with the log frequency of usage of the least frequent word in each sentence. The coefficient of correlation was .68, indicating that the frequency of usage of the least common word accounted for about half of the variance in sentence thresholds.

METHOD

English Experiment

Test materials.—The words used in the English experiment are given in Table 1. In order to control for effects of word length, only monosyllabic words were used. The frequency of usage of each word was determined from the Lorge Magazine Count of 4,500,000 words (**16**), since we considered that this count would best approximate oral usage. Words were selected in four ranges of frequency: 1–3, 10–33, 100–330, and 1000–3300. The words were drawn at random from the Psycho-Acoustic Laboratory PB lists until eight words had been selected for each of the three highest frequency categories. A few words were rejected in

---

[1] The main results of this research were presented in a paper read at the Third International Congress on Acoustics, Cambridge, Massachusetts, June 19, 1956.

[2] We wish to thank Mrs. Sheila Walsh for her aid in collecting the data of the English experiment.

[3] The French experiment was done by the first author at the Sorbonne during a sabbatical semester. We wish to thank Professor Paul Fraisse, Directeur du Laboratoire de Psychologie Expérimentale, without whose generous aid and hospitality this research could not have been done.

[4] The frequency count used by Black was the 1931 Thorndike list (**15**) which is weighted heavily with children's books.

order to avoid too great similarity among items. After the experiment had been run, we discovered that, due to a clerical error, seven words had been included in the 10–33 range and nine words in the 100–330 range. Therefore the scores for these ranges were weighted appropriately in the statistical analyses. Since most low-frequency words had been eliminated from the PB lists during their construction, we obtained monosyllables of frequencies 1–3 by drawing at random from the Lorge Magazine Count. The 32 words were arranged in seven randomly ordered lists. A different additional word was placed at the beginning of each list to act as a buffer word in the test. The lists were then tape recorded. Each word was preceded by a number and by the carrier phrase, "You will write." The speaker monitored his voice level on the carrier phrase. Immediately after the number of the word was given, white noise was introduced into the recorder, masking the carrier phrase and the test word. The first list was recorded at a signal-to-noise ratio of −12 db. Each successive list was masked by 4 db less noise, so that the lists became progressively more intelligible. The seventh list was recorded in the quiet. The words were given at 10-sec. intervals; the lists were separated by 30-sec. intervals.

Subjects.—The Ss were 109 students in summer session courses in psychology at the University of California. They were run in groups of 15 to 20. They did not know the purpose of the experiment.

Procedure.—The Ss were told that they would hear words in the presence of noise, and they were instructed to write in the appropriate space on their answer sheets whatever they heard at each stimulus presentation. They could write a word, a part of a word, or nothing at all. Before the test, examples were given of two words masked by rather intense noise and of the same words masked by rather weak noise. A separate answer sheet was provided for each of the seven lists. At the end of the experiment, S was instructed to turn over his booklet of answer sheets and to write on the back sheet all of the words that he could remember from the test. This procedure was added because we were interested in the effects on recall of the initial familiarity of the items and of the frequency of recognition during the threshold experiment. Five minutes were allowed for the recall test.

Following the recall test, S was instructed to write the name of his native language on his booklet. Eighty-seven Ss gave English as their native language; we shall refer to this group as the English Group. Twelve gave some other language; this group will be designated

TABLE 1

STIMULUS WORDS AND THEIR FREQUENCIES OF USAGE

English Experiment		French Experiment	
Word	Frequency per 4,500,000	Word	Frequency per 312,000
Flange	1	Guidon	1
Prism	1	Hernie	1
Dram	2	Notice	1
Larch	2	Pliant	1
Thrall	2		
Tithe	2		
Cull	3		
Hoot	3		
Cud	10	Visage	9
Jab	13	Bouton	10
Foe	18	Cabine	10
Pelt	20	Niveau	10
Pew	24		
Gem	30		
Hash	32		
Cheat	102	Besoin	85
Ridge	111	Malade	87
Rouse	115	Dedans	91
Lump	117	Argent	98
Apt	132		
Barn	176		
Curve	202		
Bean	265		
Ray	325		
Age	1022	Enfant	305
Price	1026	Jamais	325
Chair	1298	Petite	332
Reach	1457	Moment	337
Walk	2084		
Next	2321		
Find	2698		
Put	2896		

the Foreign Group. Ten gave both English and another language; this group will be called the Bilingual Group.

Scoring procedure.—To determine thresholds, the first correct transcription of each word was scored for each S. Thus, for each S, the word was given a score that ranged from 1 to 7, the number being that of the trial on which the word was first reported correctly. If S never reported the word correctly, it was scored 8. In addition, each response was assigned to one of four categories: C—a correct response; M—a meaningful word, but an incorrect response; N—a nonsense response, i.e., a letter or sequence of letters without dictionary meaning; B—a blank, i.e., a failure to respond.

TABLE 2

SCORES OF RECOGNITION FOR THE FOUR FREQUENCY RANGES OF STIMULI

English Experiment

Ss	N	Frequency Ranges							
		1–3		10–33		100–330		1000–3300	
		Mean	SD	Mean	SD	Mean	SD	Mean	SD
English	87	6.87	.52	6.10	.52	41.41	4.73	4.08	.63
Bilingual	10	7.15	.40	6.16	.71	5.54	.54	3.92	.46
Foreign	12	7.44	.42	6.84	.70	5.87	.71	4.51	.61

French Experiment

Ss	N	Frequency Ranges							
		1		10		100		330	
		Mean	SD	Mean	SD	Mean	SD	Mean	SD
French	60	6.72	.48	6.16	.63	5.22	.47	5.48 (5.28)*	.58 (.59)*

* Liberal scoring of response to *Petite*.

French Experiment

Test materials.—The French experiment was similar to the English one but was less extensive. The words used are given in Table 1. They are disyllabic words, six letters long, selected from the count of oral usage made for *Le Français Elémentaire* (3).[5] The French count is based on only 312,000 running words, and we could use a range of only two and one-half log units of frequency for the experiment. The words were chosen to have frequencies as close as possible to 1, 10, 100, and 330, while avoiding undue similarity among items. Four other words were used as fillers. The 20 words were arranged in seven randomly ordered lists. Starting with a signal-to-noise ratio of −12 db for the first list, the masking noise was reduced by 3 db for each successive list; the last list was recorded in the quiet. The word *Ecrivez* was used as the carrier phrase. The recording was made by a professional French actor at the studios of the Centre d'Etudes de Radio-Télévision in Paris.[6]

In order to present the test to the main group of Ss at the Sorbonne, it was necessary to re-record the tape, and some noise and distortion were unfortunately introduced at this step. A preliminary test had been made with six Ss, using the original tape in the recording studio. Comparison of their results with those of the main group show that the re-recording raised thresholds by about 5 db.

Subjects.—The Ss were students in a course in experimental psychology at the Sorbonne. They were run in a single group. The Ss did not know the purpose of the experiment. The answer sheets were scored for only those students whose native language was French—a total of 60 Ss.

Procedure.—The instructions—similar to those in the English experiment—were recorded by the speaker, and examples of words masked by noise were also given before the test. No recall test was given to this group. The scoring procedure was the same as for the English experiment.

[5] This word count, then unpublished, was made available to us by Professeur G. Gougenheim, Directeur du Centre d'Etude du Français Elémentaire. We are grateful to him and to Professeur P. Rivenc, Directeur-adjoint, for helping us to use the materials prepared by the Centre.

[6] We are grateful to Monsieur Jean Tardieu, Director du Centre d'Etudes de Radio-Télévision, at whose studios the recording was made.

RESULTS

Thresholds

English experiment.—Thresholds were computed separately for the English Group, the Bilingual Group, and the Foreign Group. The sum of the thresholds for all of the words of a frequency range was determined for each *S*. The mean threshold per *S* per word for each frequency range is presented in Table 2. Let us consider first the English Group which formed the bulk of the *S*s. Their thresholds decrease steadily with increasing frequency of usage. An analysis of variance of their threshold scores showed that the differences among words of the four frequency ranges were highly significant (3 and 258 *df*; $F = 503.67$; $P < .001$). Using Tukey's gap test (9), we found that each of the successive differences was significant.

The thresholds of the Bilingual and Foreign Groups are higher than those of the English Group, but the relationships between thresholds and word frequency are similar in all groups. An analysis of variance was made to compare the three groups.[7] The variance due to groups of *S*s was highly significant (2 and 106 *df*; $F = 13.76$; $P < .001$). The interaction between groups and frequency ranges fell short of significance. In order to test the significance of the differences between individual group means, we used the method of allowances (cf. 9, pp. 304–307). The difference between the English and the Foreign Groups was significant beyond the .01 level; between the Bilingual and Foreign Groups, at the .01 level.

[7] The numbers of *S*s in the three groups are, of course, quite different. However, since the subclass numbers are proportional, it is possible to perform a conventional analysis of variance (see Snedecor [14, p. 281]).

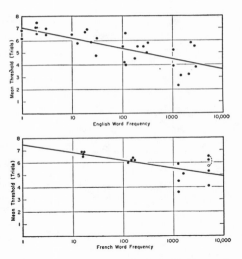

FIG. 1. Thresholds of individual words versus their frequencies of usage, plotted separately for the English and French experiments.

The difference between the English and Bilingual Groups was not significant.

The thresholds of native speakers for all words are shown in Fig. 1. In the English experiment the least frequent words were perceived correctly, on the average, only on the last trial. The most frequent words were perceived, on the average, on about the fourth trial. Thus it appears that the most frequent words could be perceived, on the average, through about 12 db more noise than could the least frequent words, though it must be recognized that the sequential nature of the trials may have influenced this result. The relation between threshold and log frequency is approximately linear. The correlation between threshold and log frequency is $-.78$.[8] It may be interesting to consider only the words drawn from the Psycho-Acous-

[8] This correlation is similar to correlations ranging from $-.68$ to $-.75$ reported by Howes and Solomon (5) between frequency of usage and *visual* thresholds.

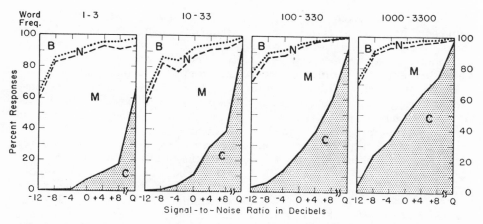

FIG. 2. Percentages of responses in the English experiment falling into each of the four response categories, graphed separately for each frequency range of stimuli. Each curve represents the sum of all the categories whose initials lie below the curve.

tic Laboratory PB lists (the three categories of highest frequency), since these lists are phonetically balanced and are used widely in articulation testing. This selection from the experimental series of course restricts the range and lowers the correlation. In this case the correlation becomes −.62; it is significantly different from 0 beyond the .01 level.

French experiment.—The sum of the thresholds for the words of each frequency range was determined for each S. The mean thresholds per S per word for the four frequency ranges are presented in Table 2. For the first three frequency ranges the thresholds in the French experiment are similar to those in the English experiment, and there is a regular decline of threshold with frequency. For the words of highest frequency, however, there is a small increase of threshold over that of the third range. It will be noted that two mean thresholds are presented for the highest frequency range. These thresholds differ only because of the scoring of one word, the adjective *Petite* which many

Ss first heard as *Petit*. The lower threshold is based on a more liberal scoring in which either the feminine or the musculine form was counted as correct. An analysis of variance was made of these data, based on the strict scoring. As in the English experiment, the variance due to frequency ranges is highly significant (3 and 177 df; $F = 96.73$; $P < .001$). The gap test shows that all of the differences are significant, including the inversion at the last step. With a second analysis of variance using the more liberal scoring for *Petite*, frequency remains highly significant, but the final inversion is no longer significant.

The thresholds for all French words are shown in the lower graph of Fig. 1. To make word frequencies in the two experiments roughly comparable on the graphs, the frequencies of the French words, based on a sample of 312,000 have been multiplied by 14.4 in order to approximate the 4,500,000 word base of the English sample. The least frequent words in the French experiment had a mean threshold of about 7; words of the two categories of highest frequency had mean thresholds of about 5. The correlation between threshold and log frequency is −.65, which is significantly different from 0 at the .01 level. With the more liberal scoring of "Petite," the correlation between thresholds and log frequency becomes −.71; this is very close to the correlation we found in the English experiment.

Distribution of Responses

English experiment.—Fig. 2 presents the results obtained in the English experiment when the responses were categorized as C (correct), M (meaningful but incorrect), N (nonsense), and B (blank). A separate graph has been drawn for the responses to stimuli of each frequency range. The solid curves show the percentage of correct responses on the successive trials. Without exception, each solid curve lies above the preceding one at every point. The dashed curves show the sum of the correct and the meaningful responses, that is, the percentages of all English responses. Note that these curves are similar

in height and shape for all four frequency ranges of stimuli. In other words, Ss showed about the same number of English responses for all groups of stimuli, but there was a greater tendency for these responses to be *correct* when the stimuli were frequent than when they were infrequent.

French experiment.—Figure 3 presents the results of the French experiment when the same four response categories were used. The curves are similar to those of Fig. 2, except that there is a larger proportion of blanks. The initial masking effect was greater in the French experiment, and this may also have reduced the set to give words in the later lists. The dashed curves show the percentage of responses that were French words, whether correct or incorrect. As in the English experiment, these curves are similar for all four frequency ranges of stimuli.

Nonsense Responses

English experiment.—Only 3% of all responses in the English experiment were nonsense responses. The graphs

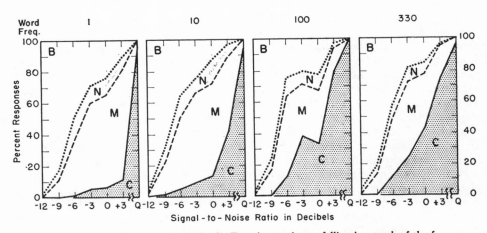

FIG. 3. Percentages of responses in the French experiment falling into each of the four response categories, graphed separately for each frequency range of stimuli.

TABLE 3

MEAN FREQUENCY OF RECOGNITIONS PER
SUBJECT FOR WORDS RECALLED
AND NOT RECALLED

	High-Frequency Words		Low-Frequency Words		All Words	
	Mean	SD	Mean	SD	Mean	SD
Recalled	3.35	.67	2.00	.63	5.35	1.04
Not Recalled	2.83	.55	1.53	.35	4.36	.70

in Fig. 2 indicate that somewhat more nonsense responses were given to the stimuli in the lower two frequency ranges than to those in the higher two ranges. To test the significance of this difference we performed an analysis of variance. The distribution of the rather rare nonsense responses approximated a Poisson distribution, and the Freeman-Tukey transformation ($\sqrt{X} + \sqrt{X + 1}$ [9]) was used to remove heterogeneity of variance. In the case of a Poisson distribution, the error variance ideally becomes approximately 1.00 under this transformation (9, p. 326). For our data, the error variance of the transformed data is .92. The difference indicated by the graphs between words of lower and higher frequency is highly significant (3 and 258 df; $F = 17.70$; $P < .001$). Apparently it is somewhat easier to base a nonsense response on a discriminated fragment of a low-frequency word than on a discriminated fragment of a high-frequency word.

French experiment.—In this experiment the nonsense responses were again rather rare, accounting for about 6% of all responses. As in the English experiment, Fig. 3 indicates the nonsense responses to have been given somewhat more frequently to stimuli of the two lower frequency ranges. We performed an analysis of variance of these data, using the Freeman-Tukey transformation. Here again the results of the English experiment are closely paralleled.

Meaningful Responses

English experiment.—The meaningful but incorrect responses were listed for each of the stimuli in the English experiment. The frequency of each meaningful response was then found in the Lorge Magazine Count. In general these responses were found to be of rather high frequency of occurrence in the language. Thirty-four per cent had frequencies equal to or greater than 1000 per 4,500,000. Such a high frequency is shown by only 512 words of the total of 30,000 in the Lorge Count. These results indicate that Ss tended strongly to restrict their responses to words of high frequency of usage.

French experiment.—The meaningful responses were analyzed as in the English experiment. Since the French stimuli were bisyllables and word frequency decreases with word length, it was expected that the meaningful responses would be of lower frequency of occurrence than those of the English experiment. It was found that 15% had frequencies equal to or greater than 1000 per 4,500,000. This high a frequency was found for only 417 words in the French count. Here too, then, Ss tended to limit their responses to rather common words.

Recall Test

The results of the test of recall given at the end of the threshold test are presented in Table 3. The stimulus words were divided into four classes for each S: (a) Recalled words of high frequency (frequency ≥ 100); (b) Non-recalled words of high frequency; (c) Recalled words of low frequency (frequency ≤ 33); and (d) Non-recalled words of low frequency. For each S, we calculated the mean number of times that he had recognized words of each of these classes. Table 3 presents the mean numbers of recognitions per S. It will be seen that within each of the two frequency categories, recall accompanied greater frequency of recognition, and these differences were found to be significant in an analysis of variance. At the same time, it should be noted that the high frequency words that were *not* recalled had been recognized, on the average, one-third more often than the low-frequency words that *were* recalled; i.e., recall increased more slowly with exercise for high-frequency words than for low-frequency words. These results suggest that frequency of usage played a dual role in determining the recall scores of the stimuli: (a) On the one hand, the more frequent words were recognized more often than the less frequent words during the threshold tests, and this greater exercise favored recall. (b) On the other hand, the more frequent words were probably subjected to more interference than the less frequent words during the threshold test. Most of the responses in the threshold test were words of high frequency, and maximal retroactive inhibition is favored by approximate equality of learning of original and interpolated material (6, p. 417) and by similarity in their association values (13). The two hypothesized effects of frequency of usage presumably canceled each other out in this situation. The percentage of recall, among Ss who had recognized a word at least once, was 37.4

or the high-frequency words and 37.0 for the low-frequency words.

DISCUSSION

Role of frequency of usage.—In both the English and the French experiments, frequency of usage is clearly the most important factor determining the differences among thresholds, since it accounts for about half the variance. Furthermore, this is probably an underestimate of the effect of frequency. The only measures of frequency that we could use are population averages, and they do not reflect individual differences in frequency of usage. It is also pertinent to note that the frequency measure in the English experiment had to be based on *written* usage, since no adequate count of oral usage in English is available. Nevertheless, the correlation between written frequency and auditory thresholds is high. There are two reasons for expecting written frequency to approach auditory frequency as a predictor of auditory thresholds: (a) Counts of written and oral frequencies made in French show fairly close correspondences, although there are characteristic differences (3). (b) In an earlier experiment, we have shown a significant relation between the frequency of visual training and auditory thresholds (12). It may nevertheless be asked why the French experiment, which did utilize an oral count of frequency, did not show a somewhat higher correlation between threshold and frequency than the English experiment. We may note two factors which tended to reduce the correlation in the French experiment relative to that of the English experiment: (a) The sample of items in the French experiment was only half as large as that in the English experiment, and it would therefore be expected to be less reliable. (b) The range of frequency in the French experiment was only two and one-half log units as compared with three and one-half in the English experiment. We have already seen that restricting the range to two and one-half units in the English experiment reduced the correlation to a value below that of the French experiment.

As to the mechanism of the effect of frequency, we would offer these considerations: When the word is heavily masked, it is likely that only a part of it will be discriminated. The *S* bases his report on this fragmentary perception and his knowledge of the language. The responses in most cases were either correct or meaningful but incorrect; i.e., *S* had no difficulty in giving responses that both resembled the stimulus and conformed to his language. Furthermore, the responses tended to be of relatively high frequency of occurrence in the language, and, for each stimulus, a few words tended to account for a rather large proportion of the meaningful but incorrect responses. Thus it appears that the masked stimulus plus *S*'s language habits tend to favor a small number of competing responses of relatively high frequency. If the stimulus word is itself of relatively high frequency of occurrence in the language, it will tend to be prominent among these competitors, and thus it will tend to be reported on an early trial. If, on the other hand, the stimulus is of relatively low frequency of occurrence, it is unlikely to be among the main competing responses on the early trials. In this case more information—a less ambiguous stimulus of the later lists— will be needed to secure recognition of the rarer stimulus word.

Effects of word length.—Since intelligibility has been shown to increase with word length (2), we selected for each experiment test items that were homogeneous in syllabic length—monosyllables in the English experiment and bisyllables in the French experiment. Howes (4), although he does not mention this point, also used a relatively homogenous group of items. The words he used for his analysis—the least frequent words in the sentences of Mason and Garrison (8)—were almost all bisyllables. Using items that were homo-geneous in length, both Howes and we found word frequency to account for about half the variance in thresholds. Black (1), on the other hand, used items that were heterogeneous in length, and he did not control for word length in his analysis of the effect of frequency. Though concluding that frequency of usage was a significant source of variance, he did not find it to account for a large proportion of the variance. The difference between his results and ours may thus be due to uncontrolled effects of word length in Black's experiment.

It is interesting to note that although length of words is correlated negatively with their *auditory* thresholds, it is correlated positively with their *visual* thresholds (7). This difference may be related to a previous observation: "Auditory discrimination of verbal stimuli tends to be made in units such as syllables. Visual discrimination is more analytic. The *S* can effectively attend to units of different sizes" (12, p. 218). Thus a perceived fragment of an auditory stimulus tends to be completed in the response; the longer the auditory stimulus word, the greater the chance that *S* will perceive at least part of it and then complete the rest. A perceived fragment of a visual stimulus tends to be reported as such; the longer the visual stimulus word, the greater the chance that part of it will not be perceived and that the report will be incomplete.

Applications.—Since frequency of usage is the major determinant of threshold variance, it should be controlled in experiments designed to test the effects on intelligibility of other factors such as word length, phonetic composition, and length of the test list. Articulation tests might also be examined from this point of view. A sample of three of the PAL PB lists (Numbers 1, 10, and 20 [2]) indicates that they are similar in frequency composition: About 8% of the words have frequencies of less than 10 on the Lorge Magazine Count. The ranges 10–33, 100–330, and 1000–3300 all contain about equal numbers of items. While the lists seem satisfactorily similar to each other, the test might be made more discriminating for acoustic factors if the range of frequency of the items was reduced. This point seems especially pertinent when the articulation test is given to *S*s who have had little or no preliminary training with the word lists, as in clinical audiometry. When considerable training with the test lists has been given, frequency of usage may be less important in determining the thresholds.

Lists of highly intelligible words are sometimes required for various purposes, e.g., alphabetic equivalents for telephonic, aviation or military use. In the preparation of such lists, an initial screening might be done in terms of relative frequency of usage.

Recall test.—According to Osgood (11) an interference theory of forgetting must predict that meaningful items will be recalled less well than nonsense items. Meaningful material occurs more often than nonsense material, and thus the meaningful items of a test should suffer greater interference from preceding or interpolated material. Underwood and Richardson (17) have recently presented data that tend to support this hypothesis, using nonsense syllables of high and low association values. The stimuli that we used can be considered to vary in meaningfulness in the sense that the words of higher frequency are more familiar and have greater "meaning value" (10) than do words of lower frequency. Since our data suggest that susceptibility to interference varies directly with frequency of usage, our findings are in agreement with Osgood's analysis and with the results of Underwood and Richardson.

SUMMARY

Parallel experiments were performed in English and French in order to determine whether the intelligibility of words masked by noise varies with the frequency of usage of the words. In each experiment, the items were homogeneous in syllabic length. Correlations between intelligibility scores and log frequency were −.78 and −.65 in the respective experiments, indicating that frequency of usage accounts for about half the variance of the thresholds.[9] Nonsense responses were rare, but in both experiments they were given significantly more often to stimuli of low frequency than to stimuli of high frequency. Most of the incorrect responses were meaningful words, and these tended to be of high frequency of usage. In the English experiment, *S*s attempted to recall the stimuli at the end of the threshold test. The high-frequency words, though they had been recognized more often during the threshold test, were not recalled better than the low-frequency words. This effect is attributed to interference among the many high-frequency responses made during the threshold test.

REFERENCES

1. BLACK, J. W. Accompaniments of word intelligibility. *J. Speech Hearing Disorders*, 1942, **17**, 409–418.
2. EGAN, J. P. Articulation testing methods. *Laryngoscope*, 1948, **58**, 955–991.
3. GOUGENHEIM, G., RIVENC, P., MICHÉA, R., & SAUVAGEOT, A. *L'Elaboration du Français Elémentaire*. Paris: Didier, 1956.
4. HOWES, D. The intelligibility of spoken messages. *Amer. J. Psychol.*, 1952, **65**, 460–465.
5. HOWES, D. H., & SOLOMON, R. L. Visual duration threshold as a function of word-probability. *J. exp. Psychol.*, 1951, **41**, 401–410.
6. McGEOCH, J. A., & IRION, A. L. *The psychology of human learning*. New York: Longmans, Green, 1952.
7. McGINNIES, E., COMER, P. B., & LACEY, O. L. Visual-recognition thresholds as a function of word length and word frequency *J. exp. Psychol.*, 1952, **44**, 65–69.
8. MASON, H. M., & GARRISON, B. K. Intelligibility of spoken messages; liked and disliked. *J. abnorm. soc. Psychol.*, 1951, **46**, 100–103.
9. MOSTELLER, F., & BUSH, R. R. Selected quantitative techniques. In G. Lindzey

[9] Word frequency has been found to account for an average of 69% of intelligibility variance for words of 3 to 11 letters in length, according to an article which appeared after the present paper had been accepted. See D. Howes, "On the Relation Between the Intelligibility and Frequency of Occurrence of English Words." *J. acous. Soc. Amer.*, 1957, **29**, 296–305.

(Ed.), *Handbook of social psychology.* Vol. 1. *Theory and method.* Cambridge, Mass.: Addison-Wesley, 1954.

10. NOBLE, C. E. An analysis of meaning. *Psychol. Rev.*, 1952, **59**, 421–430.

11. OSGOOD, C. E. *Method and theory in experimental psychology.* New York: Oxford Univer. Press, 1953.

12. POSTMAN, L., & ROSENZWEIG, M. R. Practice and transfer in the visual and auditory recognition of verbal stimuli. *Amer. J. Psychol.*, 1956, **69**, 209–226.

13. SISSON, E. D. Retroactive inhibition: the influence of degree of association value of original and interpolated lists. *J. exp. Psychol.*, 1938, **22**, 573–580.

14. SNEDECOR, G. W. *Statistical methods applied to experiments in agriculture and biology.* (4th ed.) Ames, Ia.: Collegiate Press, 1946.

15. THORNDIKE, E. L. *A teacher's word book of 20,000 words.* New York: Teachers Coll., Columbia Univer., 1931.

16. THORNDIKE, E. L., & LORGE, I. *The teacher's word book of 30,000 words.* New York: Teachers Coll., Columbia Univer., 1944.

17. UNDERWOOD, B. J., & RICHARDSON, J. The influence of meaningfulness, intralist similarity, and serial position on retention. *J. exp. Psychol.*, 1956, **52**, 119–126.

(Received November 16, 1956)

10

Reprinted from *Can. J. Psychol.* **15**(3):166–171 (1961)

CEREBRAL DOMINANCE AND THE PERCEPTION OF VERBAL STIMULI[1]

DOREEN KIMURA[2]
McGill University

IN A PREVIOUS STUDY (Kimura, 1961) the writer demonstrated that, when different digits are presented simultaneously to the two ears, the following results are obtained:

(1) Unilateral temporal lobectomy impairs the recognition of digits arriving at the ear contralateral to the removal, a finding in agreement with other studies (Jerger & Mier, 1960; Sinha, 1959).

(2) Over-all efficiency, as measured by the total number of digits correctly reported from both ears, is affected by left temporal lobectomy but not by right temporal lobectomy. Both before and after operation patients with lesions of the left temporal lobe are inferior to those with lesions of the right, even when the groups are matched for digit span.

These facts were interpreted to mean that the crossed auditory pathways in man were stronger or more numerous than the uncrossed and that the left temporal lobe played a more important part than the right in the perception of spoken material.

For all groups of subjects studied, regardless of the site of the lesion, the preoperative score was higher for the right ear than for the left. Since the right ear was presumably more strongly connected to the left temporal lobe than was the left ear, this finding suggested that verbal material arriving along this pathway had an advantage in being more reliably transmitted to the hemisphere which was dominant for speech representation. It would then follow that, in subjects with speech represented in the right hemisphere, recognition of verbal material arriving at the left ear should be more efficient. This was the hypothesis investigated in the present study.

METHOD

Subjects

The Ss were 120 patients at the Montreal Neurological Institute with epileptogenic lesions of various parts of the brain. Of these, 107 had speech represented in the left

---

[1]This research was supported by Grant 9401-11 to Dr. D. O. Hebb from the Defence Research Board, Ottawa, with assistance from Grant B-2831 to Dr. Brenda Milner from the U.S. Public Health Service. I wish to thank Dr. Milner for her guidance throughout the investigation and in the preparation of this paper. Thanks are also due to Dr. Wilder Penfield and Dr. Theodore Rasmussen for permission to work with their patients.

[2]Now at the Montreal Neurological Institute.

hemisphere, 13 in the right hemisphere. The 13 subjects in the second group were found to have speech on the right by the technique of injecting sodium amytal into the internal carotid artery of one side, thereby temporarily disrupting the functions of that hemisphere (Wada & Rasmussen, 1960). The right and left sides were injected on different days, with contralateral hemiplegia and hemianopia resulting from each injection. Dysphasia, however, occurred only after injection of the dominant hemisphere.[3]

In the left-dominant group not all subjects were given the sodium amytal test, since it was administered only in doubtful cases. It is possible therefore that one or two subjects are included in this group who actually have speech represented on the right. (Any such cases would tend to minimize differences between groups rather than enhance them.) All left-handers were given the test, however, and the proportion of right-handers with speech on the right is very low in this patient population (Penfield & Roberts, 1959).

Thirteen normal control subjects were also tested. They were all right-handed.

Procedure

The procedure has been described in detail in the previous paper (Kimura, 1961). A dual-channel tape-recorder with stereophonic ear-phones was used for the test. Digits were presented through these ear-phones in groups of six in such a way that half the digits came to the left ear, half to the right. After each group of six numbers, the subject reported everything he had heard, in any order he liked. For the greater part of the test the six numbers were presented as three pairs, that is, two different numbers were presented simultaneously to the two ears, in a manner first introduced by Broadbent (1956). In all cases, different material was presented to each ear. There were 32 groups of six digits, making a total possible score of 96 for each ear.

RESULTS

Table I presents data for five groups of subjects classified according to the origin of their seizures, and for a group of normal control subjects. It demonstrates clearly that the right ear is more efficient than the left regardless of the site of the lesion. This effect was confirmed for the normal group also ($p < .02$, difference t test) but it is somewhat less marked, due perhaps to the higher over-all efficiency. The five groups in Table I, exclusive of normal controls, make up the left-dominant group. Table II compares the relative efficiency of right and left ears for this group and

TABLE I
PREOPERATIVE MEAN SCORES

Group	Left ear	Right ear
Left temporal	76.8	81.5
Right temporal	83.4	88.0
Bitemporal	77.9	80.2
Frontal	82.7	86.4
Subcortical	76.5	85.5
Normal	90.25	92.25

[3]Throughout this paper the term "dominant" will be used to refer to the hemisphere in which speech is represented.

TABLE II

HEMISPHERE DOMINANCE AND MEAN SCORES FOR THE TWO EARS

Locus of speech	N	Left ear	Right ear	Right minus left
Left hemisphere	107	76.64	83.01	6.37
Right hemisphere	13	85.00	74.85	−10.15

for the 13 subjects with speech in the right hemisphere. These data indicate that when speech is represented in the left hemisphere, the right ear is more efficient, and when speech is represented in the right hemisphere, the left ear is more efficient.

It also happens that most of the subjects with speech on the left were right-handed, and most of the subjects with speech on the right were left-handed. It therefore seemed important to determine the relation, if any, between handedness and the relative efficiency of the two ears. Accordingly, these two groups were broken down into two more groups on the basis of handedness, and the results are shown in Table III.

TABLE III

SPEECH VERSUS HANDEDNESS
(MEAN SCORES)

Handedness	N	Left ear	Right ear
Left-dominant group			
Right-handed	93	77.03	83.73
Left-handed	10	72.50	77.00
Right-dominant group			
Right-handed	3	83.67	81.67
Left-handed	9	85.00	71.44

Ambidextrous subjects were omitted from this analysis. It is clear that the ear opposite the dominant hemisphere is more efficient, irrespective of handedness. This is borne out by a statistical analysis of the difference scores between ears. A simple analysis of variance of this difference score for the four groups yields an F ratio of 10.42 ($p < .001$). Subsequent t tests demonstrate a significant difference between the two left-handed groups with speech in opposite hemispheres ($p < .001$) and no difference between the two left-dominant groups with opposite handedness ($.40 < p < .50$). Thus handedness is not a factor in producing these results.

In the group of 13 subjects with speech on the right, nine had widespread damage to the left hemisphere. This was presumably an important influence in producing the development of speech on the right, since the proportion of left-dominant subjects with such damage is very low.

The right hemisphere in these nine cases is both the dominant hemisphere and the intact one, and the superiority of the left ear may be due to either of these factors. That is, the left ear may be more efficient in the right-dominant group because the large lesion in the left hemisphere has depressed performance on the contralateral (right) ear. There are two points against this. First, two of the right-dominant subjects had damage only to the right, the dominant hemisphere, and two more had only minor damage to the left hemisphere. All four of these subjects were more efficient on the left ear. Secondly, seven subjects were selected from the left-dominant group because they had widespread damage to the left hemisphere, and three of the thirteen subjects were dropped from the right-dominant group because they had a high degree of such damage as judged by the presence of weakness or smallness on the right side of the body. These two selected groups were then compared for the relative

TABLE IV

MEAN SCORES OF TWO GROUPS MATCHED FOR LEFT-HEMISPHERE DAMAGE

Locus of speech	N	Left ear	Right ear	Right minus left
Left hemisphere	7	70.7	83.0	12.3
Right hemisphere	10	84.4	78.4	−6.0

efficiency of right and left ears (Table IV). Again, it is apparent that the ear opposite the dominant hemisphere is the more efficient despite the presence of severe left-hemisphere damage in both groups ($p < .02$).

DISCUSSION

It appears that when different verbal stimuli are presented to the two ears, those stimuli which arrive at the ear opposite the dominant hemisphere are more efficiently recognized. This is consistent with the view presented in a previous paper that the crossed auditory pathway is the more efficient one, and that the dominant temporal lobe plays an important part in the elaboration of speech sounds. Stimuli arriving at the right cochlea will presumably send more impulses to the left Heschl's gyrus, and hence to the rest of that hemisphere, than to the right hemisphere, and these stimuli will therefore be more reliably identified. Under normal hearing conditions, both cochleas receive the same stimuli, and there is no competition between the pathways from the two ears. This might explain why the greater efficiency of the right ear for speech sounds has so far gone undetected. Another reason for this may be that, in normal subjects, both pathways are very efficient, and only material of a certain level of difficulty will permit the detection of a difference between ears.

If the relation suggested here between the identification of verbal stimuli and the hemisphere at which they arrive is correct, one might expect a similar effect with visually presented verbal material. That is, since material in the right field first excites the left hemisphere, it should perhaps be perceived more accurately than the same material in the left field. Unfortunately verbal material presented visually is subject to some very strong influences in the form of reading habits. These tend under some circumstances to make recognition of alphabetical material better in the left visual field (Bryden, 1960; Heron, 1957). Nevertheless, alphabetical material is recognized more efficiently in the right field under a wider variety of conditions (Bryden, 1958; Forgays, 1953; Heron, 1957; Kimura, 1959; Mishkin & Forgays, 1952).

Forgays' developmental data on the greater accuracy of recognition in the right visual field are in agreement with generally held views on the age range in which speech is taken over by one hemisphere. An interesting point is that, under conditions which make the right field more efficient for verbal material, geometric and nonsense forms are recognized equally well in both fields (Bryden, 1960; Heron, 1957; Terrace, 1959). There is of course the possibility that the increased efficiency of the right field for verbal material is also due to reading experience rather than the dominance of one set of pathways. This suggestion has been made by Mishkin and Forgays, and by Heron, and it derives some support from the finding of Orbach (1952) that experience with Hebrew, which is read in a direction opposite to English, tends to make the left field more efficient. This effect is not entirely achieved, however, and Orbach's data, though incomplete, suggest that the right field may in fact be the prepotent one.

A further test of the hypothesis proposed here might be provided by the presentation of non-verbal material in the same way that digits were presented, since with non-verbal material the right ear should be no more efficient than the left. It would also be of interest to discover at what age the right-ear effect first appears, for such information would have direct relevance for the subject of cerebral dominance. Both these problems are now being investigated.

SUMMARY

Patients with epileptogenic foci in various parts of the brain were given an auditory test in which different verbal material was presented to the two ears. One group of subjects had speech represented in the left hemisphere, the other in the right. Stimuli arriving at the ear contralateral to the dominant hemisphere were more efficiently recognized than stimuli arriving at the ipsilateral ear, that is, in the left-dominant group the right ear was more efficient, and in the right-dominant group the left ear was more efficient. This effect was independent of handedness and of the locus of epileptic discharge. The results are consistent with earlier suggestions that the crossed auditory pathways are stronger than the uncrossed, and that the dominant temporal lobe is more important than the non-dominant in the perception of spoken material.

REFERENCES

BROADBENT, D. E.   Successive responses to simultaneous stimuli. *Quart. J. exp. Psychol.*, 1956, **8**, 145–62.

BRYDEN, M. P.   The role of eye movements in perception. Unpublished master's thesis, McGill University, 1958.

——— Tachistoscopic recognition of non-alphabetical material. *Canad. J. Psychol.*, 1960, **14**, 78–86.

FORGAYS, D. G.   The development of differential word recognition. *J. exp. Psychol.*, 1953, **45**, 165–8.

HERON, W.   Perception as a function of retinal locus and attention. *Amer. J. Psychol.*, 1957, **70**, 38–48.

JERGER, J. F., & MIER, M.   The effect of brain stem lesions on auditory responses of humans. Paper read at Psychonomic Society, September, 1960, Chicago.

KIMURA, DOREEN.   The effect of letter position on recognition. *Canad. J. Psychol.*, 1959, **13**, 1–10.

——— Some effects of temporal-lobe damage on auditory perception. *Canad. J. Psychol.*, 1961, **15**, 156–65.

MISHKIN, M., & FORGAYS, D. G.   Word recognition as a function of retinal locus. *J. exp. Psychol.*, 1952, **43**, 43–8.

ORBACH, J.   Retinal locus as a factor in the recognition of visually perceived words. *Amer. J. Psychol.*, 1952. **65**, 555–62.

PENFIELD, W., & ROBERTS, L.   *Speech and brain-mechanisms.* Princeton: Princeton University Press, 1959.

SINHA, S. P.   The role of the temporal lobe in hearing. Unpublished master's thesis, McGill University, 1959.

TERRACE, H. S.   The effects of retinal locus and attention on the perception of words. *J. exp. Psychol.*, 1959, **58**, 382–5.

WADA, J., & RASMUSSEN, T.   Intracarotid injection of sodium amytal for the lateralization of cerebral speech dominance. Experimental and clinical observations. *J. Neurosurg.*, 1960, **17**, 266–82.

11

Reprinted from *Acoust. Soc. Am. J.* **48**(2), Pt. 2:599–602 (1970)

Opposed Effects of a Delayed Channel on Perception of Dichotically and Monotically Presented CV Syllables

M. Studdert-Kennedy,* D. Shankweiler,† and S. Schulman

Haskins Laboratories, 270 Crown Street, New Haven, Connecticut 06510

We investigated the effects upon perception of delaying one channel during the dichotic presentation of pairs of CV syllables differing in initial stop consonant. Unexpectedly, the time advantage accrued not to the leading, but to the lagging syllable. The situation was exactly reversed with monotic presentation; that is, the advantage accrued to the leading syllable. While the latter result may be interpreted as an instance of peripheral simultaneous masking, the dichotic result would seem to be of central origin.

WE WISH TO REPORT A NEW PHENOMENON IN BINAURAL SPEECH listening that we have termed the "lag effect." The effect is seen in the greater accuracy with which subjects identify the lagging member of a pair of temporally overlapped syllables presented to opposite ears. Earlier experiments had shown that if CV or CVC syllables, differing only in their initial or final consonants, were presented in dichotic competition, those presented to the right ear were correctly reported significantly more often than those presented to the left.[1,2] As part of a general program of research into

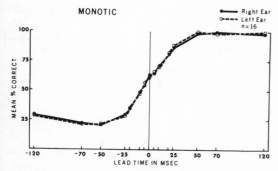

MONOTIC

● Right Ear
○--- Left Ear
n = 16

FIG. 1. Mean percent correct by ear on monotically presented CV syllable pairs as a function of temporal lead in milliseconds, for 16 subjects.

the conditions of this right-ear advantage for consonants, we undertook to titrate the effect in temporal units; our plan was to estimate the number of milliseconds by which the left-ear syllable should lead the right-ear syllable for the right-ear advantage to be abolished. In that event, we found that the right-ear advantage was more readily abolished by a left-ear lag than by a left-ear lead. The effect has now been repeatedly confirmed both at our own laboratory and elsewhere.[3],[4] Here we wish simply to report some of its conditions as uncovered in the original experiment.

The stimuli were formed from the syllables /ba, da, ga, pa, ta, ka/, each 250 msec long, synthesized on the Haskins Laboratories parallel formant synthesizer. Syllables were recorded in pairs, one on each channel of a balanced two-track tape recorder. By means of a computer-aided routine, two 240-pair random-order tapes were prepared; the onset of one member of each pair was made to lead (or lag) the onset of the other by 0, 5, 10, 20, 25, 50, 70, or 120 msec. The two tapes provided a fully balanced 480-item test in which each syllable occurred equally often on each channel, paired with each syllable other than itself. There was a total of 30 presentations at each lead and lag value other than zero, at which there were 60 presentations. These tapes were intended for dichotic presentation. A second pair of tapes was prepared for monotic presentation by mixing the two channels of the dichotic tape electronically and recording the output on a single track.

The subjects were 16 right-handed undergraduate women, all of whom had scored 95% or better on both ears in monaural identification tests of the synthetic syllables. As in previous dichotic studies,[1],[2] appropriate counterbalancing procedures distributed all effects due to recorder channels, earphone characteristics, positions of earphones on the head, or sequence of testing equally over the ears of the entire group of subjects. Subjects were instructed to record two from the set of six consonants on each trial, writing on an answer sheet and guessing if necessary.

As a baseline against which the dichotic data may be judged, we first present the group monotic data; in Fig. 1, mean-percentage correct is plotted as a function of temporal lag (negative) and lead (positive) in milliseconds, for right and left ears. Each point is based on 480 judgments (960 at 0 msec). The two ears give essentially identical results: performance is at chance level for syllables with onsets that lag by 25 msec or more, but then rises steadily to virtually perfect performance for syllables that lead by 50 or more. The functions were similar for all subjects; every one of the 16 reached at least 95% correct for a lead of 50 msec.

The results seem open to a straightforward peripheral-masking interpretation. Although each syllable was approximately 250 msec long, the important cues for the identification of its initial consonant occur in the first 50 msec, during which the syllable is also rising to its maximum amplitude. As lead time is increased

from zero, more and more of the crucial portion of the syllable is presented without interference from the lagging syllable, until, at 50 msec, all needed consonantal information in the leading syllable is freely available, and performance is almost perfect. On the other hand, as lag time is increased from zero, more and more of the crucial portion of the lagging syllable occurs during the period of maximum amplitude of the leading syllable, until, at − 50 msec, the important cues in the lagging syllable are fully masked, and performance drops to chance. This account squares with the subjective impression of the monotic pairs at the longer lead/lag values: one hears a single syllable with a superimposed click.

The dichotic results present a quite different picture. Figure 2 displays the group dichotic results plotted on the same coordinates as Fig. 1. On this plot, the difference between levels for left and right ears is a measure of the ear advantage (laterality effect), and the slopes of the functions from their minima measure the advantages accruing from changes in lead or lag time. Where the two functions are parallel, laterality effect and temporal effects are additive; significant deviations from the parallel indicate some interaction between the two effects.

We note first the laterality effect. Right-ear performance is superior to left at every lag/lead value other than − 120 msec. Ten of the 16 subjects show significant right-ear advantages by matched pair t-tests over the lag/lead range; four show no significant ear advantage; two show significant left-ear advantages. Subject-according-to-ear interaction is significant by analysis of variance; hence, the over-all ear effect is not significant. Individual differences of this order are common in dichotic experiments and may be related to differences in cerebral language dominance. Figure 3 gives some idea of the variability; see the example of a clearly right-eared subject (above) and of a subject showing no significant ear advantage (below).

Second, we note that increases in the amount of lag yield, for both ears, increases rather than decreases in performance. Furthermore, the functions are not symmetrical; they reach their minima at lead values of 20 or 25 msec, rather than at zero; they reach their maxima at a lag value of − 70 msec, where performance is superior by some 20% to performance at the corresponding lead value. In other words, the functions climb more rapidly over the lag than over the lead range. And this is true of every subject, despite considerably greater intersubject variability in the dichotic than in the monotic data. The over-all effect of temporal offset is highly significant by analysis of variance, and there is no significant subject by temporal-offset interaction.

The advantage of the lagging over the leading syllable may be more clearly seen if we replot the data of Fig. 2 so that each pair of points shows the mean percent correct by ear for all trials of a given type. For example, the pair of points at the extreme left in Fig. 4 gives performance for trials on which the left ear lagged by 120 msec, and the corresponding pair at the extreme right

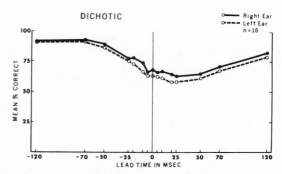

DICHOTIC

○── Right Ear
○--- Left Ear
n = 16

FIG. 2. Mean percent correct by ear on dichotically presented CV syllable pairs as a function of temporal lead in milliseconds, for 16 subjects.

gives performance for trials on which the right ear lagged by 120 msec. (Figure 4 may be generated by rotating the right-ear function of Fig. 2 through 180° in a plane vertical to the page.) We see immediately that the ear to which the lagging syllable is presented almost invariably has the advantage over the leading ear. The exception is over the short left-ear lags (0–10 msec), where the right-ear advantage under dichotic stimulation is sufficient to cancel the left-ear advantage from lag. In fact, for these group data, 10 msec is the titration value that we originally sought, that is, the temporal advantage to the left ear necessary to cancel the dichotic advantage to the right. However, the value is not reliable across subjects.

Cancellation of the right-ear advantage by an appropriate left-ear lag suggests that the laterality and lag effects are independent phenomena. The same conclusion is suggested by the asymmetry of Fig. 4; the wider separation of the two curves over the right lag range than over the left is due to the fact that the right ear, whether leading or lagging, has an over-all higher level of performance than the left. The generally parallel courses of the two curves in Fig. 2 makes the same point, and analysis of variance shows no significant interaction between ear and temporal offset.

We may now pose fairly precisely the problem raised by the dichotic lag effect. From Fig. 2, it is evident that there is little variation in performance between −5 and +50; within this range, the functions for both ears reach a broad minimum. For 15 out of 16 subjects, this is the range within which both ears reach their minima; the 16th subject gives her minima at +70 msec. Thus, for every subject, dichotic performance is at its worst in the very range of lead values over which monotic performance is at, or rising to, its peak. The paradox sharpens when we recall that the conditions of presentation for the leading portion of the leading syllable are identical under monotic and dichotic presentation. For example, under both conditions, the initial 50 msec of a syllable leading by that amount are presented without interruption to a single ear. These 50 msec carry all the information needed for

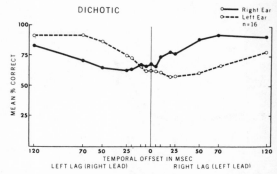

FIG. 4. Mean percent correct by ear on left lag and right lag CV syllable pairs, dichotically presented, for 16 subjects.

identification of the initial consonant, and, under monotic conditions, virtually perfect identification is achieved by every subject, while performance on the syllable that lags by 50 msec drops to chance. Under dichotic conditions, on the other hand, performance on the leading syllable is, for every subject, close to her function minimum and on the lagging syllable close to her function maximum.

What gives rise to this reversal of the direction of the effect under dichotic conditions? The question is of interest for the light that its answer may throw on the processes of speech perception. For while the monotic lead effect may be interpreted as an instance of peripheral simultaneous masking, the dichotic lag effect seems to be of central origin, possibly analogous to metacontrast effects in vision. Werner[5] showed that perception of a disk flashed on a screen might be blocked, if rapidly followed by presentation of a ring having the same internal diameter as the disk. He attributed the effect to interference by the ring with development of the disk's contour. Later work (for example, Kolers and Rosner[6]) showed that a similar effect might be obtained dichotically, and therefore involved central mechanisms.

Interpretation of the dichotic lag effect along analogous lines would assume processing of the important cues in the leading stimulus to be incomplete at the time the lagging stimulus arrived along a different channel to compete for, and frequently capture, the processors. Occlusion of the leading syllable by a switch in channels just as the crucial information in that syllable is being processed recalls the finding of Huggins[7] that the rate of across-ears switching, which is most disruptive to speech perception, is roughly equal to the syllable rate. A similar disruption does not occur when the lagging syllable is presented along the same channel in wake of the first, presumably because it is masked at a peripheral point in the pathway.

The notion that the lag effect reflects interruption of speech processing is further suggested by control data. Studies with nonspeech have not yet been completed, but Porter, Shankweiler, and Liberman[8] have reported that, if the stimuli are steady-state synthetic vowels, the advantage tends to the leading rather than to the lagging stimulus. Given that such stimuli have been found, under other experimental conditions, to be perceived in the manner more of nonspeech than of speech,[1,2,9,10] we may reasonably suspect that the lag effect is tied to speech, and, specifically, to those components of the speech stream for which a relatively complex decoding operation is necessary.

However, an adequate account of the effect and of its implications for speech perception calls for much further study. Several experiments are already under way at Haskins Laboratories. These include studies of individual differences, nonspeech controls, attention switching, channel tracking, and consonant-feature errors.

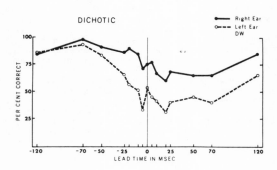

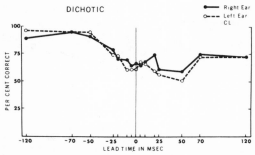

FIG. 3. Percent correct by ear for two subjects on dichotically presented CV syllable pairs as a function of temporal lead in milliseconds.

Acknowledgment: Research for this paper was supported by grants from the National Institute of Child Health and Human Development and the National Institute of Dental Research.

* Also at Queens College, City Univ. of New York.
† Also at the Univ. of Connecticut.

[1] D. Shankweiler and M. Studdert-Kennedy, "Identification of Consonants and Vowels Presented to Left and Right Ears," Quart. J. Exp. Psychol. **19**, 59–63 (1967).

[2] M. Studdert-Kennedy, and D. Shankweiler, "Hemispheric Specialization for Speech Perception," J. Acoust. Soc. Amer. **48**, 579–594 (1970).

[3] C. I. Berlin, M. E. Willett, C. Thompson, J. K. Cullen, and S. S. Lowe, "Voiceless versus Voiced CV Perception in Dichotic and Monotic Listening," J. Acoust. Soc. Amer. **47**, 75(A) (1970).

[4] S. S. Lowe, J. K. Cullen, C. Thompson, C. I. Berlin, L. L. Kirkpatrick, and J. T. Ryan, "Dichotic and Monotic Simultaneous and Time-Staggered Speech," J. Acoust. Soc. Amer. **47**, 76(A) (1970).

[5] H. Werner, "Studies in Contour: I. Quantitative Analyses," Amer. J. Psychol. **47**, 40–64 (1935).

[6] P. Kolers and B. S. Rosner, "On Visual Masking (Metacontrast): Dichoptic Observation," Amer. J. Psychol. **73**, 2–21 (1960).

[7] A. W. F. Huggins, "Distortion of the Temporal Pattern of Speech: Interruption and Alternation," J. Acoust. Soc. Amer. **36**, 1055–1064 (1964).

[8] R. Porter, D. Shankweiler, and A. M. Liberman, "Differential Effects of Binaural Time Differences in Perception of Stop Consonants and Vowels," Proc. 77th Annual Convention of the Amer. Psychol. Ass. (1969).

[9] A. M. Liberman, F. S. Cooper, D. Shankweiler, and M. Studdert-Kennedy, "Perception of the Speech Code," Psychol. Rev. **74**, 431–461 (1967).

[10] M. Studdert-Kennedy, A. M. Liberman, K. S. Harris, and F. S. Cooper, "The Motor Theory of Speech Perception: A Reply to Lane's Critical Review," Psychol. Rev. **77**, 234–249 (1970).

Part III

THE STATISTICS OF SPEECH AND THE PREDICTION OF SPEECH INTELLIGIBILITY

Editor's Comments
on Papers 12, 13, and 14

12   FRENCH and STEINBERG
Excerpt from *Factors Governing the Intelligibility of Speech Sounds*

13   KRYTER
Validation of the Articulation Index

14   JANSSEN
A Method for the Calculation of the Speech Intelligibility Under Conditions of Reverberation and Noise

Speech intelligibility tests are undertaken only because they offer the most convincing and trustworthy method of measurement of the ability to understand speech. They are expensive and time consuming; they require several subjects, some equipment, and a skilled experimenter; and, even worse, they are difficult to replicate in other laboratories or at other times. Therefore, almost from the beginning physicists and engineers have tried to find ways to predict the results from simpler, swifter, more reliable instruments that are not subject to fatigue, ennui, or head colds. No prediction method has been found that is suitable for all conditions, but several have been developed that have rather wide applications. All are based on the statistics both of speech and of the interfering condition, such as noise, reverberation, or processing. This part treats the statistics of speech and the methods of predicting intelligibility for listeners with normal hearing; prediction of speech thresholds and of hearing loss for speech is deferred until Part VI.

Establishing the statistics of speech has proved to be difficult. There are wide variations among speakers, languages, speech samples, rates and levels of speaking, and methods of measurement. Furthermore, it is not at all clear just what data should be contained in the statistics one should collect and use. The early investigators concentrated on the physical acoustics of the speech waveform, i.e., energy-frequency distribution, peak distribution, and signal durations. The seminal paper by Dunn and White was cited in Part I. There are several other papers on speech statistics in the bibliography for this part, including a fine paper by Chang (1951), which deals with the autocorrelation functions and the zero crossing information prized by investigators who use computers for speech synthesis and analysis. Tarnóczy (1962, 1971), Borovičková (1963), and Zalewski (1971) show some of the differences among the statistics of different languages. Falter's (1967) excellent review is recommended.

The very method of measuring speaking level is a challenging problem. A common fault of papers describing speech intelligibility measurements is a lack of sufficient information concerning the place, means, and method of measuring the speaking level to permit readers to replicate the experimental levels and to calculate the Articulation Index. The talker usually monitors his speaking level on the swinging pointer of a meter that does not measure either peaks, peaks in one-eighth-second intervals, long term rms. pressure, or rms. pressure in one-eighth-second intervals. The conversions that are necessary for the data that are collected require acceptance of assumptions that may not be valid for the particular experiment. Several papers in the bibliography treat the problem of monitoring and measuring speaking level. Readers are directed especially to the papers of Brady (1965, 1968, 1971), Bricker (1965), and Shearme (1954). Now, with on-line computers, experimenters can measure the rms. noise levels and the peak levels in one-eighth-second intervals directly.

French and Steinberg's classic paper on the prediction of intelligibility from physical measurements is reproduced here nearly in full as Paper 12. It presents the Articulation Index (AI) method of prediction. (The portions that are missing concern the effects of hearing loss and some examples of the applicability of the method.) In a later monograph based on the same Bell Labs data, Fletcher and Galt (1950) took a somewhat different approach to the prediction of telephone intelligibility, and later Fletcher (1952) added an extension to cover the case of persons with hearing impairments. The monograph is too long and difficult to permit extraction of a useful and readable portion for reproduction here, but it is recommended to the reader who wishes a thorough understanding of the process of prediction of intelligibility. Lehmann (1962) repeated much of the Bell Labs and Harvard Psycho-Acoustics Laboratory research with more modern instruments and the French language. He and Saito (1961) have tried to take into account the spread of masking outside the frequency bands for which the index is being calculated.

The AI has been attacked as unsoundly based, too difficult, time consuming, limited, and inaccurate. Licklider (1959) has summarized elegantly the theory of the AI and the evidence by Hirsh (1954, citation in Part II), Kryter (1956), and Licklider (1957, citation in Part II) that the theory is unsound. On the other hand about a dozen papers in the bibliography to this section attest to the AI's accuracy and usefulness. It works well for a wide range of commonly encountered problems and is sufficiently accurate to use as a design tool. In the editor's experience the AI will always predict correctly the direction and relative size of the differences in speech intelligibility of two systems under comparison at the same time in the same laboratory by the same test team. Kryter (1956) and Hawley (1957) present a straightforward but laborious method of calculating the AI; Kryter (1962) improved and expanded the method,* and in a paper which is reproduced here (Paper 13) he shows the validity of AI methods and treats some difficult conditions.

The reports by Licklider (1959), Goldberg (1963), and Kryter (1966) describe devices that have been developed to do the predictions automatically for communication systems with frequently encountered disturbances. Several simplifications of the AI method have been proposed for specific situations. Paper 14 by Janssen is a good example of a simplification for architectural use. Most of these simplifications reduce the number of frequency bands, compare readings on commonly used instruments, and assume good behavior in several places for which the AI method permits nonlinearity and variations from the average values. Bowman (1974), Cluff (1969), Golikov (1958, 1961), Houtgast (1971, 1973), Tkachenko (1955), and Webster (1968) all have alternatives to the AI that are worthy of consideration.

The most useful and widely used alternate to the AI is the Speech Interference Level (SIL). Scientists and engineers whose major interest is in noise control are also concerned about the effects of noise on the intelligibility of speech, usually in face-to-face communication or at one end of a telephone conversation. They approach the problems of signal-to-noise determinations with different instruments from those of the communications engineer or the speech scientist and with satisfactory speech communication as only one of their objectives in noise control. These scientists have developed a whole set of measures† for noise of which the SIL is the most useful for the speech intelligibility situa-

---

* The American National Standards Institute (1969) publication uses this method.

†These topics will be treated in a companion volume on noise in the series of Benchmark Papers in Acoustics.

tion. The SIL is simply the mean of the sound pressure levels in the three octave bands now with their geometric means centered at frequencies of 500, 1000, and 2000 Hz. If one carefully observes the cautions stated by Beranek (1960, 1971, citations in Part V), and other texts, the SIL is an accurate descriptor of the behavior of many kinds of noise. If one then assumes that the talkers adjust their levels as described by Webster (1968), one successfully can use the SIL as a criterion for predicting speech intelligibility in many commonly encountered situations. Part V contains additional discussion and citations regarding speech in noisy rooms.

BIBLIOGRAPHY

American National Standards Institute, *Methods for the Calculation of the Articulation Index*, S3.5-1969, American National Standards Institute, New York (1969).

Banuls-Terol, V., "Weighted Average Spectrum of Human Speech: An Approach," *Proc. 7th Int. Cong. Acoust.*, Akadémiai Kaidó, Budapest (1971), **3**, pp. 253–256.

Beranke, L. L., "Revised Criteria for Noise in Buildings," *Noise Control* **3**, no. 1:19–27 (Jan. 1957).

Bilger, R. C., and I. J. Hirsh, "Masking of Tones by Bands of Noise," *J. Acoust. Soc. Am.* **28**:623–630 (1956).

Borovičková, B., and V. Maláč, "Technische Angaben zur Frage der Feststellung des Erkennbarkeitsindexes der tschechischen Sprache," *Phonetica* **9**:220–232 (1963).

Bowman, N. T., "The Articulation Index and Its Application to Room Acoustics Design," *J. Sound Vibr.* **32**:109–130 (1974).

Brady, P. T., "A Statistical Basis for Objective Measurement of Speech Levels," *Bell Syst. Tech. J.* **44**:1453–1486 (1965).

Brady, P. T., Equivalent Peak Level: A Threshold-Independent Speech-Level Measure," *J. Acoust. Soc. Am.* **44**:695–699 (1968).

Brady, P. T., "Need for Standardization in the Measurement of Speech Level," (L) *J. Acoust. Soc. Am.* **50**:712–714 (1971).

Brady, P. T., "Equivalent Peak Level: A Threshold-Independent Speech-Level Measure," *J. Acoust. Soc. Am.* **44**:695–699 (1968).

Brandt, J. F., K. F. Ruder, and T. Shipp, Jr., "Vocal Loudness and Effort in Continuous Speech," *J. Acoust. Soc. Am.* **46**:1543–1548 (1969).

Braun, K., and W. Schobel, "Messungen der statistischen Verteilung des Sprachvolumens in Fernsprechkanälen," *NTZ-Nachrichtentech. Z.* **12**:291–296 (1959).

Bricker, P. D., "Technique for Objective Measurement of Speech Levels," (L) *J. Acoust. Soc. Am.* **38**:361–362 (1965).

Chang, S.-H., G. E. Pihl, and M. W. Essigmann, "Representations of Speech Sounds and Some of Their Statistical Properties," *Proc. IRE* **39**:147–153 (1951).

Chavasse, P., "Sur la structure et la forme de l'emission vocale au cours de la conversation téléphonique," *C. R. Acad. Sci. Paris* **250**:4457–4458 (1960).

Chinn, H. A., D. K. Gannett, and R. M. Morris, "A New Standard Volume Indicator and Reference Level," *Proc. IRE* **28**:1–16 (1940).

Cluff, G. L., "A Comparison of Selected Methods of Determining Speech Interference Calculated by the Articulation Index," *J. Aud. Res.* **9**:81–88 (1969).

Denes, P., "On the Statistics of Spoken English," *J. Acoust. Soc. Am.* **35**:892–904 (1963).

Falter, J. W., and K. W. Otten, "Cybernetics and Speech Communications: A Survey of Russian Literature," *IEEE Trans. Audio Electroacoust.* **AU-15**:27–36 (1967).

Flanagan, J. L., "Analog Measurements of Sound Radiation from the Mouth," *J. Acoust. Soc. Am.* **32**:1613–1620 (1960).

Flanagan, J., and H. Levitt, "Speech Interference from Community Noise," in *Proc. of the Conference on Noise as a Public Health Hazard*, W. D. Ward, and J. E. Fricke, eds. American Speech and Hearing Assn., Washington (1969), pp. 167–174.

Fletcher, H., "The Perception of Speech Sounds by Deafened Persons," *J. Acoust. Soc. Am.* **24**:490–497 (1952).

Fletcher, H., and R. S. Galt, "The Perception of Speech and Its Relation to Telephony," *J. Acoust. Soc. Am.* **22**:89–150 (1950).

Fujisaki, H., *et al.*, "Statistical Properties of Speech Sounds," in *Rep. of 6th Int. Cong. Acoust.*, Y. Kohasi, ed., Maruzen, Tokyo (1968), pp. B59–B62.

Gardner, M. B., "Factors Affecting Individual and Group Levels in Verbal Communication," *J. Aud. Eng. Soc.* **19**:560–569 (1971).

Giacomelli, L., and A. Roveri, "An Experimental Evaluation of Some Parameters Characterizing the "Time Occupancy of Spectrum Channels" of Speech Signals," *Alta Freq.* **40**:347E–363E (1971).

Goldberg, J. M., "The Voice Interference Analysis Set, an Instrument for Determining the Degradation of Signal Quality of a Voice Communications Channel," *J. Aud. Eng. Soc.* **11**:115–119 (1963).

Golikov, E. E., "Apparatus for Measuring Articulation in Rooms," (L) *Sov. Phys.—Acoust.* **4**:373–375 (1958).

Golikov, E. E., "Calculating the Articulation in Noisy Rooms," *Sov. Phys.—Acoust.* **6**:407–408 (1961).

Green, D. M., C. Williams, and K. D. Kryter, "Peak VU Deflection and Energy for Monosyllabic Words," *J. Acoust. Soc. Am.* **31**:1264–1265 (1959).

Hawley, M. E., and A. H. Kettler, "The Apparent Source of Speech in the Mouth," *J. Acoust. Soc. Am.* **22**:365–369 (1950).

Hawley, M. E., and K. D. Kryter, "Effects of Noise on Speech," in *Handbook of Noise Control*, C. M. Harris, ed., McGraw-Hill, New York (1957).

Houtgast, T., and H. J. M. Steenken, "Evaluation of Speech Transmission Channels by Using Artificial Signals," *Acustica* **25**:355–367 (1971).

Houtgast, T., and H. J. M. Steenken, "The Modulation Transfer Function in Room Acoustics as a Predictor of Speech Intelligibility," *Acustica* **28**:66–73 (1973).

IRE Standards Committee, "IRE Standards on American Recommended Practice for Volume Measurements of Electrical Speech and Program Waves, 1953," *Proc. IRE* **42**:815–817 (1954).

Januška, I., "Experimentally Stated Correlation between Objective Echograms Evaluation and Speech Intelligibility," *Arch. Akust.* **3**:139–152 (1968).

Kopra, L. L., and D. Blosser, "Effects of Method of Measurement on Most Comfortable Loudness Level for Speech," *J. Speech Hear. Res.* **11**:497–508 (1968).

Kryter, K. D., "On Predicting the Intelligibility of Speech from Acoustical Measures," *J. Speech Hear. Disord.* **21**:208–217 (1956).

Kryter, K. D., "Noise Control Criteria for Buildings," *Noise Control* **3**, no. 6:14–20 (Nov. 1957).

Kryter, K. D., "Methods for the Calculation and Use of the Articulation Index," *J. Acoust. Soc. Am.* **34**:1689–1697 (1962).

Kryter, K. D., and J. H. Ball, "SCIM—A Meter for Measuring the Performance of Speech Communication Systems," Decision Sciences Lab. Electronic Systems Div., Air Force Systems Command Rpt. ESD-TR-66-667 (Dec. 1966).

Küpfmüller, K., "Regelungsvorgänge beim Sprechen und Hören," in *Proc. 3rd Int. Cong. Acoust., Stuttgart, 1959*, L. Cremer, ed., Elsevier, Amsterdam (1961), pp. 171–187.

Lane, H. L., "The Role of Hearing in Speech: Communication with Alterations in the Signal-to-Noise Ratio, Timing, and Spectrum of Sidetone," in *Proc. 7th Int. Cong. Acoust.*, Akadémiai Kiadó, Budapest (1971), **3**, pp. 221–224.

Lehmann, R., "Détermination théoritique de l'intelligibilité du langage en presence d'un bruit de masque," *C. R. Acad. Sci. Paris* **254**:3253–3255 (1962).

Lehmann, R., "Étude psychophysique de l'intelligibilité du langage," *Ann. Télécommun.* **17**:242–267, 286–303 (1962).

Lehmann, R., "Effet de masquage et indice de netteté," *Rev. Acoust.* **1**:167–170 (1968).

Levitt, H., and P. D. Bricker, "Reduction of Observer Bias in Reading Speech Levels with a VU Meter," *J. Acoust. Soc. Am.* **47**:1583–1587 (1970).

Levitt, H., and L. R. Rabiner, "Predicting Binaural Gain in Intelligibility and Release from Masking Noise," *J. Acoust. Soc. Am.* **42**:820–829 (1967).

Licklider, J. C. R., "Three Auditory Theories," in *Psychology: A Study of a Science*, S. Koch, ed., vol. 1, McGraw-Hill, New York (1959).

Licklider, J. C. R., A. Bisberg, and H. Schwartzlander, "An Electronic Device to Measure the Intelligibility of Speech," *Proc. Nat. Electr. Conf.* **15**:329–334 (1959).

Lochner, J. P., and J. F. Burger, "The Intelligibility of Speech under Reverberant Conditions," *Acustica* **11**:195–200 (1961).

Lochner, J. P. A., and P. Meffert, "Sound Energy Integrator with an Electrostatic Squaring Device," *J. Acoust. Soc. Am.* **32**:267– 273 (1960).

Maack, A., "Höchstlautstärke und Durchschnittlautstärke," *Z. Phonetik* **7**:213–230 (1953).

McAdoo, K., "Speech Volumes on Bell System Message Circuits, 1960 Survey," *Bell Syst. Tech. J.* **42**:1999–2012 (1963).

Maeda, K., "Relation between Articulation, Intelligibility, and Entropy of Spoken Words," *J. Inst. Electr. Commun. Eng. Japan* **37**:359–365

(1954). in Japanese, English abstract.

Martin, D. W., "Uniform Speech-Peak Clipping in a Uniform Signal-to-Noise Spectrum Ratio," *J. Acoust. Soc. Am.* **22**:614–621 (1950).

Mikhailov, V. G., "Formant Distribution of Russian Speech for Male Voices," *Sov. Phys.—Acoust.* **18**:49–52 (1972).

Peterson, G. E., and N. P. McKinney, "The Measurement of Speech Power," *Phonetica* **7**:65–84 (1961).

Pfretzschner, J., and A. Jover, "Influence de la distorsion harmonique d'un systeme de transmission sur l'intelligibilité," in *Reports of the 6th Int. Cong. Acoust.*, Y. Kohasi, ed., Maruzen, Tokyo (1968), pp. C5–C8.

Pickett, J. M., and I. Pollack, "Prediction of Speech Intelligibility at High Noise Levels," *J. Acoust. Soc. Am.* **30**:955–963 (1958).

Richards, D. L., and R. B. Archbold, "A Development of the Collard Principle of Articulation Calculation," *Proc. Inst. Electr. Eng.* **103B**:679–691 (1956).

Rozhanskaja, E. V., "The Mathematics of the Theory of Intelligibility of Speech," *Trud. Komiss, Akust.* no. 7:53–60 (1953). in Russian.

Rudmose, H. W., K. C. Clark, F. D. Carlson, J. C. Eisenstein, and R. A. Walker, "Voice Measurements with an Audio Spectrometer, " *J. Acoust. Soc. Am.* **20**:503–512 (1948).

Saito, S., and S. Watanabe, "Normalized Representation of Noise-Band Masking and Its Applications to the Prediction of Speech Intelligibility," *J. Acoust. Soc. Am.* **33**:1013–1021 (1961).

Schwartz, M. F. "Power Spectral Density Measurements of Oral and Whispered Speech," *J. Speech Hear. Res.* **13**:445–446 (1970).

Shearme, J. N., and D. L. Richards, "The Measurement of Speech Level," *Post Office Elect. Eng. J.* **47**:159–161 (1954).

Sjögren, H, "Objective Measurements of Speech Level," *Audiology* **12**:47–54 (1973).

Stevens, S. S., J. P. Egan, and G. A. Miller, "Methods of Measuring Speech Spectra," *J. Acoust. Soc. Am.* **19**:771–780 (1947).

Stuckey, C. W., and R. W. Robertson, "Investigation of an Automatic Voice Intelligibility Concept," *IEEE Trans. Audio* **AU-12**:3–8 (1964).

Tarnóczy, T. H., "Determination of the Speech Spectrum through Measurements of Superposed Samples," *J. Acoust. Soc. Am.* **28**:1270–1275 (1956).

Tarnóczy, T., "Sprachliche Verschiedenheiten erhalten durch Sprechchormethode," G27 in *Proc. 4th Int. Cong. Acoust.* Copenhagen (1962).

Tarnóczy, T., "Das durchschnittliche Energie-Spektrum der Sprache (für sechs Sprachen)," *Acustica* **24**:57–74 (1971).

Tkachenko, A.D., "Tonal Method for Determining the Intelligibility of Speech Transmitted by Communications Channels," *Sov. Phys.—Acoust.* **1**:182–191 (1955).

Torii, N., "An English Articulation Test Using Japanese Students," *J. Acoust. Soc. Japan* **11**:108–114 (1955). in Japanese, abstract in English.

Vasil'ev, V. P., and G. V. Zibin, "Experimental Investigation of the Statistical Characteristics of a Telephone Signal," *Sov. Phys.—Acoust.* **15**:175–178 (1969).

Voelker, C. H., "Phonetic Distribution in Formal American Pronunciation," *J. Acoust. Soc. Am.* **5**:242–246 (1934).

Webster, J. C., "Relations between Speech-Interference Contours and Idealized Articulation-Index Contours," *J. Acoust. Soc. Am.* **36**:1662–1669 (1964).

Webster, J. C., "Frequency Weighting Contours for Predicting the Speech Interfering Aspects of Noise," *Philos. Trans.* **263**:315–323 (1968).

Webster, J. C., "Effects of Noise on Speech Intelligibility," in *Noise as a Public Health Hazard,* Am. Speech Hearing Assn., Washington (1969), pp. 49–73.

Webster, J. C., "Updating and Interpreting the Speech Interference Level (SIL)," *J. Aud. Eng. Soc.* **18**:114–118 (1970).

Webster, J. C., and R. G. Klumpp, "The Effect of Room Noise and Number of Competing Talkers upon Talker Output," in *Proc. 3rd Int. Cong. Acoust. Stuttgart, 1959,* L. Cremer, ed., Elsevier, Amsterdam (1961), pp. 246–247.

Webster, J. C., and R. G. Klumpp, "Articulation Index and Average Curve Fitting Methods of Predicting Speech Interference," *J. Acoust. Soc. Am.* **35**:1339–1343 (1963).

Zalewski, J., and W. Majewski, "Polish Speech Spectrum Obtained from Superposed Samples and Its Comparison with Spectra of Other Languages," *Proc. 7th Int. Cong. Acoust.* Akadémiai Kiadó, Budapest (1971), **3**, pp. 249–252.

12

Reprinted from pp. 90–114 of *Acoust. Soc. Am. J.* **19**(1):90–119 (1947)

Factors Governing the Intelligibility of Speech Sounds

N. R. Fᴇɴᴄʜ ᴀɴᴅ J. C. Sᴛᴇɪɴʙᴇʀɢ

Bell Telephone Laboratories, New York, New York

(Received November 22, 1946)

The characteristics of speech, hearing, and noise are discussed in relation to the recognition of speech sounds by the ear. It is shown that the intelligibility of these sounds is related to a quantity called articulation index which can be computed from the intensities of speech and unwanted sounds received by the ear, both as a function of frequency. Relationships developed for this purpose are presented. Results calculated from these relations are compared with the results of tests of the subjective effects on intelligibility of varying the intensity of the received speech, altering its normal intensity-frequency relations and adding noise.

1. INTRODUCTION

THIS paper discusses the factors which govern the intelligibility of speech sounds and presents relationships for expressing quantitatively, in terms of the fundamental characteristics of speech and hearing, the capability of the ear in recognizing these sounds. The relationships are based on studies of speech and hearing which have been carried on at Bell Telephone Laboratories over a number of years. The results of these studies have in large measure already been published. The formulation of the results into relationships for expressing speech intelligibility, which has also been in progress for a number of years, has not been previously published. The purpose of this paper is to bring the relationships and basic data together into one report.

Speech consists of a succession of sounds varying rapidly from instant to instant in intensity and frequency. Assuming that the various components are received by the ear in their initial order and spacing in time, the success of the listener in recognizing and interpreting these sounds depends upon their intensity in his ear and the intensity of unwanted sounds that may be present, both as a function of frequency. The relationships presented here deal with intelligibility as a function of these intensities. Relationships having the same objective were formulated about 25 years ago by H. Fletcher. While the present relationships are based largely on data not then available, their development has employed to a considerable extent the concepts of the earlier formulation.

Before proceeding with the subject matter of the paper a word concerning applications of the material may be in order. Material of this type has, of course, been of considerable service for many years in the Bell System. It has, for example, helped to guide the direction of development work on transmission instrumentalities and has aided the preparation of the quantitative transmission data used in engineering the telephone plant.[1] Other factors, however, in addition to those discussed here, often need to be considered in appraising the transmission performance of a speech communication system. For example, echoes, phase distortion, and reverberation may affect intelligibility.[2,3] The naturalness of the received speech may need consideration as a separate item. This is also true of loudness because speech may be too loud for comfort or so faint that the effort of concentrating on the sounds is excessively annoying, even though the sounds are intelligible.

In addition, there is usually the question whether some of the data used in applying the computational methods or, for that matter, in testing the transmission performance of speech communication systems in the laboratory, are truly representative of the conditions of actual use. In either case the value of the results depends upon the degree to which these conditions and the reactions of the users to them can be specified. This information is often difficult to obtain. It is desirable, therefore, in applying the results of computational methods or laboratory tests, to check any modifications of speech communication systems by testing them under actual service conditions and determining their effect on over-all performance as judged by the users. The

reasons for such a procedure are indicated briefly below and in more detail in a paper by W. H. Martin.[4]

The intensity of the speech received by the ear at each frequency depends on the intensity of the original speech sounds, the position of the mouth of the talker with respect to the microphone, the efficiency at each frequency of the latter in converting to electrical form the speech sounds which reach it, the transmission characteristics of the circuit intervening between the microphone and receiver, the efficiency of the latter in reconverting the speech waves to acoustical form and finally the coupling between the receiver and the ear. It is important to note that those items which are under the control of the user are subject to large variations. For example, there are large natural differences between the intensities of the same sounds spoken by different people or by the same people at different times. In addition, a person tends to adjust the output of his voice in part by the loudness with which he hears his own speech and the incoming speech, both being functions of the response characteristics of the communication system employed. Speech intensities also depend on the intensity of unwanted sounds, such as ambient noise in which the speaker may be immersed. These same factors also partly control the speaker's position with respect to the microphone and the way in which the listener holds the receiver to his ear.

Unwanted sounds in the ear have a masking effect on speech and constitute another major variable. They may arise from electrical disturbances originating within or without the communication system or from ambient noise. The latter may reach the ear by several paths: (1) by leakage between the receiver cap and the ear, or directly when loud speakers are used; (2) by being picked up by the microphone at the listening location and transmitted to the local receiver by sidetone; and (3) by transmission from the distant microphone.

Summarizing, it can be seen that the speech and noise received by a listener are the net result of a large number of factors of which several different types can be discerned: (1) the basic characteristics of speech and hearing, (2) the

[1] F. W. McKown and J. W. Emling, Bell Sys. Tech. J. 12, 331 (1933).
[2] V. O. Knudsen, J. Acous. Soc. Am. 1, 56 (1929).
[3] J. C. Steinberg, J. Acous. Soc. Am. 1, 121 (1929).

[4] W. H. Martin, Bell Sys. Tech. J. 10, 116 (1931).

electrical and acoustical characteristics of the instruments and circuits intervening between talker and listener, (3) the conditions under which communication takes place, and (4) the behavior of the talker and listener as modified by the characteristics of the communication system and by the conditions under which it is used.

By expressing the intelligibility relationships in terms of the intensities of speech and noise in the ear of the listener, the complicating factors discussed in the previous paragraphs do not appear explicitly in the relations. They appear only when the speech and noise intensities in the listener's ear are required in order to apply the relationships to the solution of a particular problem. There is also the question of the effect of variations in the acuity of hearing of the listeners. The relationships presented here apply specifically to young men and women who have good hearing but in general, as discussed later, their field of application is broader than this.

There are a set of consistent and well-defined concepts which underlie the intelligibility relationships. As these may be lost sight of in the details of formulation given in the succeeding pages, they are summarized briefly in the next section.

2. BASIC CONCEPTS

The intelligibility of the received speech sounds is related to a quantity which has been called the articulation index and designated A. It is a quantity such that increments ΔA carried by increments Δf of the speech frequency range may be added together to obtain the total A. The maximum possible value of A is assigned a value of unity; the minimum value is zero.

Any increment Δf of the speech frequency range may at best carry a maximum value of ΔA designated as ΔA_m. When conditions are not optimum for hearing speech in the increment Δf, this increment contributes only a fractional amount W of its maximum, or $\Delta A = W \cdot \Delta A_m$. For convenience in making computations, the frequency range may be divided into twenty bands whose frequency limits are so chosen that the ΔA_m of each band is 0.05, i.e., one-twentieth of the articulation index of the full band under optimum conditions. The general procedure for computing articulation index involves the de-

termination of a value of W for each of the twenty bands, the addition of these twenty values of W and the division of this sum by twenty.

The particular value of W for any one band of speech depends upon a quantity E called the effective sensation level of the band in the ear of the listener, which is simply the sensation level of the band minus the total masking. The sensation level of a speech band is the attenuation needed to reduce the band to the threshold of hearing in the absence of noise and is determined from the intensities of the speech components within the band at the ear of the listener and the acuity of hearing. The total masking is the shift in threshold due to the presence of noise and is the resultant of three kinds of masking: (a) residual masking due to components of preceding speech sounds within the band, (b) interband masking due to speech components in adjacent bands, and (c) masking from extraneous noise components. The factor W is equal to the fraction of $\frac{1}{8}$th second time intervals in which the speech intensity in the particular band is of sufficient intensity to be heard. Stated differently, it is the fraction of these intervals in which the speech intensity in a band exceeds the intensity which corresponds to an effective sensation level of 0 db.

In this paper the relationship between ΔA_m and Δf is obtained empirically from the results of articulation tests on appropriate high pass and low pass filter systems. However, Mr. R. H. Galt has shown, in an unpublished memorandum, that this relationship can be derived from data on the differential pitch sensitivity of the ear. This suggests that the articulation index has a more fundamental significance than might be indicated by its empirical derivation.[5]

Although the response characteristics of a telephone system and its component parts do not enter explicitly into the articulation relationships, they are required in applications of the latter to particular problems. To serve the desired purpose the basic speech, noise, and hearing data and the over-all response of the telephone system must be so specified that they can be combined to obtain intensities received in the listener's ear. The type of response needed is obviously not one based

---

[5] W. A. Munson, J. Acous. Soc. Am. **17**, 103A (1945).

alone on physical measurements of microphone, circuit, and receiver apart from voice and ear. It should include the effects of using real voices and ears. The methods of expressing response characteristics and the characteristics of speech and hearing which underlie the articulation index relationships, are essentially interdependent. Consequently, these subjects are discussed in the following two sections prior to the derivation and detailed discussion of the articulation index relations.

The following are the principal symbols used in this paper. A number of the symbols represent intensity levels; these are in db above 10^{-16} watt/cm².

A articulation index,

ΔA increment of articulation index carried by an increment Δf of the speech frequency range,

ΔA_m maximum possible value of ΔA,

W fractional part of ΔA_m obtained when listening conditions are not optimum,

S syllable articulation,

R over-all orthotelephonic response,

β intensity level of a single frequency tone,

β_0 threshold intensity level of a single frequency tone,

K $10 \log_{10}\Delta f_c$,

Δf_c width of critical bands of the ear in cycles,

X $(\beta_0 - K)$,

B the long average intensity per cycle level of the noise received from all sources,

B_f component of B produced in a particular frequency region by speech in the same region,

B_n component of B produced in a particular frequency region by speech in other frequency regions,

B_E component of B from all sources other than speech,

Z level above threshold of a critical band of noise, i.e., effective level,

M masking, i.e., shift of threshold caused by noise,

m $(M-Z)$ for values of Z greater than 50 db,

B_s' the long average intensity per cycle level of an idealized spectrum of speech at one meter from the lips (Fig. 2),

B_s the long average intensity per cycle level of the speech received over a communication system,

V the actual speech level, for any talker, at two inches from the lips, as measured with a sound level meter with 40-db weighting,

H level of a critical band of speech above its threshold level in the absence of noise, i.e., band sensation level,

E the effective sensation level of a band of speech, and

p difference in db between the intensity in a critical band exceeded by 1 percent of ⅛th second intervals of received speech and the long average intensity in the same band.

3. CHARACTERISTICS OF SPEECH AND HEARING

3.1 The Spectrum of Speech

Figure 1 shows the results of several sets of measurements of the intensity of speech as a function of frequency. Curve A represents the average spectrum of four men and four women members of the testing crew used in carrying out the last extensive program of fundamental articulation tests. The spectrum is at a point two inches directly in front of the lips and is expressed in terms of the long time average intensity per cycle, in db relative to 10^{-16} watt/cm². Curves B and C are the spectra given for six men and five women in Fig. 10 of a paper by Dunn and White.[6] In the present paper the latter spectra have been shifted to change from 30 cm, the point of measurement, to the 2-inch position at which curve A applies. In order to provide a better basis for comparing shapes, the curve for the women has been shifted upward an additional 3 db because their total power was that much less than the men's.

It will be observed that there is an appreciable difference between the shapes of the Dunn and White spectra and the spectrum of the articulation testing crew. Because of the long interval (several years) between the two sets of measurements, it has been impracticable to determine whether the differences are real or result from one or more of the numerous differences in the testing arrangements and procedures. In view of this and the substantial differences which may exist between the spectra of individual voices, the smoothed and somewhat arbitrary compromise

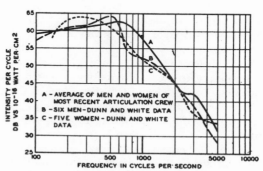

FIG. 1. Comparison of speech spectra at two inches from lips.

[6] H. K. Dunn and S. D. White, J. Acous. Soc. Am. 11, 278 (1940).

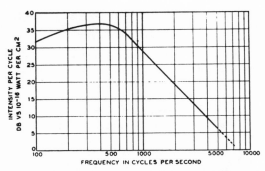

FIG. 2. Idealized long average speech spectrum at one meter from lips in a sound field free from reflections.

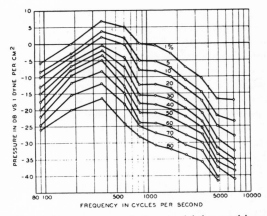

FIG. 3. R.m.s. pressure, during one-eighth second intervals, of speech at 30 cm from lips. Dunn and White composite data for six men (reference 6). Each curve shows the pressure exceeded in the indicated percentage of intervals.

spectrum of Fig. 2 has been adopted for use in this paper. For reasons which will appear later, this spectrum is given at a distance of one meter from the lips. The intensity of this spectrum, integrated over the entire frequency range, amounts to 65 db relative to 10^{-16} watt/cm². The corresponding figure at 2 inches from the lips, which is a more accurate point of measurement, is 90 db. If the speech level of a speaker having this idealized spectrum were measured by a sound level meter,[7] using flat weighting, with the microphone at 2 inches from the lips, the observed level would be about 3 db higher than the integrated value or around 93 db. This difference would occur because readings of rapidly varying material tend to be taken on the frequent peaks. With 40 db weighting the observed level should be close to the integrated level or 90 db.

3.2 Level Distribution of Speech

The spectra of speech which have just been discussed represent the average intensity over an appreciable period of time. From moment to moment the intensity of speech fluctuates rapidly above and below this average curve giving rise, at any frequency, to a level distribution of speech as a function of time. This distribution is one of the factors affecting the intelligibility of speech and consequently enters into the relationships presented later. In Fig. 3, taken largely from Fig. 3 of the previously mentioned paper[6] by Dunn and White, are shown the results of level distribution measurements made on a number of male voices.

[7] "ASA—American Standard—Sound Level Meters for Measurement of Noise and Other Sounds" (Z24.3—1944) July 28, 1944.

The same paper shows a similar set of data for women's voices. These charts show the distribution of ⅛ second intervals (roughly the duration of a syllable) with respect to the r.m.s. pressure measured during these intervals in the frequency bands indicated along the abscissa. The differences between levels which are exceeded by 1 percent and 50 percent of the intervals in the bands are shown in Table I for both the men and women talkers. It can be inferred from this table that the range over which the speech intensity fluctuates and the relative occurrence of intervals of different intensities are roughly the same for all bands and for both men and women. Taking all the bands to be alike in these respects results in certain simplifications of the relationships which are presented.

To determine the actual form of the speech level distribution, the data taken with male voices and the 1000–1400 cycle band have been used.

TABLE I. Difference in db between r.m.s. pressures of speech exceeded in 1 percent and in 50 percent of one-eighth second intervals.

Frequency band	Men's voices	Women's voices
250– 500	12 db	15 db
500– 700	18	18
700–1000	21	21
1000–1400	20	21
1400–2000	19	21
2000–2800	18	20
2800–4000	18	20

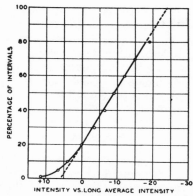

The first step was to compute the long average intensity by integrating over all of the $\frac{1}{8}$ second intervals in this band. Then the level difference between this long average intensity and the average intensity which was exceeded in 1 percent of the intervals was determined. The value of 1 percent was then plotted against this level difference to determine the point at the lower left corner of Fig. 4. The other points in the figure were obtained by the same process, using the levels exceeded in 5 percent, 10 percent, etc., of the intervals. It will be seen from the resulting curve that 1 percent of the intervals have average intensities 12 db or more above the long average intensity. It will be noted further that over the range between the 20 percent and the 80 percent points of Fig. 4, the distribution can be closely represented by a straight line. Although no accurate data are available to show the shape of the curve above the 80 percent point, it will be

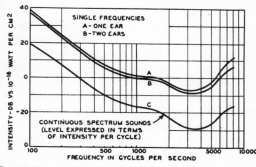

FIG. 5. Zero loudness contours for open air borne sounds.

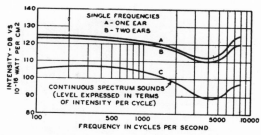

FIG. 6. 120-db loudness contours for open air borne sounds.

advantageous for reasons discussed later to assume that the distribution continues as a straight line up to 100 percent as shown by the dotted line.

If the same procedure is followed for the other bands and for women's voices it will be found that the resulting curves are similar to the curve of Fig. 4, although they tend to be somewhat steeper in slope. On the other hand it would be desirable for the purpose of this paper to measure the level distribution with bands approximating the critical band widths of the ear (Section 3.4), which are narrower bands than those used in the above measurements. This would cause some reduction in the slope of the curves. Figure 4 appears to be a reasonable compromise between these two offsetting factors. In the development of simple relationships it will be convenient and reasonably accurate to use the single curve of this figure as applying to all frequency regions.

3.3 Zero and 120 db Loudness Contours

Curves A and B of Fig. 5 show the thresholds of audibility for single frequency tones when listening with one and two ears. These curves apply to the most acute ears and indicate about the absolute minimum of sound that can be heard. The two ear curve is identical with the zero loudness contour of the "American Standard for Noise Measurement."[8] The one ear curve is the two ear curve increased by the curve of Fig. 9. In communicating by speech many of the sounds, both wanted and unwanted, tend to approach the continuous spectrum type instead of being discrete frequencies. Under these conditions the application of the single frequency threshold

[8] "ASA—American Standard for Noise Measurement (Z24.2—1942) J. Acous. Soc. Am. 13, 102 (1942).

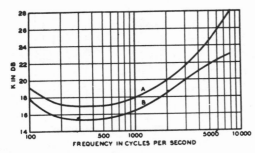

FIG. 7. Critical band widths (K) of ear. In db, $K = 10 \log_{10} W_c$, where W_c is the width of a critical band in cycles. Curves A and B are, respectively, for one- and two-ear listening.

curves requires the specification of a band width over which the intensity of the continuous spectrum sound is integrated. This is discussed later. For the present it is sufficient to note that curve C of Fig. 5 may be considered as a threshold curve for sound of the continuous spectrum type, when its level is expressed in terms of the intensity per cycle.

Curve B of Fig. 6 shows the two ear 120-db loudness contour for single frequency tones taken from the same source as curve B of Fig. 5. Curve A of Fig. 6 for one ear listening was obtained by adding to curve B of the same figure the curve of Fig. 9. The significance of the 120-db loudness contours lies in the fact that more intense sounds lying in the region above these curves are apt to annoy the listener, produce a sensation of feeling or, if of sufficiently high level, produce an actual sensation of pain. Curve C applies to sounds of the continuous spectrum type. This figure is of interest primarily in situations where there is extremely intense noise at the receiving position and higher than normal levels of received speech are required for the attainment of adequate intelligibility.

When there are no unwanted sounds in the ear the practical limits within which the wanted sounds should lie are bounded by the region just above the 120-db loudness contour and the threshold of audibility. These curves apply to the case where the sound waves arrive from a source at some distance from the observer who faces the source in a place free of reverberation. The intensities are measured with the observer out of the sound field, but at the position he takes in listening. Thus they do not represent the in-

tensities which actually exist in the ear except over the lower part of the frequency range. To use these curves in applications in which the listening is done with head receivers, it is necessary to express the output of the receiver in terms of the intensity of open airborne sounds which produce the same sensation as the sounds from the receiver.

3.4 Masking

In most problems involving speech reception, unwanted sounds are present in the ear of the listener and reduce the sensitivity of the ear to other sounds. This reduction in sensitivity is known as masking and at any frequency the amount of the masking M is equal to the difference between the levels β and β_0 of a single frequency tone which are just audible in the presence of the noise and in the total absence of noise, or

$$M = \beta - \beta_0. \tag{1}$$

The plot of M as a function of frequency is known as the masking spectrum of the noise. In general, interfering noises in the ear of a listener are of the continuous spectrum type, such as room noise. The masking relations provide a means for computing the masking caused by noise of this type when its spectrum affecting the ear is known. The amount of masking which is given by these relations is the threshold shift which would be observed by a highly idealized group of individuals whose thresholds β_0 in the absence of noise are given by the curves of Fig. 5. Actually, the threshold varies greatly among individuals depending upon such factors as fatigue, health, and age, the chosen curves representing about the absolute minimum of sound that can be heard by the most acute ears. The formula will thus, in general, compute a masking figure which is somewhat larger than would be observed by a random crew of observers. This, however, will usually be of no practical importance because computed levels of wanted sounds, above the same threshold, will be too large by the same amount. The margin of the wanted sounds above the unwanted ones is largely independent of the absolute threshold of the observer provided the noise is above the actual threshold. Observed tone levels which can just be heard in the presence of appreciable amounts of noise should be in good agreement with computed tone levels obtained by adding computed maskings to the idealized threshold curve, regardless, within fairly large limits, of the absolute thresholds of the observers.

Tests have shown that the masking effect on single frequency tones of noises having continuous spectra, which do not change in intensity too rapidly with frequency, is dependent only upon the level difference in db between (1) the intensity of the noise integrated over a narrow frequency band whose frequency limits are somewhat below and above the frequency of the masked tone, and (2) the single frequency threshold intensity in the absence of noise. These narrow bands are known as critical bands[9] of the ear and the above level difference at any frequency is referred to as the effective level of the noise at that frequency. The width of the critical bands is a function of frequency, varying from about 30 cycles at low frequencies to several hundred cycles at high frequencies.

The level difference in db between the noise intensity integrated over a critical band and the single frequency threshold (β_0) is given by

$$Z = (B+K) - \beta_0 = B - (\beta_0 - K), \qquad (2)$$

where

Z = level above threshold of a critical band of noise, i.e., effective level,

B = the long average intensity per cycle level of the noise received from all sources, expressed in db above 10^{-16} watt/cm^2,

$K = 10 \log_{10} \Delta f_c$, where Δf_c is the critical band width in cycles.

The values of K for one and two ear listening, as derived from masking tests, are shown by Fig. 7. The above expression for effective level is equivalent to referring the noise B to a new threshold which is K db lower than the single frequency threshold. Thus, instead of always being obliged to add a quantity K to the noise spectrum, it will be more convenient, where the noise spectrum is expressed in terms of the intensity per cycle, to subtract from B a new threshold X where

$$X = \beta_0 - K \qquad (3)$$

and then

$$Z = B - X. \qquad (4)$$

[9] H. Fletcher and W. A. Munson, J. Acous. Soc. Am. 9, 1 (1937).

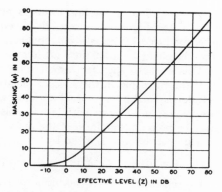

Fig. 8. Relation between the effective level of noise in any frequency region and the resulting masking in the same region.

The value of X is shown by the bottom curve of Fig. 5. It may be noted that the differences between the one- and two-ear single frequency threshold curves in Fig. 5 are identical with the differences between the one- and two-ear K's of Fig. 7. As a result, a single value of X applies to both one- and two-ear listening.

When the value of the effective level Z is known, the amount of masking M that is produced can be read from the curve* of Fig. 8. As a matter of interest, it will be noted that the masking and the effective levels are equal over the range of 20 to 50 db masking. Within this range a tone can just be heard through a steady noise when the intensity of the former is equal to the intensity of the noise integrated over the critical band in the region of the tone. However, as the effective level in a band increases above 50 db the resulting masking increases at a somewhat faster rate. The tests which gave this result used noises covering a broad frequency range as they generally do in communication problems. This upturn in the masking curve under such conditions has a bearing on some practical problems. For example, consider a case where the only important noise affecting a listener is transmitted along with a signal and the absolute level of reproduction can be varied. Under these conditions, where the signal-to-noise ratio remains constant, the signal may not be heard as well at an intense level of reproduction as at some lower

* The values of K and M vs. Z of the present report differ slightly from those given in reference 9 as a result of additional experimental data.

level. The effect of noise at low levels is also worthy of note. Figure 8 shows that some masking is produced by noise even though it is below the threshold of audibility (Z less than zero db). This is exactly the effect which would be obtained if the threshold in the absence of noise were itself determined by a residual noise, which combines on a power basis with other noises which may be present. The form of the masking curve over its entire range is given by

$$M = (B(+)X) - X + m, \qquad (5)$$

where $(+)$ represents power addition of the quantities B and X, and m is the amount, in db, that the masking exceeds the effective level of the noise. Values of m for effective levels greater than 50 db are given in Table II; for values of Z less than 50 db, m is zero.

At this point it may be of interest to indicate the reasons why the differences between the one- and two-ear thresholds and the one- and two-ear K's are taken to be alike. Figure 9(A) shows observed differences in the acuity of hearing of the best ear and the average of both ears, taken from Fig. 20 of a paper[10] by Fletcher and Munson. The effect of one- vs. two-ear listening on K was determined by adjusting the levels of single frequency tones until they could just be heard in the presence of a noise of the continuous spectrum type. This was done alternately with one- and two-ear listening, while maintaining the same noise level for both conditions. These tests showed that higher tone levels relative to the noise levels were required when listening with one ear as compared to two. These differences, which will be shown to represent the differences in K for the two conditions are indicated by Fig. 9(B). It will be seen that a single curve represents these masking data and also the audibility data of Fig. 9(A). That the

TABLE II. Values of m to the nearest db.

Z in db	m in db	Z in db	m in db
54–60	1	78–80	6
61–65	2	81–83	7
66–70	3	84–86	8
71–74	4	87–89	9
75–77	5	90–91	10

[10] H. Fletcher and W. A. Munson, J. Acous. Soc. Am. 5, 82 (1933).

differences in tone levels for one- and two-ear listening represent the differences in their K's can be shown by noting that the level of a tone which can just be heard in the presence of noise is, from Eq. (1), given by

$$\beta = M + \beta_0.$$

From Eq. (2) the effective level of the noise is

$$Z = B + K - \beta_0.$$

Also, for the levels used in the above tests, the masking M is numerically equal to the effective level of the noise; thus Z in the second equation can be substituted for M of the first equation, which can then be written

$$\beta = B + K. \qquad (6)$$

In this equation B is the intensity level per cycle of the noise and β the intensity level of the tone which can just be heard. It follows that, if the tone level β is greater with one ear listening than with two, the value of K must increase by the same amount since B was constant for the two conditions.

4. RESPONSE CHARACTERISTICS

An over-all response which has been called "orthotelephonic[11] response" is used for applying the information of the preceding section to the derivation of the intensity of speech received over a communication system. This response may be thought of as a usage response, in that it includes the effects on the received speech of distance and coupling between the microphone and the speaker's mouth and the coupling of the receiver to the ear. By definition a telephone system has an orthotelephonic response of zero db at all frequencies when it can be replaced by a one-meter air path, between talker and listener, without changing the loudness of the received speech at any frequency. The speaker and listener face each other in an otherwise unobstructed sound field. Listening to the sound over the air path is done with either one or two ears, depending upon whether one or both ears are used with the communication system.

A telephone system having the above characteristics is designated as an orthotelephonic system. It is convenient to specify the output of such

[11] A. H. Inglis, Bell Sys. Tech. J. 17, 358 (1938).

a system, at any frequency, in terms of the intensity, at the same frequency, of the speech received over the air system, but measured before insertion of the listener's head into the sound field. As a result, the speech received over an orthotelephonic system is identical to that received over the air system in loudness and intensity when the talker speaks at the same level in both cases. Specifying the intensity of the received speech in this manner is in conformity with the manner of expressing the zero and 120-db loudness contours discussed in the previous section.

If a telephone system, which is not an orthotelephonic system, has an orthotelephonic response of R db at any frequency, this means that the speech received over an orthotelephonic system, at the same frequency, must be raised R db in intensity to be as loud as that heard over the telephone system in question. Thus the intensity level of speech received over a telephone system at any frequency is the sum of the intensity level of speech at one meter from the lips and the orthotelephonic response of the system.

In general, a person will talk at a different level than that corresponding to the idealized spectrum of Fig. 2. Correction for this can be made by raising the spectrum by an amount $V-90$, where

V = the actual speech level, for any talker, at two inches from the lips in db vs. 10^{-16} watt/cm², as measured with a sound level meter using 40 db weighting,
90 = the corresponding level for the idealized speech spectrum of Fig. 2 when shifted to the two inch point.

The above information can be combined into the following equation for computing the intensity levels of received speech:

$$B_s = B_s' + (V-90) + R, \qquad (7)$$

where

B_s = the long average intensity per cycle level of the speech received over a communication system, expressed in db vs. 10^{-16} watt/cm²,
B_s' = the long average intensity per cycle level of an idealized spectrum of speech (Fig. 2) at one meter from the lips in a place free of reverberation, expressed in db vs. 10^{-16} watt/cm².

The intensity level of the received speech B_s is, of course, in terms of the free field intensity which produces, in the uncovered ear of an observer placed in the sound field, the same sensation ob-

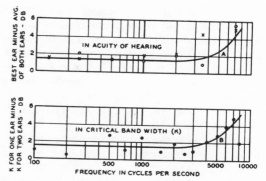

Fig. 9. Differences between one-ear and two-ear listening.

tained with speech delivered by a telephone receiver. It is equally important to note that the intensity level of received noise B, discussed previously, is also expressed in the same terms.

In concluding this section it may be in order to bring out some of the practical aspects of the problem of obtaining the orthotelephonic response of a telephone system. The over-all response is not usually measured as a whole in accordance with the above description but is derived from separate measurements of the response of microphone, electrical circuit, and receiver. The circuit responses are derived from purely physical measurements using single frequency tones. The real ear responses of receivers are also determined with single frequency tones by balancing the tone heard in the receiver against a comparison tone of the same frequency transmitted over a one-meter air path. The intensity of the output of the receiver is specified, exactly as described above, in terms of the intensity of the comparison tone, measured in the free sound field. The input to the receiver is measured in any suitable terms which will combine properly with the measurements of circuit response up to the receiver. Receiver measurements made in this way are usually accompanied by purely objective measurements, using mechanical couplers for example, from which conversion factors are obtained which do away with the need for further real ear measurements on other receivers of the same type.

The real voice response of a linear microphone can be obtained from two sets of measurements. In one, a person speaks into the microphone, taking whatever position with respect to it that is regarded as typical, while measurements are made of the output of the microphone in narrow frequency bands throughout the entire frequency range. In the other, a similar analysis is made of the speech intensity near the lips of the speaker, usually at two inches, the microphone having been removed from the sound field. These latter speech intensities, or these intensities reduced to one meter from the lips, are taken as the input to the microphone. Supplementing these measurements by objective response measurements using, for example, single frequency tones and an artificial voice, provides conversion factors which enable real voice responses of other microphones of the same type to be derived from purely objective measurements. These conversion factors allow for the interaction effects and distance losses between the artificial source and microphone relative to these effects between a real voice and the microphone. The application of this method without modification, to non-linear microphones, can give results which may be somewhat in error due to modulation products, generated by the microphone when complex waves of speech are impressed upon it. This may be avoided by a more complicated procedure beyond the scope of this paper to describe. It is also beyond the scope of the paper to go into details concerning the responses needed for determining the levels of noise in the ear. It should be sufficient to point out that the basic noise data and the response of each separate path by which noise can enter the ear should be so coordinated and expressed that they can be combined to give the noise intensity in the ear in the same terms as the received speech.

5. ARTICULATION INDEX

5.1 General

A distinguishing characteristic of speech is movement. Conversation at the rate of 200 words per minute, corresponding to about four syllables and ten speech sounds per second, is not unusual. During the brief period that a sound lasts, the intensity builds up rapidly, remains comparatively constant for a while, then decays rapidly. The various sounds differ from each other in their build-up and decay characteristics, in length, in total intensity, and in the distribution of the intensity with frequency. With the vowel sounds

the intensity is carried largely by the harmonics of the fundamental frequency of the voice and tends to be concentrated in one or more distinct frequency regions, each sound having its own characteristic regions of prominence. The consonant sounds, as a group, have components of higher frequency and lower intensity than the vowel sounds. In addition, the intensity tends to be scattered continuously over the frequency region characteristic of each sound. Thus when the elementary sounds are combined in sequence to form syllables, words, and phrases, there is a continuous succession of rapid variations in intensity, not only in particular frequency regions but also along the frequency scale. The interpretation of speech received by the ear depends upon the perception and recognition of these constantly shifting patterns.

The importance of the different regions of intensity and frequency to the recognition process was determined, in the investigation described here, by articulation tests, using a test circuit into which electrical networks and different amounts of attenuation were introduced to alter the intensity-frequency distribution and level of the called material prior to its reception by the listeners. The material consisted of meaningless monosyllables of the consonant-vowel-consonant type. The results were expressed as the percentage of syllables of which all three component sounds were perceived correctly. This percentage is designated as the syllable articulation, or simply the articulation, of the condition tested. The sounds used in these syllables include those commonly used in conversation.[12] A detailed description of this method, including the reasons for its choice, is given in other papers.[13, 14]

Syllable articulation, in common with all other known subjective measures of intelligibility such as word or sentence intelligibility, has certain limitations which impair its usefulness as a basic index. First, the value obtained from tests is not independent of the skill and experience of the testers. This difficulty can be partially overcome by calibrating a crew and correcting the results

[12] N. R. French, C. W. Carter, Jr., and W. Koenig, Jr., Bell Sys. Tech. J. 9, 290 (1930).
[13] H. Fletcher and J. C. Steinberg, Bell Sys. Tech. J. 8, 806 (1929).
[14] T. G. Castner and C. W. Carter, Jr., Bell Sys. Tech. J. 12, 347 (1933).

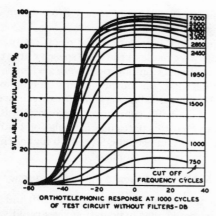

FIG. 10. Smoothed results of 1928–1929 articulation tests on low pass filters having the indicated cut-off frequencies.

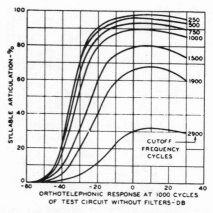

FIG. 11. Smoothed results of 1928–1929 articulation tests on high pass filters having the indicated cut-off frequencies.

by methods described elsewhere.[13] Of more importance is the fact that syllable articulation, in common with other subjective measures, is not an additive measure of the importance of the contributions made by the speech components in the different frequency regions. Stated differently, the articulation observed with a given frequency band of speech is not equal to the sum of the articulations observed when the given band is subdivided into narrower bands which are then individually tested. For the purpose of establishing relations between the intelligence carrying capacity of the components of speech and their frequency and intensity, a more fundamental index free of the above defects is needed. Such an index, called "articulation index," can be derived from the results of articulation tests. The magnitude of this index is taken to vary between zero and unity, the former applying when the received speech is completely unintelligible, the latter to the condition of best intelligibility.

The articulation index is based on the concept that any narrow band of speech frequencies of a given intensity carries a contribution to the total index which is independent* of the other bands with which it is associated and that the total contribution of all bands is the sum of the contributions of the separate bands. Letting ΔA represent the articulation index of any narrow

---

* Not absolutely true; the contribution of a band may be modified somewhat by masking produced by intense speech in neighboring bands.

band of speech frequencies and n the number of narrow bands into which the total band is subdivided for computational purposes, the articulation index A of the total band reaching the listener is

$$A = \sum_1^n \Delta A. \tag{8}$$

The value of ΔA, which is carried by any narrow frequency band, varies all the way from zero to a maximum value ΔA_m as the absolute levels of speech and noise in the ear are independently varied over wide ranges. Letting W represent the fractional part of ΔA_m which is contributed by a band with a particular combination of speech and noise, the value of articulation index for that band is given by

$$\Delta A = W \cdot \Delta A_m. \tag{9}$$

Hence,

$$A = \sum_1^n W \cdot \Delta A_m. \tag{10}$$

The establishment of relations for computing A thus involves two main steps: (1) the determination of the increments of frequency which give equal values of ΔA_m throughout the frequency range and (2) the determination of relationships between W and the levels of speech and noise in the ear.

The desired relations are derived below from the results of articulation tests on a broad-band transmission system into which high pass and low pass filters were inserted. The system included distortionless attenuators and amplifiers for varying the absolute level of the received speech.

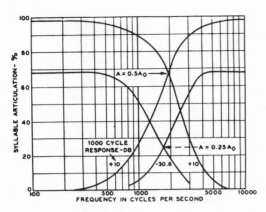

FIG. 12. Syllable articulation *versus* cut-off frequency of high pass and low pass filters at two different settings of test circuit. A_0 is articulation index of test circuit at its optimum setting.

The orthotelephonic response of the system with particular settings of attenuators and amplifiers is shown by curve A of Fig. 28. The departures of this response from flatness largely reflect usage factors and the method adopted for specifying the receiver output, which were discussed earlier in the paper. For example an imperfect seal between a receiver and the ear provides a shunting leakage path to the outside air and causes the drop in response noted at low frequencies.

The results of a few articulation tests with the frequency band limited by filters appear in a previous paper[3] by one of the writers. The smoothed results of more comprehensive tests, which provide the basis for the following relations, are given by Figs. 10 and 11. The former applies to low pass and the latter to high pass filters. The results are composite data taken with men's and women's voices. The ordinate of the curves represents the percentage of syllables which were recorded correctly. The abscissa is the ortho-telephonic response at 1000 cycles of the test circuit before insertion of the filters. The filters introduced a negligible loss within their passed bands and also caused practically complete suppression of the speech components beyond their cut-off frequencies. Thus the abscissa of Figs. 10 and 11, in combination with the response Curve A of Fig. 28 and the cut-off frequency of the filters, permits the determination of the response, at all frequencies, of the test condition corre-

sponding to any value of articulation shown on these figures.

During each articulation test electrical measurements were made of the total speech output of the microphone. Computations were also made to determine what the output of the microphone would be with a talker having the speech spectrum of Fig. 2. By comparing these results it is estimated that this particular articulation testing crew talked at an acoustic level 4 db higher than that to which Fig. 2 applies.

5.2 Relation between ΔA_m and Frequency

Referring now to the curves of Figs. 10 and 11, it will be noted that articulation rises rapidly as the circuit response is varied to raise the level of the received speech and reaches a maximum value at about the same setting of the system with each of the filters. The 1000-cycle orthotelephonic response of the system at this generally optimum setting is $+10$ db. The articulation values indicated for the different filters at this setting, plotted against the filter cut-off frequencies, are shown by the top pair of curves of Fig. 12. Now letting S_1 represent the indicated value of syllable articulation when the frequency range below a certain cut-off frequency is transmitted and S_2 the syllable articulation when the range above the same cut-off frequency is transmitted, it will be noted that the sum of S_1 and S_2 is generally greater than the articulation S_3 observed when both bands are transmitted together. In other words, the articulation of 27 percent for a 1000-cycle low pass filter, when added to 89 percent for the complementary high pass filter, does not yield the value of 98 percent which was observed for the full band. It follows, therefore, that syllable articulation is not an additive index. This is also true for observed values of letter articulation, word articulation and sentence intelligibility. However, the curves of Figs. 10 and 11 offer a means of deriving an additive index from the articulation test data, as described below.

Since the full-band system which was used may not be an optimum system for articulation, the articulation index of the speech received over it, which is presumably close to but not necessarily equal to unity at the optimum level, is here designated A_0. For this value of articulation index the syllable articulation is that observed for the full-band at a setting of +10 db, or $S = 98$ percent. It will be noted also from Fig. 12 that the high pass and low pass filter curves for this +10-db condition intersect at about 1900 cycles; this means that for this particular system half of the articulation index carried by the full-band of received speech is below and half above this frequency. At the point of intersection the observed value of S was 68 percent and consequently a syllable articulation of 68 percent for this particular testing group corresponds to an articulation index of $0.5A_0$.

If the top curve of Fig. 10 is now referred to, this curve applying to a 7000-cycle low pass filter and also to the unrestricted band, it will be noted that, by increasing the attenuation of the system, the S of the full band can be reduced to 68 percent which, as previously noted, corresponds to an articulation index of $0.5A_0$. The 1000-cycle response of the system at which this occurs is −30.6 db. If the syllable articulation obtained with the different filters at this setting of the system is now plotted against the cut-off frequency of the filters, another pair of intersecting curves will be obtained as shown in the lower part of Fig. 12. The articulation index of each of the two complementary bands, below and above the frequency of intersection (1700 cycles), consequently has by definition an articulation index of $0.25A_0$ and the corresponding value of S is 25 percent. This procedure may be followed further

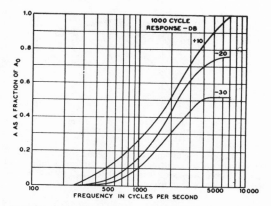

FIG. 14. Relation between articulation index and cut-off frequency at three different settings of the test circuit. Articulation index is expressed as a fraction of the articulation index (A_0) of test circuit at its optimum setting.

to find that a syllable articulation of 8 percent corresponds to an articulation index of $0.125A_0$.

Knowing from the above that a syllable articulation of 25 percent corresponds to an articulation index of $0.25A_0$ reference is again made to the +10 db curves of Fig. 12. It will be seen that a low pass filter (about 950 cycles) yielding an articulation index of $0.25A_0$ has as its complement a high pass filter having a syllable articulation of 90 percent. Since the contributions of these two complementary filters must add to A_0 it follows that $S = 90$ percent corresponds to an articulation index of $0.75A_0$. By following these procedures a sufficient number of points may be found to determine satisfactorily the curve shown in Fig. 13. This curve shows the relationship between syllable articulation and articulation index expressed as a fraction of the articulation index A_0 of the full-band of the speech received at its optimum level over the system which was tested.

Having obtained the relationship shown in Fig. 13, it is now possible to construct a set of curves showing, for each of several levels of the full-band of speech, the cumulative total of articulation index, expressed as a fraction of A_0, as the upper end of the passed band is increased in frequency. This is accomplished by reading from Fig. 10 the syllable articulation values obtained with all the filters at each of several fixed settings of the full band system, converting these values of S into fractional values of A_0 by means of the curve of Fig. 13 and plotting the

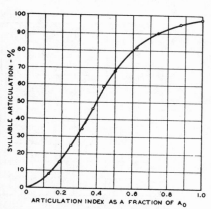

FIG. 13. Relation between syllable articulation and articulation index. The latter is expressed as a fraction of the articulation index (A_0) of the test circuit at its optimum setting.

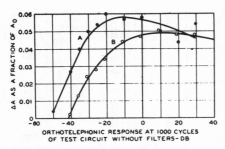

FIG. 15. Fractional values of A_0, the articulation index of the test circuit at its optimum setting, carried by individual bands. Curve A—band from 1300 to 1520 cycles. Curve B—band from 490 to 620 cycles.

results against the cut-off frequency of the filters. The results of this operation are shown in Fig. 14.

The next step is to separate the frequency range into a large number of bands (20 were used) having equal fractional values of A_0. The +10-db curve of Fig. 14 is used for this purpose since this is the optimum setting of this system with the full band. Having established by this method the frequency limits of bands of equal importance (.05A_0) *in the system tested*, the contribution of these bands at other levels can be read from a complete family of curves like those of Fig. 14. The resulting values are then plotted against the orthotelephonic response of the system at 1000 cycles* to obtain, for each of the twenty bands, curves of the type illustrated by Fig. 15. These curves show that the increment ΔA, carried by a band, first increases as the gain of the system is increased, then reaches a maximum value after which it drops off slowly as the gain is further increased. If the system tested had been an optimum system, the maximum contribution of each of the twenty bands should be .05, since the frequency limits of the bands were selected on the basis of a 5 percent contribution by each band at the optimum setting of the system. Also the maximum contribution of each band should occur at the same setting of the system. Inspection of the curves of Fig. 15 shows that neither of these expectations is precisely fulfilled, thus indicating that the testing system fell somewhat short of being an optimum system. Actually, a summation of the maximum values of ΔA_0 of the twenty curves gives a value about 3

* Any other parameter which reflects changes in received level, such as the response of the system within each of the 20 bands, could be used equally well.

percent above unity. If a value of unity is assigned to the articulation index of the speech received over an optimum system, this means that the speech received over the system tested had an articulation index of 0.97, or $A_0 = 0.97$. With this information the curve of Fig. 13, showing the relation of syllable articulation to articulation index as a fraction of A_0, can be converted to a relation between syllable articulation and absolute values of articulation index by multiplying the abscissa by 0.97. The resulting curve is shown on Fig. 23. Although this curve may be lacking in general interest the detailed description of how it was obtained is of general interest since the same method could be used by others who might start with a system having different response characteristics from that used in the tests which have been described.

We are now in a position to draw up a cumulative curve of the absolute value of articulation index *versus* frequency when all bands are simultaneously at their optimum settings. The maximum value of articulation index which can be contributed by each of the twenty bands discussed above is obtained by multiplying the maximum value of each of the twenty curves, like those of Fig. 15, by 0.97. The resulting value for the band of lowest frequency, plotted against the upper frequency limit for this band, provides one point on the desired curve. By adding successive bands, one at a time, the final relation, shown by the curve of Fig. 16 is obtained. It differs only slightly from the top curve of Fig. 14 which

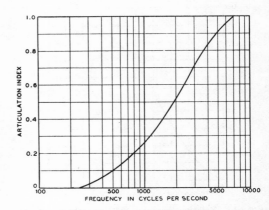

FIG. 16. Articulation index *versus* cut-off frequency. All bands are at their optimum levels. Curve is based on about equal numbers of men's and women's voices.

applied when the system used was tested at its optimum setting. In fact, the differences between the two curves are so small that it is open to question whether the data are sufficiently precise to justify the above operation in this case. It is believed, however, that the operation will be of interest in the event of additional basic studies of this nature which, caused by the particular characteristics of the circuits which may be employed, may require greater corrections.

The derivative or slope of the curve of Fig. 16 at any frequency shows the importance of that frequency with respect to its maximum possible contribution to articulation index. At any frequency the product of the slope of this curve and the factor W, discussed in the next section, represents the contribution of this frequency to the total articulation index. In general, the levels of speech and noise in the ear, and hence W, will vary sufficiently slowly with frequency to permit the use of a single value of W over a considerable frequency range. For the general run of computations twenty values of W at suitably selected frequencies should be adequate. For this purpose, it is convenient to divide the frequency range into twenty parts or computation bands such that the maximum possible contribution of each band is equal to that of the others and to determine W at the mid-frequency of each band. The limits of the twenty bands chosen in this way are obtained by reading from the continuous curve of Fig. 16 the frequencies corresponding to all the articulation indices which are multiples of .05. These band limits are given in Table III.

The importance curve of Fig. 16 is based on composite data taken with about equal numbers

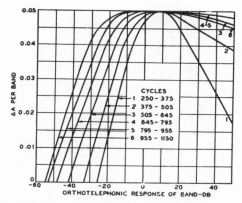

FIG. 17. Effect of level variations on articulation index carried by narrow bands. Band limits are so chosen that the articulation index of each band is 0.05 at its optimum level.

of men and women talkers. Men's voices are about an octave lower in pitch than women's and the latter tend to be somewhat richer in high frequency sounds. As a result it is probable that separate importance curves for men's and women's voices would approximate the curve of Fig. 16 in shape but be shifted somewhat toward lower and higher frequencies, respectively.

5.3 Variation of ΔA with Level

Having obtained the frequency limits of the twenty bands which individually contribute 0.05 to articulation index when each band is making its maximum possible contribution, the next step is the determination of the contribution of each band under other than optimum conditions. This includes the specification of the conditions in usable terms. The starting point is the twenty curves illustrated by the two curves of Fig. 15. The ordinates of these curves are first multiplied by 0.97 to convert to absolute values of articulation index, as discussed previously. They are then used to draw up additional curves of cumulative articulation index *vs.* frequency, similar to the curve of Fig. 16 but for levels 10, 20, 30, etc., db below the optimum level of each band, or above the reasonably well-defined settings at which the contribution of the individual bands drops to zero. After smoothing these curves, one for each relative level, they are divided into bands having the frequency limits of Table III. The contribution of each of these bands at each level is then obtained from the new set of curves (not shown)

TABLE III. Frequency bands making equal (5 percent) contributions to articulation index when all bands are at their optimum levels. Composite data for men's and women's voices.

Band	Frequency limits cycles	Band	Frequency limits cycles
1	250–375	11	1930–2140
2	375–505	12	2140–2355
3	505–645	13	2355–2600
4	645–795	14	2600–2900
5	795–955	15	2900–3255
6	955–1130	16	3255–3680
7	1130–1315	17	3680–4200
8	1315–1515	18	4200–4860
9	1515–1720	19	4860–5720
10	1720–1930	20	5720–7000

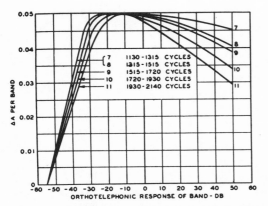

FIG. 18. Effect of level variations on articulation index carried by narrow bands. Band limits are so chosen that the articulation index of each band is 0.05 at its optimum level.

and plotted to obtain the twenty curves of Figs. 17–20, inclusive. These show the effect of level changes on the articulation index carried by each of the twenty equally important bands. The abscissa of each curve is the orthotelephonic response of the transmission system at the mid-frequency of the particular band. The specification of the response of each band in this way was accomplished by shifting the abscissa of the curves illustrated by Fig. 15 by the amount that the orthotelephonic response at the band frequencies exceeds the orthotelephonic response at 1000 cycles, Curve A of Fig. 28 providing the necessary data.

The absolute placement of the curves applies only to the particular acoustic talking level used in the basic articulation tests. However, the curves can obviously be specified on an absolute basis, if desired, in terms of the absolute intensity of the received speech, by adding to the abscissa the intensity, in each band, of the crew's speech at one meter. Such a group of curves could be used for computational purposes. A different procedure is followed, however, to obtain a solution which will not only more readily handle problems involving noise but also more clearly bring out the nature of the relationships.

The fraction of the maximum possible contribution which a band makes when it is not at an optimum level is designated by W. Curves of W against level would consequently be identical in shape to the curves of Figs. 17–20. It will be noted that these curves are essentially straight

lines except in the region where the articulation index is approaching a maximum and that the slopes of the straight line portions are approximately alike and equal to about 3 db for a change of 10 percent in W. This is the same slope that was derived earlier for the level distribution of speech in narrow bands (Fig. 4).

When speech, which is constantly fluctuating in intensity, is reproduced at a sufficiently low level only the occasional portions of highest intensity will be heard, but if the level of reproduction is raised sufficiently even the portions of lowest intensity will become audible. Thus the similarity in slope of the straight line portions of the W curves and the speech distribution curve suggests that W is equal to the fraction of the intervals of speech in a band that can be heard. It will be noted, of course, that the shapes of the W and speech curves are different in the region where W is approaching zero. Actually the W curves in this region cannot be determined accurately and probably do taper off in much the same manner as the speech level distribution (low portion of curve of Fig. 4).

As regards the upper part of the curves of Figs. 17–20 it will be seen that their shapes in this region do not agree with the speech level distribution of Fig. 4. As pointed out previously the latter was extrapolated in the 80–100 percent region and consequently may be in error. For reasons which will be pointed out later, it appears advantageous to assume that the straight line of

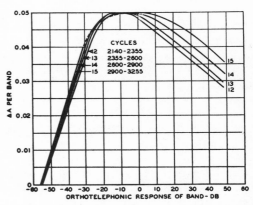

FIG. 19. Effect of level variations on articulation index carried by narrow bands. Band limits are so chosen that the articulation index of each band is 0.05 at its optimum level.

Fig. 4 represents the true speech level distribution up to 100 percent (i.e., down to the lowest level intervals) and to offer a different explanation for the bending over of the ΔA curves, and hence of W, as the level of maximum contribution is approached. This is taken up later as the explanation to be given involves a consideration of the effects of noise.

If W is equal to the fraction of the time intervals that speech in a critical band can be heard, it should be possible to derive W from the characteristics of speech and hearing and to use Figs. 17–20 for testing the method. The first step in this process is the definition of a new term H, where

H = the level of a critical band of speech above its threshold level in the absence of noise. This is termed the band sensation level.

The band sensation level of speech is given by

$$H = B_S + p + K - \beta_0 = B_S + p - X. \quad (11)$$

The terms B_S, K, β_0, and X have been defined previously. The term p is the difference in db between the intensity in a critical band exceeded by 1 percent of $\frac{1}{8}$th second intervals of received speech and the long average intensity in the same band.

Tests have shown that speech does not become inaudible until its long average intensity per cycle is reduced to about 30 db below the single frequency threshold β_0. This results from two causes which bring about the introduction of the p and K terms in the above equation. Since speech is far from constant in intensity its threshold level in any frequency region is determined by the most intense sounds in that region. As pointed out previously, the intensity of these sounds integrated over $\frac{1}{8}$th second time intervals and over frequency bands which approximate the critical bands in width, is about 12 db above the long average intensity within the same bands; hence $p = 12$ db. Actually this difference varies somewhat from band to band and in the direction of smaller values at low frequencies. In the interests of simplicity it is here considered to be independent of frequency.

The need for the K term, which is of the order of 20 db, has already been pointed out in connection with the discussion of masking of continu-

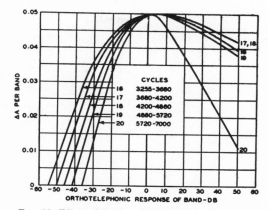

FIG. 20. Effect of level variations on articulation index carried by narrow bands. Band-limits are so chosen that the articulation index of each band is 0.05 at its optimum level.

ous spectra sounds. While speech is not rigorously of this type, the spacing of its single frequency components, which are constantly varying up and down the frequency scale, corresponds roughly to the width of the critical bands over which the intensity has to be integrated to obtain a true measure of the sensation which is produced. Therefore, without much loss of accuracy, the same values of K and hence X, which have been determined for sounds having continuous spectra can be applied to speech.

Now referring back to Figs. 4 and 17–20 it will be appreciated that there are certain consequences that can be tested if the hypothesis is correct that W is equal to the proportion of the intervals of speech in a band which can be heard. These are

(1) The computed sensation levels of the speech received in the 20 bands should be substantially alike when these bands all have the same value of W.

(2) The computed sensation level in each band for the zero point of the twenty ΔA curves, which are drawn down to the zero point as straight lines, should be 6 db. This results from the shape of the speech level distribution (Fig. 4) and the choice of the 1 percent highest intervals for expressing the sensation level of the speech in a band.

The sensation level corresponding to $W = 0$ is desired for each of the twenty frequency bands of Figs. 17–20. Although these bands are wider than the critical bands their sensation levels are nevertheless given correctly by Eq. (11). This equation involves B_S which in turn is given by

TABLE IV. Computation of the sensation level (H) of the received speech at which $W=0$ in the 1928–1929 articulation tests. For the particular crew, $H=B_{s'}+16+R-X$.

Band	$B_{s'}$ (db)	R (db)	X (db)	H (db)
1	36.5	−26	−1.5	28
2	36.6	−33.5	−8.0	27
3	35.7	−42	−11.6	21
4	33.4	−48.5	−14.1	15
5	30.7	−53.5	−15.7	9
6	28.3	−55	−16.7	6
7	26.0	−55	−17.5	5
8	24.0	−55	−18.3	3
9	22.1	−55	−19.4	2
10	20.4	−55	−21.0	2
11	18.9	−55	−23.3	3
12	17.5	−55.5	−25.2	3
13	16.1	−56	−26.6	3
14	14.6	−56	−27.8	2
15	13.0	−56	−28.5	2
16	11.3	−55.5	−28.9	1
17	9.5	−50.5	−28.8	4
18	7.5	−46	−27.8	5
19	5.1	−41.5	−25.1	5
20	2.5	−36	−19.7	2

Eq. (7). Combining Eqs. (7) and (11) we obtain

$$H = B_{s'} + (V-90) + p + R - X.$$

The term $(V-90)$ represents the acoustic talking level of the particular articulation test crew relative to the talking level corresponding to the idealized spectrum of Fig. 2; hence $(V-90)$ is +4 db as mentioned previously. Also p is +12 db as discussed above. Combining these numerical values, the values of H for this particular crew are given by:

$$H = B_{s'} + 16 + R - X.$$

This equation has been applied to the computation of H for each of the twenty bands whose frequency limits are given on Figs. 17–20. The values of $B_{s'}$ and X, at the mid-frequencies of the bands, were taken from Fig. 2 and curve C of Fig. 5. The values of the orthotelephonic response R of the circuit were read from the abscissa of Figs. 17–20 at the points of zero contribution of the twenty bands. The results of the computations are given in the last column of Table IV. For bands 5 to 20, inclusive, the computed levels are all within a range of 8 db and the average level for these bands is within $2\frac{1}{2}$ db of the required value of 6 db. In view of the many sources of error, involving the measurement of the acoustic level of the talkers, the real voice and ear calibrations of microphone and receivers and

TABLE V. Values of W for values of E between 0 and +12 db.

E in db	W	E in db	W
1.0–2.2	.01	8.4–8.7	.11
2.3–3.1	.02	8.8–9.1	.12
3.2–3.9	.03	9.2–9.5	.13
4.0–4.6	.04	9.6–9.9	.14
4.7–5.3	.05	10.0–10.3	.15
5.4–6.0	.06	10.4–10.7	.16
6.1–6.6	.07	10.8–11.1	.17
6.7–7.2	.08	11.2–11.5	.18
7.3–7.8	.09	11.6–11.8	.19
7.9–8.3	.10	11.9–12.1	.20

possible differences in the manner in which the latter were talked into and held to the ear in the calibrating and articulation tests, the results for bands 5–20 are considered to be in reasonable agreement with the requirements which are being tested.

The levels computed for bands 1 to 5, inclusive, are too high. However, they are qualitatively in agreement with what would be expected if there had been a low level of room noise in the listening booth during the tests, resulting in masking of the speech. Since room noise usually falls off rapidly with increasing frequency and the shielding effect of receivers held against the ear increases with frequency, extraneous low level noise would have its greatest masking effect in the lowest bands, and negligible effects above 1000 cycles or so. One of several possible sources of noise is the movements of the four observers who were in the booth at the same time. Another uncertainty at the lower frequencies lies in the manner in which the receiver is held to the ear. The above computation of absolute levels in the ear involves the real ear response of the receiver, and consequently the tacit assumption that the coupling between receivers and ears in the articulation tests was the same as in the subjective determinations of the receiver response. Here again any differences which may exist between the responses in the two cases are likely to be greatest at low frequencies. In view of these various effects it is believed that the computed absolute levels are sufficiently close to those required by the above hypothesis of the significance of the W factor, to justify it as a working basis in the formulation of a method for computing the articulation index of received speech.

5.4 Derivation of W—Noisy Conditions

It is apparent that values of W over the range from 0 to about 0.7 can be determined closely, for speech reproduced over linear systems and listened to under quiet conditions, by computing the fractional part of the speech distribution of Fig. 4 which is above threshold. When more than about 70 percent of the speech distribution is above threshold in the absence of noise, an additional factor is included to account for the rounded portion of the ΔA curves of Figs. 17–20, covering values of W in the range from about 0.7 to unity. This part of the curves can be arrived at on the basis of a fatigue effect which may be considered as self-masking. On this basis the hearing of the relatively infrequent low level sounds in a band is considered to be impaired through a temporary loss of sensitivity owing to the preceding sounds of higher level in the same band. This loss of sensitivity will be treated as equivalent to the effect of noise. It is necessary, therefore, to develop relations for noisy conditions before the development for quiet condition can be completed.

If there were no such loss of sensitivity and no other source of masking, and if the speech level distribution is taken to be a straight line, the value of W for any speech band would be given by the fraction of the speech intervals which have sensation levels above 6 db, or

$$W = (H - 6)/30 \qquad (12)$$

for sensation levels between 6 and 36 db. To provide a basis for accounting for the gradual tapering off of the twenty ΔA curves as $W = 1$ is approached, and also for evaluating the effects of noise generally, this equation will be rewritten as follows:

$$W = (E - 6)/30, \qquad (13)$$

where E is a new term called the effective sensation level of a band of speech, given by the following equation:

$$E = H - M, \qquad (14)$$

where M is the masking resulting from all sources of interference, including the masking of speech on itself. By application of Eq. (11) this becomes

$$E = (B_s + p - X) - M. \qquad (15)$$

This can be written in the following more convenient form for computations by replacing M by its equivalent from Eq. (5), or

$$E = B_s + p - m - (B(+)X). \qquad (16)$$

To obtain W, this expression is substituted in Eq. (13), and

$$W = 1/30[B_s + p - 6 - m - (B(+)X)]. \qquad (17)$$

This is the equation ordinarily used for computing W. Actually it is an approximation for values of W less than 0.2 (effective sensation levels less than 12 db). In cases where reception is poor and the effective sensation levels of the

TABLE VI. Values of β_0, X, K, and B_s' at selected frequencies. Values of K are in db; other quantities are in db vs. 10^{-16} watt/cm².

Bands for which ΔA_{max} =0.05	Band center cycles	One ear		Two ears			
		β_0	K	β_0	K	X	B_s'
1	310	15.5	17.0	14.0	15.5	− 1.5	36.5
2	440	9.0	17.0	7.5	15.5	− 8.0	36.6
3	575	5.5	17.1	4.0	15.6	−11.6	35.7
4	720	3.3	17.4	1.8	15.9	−14.1	33.4
5	875	2.0	17.7	0.5	16.2	−15.7	30.7
6	1040	1.4	18.1	−0.1	16.6	−16.7	28.3
7	1225	.9	18.4	−0.6	16.9	−17.5	26.0
8	1415	.5	18.8	−1.0	17.3	−18.3	24.0
9	1615	− .2	19.2	−1.7	17.7	−19.4	22.1
10	1825	−1.4	19.6	−2.9	18.1	−21.0	20.4
11	2035	−3.3	20.0	−4.8	18.5	−23.3	18.9
12	2250	−4.8	20.4	−6.3	18.9	−25.2	17.5
13	2475	−5.9	20.7	−7.4	19.2	−26.6	16.1
14	2750	−6.6	21.2	−8.2	19.6	−27.8	14.6
15	3080	−6.9	21.6	−8.5	20.0	−28.5	13.0
16	3470	−6.7	22.2	−8.6	20.3	−28.9	11.3
17	3940	−5.9	22.9	−8.0	20.8	−28.8	9.5
18	4530	−4.1	23.7	−6.5	21.3	−27.8	7.5
19	5300	−0.3	24.8	−3.3	21.8	−25.1	5.1
20	6350	+6.5	26.2	+2.6	22.3	−19.7	2.5

TABLE VII. Values of $(B(+)X) - X$ as a function of $B - X$.

$B - X$ (db)	$(B(+)X) - X$ (db)
−9	0.5
8	0.6
7	0.8
6	1.0
5	1.2
4	1.5
3	1.8
2	2.1
−1	2.5
0	3.0
+1	3.5
2	4.1
3	4.8
4	5.5
5	6.2
6	7.0
7	7.8
8	8.6
+9	9.5

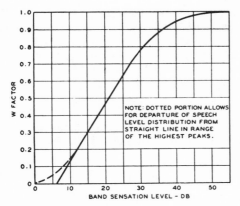

FIG. 21. The W factor for quiet conditions.

below B_S, where B_S is the long average intensity per cycle level of speech. This equivalent noise, designated by B_f, is

$$B_f = B_S - 24. \qquad (18)$$

Substituting this value of B_f for B in Eq. (17) it follows that, for quiet conditions,

$$W = 1/30[B_S + p - 6 - m - ((B_S - 24)(+)X)]. \qquad (19)$$

The relationship between W, as computed by this equation, and the sensation level of a speech band, as computed by Eq. (11), is shown by the continuous curve of Fig. 21. This curve applies to the case where there is no noise and no non-linear elements are between the voice and the ear to change the form of the time variation of speech received in a band from that of the original speech. If this curve is compared with the twenty curves of Figs. 17–20, it will be seen that it is a reasonable representation of their shapes over the entire range below their maximum values. It may be worth noting here that the self-masking factor, which produces the tapering effect as W approaches unity under quiet conditions, will also produce the same sort of an effect when other noises are present, and when the speech is raised to a level considerably above the noise level.

Figure 21 indicates that the maximum contribution of a band of speech under quiet conditions, except for the equivalent noise of self-masking B_f, is reached at a band sensation level of 50 db. At this speech level the effective level Z of the noise having an intensity per cycle level of B_f is only 14 db since B_f is 24 db below B_S and the sensation level of a speech band is determined by the levels of speech $p = 12$ db above B_S. The value of m in Eq. (19) is consequently zero over the range of the curve of Fig. 21.

Referring now to Fig. 8, it will be noted that masking does not start to increase faster than the effective level of noise until the latter exceeds 50 db. Consequently, when self-masking is the only source of masking, the value of m in Eq. (19) does not change from zero until the sensation level of speech in a band rises above 86 db. It follows that W for quiet conditions, as given by the above equations, has a value of unity for band sensation levels of speech ranging between 50 and 86 db. Thus the relations do not account for the reduc-

speech in a number of computation bands are less than 12 db, computations can be improved in accuracy by using Eq. (16) and Table V for these particular bands to allow for the departure of the most intense part of the speech level distribution from a straight line (Fig. 4). Values of m are given in Table II for values of Z above 50 db; at lower levels m is zero. Values of B_S', from which B_S is derived, and of X are given by Table VI. Values of $(B(+)X)$ relative to X are given by Table VII as a function of $(B-X)$. Outside the range for which values are given, $(B(+)X)$ equals either B or X, depending upon which is the larger.

In the above equations B represents the level above 10^{-16} watt/cm² of the combined intensity per cycle of all the various noises reaching the ear at any particular frequency. In addition to the usual sources of noise, B includes the noise equivalent in its effect to the self-masking of a band of speech on itself and also the noise equivalent in its effect to the masking of one speech band on another. These are all combined on a power basis and the sum then expressed in db. Self-masking and interband masking are further considered in the following sections.

5.5 Derivation of W—Quiet Conditions

It is now possible to consider self-masking and its effects on the form of the ΔA curves. Referring back to Eq. (13) it will be seen that if W is not to exceed unity the effective sensation level must not exceed 36 db. This is accomplished by taking the equivalent noise of self-masking as 24 db

tion of A at high speech levels as shown on Figs. 17–20. Overloading in the ear, resulting in the generation of intermodulation products, which could act as noise, is a possible explanation of this reduction. If the noise equivalents of these products could be determined their effects could be allowed for, presumably, in the same manner as other noises. It is possible that the downward droop of the curves of Figs. 17–20 above the optimum levels is excessive. Because of the small variation of the measured values of articulation with level above the optimum level with the various filters, the derivation of the variation of the contributions of the individual bands with level in this region is not at all precise.

The unimportance of m, as discussed above, applies specifically to quiet conditions. In problems involving high levels of extraneous noise the inclusion of m in the above equations may have a considerable effect on W.

5.6 Interband Masking of Speech

Articulation tests have shown that at high received levels the articulation tends to decrease as the level is increased. The effect is most evident in systems that contain pronounced peaks or frequency regions that are partially suppressed. The effect is believed to be caused in part by speech in one frequency region masking the speech sounds in other frequency regions. One rather elaborate method for allowing for this

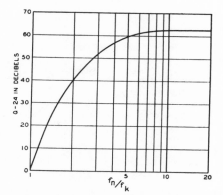

FIG. 22. Function used in determining the masking of speech by speech in lower bands.

effect has been developed but is too lengthy to describe here and also too laborious in applications involving many computations. This method involves, for example, the determination of the effect of each band of speech on each of the other bands. These effects are functions of the levels in each of the bands. In the computational method described here a simpler but presumably less accurate procedure has been followed. One simplification is to consider the effect of a speech band on only those bands which are of higher frequency. As in the case of self-masking, it will be convenient to consider the interband masking as equivalent to the masking produced by a noise B_n in the speech band being masked. The estimated intensity level of this equivalent noise B_{nk}

TABLE VIII. Q, i.e., the number of db that the noise produced in any band, by speech in any lower band, is below the long average intensity of the speech in the lower band.

Producing band	2	3	4	5	6	7	8	Band in which the noise is produced											
								9	10	11	12	13	14	15	16	17	18	19	20
1	49	62	70	75	78	81	83	85	85	85	86	86	87	87	87	87	87	87	87
2		44	56	64	70	74	78	80	82	83	84	85	85	86	86	87	87	87	87
3			42	52	61	67	71	75	78	79	81	83	84	85	85	86	86	87	87
4				40	50	57	64	68	71	75	78	79	81	82	83	84	85	86	87
5					38	49	56	62	66	70	72	75	78	79	81	83	85	85	86
6						36	46	54	59	64	67	70	72	75	77	80	82	84	85
7							35	45	51	56	61	65	69	72	75	77	79	81	84
8								35	43	50	55	59	64	67	71	74	77	80	83
9									35	42	47	52	57	63	67	71	74	78	81
10										34	41	47	52	57	63	67	71	76	79
11											33	40	46	52	57	63	68	72	77
12												33	40	47	54	60	65	71	75
13													34	41	50	55	61	67	72
14														34	42	49	56	64	70
15															35	43	51	59	65
16																35	45	54	61
17																	35	46	56
18																		36	49
19																			39

produced in band n by speech in band k is given by:

$$B_{nk} = B_{sk} - Q, \qquad (20)$$

where

B_{sk} = the intensity level of speech in band k which is doing the masking,

f_k = the mid-frequency of band k, and

f_n = the mid-frequency of the band n in which speech is being masked.

The quantity Q, derived empirically, is given on Fig. 22 as a function of (f_n/f_k). Values of Q for the particular frequency bands of Table III are given in Table VIII. To simplify the computations Q is here taken to be independent of the absolute level of B_{sk}.

Assuming the equivalent noises from the various bands to combine on a power basis, the total equivalent noise in band n produced by speech from all lower bands is given by

$$B_n = B_{n1}(+)B_{n2}(+)\cdots(+)B_{n,\,n-1}. \qquad (21)$$

In cases where very high levels of speech are necessary to ride over excessive levels of noise, and the response of the communication system contains sharp peaks or dips, interband masking may be appreciably larger than these formulas indicate.

5.7 Summary of Relationships—Linear Systems

If the speech frequency range is subdivided, for computational purposes, into twenty bands having the frequency limits of Table III, the value of ΔA_m for each band is 0.05 and the articulation index of the received speech by Eq. (10) is

$$A = 0.05(W_1 + W_2 + \cdots W_{20}). \qquad (10a)$$

The subscripts refer to the individual bands of Table III. The value of W in any particular computation band is determined by the following relation in which the quantities that vary with frequency are usually specified at the mid-frequencies of the bands

$$W = 1/30[B_S + p - 6 - m - (B(+)X)]. \qquad (17)$$

The symbol $(+)$, between two terms expressed in db, indicates that they are to be combined on a power basis and then reconverted to db. This is the basic equation for determining W except

for non-linear systems, discussed in Section 5.8, or in cases where reception is poor and the effective sensation level (Eq. (16)) of the speech in a number of the computation bands is less than 12 db. In this event Eq. (16) should be used for these particular bands and the values of W read from Table V.

The quantity B_S is the level, in db $vs.$ 10^{-16} watt/cm^2, of the long average intensity per cycle of the received speech, the intensity being expressed as a free field intensity in the manner described in Section 4. B is a similar quantity but applies to the total noise per cycle received from all sources. The value of p is ordinarily taken as 12 db at all frequencies. X is a function of frequency only; its values are given in Table VI. Values of $(B(+)X)$ relative to X are given in Table VII as a function of $B - X$. The term m can be omitted unless extraneous noise of high level is present; values of m as a function of the effective level Z of the noise B are given in Table II, where

$$Z = B - X. \qquad (4)$$

The value of B_S in Eq. (17) is given by

$$B_S = B_S' + (V - 90) + R, \qquad (7)$$

where B_S' is the intensity level, at the appropriate frequency, of the idealized speech spectrum of Fig. 2, values of which are tabulated in Table VI. The symbol V represents the actual speech level of any particular talkers, at two inches from the lips, as determined by a sound level measurement using 40-db weighting. R is the orthotelephonic response of the communication system at the appropriate frequency.

The value of B in Eqs. (4) and (17) is given by a new equation

$$B = B_E(+)B_f(+)B_n, \qquad (22)$$

where B represents the intensity per cycle level of the total noise from all sources except that produced by the received speech, and

$$B_f = B_S - 24 \qquad (18)$$

and

$$B_n = B_{n1}(+)B_{n2}(+)\cdots B_{n,\,n-1}, \qquad (21)$$

where n is the number of the particular band in which the noise is being determined and the subscripts 1, 2, etc., refer to the bands, one to

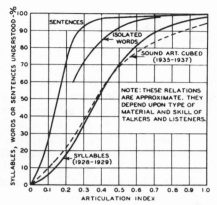

FIG. 23. Approximate relations between articulation index and subjective measures of intelligibility.

$(n-1)$, from which the noise arises because of the speech in these bands. The values of B_{n1}, B_{n2}, etc., relative to the levels B_S of speech in bands $1, 2 \cdots (n-1)$, can be read from Table VIII.

In applying these relations it should be noted that the equivalent noises B_f and B_n vary with the level of the received speech B_S. B_n can usually be omitted entirely unless the response of the communication system falls off rapidly with increasing frequency or has sharp peaks and valleys.

5.8 Non-Linear Relation between Original and Received Speech

The above derivation of the W factor applies to cases where the intensity of the received speech in any band is proportional to the initial speech. It is now necessary to consider whether the same relations which specify the W factor in such cases will hold for cases where the speech is transmitted through systems containing a non-linear element, such as a carbon transmitter. Tests have shown that for a given value of received talking volume the articulation obtained with a carbon transmitter may be somewhat less than that obtained with a linear transmitter which has the same shape of frequency response characteristic. Attempts have been made to explain this effect by considering as noise the resulting inter-modulation products of speech. While there probably is such an effect, the reduction in articulation can also be accounted for by self-masking in conjunction with the effect

of the non-linear device in altering the level distribution of the speech sounds. In some cases the output of a carbon transmitter changes r db for each db change in input, where r is nearly constant over a considerable range of levels and is usually greater than unity. It follows that the level distribution of the output of such a transmitter in a speech band would cover a range which is broader by the factor r than that of the original speech. Consequently on the basis of the self-masking theory, a greater fraction of the lower level intervals of speech would be masked by speech of higher levels in the band, thus reducing the maximum possible value of W.

The effect of such an expanding action where the output-input characteristic on a db basis is approximately linear, but with a slope different from unity, can consequently be computed from the relations which have already been given, by considering the basic speech level distribution to be r times as broad as that shown in Fig. 4 and then proceeding with the computations exactly as if the instrument were a linear one. The relationship between effective sensation level and the W factor has already been given, as follows:

$$W = (E - 6)/30. \qquad (13)$$

In this equation the number 30 represents the range between the maximum and minimum levels of speech in a band, assuming a straight line

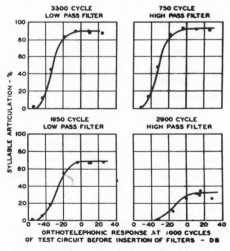

FIG. 24. Comparison of observed and computed results for 1928–1929 articulation tests. Points show observed data.

151

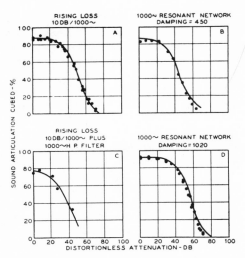

FIG. 25. Comparison of observed and computed results for 1935–1936 articulation tests. Points show observed data.

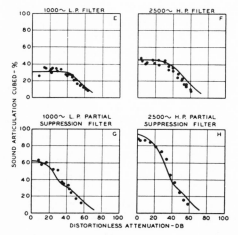

FIG. 26. Comparison of observed and computed results for 1935–1936 articulation tests. Points show observed data.

relationship between percentage of intervals and levels over the entire range. Consequently with an expanding type device the range is $30r$ and Eq. (13) can be rewritten as follows:

$$W = (E-6)/30r. \tag{23}$$

The values of the effective sensation levels are computed by Eq. (16) as before. This equation contains a peak factor p, representing the level difference between the intensity exceeded by 1 percent of $\frac{1}{8}$th second intervals of speech and the long average intensity of all intervals, which may be changed in value by the expanding action from the 12-db figure which applies to the ordinary distribution of speech levels. This can be easily computed for any value of r, but for values of r between 1 and 1.2 the values of p are practically constant at 12 db.

In cases of compression, large ratios of expansion or expansion that varies with level, it is necessary to calculate the level distribution of the received speech sounds from the characteristics of the non-linear device and the level distribution of speech shown in Fig. 4. The lower curved portion of this distribution, rather than the straight line approximation, should be used in cases of compression. Then W can be computed by determining the fraction of sounds in the modified distribution that are audible. It can be seen that, in general, this procedure will be laborious and cannot be expressed in a convenient mathematical form.

At the present time this treatment of non-linearity should be regarded primarily as an hypothesis. It has, however, been successful in explaining qualitatively the results obtained with a few systems containing non-linear elements, but other complicating factors are also involved. For example, in computations involving non-linear elements the conception of response is not as clear as it is in the case of linear elements and the shape of the response characteristic that is obtained may vary widely, depending upon the type of measurement that is made. Considerable caution must, therefore, be used in interpreting the results of computations of the articulation index of speech, received over systems containing non-linear elements.

[Editor's Note: Material has been omitted at this point.]

Reprinted from *Acoust. Soc. Am. J.* **34**(11):1698–1702 (1962)

Validation of the Articulation Index

Karl D. Kryter

Bolt Beranek and Newman Inc., Cambridge, Massachusetts

(Received July 9, 1962)

French and Steinberg proposed the basic concept and method of calculating the Articulation Index (AI) approximately 15 years ago. Although improvements and modifications of AI have been made over the years, it has not been generally accepted, perhaps because of insufficient evidence as to its validity. On the basis of studies reported in the literature and on new studies herein reported, it is shown that AI is a valid predictor of the intelligibility of speech under a wide variety of conditions of noise masking and speech distortion.

INTRODUCTION

THE so-called Articulation Index (AI) as developed by French and Steinberg[1] and later modified by various investigators[2,3] is believed to be a fairly accurate way of predicting from purely physical measures of a communications system what the intelligibility of speech will be when transmitted over that system. Indeed, the state of the art has reached the stage where detailed procedures for the calculation of the Articulation Index by several methods have been prepared. These procedures are presented in a separate companion article in this issue of JASA.[3]

One purpose of the present paper is to report the results of some experiments we have conducted that can serve to some extent as validation tests of AI. These studies, perhaps of some interest in their own right, are concerned with the effects of "remote" and upward spread of masking due to noise and intense low-frequency tones and the effects of single and multiple bandpass filtering upon speech intelligibility.

A second purpose of this paper is to present the results of calculations we have made of the relations between AI and the test scores obtained in studies conducted by other investigators on the effects of speech filtering and noise masking upon speech intelligibility.

NEW STUDIES

Experiment No. I—Narrow Bands of Speech and Noise

Nonsense-syllable tests were administered to a crew of three trained listeners seated in a sound-proofed room. Each test list contained 100 consonant-vowel-consonant (CVC) syllables. Ten consonants[4] and ten vowel[5] sounds were used; in each list each vowel

TABLE I. Speech system and noise conditions.

System No.	Speech	Noise
1	1700 cps low pass	None
2	1700 cps low pass	2400–3400 cps band, various signal-to-noise ratios
3	1700 cps high pass	None
4	1700 cps high pass	200–1200 cps band, various signal-to-noise ratios
5	1200–2400 cps passband	None
6	1700–2400 cps passband	None
7	1200–1700 cps passband	None

| System No. | Speech passbands | | | Noise |
	A	B	C	
8	0–600	1200–2400	4800–9600	None
9	0–600	1700–2400	4800–9600	None
10	0–600	1200–1700	4800–9600	None
11	0–600	1200–2400		None
12	0–600	1700–2400		None
13	0–600	1200–1700		None

The speech and noise passbands are given to the 6-dB down points of the filter skirts; the filter skirts fell off at the rate of about 60 dB per octave beyond the 6-dB down points indicated.

[1] N. R. French and J. C. Steinberg, "Factors Governing the Intelligibility of Speech Sounds," J. Acoust. Soc. Am. **19**, 90–119 (1949).

[2] L. L. Beranek, "The Design of Speech Communication Systems," Proc. Inst. Radio Engrs. **35**, 880–890 (1947).

[3] K. D. Kryter, "Methods for the Calculation and Use of the Articulation Index," J. Acoust. Soc. Am. **34**, 1689 (1962).

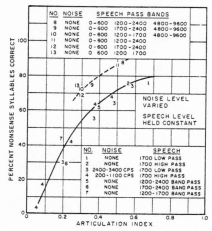

FIG. 1. Comparison of obtained and predicted test scores for bands of speech and noise.

[4] P, K, f, th (thin), d, g, z (size), z (azure), m, n.

[5] i (fit), eh (bet), ee (beet), a (fat), ay (gate), ah (father), au (taught), oh (joke), oo (moon), uh (but).

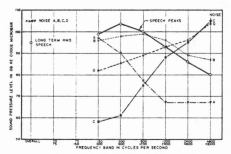

FIG. 2. Noise and speech spectra present during tests reported in Fig. 3.

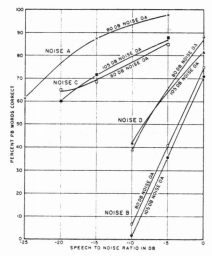

FIG. 3. PB word scores obtained with different signal-to-noise ratios and noise levels. Each point represents the average score of a listening crew of six trained college students for two lists of PB words (50 words per list) read by a male talker over a communication system having essentially a flat frequency response (±5 dB) from 100 to 6000 cps. The noise and speech were mixed electrically at the listeners' earphones (from Kryter, Flanagan, and Williams[7]).

appeared ten times and each consonant appeared ten times in the initial position and ten times in the final position. For present purposes, we will report only the percentage of syllables correctly recorded by the listeners. The tests were read over the systems listed in Table I. The noises indicated in Table I were mixed with the speech signal after the speech had been filtered.

Two to four tests of 100 nonsense syllables each were administered for each system and each noise condition. Two male talkers read the test items. Each test list represented a different "scrambling" of 100 syllables selected from the total sample of 1000 items according to the rules mentioned above.

Except for the filtering characteristic indicated in Table I, the remainder of the communication system used in these tests—microphone, tape recorder, amplifiers, and headphones—had an over-all frequency response that was flat ±2 dB from about 200 cps to about 6000 cps.

Results. In Fig. 1 the AI's calculated in accordance with the 20-band method[3] for each system and noise condition are plotted against the percent syllables correct.

The solid line represents the relation we believe to be expected between AI and percent syllables correct for the particular test crew and test material used in this study.

It is seen that the performances of all the systems, except the 3 passband systems, fall reasonably close to the performance line predicted by AI. It is therefore concluded that, at least for the conditions tested, AI adequately predicts the relative intelligibility of speech as it is influenced by noise masking, high-, low-, or single-passband filtering.

The strong increase in measured intelligibility over predicted intelligibility for the multiple-passband system would seem to indicate that AI as formulated does not properly cope with communication systems of that sort. Further, it is not readily apparent how to modify AI-calculation procedures to make it work for multiple-passband systems; from a practical point of

view, because of the relative novelty of such a communications system, an attempt at modification of AI for this purpose is probably not justified. Further data on and discussion of the intelligibility of speech through multiple-passband systems can be found elsewhere.[6]

Experiment No. 2—Broad-Band Noise

This study was designed to test the ability of AI to evaluate the masking effects upon speech of continuous-spectrum noises that have widely different slopes. Included among the noises were two that had spectral shapes similar to those found from some piston-engined and jet-engined aircraft. The spectra of the noises tested are shown in Fig. 2 and results of the PB-word-intelligibility tests and the test conditions are given in Fig. 3. Further details of this experiment can be found in reference 7.

Calculation of AI. AI's were calculated by the 20-band method for each noise at each signal-to-noise ratio tested in accordance with recently proposed procedures.[3] The AI's are plotted in Fig. 4 against the percent-PB

[6] K. D. Kryter, "Speech Bandwidth Compression through Spectrum Selection," J. Acoust. Soc. Am. 32, 547–556 (1960).
[7] K. D. Kryter, G. Flanagan, and C. Williams, "A Test of the 20-Band and Octave-Band Methods of Computing the Articulation Index," ESD-TDR-62-4, U. S. Dept. of Commerce, Office of Technical Services, Washington 25, D. C.

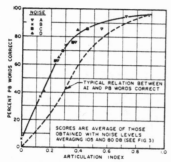

FIG. 4. Comparison of obtained and predicted intelligibility-test scores for broad-band speech in wide-band noises of differently sloped spectra.

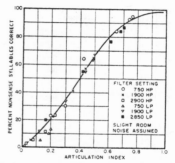

FIG. 5. Comparison of obtained and predicted test scores for speech passed through various high-pass and low-pass filters (after French and Steinberg[i]).

scores obtained at several speech-to-noise ratios. It is to be noted that the points for the various noise conditions can be closely fitted by a single line. This would seem to demonstrate that the calculated AI's accurately predicted, relative to each other, the masking effects of the various noises. The absolute values of the PB scores obtained are rather high compared to those usually reported for communication systems under comparable AI's. The most probable reason is that the crew was so thoroughly experienced in taking PB word tests from the particular talker who recorded the tests.

Attention is invited to the differences between Figs. 3 and 4. It is obvious, as has of course been previously demonstrated, e.g., by Miller,[8] that signal-to-noise ratio, the abscissa of Fig. 3, does not provide a meaningful index to the intelligibility of speech to be expected under different noise conditions. For example, at a signal-to-noise ratio of −10 dB, a percent-PB word score of 95% is realized in noise A, whereas at a signal-to-noise also of −10 dB, a score of about only 5% is obtained with the same communication system used with noise B. This is in sharp contrast to Fig. 4 wherein we find about the same intelligibility-test scores regardless of noise condition for equal values of the abscissa AI.

RELATED STUDIES

We have calculated the AI's using the 20-band method for a selected group of systems and noise conditions reported in the literature and then attempted to relate the AI's to the obtained speech-intelligibility or articulation test score. The method used for calculating was that outlined in reference 3, except in one case.

High-Pass and Low-Pass Filtering of Speech

French and Steinberg to a large extent based their derivation of AI upon the results of articulation tests conducted to determine the effects of high-pass and

low-pass filtering of speech. For this reason we have calculated AI for a number of their test conditions by the newly proposed methods. The results of these calculations are plotted against percent nonsense syllable correct in Fig. 5.

It might be noted that the calculated AI values fall reasonably close to the solid curve in Fig. 5. The solid curve shows the relation to be expected between AI and percent nonsense syllables correct for these particular tests. AI's calculated by the original French and Steinberg method give almost identical results for these data. The original French and Steinberg procedures, however, were not designed to handle as wide a variety of noise and distortion conditions as can be encompassed by the recently proposed procedures for the calculation of AI.

Single-Bandpass Filtering of Speech

Egan and Wiener[9] measured by intelligibility-testing methods the performance of bands of speech presented to the listeners along with two types of broad-band noise. Noise A had essentially a flat spectrum throughout the audible frequency range and noise B had a spectrum with a negative slope in cycles per second of about 12 dB/octave above 600 cps. The test scores obtained in the two noises are plotted against AI in Fig. 6 and Fig. 7. The closeness of the various points to a single line would seem to again attest to the general validity of the Articulation-Index concept.

Bands of Noise

One of the most instructive studies of the masking effects of noise upon speech was that conducted by Miller.[8] Miller varied width, location on the frequency scale, and intensity level of a band of noise filtered from a broad-band "white" noise.

[8] G. A. Miller, "The Masking of Speech," Psychol. Bull. 44, 105–129 (1947).

[9] J. P. Egan and F. M. Wiener, "On the Intelligibility of Bands of Speech in Noise," J. Acoust. Soc. Am. 18, 435–441 (1946).

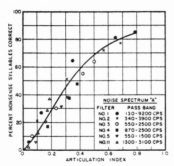

FIG. 6. Comparison of obtained and predicted test scores for speech passed through a bandpass filter and heard in the presence of a broad-band, "flat" spectrum noise set at various intensity levels (after Egan and Wiener[7]).

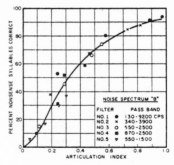

FIG. 7. Comparison of obtained and predicted text scores for speech passed through a bandpass filter and heard in the presence of a broad-band, negatively sloped spectrum noise set at various intensity levels (after Egan and Wiener[7]).

Because some of his bands of noise were relatively narrow they permit upward and downward (remote) masking to play a significant role in degrading the intelligibility of speech. In the perhaps more typical case of a broad-band or continuous-spectrum noise, the masking at any one point on the frequency scale is usually controlled by the noise energy at that point and not by masking due to energy at some remote frequency.

In spite of the severity and diversity of the noise conditions tested, we find, as is shown in Fig. 8, that, except for perhaps one or two data points, the calculated AI values follow with reasonable closeness a single curve relating these values to percent words correct.

We found, incidentally, that without making allowance for the nonlinear effects of masking at the higher intensity levels of noise and particularly the effects of upward and downward remote masking, as is done in the newly proposed methods for calculating AI, the prediction by AI of Miller's results was very poor.

Broad-Band Noise at High Levels

Pickett and Pollack[10] measured the intelligibility of speech in the presence of three types of broad-band noise—noises having a +6, 0, and −12 dB/octave spectral tilt. They varied the noises and the speech as well, over a very wide range of intensities.

The importance of Pickett and Pollack's study lies in their determination of the growth of the speech-masking effectiveness of noise as a function of its intensity level. In particular, they found that as the noise exceeds 50-dB sensation-level masking is proportionally greater than it is below a sensation level of 50 dB. (A functional relation between the sensation level of a noise and masking effectiveness has been incorporated in the proposed methods for calculating

---

[10] J. M. Pickett and I. Pollack, "Speech Intelligibility at High Noise Levels," J. Acoust. Soc. Am. 30, 955–963 (1958).

AI. The function used in the newly proposed methods[3] is similar in general shape but differs from that recommended by Pickett and Pollack in the point on the sensation-level scale at which masking effectiveness supposedly becomes nonlinear.)

Pickett and Pollack, using their method, calculated AI for their test conditions and plotted the results against measured intelligibility. They found, Fig. 9, that AI, as calculated, adequately predicts the test scores.

DISCUSSION

We feel that the above results amply demonstrate the general validity of AI calculated by the 20-band method according to procedures presented in reference 3. At least the effects on the intelligibility of PB words and some nonsense syllables of noise masking, most types of speech filtering, and combinations of masking and filtering are predictable from a knowledge of AI calculated by the 20-band method. The general accuracy of

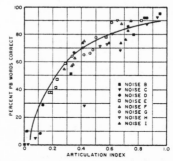

FIG. 8. Comparison of obtained and predicted test scores for broad-band speech in the presence of narrow bands of noise set at various intensity levels (after Miller[6]).

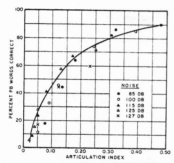

FIG. 9. Comparison of obtained and predicted test scores for broad-band speech in the presence of two different broad-band noise spectra set at the intensity levels indicated (from Pickett and Pollack[8]).

using the octave-band method for predicting the effects on intelligibility of broad-band noise has also been reported.[7]

AI should also properly evaluate the effects of some types of amplitude distortion of the speech signal, effects of speech level, vocal effort and reverberation, and intermittency of a masking noise if certain correction procedures outlined in reference 3 are followed. However, the secondary corrections that are provided in the calculation of AI to take these factors into account are based on one-of-a-kind experiments and cannot, at present, be validated against independent studies.

It is to be understood, of course, that this invariant relation between AI and intelligibility holds only when the abilities of the talkers and listeners and the difficulty of the test materials are kept constant. Test scores of "percent correct" are essentially meaningless unless the type of material, size-of-message set, and talker-listener training are known.

There is clearly a need for some valid procedure for making comparisons among the intelligibility scores obtained in different experiments. One method might be to include in all speech-intelligibility test programs a standardized reference system; the results obtained with the reference system could be used to "calibrate" or "correct," so to speak, the absolute score values to a common base of test-material difficulty and test-crew proficiency.

An alternative approach is to interpret directly the AI values to be found for any given communication system. This would allow the rank ordering of different speech-communication systems within a common scale of merit. In this regard, Beranek[2] has estimated that a system with an AI of less than 0.3 should be considered unsatisfactory for everyday speech communications, a system with an AI of between 0.3 and 0.5 should be considered barely acceptable, and systems with an AI of 0.5 or greater should be rated as satisfactory.

CONCLUSIONS

It is concluded that the Articulation Index calculated according to the newly proposed procedures[3] is an accurate method for estimating or predicting the relative intelligibility of speech under a wide range of noise, speech filtering, and other stressful conditions.

If properly used, AI should obviate, under many conditions, the need for speech-intelligibility testing, and would provide a quantitative and common frame of reference for evaluating the relative abilities of most communication systems to transmit intelligible speech.

ACKNOWLEDGMENTS

This paper was sponsored by the Electronic Systems Division, U. S. Air Force Systems Command under Contract AF 19(604)-4061 with Bolt Beranek and Newman Inc. This paper is identified as ESD Technical Document Report 62-3. Further reproduction is authorized to satisfy the needs of the U. S. government.

14

Reprinted from *Acustica* **7**(5):305–310 (1957)

A METHOD FOR THE CALCULATION OF THE SPEECH INTELLIGIBILITY UNDER CONDITIONS OF REVERBERATION AND NOISE

by J. H. Janssen

Technical Physics Department, T.N.O. and T.H., Delft, Netherlands

Summary

The method of calculation reported uses the concepts of useful speech level (i. e. maximum level of the speech signal reached within 50 ms after the arrival of a speech pulse front at the ears of the listener), reverberant speech level (i. e. maximum level in the reverberation period exclusive of the first 50 ms), the disturbing (random) noise level, the reverberation time (each of them in the five octave bands from 150 to 4800 c/s) and the articulation index. Results from measurements with and without headphones, in an anechoic room, in a reverberation chamber and in churches and theatres are compared with values predicted with the aid of the method; the agreement is satisfactory. The design of speech communication systems under reverberant and noisy conditions is facilitated.

Sommaire

Dans la méthode de calcul exposée ici, on a recours aux notions suivantes: niveau utile de la parole (c'est à dire le niveau maximum atteint dans les 50 ms après l'arrivée du front d'une impulsion de parole aux oreilles de l'auditeur), niveau de réverbération de la parole (c'est à dire le niveau maximum atteint pendant la période de réverbération qui suit les premiers 50 ms), niveau du bruit parasite aléatoire, temps de réverbération (chacune de ces quantités dans les cinq bandes d'une octave, de 150 à 4800 Hz), indice d'articulation. On a comparé avec les valeurs fournies par cette méthode les résultats de mesures faites avec et sans écouteurs aux oreilles, dans une salle anéchoïque, une salle réverbérante, des églises et des théâtres; l'accord est satisfaisant. Cette méthode facilitera le calcul des systèmes de transmission de la parole en présence de réverbération et de bruit.

Zusammenfassung

Die angegebene Methode zur Berechnung der Sprachverständlichkeit benutzt folgende Begriffe: Nutzbarer Sprachpegel (Maximalpegel eines Sprachsignals innerhalb 50 ms nachdem die Wellenfront das Ohr des Hörers erreicht hat), Nachhall-Sprachpegel (Maximalpegel während des Nachhalls, die ersten 50 ms ausgenommen), Geräuschpegel und Nachhallzeit (alle in fünf Oktavbereichen von 150 Hz bis 4800 Hz), Verständlichkeitsfaktor. Die Ergebnisse von Messungen mit und ohne Kopfhörer, in einem schalltoten und einem Hallraum sowie in Kirchen und Theatern stehen in befriedigender Übereinstimmung mit den errechneten Werten. Somit ergeben sich vereinfachte Berechnungsmöglichkeiten für die Konstruktion von Sprach-Übertragungsanlagen, die durch Nachhall und Geräusch beeinflußt werden.

1. Introduction

For every consultant in room acoustics it is of extreme importance to know in advance the effect on the intelligibility of speech of certain modifica-

tions in the design of a room. In almost every room speech will be produced in order to be understood, not only in theatres, lecture rooms and churches but also in gymnasia, dance-halls and even, as experience shows, in concert halls. It is well known that for telephone systems there exist methods to compute the intelligibility of speech material like syllables, nonsense words etc [1], [2], [3]. Although a room constitutes a rather complicated "telephone" system a simplified form (using only five octave bands) of the methods mentioned could, it seemed, be applied to the case where the speaker and the listener are situated in a room of short reverberation time (< 0.2 s). In order to check this supposition the method of FRENCH and STEINBERG was modified so as to use only five octave bands. It was found that sufficient accuracy for work in room acoustics could be obtained in this way. The next step was to derive from measurements curves that would express the influence of reverberation on the speech intelligibility, because it was thought that the theoretical predictions of BOLT and MAC DONALD [4] and those of KORN [5] were not substantiated by experiment.

It turned out that the method of calculating the speech intelligibility, using the simple quantities: useful speech level, disturbing (hindering) noise level, reverberant speech level and reverberation time, each in five octave bands, could explain the values found in some lecture rooms, churches, theatres, reverberation room and anechoic room and moreover for a telephone system. The method however is confined to cases where there is no "overload" of ears or non-linearity of apparatus and where the noise level lies more than 6 dB above the threshold of audibility. Although the influence of the possible difference in direction of arrival between speech signal and noise is not incorporated, it is believed that with the method presented here and the data supplied by others [6], [7], [8] a justified design of a room with good speech intelligibility is possible, provided the physical variables entering into the problem like e. g. speech level, echo level and delay time can be computed from the architect's plans.

2. The speech material

To obtain quantitative data on the intelligibility of speech in rooms articulation tests have been in use for a long time already [9]: an announcer reads words to one or more listeners and the percentage correctly heard is called the articulation percentage.

There are several difficulties as regards differences in word material, listeners, speech level and talkers. This report is concerned with listening experiments using 900 Dutch logatoms of the monosyllabic type (e. g. tot, reng, naas, neew, maur etc., pronounced resp. as tɔt, raeɣ, naːs, neis, maur) pre-

ceded by the carrier word 'logatoom' (Louxa: 'toum, where x = ch in loch).

The logatoms were grouped in lists of 50 and recorded in an anechoic room on magnetic tape (Grundig Reporter 700 L with Agfa F.S.P. tape at 19 cm/s tape speed; distance between talker and microphone was 1 m). During the recording the talker maintained the speech level as constant as possible by observing a modulation meter. Subsequently a well known Dutch nursery rhyme * was pronounced at the same level without any pauses between the words, and recorded under exactly the same circumstances. The longtime average root mean square pressure level in the respective frequency bands of this speech material could easily be compared with filtered bands of random noise by means of the indications on a very slow electrostatic voltmeter (Hartmann and Braun). After some trials the tape could be supplied with five octave bands of noise (150 – 300 c/s, 300 – 600 c/s, 600 – 1200 c/s, 1200 – 2400 c/s, 2400 – 4800 c/s, that gave the same indications on the electrostatic voltmeter as the respective speech bands. This random noise was called the testing noise. In this paper the speech level as heard by the listener in the bands given will be the r. m. s. pressure level due to the testing noise, as measured at the listener's position in the corresponding octave bands, produced by the loudspeaker under the same conditions as the logatoms were produced, unless otherwise stated. Each listening test comprised 200 logatoms (with the exception of a few of 150), presented to the listener in groups of 50 with adequate pauses between the groups so as to prevent unreliable results by fatigue effects.

3. The method of calculation

For the speech material described it is possible to compute the logatom intelligibility (LI) by the method given below.

In an anechoic room, in the open air or for a telephone system without reverberation: determine the difference in level (defined above) in dB between the speech signal (S) and the hindering background noise signal (H) for the five octave-bands of Fig. 1 and find the corresponding articulation index contribution $(AIC)_i$ with the aid of Fig. 1. From Fig. 2 the LI is found after summation of the five $(AIC)_i$, to the total articulation index (AI).

In the case of reverberation a distinction is made between the useful speech signal and the reverberant speech signal.

---

* Zie ginds komt de stoomboot uit Spanje weer aan, hij brengt ons Sint Nicolaas, ik zie hem al staan; hoe huppelt zijn paardje het dek op en neer, hoe waaien de wimpels al heen en al weer.

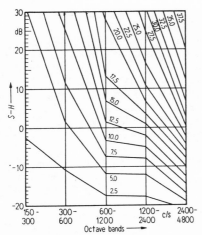

Fig. 1. The articulation index contribution $(AIC)_i$ (parameter) as a function of the octave band and the difference in level between the speech signal S and the hindering noise H; in the case of reverberation is $S = S_u$ if $S_u - S_r > -8$ dB and $S = S_r$ if $S_u - S_r \leq -8$ dB.

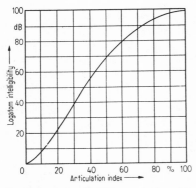

Fig. 2. The logatom intelligibility as a function of the articulation index $AI = \sum_i (AIC)_i \cdot r_i$; $i = 1, \ldots, 5$

for the five octave bands; without reverberation $r_i = 1$, with reverberation r_i is given by Fig. 3. The curve approximates the curve for S_3 according to FLETCHER [1].

The former covers 50 ms beginning at the moment of the arrival of the very first part of a speech pulse at the ears of the listener, the latter is formed by the remainder of the speech pulse, i. e. the signal arriving after the first 50 ms (for example: by reverberation or echo effects). To take account of the effect of this time distortion of the speech on the LI one firstly determines the difference in decibels $(S_u - S_r)$ of the maximum values of the speech pulse (or for each of the five frequency bands any other pulse of 10 to 20 ms duration consisting of filtered noise or a pure tone within that band) in the first

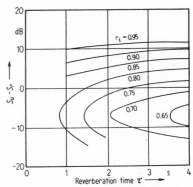

Fig. 3. The reverberation factor r_i as a function of the reverberation time τ and the difference in level $(S_u - S_r)$ between the useful and the reverberant speech signal.

50 ms and of the remainder after this time interval, as written by the Brüel & Kjær level recorder with writing speed of 1000 dB/s and with 50 dB potentiometer. Find then with the aid of Fig. 3 five so called reverberation factors r_i from the determined values of $(S_u - S_r)$ and the reverberation time τ in the five frequency bands. To determine the five $(AIC)_i$ from Fig. 1 one should proceed as follows. In the reverberant room the total speech level is formed statistically by two signals: the useful speech signal and the reverberant one originating from a preceding speech pulse. Therefore S_u can be found by subtracting from the total speech level, as defined in section 2, a correction number by means of Fig. 4. To find the five $(AIC)_i$ from Fig. 1 the difference $(S_u - H)$ is used for $(S - H)$ in the case that $(S_u - S_r) > -8$ dB. If $(S_u - S_r) \leq -8$ dB take in Fig. 1 the difference $(S_r - H)$. Finally the logatom intelligibility LI is found by means of Fig. 2 after inserting $(AI) = \sum_i (AIC)_i \cdot r_i$.

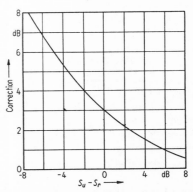

Fig. 4. From the total speech level (S_{tot}) in an octave band the useful speech level (S_u) can be derived if $(S_u - S_r)$ is known (see Fig. 3); $S_u = S_{tot}$-correction.

4. Measurements

It will be understood that the method reported here can only be approximate. As it was designed for consulting practice with the use of a T.P.D.-built simple, battery-operated, octave band sound spectrum indicator, the twenty frequency bands each contributing 5% to the total articulation index as given by FRENCH and STEINBERG [2] were reduced to five octave bands (see also section 5). The curves of Fig. 1 were found during the first part of the work. To check their validity measurements were carried out. Moreover some results of other workers [10] were examined. The results in Fig. 5 and Fig. 6 show that the method reported here is as accurate as others now in use (e. g. [3]); it is however much

simpler. The next step was to find the curves of Fig. 3. After some hit-and-miss work the best agreement with experiment was obtained with the curves shown. In Fig. 7 the results from measurements in the laboratory are given, while in Fig. 8 the observed values in churches and theatres are plotted. The agreement between theory and experiment suffices, it is thought, to justify this publication.

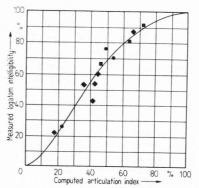

Fig. 7. Comparison of the curve ——— of Fig. 2 with the T.P.D. measurements in a reverberation chamber (156 m³); ● for 1.5 s, ■ for 2.0 s and ◆ for 3.0 s reverberation time.

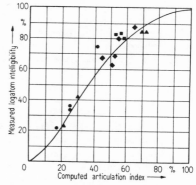

Fig. 8. Comparison of the curve ——— of Fig. 2 with the T.P.D. measurements ● in a theatre (800 seats), ◆ in a church (500 seats), ▲ in a church (600 seats) and ■ in another church (600 seats). Artificial random noise was used during these measurements, as was done in the laboratory tests (Figs. 5 and 7).

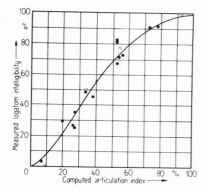

Fig. 5. Comparison of the curve ——— of Fig. 2 with the T.P.D. measurements; points on the curve agree with the theory presented in this paper, ○ in anechoic room, ● with headphones.

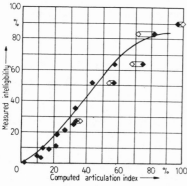

Fig. 6. From data of EGAN and WIENER [10] were computed: ◆ by means of the theory presented in this paper and ◇ by the method BERANEK [3]; corresponding points have been connected. The curve ——— according to BERANEK gives the relation between the articulation index AI and the measured intelligibility; it is seen that for different speech material different curves should be used (cf. Fig. 2).

5. Discussion

The use of the word logatom is not completely correct [11] but very simple; there will not be much difference between "official" logatoms and those used here. The latter were constructed by counting the percentages of occurrence of the various speech sounds in a Dutch pocket dictionary intended for use in conversation and combined at random as consonant-vowel-consonant sounds. The velocity of pronunciation during the recording was for the logatoms about 3 syllables per second and for the Dutch text (to determine the spectrum) about 6 syll./s. The carrier word "logatoom" enabled the talker to control his voice level during the recording and simulates reverberant speech signals during intelligibility tests. Lack of time prevented an inquiry into the influence on the LI of other carrier words. Furthermore it is possible that the stated tests would be improved with regard to naturalness by the addition of a concluding carrier word, so: logatoom-rok-logatoom. It turned out that one observer could perform a complete and reliable test; may be this was by pure accident. It is thought however that it deserves attention, because the costs of research are greatly reduced in this way while the spread in results is of the same order as that for a group of observers; this was shown by tests with five to ten observers. During recent years serious doubt has arisen as to the value of the articulation index concept [12], [13], as regards the possibility of predicting the intelligibility of different speech materials under conditions of noise and/or frequency distortion. It is thought however that for work in room-acoustics the accuracies arrived at by the present method are satisfying. Further research should be undertaken about the question whether one should characterize the useful speech signal by the maximum value of the speech sound pressure level at a writing speed of 1000 dB/s or by something like

$$\int_0^{50\,ms} p^2 \, \mathrm{d}t \,.$$

In this connection a simple experiment performed in this laboratory is worth mentioning. If one tries to mask (first test) a continuous 1000 c/s tone by an octave band $(600 - 1200 \text{ c/s})$ of noise and (second test) a 20 ms 1000 c/s pulse of the same amplitude by the same band of white noise, one will find that the first noise level needed is about 13 dB higher than the second one. If in a third test a signal is presented consisting of 20 ms, 1000 c/s, then a 10 ms time interval and again 20 ms 1000 c/s (total duration 50 ms) the masking noise level will be about 10 dB lower than the first noise level. Moreover one can find in the literature [14] (if the results are correctly interpreted by the present author) that the loudness level of a 20 ms pure tone pulse remains about 4 phons below the value for a long duration tone, whereas a 40 ms pure tone pulse reaches the final loudness level. The Brüel & Kjær high speed level recorder type 2304 behaves in about the same way at a writing speed of 1000 dB/s:

the maximum value recorded for a 20 ms pulse is about 4 dB down with respect to the long duration value whereas this difference is 0 dB for a 40 ms pulse and 1 dB for the signal 20 ms – 10 ms – 20 ms. The use of the maximum values of the speech pulse levels in the first 50 ms and in the reverberation period reached by the level recorder at the writing speed given seems to be sufficiently justified; moreover the ratio

$$D = \int_0^{50\,ms} I(t) \, \mathrm{d}t \left/ \int_0^{\infty} I(t) \, \mathrm{d}t \right.$$

as defined by THIELE [16] equals approximately $(10^{S_u/10}) / (10^{S_u/10} + 10^{S_r/10})$.

Of course the method for computing the logatom intelligibility, as reported here, has its shortcomings as regards instrumentation, physical background etc. For example, it is not well known what is the presumed minor influence of the duration and the energy distribution of the test pulse on the value of $(S_u - S_r)$ nor is it possible to compute the LI in the case of masking by pure tones.

Moreover it does not explain the curious observation made in one of the churches tested of a "linking echo". The computed LI was considerably lower than the observed one at a certain place. It was found that a strong echo at 60 ms after the first signal arrived was preceded by a weaker echo exactly at 50 ms (see also [15]). This is to say that there is no sharp line between useful and reverberant speech.

Further research is also necessary as to the question of noise and speech arriving from different directions at the listener's ears; the remaining spread in the observations might be reduced in this way.

Acknowledgment

The work described here is part of the research programme of the Technical Physics Department T.N.O. and T.H. on room acoustics. The author wishes to thank his colleagues for their helpful and indispensable advise during the course of the investigations, especially with regard to the electronic apparatus used and to the final form of this paper. He also acknowledges the valuable discussions with Mr. C. J. NEDERVEEN of the Acoustics Laboratory of the Technological University at Delft.

(Received October 27th, 1956.)

References

[1] FLETCHER, H., Speech and hearing in communication. D. van Nostrand Co., New York 1953, p. 318.
[2] FRENCH, N. R. and STEINBERG, J. C., Factors governing the intelligibility of speech sounds. J. acoust. Soc. Amer. 19 [1947], 90.

[3] BERANEK, L. L., The design of speech communication systems. Proc. Inst. Radio Engrs. 35 [1947], 880.

[4] BOLT, R. H. and MAC DONALD, A. D., Theory of speech masking by reverberation. J. acoust. Soc. Amer. 21 [1949], 577.

[5] KORN, T., Théorie générale de l'intelligibilité dans les salles. Ann. Télécommun. 5 [1950], 316.

[6] BERANEK, L. L. a. o., Speech-reinforcement system evaluation. Proc. Inst. Radio Engrs. 39 [1951], 1401.

[7] HAAS, H., Über den Einfluß eines Einfachechos auf die Hörsamkeit von Sprache. Acustica 1 [1951], 49.

[8] NICKSON, A. F. B., MUNCEY, R. W. and DUBOUT, P., The acceptability of artificial echoes with reverberant speech and music. Acustica 4 [1954], 515.

[9] KNUDSEN, V. O., Architectural acoustics. J. Wiley & Sons, New York 1932, p. 343.

[10] EGAN, J. P. and WIENER, F. M., The intelligibility of bands of speech in noise. J. acoust. Soc. Amer. 18 [1946], 435.

[11] Comm. Consult. Internat. Téléphon., Proc. XI plen. Meeting, Copenhagen 1936, p. 162.

[12] HIRSH, I. J., REYNOLDS, E. G. and JOSEPH, M., Intelligibility of different speech materials. J. acoust. Soc. Amer. 26 [1954], 530.

[13] MOL, H., Two possible decoding systems in the cochlea. P.T.T. Bedrijf 7 [1956], 46.

[14] MUNSON, W. A., The growth of auditory sensation. J. acoust. Soc. Amer. 19 [1947], 584.

[15] MEYER, E. and SCHODDER, G. R., Über den Einfluß von Schallrückwürfen auf Richtungslokalisation und Lautstärke bei Sprache. Nachr. Akad. Wiss. Göttingen IIa, Nr. 6 [1952], 31,

[16] THIELE, R., Richtungsverteilung und Zeitfolge der Schallrückwürfe in Räumen. Acustica 3 [1953], 291.

Part IV

METHODS OF MEASURING SPEECH INTELLIGIBILITY

Editor's Comments
on Papers 15 Through 19

This part concerns the design of tests and testing materials, and the methods of constructing the tests. An ideal speech intelligibility test should have the following characteristics:

1. It should have a wide range of difficulties to make it suitable to a wide range of situations.
2. It should be usable by all groups of subjects and should be free from learning effects.
3. It should be sensitive to all the factors that affect intelligibility.
4. It should be easy and quick to administer, to analyze, and to interpret.
5. It should be readily repeatable in the same situation and readily replicable in other situations.
6. The results should be seen to be closely related to the performance of the system, building, person, or procedure that is being evaluated.

No test meets all of these criteria or even most of them, although many tests have been developed with varying degrees of success.

First, several different measures of performance have been used as reported in the papers listed in the bibliography for this section.

Most tests count the fraction of correct responses, written or verbal, to speech stimuli—sounds, nonsense syllables, monosyllabic words, spondees, phrases, or sentences—but a very respectable group of experimenters advocates consideration of the confidence the listener has in his responses as well. The papers by Carterette (1958, 1962), Clarke (1960), Glanzman (1973), Pollack (1958), and Strange (1971) all present this point of view. Other investigators have counted the fraction of the messages the listeners say they think they understood [see Hughes (1942)], have measured the listener's grasp of the content of textual material, have counted the number of repetitions requested in telephone conversations, and have measured the number of words or the time required to communicate an idea. Pocock (1948) compares some of these. The editor used to amuse his children by timing them in verbally communicating enough information to produce recognizable copies of symbols such as those shown below.

Most tests consist of lists of fifty words or sounds which the listener hears and responds to under carefully controlled conditions. The classic paper on such tests by Egan has been cited more often than any other paper in the whole field of intelligibility. It is reproduced here as Paper 15, omitting only the word lists and acknowledgements. Paper 16 is a procedure for monosyllabic word intelligibility testing written by a committee of which Egan was a member. It is the only nationally adopted standard on the subject.* Beranek (1949) gives a broad presentation of the tests, but the most complete treatment is given by Pokrovsky (1962); unfortunately the latter is not so widely available.

The monosyllabic words used by Egan are well suited for testing difficult situations with a thoroughly trained crew. Campanelli (1962), Deutsch (1971), Grubb (1963 (2)), Margolis (1971), Resnick (1962), and Shutts (1964) all have papers on using shorter lists to get results of equal value more quickly. Boothroyd (1968) showed that it is less important to identify words, which are subject to vocabu-

---

* In August 1976 a draft proposal for an international standard, "Recommended Methods for the Construction and Calibration of Speech Intelligibility Tests," (ISO/DP 4870) was under consideration. Enquiries should be addressed to the Standards Secretariat, Acoustical Society of America.

lary differences and influences in listeners who are not completely trained, than it is to identify phonemes. Horiguti (1966) gives a very interesting comparison of the speech materials used as stimuli in many different languages. Paper 17 by Fairbanks describes a test which measures the ability to distinguish consonants. In modified forms, especially that of House (1965) and Voiers (see Paper 34), it has been used for speech audiometry and other applications in a closed reponse form in which the listener selects one of a small set of alternatives that are shown to him. Such a form of test is well suited to machine scoring, and several authors describe the use of computers to randomize, present, collect, score, and analyze the data from the tests. Agrawal (1974) is interesting because the method it describes copes with misspellings of the words. Lacy (1934) and Castner (1933) describe the methods used in the early Bell Labs experiments, which were considerably more thoroughly automated than the laboratories of the 1950s.

Adaptive testing, i.e., using responses to control the stimuli, is a major advance in technique. Most of the early testing permitted the scores to range widely with varying testing conditions, but the tests themselves are far less sensitive at the very high and very low score regions, and some tests, such as the ANSI Standard test, are very sensitive in the region between twenty-five and seventy-five percent or even between twenty and eighty percent. Frequently an experimenter can find nearly linear portions with slopes of a few percentage points per decibel of signal-to-noise ratio. If the purpose of the testing permits modification of the test conditions to keep the scores in this most sensitive region, fewer tests are required to get results at a given level of statistical significance. Licklider (1957) used this technique to keep scores in the region of fifty percent, and Speaks (1972) (both citations are in Part II) asked the listeners to track the signal-to-noise ratio that gave estimated scores of twenty-five, fifty, and seventy-five percent for connected discourse. Paper 18 by Levitt and Rabiner describes much more sophisticated adaptive methods. A paper by Taylor (1967) and two papers by Bode (1973, 1974) give more details on this economical technique, which in the future probably will be used whenever possible. Paper 19 by Hochhaus and Antes presents data that indicate that the incorporation of confidence data in the testing may offer even more economy.

A commercial laboratory offers intelligibility testing by means of recording tapes for portions of communications systems. The talkers and listeners and their environments are not variable parts of the tests.*

*J. Acoust. Soc. Am. **60**:761 (1976).

BIBLIOGRAPHY

Agrawal, A., and W. C. Lin, "An On-Line Speech Intelligibility Measurement System," *IEEE Trans. Acoust. Speech Sig. Proc.* **ASSP-22**: 203–206 (1974).

Ainsworth, W. A., and J. R. Millar, "A Simple Time Sharing System for Speech Perception Experiments," *Behav. Res. Method. Instrum.* **3**:2–24 (1971).

Asher, J. W., "Intelligibility Tests: A Review of Their Standardization, Some Experiments, and a New Test," *Speech Monogr.* **25**:14–28 (1958).

Balachandran, C. G., P. V. Krishnan, and P. S. Bhandari, "Speech Communications in a Highly Reverberant Hall," *Indian J. Technol.* **1**:328–330 (1963).

Balas, R. F., and G. R. Simon, "The Articulation Function of a Staggered Spondaic Word List for a Normal Hearing Population," *J. Aud. Res.* **4**:285–289 (1964).

Bell, D. W., E. J. Kruel, and J. C. Nixon, "Reliability of the Modified Rhyme Test for Hearing," *J. Speech Hear. Res.* **15**:287–295 (1972).

Benfante, H., R. Charbonneau, and A. Zinger, "Le test phonétique pour audiométrie vocale au Canada français," *Int. Audiol.* **7**:23–29 (1968).

Benitez, L., and C. Speaks, "A Test of Speech Intelligibility in the Spanish Language," *Int. Audiol.* **7**:16–22 (1968).

Benson, R. W., H. Davis, C. E. Harrison, I. J. Hirsh, E. G. Reynolds, and S. R. Silverman, "C.I.D. Auditory Tests W-1 and W-2," (L) *Laryngoscope* **61**:838–841 (1951).

Beranek, L. L., *Acoustical Measurements*, Wiley, New York (1949), pp. 761–792.

Berger, K. W., "A Speech Discrimination Task Using Multiple-Choice Key Words in Sentences," *J. Aud. Res.* **9**:247–262 (1969).

Berger, K. W., L. W. Keating, and D. E. Rose, "An Evaluation of the Kent State University (KSU) Speech Discrimination Test on Subjects with Sensori-Neural Loss," *J. Aud. Res.* **11**:140–143 (1971).

Berruecos, P., and L. Rodriguez, "Determination of the Phonetic Percent in the Spanish Language Spoken in Mexico City, and Formation of P.B. Lists of Trochaic Words," *Int. Audiol.* **6**:211–216 (1967).

Beyer, M. R., J. C. Webster, and D. M. Dague, "Revalidation of the Clinical Test Version of the Modified Rhyme Words," *J. Speech Hear. Res.* **12**:374–378 (1969).

Black, J. W., "Multiple-Choice Intelligibility Tests," *J. Speech Hear. Disord.* **22**:213–235 (1957).

Black, J. W., "Responses to Multiple-Choice Intelligibility Tests," *J. Speech Hear. Res.* **11**:453–466 (1968).

Black, J. W., and C. H. Haagen, "Multiple-Choice Intelligibility Tests, Forms A and B," *J. Speech Hear. Disord.* **28**:77–86 (1963).

Black, J. W., and W. E. Moore, *Speech: Code, Meaning and Communication*, McGraw-Hill, New York (1955).

Bode, D. L., and R. Carhart, "Measurement of Articulation Functions Using Adaptive Test Procedures," *IEEE Trans. Audio Electroacoust.* **AU-21**:196–201 (1973).

Bode, D. L., and R. Carhart, "Stability and Accuracy of Adaptive Tests of Speech Discrimination," *J. Acoust. Soc. Am.* **56**:963–970 (1974).

169

Boothroyd, A., "Statistical Theory of the Speech Discrimination Score," *J. Accoust. Soc. Am.* **43**:362–367 (1968).

Borovičková, B., and V. Malač, "Ein Beitrag zur linguistisch-phonetischen Problematik des Erkennbarkeitsindexes der tschechischen Sprache," *Phonetica* **10**:34–41 (1963).

Bowling, L. S., and B. S. Elpern, "Relative Intelligibility of Items on CID Auditory Test W-1," *J. Aud. Res.* **1**:152–157 (1961).

Broadbent, D. E., "Word-Frequency Effect and Response Bias," *Psychol. Rev.* **74**:1–15 (1967).

Brown, C. R. and H. Rubenstein, "Test of Response Bias Explanation of Word-Frequency Effect," *Science* **133**:280–281 (1961).

Bruce, D. J. "The Effect of Listeners' Anticipations on the Intelligibility of Heard Speech," *Lang. and Speech* **1**:79–97 (1958).

Campanelli, P. A., "A Measure of Intra-List Stability of Four PAL Word Lists," *J. Aud. Res.* **2**:50–55 (1962).

Campbell, R. A., "Discrimination Test Word Difficulty," *J. Speech Hear. Res.* **8**:13–22 (1965).

Cancel, C. A., "Spanish Speech Audiometry," *Int. Audiol.* **7**:206–208 (1968).

Carterette, E. C., "Message Repetition and Receiver Confirmation of Messages in Noise," *J. Acoust. Soc. Am.* **30**:846–855 (1958).

Carterette, E. C., and M. Cole, "Comparison of Receiver-Operating Characteristics for Messages Received by Eye and Ear," *J. Acoust. Soc. Am.* **34**:172–178 (1962).

Castner, T. G., and C. W. Carter, Jr., "Developments in the Application of Articulation Testing," *Bell Syst. Tech. J.* **12**:347–370 (1933).

Chavasse, P., "Essai sur la phonétique statistique de la langue française et son application à l'étude de l'intelligibilité d'une conversation," *Ann Télécommun.* **3**:5–19 (1948).

Christov, P. D., "A Semiautomatic Speech Sounds Aural Identification Procedure with Its Application to Speech Analysis," *Acustica* **29**:347–349 (1973).

Clark, L., J. B. Knowles, and A. MacLean, "The Effects of Method of Recall on Performance in the Dichotic Listening Task," *Can. J. Psychol.* **24**:194–198 (1970).

Clarke, F. R., "Constant-Ratio Rules for Confusion Matrices in Speech Communication," *J. Accoust. Soc. Am.* **29**:715–720 (1957).

Clarke, F. R., "Confidence Ratings, Second-Choice Responses, and Confusion Matrices in Intelligibility Tests," *J. Acoust. Soc. Am.* **32**:35–46 (1960).

Clarke, F. R., and C. D. Anderson, "Further Test of the Constant-Ratio Rule in Speech Communication," *J. Acoust. Soc. Am.* **29**:1318–1320 (1957).

Clarke, F. R., T. G. Birdsall, and W. P. Tanner, Jr., "Two Types of ROC Curves and Definitions of Parameters," (L) *J. Acoust. Soc. Am.* **31**:629–630 (1959).

Codd, W. A., "Transmission Ratings of Telephone Systems," *Trans. AIEE* **65**:694–698 (1946).

Davenport, W. B., "Experimental Study of Speech-Wave Probability Distributions," *J. Acoust. Soc. Am.* **24**:390–399 (1952).

Davis, H., K. C. Morrical, and C. E. Harrison, "Memorandum on Response Characteristics and Monitoring of Word and Sentence Tests Distributed by CID," *J. Acoust. Soc. Am.* **21**:552–553 (1949).

Delgado, C., "Test CIF standard pour essais d'intelligibilité en espagnol," in *Rep. 6th Int. Cong. Acoust.*, Y. Kohasi, ed., Maruzen, Tokyo (1968), pp. C1–C4.

Deutsch, L. J., and B. Kruger, "The Systematic Selection of 25 Monosyllables Which Predict the CID W-22 Speech Discrimination Score," *J. Aud. Res.* **11**:286–290 (1971).

de Wardt, R. H., "The Conduct of Articulation Measurements," *Post Office Electr. Eng. J.* **44**:159–163 (1951).

Draegert, G. L., "Intelligibility Related to Articulation," *Speech Monogr.* **13**, no. 2:50–53 (1946).

Egan, J. P., "Remarks on Rare PB Words," (L) *J. Acoust. Soc. Am.* **29**:751 (1957).

Egan, J. P., and F. R. Clarke, "Source and Receiver Behavior in the Use of a Criterion," *J. Acoust. Soc. Am.* **28**:1267–1269 (1956).

Egan, J. P., F. R. Clarke, and E. C. Carterette, "On the Transmission and Confirmation of Messages in Noise," *J. Acoust. Soc. Am.* **28**:536–550 (1956).

Falconer, G. A., "The Reliability and Validity of Monitored Connected Discourse as a Test of the Threshold of Intelligibility," *J. Speech Hear. Disord.* **13**:369–371 (1947).

Foulke, E., "Methods of Controlling the Word Rate of Recorded Speech," *J. Commun.* **20**:305–314 (1970).

Fredriksen, J. R., "Statistical Decision Model for Auditory Word Recognition," *Psychol. Rev.* **78**:409–419 (1971).

Gerber, S. E., "The Intelligibility of Speech," in *Introductory Hearing Science*, S. E. Gerber, ed., Wm. B. Sanders, Philadelphia (1974), pp. 238–260.

Giolas, T. G., "Comparative Intelligibility Scores of Sentence Lists and Continuous Discourse," *J. Aud. Res.* **6**:31–38 (1966).

Giolas, T. G., and A. Epstein, "Comparative Intelligibility of Word Lists and Continuous Discourse," *J. Speech Hear. Res.* **6**:349–358 (1963).

Gladstone, V. S., and B. M. Siegenthaler, "Carrier Phrase and Speech Intelligibility Test Score," *J. Aud. Res.* **11**:101–103 (1972).

Glanzman, D. L., and D. B. Pisoni, "Decision Processes in Speech Discrimination as Revealed by Confidence Ratings," (A) *J. Acoust. Soc. Am.* **54**:298 (1973).

Glekin, L, "Variations in Percentage of Articulation of Syllables under Influence of Repeated Exposures to Tables (of Syllables) under Conditions of Noise and Quiet," *Biofizika* **2**:452–460 (1957).

Green, D. M., and J. A. Swets, *Signal Detection Theory and Psychophysics*, Wiley, New York (1966).

Griffiths, J. D., "Rhyming Minimal Contrasts: A Simplified Diagnostic Articulation Test," *J. Acoust. Soc. Am.* **42**:236–241 (1967).

Grubb, P. A., "A Phonemic Analysis of Half-List Speech Discrimination Tests," *J. Speech Hear. Res.* **6**:271–275 (1963).

Grubb, P. A., "Some Considerations in the Use of Half-List Speech Discrimination Tests," *J. Speech Hear. Res.* **6**:294–296 (1963).

Haton, J. P., and M. Lamotte, "Étude statistique des phonèmes et diphonèmes dans le français parlé," *Rev. Acoust.* **4**:258–262 (1971).

Hawley, M. E., "Standards for Intelligibility Testing," *Mag. Stand.* **31**:327–328 (1960).

Hawley, M. E., W. Wong, and W. F. Meeker, "A Sequential Analysis for Word Articulation Tests," (A) *J. Acoust. Soc. Am.* **25**:192 (1953).

Hirsh, I. J., "Clinical Application of Two Harvard Auditory Tests," *J. Speech Disord.* **12**:151–158 (1947).

Horiguti, S., and K. Yamashito, "Comparison of Speech Audiometry Test-Words among Various Languages," *Int. Audiol.* **5**:275–279 (1966).

House, A. S., C. E. Williams, M. H. L. Hecker, and K. D. Kryter, "Articulation Testing Methods: Consonantal Differentiation with a Closed-Response Set," *J. Acoust. Soc. Am.* **37**:158–166 (1965).

Howes, D., "On the Relation between the Intelligibility and Frequency of Occurence of English Words," *J. Acoust. Soc. Am.* **29**:296–305 (1957).

Hughes, J. R., "The Comprehensive Assessment of Telephone Communications Efficiency," *J. Inst. Electr. Eng.* **89**, Pt.III:195–206 (1942).

Kreul, E. J., D. W. Bell, and J. C. Nixon, "Factors Affecting Speech Discrimination Test Difficulty," *J. Speech Hear. Res.* **12**:281–287 (1969).

Kreul, E. J., J. C. Nixon, K. D. Kryter, D. W. Bell, J. S. Lang, and E. D. Schubert, "A Proposed Clinical Test of Speech Discrimination," *J. Speech Hear. Res.* **11**:536–552 (1968).

Lacy, L. Y., "Automatic Articulation Testing Apparatus," *Bell Lab. Record* **12**:276 (1934).

Lehiste, I., and G. E. Peterson, "Linguistic Considerations in the Study of Speech Intelligibility," *J. Acoust. Soc. Am.* **31**:280–286 (1959).

Levitt, H., "Transformed Up-Down Methods in Psychoacoustics," *J. Acoust. Soc. Am.* **49**:467–477 (1971).

Lin, W. C., and A. Agrawal, "Minicomputer-Based Laboratory for Speech Intelligibility Research," *Proc. IEEE* **61**:1583–1588 (1973).

Lovrinic, J. H., E. J. Burgi, and E. T. Curry, "A Comparative Evaluation of Five Speech Discrimination Measures," *J. Speech Hear. Res.* **11**:372–381 (1968).

Macrae, J. H., P. Woodroffe, and R. H. Farrant, "Standardization of the Commonwealth Acoustic Laboratories' Recordings of Phonetically Balanced Word Lists," *J. Oto-Laryngol. Soc. Aust.* **1**:197–203 (Sept. 1963).

Margolis, R. H., and J. P. Millin, "An Item Difficulty Based Speech Discrimination Test," *J. Speech Hear. Res.* **14**:865–873 (1971).

Martin, W. H., "Rating the Transmission Performance of Telephone Circuits," *Bell Syst, Tech. J.* **10**:116–131 (1931).

Meister, F. J., "Spezielle Fragen bei der Sprachgehörprüfung und Hörhilfenanpassung," *Acustica* **4**:165–168 (1954).

Miller, G. A., *Language and Communication*, McGraw-Hill, New York (1951).

Miller, G. A., G. A. Heise, and W. Lichten, "The Intelligibility of Speech as a Function of the Context of the Test Materials," *J. Exp. Psychol.* **41**:329–335 (1951).

Miller, I., "Perception of Nonsense Passages in Relation to Amount of Information and Speech-to-Noise Ratio," *J. Exp. Psychol.* **53**:388–393 (1957).

Milner, P., "Advantages of Experienced Listeners in Intelligibility Testing," *IEEE Trans. Audio Electroacoust.* **AU-21**:161–164 (1973).

Nelson, D. A., and J. B. Shaiklin, "Writedown versus Talkback Scoring and Scoring Bias in Speech Discrimination Testing," *J. Speech Hear. Res.* **13**:645–654 (1970).

Olsen, W. O., and R. Carhart, "Development of Test Procedures for Evaluation of Binaural Hearing Aids," *Bull. Prosthetics Res.* **10-7**: 22–49 (1967).

O'Neill, J. J., "Recognition of Intelligibility Test Materials in Context and Isolation," *J. Speech Hear. Disord.* **22**:87–90 (1957).

Pederson, O. T., and G. A. Studebaker, "A New Minimal-Contrasts Closed-Response-Set Speech Test," *J. Aud. Res.* **12**:187–195 (1972).

Peterson, G. E., and I. Lehiste, "Revised CNC Lists for Auditory Tests," *J. Speech Hear. Disord.* **27**:62–70 (1962).

Pocock, L. C., "A Survey of the Telephone Transmission-Rating Problem," *J. Inst. Electr. Eng.* **95**, Pt. III:253–265 (disc. 266–270), (1948).

Pokrovskiy, N. B. *Raschet i Izmereniye Razborchivosti Rechi*, Svdaz-izdat, Moscow (1962), trans. as *Computation and Measurement of Speech Intelligibility* by Joint Publications Research Service no. 21885 (18 Nov. 1963).

Pollack, I., and L. R. Decker, "Confidence Ratings, Message Reception, and the Receiver Operating Characteristic," *J. Acoust. Soc. Am.* **30**:286–292 (1958).

Preusse, J. W., "Semiautomatic Speech Intelligibility Measurements," *IEEE Trans. Audio Electroacoust.* **AU-15**:188–191 (1967).

Resnick, D. M., "Reliability of the Twenty-Five Word Phonetically Balanced Lists," *J. Aud. Res.* **2**:5–12 (1962).

Ross, M., and D. A. Huntington, "Concerning the Reliability and Equivalency of the CID W-22 Auditory Tests," *J. Aud. Res.* **2**:220–228 (1962).

Rubenstein, H., and I. Pollack, "Word Predictability and Intelligibility," *J. Verbal Learn. Verbal Behav.* **2**:147–158 (1963).

Saito, S., "Study on the Evaluation of the Articulation Score of the Japanese Speech Sounds," *Rept. Electr. Commun. Lab. Japan* **7**:207–212 (1959).

Sapozhkov, M. A., "A Special Feature in the Intelligibility of Formants," *Sov. Phys.—Acoust.* **5**:211–213 (1959).

Schneider, H., "Zur Messung der Sprachverständlichkeit," *Frequenz* **9**:199–205 (1955).

Schubert, E. D., and E. Owens, "CVC Words as Test Items," *J. Aud. Res.* **11**:88–100 (1971).

Shutts, R. E., K. S. Burke, and J. E. Creston, "Derivation of Twenty-Five Word PB Lists," *J. Speech Hear. Disord.* **29**:442–457 (1964).

Speaks, C. A., J. Jerger, and J. Trammell, "Comparison of Sentence Identification and Conventional Speech Discrimination Scores," *J. Speech Hear. Res.* **13**:755–767 (1970).

Stark, E. W., and D. E. Hagness, "The Modified Rhyme Test As a Test of Speech Discrimination," *J. Aud. Res.* **12**:154–156 (1972).

Strange, W., and T. Halwes, "Confidence Ratings in Speech Perception Research: Evaluation of an Efficient Technique for Discrimination Testing," *Percept. Psychophysiol.* **9**:182–186 (1971).

Swaffield, J., and R. H. deWardt, "A Reference Telephone System for Articulation Tests," *Post Office Electr. Eng. J.* **43**:1–7 (1950).

Swets, J., ed., *Signal Detection and Recognition by Human Observers* Wiley, New York (1964).

Taylor, M. M., and C. D. Creelman, "PEST: Efficient Estimates on Probability Functions," *J. Acoust. Soc. Am.* **41**:782–787 (1967).

Thwing, E. J., "Effect of Repetition on Articulation Scores for PB Words," *J. Acoust. Soc. Am.* **28**:302–303 (1956).

Williams, C. E., B. W. Levin, and M. H. L. Hecker, "Effect of the Closed-Response Format on Modified Rhyme Test Scores," (L) *J. Acoust. Soc. Am.* **53**:1169–1173 (1973).

Wisch, W., "Verständlichkeits-Messungen an Übertragungssystemen mit deutschen Logotomen nach dem Magnettonverfahren," *Nachrichtentech.* **7**:342–345 (1957).

15

Reprinted from pp. 955–981 of *Laryngoscope* 58(9):955–991 (1948)

ARTICULATION TESTING METHODS.*

JAMES P. EGAN,[†][‡]

Cambridge, Mass.

There are many reasons why oral communication may be inefficient or fail completely. Although failure to understand the spoken word is commonly due to failure of context to provide adequate meaning, there are many situations in which communication is ineffective because the listener confuses certain sounds with others, or because he does not hear them at all. Distortion of speech sounds by inferior transducers, masking of these sounds by ambient or electrical noises, faulty enunciation, partial deafness — all these factors and many others may conspire to make communication uncertain and unreliable. In order to evaluate the relative importance of the various factors that influence the intelligibility of speech, methods are required by which the degree of intelligibility of speech may be determined. These methods may be classified into three groups: articulation tests, subjective appraisals and threshold tests. The present paper concerns those procedures that have been found particularly useful in the measurement of the intelligibility of speech.

A quantitative measure of the "intelligibility of speech" may be obtained by counting the number of discrete speech units correctly recorded by the listener in an articulation test. Typically, an announcer reads aloud lists of syllables, words, or sentences to a group of listeners, and the percentage of items correctly recorded by these listeners is called the articulation score. The scores obtained are dependent upon a large

*This paper concerns many of the methods used at the Psycho-Acoustic Laboratory for the study of oral communication during the war years. The research was begun under an OSRD contract and is continuing under contract with the U. S. Navy, Office of Naval Research (Contract N5ori-76). This is Report PNR-36.

†Psycho-Acoustic Laboratory, Harvard University.

‡Now at the University of Wisconsin.

number of factors that enter as parameters into every test. For convenience, these factors may be divided into two groups. One of these groups concerns the nature of the test items that constitute the discrete speech units. The other group of factors mainly concerns the procedures used in articulation testing.[1]

Although a quantitative measure of intelligibility is most completely informative, a qualitative evaluation is sometimes adequate. Frequently it is sufficient to have competent observers evaluate the quality of a given sample of speech. These observers may rank order various samples of speech in terms of the relative intelligibility of the samples, or they may describe the speech in terms of some standard of reference. If properly used, these "subjective" methods of appraisal can be employed to advantage. A brief description of these methods is included below.

For certain other purposes, it is of value to find the thresholds at which speech becomes just detectable, just perceptible, or easily intelligible. In determining these thresholds, the listener adjusts some variable, such as the intensity of a masking noise, until the appropriate threshold is reached. These procedures will be discussed later and typical results presented.

SPEECH UNITS FOR ARTICULATION TESTS.

In an articulation test the talker pronounces selected speech items and the listener records the sounds that he hears. Since the nature of the spoken items helps to determine the resulting articulation scores, the test material must be carefully selected if a proper assessment is to be made. For most testing purposes the speech sounds used should be reasonably representative of conversational speech. Furthermore, for economy of

1. For a discussion of the earlier methods employed at the Psycho-Acoustic Laboratory, Harvard University, see Stevens, S. S.; Miller, Joseph; Egan, J. P.; Waterman, T. H., and Rome, S. C.: Articulation Testing Methods, 1 February, 1942, OSRD Report No. 383. For a more detailed discussion of the present paper, see Egan, J. P.: Articulation Testing Methods, II, 1 November, 1944, OSRD Report No. 3802. (These and other OSRD reports are available through the Office of Technical Services, U. S. Department of Commerce, Washington, D. C., as PB 22916 and PB 22848, respectively.)

time and effort, it is important to group the speech units into balanced lists, each list as difficult as each other list. When lists of comparable difficulty are used, differences in articulation scores obtained with two different microphones, earphones, etc., may be interpreted as due to differences in the instruments rather than to differences in the difficulty of the lists.

1. Representation of Fundamental Speech Sounds. All, or nearly all, of the fundamental sounds into which speech can be analyzed should be represented in each list of test items. Ideally, the relative frequencies of occurrence of these fundamental speech sounds should reflect their distribution in normal speech. The desirability of a proportional representation in the test lists of the sounds that occur in everyday speech stems from a consideration of the problem of *validity*. A microphone which passed only certain types of sounds might test well with a list of words containing only such sounds, but the test would not be a valid indication of the usefulness of this instrument for ordinary conversation. For example, if a set of test lists contained no nasal sounds, it might not provide a fair test of a microphone coupled to the mouth by certain types of noise shields. As a practical matter, the actual distribution of sounds in speech depends upon whose speech it is and what is being talked about. It is possible, nevertheless, to state approximately the relative frequencies of occurrence of sounds in "average" speech, and to approach these frequencies in the distribution of sounds in each of the test lists. In any case, it must be remembered that such factors as the equipment and the type of interfering noise may alter the relative difficulty of different speech sounds.

2. Types of Test Items. Tests which measure how well speech sounds are recognized generally fall into one of three classes: *a.* single syllables made up of meaningless combinations of speech sounds; *b.* meaningful words given out of context as isolated units; and *c.* meaningful phrases or sentences, in which there are contextual relations among the words. The principal differences among these three classes depend upon the psychological factors of meaning, inflection, rhythm, etc.

Whether syllables, words, or sentences are used for testing purposes depends upon a number of considerations. The use of nonsense syllables has the advantage that the articulation score indicates more accurately the number of phonemes actually heard by the listener than do tests based on words or sentences. Also, it is quite easy to make up syllable lists of

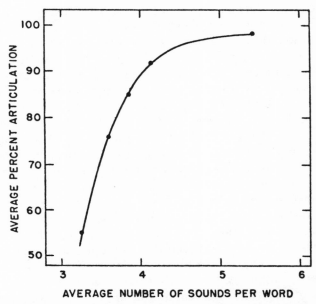

Fig. 1. Five groups of 20 words, having different average numbers of sounds per word, were read 20 times to a group of listeners. The graph shows how articulation improves when the number of sounds per word is increased.

comparable difficulty. On the other hand, the use of nonsense syllables requires that the testing crew be thoroughly trained. The announcer must pronounce the speech sounds correctly, and the listeners must record with phonetic symbols the sounds they hear. The use of words as test items does not have this disadvantage. There are large differences, however, in the relative difficulty of different words, and these differences cannot be attributed entirely to phonetic structure. Thus, short words are usually missed more frequently than long words, and a test list can be made difficult or easy by varying the proportions of short and long words. Fig. 1 shows a relation between the number of words correctly recorded and the number of sounds contained in the words. This graph shows that articulation improves markedly when the number of sounds per word is increased. When the test materials consist of lists of sentences, and when these sentences are scored in terms of the meaning conveyed, psychological factors are still more important in determining the articulation score than when single words are used. For this reason, "discrete sentence intelligiblity" is typically higher than word or syllable articulation. Even when the listener is required to record the key words of a sentence, the percentage correctly recorded depends not only upon the articulation values of these individual words, but also upon the relation they bear to the other words of the sentence.

Since the difficulty of a test list is determined not only by the difficulty of the fundamental speech sounds but also by numerous psychological factors, it is desirable to demonstrate by actual test that each test list is as difficult as each other list.

For many purposes it is important to know at least approximately the relation between the scores obtained with various types of articulation tests. Such a relation makes it possible to predict from scores obtained on one kind of articulation test the performance to be expected on a different type of test. On the other hand, since the articulation obtained with any one type of material is dependent upon the difficulty of the items selected, there is no unique relation between the scores obtained with two types of tests. The particular relation will also depend upon other factors, such as, for example, the experience of the crew and the type of equipment used; however, within the limits of experimental error, it has always been found that, when syllable articulation increases, word or sentence articulation also increases. Fig. 2 shows one relation between word and sentence articulation. This relation shows that sentence intelligibility is higher than the corresponding word articulation.

3. Difficulty and Reliability of Test Lists. It is not sufficient to make the relative frequencies of occurrence of the fundamental speech sounds correspond to those in conversational speech. In addition, the test items must be so selected that the distribution of item difficulty in each list will make possible a sensitive measuring instrument. Those items which under the conditions of the tests are always recorded cor-

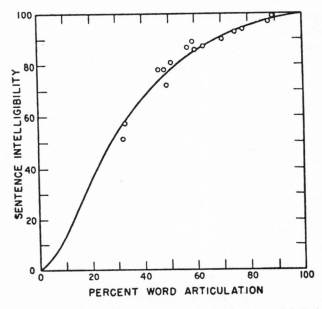

Fig. 2. Lists of words and lists of sentences were compared as to intelligibility under a wide variety of conditions. Each point on the graph represents one test of 100 words and one test of 50 sentences. The curve passing through the data was derived from results obtained at the Bell Telephone Laboratories.

rectly, or are always missed, are dead weight and may well be omitted from the test lists. There are, then, two potentially incompatible requirements for the distribution of test items with respect to difficulty, and compromise must be made between them.

a. If test lists are to be sensitive to small differences in intelligibility as well as convenient for use, the test items must be fairly closely distributed along a scale of difficulty.

b. Ideally, the distribution of difficulty should be sufficiently wide to embrace the requisite range as determined by the conditions under which the test lists will be used.

For an extensive testing program, it is convenient to have a large number of reasonably short and homogeneous test lists. When too few lists of words or sentences are used over and over, the crew of listeners tends to learn the particular grouping of items, even when the order of the items is changed each time a list is read. Short lists are desirable so that the articulation scores will not be unduly influenced by factors that tend to raise or lower the articulation score throughout the reading of a given test list. Fortunately, the reliability of the mean of a set of articulation scores can always be improved by increasing the number of tests.

The distribution of difficulty of the items in most tests follows a bell-shaped curve. For this reason, articulation tests are ordinarily not uniformly sensitive over the complete range of possible scores. The greatest sensitivity usually results when the testing conditions are so adjusted that scores near 50 per cent are obtained. This nonuniformity of the distribution of difficulty of test items implies that the variability of a test score is a function of the test score itself. Near the two extremes of the articulation scale (0 and 100 per cent) the variability of the scores is at a minimum, whereas in the middle range the variability is at a maximum; however, as mentioned above, when scores are obtained in the middle range, their reliability may be improved simply by increasing the number of tests.

AVAILABLE LISTS OF SYLLABLES, WORDS, AND SENTENCES.

Under each of the main types of test materials there are many varieties. For most purposes many of these different forms give equivalent results. For example, the *relative* effectiveness for masking speech of each of several different noises can be correctly assessed by the use of nonsense syllables, monosyllabic words, polysyllabic words, or sentences. Nevertheless, there are certain problems which are more efficiently investigated by the use of one rather than another type of test item.

1. Syllable Lists. There are several forms of nonsense syllables. One form is obtained by permuting the consonants with the vowels. Examples of syllables formed in this way are *te* and *et*. Sometimes isolated vowels and diphthongs are included. Another form of nonsense syllable consists of an initial consonant, a vowel, and a terminal consonant, as in the syllables, *zed, mōk,* and *tid.*

The construction of lists of nonsense syllables can be accomplished by a rather mechanical process. For example, one procedure followed by the Bell Telephone Laboratories[2] consists simply of drawing at random a card from each of three boxes. One box contains the initial consonants, one contains the vowels, and one contains the final consonants. Of course, certain of the syllables must be discarded: some of them are difficult to pronounce; some are very similar to other syllables; and some represent words that are taboo.

A word should be said about the selection of the phonetic alphabet employed for construction of lists of nonsense syllables. Such alphabets as the International Phonetic Alphabet make distinctions between certain phonemes which are far too fine and subtle for engineering purposes. It was found that the speech sounds in the Revised Scientific Alphabet[3] could be readily pronounced by the average speaker and consequently most of the sounds in that alphabet can be utilized.[4]

2. Monosyllabic Word Lists. In the course of its articulation testing program, the Psycho-Acoustic Laboratory constructed several sets of word lists. Since the editions and revisions through which these lists have gone are too numerous to describe here, we shall content ourselves with a

---

2. Fletcher, H., and Steinberg, J. C.: Articulation Testing Methods. Bell Syst. Tech. Jour., VIII, 806-854, 1929. It was the pioneering studies of the group at the Bell Telephone Laboratories which established articulation testing procedures as a basic method in the science of communication.

3. See Funk and Wagnall's Standard Dictionary.

4. The complete set of nonsense syllables which was used extensively at the Psycho-Acoustic Laboratory has been published as Appendix I of OSRD Report No. 3802, referred to in footnote 1.

description of the lists (PB) which represent the most recent revision.

From a large vocabulary 1200 monosyllabic words were chosen to make up what was called the RM (revised monosyllabic) lists. The exceptionally easy words were discarded from the original vocabulary, and only words in common use were retained. From this sample of 1200 words, 24 lists of 50 words each were constructed. The words were assigned to each list on the basis of the phonetic composition of the first part of the word. No attempt was made to equate these lists with respect to the phonetic structure of the final consonant or consonant compound. Although the RM lists were found reasonably satisfactory, the construction of a new set of word lists was undertaken to insure that the lists would be more nearly phonetically balanced (PB word lists). Every effort was made to make these new lists satisfy the following criteria : a. monosyllabic structure, b. equal average difficulty, c. equal range of difficulty, d. equal phonetic composition, e. a composition representative of English speech, and f. words in common usage. The PB series consists of 20 lists, each containing 50 monosyllables. They cover a wide enough range of difficulty to make them adequate for most types of articulation comparisons. The spread of difficulty is approximately the same in each list, and each list has nearly the same average difficulty.

Furthermore, the lists have very nearly the same phonetic composition, a phonetic composition quite similar to that of the English language. Rare and unfamiliar words have been avoided as much as possible, and very few of the words are extremely easy or extremely difficult under conditions in which the whole group of lists would obtain an average articulation score of about 50 per cent. Incidentally, it should be pointed out that each list contains 50 words because an attempt to satisfy the requirements listed above with lists of only 25 words met with failure.

The phonetic composition of the lists is based on Dewey's

frequency count[5] of the sounds in a sample of 100,000 words. It was found impossible to adhere strictly to the values given by Dewey, however, because of the limitations already imposed — namely, that the lists be all different and constructed of common monosyllables. According to Dewey, for instance, nearly 25 per cent of the words in his sample of 100,000 words began with short vowels. (This is due to the high frequency of such common words as *and, is, am*.) There are, however, only some 40 different common English monosyllables beginning with a short vowel. It was necessary, therefore, to limit this class of words to two per 50-word list. As a result of this and similar compromises, the resemblance of the phonetic structure of the lists to that of the language is not entirely exact.

The representation of sounds in each of the PB lists was made to follow as nearly as possible the distribution of sounds shown in Table 1. This table was derived from Dewey's counts (in compromise with the practical restrictions discussed above), and it shows the frequency of each phonetic class in each position in the monosyllables, initial, medial, and final. In each list there are about 10 compound consonants in the initial and about 10 in the final position. In Table 1 these compounds are classified in terms of the first consonant of the compound.

TABLE 1.

FREQUENCIES IN THE PHONETIC CLASSES IN THE PB LISTS.

Phonetic Class	Initial	Position of Sound in Word Medial	Final
VOWELS			
Long	2	16	2
Short	2	20	2
Diphthong		6	
CONSONANTS			
Transitional	5		5
Semivowel	9		9
Fricatives	12		12
Voiced stop	9		9
Unvoiced stop	11		11

In the construction of the lists, adherence to the frequencies

5. Dewey, Godfrey: Relative Frequency of English Speech Sounds. (Harvard University Press, Cambridge, Mass., 1923.)

184

of Table 1 was found to be most difficult for the final sounds, usually because new words were not available which satisfied all the requirements. None of the lists, however, deviates by more than a few sounds from the specified pattern.

Earlier experiments had shown that similarity of phonetic structure is no guarantee of uniform difficulty among words. As a test of this matter, the words of the preliminary PB vocabulary were read eleven times under several conditions to a crew of eleven listeners, so that it was possible to obtain approximate measures of the relative difficulty of each of the words. A few words almost always missed by all the listeners, along with several almost never missed by any of the listeners, were discarded as nondiscriminating. Then, with the words remaining, every effort was made to equate the lists both for mean difficulty and for spread of difficulty.

Among the original words tested were a number fitting the phonetic specifications but very infrequent in spoken English (thong, fop, ilk, crass). Even if it comes clearly through an interphone, an unfamiliar word is likely to be missed. Consequently, the preliminary vocabulary was read in the quiet to 23 listeners who were instructed to rate each word as 1 (familiar), 2 (somewhat unfamiliar), or 3 (quite unfamiliar). The ratings for each word were added and all words with a total rating of 35 or over were discarded as too unfamiliar to be used. This seemed the most reasonable method available for eliminating unfamiliar words.

Since the PB word lists may be of value to other investigators, the 20 lists are appended below.

3. Spondaic Word Lists. There are purposes for which it is desirable to use lists of words of homogeneous audibility, *i.e.*, lists in which each individual word is as difficult as each other word. In order to assemble such lists, experiments were conducted in which various types of words were presented to trained listeners under carefully controlled conditions. It was discovered that the class of words having the highest homogeneity contained those dissyllables spoken with equal stress on both syllables. These words are called *spondees*. Examples are *railroad, iceberg, horseshoe*. Word lists assembled from spondees have proved particularly useful in tests whose purpose is to establish accurately the level at which speech can just be heard. These homogeneous words reach the threshold of hearing, all within a narrow range of intensity, and thereby serve to determine with precision the threshold of hearing for speech.

In particular, the lists of spondees have been recorded phonographically for use as an audiometric test in the measurement of deafness.[6] The procedure for determining the threshold of a deafened ear has been greatly facilitated by recording the spondaic lists at decreasing levels of intensity on each record. The subject writes down the words he hears until the point is reached at which he can hear the words no longer. The level at which he hears half the words is usually considered the threshold of hearing for speech.

Similarly, these lists can be used to measure the relative efficiency of different earphones, or the effectiveness of different earphone cushions in coupling the earphone to the ear, etc. The electrical power required by an earphone to reach the threshold of hearing of a given ear is indicative of the sensitivity of the earphone as a transducer. *Caution:* since the spondaic words are much easier for a listener to identify than are the monosyllables (PB lists), they may sometimes be heard over a "peaked" transducer at a lower level (relative to a "uniform" transducer) than would be required for words chosen at random. Hence, the spondees are not recommended for use in the comparison of two systems which differ markedly in frequency response.

4. Sentence Lists. In testing communication equipment sentence articulation has a limited use. Under most test conditions articulation scores obtained with lists of sentences are so high that communication systems must differ considerably before substantial difference in the scores is obtained. As pointed out above, the intelligibility of sentences is favored

6. Hudgins, C. V.; Hawkins, J. E.; Karlin, J. E., and Stevens, S. S.: The Development of Recorded Auditory Tests for Measuring Hearing Loss for Speech. The Laryngoscope, 57, 57-89, January, 1947.

to a considerable degree by meaning, context, rhythm, etc. The influence of these psychological factors on the scores makes the results difficult to analyze and to interpret. Furthermore, since the listeners easily remember the sentences, a very large number of sentences is required in a testing program that employs the same listeners over and over.

There are, nevertheless, special circumstances in which sentence lists are of value. They are useful, for example, in testing the speaking ability of telephone talkers, where the utterance of a sentence provides a more complex sample of behavior than does the speaking of single words. Rate, intonation, stress pattern, and maintenance of loudness level can be tested adequately only with sentence material. Moreover, it has been observed in the course of experiments that talkers who are careless in their manner of uttering sentences may be more precise when speaking isolated words.[7]

The extensive set of sentence lists compiled at the Bell Telephone Laboratories[2] has been widely used by other laboratories. However, these lists vary considerably in difficulty, they frequently refer to details peculiar to New York City, and they are too much a test of knowledge and intelligence for use with some grades of listeners. Nevertheless, for quick appraisal of relatively poor communication systems, these lists of sentences provide a useful test material.

Another set of sentence materials available for use consists of 68 lists of 20 sentences each. Each sentence consists of five key words plus a variable number of connective words. Four of the key words are monosyllables and one is a dissyllable. An effort was made to avoid cliches, proverbs, and other stereotyped constructions, as well as the too frequent use of any one word in the lists of sentences. Since only the five key words in each sentence are scored, each list of 20 sentences contains 100 scorable items.[8]

7. Abrams, M. H.; Goffard, S. J.; Kryter, K. D.; Miller, G. A.; Miller, Joseph, and Sanford, F. H.: Speech in Noise: A Study of the Factors Determining Its Intelligibility. Psycho-Acoustic Laboratory, Harvard University, 1 September, 1944, OSRD Report No. 4023. (PB 19805.)

8. These lists are published in Appendix IV of OSRD Report No. 3802, referred to above.

Attention should be called also, at this point, to another set of sentence lists.[6] These are sentences whose comprehension can be indicated by the writing of a single word. They, like the spondaic lists, were specially devised to measure the degree to which an individual shows a hearing loss for speech. Ordinarily, sentences differ considerably with respect to the intensity level required to make them audible, and, since it is not feasible to achieve comparability by a process of selection alone, the sentences were made homogeneous by adjusting the intensity level at which a given sentence was recorded and reproduced. These adjustments were made experimentally with the aid of a crew of listeners. Then, for the final phonographic recording, each list was divided into small groups of sentences, and the intensity level of each group was successively decreased. The result of this procedure is a test which measures the threshold of hearing of a listener in terms of his ability to hear connected discourse.

METHODS OF CONDUCTING ARTICULATION TESTS.

The values of articulation scores are dependent upon a large number of factors. For example, the announcer introduces such variables as vocal quality, regional pronunciation, steadiness or variability of speech power, and other individual characteristics. If communication devices are used, the various components have their effects upon the intelligibility of the transmitted speech. Interfering noise — its presence or absence, its type, and whether it is introduced acoustically or electrically — makes for additional complications. And finally, the individuals comprising the crew of listeners differ from each other in their ability to hear speech under difficult conditions. In this array of factors are hundreds of small events — interactions among equipment, the sounds of speech, and the testing personnel — and each event contributes its small share to the overall result.

It becomes obvious, therefore, that the results of measurements of articulation cannot be interpreted in absolute terms. *All articulation scores are relative scores,* contingent upon the use of specific announcers, microphones, amplifiers, earphones, noises, listeners, and test lists. Little trust can be placed in absolute statements about articulation. In general, the only trustworthy statements regarding the effectiveness of communication systems are relative statements.

This great complexity which attaches to articulation testing makes advisable a discussion of the specific factors contrib-

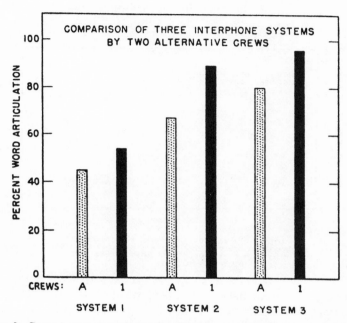

Fig. 3. Crew 1 was a trained laboratory testing crew. Crew A consisted of eight Army and Navy servicemen. All tests were made with announcer and listeners in an ambient noise (115 db). The rank order of the three communication systems as determined by the articulation scores is the same for both crews.

uting to the articulation scores and of the techniques used to control them.

1. Selection of Testing Personnel. In view of the large individual differences among talkers and listeners that are obtained under adverse conditions of communication, it is necessary to select carefully the testing personnel. For most purposes, the listeners should have reasonably normal hearing and the talkers should have no speech impediments. Experience has shown that despite differences in abilities among announcers and listeners, the relative merits of various communication systems can usually be correctly assessed. Fig. 3 shows the articulation results obtained with two different crews of listeners. Three different interphone systems were tested with each of the two crews. One crew had been given very little training before this experiment was conducted.

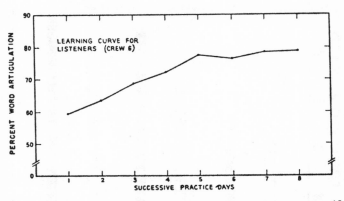

Fig. 4. Each point on the curve represents the average score on 12 tests of 100 words each with a crew of 10 listeners. The tests were read over an interphone system by three well practiced announcers. Both the announcer and the listeners were in an ambient noise (115 db).

The other crew consisted of experienced listeners trained in the laboratory. Although one crew obtained higher scores than the other, the three systems tested were ranked the same by both crews.

2. *Importance of Training and Fatigue.* Articulation scores obtained with inexperenced listeners show improvement with practice, and this improvement may be considerable under difficult listening conditions. Fig. 4 shows a typical learning curve obtained under severe acoustic stress. It is well to train a listening crew until little or no improvement results from further practice before comparisons are made among various communication devices.

In an experiment designed especially to measure the

effects of fatigue on articulation scores, tests were conducted throughout two experimental sessions of three hours each, one in the morning and the other in the afternoon of the same day.[9] In these tests, the listening crew was exposed to noise only for the interval required for the reading of the test list, and the listeners were given two 15-minute rest periods in each three-hour testing session. This entire procedure was repeated three days later, and the final results are based on both days. In all, 48 test lists of 100 words each were read to the listeners under two experimental conditions which were alternated from test to test throughout each day. For one-half the tests, both the announcer and the listeners were in an intense ambient noise (overall intensity level of 115 db) ; for the other half, a noise having a uniform spectrum was introduced electrically into the listeners' earphones. By combining the data collected on the two days of testing, it is possible to compare in Table 2 the articulation scores obtained during each of the six successive hours of testing. The low variability among these scores is evidence that articulation can be reasonably stable throughout the day. Fatigue seems to have little effect when reasonable provision is made for rest between tests.

TABLE 2.

AVERAGE ARTICULATION SCORES, HOUR BY HOUR, FOR TWO TEST CONDITIONS.

	T-17 Microphone (Ambient Noise)	BR-2S Microphone (Noise in Earphones)
A. M.		
1st hour	81	77
2nd hour	82	76
3rd hour	82	76
LUNCH		
P. M.		
4th hour	81	72
5th hour	78	78
6th hour	80	75

A temporary hearing loss acquired by listening to loud speech in the presence of noise seems to have no effect on

9. Egan, J. P.; Griffin, D. R.; Miller, Joseph; Waterman, T. H., and Stevens, S. S.: Performance of Communication Equipment in Noise. Psycho-Acoustic Laboratory, Harvard University, 1 October, 1942, OSRD Report No. 901. (PB22845.)

later tests using the same loud speech. However, if articulation tests using weak signal levels are conducted immediately after tests empoying painfully loud signal levels, the articulation scores obtained with the weak levels of received speech might be lower than the scores obtained with normal hearing.

3. Selection of Complementary Equipment. In comparing two devices with respect to the intelligibility of speech trans-

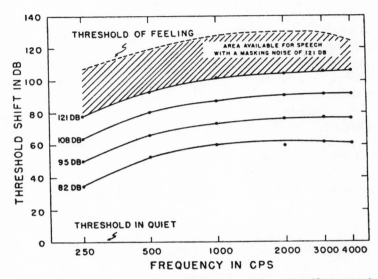

Fig. 5. These curves show how effectively a noise of uniform spectrum level (250-5000 c.p.s.) masks pure tones. The area between the curves representing the threshold of hearing in quiet and the threshold of feeling defines the auditory area available for communication in quiet. As the intensity of noise reaching the ear of a listener progressively increases, this area available for communication becomes smaller and smaller. The parameter values are the overall level of the masking noise.

mitted over them, it is important to consider the other components of communication equipment used for the test. For example, one microphone may not transduce speech frequencies above 2500 c.p.s. and another may transduce all the important frequencies of speech. If earphones which do not transduce speech frequencies above 2500 c.p.s. are used for these tests, little or no difference will be found in the articulation scores provided by the two microphones. Thus it may be stated as a general rule that the final evaluation of an instrument cannot be made apart from a consideration of its associated equipment.[9]

4. Selection of Ambient Noise Conditions. A noise reaching the ear of the listener interferes with the intelligibility of

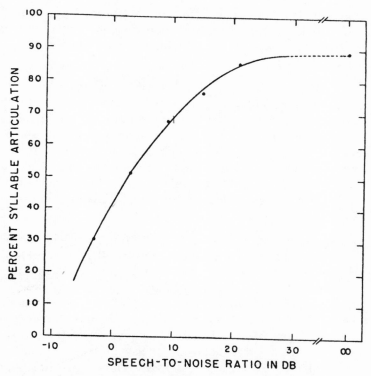

Fig. 6. Syllable articulation vs. speech-to-noise ratio. The speech level at the listeners' ears was held constant at a level of about 103 db overall. A "white noise" (random spectrum) was mixed electrically with the speech. Measurements of speech and of noise were made with a VU meter.

speech by raising the threshold of hearing so that sounds which could be heard in quiet are no longer audible. This shift in the threshold of hearing is called *masking*. The amount of masking produced by an interfering noise is the difference in decibels between the normal threshold and the masked threshold for pure tones. Fig. 5 shows several masking curves obtained by using a noise which has a uniform spectrum level. These curves show how effectively a masking noise can reduce the auditory area available for the reception of speech. They also show why the intelligibility of speech depends upon the ratio of the level of the speech signal to the level of the interfering noise. Fig. 6 shows quantitatively how articulation varies as a function of speech-to-noise ratio.[10] The particular form of this relation depends upon many factors, the most important·of which is the spectrum of the noise.[11]

If a communication system is typically used in a noisy environment, articulation tests designed to measure the intelligibility provided by that system should be conducted with the announcer or listeners, or both, in an ambient noise. Since microphones and earphones differ markedly in their ability to withstand acoustic stress, it is important that the evaluation of these devices by articulation tests be conducted under the acoustic stress which is representative of conditions of use.[9,12]

5. *Intensity of Received Speech.* Signal level is one of the most important determinants of the intelligibility of speech. For convenience, signal level in interphone communication may be considered a function of five principal variables: the voice level of the announcer, the efficiency with which the voice of the announcer is coupled to the microphone, the frequency response of the microphone, the gain of the interphone amplifier, and the frequency response of the earphone when it is coupled to the ear. These five variables are independent. In experiments designed to study the relation between articu-

10. Egan, J. P.; Miller, Joseph; Stein, M. I.; Thompson, G. G., and Waterman, T. H.: Studies on the Effect of Noise on Speech Communications. Psycho-Acoustic Laboratory, Harvard University, 25 November, 1943. OSRD Report No. 2038. (PB 22907.)

11. Miller, G. A.: The Masking of Speech. Psychol. Bull., 44, 105-129, March, 1947.

12. Waterman, T. H.: Flight and Laboratory Tests of Various Microphones and Noise Shields for Use at Low Altitudes. Joint report from the Aircraft Radio Laboratory (Memorandum Report 146) and the Psycho-Acoustic Laboratory, Harvard University (OSRD Report No. 1973), 27 December, 1943. (PB 22908.) Dr. Waterman's study shows that the articulation test is readily adaptable to the evaluation of communication devices in situ.

lation and the level of received speech it is usually practicable to vary only voice level or the gain of the amplifier. Examples of the relation between articulation and voltage gain of the amplifier are shown for three different microphones in Fig. 7.[13]

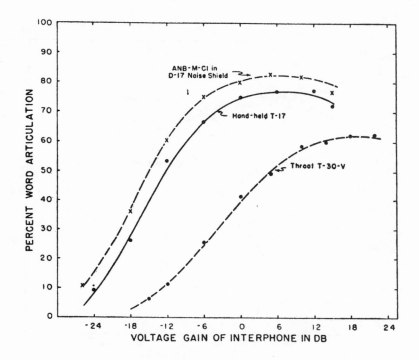

Fig. 7. Relation between per cent word articulation and voltage gain of interphone (linear system). The speech input to the microphone was held at a constant level throughout all the tests. Both the announcer and the crew of listeners were in ambient noise (airplane noise, 120 db).

Two examples of the relation between articulation and voice level are shown in Fig. 8.[13] For these experiments, the voice level of the announcer was varied over a wide range, while the gain of the amplifier was held constant.

In many experiments a system of monitoring the voice

13. Egan, J. P.; Stein, M. I., and Thompson, G. G.: The Articulation Efficiency of Nine Carbon Microphones for Use at Low Altitudes. Psycho-Acoustic Laboratory, Harvard University, 1 June, 1944, OSRD Report No. 3515. (PB 22913.)

which is independent of the system under test is desirable. By means of a magnetic throat microphone with an amplifier and output meter, a monitoring system is obtained which is satisfactory over a wide range of experimental conditions. The chief deficiency of this method is the difficulty of placing

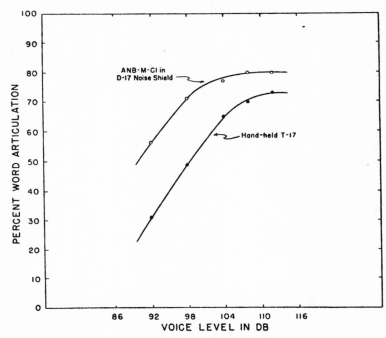

Fig. 8. Relation between per cent word articulation and voice level. The voltage gain of the interphone was held constant. The voice levels were measured by a GR Sound Level Meter (with the lips just touching the wire mesh of the microphone and the meter set to "slow" reading). Both the announcer and the listeners were in an ambient noise (airplane noise, 120 db).

a thoat microphone in the same position on the throat from test to test, but this objection can be overcome by the exercise of sufficient care. Carbon microphones do not provide a correct indication of changes in the voice level under typical conditions of testing. These microphones distort the speech signal and an effective compression occurs. Consequently, changes in the output voltage of some, if not all, carbon micro-phones are not proportional to changes in voice level.[14]

6. Use of a Carrier Sentence. In an articulation test each test item (syllable or word) is usually read as part of a sentence. For example, in the sentence, "You will write *car*," the word *car* is the only word which the listener is required to record. A carrier sentence is desirable for several reasons. *a.* The listener is prepared for the presentation of the test item, and variability in the articulation scores due to inattention or distraction is reduced. *b.* If carbon-button microphones are used, the carrier phrase preceding the test item serves to agitate the particles of carbon and reduce the variability inherent in such microphones. *c.* The carrier sentence permits the announcer to modulate his voice so as to keep the level of his voice even from word to word.

For most purposes the carrier sentence and not the test item should be used to monitor voice level. Thus, no attempt should be made to compensate for the typical differences in the speech power used in pronouncing the different sounds in the test items. When only the carrier sentence is monitored, the test item should be spoken with the same general effort as the rest of the carrier sentence.

7. Statistical Methods. When an attempt is made to repeat articulation tests under identical conditions, the articulation scores obtained are usually somewhat different. If a test is repeated a large number of times, scores of various magnitudes are obtained. Unless the mean score is very high or very low, the scores tend to be distributed according to the normal law of error. The dispersion of the distribution of average scores obtained under the "same" conditions will depend upon how well the experimental conditions have been controlled. This dispersion also depends upon the number of listeners and the length of each test list.

The differences in the articulation scores obtained under the "same" conditions arise from many sources. In addition

---

14. Kryter, K. D.: The Effect of Voice Intensity on the Output Voltage of Various Microphones. OSRD Informal Communication, IC-74. This study is incorporated in OSRD Report No. 4023. See reference 7.

to systematic errors, there are in the array of basic factors determining the articulation scores many small events which contribute their small share to the overall result. The particular combinations of these chance events determine partially the extent to which the articulation score deviates from a central value. Since different combinations of these small events are sampled upon successive tests, different articulation scores are obtained. Differences arising from this source may be considered as errors due to random sampling. Because of these errors, an experiment must be designed so that differences between articulation scores may properly be analyzed by statistical procedures. The basic principle in experimental design consists in controlling at known values as many variables as possible, and in so arranging the experimental conditions that the effects of the unknown factors are made as random as possible. By this procedure the central or average articulation score can be interpreted in terms of the known conditions, and the dispersion of the scores can be used to determine the limits of accuracy imposed by the errors of random sampling. The dispersion of the articulation scores then becomes a measure of the precision of the experiment, and an estimate of the error of measurement may be based upon this dispersion. It is then a straightforward matter to assess, by conventional statistical procedures, the reliability of the differences obtained.[15]

ABBREVIATED TESTING METHODS.

The formal articulation test based on groups of announcers and listeners may prove too cumbersome and inefficient when an articulation study involves numerous permutations of experimental conditions. It is then expeditious to devise short-cut methods.

An interesting example of an efficient procedure is one which was developed to study the effects of amplitude distor-

---

15. Goffard, S. J., and Egan, J. P.: Procedures for Measuring the Intelligibility of Speech: Sound-Powered Telephone Systems. Psycho-Acoustic Laboratory, Harvard University, 1 February, 1947, PNR-33.

tion on articulation.[16] This method may involve a single individual. The test words are recorded phonographically, and good results have been obtained with the use of a single list used over and over.

The person conducting the test has before him a written list of the words recorded on the record. These words he keeps covered with a blank card. He listens to each word in turn, and, *after* he has both heard the word and decided what he thinks it is, he moves the blank card so as to uncover the correct word. He then checks whether or not he has heard the word correctly. This procedure obviously requires care and honest judgment on the part of the listener, but control checks applied to a practiced observer have shown that the method can be made to yield valid results. Since the listener, instead of writing down the words he hears, merely checks his correct responses, he is able to work at a fast pace and the speed-up in the articulation testing is considerable.

COMPARISONS BASED UPON SUBJECTIVE APPRAISAL.

In an articulation test the evaluation of the intelligibility of speech is based upon the *number* of test items correctly recorded by the listener. In this kind of test, the listener is not required to appraise the quality of the speech, but merely to record the speech sounds that he hears. By contrast, methods of subjective appraisal require the listener to evaluate the quality of speech itself. One variation on the subjective procedure is the *method of rank order*. The listener simply judges which of two or more samples of speech is more intelligible. Another variation is the *rating scale method*, which requires him to place a sample of speech along a continuum that has been defined in advance by the experimenter. For example, the listener might be asked to use a scale which ranges from very poor to excellent. The listener may make his judgments in terms of a standard sample of speech or in terms of his previous experience in the evaluation of the intel-

16. Licklider, J. C. R.: The Effects of Amplitude Distortion Upon the Intelligibility of Speech. Psycho-Acoustic Laboratory, Harvard University, 15 November, 1944, OSRD Report No. 4217. (PB 19775.)

ligibility of speech. This method is essentially the same as the method of rank order; however, in the method of rank order the intervals between the various ranks have no particular meaning. For example, the difference between ranks one and two does not necessarily have the same meaning as the difference between ranks two and three. In the rating-scale method the observer is usually instructed to rate the speech samples on a point scale where the successive points represent distances judged to be subjectively equal. He is not required to assign different ranks to the speech samples, nor is he required to utilize all of the points of the scale.[17]

THRESHOLD METHODS.

It is frequently desirable to know the conditions under which speech is just detectable or just intelligible. Three of these threshold methods will be described.[10]

To determine the *threshold of detectability* (sometimes called the threshold of audibility) the listener adjusts some variable (usually the intensity of speech or the intensity of a masking noise) until he is just able to detect the presence of speech sounds about half the time. At this threshold level he will ordinarily be unable to identify any of the sounds themselves. This threshold of detectability is the reference level for the specification of the sensation level of speech.

About 8 db above the threshold of detectability the listener can understand, with difficulty, the gist of connected discourse. This level of received speech is called the *threshold of perceptibility*. The determination of the threshold of perceptibility is useful when the intelligibility of speech can be varied continuously from a very low to a very high value. In determining this threshold the listener adjusts some variable until, in his judgment, he is just able to understand with considerable effort the gist of the connected discourse read to him.

In an effort to determine the reliability of this procedure

17. For a detailed discussion of these psychological scaling methods, see Guilford, J. P.: Psychometric Methods. McGraw-Hill Book Company, Inc., New York, 1936.

each of three listeners made 30 determinations of the threshold of perceptibility. A high-fidelity interphone was employed and a random noise with a uniform spectrum level was mixed electrically with the speech. The speech-to-noise ratio was adjusted by the listener until he obtained his threshold. The standard deviations of these three distributions of 30 judgments each were: 1.3 db, 1.6 db, and 1.7 db. The ranges of these distributions were only 6 db, 7 db, and 6 db, respectively. Furthermore, essentially the same threshold of perceptibility was obtained by different listeners. Eight inexperienced subjects made similar judgments after receiving only brief instructions in the procedure. Table 3 shows the speech-to-noise ratios that these listeners required in order to obtain the threshold. Each entry in the table is based on the average of three judgments. Only one of the eight listeners seems to have failed to adopt the correct criterion of judgment.

TABLE 3.
THRESHOLD OF PERCEPTIBILITY FOR INEXPERIENCED LISTENERS.

Listener	Speech-to-Noise Ratio in db
AM	—5 db
SM	—6
PP	—7
RL	—7
MR	—7
IP	—8
RA	—8
JS	—8

The average for the other seven listeners is —7 db, which agrees reasonably well with the average threshold obtained with four well-trained listeners (—5.5 db).

In determining the *threshold of intelligibility* the listener adjusts some variable until, in his judgment, he is just able to obtain without perceptible effort the meaning of almost every phrase of the connected discourse read to him. This particular threshold is probably less reliable than the other two; however, listeners generally agree that this threshold is about 4 db above the threshold of perceptibility.

These thresholds are useful in determining the relative effectiveness of various types of noise in masking speech. Determination of any one of these thresholds as a function of the intensity of the masking noise shows how the intensity of speech and the intensity of noise are related so that a constant perceptual effect is maintained.[18]

ACKNOWLEDGMENT.

The writer expresses his appreciation to Prof. S. S. Stevens for his invaluable advice and criticism during the course of this study. The writer is also indebted to those members of the Psycho-Acoustic Laboratory who contributed their efforts to the methodological problems of articulation testing during the war years.

[*Editor's Note:* Material has been omitted at this point.]

---

18. For an extensive application of one of these threshold methods, see Stevens, S. S.; Miller, Joseph, and Truscott, Ida: The Masking of Speech by Sine Waves, Square Waves, and Regular and Modulated Pulses. Jour. Acous. Soc. Am., 18, 418-124, October, 1946.

16

Reprinted from pp. 6–9 of *American Standard Method for Measurement of Monosyllabic Word Intelligibility* [*S3.2-1960*], American Standards Association, Inc., 1960, 19 pp.

American Standard Method for Measurement of

Monosyllabic Word Intelligibility

Writing Group S3-W-23
M. E. Hawley, Chairman

Introduction

Speech ranks foremost among the media used by man for communication. The effectiveness of speech communication depends upon the nature of the speech material; the relevant characteristics of the talker and listener; the conditions under which the radiation, transmission, and reception of the speech waves occur; and the characteristics of the communication system. By standardizing the speech material and an intelligibility test procedure,[1] and by specifying methods for evaluating the talkers and listeners, a relative measure of the effectiveness of different communication systems under the same specified conditions of use (or the same communication system under different specified conditions) can be obtained. This is particularly useful in the development and evaluation of speech communication equipment and in the investigation of its performance under varied environmental conditions.

The method of measurement presented herein uses the PB (phonetically balanced) monosyllabic word lists given on pages 10 to 19. This choice is not intended to reject other test material or to limit future development in this field. It is rather intended to provide a yardstick for the measurement of the identification of spoken words transmitted over a communication system and to provide a standard to which other methods can be compared. Through standardization, the results of different experiments can be related.

In intelligibility testing, many of the problems that arise concern whether the talkers and the listeners should be included within the system being analyzed or whether they should be considered as part of the testing instrumentation. For example, if two intercommunication sets with individual gain (amplification) controls for the listeners are to be compared, the manner in which the talker's level and the listener's level are obtained should be specified. Whether these levels should be pre-set and held constant or whether the intelligibility crew should be allowed to

[1] The word "intelligibility" is used when the units of speech material are complete and meaningful words, phrases, or sentences; the word "articulation" is used when the units of speech material are meaningless syllables or fragments.

adjust these levels can be decided only by knowing the specific purpose of the tests.

1. Scope and Purpose

1.1 Scope. This standard describes the procedures to be followed in conducting intelligibility tests which employ monosyllabic word lists.

1.2 Purpose. The purpose of this standard is: (1) to specify the speech material and the methods to be used in these tests; and (2) to note the variables to be controlled during the measurement and to be evaluated in the report.

2. Test Procedure

2.1 General. Selected talkers shall speak the specified material in the specified manner. The speech shall be transmitted by a communication system to selected listeners who shall write down the key words they hear. The specification of the environmental conditions (e.g., ambient noise) at and between the talker and listener positions and of the training of these subjects shall be considered part of the test procedure. Results will be given in the form of percentage of test words correctly communicated. All results are relative and shall be given as a comparison with the results obtained from using one or more other systems measured at the same time as the first. Standardized intelligibility testing procedure still leaves many variables within the testing situation uncontrolled. At present it is not possible to compare with precision two systems or conditions by testing one system or condition in one laboratory and the other system or condition in another laboratory. It is hoped, however, that a standardized procedure will result in the same order of rank among a group of systems when the group is tested in several different laboratories. It occasionally happens that an approximate evaluation will suffice. In such cases, tests of a single condition may be adequate, because the comparison system consists of estimates based upon previous experience obtained under similar conditions of communication.

2.2 Test Material. The test material shall be the lists of key words given on pages 10 to 19. Each list contains 50 words so chosen that all speech sounds are represented approximately according to their frequency of occurrence in normal speech; hence, they are termed "phonetically balanced." There are 20 such lists which are approximately equivalent in difficulty. These words shall each be spoken singly in the following carrier sentence: "Would you write (key word) now." This shall be read as a simple declarative sentence. The manner of speaking shall be such as to place no unnatural stress on any word. The listener shall write, using normal spelling, only the key words on his answer sheet. A word shall be considered entirely incorrect if any one of the sounds therein is incorrectly indicated. Incorrect spellings which result in a word which sounds as originally read receive full credit. The percentage of words correctly recorded is the monosyllabic word intelligibility. If conditions change during the use of a particular list, or a test is otherwise negated, a different list shall be substituted and the test repeated. The words in each list should be given a different random arrangement each time the list is re-used.

2.3 Screening of Subjects. The method of selecting subjects (i.e., talkers and listeners) shall be described in the report. Both talkers and listeners shall meet the following criteria for auditory acuity for both ears:

Hearing loss shall average no more than 10 decibels (db) over-all with no more than 15 db at 250, 500, 1000, 2000, and 4000 cycles per second (cps) when measured with an audiometer conforming to American Standard Specification for Audiometers for General Diagnostic Purposes, Z24.5-1951. (See Section 3.)

For talkers there shall be no obvious speech defects or strong regional or national accents.

Motivation should be adequate to insure attentiveness and unbiased results. Precautions should be taken to recognize and prevent the variations (often caused by motivational changes) that can accompany lengthy, repeated psychophysical measurements.

2.4 Training and Selection of Subjects. The experimenter shall ensure that the subjects have achieved a stable level of performance under critical conditions of the test before the experiment proper is begun. The specific method of training shall be described in the report. A procedure such as the following is recommended:

The training of the subjects begins with the reading, in a quiet room, of a word list by one of the subjects. He reads aloud to the other subjects, using the carrier sentence. This is face-to-face communication without the aid of communication devices. Each listener writes the key words. At the end of the list the supervisor rereads the list, spelling out each word. The number of errors is determined for each listener and the spellings and meanings are gone over until familiarity is ensured. This procedure is then repeated with the other 19 word lists, rotating the talking assignment throughout the group. Each subject thus becomes familiar with every word. The scores of all listeners on all lists are recorded. They are examined to find the subjects (serving as talkers) for whom the listeners' scores are most consistent. These subjects are chosen as the talkers for the evaluation tests. The remaining subjects whose scores are over 90 percent with the talkers selected are chosen as listeners for the evaluation tests. Monitors and scorers are selected from the remainder of the subjects. Each talker then reads the word lists over the communication systems to be evaluated under ideal ambient conditions, until stability is obtained for several successive scores for each of the listeners. Before the evaluation tests are begun, the crew hears each talker read at least one word list under each typical condition that is to be used. The talkers and listeners are carefully instructed in the proper use of the equipment to be evaluated. Throughout this training a different randomization of each word list is used each time the list is presented. The randomizations used in training are not used in the evaluation tests.

2.5 Talker and Listener Levels. In the determination of the speech levels at the talker and listener position, the experiment must be guided by the objectives of the intelligibility tests. There are two principal conditions to be considered with regard to both the level of talking and the level of received speech.

2.5.1 *Talker Levels*

2.5.1.1 For some purposes it is desirable that the talker be considered as a part of the test instrumentation and not as a part of the system under test. Under these conditions the typical practice has been to have the talker maintain the same level and manner of talking for all conditions. For example, in experiments designed to measure the effects upon intelligibility of filters in a communication circuit, practice has usually been to keep the speech input to the system fixed at a constant level for all filtering conditions. To aid the talker in his task, it is desirable to use a monitoring system which is independent of the characteristics of the speech signal received by the listeners.

2.5.1.2 For some purposes the talker's level and manner of talking should be included as part of the system under test. Under these conditions, the talker has usually been allowed to adjust his level of talking according to whatever effects the communication devices or environmental conditions have upon him. It is still desirable to measure the level of talking but it should be done in such a manner as to have no influence upon the talkers' levels.

2.5.1.3 A different procedure could be adopted in any particular experiment as a compromise between the two procedures discussed under 2.5.1.1 and 2.5.1.2 above. For example, in preliminary tests the talker could speak in the way he selects over each of the systems or under the conditions, or both, to be tested. A talking level could be measured during these preliminary tests and then used during the experiment proper as the talking level. In such a procedure, a monitoring system might utilize its own microphone, amplifier, and indicating instrument. It is obvious that great care must be exercised when the talker is allowed to select his levels, because his level and manner of speaking may change rapidly during a given test and therefore become difficult to specify. Normally, for any one test condition, the talker shall try to maintain a uniform speech level by observing a vu (volume unit) meter[2] connected to his microphone. The talkers should try to repeat the carrier-sentence level pattern on the vu meter for each word spoken under a given condition. The speech level is defined as that of the meter readings on the three words "Would you write . . . ."[3] It is essential that the treatment of talker level during the tests be explicitly stated in the report.

2.5.2 *Listener Levels.* The considerations that apply to talker levels also apply in the setting and the measurement of the level of received speech. Again, two principal conditions arise, and the decision as to the best procedure must rest upon the particular purpose of the intelligibility test. In many cases the listener level will be determined by the

experimenter. If the equipment provides a control at the listener position for readily resetting the listening level, or if there is a special reason associated with the object of the test to permit resetting, then the levels for each condition of listening should be measured and included in the report. A change in listener level should not ordinarily be made during the reception of a single word list. However, exceptions to this rule may be advisable under particular conditions. For example, the interfering noise may fluctuate considerably from one test word to the next, and consequently maximum intelligibility scores might result only when the listener is allowed to readjust his level of received speech. In another instance, the talker level may vary because of some experimental variable, and the listener may be instructed to readjust his level for optimum reception. The details of these procedures and the results of measurements of listener levels should be given in the report of the intelligibility test results.

2.6 **Ambient Noise Fields.** Ambient noise fields shall be of a diffuse nature and shall be uniform throughout the testing area. Anomalies due to standing wave patterns shall be avoided. For certain tests special room characteristics may be required. In all cases the room characteristics shall be reported. The over-all noise level at the subject positions should be measured with an instrument meeting the requirements of American Standard Sound Level Meters for Measurement of Noise and Other Sounds, Z24.3-1944. (See Section 3.) The weighting curve and position of the microphone, of the sound level meter, and the noise spectrum should also be reported. For maximum usefulness of the results, the reverberation time and a measure of the uniformity of noise spectrum and level and of the diffuseness of the noise should be given, as well as the size and shape of the room.

In subjecting the participants to noise, reference should be made to the standard for estimates of safe limits, which it is hoped will be developed as a result of the Z24-X-2 report, "The Relations of Hearing Loss to Noise Exposure," published by the American Standards Association, Incorporated. Sessions should be sufficiently short so that bias due to fatigue will be avoided.

2.7 **Experimental Design.** In so far as is possible the various required tests shall be conducted in random order.[4] The arrangement shall be such as to give the most economical experiment, and to permit use

---

[2] See American Standard Practice for Volume Measurements of Electrical Speech and Program Waves, C16.5-1954.

[3] The average level of the key words is not the same as the average level of the first three words of the carrier sentence. When the first three words of the carrier sentence are set at 0 vu, the key words typically range from −10 to +2 vu, but average about −4 vu.

[4] For assistance in randomization, reference may be made to a standard text, e.g., EDWARDS, A. L., *Experimental Design in Psychological Research.* New York: Rinehart & Co., 1950.

of analysis of variance techniques to measure the significance of variations in data resulting from such parameters as talkers, listeners, systems, noise levels, arrangements, days, etc. Limitations on the randomization are permissible where required to avoid complicating the experiment unduly, and to avoid introducing possible bias due to such effects as (1) a run in quiet immediately after a run in high noise with the same subjects; or (2) the same word list used in two different randomizations in successive runs with the same subjects, etc.

2.8 System Usage. During the test, in so far as is possible, the system should be operated as it would be in actual practice. The following are examples of the decisions to be made:

2.8.1 For a telephone handset under evaluation, the transmitter should be either consistently covered or open during listening because, where sidetone (a channel through which the talker can hear his voice as picked up by the transmitter) is provided, noise entering the transmitter can mask the signal at the earphone.

2.8.2 Similarly, for a handset, the decision must be made whether the other ear shall be blocked or open.

2.8.3 For some microphones the distance from the talker's lips to the microphone affects the frequency response and directional characteristics; therefore, this distance will have to be decided upon; normally the manufacturer's recommendations should be followed.

It is often desirable to assign monitors to verify that the system is used in correct fashion by all subjects. The conventions adopted with respect to system usage should be included in the report.

2.9 Use of Recordings. When recorded word lists are used instead of a live talker, certain precautions such as the following should be observed:

In the recording of modified speech waves (e.g., differentiated or equalized to uniform spectrum) on equipment designed for normal speech waves, avoid overload at high frequencies resulting from the pre-emphasis normally provided in the recording amplifier.

The signal-to-noise ratio of the recording system should not be allowed to affect the results of the tests. Care should be taken that the use of recording and playback equipment does not result in either changed response-frequency characteristic, clipping, or other distortion. The experimental arrangement shall be described in the report.

2.10 Miscellaneous. An average of 15 key words per minute has been found satisfactory. The rate chosen should be uniformly maintained and should be reported.

Grading of results is best done by personnel other than the talkers or listeners. Experience has shown that errors of grading and differences between the accuracy of scorers can be important. Randomization or other protective means should be taken in scoring. If permanently employed scorers are used, random "spot" checking is recommended.

Monitors should observe that the correct word list is used and that the conditions of the test as to system, noise, etc., are in accord with the test program. They should also note any misreading of words and deviations from agreed-upon practice.

3. Revisions of American Standards Referred to in This Document

When the following American Standards referred to in this document are superseded by revisions approved by the American Standards Association, Incorporated, the revisions shall apply:

American Standard Sound Level Meters for Measurement of Noise and Other Sounds, Z24.3-1944

American Standard Specification for Audiometers for General Diagnostic Purposes, Z24.5-1951

[Editor's Note: The PB (Phonetically Balanced) monosyllabic word lists have been omitted.]

Reprinted from *Acoust. Soc. Am. J.* **30**(7):596–600 (1958)

Test of Phonemic Differentiation: The Rhyme Test

Grant Fairbanks

Speech Research Laboratory, University of Illinois, Urbana, Illinois

(Received March 10, 1958)

Materials are presented for a test of word identification in which the cues for response are confined to the initial consonants and consonant-vowel transitions. Some preliminary results are discussed.

THIS article describes a method for testing a restricted aspect of speech reception which may be referred to as *phonemic differentiation*. The test was motivated originally by need for experimental materials in which: (1) the spoken word would be the stimulus unit; (2) recognition of the word would be the response; (3) the response would depend upon the initial consonant and consonant-vowel transition; and (4) the subject's task would bear valid relation to the discrimination demands of real speech. In order that a reasonably parsimonious explanation of variance would be possible, it was desired that auditory-phonemic factors weigh heavily in the score, and that linguistic factors of higher order weigh lightly. Another requirement was that several different, but reasonably comparable forms be developed, so that subjects would remain naive with respect to vocabulary through a series of determinations. In addition, it was considered necessary that the test be short, convenient to administer, and suitable for groups.

DESIGN

The Rhyme Test is of the completion type. The stimulus words are drawn from the vocabulary of 250 common monosyllables shown in Table I. This vocabulary consists of 50 sets of five rhyming words each. To yield a single 50-item form, one word is drawn from each set. In the table the sets are shown in a usable random order that is the same for all forms. Various forms are indicated within Table I, and will be discussed below.

Within a set the five rhyming words differ in the initial consonant phoneme, in each case an element. The words of a set are also spelled alike in the rhyming portion ("stem"), and differ in the initial consonant spelling, in each case a single letter. Each spelled stem is unique. The subject's response sheet shows the 50 stems in order of stimulus, each preceded by a space in which he enters one letter to complete the spelling of the word (e.g., —ot, —ay, —op).[1] Copies of the same response sheet serve for different forms. Care has been taken to avoid spellings with variable pronunciation (e.g., *some-home, lose-pose-dose*, etc.), both within the

[1] We have found it convenient to arrange the stems in columns of 10, designated A, B, C, D, E, with a single numbering from 1 to 10 along the left margin. In the recorded versions mentioned below, the start of each column is identified by "Column A," etc. Individual items are not identified. We consider this preferable and have found it to be feasible.

stimulus words and among the possible response words outside the list. Thus, each spelled stem denotes an unmistakable class of words. Instructions are simple. The subject is told, with a couple of illustrations, that he will hear 50 words that are spelled in order on the sheet, each with its first letter omitted, and that he is to write in the letters as he hears the words. The literacy demand is close to minimal, probably less than that imposed by reading the alternatives in a multiple-choice test.

In constructing the materials, the first consideration was to pick sets that would provide, within the constraints mentioned, a number of possible *response words* for each stem, from which were to be selected five *stimulus words* for each stem that rank high in familiarity, five being the number of matched forms.

The total vocabulary of possible responses corresponding to the 50 stems finally chosen, i.e., the English words formed by one-letter additions to the stems, is estimated as 536. The matrix shows a range of 6 to 16 response words among the 50 stems, with a median of 11. When words of low stability in the working language (regional, archaic, and obscene words, rare slang, rare names) are excluded, the test taps a vocabulary of about 475 words. From words of this kind it is likely that the typical stem offers the average adult a choice of 8 to 9 alternatives. For example, the first stem would be likely to offer *cot, dot, got, hot, lot, not, pot, rot*; in most cases *jot, sot* and *tot* would also be expected, *wot* rarely. This is a larger number of alternatives than is practical in a multiple-choice test. It will be noted that the chance probability is determined by the personal vocabulary of the subject, but remains constant for him from form to form.

Selection of the stimulus words was guided by the data of Thorndike and Lorge.[2] The cumulative distribution is shown in Table II. According to that count, the 250 stimulus words are among the 9000 most frequent words of the language, 200 are among the most frequent 3000, and 112 are among the most frequent 1000. The 112 from the first 1000 are distributed among 46 of the rhyming sets; five sets consist entirely of such words. Each of the 50 sets has at least three words among the most common 4000.

The stimulus vocabulary involves 18 consonant phonemes, and their distribution is given in Table III.

[2] E. L. Thorndike and I. Lorge, *The Teacher's Word Book of 30,000 Words* (Columbia University Press, New York, 1944).

According to the data of French, Carter, and Koenig,[3] these 18 consonants account for approximately 90% of all consonant occurrences in the language. The remaining seven are eliminated by the design; /ŋ/ and /ʒ/ occur only finally, while /θ/, /ð/, /ʃ/, /tʃ/, and /hw/ take two-letter spellings, which were excluded in the interests of simplifying the response. The rank-difference correlation between order of frequency of initial consonants in the test (the order in Table III) and total occurrences (all positions) in the language is 0.65, including in the calculation the seven consonants absent

TABLE II. Cumulative distribution of word frequency, based on count of Thorndike and Lorge.[3]

Most common: (×1000)	N
9	250
8	247
7	244
6	242
5	233
4	217
3	200
2	165
1	112

TABLE I. Stimulus vocabulary. Columns: five comparable forms, matched in phonemic distributions and word familiarity. Italics: Form RT-F, biased with high word familiarity. Asterisks: Form RT-P, matched to consonant distribution of language.

	RT-1	RT-2	RT-3	RT-4	RT-5
1.	hot	got	*not	pot	lot
2.	pay	may	*day	way	say
3.	*top	hop	pop	mop	cop
4.	peel	reel	feel	*heel	keel
5.	wake	*take	make	cake	lake
6.	*law	saw	jaw	paw	raw
7.	*vile	mile	file	tile	pile
8.	*neat	seat	beat	heat	meat
9.	look	cook	hook	*took	book
10.	fill	*kill	will	till	bill
11.	*tire	hire	sire	fire	wire
12.	male	tale	*sale	pale	bale
13.	sent	rent	*went	bent	tent
14.	*moon	noon	coon	boon	soon
15.	kick	*sick	lick	tick	pick
16.	same	fame	name	*came	game
17.	*wide	tide	*lip	ride	hide
18.	rip	dip	*lip	hip	tip
19.	sore	bore	tore	*more	wore
20.	bang	*hang	sang	gang	rang
21.	men	den	hen	pen	*ten
22.	park	bark	lark	mark	*dark
23.	coil	foil	boil	*soil	toil
24.	big	wig	*dig	fig	pig
25.	rage	cage	*page	sage	wage
26.	cast	past	*fast	last	mast
27.	gain	pain	main	rain	*vain
28.	nest	west	test	best	*rest
29.	gun	nun	*run	sun	fun
30.	heal	deal	seal	*zeal	meal
31.	sin	*win	tin	din	pin
32.	bust	just	*must	rust	dust
33.	fine	mine	wine	*nine	line
34.	mink	link	*pink	wink	sink
35.	sold	*told	hold	cold	gold
36.	hit	sit	wit	*fit	bit
37.	*led	bed	red	wed	fed
38.	tend	*send	bend	lend	mend
39.	rid	bid	*kid	did	hid
40.	*back	lack	pack	jack	sack
41.	*tail	sail	mail	nail	fail
42.	fight	light	right	might	*night
43.	torn	worn	*born	horn	corn
44.	rod	*god	cod	sod	nod
45.	dock	mock	cock	lock	*rock
46.	bump	pump	lump	dump	*jump
47.	*date	rate	gate	late	hate
48.	well	fell	*tell	bell	sell
49.	set	let	get	*yet	met
50.	*luck	tuck	duck	suck	buck

TABLE III. Distributions of consonants and vowels in the stimulus vocabulary. Descending orders.

Consonants		Vowels	
/s/	27	/ɪ/	40
/t/	22	/e/	40
/b/	22	/ɛ/	35
/m/	21	/ɑ/	25
/l/	19	/ɑɪ/	25
/p/	18	/ʌ/	20
/r/	17	/i/	15
/w/	17	/æ/	15
/k/	16	/ɔ/	15
/h/	16	/ʊ/	5
/f/	15	/u/	5
/d/	13	/o/	5
/n/	10	/ɔɪ/	5
/g/	9		
/dʒ/	4		
/v/	2		
/j/	1		
/z/	1		

from the test. The distribution of the 13 vowels and diphthongs in the stems is also shown in Table III. The most ubiquitous vowel, /ə/, is excluded by restricting the words to isolated monosyllables, and /ɝ/, /ʒ/, ɑʊ/, and /ju/ are also absent. Occurrences of /e/ and /ʌ/ are relatively high in the order, but the main characteristic of the vowel distribution is that it is somewhat flatter then in the language.

The consonant-vowel transitions in the stimulus vocabulary were also tabulated, but the diversity was such that they need not be reported in detail. Among the 250 words, 129 different CV combinations were found, 63 of them occurring once only. The most frequent are /bɛ/, /tɛ/, /se/, /me/, and /wɪ/, each with five words. The total number of different combinations is 55% of the possible number for the 18 consonants and 13 vowels, and 31% of those possible in English (using 23C×18V and ignoring incompatibilities). It is concluded that transitions are adequately represented and that there are no undue biases. The diversity, incidentally, has some interesting possibilities for comparison. For example, /s/ is combined with 12 different vowels and diphthongs, /b/ with 11, /t/, /m/, /k/, /h/ with 10 each. The eight sets of words with /e/ involve 15 different initial consonants, the seven with /ɛ/ involve 14, etc.

[3] French, Carter, and Koenig, Bell System Tech. J. 9, 290 (1930).

TABLE IV. VU readings of the recorded version.

VU	RT-1	RT-2	RT-3	RT-4	RT-5	Total
0	5	6	8	7	8	34
−1	14	18	15	14	13	74
−2	22	16	18	17	18	91
−3	6	9	9	10	8	42
−4	3	1	0	2	3	9

RECORDED VERSION AND RESULTS IN NOISE

A version of the stimulus materials has been recorded on tape, with the author as speaker, and given some experimental trial. The words were spoken in isolation, clearly, naturally, and with average vocal effort. Because of the effect of vocal effort upon the consonant-vowel ratio,[4] reasonable uniformity was considered important, especially with a test of this kind. An attempt to keep the effort uniform was facilitated through use of a regular 5-sec respiratory cycle, established by light flashes, with one word uttered at the beginning of the expiratory phase of each cycle. Rhyming words were spoken consecutively and the entire list was completed without stopping. No metering was employed. The recording was made on Magnecord M-90 equipment at 7.5 ips; an Altec M-11 microphone system was used. The distribution of VU readings for the total vocabulary is shown in the last column of Table IV. The measurements were of the master version and were made with a Daven 911-B meter, reading the vowel maxima rounded to the midpoints shown. The table shows the distribution to be within a range of 5 db with a mild negative skew. The middle 125 words are within 1.5 db by interpolation.

The recorded test was studied in the following manner. The master version was divided into five stimulus tapes. The five words of each set were ordered at random and one word assigned to each tape. The same random order of sets was used for all tapes. The subjects were 40 university students, divided into two main groups of 20 (A and B), with each group divided further into five subgroups of four. With Group A five vowel-to-noise ratios, ranging from 2 to −6 db in 2-db steps, were used to bracket the point of 50% identification. For a given subgroup one tape was assigned to each V/N ratio, and the five tapes administered in a single descending series with brief rest between tapes. Each subject thus was exposed to the complete vocabulary once. Assignment of tapes to V/N ratios was varied across the subgroups in a systematic Latin square, so that all words and subjects were represented equally at each ratio. The procedure with Group B was identical, except that ratios of 15, 9, 5, 1, and −2 db were used. These were chosen to span the upper part of the identification range and overlap the values for Group A, repeating one ratio, −2 db. All tapes were administered at the same level, with the median vowel

[4] G. Fairbanks and M. S. Miron, J. Acoust. Soc. Am. 29, 621 (1957).

about 65 db above threshold. Noise (0–20 000 cps) from a Grason-Stadler generator was adjusted re the medians of the individual tapes. PDR-10 headsets were used; presentation was by subgroups of four; the method of response was as described earlier.

The results are presented in Table V. The progressions are regular, and the means from the two groups agree very satisfactorily in the range of overlap. It will be noted that from 9 db to −6 db, word recognition declined in an approximately linear manner with vowel-to-noise ratio. The slope is about 3% per db. This is similar to that usually found with PB words in noise and to that of gain functions with PBs in quiet, suggesting that the heterogeneity of the Rhyme Test might be equally suitable for discrimination functions. As would be expected from the nature of the task, the scores appear to be somewhat higher than those obtained with PBs in noise, possibly around 15% over the range studied. For 50% identification the difference should be about 5 db. In interpreting Table V it should be remembered that the ratios were established re the vowels. The average consonant-vowel ratio was probably around −15 db for the level of effort employed by the speaker.

The procedure was not planned for detailed comparison of the five random lists. At each V/N ratio, each list was heard by a different subgroup. It is possible, however, to make general comparisons by combining the data for each list, since all lists appeared at all ratios and were heard by all subjects. For the 20 subjects of Group A the lists ranged from 44 to 54% around a mean of 48%; for Group B (larger ratios) the range was 68 to 73% and the mean 71%. The grand mean for all 40 subjects was 60%, with the lists ranging from 57 to 64%. Variations of this size correspond to changes of about 2 to 3 db in V/N ratio (see Table V).

The ratio −2 db was used with both groups and yielded respective means of 49 and 51%. Thus it was possible to develop a score for each word from the responses of 8 subjects, at approximately the point of 50% identification of the mean word. These scores were pooled by consonant phonemes in order to explore their relative identifiability, the total number of responses per phoneme being 8 times the entry in Table III. The results of these tabulations are shown in Table VI,

TABLE V. Mean percentage correct for complete stimulus vocabulary at various V/N ratios. Twenty subjects in each group.

V/N (db)	Group A	Group B
15		89
9		84
5		73
2	64	
1		58
0	56	
−2	51	49
−4	38	
−6	33	

where the rank is a descending order of percentage correct. The findings are to be interpreted with due regard to the fact that only one speaker was used.

It will be seen that the over-all variation is three to one. Comparison of /m/ and /t/, both with substantial numbers of total responses, shows a difference of two to one. Each of the 21 words with /m/ was identified by at least 4 subjects; 15 of the 22 words with /t/ were identified by fewer than 4 subjects. The power of the phonemic factor is also shown by the range of variation within rhyming sets. For instance, in the first set of Table I, *hot*, etc., the words ranked 8, 8, 6, 4, 1 in number of correct identifications, a range of 7 subjects. The median range for the 50 sets was 5 subjects; in 45 sets the range was 4 subjects or greater.

Table VI also discloses that the phonemic differences are lawful as well as powerful. The nasal consonants are at the top of the order, and ⅔ of the voiceless consonants are in the bottom ⅓ of the order.[5] The following relationships may not be so evident.

$$/m/ > /n/$$
$$\lor \quad \lor$$
$$/g/ > /b/ > /d/$$
$$\lor \quad \lor \quad \lor$$
$$/k/ > /p/ > /t/$$
$$\land \quad \land$$
$$/f/ > /s/$$
$$\lor \quad \lor$$
$$/v/ = /z/$$

Rows and columns of the above arrangement designate features; within either, the contrast of any two adjacent members is minimal. A high degree of orderliness is evident in both dimensions. Probably the acoustical characteristics of the consonants *per se* are primary

TABLE VI. Mean percentage correct for the various consonants at V/N = -2 db. Descending order. Eight subjects.

	% Correct
/m/	76.2
/n/	62.3
/j/	62.3
/g/	61.1
/f/	59.2
/l/	55.9
/b/	52.3
/w/	52.2
/r/	49.3
/k/	44.5
/d/	43.3
/dʒ/	40.6
/s/	40.3
/p/	40.3
/h/	39.8
/t/	38.6
/v/	25.0
/z/	25.0

[5] Cf. G. A. Miller and P. E. Nicely, J. Acoust. Soc. Am. 27, 338 (1955). ". . . voicing and nasality are much less affected by a random masking noise than are the other features." Based on initial consonants followed by /ɑ/.

determinants of the vertical relationships, while the consonant-vowel transitions figure importantly in the horizontal progressions. This is an intriguing finding that should be followed up with more speakers. The data support the idea that the Rhyme Test intercepts the speech reception process at a stage in which a substantial portion of the variance in word identification is attributable to the distinctive features of phonemes. The systematic variations also justify the matching procedures described immediately below.

MATCHED FORMS AND SPECIAL FORMS

The columns of Table I indicate five test forms, designated as RT-1, etc., that are comparable in their phonemic distributions. As nearly as the numbers of total occurrences permit (see Table III), the distributions are matched. That is, the number of occurrences of a given consonant in any form does not differ from that in any other form by more than one. These one-word differences were offset as much as possible by "dovetailing" with similar consonants, so that the distributions of features are also comparable. After the consonants had been distributed, the CV transitions were examined. There appeared to be no undue bias. The 63 unique combinations are divided among the forms with a range of 11 to 14; the number of different combinations per form varies from 41 to 45; the maximum number of occurrences of one combination in any one form is three. The forms also are satisfactorily comparable in word frequency. They range from 20 to 27 words among the most common 1000. All 50 words of RT-3 are among the most common 6000; the form that differs most at that point has 47 words among the most common 6000. Table IV shows the distributions of VU readings for the RT forms, and the similarities will be noted. The five medians are within a range of 0.2 db by interpolation.

Two special forms are also indicated in Table I. Italics show a form, RT-F, that is loaded with familiar words and might be suitable for testing a child or semiliterate adult. All but four of the words are among the most common 1000. The other words are *sale*, *pink*, and *jump* in the second, and *luck* in the third 1000. In addition to high familiarity, RT-F meets the standards of phonemic distribution used with the numbered forms and tests 16 different consonants.

The asterisks in Table I indicate RT-P, a form that was drawn to approximate the consonant distribution reported by French, Carter, and Koenig.[6] This form includes all 18 consonants of Table III, and the rank-difference correlation between their frequency and that of all consonants in the language is 0.86. Familiarity was also a condition of selection. All words are in the first 5000, 48 in the first 3000, 41 in the first 1000. RT-P and RT-F have 34 words in common.

It will not be overlooked that a variety of other forms may be drawn which control the distributions of consonants or consonant-vowel transitions in particular ways. Study of the sets will show that one form with 48 voiceless consonants, another with no voiceless consonants, and another with 43 voiceless fricatives, for example, are possible. By subscoring, forms with controlled distributions of features should have considerable utility in analytic studies of individuals and systems. One such form might consist of 25 voiced and 25 voiceless consonants, the two halves being matched with respect to the other features. Among persons with hearing loss, degree of loss might be correlated with the voiced subscore and type of loss with the difference between the voiced and voiceless subscores, etc. Finally, it should be mentioned that the Rhyme Test stems may be used with an extended stimulus vocabulary that can serve various special purposes. Consonant phonemes that take two-letter spellings, consonant clusters, rare words, etc., are examples of controls that may be exerted within the same format.

ACKNOWLEDGMENTS

The author is grateful to Anthony Holbrook and Murray S. Miron for technical assistance. He is also indebted to the latter for conducting the experimental trials.

Reprinted from *Acoust. Soc. Am. J.* **42**(3):609–612 (1967)

Use of a Sequential Strategy in Intelligibility Testing

H. Levitt and L. R. Rabiner

Bell Telephone Laboratories, Incorporated, Murary Hill, New Jersey 07971

In a recent experiment involving intelligibility testing, the response curve (intelligibility function) was found to flatten off sharply at moderately high intelligibilities. A sequential strategy of the up–down-transformed-response (UDTR) type was used in order to concentrate observations in the symmetric region of the curve. The transformed-response curve showed the departure from symmetry at a much higher intelligibility level. Precision of estimation for the 50% level was found to be higher than for the simple up-and-down procedure. The technique is designed for situations in which it is difficult or impossible to vary the step size.

IN a recent experiment,[1] it was required that the signal level corresponding to 50% intelligibility be measured rapidly and efficiently. Preliminary trials showed that the intelligibility function was typically of the form shown in Fig. 1. The curves tended to flatten at relatively high intelligibility levels, i.e., 100% intelligibility was never obtained. Fitting a curve to such data can be difficult. One approach is to assume that the flattening is due to extraneous random errors independent of the main effect. A "correction factor" is determined from the estimated asymptote and a symmetric ogive fitted to the adjusted data using conventional procedures. Although this approach has the merit that it reduces the problem to a well-known form, it is, nevertheless, unsatisfactory for at least two reasons. The use of a correction factor is difficult to justify on theoretical grounds. The factors that prevent 100% intelligibility from being achieved can hardly be considered random, independent effects for which a "correction" is necessary. On practical grounds, the correction procedure is not recommended since it depends on the estimated asymptote and is subject to experimental error.

A sequential strategy of the up–down type appears eminently suited to a problem of this kind. Briefly, the simple up-and-down procedure[2] operates as follows. A word (the stimulus) is presented to the subject at a given signal-to-noise ratio. If a correct response is obtained, i.e., the subject correctly identifies the word, the signal-to-noise (S/N) ratio is decreased by a fixed amount. If an incorrect response is obtained, the S/N ratio is increased by the same fixed amount (the step size). As the procedure is repeated the choice of S/N ratio converges on that value at which 50% of the responses are correct. A sequence of changes in S/N

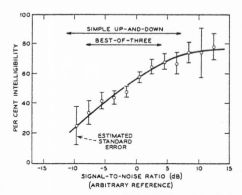

FIG. 1. Typical response curve. The curve is typical of the data obtained in the experiment of Levitt and Rabiner (1966). Intelligibilities above 80% were seldom obtained. The curve was fitted by eye. The arrows show the average range of the observations using the simple up-and-down and best-of-three procedures.

[1] H. Levitt and L. R. Rabiner, "Binaural Masking-Level Differences and Improvements in Intelligibility," J. Acoust. Soc. Am. **39**, 1232(A) (1966).

[2] W. J. Dixon and A. M. Mood, "A Method for Obtaining and Analyzing Sensitivity Data," J. Am. Statist. Assoc. **43**, 109–126 (1948).

TABLE I. Strategies for estimating midpoint. Several strategies of the UDTR type for estimating the 50% level are shown. $+$ represents a positive response; $-$ represents a negative response. The probability of a positive response is p.

Strategy	Possible response sequences		Probability of decreasing S/N
	Decrease S/N	Increase S/N	
Simple up-and-down	$+$	$-$	p
Best-of-three	$++, -++, +-+.$	$--, +--, -+-.$	$p^2(3-2p)$
Best-of-five	$+++,$ $++-+, +-++, -+++,$ $++--+, +-+-+, -++-+,$ $+--++, -+-++, --+++.$	$---,$ $+---, -+--, --+-,$ $++--, +-+--, +--+-,$ $-++--, -+-+-, --++-.$	$p^3(10-15p+6p^2)$
Best-of-seven	All permutations of 4 $+$ responses and 3 or less $-$ responses, ending with a $+$ response.	All permutations of 4 $-$ responses and 3 or less $+$ responses, ending with a $-$ response.	$p^4(35-84p+70p^2-20p^3)$

ratio in the same direction is defined as a run. The midpoint of a run is an estimate of the 50% intelligibility level. Not only does this technique ensure that observations are concentrated in the region of interest, resulting in greater precision of estimation, but it is not necessary to make any parametric assumptions about the response curve (i.e., intelligibility function). A necessary restriction is that intelligibility increase monotonically with S/N ratio.

In the particular example considered here, it is important that as many observations as possible be placed in the symmetric region of the response curve ($20\% < p < 80\%$). Frequent excursions out of this region not only reduce efficiency, but may bias the resulting estimates substantially. A highly efficient procedure is to use a large step size in order to get close to the 50% level and then gradually reduce the step size for subsequent estimates.[3] For a very small step size, several long and highly improbable runs would be required in order to get away from the 50% region of the curve. On the other hand, once outside the desired region, many observations would be wasted in order to return. It is also often not practical or convenient to vary the step size during an experiment.

An alternative procedure is to use a sequential strategy of the up–down-transformed-response (UDTR) type.[4] According to this procedure, response sequences are classified into two mutually exclusive and exhaustive groups; an "increase-S/N" group and a "decrease-S/N" group (see Table I). The procedure follows the simple up-and-down rule except that the S/N ratio is changed only after a response sequence belonging to one of the two groups is obtained. Several strategies of the UDTR type that converge on the 50% level are shown in Table I.

[3] H. Robbins and S. Monro, "A Stochastic Approximation Method," Ann. Math. Statist. 22, 400–407 (1951).
[4] G. B. Wetherill and H. Levitt, "Sequential Estimation of Points on a Psychometric Function," Brit. J. Math. Statist. Psychol. 18, 1–8 (1965).

The term "transformed response" is used in a statistical sense. If p is the probability of a correct response, then for the simple up-and-down procedure, p is also the probability of decreasing S/N ratio at the next presentation of the stimulus. For the UDTR procedure, the probability of decreasing S/N ratio at the next change in S/N ratio is a function of p and is dependent on the grouping of the response sequences. Consider, for example, the best-of-three method shown in Table I. Let a correct response be represented by $+$ and an incorrect response by $-$. The response sequences belonging to the decrease-S/N group are $++$, $+-+$, and $-++$. The probability of a response sequence belonging to this group is, therefore, $p^2+p^2(1-p)+p^2(1-p)$, which reduces to $p^2(3-2p)$. Hence, for the best-of-three method, the probability of decreasing S/N ratio at the next change in S/N ratio is $p^2(3-2p)$, as opposed to p for the simple up-and-down procedure.

Conceptually, it is convenient to think of sequential strategies of the UDTR type as being identical to the simple up-and-down procedure, except that in this case, a "response" (i.e., the transformed response) is defined as a sequence of single $+$ or $-$ responses. The effect of grouping response sequences is clearly seen in terms of the *transformed response curve*, i.e., the probability of decreasing the S/N ratio (at the next change) versus S/N ratio. The transformed-response curves for the strategies listed in Table I are shown in Fig. 2. The original (untransformed) response curve is assumed to be cumulative normal, truncated at the 80% level. The transformed curves are very nearly cumulative normal and truncated well above the 80% level. The slope is also increased by the transformation. A cumulative normal was chosen for purposes of illustration; the transformation is similar in form for other s-shaped response curves.

The performance of an UDTR strategy on the transformed-response curve is identical to that of the simple up-and-down strategy on the original (untransformed) response curve. The UDTR strategy, for example, will

TABLE II. Comparison of estimation procedures. The average range and estimated standard errors are shown for the simple up-and-down and best-of-three strategies. The estimated standard error was obtained from an analysis of variance on the data for each subject.

Subject	Strategy	Estimated standard error (dB)	Average range (dB)
DB	Simple up-and-down	0.89	16.2
DB	Best-of-three	0.83	10.3
HL	Simple up-and-down	0.94	16.7
HL	Best-of-three	1.00	12.5
AER	Simple up-and-down	1.14	19.2
AER	Best-of-three	1.08	11.5

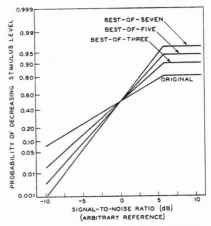

FIG. 2. Transformed response curves. The original response curve was assumed to be cumulative normal, truncated at the 80% level. The transformed response curves are very nearly cumulative normal and are truncated at a much higher level. The transformations are listed in Table I.

converge on the 50% level of the transformed-response curve (which need not be the 50% level of the untransformed curve). For the strategies considered here, the 50% level of each of the transformed-response curves is identical to that of the original response curve, hence, all these strategies converge on the untransformed 50% intelligibility level. Since the transformed-response curves truncate at a higher level, it is less likely that observations will be placed outside the symmetric region of the response curve. The strategies considered here have the practical advantage that the step size is fixed.

An important feature of the UDTR procedure is its generality. A variety of up–down strategies (for example, Zwislocki's[5] forced-choice tracking method and Campbell's[6] BUDTIFF method) may be analyzed within this framework. Although the UDTR procedure was developed primarily for estimating points on a response curve other than the 50% level, the example given here shows that the technique need not be restricted to this application.

The particular strategy used in this investigation was the second listed in Table I, i.e., the best-of-three. In starting each test, a coarse estimate of the 50% level was obtained by presenting the first word at a high S/N ratio and reducing level in large, double steps (4 dB) until the first change in response type was obtained, after which a fixed step size of 2 dB was employed. A standard Grason–Stadler recording attenuator was used, the experimenter activating the "increase attenuation" or "decrease attenuation" control according to the subject's responses. The mean value of all the runs, other than the first two, obtained in a single test was used as an estimate of the 50% level for that test. The first two runs were omitted in order to reduce starting errors. Seventy-five words, randomly selected

from two lists of 50 phonetically balanced CNC words[7] were used in each test.

A comparison was made between the best-of-three technique and the simple up-and-down method. Eight tests for each method and for each of three subjects were carried out. The results (Table II) showed that the best-of-three method was not only more effective in restricting observations to the 50% region, but was also more efficient than the simple-up-down method in estimating the 50% level. The average range (max–min value, excluding the first run) of the observations for the best-of-three method was on the order of 12 dB, whereas, for the simple up-and-down technique, the range was nearly 18 dB. The standard error of the midpoint estimate for the best-of-three method was also slightly smaller on average. This result is not surprising since efficient estimation of points on a response curve requires that observations be placed as close as possible to the point being estimated. A disadvantage of the transformed-response procedure is that more observations are required per run and, therefore, the relative cost of discarding early or incomplete runs is greater. A poor initial estimate will result in a lengthy first run, hence, it is recommended that a rough estimate of the 50% level be obtained prior to using the best-of-three method. The simple up-and-down procedure[2] may be convenient for this purpose.

[5] J. Zwislocki, F. Maire, A. S. Feldman, and H. Rubin, "On the Effect of Practice and Motivation on the Threshold of Audibility," J. Acoust. Soc. Am. 30, 254–262 (1958).

[6] R. A. Campbell, "Detection of a Noise Signal of Varying Duration," J. Acoust. Soc. Am. 35, 1732–1737 (1963).

[7] G. E. Peterson and I. Lehiste, "Revised CNC Lists for Auditory Tests," J. Speech and Hearing Disorders 27, 62–70 (1962).

A brief study of the best-of-three technique in another context is reported by Wetherill[8] (see Routine 5) who carried out empirical sampling trials on several strategies for estimating the 50% level. Of four strategies that were compared, including the simple up-and-down procedure, (ibid, Table 22) the best-of-three method showed the smallest mean-square error, given a reasonably accurate initial estimate.

Sequential procedures offer many advantages that

may be of value in intelligibility testing as well as in other areas of subjective testing. In the example given here, a method for reducing the spread of observations about the 50% intelligibility level has been described. The technique is both efficient and practical, and does not require any change in step size (although this modification can also be used).

ACKNOWLEDGMENTS

We wish to thank Dr. J. L. Flanagan, Dr. M. Treisman, and Dr. J. L. Hall for their constructive criticism.

[8] G. B. Wetherill, "Sequential Estimation of Quantal Response Curves," J. Roy. Statist. Soc. B25, 1–48 (1963).

19

Reprinted from *Percept. Psychophysiol.* **13**:131–132 (1973)

Speech identification and "knowing that you know"*

LARRY HOCHHAUS† and JAMES R. ANTES

Iowa State University, Ames, Iowa 50010

Twenty-five Ss heard a random list and a context (food-related) list of 50 words masked in white noise for a total of three trials each. The Ss were required to write the word and indicate their certainty that it was correct. Confidence rating accuracy (Type 2 d′) was greater for context than for random lists (p < .001). Probability correct also improved with context (p < .001). Unlike the context factor, repetitions led to greater probability correct (p < .001) but did not lead to changes in Type 2 d′. The results were interpreted as support for a feedback model of context and confidence rating accuracy.

Lack of research and research techniques have hampered the understanding of what Tulving and Madigan (1970) feel is "one of the truly unique characteristics of human memory: its knowledge of its own knowledge [p. 477]." A means of investigating this highly cognitive phenomenon is, however, provided by a unique signal detection analysis. Confidence ratings applied to evocative responses (e.g., speech identifications, recall memory attempts) yield a "Type 2" signal detection analysis (Clarke, Birdsall, & Tanner, 1959). As such, the Type 2 d′ is an index of the ability to discriminate correct from incorrect responses. Here, then, is a way to study an S's "knowledge of his own knowledge."

In memory tasks, variables which affect retention do not affect recall rating accuracy (Bernbach, 1967), but in word identification tasks the Type 2 d′ increases with increasing speech-to-noise ratios (Pollack & Decker, 1958). The purpose of the present experiment was to investigate the effects of another factor (context) on confidence rating accuracy.

Bruce (1956) found that random words were more difficult to perceive than lists of words constrained contextually (e.g., parts of the body, things to eat). Perhaps context forms a feedback system which provides the listener with important "knowing that you know" information. To test this hypothesis, the Bruce experiment was repeated, adding the requirement that listeners additionally rate the confidence of each speech identification attempt. It was hypothesized that confidence rating accuracy (measured by the Type 2 d′) is greater for context than for random lists.

METHOD

Subjects

The Ss were 25 undergraduate students enrolled in the introductory psychology course at Iowa State University. All Ss received course credit for their participation.

Materials

Two lists of 50 words were constructed, a context (C) list of monosyllable food-related words and a random (R) list of monosyllable words matched word for word with the C list for frequency of occurrence in the language by the Thorndike-Lorge (1944) G list and for initial phoneme. The words were recorded at a constant level at 6-sec intervals onto one track of a Wollensak stereo tape recorder, with a break between lists. White noise was then recorded on the other track from a

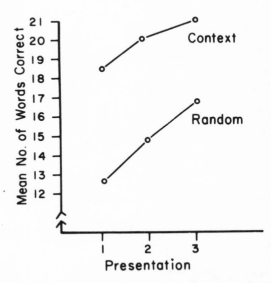

Fig. 1. Average number of words identified as a function of type of list and number of presentations.

*This research was supported, in part, by United States Public Health Service Research Grant MH 13192 to Wayne H. Bartz.
†Now at Oklahoma State University, Stillwater, Oklahoma 74074.

Table 1
Analysis of Variance Summary

Source	df	MS	F
Conditions (C)	1	977.92	77.12*
Repetitions (R)	2	137.00	10.80‡
C by R	2	9.85	.78
Ss	24	71.10	5.61

Significant at the .01 level; ‡significant at the .001 level

Grason-Stadler noise generator. The speech-to-noise ratio was adjusted to about 25% intelligibility for three trial Ss. This recording was then transcribed onto a Bell and Howell monaural tape recorder.

Procedure

Up to six Ss were seated at a common distance from the tape recorder speaker. Each list was presented alternately for a total of three times. The Ss were told only that they would hear six lists of 50 words. They were not told how many different lists there were. They were instructed to write the word they heard on a prepared sheet and to indicate their certainty that the response was correct by circling a number, 1-5, adjacent to the answer blank. A response of 5 indicated "very certain" and 1 indicated "very uncertain." The Ss were encouraged to respond to every word unless they had absolutely no response, in which case they marked an "X" in the blank. There was a short rest between lists for collection of response sheets and distribution of new ones.

RESULTS

The results, summarized by Fig. 1, were in general agreement with those of Bruce (1956). Although Bruce dismissed any repetition effect as insignificant, the figure clearly suggests one. An analysis of variance, shown in Table 1, indicates a repetition effect significant at the

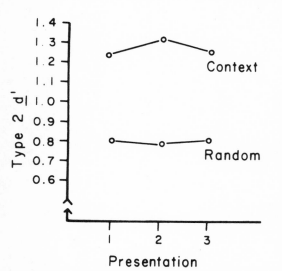

Fig. 2. Type 2 d' values as a function of type of list and number of presentations.

.001 level. The difference in the two conditions is also significant at the .001 level.

The table of Hochhaus (1972) was used to compute the values of Type 2 d' summarized by Fig. 2. The G test of Gourevitch and Galanter (1967) showed that Type 2 d' is greater for C than for R lists (p < .001), while repetitions did not affect this index (p > .10 for each of six comparisons).

DISCUSSION

There are two possible explanations for the significant repetition effect while Bruce (1956) reported none. One possibility lies in the fact that Bruce used only nine Ss. Second, the effect might conceivably be the result of the particular speech-to-noise ratio used in the present study. Subsequent studies should try more than one speech-to-noise ratio and look for a Repetition by Ratio interaction.

The finding that repeated presentations do not improve confidence rating accuracy is consistent with the results of memory experiments. Bernbach (1967) found that repetitions of paired-associate study trials did not change Type 2 d' based on recall responses, although repetitions led to better recall. It is interesting, however, that repetitions do not improve performance in a fashion analogous to changes in the speech-to-noise ratio. Pollack and Decker (1958) found that increases in the S/N ratio led to improvement in both probability correct and d'.

Also, the fact that repetitions do not change d' rules out an alternative interpretation of the higher context d' given in terms of changes in probability correct. Therefore, the context effect appears real and is taken as support for the hypothesis that contextual feedback provides a basis for "knowing that you know."

REFERENCES

Bernbach, H. A. Decision processes in memory. *Psychological Review,* 1967, 74, 462-480.

Bruce, D. J. Effects of context upon the intelligibility of heard speech. In C. Cherry (Ed.), *Information theory: Third London symposium.* London: Butterworth, 1956. Pp. 245-252.

Clarke, F. R., Birdsall, T. G., & Tanner, W. P., Jr. Two types of ROC curves and definitions of parameters. *Journal of the Acoustical Society of America,* 1959, 31, 629-630.

Gourevitch, V., & Galanter, P. A significance test for one parameter isosensitivity functions. *Psychometrika,* 1967, 32, 25-33.

Hochhaus, L. A table for the calculation of d' and β. *Psychological Bulletin,* 1972, 77, 375-376.

Pollack, I., & Decker, L. R. Confidence rating, message reception, and the receiver operating characteristic. *Journal of the Acoustical Society of America,* 1958, 30, 286-292.

Thorndike, E. L., & Lorge, I. *The teacher's word book of 30,000 words.* New York: Bureau of Publications, Teachers College, Columbia University, 1944.

Tulving, E., & Madigan, S. A. Memory and verbal learning. *Annual Review of Psychology,* 1970, 21, 437-484.

Part V

APPLICATIONS TO ARCHITECTURAL ACOUSTICS

Editor's Comments
on Papers 20 and 21

20 BOLT and MacDONALD
Theory of Speech Masking by Reverberation

21 CAVANAUGH et al.
Excerpt from *Speech Privacy in Buildings*

Greek theaters are famous, even to tourists today, for their acoustics, especially for speech, but it is unlikely that the architects used intelligibility tests. Shankland (1973) comments, "No written evidence has been found to suggest deliberate architectural design objectives relating seating geometry and acoustics, and it appears probable that the architect was concerned primarily with visual requirements." Knudsen, in the citations given in Part I, seems to have been the first to use intelligibility techniques extensively for measuring the performance of halls. The tests are not widely used now for this purpose, and there are few papers in the literature on the results of the tests. Most architectural consultants design to a reverberation curve as an objective and avoid strong echos of more than fifty milliseconds. If they achieve these goals, they can be reasonably confident that the speech intelligibility will be satisfactory. The tests are expensive, difficult to control in a hall, and do little to change the opinion of the users. Therefore, this is the briefest section in this book. Paper 20 by Bolt and MacDonald explains the relationship of room acoustics to intelligibility by use of the AI method. Nordlund (1968) gives a good description of contemporary techniques for making intelligibility measurements. The paper by Haas (1951) has given his name to the precedence effect by which sound seems to come from the direction from which it is first received, even if, within limits, the same sound, received later from another direction, is more intense. The effect was first noted by Joseph Henry in the nineteenth century and is used today in delayed speech reinforcement systems.

An interesting and general application of intelligibility principles has been to the design for privacy, where the objective is to *prevent* intelligible listening. Bürolandschaft designs for offices with open plenums and few ceiling-high partitions are common problems. The long paper by Cavanaugh et al. is the classic in this field, so the pertinent portion is reproduced here as Paper 21. Pirn (1971) and Warnock (1973) have continued to develop the application of the AI method to the speech privacy situation.

BIBLIOGRAPHY

Anonymous, *Proceedings of the Symposium on Speech Intelligibility*, Liège (1973).

Beranek, L. L., "Criteria for Office Quieting Based on Questionnaire Rating Studies," *J. Acoust. Soc. Am.* **28**:833–852 (1956).

Beranek, L. L., "Revised Criteria for Noise in Buildings," *Noise Control* **3**:19–27 (Jan. 1957).

Beranek, L. L., ed., *Noise Reduction*, McGraw-Hill, New York (1960).

Beranek, L. L., ed., *Noise and Vibration Control*, McGraw-Hill, New York (1971).

Choudhury, N. K. D., P. S. Bhandari, and R. K. Srivastava, "An Investigation on the Acoustical Conditions in Some School Buildings in Asia," *Acustica* **31**:119–123 (1974).

Erier, W., "Die Entwicklung eines Deutlichkeitsmessgerätes," *Hochfrequenztech. u. Elektroakust.* **65**:53–59 (Sept 1956).

Furrer, W., and A. Lauber, *Raum- und Bauakustik-Lärmabwehr*, 3rd ed., Birkhäuser, Basel (1972), 2nd ed. trans. as *Room and Building Acoustics and Noise Abatement*, Butterworths, Washington (1964).

Haas, H., "Über den Einfluss eines Einfachechos auf die Hörsamkeit von Sprache," *Acustica* **1**:49–58 (1951), trans. as "The Influence of a Single Echo on the Audibility of Speech," *J. Aud. Eng. Soc.* **20**:145–159 (1972).

Iida, S., "Tendency of Mishearing in Articulation Test," (L) *J. Acoust. Soc. Japan* **29**:527–534 (1973). in Japanese, figures labeled in English.

Jeffress, L. A., R. N. Lane, and F. Seay, "Articulation Scores for Two Similar, Reverberant Rooms, One with Polycylindrical Diffusers on Walls and Ceiling," *J. Acoust. Soc. Am.* **27**:787–788 (1955).

Klimesh, B., "Tests of Intelligibility of Czech Speech in Cinema Auditoriums with the Help of Syllable Legibility," *Sov. Phys.—Acoust.* **5**:426–430 (1960).

Korn, T. "Théorie generale de l'intelligibilité dans les salles," *Ann. Télécommun.* **5**:316–320 (1950).

Kuga, S., "Report on 'Articulation Test' on Three Well-Known Halls in Tokyo," *J. Acoust. Soc. Japan* **10**:271–281 (1954). in Japanese, abstract in English.

Kurtović, H. Š., "Contribution à la recherche de l'influence du son reflechi sur l'intelligibilité," G21 in *Proc. 5th Int. Cong. Acoust.* Liège (1965).

Lochner, J. P. A., and J. F. Burger, "The Intelligibility of Reinforced Speech," *Acustica* **9**:31–38 (1959).

Lochner, J. P. A., and J. F. Burger, "Optimum Reverberation Time for Speech Rooms Based on Hearing Characteristics," *Acustica* **10**:394–399 (1960).

Lochner, J. P. A., and J. F. Burger, "The Influence of Reflections on Auditorium Acoustics," *J. Sound Vib.* **1**:426–454 (1964).

Lochner, J. P. A., and P. Meffert, "Analysis of Reflection Patterns in Auditoria," *J. Acoust. Soc. Am.* **35**:1429–1431 (1963).

Moles, A., "Le taux d'intelligibilité en tant que critère de la qualité acoustique d'une salle," *Ann. Télécommun* **5**:57–64 (1950).

Moles, A., "L'Emploi de la reverberation artificielle dans le théâtre parlé," *Ann. Télécommun.* **6**:245–249 (1951).

Niese, H., "Vorschlag für die Definition und Messung der Deutlichkeit nach subjectiven Grundlagen," *Hochfrequenztech. u. Elektroakust.* **65**:4–15 (1956).

Niese, H., "Die Prüfung des raumakustischen 'Echograd-Kriteriums' mit Hilfe von Silbenverständlichkeitmessungen," *Hochfrequenztech. u. Elektroakust.* **66**:70–83 (1957).

Niese, H., "Die Messung der Nutzschall- und Echogradverteilung zur Beurteilung der Hörsamkeit in Räumen," *Acustica* **11**:201–213 (1961).

Nordlund, B., T. Kihlman, and S. Lindblad, "Use of Articulation Tests in Auditorium Studies," *J. Acoust. Soc. Am.* **44**:148–157 (1968).

Papathanasopoulos, B., "Akustische Messungen im Theater von Epidauros," G45 in *Proc. 5th Int. Cong. Acoust.*, Liège (1965).

Peutz, V. M. A., "Articulation Loss of Consonants as a Criterion for Speech Transmission in a Room," *J. Aud. Eng. Soc.* **19**:915–919 (1971).

Pirn, R., "Acoustical Variables in Open Planning," *J. Acoust. Soc. Am.* **49**:1339–1345 (1971).

Pujolle, J., "Definition d'un indice d'intelligibilité de la parole dans les salles," *Ann. Télécommun.* **4**:325–328 (1949).

Ramakrishna, B. S., and T. I. Smits, "Acoustics of Northrop Memorial Auditorium," *J. Acoust. Soc. Am.* **47**:951–960 (1970).

Ross, M., "Classroom Acoustics and Speech Intelligibility," in *Handbook of Clinical Audiology*, J. Katz, ed., Williams & Wilkins, Baltimore (1972), pp. 756–771.

Seraphim, H. -P., "Über die Wahrnehmbarkeit mehrerer Rückwürfe von Sprachschall," *Acustica* **11**:80–91 (1961).

Shankland, R. S., "Acoustics of Greek Theatres," *Phys. Today* **26**:30–35 (Oct. 1973).

Tolk, J., and V. M. A. Peutz, "Speech Intelligibility in Reverberant Rooms," A52 in *Proc. 5th Int. Cong. Acoust.* Liège (1965).

Vermeulen, R., "Auditorium Acoustics and Intelligibility," *Phillips Tech. Rev.* **3**:139–146 (1938).

Warnock, A. C. C., "Acoustical Privacy in the Landscaped Office," *J. Acoust. Soc. Am.* **53**:1535–1543 (1973).

Yamaguchi, K., "Multivariate Analysis of Subjective and Physical Measures of Hall Acoustics," *J. Acoust. Soc. Am.* **52**:1271–1279 (1972).

Young, R. W., "Re-Vision of the Speech-Privacy Calculation," *J. Acoust. Soc. Am.* **38**:524–530 (1965).

Reprinted from *Acoust. Soc. Am. J.* **21**(6):577–580 (1949)

Theory of Speech Masking by Reverberation

R. H. BOLT

Acoustics Laboratory, Massachusetts Institute of Technology, Cambridge, Massachusetts

AND

A. D. MACDONALD*

Dalhousie University and the Naval Research Establishment, Halifax, Nova Scotia

A general statistical theory is developed for the masking effect of reverberation on the intelligibility of words. Speech is considered a series of discrete pulses distributed statistically over a 30-db range in sound pressure level in a given frequency band. The articulation index is calculated as a function of reverberation time, using preliminary values of speech pulse lengths and spacings obtained from *Visible Speech* spectrograms. The percent articulation for words is then calculated from the articulation index and is compared with Knudsen's experimental values. The theoretical values agree precisely with the measured values at reverberation times less than two seconds and differ by less than 17 percent out to six seconds. The calculations are extended to include a combination of background noise and reverberation.

STUDIES of speech hearing in rooms[1] have shown that reverberation reduces the number of sounds that are heard correctly. A sound spoken in a room is prolonged, with a more or less logarithmic decay, so that it is present to mask subsequent sounds. From articulation tests performed in many rooms, Knudsen established a "reduction factor for reverberation," a number that starts at unity for zero reverberation and drops as reverberation increases above about 0.4 sec. Presumably the speech material used in Knudsen's tests corresponds approximately with the "word list percent articulation" of subsequent investigators.[2] These later studies have established the articulation index as a basic psychophysical quantity, correlatable both with physical characteristics of speech sounds and with percent articulation for syllables, words, and sentences.

The purpose of this paper is to explore the problem of calculating the influence of reverberation on speech intelligibility. At the present time some of the psychophysical data required for such a theory are available, but other information which will be needed for a completely satisfactory theory has not yet been obtained. Accordingly, the present paper is restricted to:

(a) the establishment of a general statistical approach to the problem;

(b) preliminary calculation on reverberation masking, based on presently available data and on certain assumptions regarding the distribution of speech sounds;

(c) calculation of combined effect of reverberation and noise.

The calculations included are a first approximation only and do not fully exploit the generality of the approach to the problem. In particular the simplifications involved in the articulation-area presentation[3] are implicit in the present calculations.

* Guest of Acoustics Laboratory, M.I.T., Summer, 1949.

[1] V. O. Knudsen, *Architectural Acoustics* (John Wiley and Sons, Inc., New York, 1932), p. 381.

[2] H. Fletcher and J. C. Steinberg, Bell Sys. Tech. J. **8**, 806 (1929). J. P. Egan and F. M. Wiener, J. Acous. Soc. Am. **18**, 435 (1946).

[3] N. R. French and J. C. Steinberg, J. Acous. Soc. Am. **19**, 90 (1947). L. L. Beranek, Proc. I. R. E. **35**, 880 (1947); J. Acous. Soc. Am. **19**, 357 (1947).

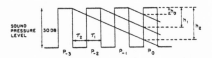

FIG. 1. Diagrammatic representation of speech pulses. Each vertical band represents a statistical distribution of intensities.

GENERAL THEORY

We assume speech to be composed of a series of discrete pulses of energy having durations τ_1 and spaces between pulses of durations τ_2 sec. These pulses are statistically distributed in sound pressure level over a range of 30 db in any given band of frequencies. We perform the analysis by considering a "statistical pulse" with a height of 30 db which is, in essence, a population of pulses occurring with equal probability at any level within the 30-db range.

We compute the articulation index by considering sequentially the way in which various sections of a statistical pulse are masked by sections of previous pulses. The sum of the unmasked portions of the statistical pulses is, by definition, the articulation index. Implicit in this last statement is, of course, the understanding that any subdivision of the statistical pulse into frequency bands would be carried out with proper weighting in accordance with the articulation area.[3] The demonstrated uniform distribution of articulation area with pressure level is automatically incorporated in the above definition of "statistical pulse."

In the analysis we shall assume that the pulse front carries the greater part of the intelligibility. This assumption is based on the following line of reasoning. If the intelligibility were carried equally by all parts of the pulse, almost all the masking effect would be due to a self-masking of most of the pulse by the initial part of the pulse. In this case the space between speech pulses would not affect intelligibility. However, experiment has shown that in a reverberant room intelligibility is greatly increased by speaking slowly. Therefore self-masking must be relatively unimportant, and we shall consider the masking of the front of one pulse by the end of previous pulses. Furthermore, experimental data on the effect of interruption of speech indicate that this viewpoint is reasonable.[4]

Consider the model given in Fig. 1. The vertical bands 30 db high, spread along a time scale, represent statistical distributions of pulse heights that vary from zero to 30 db. If we consider the probability that the pulse height lies between h and $h+dh$ as the statistical population of the band dh, then bands of equal heights have equal populations. Consider the P_0th statistical pulse and the influence on it by previous statistical pulses. The amount of P_0 that is masked is determined

[4] J. C. R. Licklider and G. A. Miller, J. Acous. Soc. Am. 20, 593 (1948).

by m, the slope of the decay of previous pulses, where

$$m = (60/T)\text{db/sec}.$$

and T is the conventionally defined reverberation time in seconds. The total fraction of the pulse front which is, on the average, free from masking is the articulation index. Consider first the band h_0 of the statistical pulse P_0. Because of the reverberation decay, this height h_0, which is equal to $m\tau_2$, is free of masking possibility and the component articulation index is given by

$$A_0 = h_0/30 = 2\tau_2/T. \tag{1}$$

Consider next the band $h_1 - h_0$ in P_0 which may or may not be masked by a band of equal height in P_{-1}. The fraction

$$f_1 = (h_1 - h_0)/30$$

of P_0's total population may be masked by a fraction f_1 of P_{-1}'s population only during that part of the time when the P_{-1} components are higher than the time-projected P_0 components in question. For a uniform level of statistically independent heights this fraction of the time is $\frac{1}{2}$; and therefore that fraction of f_1 which escapes masking is given by

$$A_1 = f_1(1 - f_1/2). \tag{2}$$

The band $(h_2 - h_1)/30$ of P_0, which is the same fraction f_1, is completely masked by P_{-1} when the height of P_{-1} is greater than $(1-f_1)30$, i.e., is completely masked by the upper f_1 of P_{-1}. It is masked by the second fraction f_1 of P_{-1} one-half of the time, on the basis of the argument used previously. Of the fraction of this band which escapes masking by P_{-1}, a fraction $f_1/2$ will be masked by the upper band of P_{-2}. Therefore the component articulation index for $h_2 - h_1$ is

$$A_2 = f_1(1 - f_1/2)(1 - \tfrac{3}{2}f_1) = A_1(1 - \tfrac{3}{2}f_1). \tag{3}$$

The same argument applied to the higher order components of the articulation index gives

$$A_n = A_{n-1}\left(1 - \frac{2n-1}{2}f_1\right), \tag{4}$$

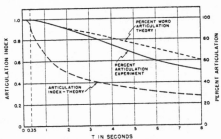

FIG. 2. Calculations of theory compared with Knudsen's experimental value of percent articulation for words. The articulation index is also shown.

where

$$f_1 = (2/T)(\tau_1 + \tau_2).$$

The articulation index A.I. is then defined as

$$A.I. = \sum_n A_n, \qquad (5)$$

where A_n is given by Eqs. (1), (2), and (4).

CALCULATION OF REVERBERATION MASKING

For the purposes of rough calculation, the lengths of speech pulses and spaces between pulses were measured on spectrograms of speech made at the Bell Telephone Laboratories.[5] A transparent grid divided into 500-c.p.s. frequency bands was placed over a speech spectrogram. In each frequency band the length of the pulses and the spaces between pulses were measured. Measurements were made of a large number of values of τ_1 and τ_2 for each of the seven frequency bands of 500 cycles width. It would be possible to calculate a component articulation index for each of these bands and add them, properly weighted, to evaluate the articulation index. However, in the present calculations the values of τ_1 and τ_2 for all frequencies were averaged, and an average articulation index computed. The different types of speech sounds such as vowels, nasals, and stops were given equal weight. The study of about 300 words in 40 sentences indicates that the average speech pulse lasts 0.13 sec., with an average interval between pulses of 0.10 sec. The average values for the individual frequency bands did not differ greatly from this.

The articulation index, calculated from Eq. (5) and using the above values for pulse lengths and intervals, is plotted as a function of reverberation time in Fig. 2. The percent articulation for words, obtained from the articulation index by the use of previously available information,[3] is also given in Fig. 2. In addition, the percent word articulation determined experimentally by Knudsen is plotted.

CALCULATION OF COMBINED REVERBERATION AND NOISE MASKING

The method of calculating the articulation index lends itself readily to the inclusion of the effect of background noise. A uniform continuous spectrum of noise over a given frequency band at a given pressure level completely masks all sounds below that level in the same frequency band. Therefore, in computing the articulation index, one need only set equal to zero all components of the articulation index which arise from statistical pulses below the noise level.

Figure 3 shows a plot of the articulation index computed for several values of the difference between level

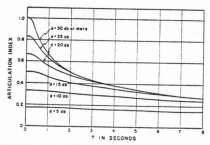

FIG. 3. Articulation index plotted as a function of reverberation time for different background noise levels. The numbers on the various curves represent the difference between speech peak level and continuous spectrum noise level, in the same frequency band.

of speech peaks** and continuous spectrum noise level in the same frequency band. If the background noise level varies with frequency, as is generally the case, the components of the articulation index may be computed for different frequency bands and averaged with proper weighting, in accordance with the articulation index frequency scale.[3] Figure 3 indicates that the influences of reverberation and of background noise cannot be computed rigorously from separable factors.***

CONCLUSIONS

We see from the data shown in Fig. 2 that the calculated word articulation coincides with Knudsen's experimental values for reverberation times from zero to 2 sec. Beyond 3 sec. the curves deviate gradually with a maximum difference of approximately 17 percent at 6 sec. This close agreement may seem somewhat fortuitous when one considers that the experimental data used in the calculations were obtained from three independent sources. Moreover, the word lists used by Knudsen and those in the speech spectrogram are not necessarily identical in their statistical representation of speech. Certain assumptions in the theory and simplifications in the averaging processes discussed above also introduce some uncertainty in the calculated values.

In spite of these discrepancies, however, it is gratifying to note that a relatively simple calculation fits the observed facts accurately over the range of reverberation times (less than 2.5 sec.) normally encountered in properly designed auditoriums. It is also interesting to note that, in agreement with Knudsen's findings, the percentage articulation is unity below some minimum value of reverberation. With the values used here, this minimum time is 0.35 sec. Regardless of the values selected for the durations and intervals of speech

---

[5] Potter, Kopp, and Green, *Visible Speech* (D. Van Nostrand and Company, Inc., New York, 1947), Bell Telephone Laboratories Series.

** The level of speech peaks is 12 db above the r.m.s. level and 30 db above the average level of speech minima. See reference 3.
*** As was done for example in Knudsen's approximate treatment of this problem in which he multiplies a factor for noise by a factor for reverberation. See reference 1.

sounds, there will obviously be some minimum reverberation time below which the articulation is in no way influenced.

There is ample evidence that, in general, the decay of sound in a room is not simply exponential, as assumed in this paper. Irregular decay, beats, and discrete reflections are often observed in practice. The general approach outlined in this paper can be extended to these more complicated cases. Other studies of interest would include the refinement of the statistical values of speech pulse lengths and spaces, perhaps taking into consideration the essential differences between vowels and consonants. Extensive measurements of articulation index under a wide range of reverberation conditions are also needed.

The authors are indebted to Dr. G. A. Miller of the Psycho-Acoustic Laboratory, Harvard University, for a critical review of this paper.

21

Reprinted from pp. 478–484 of Acoust. Soc. Am. J. **34**:475–492 (1962)

SPEECH PRIVACY IN BUILDINGS

W. J. Cavanaugh, W. R. Farrell, P. W. Hirtle, and B. G. Watters

[*Editor's Note*: In the original, material precedes this excerpt.]

(1) Background Noise

The intelligibility of intruding speech is destroyed when the speech peaks are submerged in steady background noise (or when reduced below the threshold of hearing—a rare instance). *Thus, an increase in the background level has the same effect on intelligibility as an increase in the transmission loss.*

Figure 2 shows typical measurements of steady background noise in various spaces. The lowest curve gives average evening noise levels in a hotel in a quiet section of a small city. Similarly low levels are frequently found in un-air-conditioned hospitals, dormitories, office or "professional" buildings, etc. These levels are approximately equal to the average threshold of hearing for broad-band noise. The upper curve shows measured levels typical of a general office area. Between these two extremes are shown the results of a recent survey[8] of the background-noise levels in 62 private offices. (In none of these cases was there a complaint because of the noise.) The numbers on the three dashed curves give the percentage of the data points that exceeded the respective curves in each octave band.

Figure 2 shows that background levels in the speech-frequency bands vary from building to building by 30 db or more. Thus, we would expect a comparable variation in the "effectiveness" of a given isolating structure built in these different locations. An accurate design scheme must include the accurate prediction of background levels in the completed building. While there are many sources of background noise, only a few can be relied upon to be continuously present. Most important of these are traffic ("city") noise[9] and air-conditioning terminal-device noise.

(2) Published TL Data

Unfortunately, the published TL data for sound-isolating barriers are often significantly higher than the corresponding field performance. For example, it is not uncommon to find differences in the order of 10 db or more between the advertised transmission-loss values of a partition, and the data obtained from a valid field measurement (i.e., one in which the structure in question is not flanked by other sound-transmission paths). Obviously, this degree of uncertainty cannot be permitted in any scheme which must accurately design for speech privacy in buildings. Admittedly there are knotty problems being explored by acoustical researchers to determine and define the significance of differences in TL measurements both in the laboratory and in the field.[10–12] However, since these differences do

in fact exist, it seems appropriate to reflect on some of the causes for optimistically high published values.

(A) Incomplete Test Sample

An important example is the prefabricated partition which typically consists of not only the main panels but also the base plates, headers, connectors, trimstrips, fillers, edge gaskets, etc., all of which are adjusted in place to meet the usual variances in building construction. The differences in TL of the panel and that of the entire partition assembly can easily be 10 or more db.[13] With such panel assemblies, useful TL data for building design can be derived only from a test specimen large enough to incorporate all of the essential elements of the construction in their normal proportion and with a careful simulation of the usual building irregularities at the perimeter.

(B) Test-Panel Size and Boundary Damping

The transmission loss of many walls, especially rigid ones, is influenced by the size and edge damping.[14,15] Until an adequate theoretical basis exists for relating such effects on the transmission loss of a barrier, the prudent course for the designer interested in field performance is to use test data on walls which are tested under essentially the *same* size and edge conditions as will be used in the field.

(C) Noise-Reduction or Attenuation Data Reported as Transmission Loss

Much of the manufacturers' literature contains noise-reduction or sound-reduction data taken under rather special conditions (i.e., the source or receiver room is unusual in size or sound absorption). Generally, such data are qualified in the original test report, but these qualifications are often not fully understood by the test sponsor. Such tests may be quite useful as "pilot" data in guiding the development of a structure, but the indiscriminate use of such data has resulted in many unsatisfactory situations in finished buildings.

(D) Obsolete Data

In the past, there has been no means of recalling data which have become obsolete. As a result the body of data

mission through suspended ceiling systems," J. Acoust. Soc. Am. **33**, 1523–1530 (1961).
[11] R. N. Lane and E. E. Mikeska, "Problems of field measurement of transmission loss as illustrated by data on lightweight partitions used in music buildings," J. Acoust. Soc. Am. **33**, 1531–1535 (1961).
[12] T. Mariner, "Critique of the reverberant room method of measuring airborne sound transmission loss," J. Acoust. Soc. Am. **33**, 1131–1139 (1961).
[13] R. N. Hamme, "Understanding sound transmission loss of lightweight partitions," Noise Control **6**, 13–17 (1960).
[14] M. Heckl and K. Seifert, "Untersuchungen über den Einfluss der Eigenresonanzen der Messräume auf die Ergebnisse von Schalldämmessungen," Acustica **8**, 212–220 (1958).
[15] B. G. Watters, "In-place flexural damping of walls," Session N, 62nd Meeting of the Acoustical Society of America, November, 1961.

[8] W. R. Farrell, "Evaluation of the effectiveness and acceptability of masking noise for providing speech privacy in buildings," Paper T7 presented at the 60th Meeting of the Acoustical Society of America, 1960.
[9] L. N. Miller, "A sampling of New York City traffic noise," Noise Control **6**, 39–43 (1960).
[10] R. N. Hamme, "Laboratory measurements of sound trans-

with which the designer must work is a hodgepodge. Refinements in our understanding of transmission loss have resulted in improvement of testing techniques and in some cases the building of new test facilities. Differences between the test values of barriers tested in new and obsolete facilities have been 5 db or more, yet many manufacturers continue to publish the obsolete (and usually higher) values.

Some means is needed to keep test data current and abreast of the times. One positive step in this direction is that adopted by the Acoustical Door Institute in conjunction with the Riverbank Acoustical Laboratories which regards data four or more years old as automatically obsolete.

Solutions to these problems and others related to obtaining adequate TL data in terms of field performance will require the cooperation of manufacturers, consultants, acoustical researchers, testing laboratories, and standards committees alike. Meanwhile, the burden of providing the impetus for solution falls on the data users themselves who must be critical of the data used in actual building design. Clearly they must demand as a minimum the complete details of the test data of the structure under consideration including a full description of the test sample and installation details, the test procedure, date of test, etc. Only those data which are truly representative of "field-like" TL performance can be useful in an accurate design scheme.

(3) Size, Shape, and Sound Absorption of the Rooms to be Isolated

For two adjacent rooms not too large or too "dead," the sound-pressure level incident upon the isolating wall is proportional to the average level in the source room, SPL_1

$$SPL_1 = PWL - 10 \log(S\bar{\alpha})_1 + 6 \text{ db.}$$

In similar fashion, the intruding-speech level, SPL_2, is given by

$$SPL_2 = SPL_1 - TL + 10 \log S_w - 10 \log(S\bar{\alpha})_2,$$

where $S\bar{\alpha} = (0.049 V/\bar{T})$ sq ft, $V =$ the volume of the room in cu ft, $\bar{T} =$ the reverberation time in sec, $S_w =$ the area of the transmitting wall in sq ft, $TL =$ the random incidence sound-transmission loss of the wall in db, SPL_1 and $SPL_2 =$ the rms sound pressures averaged over the volume of the source room and receiving room, expressed in db re 2×10^{-4} d/cm^2, $PWL_1 =$ the sound-power level of the speech source in db re 10^{-13} w.

The sound-absorbing area $S\bar{\alpha}$ is determined not only by the absorption coefficient and area of acoustical materials in the room, but also by the location of the materials,[16,17] the absorption of carpets, drapes, furnish-

[16] L. L. Beranek, "Acoustic impedance of commercial materials and the performance of rectangular rooms with one treated surface," J. Acoust. Soc. Am. 12, 14–23 (1940).
[17] D. Fitzroy, "Reverberation formula which seems to be more accurate with nonuniform distribution of absorption," J. Acoust. Soc. Am., 31, 893–897 (1959).

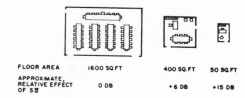

FLOOR AREA	1600 SQ.FT	400 SQ.FT	50 SQ.FT
APPROXIMATE, RELATIVE EFFECT OF $S\bar{\alpha}$	0 DB	+6 DB	+15 DB

FIG. 3. The buildup of speech levels in rooms of various sizes.

ings, and people, and by the coupling of the various room modes provided by large objects such as desks, chairs, and file cabinets. To our knowledge, no practical theory presently available permits the calculation of $S\bar{\alpha}$ taking into account all of the above factors. *Fortunately, if unusually "live" and unusually "dead" rooms are neglected, field data show $S\bar{\alpha}$ to be approximately equal to the floor area of the room, in the speech frequency range, for rooms of moderate size.*

Using this result, it is easy to see the effect of neglecting the room size when calculating the intruding-speech level. Figure 3 shows a range of talker-room sizes from a small 6 ft×8 ft office or interview room to a 40 ft×40 ft classroom or board room. Assuming a constant speech power, the corresponding range in reverberant speech levels is 15 db. An accurate analysis scheme must take this effect into account.

Figure 4 shows a range of *ratios* of wall area to listener-room floor area from $\frac{1}{2}$ to 2; the corresponding variation in transmitted levels is 6 db. An accurate design scheme must take this additional effect into account as well.

(4) Expected Speech Activity

As talkers move from one environment to another, we should expect changes in their *average* speech level. For example, the average talker might be expected to use "normal" or "conversational" speech effort when talking to someone a few feet away (as in a small office or in a hotel room). The same average talker would

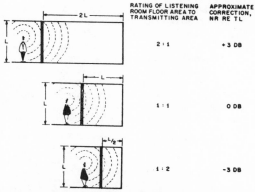

FIG. 4. The relationship of NR and TL in rooms of various shapes.

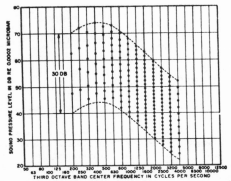

FIG. 5. Graphical representation of normal speech levels in a 100 sabine room. Number of dots in each third-octave band signifies relative contribution to articulation index. The data are obtained from Fig. 2 of reference 22 using the directivity-index data given by Beranek (reference 21) after H. K. Dunn and D. W. Farnsworth [J. Acoust. Soc. Am. 10, 184 (1939)]. The peak factor of speech is taken to be +12 db at all frequencies.

probably increase his speech effort to a "raised voice" when speaking to a group of people in a conference room. In some unusual conditions (for example, in psychiatric interviewing offices), the speech effort might occasionally increase further to a "loud voice." The sound levels for a "raised voice" are about 6 db higher than those for conversational speech; a "loud voice" is about 12 db higher.[18]

(5) Kind of Privacy Required

The degree of speech privacy required by the occupant of a room depends on his activity. As an example, consider the case of an engineer or other technical person. During most of his work day, his desire for speech isolation is set by his wish for freedom from distraction. We have called this "normal" privacy. However, if he should be called into the office of his supervisor or employer to discuss salary or personal matters, the need for speech isolation is different. It no longer is the freedom from distraction, but now becomes the assurance of not being overheard. This kind of privacy we have called "confidential." Let us further imagine that a part of his work concerns a highly classified project. Conferences he may have in this connection may need to be truly secret.[19]

In laboratory tests described in Sec. V, where a private office environment was simulated, the more critical occupants desired a fairly low intelligibility of intruding speech when their work was confidential and permitted a higher intelligibility when their work re-

[18] L. L. Beranek, *Acoustics* (McGraw-Hill Book Company, Inc., New York, 1954), p. 338.
[19] True secrecy is much more complicated than the "confidential" requirement just mentioned. For example, if an eavesdropper is free to place his ear to the wall and thus shut out the airborne background noise, the problem becomes one of the signal-to-noise ratio of the vibration levels in the wall structure. True secrecy is not considered here.

quired only freedom from distraction. Generally, this amounted to a 6-db difference in the ratio of speech signal to background noise.

V. EXPERIMENTS ON THE RELATIONSHIP BETWEEN SPEECH INTELLIGIBILITY AND SPEECH PRIVACY

It is a matter of simple observation that even though the background-noise level around us is well above our threshold of hearing, we almost invariably become accustomed to it, accept it, and, most of the time, are altogether unaware of it. On the other hand, we sometimes express strong dissatisfaction at intruding speech whose rms levels are no greater than those of the background noise.

One possible explanation for the above observations is that speech privacy is related to speech intelligibility. Speech intelligibility, we know, is determined not by the level of the speech but rather by the ratio of speech to noise. Our experimental work has looked for confirmation of this assumed relationship. We found that each subject had a precise personal criterion for the speech-to-noise ratio which for him just constituted privacy, that there is a wide variation (10 db or so) in the criteria of various subjects, but that the assumed relationship of intelligibility and privacy seemed to be consistent with the experimental results.

A. Review of Speech-Intelligibility Theory

A general theory of speech intelligibility was developed about 20 years ago by the Bell Telephone Laboratories[20] and has been expanded by Beranek[21] and

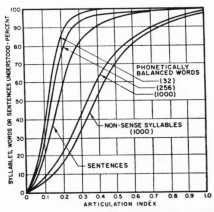

FIG. 6. Approximate relationship between articulation index and intelligibility for skilled talkers and listeners. The numbers in parentheses give the size of the test vocabulary.

[20] N. R. French and J. C. Steinberg, "Factors governing the intelligibility of speech sounds," J. Acoust. Soc. Am. 19, 90 (1947).
[21] L. L. Beranek, "Design of speech systems," Proc. IRE, 35, 880–890 (1947).

others. Although more recent studies[22] have cast doubt on its exactness, it remains the most generally useful theory available today.

Some important aspects of this theory are:

(1) The intelligible part of speech energy lies roughly between 200 and 6000 cps.

(2) Most of the energy of speech is in the frequency range below 800 cps; most of the contribution to intelligibility above 800 cps.

(3) In each frequency band, speech has a dynamic range of about 30 db; the peak values lie about 12 db above the long-time rms levels.

(4) Any frequency band in the range 200 to 6000 cps may be considered to make a contribution to intelligibility that is proportional (a) to the fraction of its 30-db dynamic range which is greater than the masking noise (or threshold of hearing), (b) to the bandwidth, and (c) to the "importance function" for that band. The importance function is a maximum at about 2000 cps.

These facts are symbolized in Fig. 5, where the useful speech signal is shown as a dot field beginning at 200 cps and extending to 6000 cps. Each dot signifies a possible ½% contribution to the articulation index. The field is 30 db "high" and the greatest density of dots is at 2000 cps. The dot field is drawn for an average talker using "conversational" speech effort. The upper envelope of the field gives the approximate peak sound-pressure level in a room with 100 sabines of sound absorption.

If on Fig. 5 we plot the background-noise level in ⅓-octave bands then the ratio of the number of dots which lie above the plot to the total number is approxi-

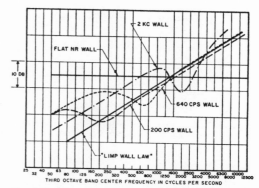

Fig. 8. Relative noise-reduction characteristics of test walls.

mately equal to the articulation index (AI). This objective quantity has been empirically related to the intelligibility of various kinds of speech (i.e., unrelated words, sentences, etc.) as shown in Fig. 6. Our study tried to determine if this same quantity could also be related to the feeling of speech privacy.

B. Some Experimental Results

Most of our experiments were conducted in simulated private-office environments having the elements shown in Fig. 7. Usually the test subject was provided with a desk, chair, and reading matter.

The intruding speech was generated with a loudspeaker and tape recorder in the adjacent room. The speech signal used was a shorthand-training recording;[23] the talker gave dictation at a rate of 100 wpm at a fairly constant level. The distribution of average levels existing in 150-msec intervals was measured.

The isolation was provided partly by the actual physical wall separating the two test rooms and partly by a spectrum-shaping ⅓-octave filter and a 2 db-per-step attenuator controlled by the experimenter. In one set of experiments, for example, the filter was adjusted so that the total isolation was equal, successively, to each of the five curves in Fig. 8.

These curves are representative of commonly used partitions. The "flat" curve is often found when a partition is seriously flanked by air leaks. The 6-db per octave "limp" wall curve is approximated by single, thin sheets of steel, lead, or plastic. The 200-, 640-, and 2000-cps curves are characteristic of walls having these critical frequencies. Hollow masonry block, solid studless plaster, and plasterboard or plywood are examples, respectively.

Care was taken to ensure a steady, consistent background noise. In one experiment, for example, the noise was established by a 2-channel tape recording of traffic and diffuser noise. The diffuser-noise loudspeaker was

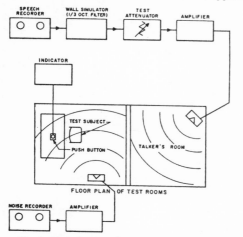

Fig. 7. Block diagram of speech-privacy test setup simulating private-office environment.

[22] J. C. R. Licklider, "Three auditory theories," in *Psychology: A Study of a Science*, edited by S. Koch (McGraw-Hill Book Company, Inc., New York, 1959).

[23] Sustained Dictation Record, No. SD-2, Gregg Publishing Division, Bus. Ed. Div., McGraw-Hill Book Company, Inc., New York, Dictation Speed, 100 wpm.

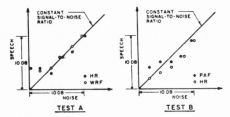

FIG. 9. Results of test showing dependence of tolerated speech levels on background-noise level.

hidden in the ceiling above a real air diffuser; the traffic-noise loudspeaker was placed near a window. The noise levels approximated the NC-35 contour in the speech-frequency range and were held constant throughout the experiment. The reaction of the test subject was generally transmitted by a push button mounted on his desk. The sound-pressure levels of both the background noise and of the intruding speech were measured in $\frac{1}{3}$-octave bands using a nondirectional microphone at several points near where the test subject was to be seated.

Two sets of written instructions were normally given to the test subjects as shown below. The instructions for Test B were given to the subject after completion of Test A.

The purpose of these tests is to measure the amount of sound isolation people consider adequate for their offices.

Test A

In the office adjacent to the room you are in, we will reproduce through a loudspeaker various types of speech signals that will gradually increase in intensity until you can hear them. When the speech reaches a level that you consider bothersome, please push the button-switch on the table before you. During this test, imagine, if you will, that you are doing your normal work, including conferences, in your own office. In other words, push the switch when you believe the speech from the office adjacent to yours first reaches a level that, day in and day out, would interfere with the performance of your average, normal work.

As soon as you have pressed the switch, the intensity of the speech signal will again be reduced to an inaudible level and then slowly increased until you can hear it. Each time, please press the switch when the speech just reaches the level you feel would be bothersome to your work routine. This sequence will be repeated a number of times. You will be told by the experimenter when test A is completed.

Test B

During test B, respond to the speech coming from the office next door in somewhat the same way as in the previous test. However, this time, please judge the privacy that you require for the most sensitive or confidential work you do in your office. For example, the discussion of company-classified material, personnel matters, etc. For test B bear in mind that conversation in your office will be heard outside to the same degree you are able to hear speech coming from the adjacent office.

As soon as you have pressed the switch, the intensity of the speech signal will be reduced to an inaudible level and then slowly increased until you can again hear it. Please press the switch again

at what you consider the proper time. This sequence will again be repeated several times. You will be told by the experimenter when test B is completed.

A brief preliminary test was run to see if the absolute level of the background noise influenced the test results. The data of Fig. 9 show that on the average our test subjects responded with a constant signal-to-noise ratio as the background levels varied. The fairly narrow range of test background levels in this case was imposed by the real background (about NC-20) and the desire to keep the test levels below about NC-35.

As stated in the instructions, the 2-db per step gain control which controlled the level of the intruding speech was increased in a cyclic fashion; beginning well below the response level of the subject, increasing gradually (in 2-db steps), and remaining constant for 10 sec on at least the last step below the setting which invoked a response.

The short-time variability of almost all subjects was small. For example, during one day of testing, 13 subjects made 356 judgments of privacy. The rms variation from their average responses was 1.3 db. A significant part of this variation probably is the result of the fact that the speech levels could not be varied in steps smaller than 2 db.

The learning process of most subjects appeared to be very rapid. In general, the testing was continued until the subject appeared to give a consistent response; about four responses were normally found to be adequate. The 1.3-db variation above includes any learning effect.

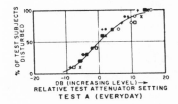

ZERO DB CORRESPONDS TO ATTENUATOR SETTING OF		
	TEST A	TEST B
• FLAT	32 DB	26 DB
+ LIMP	29 DB	21 DB
o 200	28 DB	22 DB
x 640	27 DB	21 DB
□ 2 KC	30 DB	23 DB

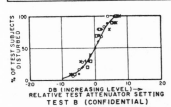

FIG. 10. Relative speech levels required to just-cause annoyance for the (A) (everyday) and (B) (confidential) tests.

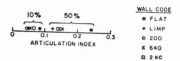

Fig. 11. Calculated articulation index of normal speech transmitted through the five walls of Fig. 17. The speech level is that required to induce a reaction by 10 and 50% of the test subjects.

We have little data on the long-time variability of response. In one experiment with two test subjects, a repeat test after an hour's delay gave no change in response. For a second subject, a day's delay produced an apparent 2-db shift. The response level of one of the authors was found to be within about 2 db of its initial value after an 18-month time lapse.

While any one subject had a definite idea of what constituted speech privacy, not all subjects agreed on the *same* definition. Figure 10 shows the variation in response levels of a group of about 10 test subjects drawn from a business-office environment. The five symbols in the figure are for the five different simulated transmission-loss curves shown in Fig. 8. Each subject was tested with speech intruding through each of the five simulated walls, first following the instructions for test A (everyday privacy) and then assuming the need for confidential privacy (test B). The data for each transmission-loss curve have been shifted arbitrarily as a set so that all data coincide at the 50% level of reaction.

When asked to define "normal" or everyday privacy, the least critical subject allowed 20-db higher speech levels than the most critical. When defining "confidential" privacy, the maximum variation among subjects was about 10 db. There was a shift of about 6 db between the definitions of "normal" and "confidential" privacy as given by the most critical subjects.

Figure 10 is characteristic of all the data we have obtained. However, just as the various subjects for this test differed in their concept of privacy, various groups will differ. The subjects for Fig. 10 were somewhat less critical than others we have tested, and the slopes of the curves are more gradual than for other groups.

The different transmission-loss curves of Fig. 8 result in different spectra for the intruding speech. Since our subjects were tested with these different spectra, we can check the computed articulation index for each spectrum against the subjects' response levels. Such a comparison is shown in Fig. 11 for the 10 and 50% levels of annoyance for the subjects of Fig. 10 tested for "confidential" privacy. It appears that both the most critical 10% of the subjects and the average subject tolerated a higher articulation index for the "flat" wall, the wall with relatively weak low-frequency speech components. However, it should be noted that although the articulation index for the "flat" wall is nearly double that for the other walls, a reduction of only 3 db in the "flat" speech levels would have reduced the articulation

index to that for the other walls. The over-all precision of the experiment is probably no greater than 3 db.

Although the results of Fig. 11 seem to be fairly well explainable in terms of the calculated intelligibility of the intruding speech, it is interesting to speculate on the actual basis for judgment by our subjects. To this end, we talked with some of the subjects after the experiment was completed. It is clear that real or apparent intelligibility is involved in the judgments of many if not most of them. A typical comment was that the subject reacted when he could just begin to understand the intruding speech. Some of the less critical subjects said that they reacted when the intruding speech distracted them from the work (reading) they were performing. Usually this occurred at a fairly high level of intelligibility.

Some of the most critical subjects appeared to react when the speech sounds became recognizable as such, even though the intelligibility of the speech was virtually zero. One explanation put forth was that the very tone of voice used by the talker (if he were someone well known to the listener) could convey intelligibility. More or less at the opposite extreme, some subjects accepted a moderately high degree of intelligibility of intruding speech even for the "B" or confidential test. One subject told us that even though the intruding speech levels were clearly intelligible, he knew that he could carry on a private conversation in his own office by the simple

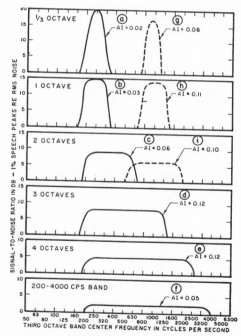

Fig. 12. Approximate 1% peak speech levels judged by one subject to be equally annoying. (Background noise approximately N33, see Sec. VII.)

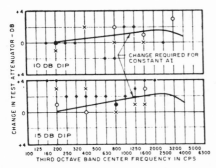

FIG. 13. Change in test attenuator required to compensate for ⅓-octave-wide TL dip. Intruding speech spectrum otherwise has equal signal-to-noise ratio in all bands.

expedient of lowering his voice, and apparently was willing to do so.

A critical question arises concerning the importance of sharp dips in the TL curve of a sound-isolating structure.[24] A good example is the plaster partition of Fig. 16. We conducted some exploratory experiments to see if the AI relates to structures with sharp dips in the same way it relates to the more usual structure. These experiments were conducted along the lines described earlier. The Gregg-shorthand recording was played through a loudspeaker in an adjoining room after first being passed through a ⅓-octave spectrum-shaping filter. The background noise for these tests was generated by a ceiling air diffuser.

We began with the intruding-speech sound filtered through the single 250-cps ⅓-octave as shown in Fig. 12 [spectrum (a)]. The over-all level was increased until the subject reacted. The bandwidth was then increased to a full octave, centered on 250 cps as shown by spectrum (b). The signal-to-noise ratio throughout the octave was approximately independent of frequency. The over-all level was again adjusted until the subject reacted. As shown by spectra (c) through (f), the bandwidth was further increased in steps until the full range from 200 to 4000 cps was covered. The signal-to-noise ratio, expressed in decibels, was determined for each bandwidth. A similar experiment began with the 1000 cps, ⅓-octave band [spectra (g) through (i)]. One of the authors was the subject tested.

While this was purely a preliminary experiment, some interesting points may be noted. First, for the single ⅓-octave bands and for the octave band centered on 250 cps, the subject found the intruding speech signal

<hr />

[24] Another reason for considering this problem is to determine the relevance to the speech-privacy problem of single-number rating schemes which may rate a wall solely upon the TL measured at the depth of such a dip. The new Sound Transmission Class (STC) scheme as described in the ASTM standard E90-61T tends to give a very high weighting to sharp dips in TL curves. In contrast, the British "grade" scheme and the German DIN rating method tend to smooth or to average out dips in the TL curve. The AI scheme developed in this paper uses a weighted averaging technique.

to be almost completely unintelligible although it could be recognized as speech. There was increasing intelligibility for the wider-band tests. Thus, we do find annoyance caused by unintelligible, narrow-band speech, especially at the low frequencies. The calculated AI's for the various bandwidths confirm this. The AI for the 250 cps, ⅓-octave was only 2% when the subject responded. This compares with 5-10% for the wider bandwidths.

The more compelling point, however, is *the relatively small importance of a narrow band of intruding speech.* While the observed importance is greater than given by the articulation index, we found that the signal-to-noise ratio for the single 250-cps ⅓-octave band could be about *18 db greater* than for the full frequency range.

A further experiment was designed to more nearly simulate the conditions of a wall with a sharp TL dip. In this experiment, the spectrum-shaping filter was first adjusted for equal signal-to-noise ratio in all bands from 200 through 4000 cps. The test attenuator was then adjusted until the subject responded. Next, the level of one one-third octave band was raised 10 db above its previous setting. As can be recognized, this 10-db adjustment corresponds to a 10-db dip in the TL of a structure which otherwise provides an equal signal-to-noise ratio throughout the entire range of speech-intelligibility frequencies. Finally, the test attenuator was again adjusted until the subject responded. Three of the authors were subjects for this experiment. The data are given in the upper part of Fig. 13. As may be seen, a 10-db dip only one-third octave wide was judged to be relatively unimportant. Indeed, the importance was fairly well predicted by the contribution to the articulation index of the dip.

The experiment was again run but with a 15-db dip. The results are given in the lower portion of Fig. 13. As may be seen, there is a response which at the lower frequencies is not predicted by the change in the articulation index caused by the dip. During the lower-frequency tests, the subjects were aware of two separate sources of annoyance. One was the just-intelligible broad-band speech signal; the other was a narrow band of noise, which could, however, be recognized as being caused by the speech signal. It was also noted that the subjects most critical of wide-band intruding speech gave more importance to low-frequency TL dips.

It is clear that dips in the TL curve of a structure can, if they are deep enough, cause annoyance which is not explainable in terms of speech intelligibility. Stated another way, the function which relates *annoyance* to signal-to-noise ratio is larger, in the case of low-frequency narrow bands of speech, than the function which relates *intelligibility* to the signal-to-noise ratio. This effect deserves more-careful study. However, it is even more apparent that the effect of a narrow TL dip is small, and, for the great majority of TL curves encountered, the effect is accounted for by the articulation-index rating scheme proposed here.

[*Editor's Note*: Material has been omitted at this point.]

Part VI

APPLICATIONS TO AUDIOLOGY

Editor's Comments
on Papers 22, 23, and 24

22   LICHTWITZ
On the Application of the New Edison Phonograph to General Hearing Measurements

23   HIRSH et al.
Development of Materials for Speech Audiometry

24   WITTICH, WOOD, and MAHAFFEY
Computerized Speech Audiometric Procedures

This part concerns the uses of intelligibility testing to detect the magnitude and nature of hearing losses and to assist in the selection of corrective surgery or prescription of a hearing aid. This part differs from others in the book because in the other parts the items under evaluation are rooms, communications systems, hearing aids, or speech synthesis or analysis devices and the humans are used as instruments with representative characteristics; in this part people are being evaluated and the uniqueness of their behavior is being measured. The differences are great, so some of the literature on test materials, on prediction of intelligibility scores, and on the methods of testing which are peculiar to this application are concentrated in this part. It is the only part in which the listeners do not have normal hearing. It is also the only part in which medical doctors and journals are cited often. They have traditions, safeguards, and concerns with which engineers, psychologists, and physicists are seldom involved. The clinician writes to assist other practicing otologists and audiologists in coping with the problems encountered in daily meetings with many patients for short periods. His subjects never have a chance to become fully trained listeners and may be malingering. He treats his patients one at a time, not as a class of users of a building or a device, and his relations with them must be different from those of an experimenter using subjects as cooperative instruments. For these reasons the reader may find the literature that is cited is different in tone, in investigative procedures, in statistical analysis of the results, and in the conclusions from the majority of the literature in the other parts.

Lidén (1954), in his fine and comprehensive monograph, says that hearing tests with spoken words were mentioned in the literature in the sixteenth century. Certainly they seem to have preceded the tuning fork for the measurement of hearing. Spoken and whispered words continued to be used after the vacuum tube pure tone audiometer was invented by Guttman in 1921 and by Fowler and Wegel in 1922. Bunch (1941) gives the history of the audiometer. The first speech audiometers were invented by Lichtwitz in 1889 and by Bryant in 1904. Lichtwitz's paper appeared in French and German; the French version is cited in the bibliography and a translation of the German version is printed for the first time as Paper 22. Lichtwitz seems to have been way ahead of his time, and Bryant (1904) gives no indication of having read Lichtwitz's paper. Bryant also used an Edison phonograph and wrote jubilantly, "The phonograph acoumeter invented by me overcomes all difficulties, for it can be manufactured in large numbers with perfect accuracy, and the pitch and intensity of its mechanical human voice do not vary."* His selection of test materials was prophetic, for he says, "Records are made from carefully selected monosyllabic words in common use, with special reference to the logographic value of their consonants."

Bryant's attenuators were valves (including a malingerer's valve) in the tubes leading from the box around the gramophone to the patient's ears. The valves were not reliable and the device was not popular. MacFarlan (1945) gives a good history of the development of speech audiometry. He says that by 1926 William A. Bristol was using a phonograph to test children's hearing at the Lexington Avenue School for the Deaf in New York. The first widely used speech audiometers in the United States were mentioned in Part I. In Manchester, England, Sir David Monro and A. W. G. Ewing developed carrier sentences and nonsense syllables for testing children. The latter author, with I. R. Ewing, T. S. Littler, and P. A. T. Kerridge, composed other lists of test words and sentences. In 1938 in the United States Arthur M. Wengel developed a consonant-vowel-consonant paired rhyme test for testing hearing, and at Washington University Alfred R. Thea developed in 1941 a list of phonetically balanced words for closed response hearing tests. None of these tests was widely adopted by individual clinicians, who continued to use spoken and whispered numbers or words in a corridor, moving forward to increase sound intensity at the patient's ear. Curry (1949 (2)), Flottorp (1955), Glorig (1949), Goldman (1944), Harris (1946, 1949), and King (1953)

Acoumeter was a nineteenth century term applied to any device used to measure hearing.

denounced these tests as inaccurate, inadequate, and misleading. Glorig's philippic is the most devastating: "The 'spoken voice' test has inherent faults that make it impossible to arrive at even approximate hearing thresholds."

During the decade following World War II there was a sudden increase in concern for and investigation of hearing. Money for treatment of war veterans, a greater general appreciation of and support for science, a reservoir of trained manpower, better transducers, new subminiature tubes for hearing aids, and greater recognition of hearing loss as a compensable disability all contributed to improved protective and corrective hearing programs. The field of audiology emerged as a recognized separate discipline with the first international conference under that name in 1948. The term was coined by Willard B. Hargrave in 1938 and made popular by Norton Canfield and Raymond Carhart in 1945.* Canfield wrote, "Audiology considers everything that can be of aid or detriment to life, from sounds which can or should be heard." †

The bibliography for this part contains papers primarily on the following subjects:

factors affecting intelligibility for listeners with impaired hearing

prediction of speech reception thresholds and discrimination losses from pure tone audiograms

testing materials, including material in various national and regional languages

diagnostic testing materials and techniques

tests for malingering

standardization and validation of tests and equipment

measurements to help select hearing aids

value of binaural hearing aids

It is especially difficult to select papers for reproduction in this part because most of the outstanding and enduring ones are far too long to include, and extracts from them would miss the important points. Paper 23 by Hirsh et al. was the first description of the materials most widely used for speech audiometry today. Hirsh (1952), pp. 119–153, properly places these materials in their clinical context. Davis (1970) presents nine different sets of materials and explains the usefulness of each. These and other texts cited in the bibliography put speech audiometry in its proper perspective relative to other techniques for various applications. Paper 24 by Wittich, Wood, and Mahaffey has been selected because it is the first to describe the automation of speech audiometry, using tech-

* *Audiology* **10**:1 (1971).

† *Ibid.*

niques that are bound to be emulated widely as a very good method of saving the time of professional people for truly judgemental activities.

Although they are not reproduced here, the reader is directed to several excellent papers, including reviews, by Carhart (1951) and by Coles (1973), Hahlbrock (1953), Kroath (1958), Lidén (1954 [2]), Palva (1965), and Silverman (1950). Palva's monograph of 1952 contains descriptions of the author's extensive investigations with his own patients and has a large bibliography. Ventry's (1965) bibliography contains over 400 citations on the subject. Davis (1948) proposed a Social Adequacy Index based on the intelligibility of the Harvard phonetically balanced word lists spoken at an average level. It was a major step in recognition that a partial loss of the ability to understand speech under everyday conditions is a separate, measurable disability. Utley (1944) describes good experimental techniques that were ahead of their time. Noble (1973) gives a very recent review of his subjects. Pestalozza (1954) reports on the validity of filtering noise to normal subjects to simulate different kinds of deafness. Stevenson (1975) describes some of the most modern techniques of displaying a closed set of alternatives just before the stimulus is presented, adapting the level of the stimulus to the results of previous responses, and having the listeners respond by shadowing, i.e., repeating after the stimulus. The long report by Davis (1946) was a major step in applying science to the selection of hearing aids.

BIBLIOGRAPHY

Alusi, H. A., R. Hinchcliffe, B. Ingham, J. J. Knight, and C. North, "Arabic Speech Audiometry," *Audiology* **13**:212–230 (1974).

American Academy of Ophthalmology and Otolaryngology, Committee on Conservation of Hearing," Guide for the Evaluation of Hearing Impairment," *Trans. Am. Acad. Ophthalmol. Otolaryngol.* **63**:236–238 (1959).

Amersbach, K., and F. J. Meister, "Ein Wortkatalog für isophone Sprachgehörprüfung," *Arch. Ohr usw. Heilkd. u. Z. Hals. usw. Heilkd.* **157**:352–358 (1950).

Amersbach, K., and F. J. Meister, "Grundlagen der isophonen Sprachgehörprüfung," *Arch. Ohr usw. Heilkd. u. Z. Hals. usw. Heilkd.* **157**:412–417 (1951).

Azoy, A., M. G. Pomareda, and L. Sabata, "Audiometria Verbal," *Arch. Med. ex. Madrid* **14**:75–101 (1951).

Azzi, A., "Prove di acumetria vocale per la lingua italiana," *Arch. Ital. di Oto-Rino. e Laringol.* **61**, Suppl. 5:45–84 (1950).

Balas, R. F., "Staggered Spondaic Word Test: Support," *Ann. Otol. Rhinol. Laryngol.* **80**:132–134 (1971).

Beasley, W. C., and H. Rosenwasser, "Determining Factors in Composing and Analyzing Speech-Hearing Tests," *Laryngoscope* **60**:658–679 (1950).

Berger, K. W., "Speech Audiometry," in *Audiological Assessment*, D. E. Rose, ed., Prentice-Hall, Englewood Cliffs, N. J. (1971), pp. 207–240.

Berruecos, V., C. Oldini, A. Staffieri, and G. P. Theatini, "La reduccion de la redundancia semantica en la audiometria vocal con frases," *Acta Audiol. Foniatr. Hispanoamer.* **9**:1–12 (1972).

Bocca, E., C. Calearo, and V. Cassnari, "A New Method for Testing Hearing in Temporal Lobe Tumors," *Acta Oto-Laryngol.* **44**:219–221 (1954).

Bocca, E., and A. Pellegrini, "Possibilita di calcolare il deficit di percezione della voce in base alla soglia uditiva per i toni puri," *Arch. Ital. di Oto-Rino. et Laringol.* **61**, Suppl. 5:103–115 (1950).

Breakey, M. R., and H. Davis, "Comparisons of Thresholds for Speech: Word and Sentence Tests; Receiver vs. Field and Monaural vs. Binaural Listening," *Laryngoscope* **59**:236–250 (1949).

Bryant, W. S., "A Phonographic Acoumeter," *Arch. Otol. Laryngol.* **33**:438–443 (1904).

Bunch, C. C., "The Development of the Audiometer," *Laryngoscope* **52**:1100–1118 (1941).

Calearo, C., and A. Lazzaroni, "Speech Intelligibility in Relation to the Speed of the Message," *Laryngoscope* **67**:410–419 (1957).

Carhart, R., "Tests for Selection of Hearing Aids," *Laryngoscope* **56**:780–794 (1946).

Carhart, R., "The Clinical Application of Bone Conduction Audiometry," *Trans. Am. Acad. Ophthalmol. Otolaryngol.* **54**:699–707 (1950).

Carhart, R., "Basic Principles of Speech Audiometry," *Acta Oto-Laryngol.* **40**:62–71 (1951–1952).

Carhart, R., "Problems in the Measurement of Speech Discrimination," *Arch. Otolaryngol.* **82**:253–260 (1965).

Carhart, R., and T. W. Tillman, "Interaction of Competing Speech Signals with Hearing Losses," *Arch. Otolaryngol.* **91**:273–279 (1970).

Casella, B., "I metodi moderni di audiometria vocale nell'esame del personale aeronavigante," *Riv. Med. Aeronaut.* **14**:314–324 (1951).

Chichcov, L., "Verbal Audiometry in the Bulgarian Language—Monosyllable Test," *Khirurgia* (Sofia) **12**:889–903 (1959). in Bulgarian.

Chistovich, L. A., I. A. Klaas, and I. N. Kuzmin, "The Process of Speech Sound Discrimination," *Vopr. Psikhol.* no. 6, 26–39 (1962). in Russian, abstract in English.

Clemis, J. D., and W. F. Carver, "Discrimination Scores for Speech in Menière's Disease," *Arch. Otolaryngol.* **86**:614–618 (1967).

Coen, R., and M. Ghirlanda, "Impiego della voce femminile in audiometria vocale," *Valsalva* **32**:201–226 (1956).

Coles, R. R. A., A. Markides, and V. M. Priede, "Uses and Abuses of Speech Audiometry," in *Disorders of Auditory Function*, W. Taylor, ed., Academic Press, London (1973), pp. 181–202.

Coles, R. R. A., and A. R. D. Thornton, "Audiology Research in the I.S.V.R.'s First Decade," *J. Sound Vib.* **28**:313–332 (1973).

Conn, M., I. M. Ventry, and R. W. Woods, "Pure-Tone Average and Spondee Threshold Relationships in Simulated Hearing Loss," *J. Aud. Res.* **12**:234–239 (1972).

Constantineşçu F., "The Value of Vocal Audiometry," *Oto-Rino-Laryngol.* **15**:321–324 (1970). in Roumanian.

Curry, E. T., "Relation between Hearing Loss for Specific Frequencies and the Distance at Which Speech Can Be Identified," *Ann. Otol. Rhinol. Laryngol.* **58**:33–39 (1949).

Curry, E. T., "A Study of the Relationship between Speech Thresholds and Audiometric Results in Perception Deafness," *J. Speech Hear. Disord.* **14**:104–110 (1949).

Davis, H., ed., *Hearing and Deafness: A Guide for Laymen*," Murray Hill Books, New York (1947).

Davis, H., "The Articulation Area and the Social Adequacy Index for Hearing," *Laryngoscope* **58**:761–778 (1948).

Davis, H., C. V. Hudgins, R. J. Marquis, R. H. Nichols, Jr., G. E. Peterson, D. A. Ross, and S. S. Stevens, "The Selection of Hearing Aids," *Laryngoscope* **56**:85–115, 135–163 (1946).

Davis, H., and S. R. Silverman, eds., *Hearing and Deafness*, 3rd ed., Holt, Rinehart, and Winston, New York (1970).

Davis, H., S. S. Stevens, R. H. Nichols, Jr., C. V. Hudgins, R. J. Marcus, G. ʷ. Peterson, and D. A. Ross, *Hearing Aids—An Experimental Study of Design Objectives*, Harvard Univ. P., Cambridge, Mass. (1947).

Decroix, G., and J. Dehaussy, *Stéréaudiométrie et appareillages stéréophonique, notions nouvelles sur la correction audioprothétique des surdité*, 2nd ed., Arnette, Paris (1965).

Demanez, J. P., F. L. Dittrich, and A. Ledoux, "DAF—Test: A New Recording and Analyzing Device," *Int. Audio.* **5**:91–96 (1966).

de Quiros, J., "Accelerated Speech Audiometry, and Examination of Test Results," *Trans. Beltone Inst. Hear. Res. No. 17*, Chicago (1964).

Dickson, E. D. D., "Hearing-Problems Involved in Systems of Intercommunication," *Brit. Med. Bull.* **5**:53–54 (1947).

Eggenschwiler, E., and K. Tanner, "Sprechaudiometrie und Wörterteste," *Pract. Otorhinolaryngol.* Basel **20**:96–103 (1958).

Elliott, L. L., "Prediction of Speech Discrimination Scores from Other Test Information," *J. Aud. Res.* **3**:35–45 (1963).

Ewertsen, H. W., "Delayed Speech Test," *Acta Oto-Laryngd.* **45**:383–387 (1955).

Falconer, G. A., and H. Davis, "The Intelligibility of Connected Discourse as a Test for the Threshold of Speech," *Laryngoscope* **57**:581–595 (1947).

Falconnet, P., "Les constantes phonétiques du langage et la constitution de tests parlés," *J. fr. Oto-Rhino-Laryngol.* **8**:31–35 (1959).

Fant, G., ed., *Proceedings of Symposium on Speech Communication Ability and Profound Deafness*, A. G. Bell Assn., Washington (1972).

Farrimond, T., "Prediction of Speech Hearing Loss for Older Industrial Workers," *Gerontologia* **5**:65–87 (1961).

Feldmann, H., "Untersuchungen über das binaurale Hören unter Einwirkung von Störgeräusch," *Arch. Ohr usw. Heilkd. u. Z. usw. Heilkd.* **181**:337–374 (1963).

Feldmann, H., "A History of Audiology," *Trans. Beltone Inst. Hearing Res. No. 22* (1970).

Ferrer, O., "Speech Audiometry: A Discrimination Test for Spanish Language," *Laryngoscope* **70**:1541–1551 (1960).

Finzi, A., "Rilievi audiometrici tonali e vocali nella presbiacusia," *Arch. Ital. di Oto-Rino. e Laringol.* **68**:211–227 (1957).

Fletcher, H., "A Method of Calculating Hearing Loss for Speech from an Audiogram," *J. Acoust. Soc. Am.* **22**:1–5 (1950).

Flottorp, G., "Experimental Sound Levels during Voice Tests," *Acta Oto-Laryngol.* **45**:323–338 (1955).

Fowler, E. P., "Method of Measuring the Percentage of Capacity for Hearing Speech," *J. Acoust. Soc. Am.* **13**:373–382 (1942).

Fowler, E. P., and H. Fletcher, "Three Million Deafened School Children," *J. Am. Med. Assn.* **87**:1877–1882 (1926).

Frank, T., and R. S. Karlovich, "Effect of Contralateral Noise on Speech Detection and Speech Reception Thresholds," *Audiology* **14**:34–43 (1975).

Fricke, J. E., "Syllable Duration and the Lombard Effect," *Int. Audiol.* **9**:53–57 (1970).

Fry, D. B., "Word and Sentence Lists for Use in Speech Audiometry," *Lancet* 197–199 (22 July 1961).

Fry, D. B., and P. M. T. Kerridge, "Tests for the Hearing of Speech by Deaf People," *Lancet* **1236**:106–109 (1939).

Gengel, R. W., "On the Reliability of Discrimination Performances in Persons with Sensorineural Hearing-Impairment Using a Closed-Set Response," *J. Aud. Res.* **13**:97–100 (1973).

Giolas, T. G., "Speech Audiometry," in *Auditory Assessment of the Difficult-to-Test*, R. T. Fulton and L. L. Lloyd, eds., Williams & Wilkins, Baltimore (1975), pp. 37–70.

Gjaevenes, K., "Estimating SRT for Norwegian PB Monosyllables from the Pure-Tone Audiogram in Conductive Hearing Loss," *J. Aud. Res.* **14**:61–64 (1974).

Glorig, A., "Hearing Evaluation by Low Conversational Voice Tests," *Ann. Otol. Rhinol. Laryngol.* **58**:394–402 (1949).

Goldman, J. L., "A Comparative Study of Whisper Tests and Audiograms," *Laryngoscope* **54**:559–572 (1944).

Gormley, J. C., and G. J. Gormley, "A Critical Review of the Literature on the Validity and Reliability of the Audiogram," *Speech Monogr.* **13**:66–80 (1946).

Graham, A. B., ed., *Sensorineural Hearing Processes and Disorders*, Little, Brown, Boston (1967).

Greenberg, G. I., G. V. Dorfman, and M. G. Visleveva, "Tables of Russian Words Used in Clinical Hearing Tests by the Speech Audiometer," *Vestnik. Oto-Rino-Laringol.* **3**:78–83 (1957). in Russian, summary in English.

Grisanti, G., "L'Intelligibilitá della parola in presenza di rumore ambientale," *Valsalva* **42**:348–372 (1965).

Groen, J. J., "Speech Audiometry as a Means for Establishing the Social Significance of Deafness," *T. Soc. Geneeskd.* **45**:418–421 (1967). in Dutch, abstract in English.

Groen, J. J., and A. C. M. Hellema, "Binaural Speech Audiometry," *Acta Oto-Laryngol.* **52**:397–414 (1960).

Groen, J. J., and A. C. M. Hellema, "Binaural Speech Audiometry," *Int. Audiol.* **1**:218–221 (1968).

Guberina, P., "L'Audiométrie verbo-tonale," *Rev. Laryngol.* **77**:20–58 (1956).

Hahlbrock, K. H., "Über Sprachaudiometrie und neue Wörterteste," *Arch. Ohr. usw. Heilkd. u. z. Hals. usw. Heilkd.* **162**:394–431 (1953).

Hahlbrock, K. H., *Sprachaudiometrie*, G. Thieme, Stuttgart (1957).

Hahlbrock, K. H., "Knochenleitungs-Sprachaudiometrie als zusätzliche Messmethode vor hörverbessernden Operationen," *Acta Oto-Laryngol.* **53**:365–373 (1961).

Hanson, G., "A Further Factorial Investigation of Speech Sound Perception," *Scand. J. Psychol.* **5**:117–122 (1964).

Harris, J. D., "Free Voice and Pure Tone Audiometry for Routine Testing of Auditory Acuity," *Arch. Otolaryngol.* **44**:452–467 (1946).

Harris, J. D., "Some Suggestions for Speech Reception Testing," *Arch. Otolaryngol.* **50**:388–405 (1949).

Harris, J. D., "Speech Audiometry" in *Audiometry: Principles and Practices*, Williams & Wilkins, Baltimore (1965).

Hinchcliffe, R., and L. Wheeler, "An Investigation of the Effect of Flying on Speech Intelligibility in Noise," *J. Aviat. Med.* **28**:277–280 (1957).

Hipskind, N. M., and W. F. Rintelmann, "Effects of Experimental Bias upon Pure-Tone and Speech Audiometry," *J. Aud. Res.* **9**:298–305 (1969).

Hirsh, I. J., *The Measurement of Hearing*, McGraw-Hill, New York (1952).

Hood, J. D., "Speech Discrimination and Its Relationship to Disorders of the Loudness Function," *Int. Audiol.* **7**:232–238 (1968).

Horiguti, S., "Do Phonemic and Linguistic Differences among Languages Interfere with Speech Audiometry?" *Int. Audiol.* **3**:237–245 (1964).

Hudgins, C. V., "An Investigation of the Intelligibility of the Speech of the Deaf," *Genet. Psychol. Monogr.* **25**:289–392 (1942).

Hudgins, C. V., J. E. Hawkins, J. E. Karlin, and S. S. Stevens, "The Development of Recorded Auditory Tests for Measuring Hearing Loss for Speech," *Laryngoscope* **57**:57–89 (1947).

Huizing, H. C., R. Kruisinga, and M. Taselaar, "Triplet Audiometry: An Analysis of Band Discrimination in Speech Reception, *Acta Oro-Laryngol.* **51**:256–259 (1960).

Huizing, H. C., and J. A. Reyntjes, "Recruitment and Optimum Speech Intelligibility," *Rev. Laryngol. Bordeaux*, **Suppl.** 215–218 (May 1951).

Jerger, J., ed., *Modern Developments in Audiology*, 2nd ed., Academic Press, New York (1972).

Kapteyn, T. S., "Automatic Speech Audiometry," *Int. Audiol.* **9**:176–183 (1970).

Katz, J., "The SSW Test: An Interim Report," *J. Speech Hear. Disord.* **33**:132–146 (1968).

Katz, J., ed., *Handbook of Clinical Audiology*, Williams & Wilkins, Baltimore (1972).

Keller, F., "Technische und akustische Grundlagen der Sprachaudiometrie," *Z. Inst.* **74**:89–96 (1966).

King, P. F., "Some Imperfections of the Free Field Voice Tests," *J. Laryngol. Otol.* **67**:358–364 (1953).

Kinstler, D. B., J. G. Phelan, and R. W. Lavendar, "The Stenger and Speech Stenger Tests in Functional Hearing Loss," *Audiology* **11**:187–193 (1972).

Kirikae, I., et al., "A Study of Hearing Test Using Interrupted Speech," *J. Oto-Rhino-Laryngol. Soc. Japan* **67**:245–254 (1964). in Japanese, abstract in English.

Kiyosawa, H., "A Few Problems of Articulation Testing Method by Loudspeaker System," *Otol. Fukuoka* **11**:31–45 (1965). in Japanese, summary in English.

Konig, E., "Das Problem des Sprechaudiometrie im deutschweizerischen Sprachgebiet," *Pract. Otorhinolaryngol.* **28**:39–63 (1966).

Korsan-Bengsten, M., "Distorted Speech Audiometry," *Acta Oto-Laryngol.*, Suppl. 310 (1973).

Kroath, F., and F. Doubek, "Prüfung des Lautverstandnises als Ergänzung zu den üblichen Sprachverständnistesten," *Arch. Ohr. usw. Heilkd. u. Z. Hals. usw. Heilkd.* **173**:474–479 (1958).

Kryter, K. D., "Hearing Impairment for Speech," *Arch. Otolaryngol.* **77**:598–602 (1963).

Lafon, J. -C., *Le test phonétique et la mesure de l'audition*, Dunod, Paris (1964). trans. as *The Phonetic Test and the Measurement of Hearing*, Centrex, Eindhoven (1966).

Langenbeck, B., *Leitfaden der Praktischen Audiometrie*, 3rd ed. G. Thieme, Stuttgart (1965). Translated as *Textbook of Practical Audiometry*, Williams & Wilkins, Baltimore (1965).

Lehmann, R., *Elements de physio- et phychoacoustique*, Dunod, Paris (1969).

Leisti, T., "On Speech Audiograms," *Acta Oto-Laryngol.* **37**:256–260 (1949).

Lichtwitz, L., "De l'emploi du nouveau phonographe d'Edison comme acoumètre universel," *Ann. des mal. de l'oreille, etc.* Paris **15**:622–632 (1889).

Lidén, G., "Speech Audiometry: An Experimental and Clinical Study with Swedish Language Material," *Acta Oto-Laryngol.*, Suppl. 114 (1954).

Lidén, G., and G. Fant, "Swedish Word Material for Speech Audiometry and Articulation Tests," *Acta Oto-Laryngol.*, Suppl. 116, 189–204 (1954).

Lindeman, H. E., "Application of Speech Audiometry in Industrial Plants," *T. Soc. Geneeskd.* **45**:422–424 (1967). in Dutch, summary in English.

Linden, A., "Distorted Speech and Binaural Speech Resynthesis Tests," *Acta Oto-Laryngol.* **58**:32–48 (1964).

Lüscher, E., and C. Baud, "Die Sprechaudiometrie," *Arch. Ohr. usw. Heilkd. u. Z. Hals. usw. Heilkd.* **157**:549–561 (1951).

MacFarlan, D., "Speech Hearing and Speech Interpretation Testing," *Arch. Otolaryngol.* **31**:517–528 (1940).

MacFarlan, D., "Speech Hearing Tests," *Laryngoscope* **55**:71–115 (1945).

MacFarlan, D., "Testing Speech-Hearing and the Efficiency of Hearing Aids," *Ann. Otol. Rhinol. Laryngol.* **57**:444–452 (1948).

Matsui, R., "Studies in Speech Audiometry," *Hirosaki Med. J.* **11**:414–441 (1960). in Japanese, abstract in English.

Meister, F. J., *Akustische Messtechnik der Gehörprüfung*, G. Braun, Karlsruhe (1954).

Meister, J. J., "Sprachanalyse und Sprachgehörprüfung," *Z. Phonetik u. allg. Sprachwiss.* **8**:108–122 (1954).

Mullins, C. J., and J. L. Bangs, "Relationships between Speech Discrimination and Other Audiometric Data," *Acta Oto-Laryngol.* **47**:149–157 (1957).

Neely, K. K., "The Measurement of the Effectiveness with Which Hard-of-Hearing Individuals Discriminate Speech," *Int. Audiol.* **6**:431–435 (1967).

Neil, J. H., "Testing the Acuity of Hearing," *N. Z. Med. J.* **40**:223–230 (1941).

Noble, W. G., "Pure-Tone Acuity, Speech Hearing Ability, and Deafness in Acoustic Trauma: A Review of the Literature," *Audiology* **12**:291–315 (1973).

Owens, E., and E. D. Schubert, "The Development of Constant Items for Speech Discrimination Testing," *J. Speech Hear. Res.* **11**: 656–667 (1968).

Palva, A., "Filtered Speech Audiometry. I. Basic Studies with Finnish Speech toward Creation of a Method for the Diagnosis of Central Auditory Disorders," *Acta Oto-Laryngol.*, Suppl. 210 (1965).

Palva, T., "Finnish Speech Audiometry: Methods and Clinical Applications," *Acta Oto-Laryngol.*, Suppl. 101 (1952).

Pestalozza, G., and A. Lazzaroni, "Noise Effect on Speech Perception in Clinical and Experimental Types of Deafness," *Acta Oto-Laryngol.* **44**:350–358 (1954).

Pirodda, E., "I tests audiometrici par la voce nelle attuali applicazioni cliniche," *Bull. Sci. Med. Bologna* **122**:484–496 (1950).

Quist-Hanssen, S., and E. Steen, "Observed and Calculated Hearing Loss for Speech in Noise-Induced Deafness," *Acta Oto-Laryngol.*, Suppl. 158: 277–285 (1960).

Révész, G., O. Ribári, and I. Martikány, "The Effects of Noise on Speech Intelligibility and Other Psychophysiological Factors," in *Proc. 7th Int. Cong. Acoust.*, Akadémiai Kiadó, Budapest (1971) **3**, pp. 149–152.

Rhodes, R. C., "Discrimination of Filtered CNC Lists by Normals and Hypacusics," *J. Aud. Res.* **6**:129–133 (1966).

Robinson, M., and S. D. Kasden, "Bone Conduction Speech Audiometry: A Calibrated Method to Predict Post-Stapedectomy Discrimination Scores," *Ann. Otol. Rhinol. Laryngol.* **79**:818–824 (1970).

Röser, D., "Hörweitenbestimmung und Sprachaudiometrie in der Praxis," *Z. Laryngol.* **38**:116–127 (1959).

Ross, M., and T. G. Giolas, "Effect of Three Classroom Listening Conditions on Speech Intelligibility," *Amer. Ann. Deaf* **116**:580–584 (1971).

Sambataro, C., and G. Pestalozza, "Masking and Fatigue Effect of White Noise in Connection with Speech Tests," *Laryngoscope* **62**: 1197–1204 (1952).

Schubert, K., "Auf Wegen zu neuen Hörprüfgeräten," *Arch. Ohr. usw. Heilkd. u. Z. Hals. usw. Heilkd.* **155**:656–666 (1949).

Schubert, K., *Sprachhörprüfmethoden*, G. Thiem, Stuttgart (1958).

Schubert, K., ed., *Theorie und Praxis der Hörgeräteanpassung sowie Probleme der Begutachtung*, G. Thieme, Stuttgart (1960).

Schultz, M. C., "A Critique of Speech Recognition Testing Preliminary to Hearing Therapy," *J. Speech Hear. Disord.* **37**:195–202 (1972).

Siegenthaler, B. M., and R. Strand, "Audiogram-Average Methods and SRT Scores," *J. Acoust. Soc. Am.* **36**:589–593 (1964).

Silverman, S. R., "Use of Speech Tests for Evaluation of Clinical Procedures," *Arch. Otolaryngol.* **51**:786–797 (1950).

Silverman, S. R., and I. J. Hirsh, "Problems Related to the Use of Speech in Clinical Audiometry," *Ann. Otol. Rhinol. Laryngol.* **64**:1234–1244 (1955).

Simonton, K. M., and L. D. Hedgecock, "A Laboratory Assessment of Hearing Acuity for Voice Signals against a Background of Noise," *Ann. Otol. Rhinol. Laryngol.* **62**:735–747 (1953).

Stevenson, P. W., "Responses to Speech Audiometry and Phonemic Discrimination Patterns in the Elderly," *Audiology* **14**:185–231 (1975).

Sugaya, K., "Objections to Using Two Syllable Sounds in Articulation Tests," *Otolaryngol.* (Tokyo) **26**:187–189 (1954).

Tato, J. M., M. V. A. Chavez, and M. S. Sarrail, "Discriminación auditiva de sonidos, palabras y oraciones, reproducidos una octava mas un intervale de tercera por debajo del tono de grabación," *Otolaringol.* (Buenos Aires) **3**:75–83 (1952).

Tato, J. M., and J. B. de Quiros, "Die sensibilisierte Sprachaudiometrie," *Acta Oto-Laryngol.* **51**:593–614 (1960).

Utley, J., "The Relation between Speech Sound Discrimination and Percentage of Hearing Loss," *J. Speech Disord.* **9**:103–113 (1944).

Van Leeuwen, H. A., "Speech Audiometry in Industry," *T. Soc. Geneeskd.* **50** Suppl. 2:44–45 (Apr. 1972). in Dutch, abstract in English.

Van Zyl, F. J., and V. J. Brasier, "A Comparison of Monaural and Binaural Speech Discrimination Curves," *Brit. J. Audiol.* **7**:69–71 (1973).

Ventry, I. M., et al., "Bibliography of Functional Hearing Loss," *J. Aud. Res.* **5**:262–272 (1965).

Watson, L. A., and T. Tolan, *Hearing Tests and Hearing Instruments*, Williams & Wilkins, Baltimore (1949).

Webster, J. C., "Important Frequencies in Noise-Masked Speech," *Arch. Otolaryngol.* **80**:494–504 (1964).

Wells, W. A., "Facts and Fallacies of Hearing Tests," *Laryngoscope* **48**:137–146 (1938).

Wendt, K., "Die Wortverständlichkeit bei zweiohrigem Hören," *Nachrichtentech. Fachber.* **15**:21–24 (1959).

Wolf, O., "Hörprüfungsworte und ihr differentiell-diagnostischer Werth," *Arch. f. Ohrenheilkd.* (Leipzig) **29**:85–86 (1889–1890), trans. as "Words As Tests of the Hearing Power and Their Differential Diagnostic Value," *Arch. Otolaryngol.* **19**:298–304 (1890).

Wright, H. N., and R. Carhart, "The Efficiency of Binaural Listening among the Hearing-Impaired," *Arch. Otolaryngol.* **72**:789–797 (1960).

Zangmeister, H. E., "Zur Sprachaudiometrie," *Z. Laryngol. Rhinol. Otol.* **31**:335–338 (1952).

22

ON THE APPLICATION OF THE NEW EDISON PHONOGRAPH TO GENERAL HEARING MEASUREMENT

L. Lichtwitz

This article was translated expressly for this Benchmark volume by Mones E. Hawley from "Über die Anwendung des neuen Edison'schen Phonographen als allgemeinen Hörmesser," in Prager med. Wochenschr. **14**:547–549 (1889).

The functional measurement of hearing is of great importance for the diagnosis and prognosis of diseases of the ear. It is more important to the otologist than the determination of visual acuity is to the ophthalmogist. With his ophthalmoscope the latter can determine perfectly the condition of the refractive medium, the choroid, the retina, and the optic nerve. The aurist,* on the other hand, with his otoscope is permitted to examine only a part of the hearing apparatus (tympanic membrane, and part of the middle ear), while the inner walls of the tympanic cavity and especially the labyrinth are concealed from direct examination, so that afflictions of the hearing organs can be determined only from subjective indications and especially from the functional hearing examination.

In the hearing examination it is important to distinguish the perceptive faculty for which the labyrinth receives sound waves through the air from the perceptive faculty for which tones and noise are conducted by the tympanic-cranial path. The examination of the perception by cranial conduction often gives us valuable indications of the location of the affliction, while the measurement of the air conduction perception allows us to measure the degree of hearing impairment and permits us to control the effects of treatment. When one speaks ordinarily of hearing acuity, he means only the results of air conduction measurements.[1]

---

* The author uses the terms *Otologe* and *Ohrenarzt* interchangeably in this paper; in the French version *l'auriste* is used for both. *Aurist* was used in the American literature of the time in connection with examination but not with surgery. I have followed American terminology of 1890. [Trans.]

[1] Some authors do not give a precise definition of auditory acuity. The majority implicitly seem to assume that they will measure only the degree of conduction through the air path. Nevertheless, strictly speaking, auditory acuity is an expression that applies as much to sensitivity for air conduction as for bone conduction.

A wide variety of devices have been invented and used which emit various tones and noises to measure hearing capability, but none of these sound sources satisfies the requirements of a good acoumeter. We will review briefly the various acoumeters which have been applied throughout the world and mention their shortcomings. All of these determine the hearing acuity for air conducted tones, and only a few such as the tuning fork, the watch, and Politzer's acoumeter can be used also to measure the bone conduction acuity.

[The author then reviews briefly the devices most commonly used for pure tone and noise audiometry and their disadvantages. He notes that the watch tick is the most commonly used device, although it is not standardized in emission and does not correlate well with speech perception in many cases. Tuning forks and electrically driven sources are a great improvement, but the acuity for these sounds does not always correspond with the acuity for speech materials. *Trans.*]

It was therefore quite natural to use speech itself as the most perfect source for hearing measurements. Speech, which covers eight octaves, by this fact would give us the best idea of auditory acuity. Also the hearing capability for speech is of the greatest interest to patients. In his treatise on practical ear therapy Roosa[2] cites the characteristic response of a deaf child which he had occasion to examine in the course of treatment. After the child had submitted with good grace to the lengthy examination of his hearing by means of watch ticks, he finally asked, "What difference does it make whether I hear the watch, I want to hear what people say to me."

Although the usefulness of speech for the determination of hearing acuity will be recognized by all aurists, speech has been used only in a limited degree for the following reasons. Firstly, if one subjects a normal or an impaired ear to a speech test, he finds that the various words and syllables will be heard at different distances. The detailed experiments of O. Wolf gave the explanation for this fact.[3] He showed that each of the vowels and consonants was perceived at a different distance and that in general the vowels are understood better than the consonants. This author also has prepared a schematic presentation of the relative intensities of speech sounds in which the various letters of the alphabet are grouped according to their perceptibility. From this research it follows that for different words and syllables, although pronounced with the same intensity, each represents a particular acoustical value. From these data one can easily construct tables which contain words with the same acoumetric values; but the same doctor can not pronounce the same words at different times with the same intensity, and even less can one find that different doctors give the same intonation to permit the comparison among themselves of the results

[2] Roosa, D. B. S., *Lehrbuch der praktischen Ohrenheilkunde* [deutche Übersetzung von L. Weissof, 6th ed., W. Wood & Co. New York (1885)] (1889), p. 3.
[3] Wolf, O., *Sprach und Ohr*, F. Vieweg & Sohn, Braunschweig (1871).

of different hearing examinations.[4] Furthermore in order to measure the hearing acuity for speech in cases of moderate deafness one will have to have very large rooms, for the whispered voice can be heard by a normal ear at a distance of twenty to twenty-five meters.

From the previously stated critical remarks concerning various sound sources we can now deduce the characteristics that should be combined in a good acoumeter.

1. The acoumeter should reproduce all the sounds and noises perceptible by a normal ear and especially speech with all inflections.

2. It should be a constant sound source in order to permit comparison of the hearing acutiy of different patients and of the same patients at different times of his affliction.

3. It should be a uniform apparatus with fixed construction in order to make its adoption universal for aurists in different countries and to publish hearing acuity in an easily understandable way, as the ophthalmogists do for the visual acuity.

4. Its use should be simple and should not require much time or space.

5. It should be possible to measure hearing sensitivity both for the air conduction path and for the bone conduction path.

The new Edison phonograph possesses, if not all of these qualities, at least the first two which are the essentials of a good acoumeter, and it will be possible with some improvements to give it all of them.

1. "The new phonograph," according to the description which Richet gives of it in *Revue scientifique* for 4th May 1889, "consists essentially of a rotating cylinder over which one fits a hollow roll made of a material which appears to be wax-like. On this roll, which is set in motion by an electric motor of great precision, the oscillations of a light stylus are inscribed. The vibrations of the voice move a membrane which moves the stylus, and thus the stylus oscillations inscribe on the wax. After the sound vibrations have been inscribed, if one lets the stylus trace the same path, the shaking of the stylus vibrates the membrane which communicates to the external air a sound absolutely identical to the original."

Gournaud,[5] entrusted by Edison with presenting the phonograph to the Academy of Sciences in Paris, says in his report that the perfected phonograph records and reproduces with the greatest fidelity all the sounds and all the noises which can be perceived by the human ear, all the sounds of music, all the sounds produced in the languages of all the peoples of the whole world with all their variations in intensity,

---

[4] Lucae has built the so-called Maximalphonometer by means of which he measures the intensity of the voice from the measurement of the pressure of the expired air. Later Politzer (*Lehrbuch der Ohrenheilkunde*, 2nd edition, (1887) p. 113) has said that this apparatus has little practical value because speech intensity does not correspond adequately to expiration pressure.

[5] Gouraud, Col., *Comptes rendus de l'Academie des sciences*, pp. 841–845, 23 Apr. 1889.

timbre, etc. With the assistance of this apparatus it will be possible to prepare some phonograms which can serve as acoumetric scales according to the model of optometric scales. These scales will bear the impressions of vowels, consonants, syllables, words, and phrases according to their intensities and grouped by their acoustic values as established by O. Wolf. They will also be inscribed with the tones of all the octaves. Thus the first desideratum of a good acoumeter has been realized, because with the scales one will be able to examine the ear from the point of view of perception of the selected sounds and noise.

2. Another quality of the new phonograph consists of its being able "to reproduce an almost unlimited number of times the inscribed word without sensible alteration."[6] It is thus possible to let our patients hear the same phonogram every time reproduced in the same way. We have seen previously that the constancy of sound source is the second fundamental quality of a good acoumeter.

3. According to a personal communication from the representative of the Edison Company in London, all the apparatuses are of the same construction. Thus they will reproduce with the same intensity and the same timbre the phonograms adopted as uniform acoumetric scales. To obtain these uniform phonograms it will be sufficient to set up at a given distance from a phonograph reproducing a standard phonogram a second phonograph on which one can produce a considerable number of identical phonograms which will serve the aurists. Thanks to the uniformity of the phonographs and the phonogram scales, the aurists in all countries can compare the results of their hearing examinations one with another.[7]

There remains only one difficulty; this is the preparation of the standard phonogram, which should follow a regularly decreasing progression and which should be constructed on a uniform scale. This difficulty lies less in the imperfection of the machine than in that there does not exist in physics any means to measure and grade exactly the intensity of sounds. However, otologists do not need absolute acoustical values, but only the relative values, and the phonograms constructed in the following fashion will be able to produce acoumetric scales: one should pronounce in front of the mouthpiece of the phonograph at regularly increasing distances the particular words or the letters with an intensity which one can maintain constant during the short period which is sufficient for the experiment. The phonograms thus obtained will furnish a scale of decreasing speech intensity, largely sufficing for the purposes that we have stated.[8]

[6] Jansen, J., "Sur le phonographe de M. Edison," *Ibid.*, pp. 832–835.

[7] We have not been able to determine up to this point just how much the actual apparatus will possess the uniformity which is possible in principle. If the ideal should not be completely realized, it will not be difficult to find a coefficient for each apparatus which will permit the establishment of the relative intensities between the phonograph in question and a standard phonograph.

[8] By this means we have prepared a phonogram which we have demonstrated to the International Congress of Otology and Laryngology. The phonograph returns with a regularly decreasing intensity the words that we had spoken into

4. The use of the phonograph will be easier and will take less time than the methods now in use. It will be like the methods used by oculists to measure visual acuity. The ear which is to be measured is connected to the phonograph by a tube. One lets the patient listen to one phonogram after another. Thus one descends the phonogram scale until one arrives at the phonogram which the patient can no longer hear and which indicates the limit of auditory acuity.[9] This method differs from those used at present in that the sound source remains always at the same distance and it is the intensity of the sound alone that varies. The phonograph will be able to be employed in small clinic rooms and doctors' consultation chambers, and it will also have the advantage that ambient noise will not trouble the results of the examination. Furthermore, the examination will be limited to one ear, and it is well known how difficult it is in the case of unilateral deafness to prevent the voice or the acoumeter sound from being heard in the normal healthy ear if it is not blocked off completely.

5. In its present form the phonograph will give us information only on the perception of airborn sound. Perhaps it also will be possible by means of an auxilliary apparatus to apply it to the measure of perception through the cranium.

In closing I should like to meet an objection that one could raise against the universal use of the phonograph, which relates to its high price. If one but thinks about the general usage that the phonograph will receive in commerce, industry, and journalism,[10] then he can hope that the price will be reduced sufficiently for all aurists to obtain a phonograph which will replace all their other instruments for hearing examinations.[11]

Not only otologists will need the phonograph, but it will be used also by other branches of medicine. Already William Porter of St. Louis,[12] Mount Bleyer of New York,[13] and, recently, Marcel Baudouin

the apparatus at the regularly increasing distances. Notwithstanding the short time which we had to experiment with the phonograph and in spite of unfavorable circumstances of ambient noise and insufficient preparation for investigation, etc., we were able to assure ourselves of the validity of our theoretical deductions and of the possibility that useful phonograms can be constructed observing the care that such delicate experiments require. The Edison Co. of London will soon put an apparatus at our disposal. As soon as we have finished our experiments, we will give the results of them.

[9] The apparatus is constructed so that one can interrupt, speed, or slow the emission of the sound immediately and at will.

[10] I believe that the phonograph will also be able to render great service in the instruction of foreign languages, expecially those in which pronunciation can be obtained only by the live voice, English, for example.

[11] Already the *Review scientifique* of 27th April of this year indicates that truly the price of the apparatus will be less than 200 Fr.

[12] W. Porter, *Weekly Medical Review* No. 10, 1888.

[13] Mount Bleyer, "The Phonograph in Physical Diagnosis, with Experiments, and Its Future," *N.J. Medical Record* 17 Nov. 1888.

of Paris[14] have proposed its use to register the physical signs and noises that are produced in the heart and lungs. We also believe that one will also be able to use it to register the different disturbances of interior language (dysphasia) and those of exterior language (dyslalia). For the last, one will be able to control the good effects produced on speech articulation by plastic surgery on the palate or by removal of tumors from the rear nasal chambers (enlarged adenoids, naso-pharyngial polyps). The phonograph will also be able to register the troubles of the emission of sounds because of different diseases of the larynx (catarrh, tumors, distruction and paralysis of the vocal cords).

Further ahead, the new phonograph will enable us to complete our knowledge of the resonance of membranes and will give us a more exact definition of the sounds which compose speech than that which was possible with the old phonographs.[15,16] There exists a vast field for the application of the phonograph to the physical and medical sciences.

[14] M. Baudouin, "Des applications du phonographe aux sciences médicales," *Progrès méd.* No. 22 (1 June 1889).

[15] A. M. Mayer, *Sound*, New York (1878).

[16] O. Wolf, "Versuche mit dem Edison'schen Phonographen," *Z. f. Ohren-heilkd.* **8**:12–17 (1879).

23

Reprinted from *J. Speech Hearing Disord.* **17**(3):321–337 (1952)

Development Of Materials For Speech Audiometry

Ira J. Hirsh

Hallowell Davis

S. Richard Silverman

Elizabeth G. Reynolds

Elizabeth Eldert

Robert W. Benson

THE SOUNDS of speech have come to occupy an important place among the auditory stimuli that are used in clinical audiometry. By measuring a patient's ability to use his hearing in ways that are closer to everyday auditory experience, speech audiometry has not only added a kind of validity to pure-tone audiometry, but also certain speech tests have appeared to have diagnostic and prognostic value as well (*10*). The growth in the general acceptance and use of speech audiometry is accompanied by a need for

Ira J. Hirsh (Ph.D., Harvard, 1948) is Research Associate, Hallowell Davis (M.D., Harvard, 1922) is Director of Research, S. Richard Silverman (Ph.D., Washington Univ., 1942) is Director, Elizabeth G. Reynolds (B.A., Mt. Holyoke, 1949) is Research Assistant, and Robert W. Benson (Ph.D., Washington Univ., 1952) is Research Associate, Central Institute for the Deaf; and Elizabeth Eldert (M.A., Northwestern Univ., 1948) was formerly Audiologist, Department of Otolaryngology, Washington University School of Medicine. These materials were developed under contracts with the Veterans Administration (Contract V1001M-577) and the Office of Naval Research (Contract N6onr-272, Project No. NR142-170, Task Order III.)

standardization so that the test results in one clinic can be compared with those of another clinic. The present article deals with modifications of existing recorded auditory tests that yield new auditory tests, which appear to satisfy some clinical needs that were not fulfilled by older tests. In particular, tests will be described that permit the measurement of two clinical quantities: *hearing loss for speech* and *discrimination loss.*

Background

During World War II, considerable effort was expended in the development of articulation testing methods for the evaluation of various types of military communications equipment. It turned out that certain of these tests, developed at the Psycho-Acoustic Laboratory, Harvard University, were applicable to the clinical evaluation of hearing.

Psycho-Acoustic Laboratory (PAL) Auditory Tests No. 9 and No. 12, for measuring the threshold of intelligibility for spondaic words and for sentences, respectively, were made available on phonograph records for clinical use—first for military rehabilitation centers and then for more general use. These two recorded tests permitted a quick and reliable measure of the threshold of intelligibility and its related clinical measure, the hearing loss for speech. They have been described by Hudgins *et al* (*11*), by Hirsh (*9*), and others.

In a study of patients who were evaluated with respect to suitability for the fenestration operation, Davis (*2*) and his co-workers have formulated a general estimate of a patient's ability to hear speech by coupling the results on the threshold of intelligibility (or the hearing loss for speech) with a measure of the ability to discriminate among speech sounds at levels considerably above the threshold. This latter ability was measured by using the Psycho-Acoustic Laboratory's PB-50 lists, which are the phonetically balanced lists described by Egan (*5*). It appears that both types of tests are clinically useful and, indeed, that the latter measure of discrimination loss is the more useful clinical datum because the former, hearing loss for speech, can be predicted so reliably from the audiogram (*1, 6, 8*).

Several years have passed during which many audiometrists have had a chance to try out the spondee words and the PB-lists both by live-voice techniques and by way of phonograph records. During these years, reports have accumulated of several deficiencies in the Harvard tests, deficiencies mostly with respect to clinical use. Specifically, it has been reported informally that certain of the records of Auditory Test No. 9 yield slightly different thresholds from other of these records. Further, the large vocabulary that was assembled for the 20 PB-lists [published in Egan (*6*)] was too large for many clinical patients. The vocabulary appeared to need restriction in the dimension of familiarity. Finally, recorded versions of the PB-lists have not been available in suitably standard form.

This article does not purport to reveal any basically new concepts or techniques. It represents, rather, a report of modifications of these earlier tests in order to correct or eliminate some of these deficiencies that have been found as the tests have been used clinically.

Two basic improvements, from the clinical point of view, have been made. *First*, the vocabulary for the spondee lists and the PB-lists has been restricted so as to include only those words that meet certain criteria of familiarity. Furthermore, the vocabulary in each PB-list has been more rigidly phonetically balanced. The more rigid application of criteria of phonetic balance has resulted in a smaller test vocabulary, but one that appears to be sufficiently large for the small samples of lists that characterize clinical use. A *second* major improvement has been made possible by the use of recording on magnetic tape. With this recording technique it was possible to speak a given test word only once and then to copy it as many times as necessary to have it appear on different versions of a given test list. In the older tests, for example, the word *hothouse* appeared in each of six scramblings (word orders) of one spondee list. Since the test was made from original disc recordings, the word had to be spoken six times, once within each scrambling. With tape, one would have to speak the word only once, copy it six times, and cut and resplice the actual tapes in order to produce the word in its proper place in each of the six word orders.

An improved version of the Auditory Test No. 9 for clinical use is

C.I.D. Auditory Test W-2 (spondees at descending levels). The comparable modification of Auditory Test No. 14 is C.I.D. Auditory Test W-1 (spondees at constant level). Finally, recorded versions of the modified PB-lists appear as C.I.D. Auditory Test W-22. A general description, method of construction, and preliminary test results for each of these three tests follows.

Description and Development

C.I.D. Auditory Test W-1. Test W-1 consists of six scramblings of a single list of 36 spondaic words. These are recorded at a constant level, each word at a level 10 db below the level of an introductory carrier phrase, 'Say the word . . .' On the inside of each of the six record faces, a *1000 cps tone has been recorded at the level of the carrier phrases, that is, 10 db above the test words.* Since it was desirable that the carrier phrases be well above the level of the test words, especially for those playback levels at which the test words would be just barely intelligible, the tone could not be recorded at the level of the test words without endangering the monitoring meter of the test user. If, for example, the tone were recorded at the same level as the test words, and a playback were adjusted so that an ordinary VU meter read '0 VU,' the carrier phrases would force the indicator to hit the pin at the right side of the scale.

Use of Test W-1. In general, Test W-1 permits the measurement of the threshold of intelligibility, the level at which a listener repeats correctly 50% of the words of a given list, by traditional methods of articulation testing. In clinical application, it may be used by the audiometrist who wishes to control manually (with an attentuator that is variable in decibel or some multiple of decibel steps) the intensity of the words presented to a listener.

Construction of Test W-1. The starting point for vocabulary was the group of 84 spondee words in PAL Test No. 9 (and No. 14). The most familiar spondees were obtained from ratings of judges who, working independently, rated the words in the Harvard tests on a three-point scale of familiarity. The words rated most familiar were spoken by an adult male and were recorded on a phonograph disc.

Two acetate discs were cut simultaneously, one for future rerecording and one for preliminary use. The talker monitored the carrier phrase 'Say the word,' carefully on a VU meter, and then spoke the following test word with 'equal effort.' When spoken in this manner the words varied from each other in intensity level by about ± 2 db. Some words were spoken several times until the talker felt that a satisfactory rendition had been obtained.

In a preliminary experiment, six listeners with normal pure-tone audiograms listened monaurally to the words through standard playback equipment (See Appendix A). The group included both experienced and inexperienced listeners. Instructions were as follows:

> You are going to hear a list of two-syllable words, like 'baseball' and 'armchair.' A man's voice will say 'Say the word' before each word. Listen for the word following. Some groups of words are louder, some are softer than others. Repeat through the microphone what you hear. If you hear only unintelligible sound after 'Say the word,' let me know by saying 'Check.'

Individual thresholds for speech (in db re 0.0002 microbar) were obtained for the spondaic word lists in the PAL Test 9. The method of scoring was that described in Hudgins *et al* (*11*).

Each listener then listened to the disc recording of the more familiar (CID) spondees at +4, +2, 0, −2, −4, and −6 db relative to the threshold that had been obtained for PAL Test 9. The order in which the lists were presented was the same for each listener. The order in which the different levels appeared, however, was varied for each listener and each list according to a random Latin Square design. In this design, dependent variables, such as learning and fatigue, are presumably weighted equally at each level in the averaged data for six listeners. All data for each listener were obtained in one listening session.

Raw data were recorded in terms of the number of errors per word for each listener. One word, relatively much easier than the others, might be repeated correctly even at levels 4 and 6 db below the threshold. Consequently, there would be very few errors for that word. And conversely, a difficult word might not be heard correctly, even at levels 2 and 4 db above the threshold, and would have many errors. In the analysis of this preliminary data an easy word was defined as one missed once or less by all six listeners. A difficult word was one missed five or more times by all six listeners. Words falling in both of these extreme categories were eliminated, and also the words that five of the six listeners found difficult or easy. In the 36 words left, a group of equally intelligible spondees was approximated.

The original disc reserve was then dubbed to tape. The 36 chosen words were cut out and spliced together with enough blank tape between words to facilitate the separate attenuation of individual words. This was called the *master tape* and all subsequent versions of the 36 words were recorded from this tape. One carrier phrase was recorded with good quality and even monitoring. This carrier was recorded separately from the words and therefore sounds qualitatively different from the words. This difference, however, in no way affects the results of the tests and is not very noticeable at levels around threshold where the test is given. This was called the *master carrier phrase*. It could be rerecorded any number of times by making a loop of it and running the tape around and around on the recording head of the tape recorder.

Six different word orders of the same 36 words were put together in the following manner. The master tape was dubbed to tape again six times. The order of the words in five dubbings was changed by cutting the words apart and resplicing them in different positions within each list. The master carrier phrase was then recorded once for each of the 216 words in the six lists at +10 db relative to the words. A carrier phrase was spliced in front of each word and the timing made such that one carrier phrase plus the word following plus the pause for a listener's response took six seconds. The six word orders were designated as Lists A, B, C, D, E, and F of W-1 and an appropriate recorded introduction was spliced in front of each. A copy of these lists as just described was made for experimental purposes and the original spliced version was held in reserve.

An experiment similar to the preliminary testing was then run. One Latin Square was done with inexperienced listeners, however, and another with experienced listeners. The six word orders were given to all listeners in the same sequence, although the levels at which different listeners heard different word orders were determined by a random Latin Square. Tentative speech thresholds were determined this time by using one of the experimental word lists. The words were presented at this threshold (0 db) and +4, +2, −2, −4, and −6 db. Raw data for each group of subjects were scored as errors for each word at each of the presentation levels.

Performance on the separate words varied little between the experienced and inexperienced listeners. For present purposes, therefore, their data were treated together. An inspection of the data showed that some words were still more difficult, some easier, than others in spite of the initial attempt to get a group of words homogenous with respect to intelligibility. The degree of difficulty of a word was correlated with the intensity reading of the word on a VU meter. The easy words monitored at higher levels, the more difficult words at lower levels, relative to the average intensity reading for the 36 words. This correlation existed even though originally the words were spoken with 'equal effort' and varied only ± 2 db from an average intensity reading. It was therefore decided to push the more difficult words up 2db and the easier words down 2 db.

A second set of the same six word orders was made from the master tape changing the levels of the more difficult or easier words by ± 2 db in each rerecording of the master tape. The experiment described above was repeated. An analysis of the data showed that the words were now more homogenous with respect to intelligibility and variations in the thresholds of individual words were, as adequately as could be measured by this method, chance variations. Since tape reproducers are not in general clinical use, and since there is no good way of copying large numbers of tape recordings, this last version of the six word lists was recorded on discs as Auditory Test W-1.

This final recording was done at the Technisonic Recording Studios. The word lists were recorded both at 78.26 rpm and 33⅓ rpm with the NARTB recording characteristic (14). A half-minute of a 1000 cps calibration tone, at the level of the carrier phrase, was put at the inner edge of each record so that individual operators can set their levels on a constant signal.

Preliminary Test Results for Test W-1. The articulation - vs. - gain function for Test W-1 as recorded on the final tapes is shown in Figure 1. The function represents the data of all listeners, six inexperienced and six experienced, and was drawn as the most representative curve for the series of individual curves superposed on each other at 0 db, or threshold. Therefore the function is to be interpreted as showing slope relative to threshold with no indication of the absolute levels involved.

The articulation score rises from 0 to 100% within a range of about 20 db. There is an increase from 20 to 80% within a range of 8 db and throughout this range the slope or rate of rise in score is about 8% per db. Since the threshold falls on the

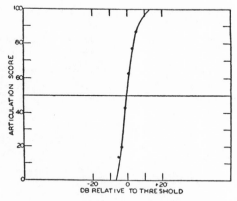

FIGURE 1. Articulation score as a function of level relative to individual threshold (Auditory Test W-1). Points represent average scores for 12 listeners.

steepest part of the function, it is crossed very abruptly and, therefore, can be very sensitively determined with this test. There is a definite 'tail' on the upper end of the curve. The rate of rise of the curve tapers off above 80% and does not reach the 100% point until about +14 db above threshold. Much of this tapering is due to the performance of the inexperienced listeners at levels above threshold. They were not familiar with the words or the listening situation and therefore continued to miss a few words even at levels above threshold where their scores should have been nearer 100%. Momentary inattention on the part of all listeners also contributed to the flattening of the function at the upper end. Below threshold the words drop out very quickly and there is little if any 'tail' at this end of the curve.

The absolute thresholds for the experienced and inexperienced listeners were approximately the same, 20 db and 21 db re 0.0002 microbar, respectively. The difference between the two thresholds was not significant.

Preliminary checks were also made with the first disc recordings of Test W-1. Fourteen listeners (in groups of four or five) listened monaurally to all six scramblings at each of two levels, one below threshold and the other above. These levels were not the same for all listeners as each earphone used had a correction factor of its own which changed the output level. The two points obtained in each case were connected by a straight line, the slope of which was close to 8% per db, and the approximate threshold was interpolated from this straight line function. The mean absolute threshold obtained in this way was 14.3 db re 0.0002 microbar and the standard deviation of the individual mean thresholds around this mean was 2.2 db.

It should be stressed here that the above results with the new W-1 disc recordings are tentative and await confirmation from those who use the test according to the instruction manual issued with the test.

C.I.D. Auditory Test W-2. Test W-2 employs the 36 words that were used in W-1 and also the same six word orders. Test W-2 differs from W-1, however, in that the intensity of the words is attenuated within each list at the rate of 3 db every three words. In the older PAL Test 9 the rate of attenuation was 4 db every six words. In the present test, it was attempted to employ a faster pace and also to avoid the necessity of a table for scoring by letting each word represent 1 db of attenuation on the average.

Use of Test W-2. This test is designed specifically for a rapid estimate of the threshold of intelligibility. The six word orders, labelled lists A through F, are the same as those of Test W-1. Instead of presenting a whole list or a portion of a list at a fixed intensity or several intensities, this test sweeps through an intensity range of 33 db by attenuating the level of the test words 3 db every three words. The rationale for this procedure consists of sampling three-word portions of the list at intensity levels that are 3 db apart. Ideally the intensity level at which a listener repeats 50% of a group (i.e., 1.5 words) would be the threshold. Actually, the threshold is approximated by assuming that the words are attenuated at an average rate of 1 db per word and that the threshold is the level at which the first group of three words is presented minus the number of words (or of decibels) that the listener repeats correctly.

Of course, a threshold calculated in this way will be in error because the 50%-criterion is not fully met unless 50% of the first group (i.e., the first 1.5 words) is first subtracted out of the total. The 1.5-db error involved is a constant of small magnitude relative to ordinary test results and may be neglected in clinical use. The absolute thresholds to be given below have taken this correction into account and represent, therefore, the best approximation to a 50%-response level. In general, the clinical norms, if established without this correction, should be 1.5 db lower.

Construction of Test W-2. When the master tape was dubbed again to tape for this test, the initial relative level of the same words was changed ± 2 db in each rerecording as they had been for the final version of Auditory Test W-1. In addition, in each rerecording every word was separately attenuated in such a way that when the words were spliced together in the same order as in W-1 the intensity within each list decreased 3 db every three words.

Two hundred sixteen copies of the master carrier phrase were made, one for each word in W-2. The first nine carriers for each list were recorded at the level of the first three words. The intensity of the rest of the carrier phrases for each list was decreased 3 db after every three carrier phrases. In the final spliced version of the test, therefore, the first nine carrier phrases are at the starting level of the test even though the intensity of the test words in these first three groups is already being attenuated. From the tenth item on, the carrier phrases are progressively attenuated, each carrier phrase remaining 6 db above the word that follows it.

A carrier phrase at the correct relative level was then spliced in front of each word. The lists were designated as lists A, B, C, D, E and F of W-2, corresponding to the same lists in W-1. Appropriate introductions

were then spliced in front of the lists. Finally, copies of this original spliced version were made for experimental purposes.

The experimental problem was to find out if there were any differences in difficulty among the lists. A group of six experienced listeners were given the six word orders of Auditory Test W-2. The tests were started at 40 db above 0.0002 microbar so that, assuming that the thresholds would be around 20 db, a listener would repeat approximately half the list before reaching threshold. Instructions to the listener were the same as for the experiments with Auditory Test W-1. The order in which each listener heard the W-2 lists was determined by a random Latin Square design.

An analysis of variance showed that different thresholds obtained by using different word orders varied no more than would be expected by random error. There were differences, however, in the average thresholds for six listeners as obtained with the different lists. Differences were of the order of ± 1 db. It appears that the lists of words are not equal in difficulty unless each entire list is heard. When only part of the list is heard the difficulty of the list depends on which part is heard. For a given listener it cannot be said that all parts of the lists are equal in difficulty.

The six word lists were then recorded on discs at the Technisonic Recording Studios. These lists were also recorded at 78.26 rpm and at 33⅓ rpm with the NARTB recording characteristic (14). Again, as for W-1, a 1000 cps calibration tone was put at the inner edge of each record. This calibration tone is at the average level of the first nine carrier phrases and of the first three words.

Preliminary test results. The same 14 listeners who listened to the W-1 disc recordings also listened to the

W-2 recordings. Each of the listeners heard all six scramblings of W-2 and individual thresholds were taken as the mean of the six scores for each listener. Lists were started at a level of 35 db re 0.0002 microbar and, as described, the level of each successive three words decreased 3 db. When the test is started at 35 db for normal ears half or more of the test is heard before threshold is reached.

The mean absolute threshold for 14 listeners was 17.7 db re 0.0002 microbar. (This includes the 1.5 db correction mentioned earlier.) The standard deviation of the individual thresholds was 2.6 db. The difference between the W-1 and the W-2 thresholds of about 3.5 db in favor of W-1 may result from presenting all 36 words at a given level instead of only three. In actual clinical practice Test W-1 should be administered, as described in the manual, by 'bracketing' the threshold using small samples of four or five words at levels around threshold. Thresholds obtained in this manner will undoubtedly be closer to those obtained with W-2.

An analysis of variance showed that there were no significant differences in difficulty between the W-2 lists as they were recorded on disc. Again, however, as with the tape versions, there were differences of the order of ± 1 db.

C.I.D. Auditory Test W-22. Test W-22 consists of a vocabulary of 200 monosyllabic words divided into four lists of 50 words each. Each list is phonetically balanced; that is, the speech sounds within the list occur with the same relative frequency as they do in a representative sample of English speech. Six scramblings of each list are available. The words have been spoken with the carrier phrase, 'You will say,' and the 1000 cps calibration tone on the inner face of every record is at the average level of the carrier phrases.

Use of Test W-22. This test is used to determine a patient's discrimination loss for speech. The discrimination loss for speech is the difference between 100 per cent and the percentage of given speech material that a listener repeats correctly at a level that is sufficiently high so that a further increase in intensity is not accompanied by a further increase in the amount of speech material repeated correctly. Low discrimination scores, i.e., large discriminations losses, have been found to yield important diagnostic distinctions (2).

Construction of Test W-22. The most important task was the selection of the vocabulary to make up the phonetically balanced word lists. The following criteria for the vocabulary were set up. First, all the words must be one-syllable words with no repetition of words in the different lists. Second, any word chosen should be a familiar word. This second criterion is to minimize the effect of differences in the educational background of subjects. Third, the phonetic composition of each word list should correspond to that of English as a whole as closely as possible.

This third criterion was the most difficult one to satisfy because there are no satisfactory studies of spoken English in the literature. The sources used were Dewey's study (4) of the phonetic composition of newsprint and the Bell Telephone Laboratories' study (7) of business telephone calls in New York City. The two sources were given equal weight in the determination of the phonetic criteria for the word lists.

The sources were followed as closely as possible. First the distribution of syllable types (vowel-consonant, consonant-vowel-consonant, etc.) was determined. Then the distribution of vowels and consonants within each list was planned. Here the frequency of occurrence of consonants and consonant compounds in initial and final positions was considered. All distributions of phonetic elements were based on distributions of individual speech sounds rather than on groups of sounds.

The vocabulary of the 20 Psycho-Acoustic Laboratory PB-50 lists, a total of 1000 words, was used as a pool from which words were drawn for Auditory Test W-22. From this pool 120 words were used. The remainder of the vocabulary (80 words) was not drawn from any specific source.

Five people independently rated the entire PAL vocabulary for familiarity. They were instructed to rate about half the words in each PB-50 list as 1 (most familiar), about 25% as 2 (fairly familiar), and approximately 25% as 3 (very unfamiliar). Agreement among the five raters was good. A final rating in familiarity, based on the rating given by the majority of the raters, was then assigned to each word. Of the 120 words from the PAL lists used in Auditory Test W-22, 112 were rated as 1, 7 as 2, and only one, 'isle,' as 3.

The entire W-22 vocabulary, a total of 200 words, was checked with the Thorndike list (15). All words except 'ace' appear on the Thorndike list. According to Thorndike, 190 are among the 4000 most common English words; 171 are among the 2000 most common words; and 144 are among the 1000 most common words. The W-22 vocabulary was also checked with the Dewey list (4). Of the 200 words, 128 appear on this list. All of these 128 words are among the first 2000 most common words on the Thorndike list.

The only words of doubtful familiarity are 'ace,' 'ale,' and 'pew.' These

TABLE 1. W-22 distribution of syllable types.

Type	Percentage of words
VC	20
CV	22
CVC	36
VCC	4
CCV	2
CVCC	10
CCVC	4
CCVCC	2

words received a rating of 2 by the board of judges and are relatively unfamiliar according to the Thorndike lists. 'Isle,' which was given a rating of 3 by the judges, is among the 3000 most common words according to Thorndike; as 'aisle' it is in the first 5000; and as 'I'll' it is in the first 2000. In general, the vocabulary consists of very common words.

The third criterion states that the phonetic composition of the lists shall correspond as closely as possible to that of English as it is generally spoken.

The first step in setting up a plan for phonetic balance was to decide on percentages for the various consonant-vowel arrangements found in monosyllabic words (Table 1). This decision was based on the analysis of syllable types in the study by French, Carter and Koenig (7), with the following modifications. All vowel words were omitted. The high frequency of their occurrence depends on two words, 'I' and 'you.' The percentage of consonant-vowel-consonant words was increased slightly and the percentage of words containing consonant compounds (two or more consonants in a row) was increased from 14.7% to 22%. The distribution of syllable types followed the French, Carter and Koenig study as closely as was practicable. In each W-22 list there were four initial consonant compounds and eight final compounds.

The next step was to decide on the distribution of vowels within each list (Table 2). The mean of the percentages given by Dewey (4) and by French, Carter and Koenig (7) for the frequency of occurrence of each vowel was followed as closely as possible. The following modifications were made. The neutral vowel was omitted from the distribution, since this vowel does not ordinarily appear in monosyllabic words. The percentages for the other vowels were increased, therefore, by an appropriate amount to make up for the absence of the neutral vowel from the distribution. Percentages for long vowels were also increased in order to fulfill requirements for syllable distribution. In general, a plan for the distribution of vowel sounds was worked out which

TABLE 2. W-22 vowel distribution.

Vowel Sound	Per cent occurrence in each W-22 list
ɪ	12
æ	10
ɛ	10
ɑ	8
ʌ	8
i	10
e	10
o	6
u	6
ɑɪ	6
ɔ	4
ʊ	4
ɑʊ	2
ɪʊ	2
ɔɪ*	1
ɝ*	1

*The ɔɪ vowel occurs once in two lists and the ɝ sound in the other two lists.

TABLE 3. W-22 consonant distribution.

Sound	Number of occurrences in each PB list	
	Initial	Final
t	4	7
n	3	7
r	2	7
d	3	3
l	2	4
s	3	3
m	2	3
k	3	1
w	4	0
z	0	4
v	0	3
ð	2	1
h	3	0
f	1	1
p	1	1
b	2	0
j	2	0
ŋ	0	1
g	1	0
ʃ	1	0
θ	1	0
tʃ	1	0
dʒ	1	0
ʒ	0	0
	—	—
	42	46

was practicable, and it was followed exactly in each list.

Finally, the distribution of consonants was determined (Table 3). As for the vowel sounds, the mean of the percentages given by Dewey and by French, Carter and Koenig for the frequency of occurrence of each consonant sound was followed. The percentage for each consonant was divided into a quota for appearance of that consonant in initial and final positions. This was done by referring to both Dewey and the French, Carter and Koenig study and following their

262

divisions roughly. The number of words in each PB-list (50 words) is too small to permit precise division of the consonants into quotas for initial and final positions.

Once the four PB-lists, each containing 50 different monosyllabic words, had been chosen they were recorded on magnetic tape. The talker used the carrier phrase 'You will say.' He monitored this phrase on a VU meter and then spoke the word as it would naturally follow in the phrase.

The four lists dubbed from live voice to magnetic tape were the master lists. Each list was then rerecorded six times and the words were cut and spliced in different orders to give six different word orders for each of the lists. There was no master carrier. Each phrase was kept intact as it had been spoken. The lists were designated Lists 1, 2, 3, and 4 and the word orders for each were lettered A through F. Appropriate introductions were then spliced into the recording. Copies on tape of the spliced version were made for experimental purposes and the original was kept for rerecording onto disc.

Trouble was encountered with signal transfer from one layer of tape to the layer directly underneath on the reel both on the original recording and on the copies. This phenomenon is recognized by the tape manufacturer but usually the level of the transfer signal is very low and is not noticeable in a continuous recording. The transfer signal on the recordings was 45 to 50 db below the signal and below threshold at lower playback levels. At the highest playback levels used in the experiment, however, particularly at 100 db, the 'echo' was above threshold in the pauses between phrases. In the following experiments, the words were presented at a level 20 db above an intermixed white noise.

The noise effectively masked the echo but did not interfere with the intelligibility of the words. When the lists were dubbed to disc the cutting head on the recording lathe was short-circuited between each phrase so that none of the echo was recorded.

An experimental check was made to determine whether the four lists were equal in difficulty. It was assumed that there would be no differences in difficulty among different word orders of the same list. Three groups of five listeners, a total of 15 in all, were used. They were screened at +10 db relative to normal threshold for all test frequencies on the Maico puretone audiometer. Each group of five came on eight consecutive evenings (Saturdays and Sundays excluded) and listened each evening for 2½ hours including two or three rest periods.

Instructions were as follows:

You are going to hear lists of one-syllable words. All the words you will hear are on the printed sheet I have just given you. At the beginning of each session you will be given the chance to look at this list. Some lists will be very loud and others will be very soft. Listen carefully and write down as many words as you can.

Group I first listened monaurally to all 24 lists (six word orders of each of four lists) at 100 db re 0.0002 microbar. This procedure gave the listeners an indoctrination period in which the words were presented at a high level. Then they heard each of the 24 word lists at levels 10 db apart from 20 to 70 db re 0.0002 microbar. Lists and levels were randomized with the exception that no list was ever heard twice at the same level.

Group II listened under the same conditions. The lists and levels were in a different order, however, and an eighth level of 15 db re 0.0002 microbar was also used when it was found that not enough low scores at 20 db were being obtained to determine the bottom of the articulation curve. Group III first listened to all lists at 100 db. Then they listened to each word order at 50, 40, 30, 20 and 15 db re 0.0002 microbar. The scores from the first two groups were consistently near 100% correct above 50 db and it was felt that the shape of the upper part of the curve was well determined without running Group III at 60 and 70 db.

The articulation scores for each list are plotted as a function of sound pressure level in Figure 2. At higher levels there are no significant differences between the list scores. From 40 db down, however, there are greater differences. The gain function for List 1 was consistently lower than for the other lists. A second articulation curve (the broken curve) drawn through the scores for List 1 alone is shifted over on the scale approximately 2 db. A calculation of the average relative intensity of the words in each list as

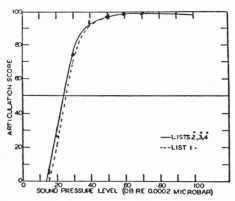

FIGURE 2. Articulation score (Auditory Test W-22) as a function of sound pressure level (experimental tape versions). Each point is the average of 15 listeners' scores on all six word orders of a list. The solid curve is drawn through points for Lists 2, 3, and 4. The broken curve is drawn through the points for List 1.

read from a VU meter showed that the words in List 1 were on the average 2.5 db lower than the words in any other list. Therefore, in the final recordings from magnetic tape to disc the intensity of List 1 was increased 2 db relative to the intensity at which the other three lists were recorded.

The threshold (50%-response) for these new PB-lists as determined from the experimental curve in Figure 2 is 24 db re 0.0002 microbar.

After inspection of the above data and the subsequent decision to raise the relative level of List 1 2-db, the six word orders of each list were recorded onto disc from tape. The lists were recorded at 33⅓ rpm and 78.26 rpm. A calibration tone at the average level of the carrier phrase 'You will say' was put on the inner band of every record.

Preliminary Test Results for Test W-22. The articulation function for Test W-22 has already been discussed under the construction of the test and is shown in Figure 2. This function was obtained using the experimental tapes. After the tapes were dubbed to disc for the final version of the test the articulation function was checked at two points using the disc recordings. The disc recordings were played to 15 listeners (in groups of 5) at 80 db re 0.0002 microbar to check the maximum articulation score and at 25 db to check scores close to threshold.

The average score at 80 db using the disc recordings was 98% as compared to a score of approximately 99% at 80 db read from the articulation function. At 25 db scores were higher with the 78 rpm recordings than with the 33⅓ rpm recordings. The average score for the 78 rpm's was 63.4%, for the 33⅓ rpm's, 56.3%. The 33⅓ score agrees closely with the articulation score that would have been obtained at 25 db with the experimental tapes (see Figure 2).

Although the same word orders of a list monitor alike on both the 78 and the 33⅓ rpm recordings, it is very possible that the high frequencies were given a boost of a few db on the 78 rpm recordings. This boost does not show up in the monitoring as the VU meter is responding primarily to the energy around 250 cps which is the peak energy of the speaker's voice. Since the high frequencies are important in the discrimination of many consonants a high frequency boost in the recording might be accompanied by an increased articulation score for the recordings affected.

These data showed no consistent differences between scores on the four different lists. All listeners were given ample opportunity to study alphabetical lists of the words, however, and heard scramblings of each list as least three times. In a shorter clinical procedure where listeners may hear scramblings of two different lists once, some sort of differences between lists may appear from listener to listener. It can only be said that the averaged data of several listeners from several tests showed no consistent difference between lists.

As with the W-1 and W-2 results these results await verification from several clinics using a large number of listeners.

Discussion

Although this report is intended to be only a description of some new auditory tests, it seems appropriate to discuss the relations among these tests and their predecessors. This discussion is supported by experimental data on

a relatively few listeners. Most of the conclusions must remain tentative until a larger amount of clinical information is available.

Relations Among The New Tests. There are two outstanding relations that have been established with groups of normal listeners: one concerns the relation between W-1 and W-2 and the other between W-1 and W-22.

Descending-Level vs. Constant-Level Spondees. It has already been shown that the threshold for W-2 is about 4 db above the threshold for W-1. That this difference is real is attested by some observations in which W-1 recordings were used as if they were W-2. Otherwise said, the W-1 recording was begun at a certain sound pressure level and the experimenter attenuated the words by 3 db every three words. The results of this procedure yielded thresholds of the order of 18 db re 0.0002 microbar, the tentative standard threshold for W-2 It seems fair to conclude that the difference between the thresholds for W-1 and W-2 is attributable to the number of words that are presented at each level. From a restricted point of view, the W-1 threshold, at about 14 db, represents the experimental ideal. When W-1 is put to clinical use, however, the tester ordinarily presents only four or five words at each level. Thus, in clinical use, when all 36 words are not presented at each test level, the expected threshold will be more nearly 18 db, as for W-2.

Spondees vs. Monosyllables. Figure 3 shows the articulation-vs.-gain functions for all versions of W-1 and W-22. Two generalizations may be made: (1) The intelligibility of the spondee words (W-1) increases more rapidly with increase in intensity than does the intelligibility of the monosyllabic

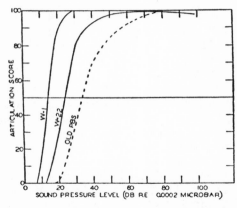

FIGURE 3. Relations between Auditory Test W-1, W-22, and the old PB-50 lists recorded at Technisonic Studios. The broken curve refers to the older version of the PB-lists. The solid curve labelled W-1 is the same curve found in Figure 1, but drawn relative to the average absolute threshold for 12 listeners. The curve labelled W-22 is the curve drawn for Lists 2, 3, and 4 in Figure 2.

words of the PB-lists (W-22), and (2) the level at which a listener can repeat correctly 50% of a list of spondees is lower than for one of the PB-lists of monosyllables. The reasons for the lower spondee threshold have been treated adequately elsewhere (5, 11, 12, 13.) It should be pointed out here, however, that the threshold for the present PB-lists (W-22) is much closer to the spondee threshold than have been the thresholds for previous PB-lists (see below).

Relations Between Present and Former Recorded Tests. It is clear that the results for normal listeners with these new recorded tests are not the same as the results for the older tests. Some of these differences need to be pointed out in detail.

Relation Between W-2 and PAL Auditory Test No. 9. The present W-2 threshold of 18 db is somewhat lower than the threshold for Test

No. 9 (22 db). The reasons for this difference cannot be attributed entirely to the new recording procedure. First, the old threshold at 22 db is a clinical threshold, somewhat higher than experimental ones. Furthermore, the total spondee vocabulary in W-2 is only 36 words while the total vocabulary for Auditory Test No. 9 is 84 words, or 42 words on either version. In view of the relation between the intelligibility of a given list of words and the size of the vocabulary for the list, which has been pointed out by Miller, Heise and Lichten (13), it is not surprising that the threshold for the new tests with a smaller vocabulary should be lower. Again, it must be kept in mind that these thresholds are restricted to a psychophysical procedure in which only a few words are presented at each level. The low threshold that is obtained for W-1 indicates the order of difference that may be accounted for by these variations in the testing procedure.

Relation between W-22 and the older PB-lists. For some time a set of recordings of some of the PB-lists published by Egan has been available for distribution from the Technisonic Studios. These have enjoyed sufficient clinical use so that some tentative standards have become available. The articulation-vs.-gain function for these recordings is shown as a third curve in Figure 3. It is clear that the intelligibility of these older recordings at any given level is lower than for W-22 and that the function for the older recordings is not nearly so steep as that for W-22. Several reasons may be given for this difference. It has already been shown, in the above discussion of the development of Test W-1, that the intelligibility of a word is markedly dependent on its intensity relative to the other words in a list. The monitoring in W-22 is such that all of the words are much closer to each other in intensity than they were on the older recordings of the Egan lists. Furthermore, the vocabulary for W-22 consists of a total of 200 words while the total vocabulary in the Egan list was 1000 words. Again, noting the relation between intelligibility and vocabulary size (13), it is not surprising that the intelligibility of the smaller vocabulary should be higher at any given level than for the larger vocabulary.

There are certain clinical questions that arise concerning the usefulness of W-22 in measuring discrimination loss. The smaller vocabulary makes W-22 an 'easier' test than the older PB-lists. Both the vocabulary and the greater internal homogeneity contribute to a steeper gain function for W-22 than for the older PB-lists (12) (see Figure 3). There is not available as yet sufficient clinical information to predict whether this higher intelligibility and steeper gain function will make the use of W-22 more limited in the measurement of discrimination loss than the use of the older PB-lists.

Summary

Three new recorded tests for the hearing of speech have been described. Tests W-1, W-2 and W-22 have been constructed to take the place of recorded versions of PAL Auditory Tests 14 and 9 and the PB-lists published by Egan respectively. Two novel techniques have been introduced: (1) The use of magnetic tape recording has permitted the construction of several versions or word orders of a given test list in which all occurrences of a test item in the several versions are physically identical; (2) The criterion

of phonetic balance in W-22 and the criterion of familiarity of test items in both tests have been more rigidly followed, resulting in easier, more homogeneous lists, but with a more limited vocabulary.

Preliminary results have been presented in which the intelligibility for these new tests is shown as a function of intensity. Furthermore, a relation between intelligibility for these new tests and their analagous predecessors has been established. The authors' recommendation for the clinical adoption of these tests is tentative, pending the accumulation of results on larger groups of listeners in both clinical and laboratory situations.[1]

Appendix A

Equipment

The equipment necessary for reproducing the recordings of Auditory Tests W-1, W-2, and W-22 is represented by the American Standard Speech Audiometer[2] and includes the following elements:

1. A turntable and phonograph pickup with NARTB (National Association of Radio and Television Broadcasters) playback characteristic.
2. An amplifier.
3. A meter for monitoring the output of the amplifier.
4. An attenuator.
5. A calibrated earphone or loudspeaker.

[1] While this paper was in preparation clinical trials of W-2 and W-22 were conducted in the Hofheimer Audiology Laboratory (Washington University) and in the Hearing Clinic of Central Institute for the Deaf. Experience to date indicates (1) that W-2 is very satisfactory for determining the threshold for speech, but (2) that W-22 does *not* satisfactorily separate patients with mixed deafness from patients with pure conductive deafness. The older recordings of the Egan lists are more effective in this respect. The reasons for this difference are now being sought.

[2] *American Standard Specification for Speech Audiometers.* New York: American Standards Association (in preparation).

The components are shown in the block diagram below:

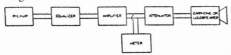

The turntable should be capable of playing recordings at a speed of 33⅓ rpm or of 78.26 rpm. The pickup should exert a force not greater than 10 grams. The pickup should be equalized so that it reproduces the frequencies in accordance with the NARTB characteristic.

Appropriate amplifiers should be used in order to obtain the power level necessary to drive either the earphone or the loudspeaker. The output noise of the amplifier should be at least 50 db below the signal under all conditions. The meter should be provided to indicate the rms value of a 1000 cps tone. A VU meter is very convenient but it is not essential.

An attenuator should be provided with a maximum insertion loss of at least 110 db with indicated steps of 5 db or less. If the indicated steps are 5 db, an accessory vernier attenuator with steps of 2 db or 1 db is very desirable.

The earphone or loudspeaker should be of good quality in order to meet the following requirements. The over-all response characteristic including the pickup and equalizer, amplifier, attenuator and earphone or loudspeaker should not deviate more than plus or minus 5 db from the NARTB characteristic over the frequency range from 200 to 5000 cps. Furthermore, at no frequency from 50 cps to 10,000 cps should the pressure exceed the pressure at 1000 cps by more than plus 5 db.

Appendix B

The following lists of words constitute the vocabulary of the three Auditory Tests described in this report. Only an alphabetical order is given here. The ideal test lists used in the recorded versions are randomized orders of these words. The reader can make up equivalent test lists from these alphabetized orders by suitable scrambling.

Alphabetical List of the Spondaic Words Used in Auditory Tests W-1 and W-2

1. airplane
2. armchair
3. baseball
4. birthday
5. cowboy
6. daybreak
7. doormat
8. drawbridge
9. duckpond
10. eardrum
11. farewell
12. grandson
13. greyhound
14. hardware
15. headlight
16. horseshoe
17. hotdog
18. hothouse
19. iceberg
20. inkwell
21. mousetrap
22. mushroom
23. northwest
24. oatmeal
25. padlock
26. pancake
27. playground
28. railroad
29. schoolboy
30. sidewalk
31. stairway
32. sunset
33. toothbrush
34. whitewash
35. woodwork
36. workshop

Alphabetical Lists of the Words in Auditory Test W-22

List 1	List 2
1. ace	1. ail
2. ache	2. air
3. an	3. and
4. as	4. been
5. bathe	5. by
6. bells	6. cap
7. carve	7. cars
8. chew	8. chest
9. could	9. die
10. dad	10. does
11. day	11. dumb
12. deaf	12. ease
13. earn	13. eat
14. east	14. else
15. felt	15. flat
16. give	16. gave
17. high	17. ham
18. him	18. hit
19. hunt	19. hurt
20. isle	20. ice
21. it	21. ill
22. jam	22. jaw
23. knees	23. key
24. law	24. knee
25. low	25. live
26. me	26. move
27. mew	27. new
28. none	28. now
29. not	29. oak
30. or'	30. odd
31. owl	31. off
32. poor	32. one
33. ran	33. own
34. see	34. pew
35. she	35. rooms
36. skin	36. send
37. stove	37. show
38. them	38. smart
39. there	39. star
40. thing	40. tear
41. toe	41. that
42. true	42. then
43. twins	43. thin

44. up
45. us
46. wet
47. what
48. wire
49. yard
50. you

List 3

1. add
2. aim
3. are
4. ate
5. bill
6. book
7. camp
8. chair
9. cute
10. do
11. done
12. dull
13. ears
14. end
15. farm
16. glove
17. hand
18. have
19. he
20. if
21. is
22. jar
23. king
24. knit
25. lie
26. may
27. nest
28. no
29. oil
30. on
31. out
32. owes
33. pie
34. raw
35. say
36. shove
37. smooth
38. start
39. tan
40. ten
41. this
42. three
43. though
44. tie
45. use
46. we
47. west
48. when
49. wool
50. year

44. too
45. tree
46. way
47. well
48. with
49. young
50. your

List 4

1. aid
2. all
3. am
4. arm
5. art
6. at
7. bee
8. bread
9. can
10. chin
11. clothes
12. cook
13. darn
14. dolls
15. dust
16. ear
17. eyes
18. few
19. go
20. hang
21. his
22. in
23. jump
24. leave
25. men
26. my
27. near
28. net
29. nuts
30. of
31. ought
32. our
33. pale
34. save
35. shoe
36. so
37. stiff
38. tea
39. tin
40. than
41. they
42. through
43. toy
44. where
45. who
46. why
47. will
48. wood
49. yes
50. yet

References

1. CARHART, R. Speech reception in relation to pattern of pure tone loss. *JSD*, 11, 1946, 97-108.
2. DAVIS, H. The articulation area and the social adequacy index for hearing *Laryngoscope*, 58, 1948, 761-778.
3. DAVIS, H., MORRICAL, K. C. AND HARRISON, C. F. Memorandum on response characteristics and monitoring of word and sentence tests distributed by CID. *J. acoust. Soc. Amer.*, 21, 1949, 552-553.
4. DEWEY, G. *Relative Frequency of English Speech Sounds.* Cambridge, Mass.: Harvard Univ. Press, 1923.
5. EGAN, J. P. Articulation testing methods. *Laryngoscope*, 58, 1948, 955-991.
6. FLETCHER, H. A method of calculating hearing loss for speech from an audiogram. *J. acoust. Soc. Amer.*, 22, 1950, 1-5.
7. FRENCH, N. R., CARTER, C. W. AND KOENIG, W. The words and sounds of telephone conversations. *Bell Syst. tech. J.*, 9, 1930, 290-324.
8. HARRIS, J. D. Free voice and pure-tone audiometry for testing of auditory acuity. *Arch. Otolaryng., Chicago*, 44, 1946, 452-467.
9. HIRSH, I. J. Clinical application of two Harvard auditory tests. *JSD*, 12, 1947, 151-158.
10. ———. *The Measurement of Hearing.* New York: McGraw-Hill, 1952.
11. HUDGINS, C. V., HAWKINS, J. E., KARLIN, J. E. AND STEVENS, S. S. The development of recorded auditory tests for measuring hearing loss for speech. *Laryngoscope*, 57, 1947, 57-89.
12. LEVIN, R. The intelligibility of different kinds of test material used in speech audiometry. M.A. Thesis, Washington Univ., 1952.
13. MILLER, G. A., HEISE, G. A. AND LICHTEN, W. The intelligibility of speech as a function of the context of the test materials. *J. exp. Psychol.*, 41, 1951, 329-335.
14. *Recording and Listening Test Standards.* Washington, D. C.: Nat. Ass. Radio Telev. Broadcast., 1950.
15. THORNDIKE, E. L. *A Teacher's Word Book Of The Twenty Thousand Words Found Most Frequently and Widely In General Reading For Children And Young People.* New York: Teachers Coll., Columbia Univ., 1932.

24

Reprinted from *J. Aud. Res.* **11**:335–344 (1971)

COMPUTERIZED SPEECH AUDIOMETRIC PROCEDURES

WALTER W. WITTCH,[1] THOMAS J. WOOD[2] and ROBERT B. MAHAFFEY[3]
University of Southern Mississippi, Hattiesburg

INTRODUCTION

Conventional clinical procedures require that the audiologist devote a significant portion of his clinical time to the administration of a battery of audiometric tests to assess the functional status of the hearing mechanism. The audiometric procedures routinely employed for this purpose determine pure-tone air-conduction (ac) and bone-conduction (bc) thresholds, speech reception thresholds (SRT), and speech discrimination scores (DS). The audiometric tests used to evaluate these parameters of hearing are, for the most part, administered manually.

Although the mechanics of administering these audiometric tests have been standardized, considerable intra- and inter-examiner variation can often be observed in their administration. When the variable of masking is introduced into the testing procedure, an even greater disparity evolves between individual examiner's criteria for determining the need for masking and the amount of masking to be used (Martin and Pennington, 1971). Consequently, it is suspected that the values recorded on the audiogram may not always reflect the product of "standardized" audiometric techniques.

Because SRT and DS testing procedures have been standardized in terms of instrumentation, of stimuli, and of the mechanics of administration, the consistent and detailed logic required for computer programming should be applicable to speech audiometry. It was hypothesized that the variable of examiner subjectivity would be removed from the audiometric testing procedure because of the consistency with which testing criteria would be applied by the computer.

While use of the computer as a research tool in acoustics has increased significantly during the past decade (Schroeder, 1969), the application of computer technology to the administration and analysis of clinical audiometry has remained minimal. A limited clinical application of computers has been reported in the area of average evoked response (AER) audiometry (for example, Goldstein and Price, 1966; Hogan and Graham, 1967; Lowell et al, 1961; McCandless, 1967). In terms of direct clinical applicability, Rudmose (1963) described an automatic computing audiometer developed by Weiss; however, the instrumentation afforded by this audiometer was limited to the determination of unmasked pure-tone ac thresholds. A later study (Wood et al, 1972) investigated the computerization of pure-tone ac and bc audiometrics employing available masking contingencies. Preliminary research has also been conducted to determine the computer

[1] Present adress: VA Hospital, 13000 North 30th St., Tampa, Florida, 33612

[2,3] Present address: Institute of Speech and Hearing Sciences, Univ. of North Carolina, Chapel Hill

applicability of meeting audiometric calibration and monitoring needs (Wood, 1971). However, a review of the literature has failed to reveal reports of research devoted to the application of computer techniques in the clinical administration of speech audiometry.

The purpose of the present study was to develop a computer program and the interfacing systems which would permit a digital computer to (1) control the administration of SRT and DS tests; (2) recognize the need for masking, determine the appropriate masking level, and regulate the presentation of the masker to the nontest ear; (3) analyze subject responses for the purpose of regulating the rates and intensities of stimuli presentation; and (4) present the SRTs, DSs, and masking levels used, if any, in an audiogram format at the conclusion of the computerized testing procedure. The validity of the computerized procedures were evaluated, statistically, in terms of Pearson r's computed between the SRT and DS values obtained by the computer and those recorded by an experienced audiologist while testing the same hypacusic Ss.

METHOD

Stimuli. The computerization of speech audiometry required that test stimuli be employed compatible with an automated procedure of identifying and recording subject responses; consequently, it was necessary to employ a closed-set format for both SRT and DS testing. Two tape recordings of the CID W-1 lists A, B, C, D, and E were made from previously unused records (Technisonic Studios, Inc.). The result was a list of 180 spondee words, all recorded at the same level with a marking signal for tape-movement control recorded on Track Two of the tape immediately after each spondee recorded on Track One.

It was decided that discrimination testing materials be employed which correlate highly with results obtained from the CID W-22 lists since the latter are commonly employed in clinical DS testing. The rhyme test developed by Fairbanks (1958) was selected because previous research conducted by Kopra and Blosser (1968) has indicated the comparability of this test to the CID W-22 lists.

For discrimination testing, two recordings of the Fairbanks Rhyme Test (FBRT) Lists RT-1, -2, -3, and -4 were dubbed from a tape recording spoken by Grant Fairbanks. The four lists of one copy were placed on separate, identified reels for use in manual DS testing. On Track Two of the second recording, a marking signal was recorded immediately after each monosyllabic word occuring on Track One.

Computer Instrumentation. Interfacing of Ss with the PDP/8-I digital computer was accomplished through a Digital Equipment Corp. AXO8 Laboratory Peripheral Unit (LPU). Digital outputs from the LPU controlled an Ampex Series 350-3 tape recorder, a Lafayette 303b3 memory drum, and a Beltone Model NB 101 masking generator. A block diagram of the instrumentation is shown in Fig. 1.

Ten of the twelve bits in the buffered external register of the LPU were used to control signal and masking attenuation. The remaining two bits controlled the mode of signal presentation (i.e., ac or bc) and the selection of the earphone to which the signal and masker were presented. Each of the two digital attenuators, consisting of relays and T-pads, provided a 115 db attenuation range in 5-db steps.

The Channel I of the tape recorder, after amplification, served as an input to a Grason-Stadler Model 829E electronic switch. The output of the switch passed through one of the digital attenuation bridges and terminated in a pair of matched 600-ohm TDH-39 earphones mounted in MX-41/AR cushions and located in an IAC Model 1205-A sound-treated room. A digital output from the computer determined the output mode of

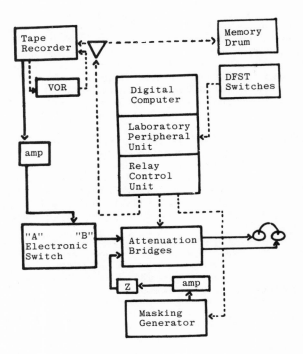

Fig. 1. Simplified block diagram of instrumentation for computerized speech audiometry.

the electronic switch. A second digital output controlled two parallel relays. The first of these was connected to the remote START of the tape recorder; the second to the stepping relay of the memory drum. When the relays were energized the tape recorder was started and the memory drum advanced one frame.

The Channel II output of the tape recorder served as an input to a Grason-Stadler Model E 7300 A-1 voice operated relay (VOR). The VOR was connected to the remote STOP of the tape recorder so that the marking signals recorded on Track Two of the tape recordings stopped the recorder after each stimulus presentation.

Subject responses were sampled by a contingency register associated with the computer. Input to the contingency register was provided by 5 push-button switches positioned beneath the window of the memory drum. When one of these switches was depressed, the corresponding bit in the contingency register was set.

As each stimulus was presented, a closed-set of 5 response words advanced into the memory-drum window. S designated his choice, after hearing the stimulus, by depressing one of the 5 switches. This system provided a multiple-choice method for S to designate his perception of the stimulus. The computer then determined if the response was "correct" or "incorrect" by comparing the response with a stored "correct response" table. Following the presentation of each speech stimulus, the memory drum was advanced to provide synchrony between the acoustic stimulus and the forced-choice alternatives presented by the memory drum. The same procedure was used for SRT and DS testing. The SRT response-choice form used on the memory drum was constructed from randomized orders of the 36 spondee words of the CID W-1 lists. The same procedure was followed for the DS form except that there were 50 words in each list.

A resistance-capacitance clock in the LPU provided an inter-stimulus interval of 7 sec. If S did not respond within this time interval, his response was considered incorrect.

The wide-band noise from the masking generator was amplified with a Hewlett-Packard Model 450 A amplifier before entering the second attenuation bridge and proceeding on to the earphones.

Calibration. A Hewlett Packard 400AB vacuum tube voltmeter was used to voltage-calibrate the T pads comprising each attenuation bridge. Acoustic calibration was performed with a General Radio Type 1551-C sound level meter and a standard 6cc coupler. The circuit was adjusted so that when maximum attenuation was applied by the attenuation bridge, audiometric zero for speech was equal to 19 db re: 2×10^{-4} microbar. Since a correction factor of +15 db had to be inserted into the computer program to achieve this reference standard, the maximum hearing level (HL) available during speech audiometry was 100 db HL.

The masking noise was calibrated in units of effective masking for speech employing a procedure proposed by Martin (1967, 1972) and Studebaker (1967).

Manual Instrumentation. A Beltone CR 5000 twin-channel audiometer was used for all manual SRT and DS testing. Audiometric zero (i.e., 0 db HL) for speech was equal to 19 db re: 2×10^{-4} microbar.

The tape recordings described earlier were played on a Viking Model 22 tape deck, the output of which terminated in a pair of TDH-39 earphones located in an IAC, Model 404A sound-treated room.

S was required to repeat the stimulus words during SRT testing. The audiologists monitored these oral responses via a talk-back circuit. Since the FBRT was used as a closed multiple-choice test, S was instructed to choose the word he heard from a set of five rhyming words printed on a response sheet. His choice was indicated by circling or underlining the appropriate word in each set.

The wide-band noise of the audiometer was calibrated in units of effective masking for speech following the same procedure employed in calibrating the computerized system.

Subjects. Since the maximum HL permitted by the computer-controlled instrumentation was 100 db, the use of a 30-db SL for DS testing meant that an S was acceptable if his pure-tone average for the frequencies .5, 1, and 2 Kc/s did not exceed 70 db HL. Furthermore, each S had to demonstrate at least an elementary reading ability since the computerized testing procedure required that he respond by pushing buttons corresponding to printed words appearing in the memory-drum window.

16 hypacusics meeting these general criteria were randomly assigned to one of two groups; 7 M and 1 F assigned to Group I had a mean age of 36.9 yrs; 3 M and 5 F assigned to Group II had a mean age of 38.9 years.

SRTs and DSs were obtained twice in both ears of each Group I S; once by each of the two Ph.D.-level audiologists who were relatively naive to the computerized procedures. The same measurements were obtained on each of the Ss in group II by the computer and one of the audiologists who had also tested Group I Ss. Hereafter, the audiologist who tested Ss in both groups will be referred to as A_1. The other audiologist will be referred to as A_2. Hence, Group I Ss were assigned to the A_1-A_2 condition, whereas Group II Ss were assigned to the C-A_1 condition.

To insure that the results were not systematically biased by the order of testing, the testing order of Ss in each group was counterbalanced. Also, each S was exposed to the 36 W-1 spondee words prior to actual SRT testing in order to decrease a familiarization effect.

PROCEDURES

Computerized SRT. SRT testing was initiated by depressing either "R" (right ear) or "L" (left ear), then "C" (continue) on the teletype keyboard. The first spondee was presented at 50 db HL. The intensity of subsequent stimuli was either increased or decreased, depending upon whether S responded correctly or incorrectly to the first stimulus. If he responded correctly, the signal was attenuated in 5-db steps with one word presented at each level until he responded incorrectly or gave no response. The computer then increased the HL of the stimulus 10 db above that level. Having bracketed the assumed threshold, the computer began the SRT determination procedure using the descending method proposed by Chaiklin and Ventry (1964).

The computer was programmed to employ a 50% correct-response criterion for threshold. A maximum of 6 or a minimum of 3 spondees were presented at each HL during the threshold determination. In order to avoid premature threshold designations, the computer continued to attenuate the signal in 5-db steps until S failed to meet the threshold criterion at two consecutive HLs. The lowest HL at which S met the 50% criterion was recorded as the SRT. However, programming contingencies also provided for the determination of 0 db and NR (no response) thresholds in the event S consistently responded at 0 db in the initial bracketing procedure or failed to respond within the maximum output afforded by the testing system.

Inconsistency in S's response pattern was another contingency provided for, by comparing the starting point for the threshold descent to the assumed threshold as defined by the original bracketing procedure. If this comparison revealed a disparity, the computer terminated the initial threshold search and repeated the entire procedure a second time. If this second SRT search met with the same response-pattern inconsistency, the procedure was terminated in that ear, a question mark (?) was recorded, and testing was begun in the other ear. Fig. 2 presents two examples of how the computer responded to inconsistencies in the response patterns.

After the unmasked SRTs had been recorded, the computer determined whether it was necessary to retest these thresholds in either ear with masking. The procedure followed for masked SRT testing was essentially that proposed by Martin (1967, 1972) and Martin et al (1965). If the difference between the SRT and each of the contralateral bc values did not exceed 40 db for either ear, masking was considered unnecessary and the computer halted the testing procedure. This permitted an indefinite period of time to cue the tape recording, change the memory-drum sleeve, and give instructions to S before the DS tests were begun.

If the computer determined masking to be necessary, initial testing employed the procedure of minimum effective masking (Martin, 1967, 1972). In the event a threshold was not obtained as a result of minimum effective masking, the computer proceeded to the plateau method of threshold determination (Hood, 1957). Additional contingencies within the program allowed the computer to determine insufficient signal intensity, insufficient masking, and the possibility of overmasking.

SRT L.E.				SRT R.E.			
50 Db IC		50	IC	50 Db IC		50 Db IC	
60	C	60	IC	60	C	60	IC
70	C	70	C	55	C	70	C
65	IC	65	C	50	C	65	C
75	IC	60	C	45	IC	60	C
75	IC	55	IC	55	IC	55	C
75	C	65	C	55	IC	50	C
75	IC	65	C	55	C	45	NR
75	IC	65	IC	55	IC	55	IC
		65	C	55	C	55	C
		60	IC	55	IC	55	IC
		60	NR			55	IC ?
		60	IC				
		60	NR				
		55	NR				
		55	NR				
		55	NR				
		55	NR 65 Db				

Fig. 2. Two examples of how the computer was programmed to accommodate inconsistency in subject's response pattern during the SRT testing procedure (C = correct response, IC = incorrect response, NR = no response.)

Computerized DS Testing. During discrimination testing the computer was programmed always to test the R ear first. A 30-db SL (re: SRT) was employed in assessing discrimination abilities. Contingencies were incorporated into the computer program which allowed testing in either the masked or unmasked condition. The need for masking was determined by subtracting the interaural attenuation (40 db) from the DS HL and comparing the remainder to the best bc thresholds for .5, 1, and 2 Kc/s in the nontest ear.

In the event masking was determined necessary, the computer was programmed to provide the level of effective masking according to the calculation (EM = PBHL − IA + ABG) proposed by Martin (1972).

The computer alternately tested the R and L ears by presenting 50 monosyllabic words. When masking was employed, 5 db was added to the FBRT presentation level to compensate for the central masking effect. Comparison of each response to previously stored values permitted them to be stored in memory as "correct" or "incorrect." When the 50 stimuli had been presented, the DS was recorded in total percent correct by assigning a value of 2% to each correct response.

As in the case of SRT testing, the computer program was designed to accommodate and react accordingly for cases of insufficient intensity, insufficient masking, or overmasking. If the possibility of overmasking occurred, the computer printed "OM" on the teletype and DS testing was not attempted in that ear. Similarly, "IM" and "II" designated insufficient masking and insufficient intensity, respectively.

At the conclusion of the DS test, the computer typed out an audiogram containing a complete summary of the results obtained. These included the SRTs, the DS for each ear, and related masking levels.

Manual Testing. The two audiologists were not restricted in their testing procedures. In fact, they were encouraged to use the methods they typically employed during clinical testing. However, since the audiometer used for manual testing offered 1-db increments while the computer was capable of providing only 5-db increments, the values recorded by the audiologists were rounded to the nearest 5 db, when necessary, for purposes of statistical treatment. Also, the audiologists were directed to perform DS testing at 30 db SL and they were required to record masking levels employed during SRT and DS testing.

RESULTS AND DISCUSSION

The efficacy of the computerized speech audiometric procedures was evaluated in terms of Pearson r's computed between SRTs and DSs obtained by the computer and audiologist A_1 on the same 8 hypacusics (C-A_1). Since C-A_1 correlations, within a concurrent validity type of study, lack relative significance until they are compared with results obtained by conventional clinical methods, the SRTs and DSs of 8 different hypacusics tested by two audiologists were also submitted to a correlational analysis (A_1-A_2).

SRTs. A strong relationship between unmasked and masked SRTs was revealed by correlations of .92 and .93 for the A_1-A_2 and C-A_1 conditions, respectively. Investigation of the A_1-A_2 data in terms of a masked-unmasked dichotomy revealed that A_1 and A_2 agreed that masking was unnecessary while determining the SRT in 11 of the 16 ears tested. The correlation for these 11 unmasked SRTs was .98. There was lack of agreement between the two examiners regarding the need for masking in 4 of the ears evaluated. That is, either A_1 or A_2, but not both, applied masking while measuring the SRT in these 4 ears. The correlation of .32 for these 4 SRTs must be interpreted with caution since 3 of the paired SRTs differed only by 5 db. The 20-db discrepancy existing between the fourth SRT-comparison undoubtedly accounts for this low statistic.

Since A_1 and A_2 agreed that masking was indicated during only 1 of the 16 SRT determinations, a correlation could not be computed. However, the SRTs obtained in this ear were 30 db and 50 db for A_1 and A_2, respectively.

A masked-unmasked dichotomization of the C-A_1 data revealed that the computer and A_1 agreed that masking was not indicated during 15 of the 16 measurements performed; the obtained correlation was .92. In determining the SRT of the 16th ear, A_1 applied masking while the computer did not. Both recorded an SRT of 40 db.

Speech Discrimination. A relatively strong relationship between the 16 FBRT scores existed in the A_1-A_2 condition ($r = .73$). That this correlation is not higher is difficult to explain since both examiners used the same FBRT recordings, presentation levels (i.e., 30 db SL), and audiometric equipment. Generalizations are admittedly risky in speaking of DS testing, but the correlation obtained might reflect a difference in the ability of the individual FBRT lists to assess the DS function.

For one of the C-A_1 subjects, the computer determined that the level of effective masking required for both ears constituted possible overmasking. Since the computer was programmed to omit DS testing upon encountering this contingency, the DSs recorded by A_1 for this S had to be omitted from the correlational analysis. An r of .82 was obtained for the remaining 14-paired FBRT scores, thus indicated a somewhat stronger relationship than was seen for the A_1-A_2 condition. However, the application of Fischer's zr transformation (Ferguson, 1966) revealed that the difference between the A_1-A_2 and C-A_1 correlations was not statistically significant ($z = .56$).

Both examiners decided that masking was unnecessary when testing 10 of the 16 ears in the A_1-A_2 condition. The correlation for these unmasked DSs was .81. For the masked FBRT scores a correlation of .53 was obtained. This discrepancy between masked and unmasked correlations might be attributed to the difference in masking levels used by the examiners. An r of .20 indicates that there was very little relationship between the masking levels employed by each examiner.

The computer and A_1 agreed that masking was unnecessary while determining the DS in 6 ears ($r = .97$). Agreement between the computer and A_1 relative to the need for masking occurred twice. A meaningful correlation could not be computed for these two scores; however, the difference was only 2% for one ear, but 24% for the other ear. The disparity encountered in the latter ear is paradoxical since the C-A_1 SRTs were identical (40 db HL) and the masking levels employed differed by only 5 db.

The mean level of masking employed by the computer for DS testing was 35 db as compared to an average of 60 db for A_1. A correlated t computed on these 7 paired masking levels failed to reach the .05 significance level ($t = 2.61$). Further evidence of the relatively weak relationship between these masking levels is offered by a correlation of .53.

CONCLUSIONS

Despite the differences apparent in the criteria employed by each audiologist and the computer in determining the need for masking and masking levels, significantly high over-all correlations were found between computer-obtained SRTs and DSs and those recorded by examiner A_1. Equally strong relationships were found between the data recorded by the two audiologists when each tested the 8 hypacusics assigned to a second group (A_1-A_2).

Examination of the masked SRTs, DSs and the masking levels employed, revealed diminished agreement between the computer and audiologist and between audiologists. Further investigation into the standardization of criteria concerning clinical masking seems warranted.

In general, the results of this study indicate that SRT and DS testing procedures are amenable to an automated treatment. The results further indicate that the computerized procedures used to determine SRT and DS are a clinically feasible means of assessing these auditory functions.

SUMMARY

A PDP/8-I digital computer was programmed to (1) administer SRT and DS tests, (2) recognize the need for masking, determine the appropriate masking level, and regulate the presentation of the masker to the nontest ear, (3) analyze the subject's responses for the purpose of regulating the rates and intensities of stimuli presentation, and (4) present SRTs, DSs, and masking levels used, if any, in an audiogram format at the conclusion of the testing procedure. The efficacy of this automated design was evaluated in terms of Pearson r's between the SRTs and DSs recorded by a computer and an audiologist when each performed these tests on the same 8 hypacusics. The results indicate that the computerized procedures employed in this study offer a clinically feasible means of assessing these auditory functions.

ACKNOWLEDGEMENT

This article is based upon the first-named author's doctoral thesis completed under the direction of Dr. Julia Davis at The University of Southern Mississippi.

REFERENCES

1. Chaiklin, J.B., and Ventry, I.M. Spondee threshold measurements: a comparison of 2-db and 5-db methods. J. Speech Hear. Dis., 1964, 29, 47-59.
2. Fairbanks, G. Test of phonemic differentiation: the rhyme test. J. Acoust. Soc. Amer., 1958, 30, 596-600.
3. Ferguson, G.A. *Statistical Analysis in Psychology and Education*. New York: McGraw-Hill, 1966.
4. Goldstein, R., and Price, L.L. Clinical use of EEA with an average response computer: a case report. J. Speech Hear. Dis., 1966, 31, 75-78.
5. Hogan, D.D., and Graham, J.T. The use of the summing computer for analyzing auditory evoked responses of mentally retarded children. J. Aud. Res., 1967, 7, 1-13.
6. Hodd, J.D. The principles and practice of bone-conduction audiometry. Proc. Roy. Soc. Med., 1957, 50, 689-697.
7. Kopra, L.L., and Blosser, D. Comparison of Fairbanks rhyme test and CID auditory test W-22 in normal and hearing impaired listeners. J. Speech Hear. Res., 1968, 11, 735-739.
8. Lowell, E., Williams, C.T., Ballinger, R.M., and Alvig, D.P. Measurement of auditory threshold with a special purpose analog computer. J. Speech Hear. Res., 1961, 4, 105-112.
9. McCandless, G. Clinical application of evoked response audiometry. J. Speech Hear. Res., 1967, 10, 468-478.
10. Martin, F.N. A simplified method of clinical masking. J. Aud. Res., 1967, 7, 59-62.
11. Martin, F.N. *Clinical Audiometry and Masking*. Indianapolis: Bobbs-Merrill, 1972.
12. Martin, F.N., Bailey, H.A.T., and Pappas, J.J. The effects of central masking on thresholds for speech. J. Aud. Res., 1965, 5, 293-296.

13. Martin, F.N., and Pennington, C.D. Current trends in audiometric practices. Asha, 1971, 13, 671-677.
14. Rudmose, W. Automatic audiometry. In J. Jerger (Ed.), *Modern Developments in Audiology*. New York: Academic Press, 1963.
15. Schroeder, M.R. Computers in acoustics: symbiosis of an old science and a new tool. J. Acous. Soc. Amer., 1969, 45, 1077-1088.
16. Studebaker, G.A. Clinical masking of the nontest ear. J. Speech Hear. Dis., 1967, 32, 360-371.
17. Wood, T.J. A computerized audiometric system for the fail-detect monitoring and self-calibration of frequency and hearing level. J. Aud. Res., 1971, 11.
18. Wood, T.J., Wittich, W.W., and Mahaffey, R.B. Computerized pure-tone audiometric procedures. J. Speech Hear. Res., 1972, 15.

Part VII

APPLICATIONS TO COMMUNICATIONS ENGINEERING

Editor's Comments
on Papers 25 Through 28

Much research and development on speech intelligibility has been undertaken to permit better or faster evaluations of communications systems and devices. This part concerns such evaluations. Most of the books and papers cited in the bibliography deal with one or more of five topics:

Systems—telephones, broadcasting, point-to-point radio, aircraft and vehicular interphones, shipboard interior communications

Equipment—ear defenders, earphones, loudspeakers, amplifiers, compressors, limiters, clippers, filters, storage devices, microphones

Techniques—training, listening to competing messages

Environments—high altitudes, space, helium-oxygen mixtures, underwater (both for divers and vehicles), very loud noise

Hearing aids—monaural and binaural, ear inserts, processors for the hard of hearing

The outstandingly authoritative paper in this part is Paper 25, which is reproduced in full here. It is comprehensive and clear, brings together much Bell Labs and World War II research and development, and shows a creative approach to a broad systems problem. Paper 26 by Cherry and Wiley presents an ingenious experiment in which adding noise improved intelligibility. In Paper

27 the authors successfully apply the AI method to an important case for which it was not intended, that of fading radio communications. Paper 28 by Kretsinger and Young is one of the best descriptions of the use of speech intelligibility testing to compare the performance of electronic processing techniques.

Among the notable papers that could not be included as reproductions is one by Baxter (1966) which describes an unusual use of a confusion matrix for speech sounds and logatoms to evaluate a communications channel. Black (1946[2]) showed that large increases in the intelligibility of talkers could be obtained with practice and instruction, but that after three hours there was little additional improvement. Bode (1971) shows the relationship between the harmonic distortion in hearing aids and the deterioration in the intelligibility of consonants heard by listeners without hearing impairments. Brady (1965) treats the problems of voice actuated devices and telephone circuits with long time delays. Cahn (1960) shows how to determine the amount of peak clipping that will give the highest signal-to-noise ratio. Edgardh (1951–1952) combined extreme compression of the dynamic range of speech with very short release times to confine most speech within a 3-db range without serious loss of intelligibility, and Endres (1969) retained almost all the original intelligibility after shortening logatoms by fifty percent or after removing half their frequency components.

Hirsh's (1950) paper was an important early statement that the advantages of binaural hearing aids are for localization only. Several later investigators have emphasized the importance of localization for satisfactory face-to-face communications amid other voices and noise. The papers by Jerger are recommended to the reader who is interested in careful, thoughtful reports on hearing aid selection and performance. Kryter's (1946) paper is a milestone, for here he first noted that speech intelligibility could be improved by wearing ear plugs. Papers by Makinson (1947) and by Radley (1948) are noteworthy because they describe the British research and development efforts during World War II to improve speech communications in aircraft and in armoured vehicles. Morrow's (1971) papers are particularly good on the problems of communications from diving masks. Pickett (1958) presents the results, unique in the literature, of experiments with the simple megaphone.

BIBLIOGRAPHY

Barducci, I., and G. Ibba, "Influenza della curva di riposta del ricevitore sulla intensità comprehensibità e qualità del segnale telefonico," *Alta Freq.* **33**:580–583 (1964).

Barrasch, G., "Die Verständlichkeit der Sprachlaute bei der Übertragung über verschiedenartige Systeme," *Hochfrequenztech. u. Elektroakust.* **71**:115–123 (1962).

Baxter, D. D., and B. E. Keiser, "A Speech Channel Evaluation Divorced from Talker-Listener Influence," *IEEE Trans. Commun. Tech.* **14**:101–112 (1966).

Beitscher, H. R., and J. C. Webster, "Intelligibility of UHF and VHF Transmissions at Fifteen Representative Air Traffic Control Towers," *J. Acoust. Soc. Am.* **28**:561–564 (1956).

Bertsch, W. F., J. C. Webster, R. G. Klumpp, and P. O. Thompson, "Effects of the Two Message-Storage Schemes upon Communications within a Small Problem-Solving Group," *J. Acoust. Soc. Am.* **28**:550–553 (1956).

Black, J. W., "Effects of Voice Communication Training," *Speech Monogr.* **13**: no. 2, 64–68 (1946).

Black, J. W., and H. M. Mason, "Training for Voice Communication," *J. Acoust. Soc. Am.* **18**:441–445 (1946).

Bode, D. L., and R. N. Kasten, "Hearing Aid Distortion and Consonant Identification," *J. Speech Hear. Res.* **14**:323–331 (1971).

Brady, P. T., "A Technique for Investigating On-Off Patterns of Speech," *Bell Syst. Tech. J.* **44**:1–22 (1965).

Broadbent, D. E., "Listening to One of Two Synchronous Messages," *J. Exp. Psychol.* **44**:51–55 (1952).

Broadbent, D. E., "Speaking and Listening Simultaneously," *J. Exp. Psychol.* **43**:267–273 (1952).

Brosze, O., K. O. Schmidt, and A. Schmoldt, "Versuche zur Verbesserung der Sprachverständlichkeit bei Störgeräuschen," *NTZ-Nachrichtentech. Z.* **12**:297–300 (1959).

Cahn, C. R., "Crosstalk Due to Finite Limiting of Frequency-Multiplexed Signals," *IRE Proc.* **48**:53–59 (1960).

Calearo, C., G. Pestalozza, and G. P. Teatini, "La comprensione della voce parlanta in presenza di differenti condizioni di rumore," *Arch. Ital. di Oto-Rino. e Laringol.* **70**:570–580 (1959).

Cooke, J. P., and S. E. Beard, "Verbal Communication Intelligibility in Oxygen-Helium and Other Breathing Mixtures at Low Atmospheric Pressures," *Aerosp. Med.* **36**:1167–1172 (1965).

Cooke, J. P., and S. E. Beard, "Speech Intelligibility for Space Vehicles, Using Nitrogen or Helium as the Inert Gas," *J. Acoust. Soc. Am.* **40**:1450–1453 (1966).

Copel, M., "Helium Voice Unscrambling," *IEEE Trans. Audio Electroacoust.* **AU-14**:122–126 (1966).

Craiglow, R. L., N. R. Getzin, and R. A. Swanson, "Power Requirements for Speech Communication Systems," *IRE Trans. Audio* **AU-9**:186–190 (1961).

Cunningham, W. J., S. J. Goffard, and J. C. R. Licklider, "The Influence of Amplitude Limiting and Frequency Selectivity upon the Performance of Radio Receivers in Noise,: *Proc. IRE* **35**:1021–1025 (1947).

Daguet, J., and G. Gilabert, "La parole à niveau constant dans les émetterus à bande latérale unique," *Onde Élect.* **41**, no. 410:498–509 (1961).

De Mitri, T., and C. Pasini, "La intelligibilita della parola in ambiente silente e rumoroso con l'uso di prottettori auricolari non selettivi e selettivi," *Arch. Ital. di Oto-Rino. e Laringol.* **69**:260–270 (1958).

Deveney, R. P., "Intelligibility Test of Communications Ear Defenders in an Area of Extremely High Intensity Noise," *J. Aud. Eng. Soc.* **11**:41–44 (1963).

Dodds, E., and E. Harford, "Modified Earpieces and CROS for High Frequency Hearing Losses," *J. Speech Hear. Res.* **11**:204–218 (1968).

Edgardh, B. H., "The Use of Extreme Limitation of the Dynamic Equalization of Vowels and Consonants in Hearing Aids," *Acta Oto-Laryngd.* **40**:376–382 (1951–1952).

Endres, W., "Untersuchungen zur Eigenung des Frequenzbandes für die Sprachübertragung," *Acustica* **21**:125–133 (1969).

Fawe, A. L., "Interpretation of Infinitely Clipped Speech Properties," *IEEE Trans. Audio Electroacoust.* **AU-14**:178–183 (1966).

Fawe, A. L., "A New Approach to Speech Bandwith Reduction," *IEEE Trans. Audio Electroacoust.* **AU-15**:37–39 (1967).

Gabor, D., "New Possibilities in Speech Transmission," *J. Inst. Electr. Eng.* **94 III** 369–390 (1947), **95 III** 39, 411–412 (disc.).

Gardner, H. J., "Application of a High-Frequency Consonant Discrimination Word List in Hearing Aid Evaluation," *J. Speech Hear. Discord.* **36**:354–355 (1971).

Giordano, T. A., H. B. Rothman, and H. Hollien, "Helium Speech Unscramblers—A Critical Review of the State of the Art," *IEEE Trans. Audio Electroacoust.* **AU-21**:436–444 (1973).

Goodman, J., "The Evaluation of Ear Protection Devices as Elements of a Speech Communication System," in *Proc. 3rd Int. Cong. Acoust., Stuttgart, 1959*, Elsevier, Amsterdam (1961), pp. 250–252.

Griffiths, J. D., "Optimum Linear Filter for Speech Transmission," *J. Acoust. Soc. Am.* **43**:81–86 (1968).

Harris, J. D., H. L. Haines, P. A. Kelsey, and T. D. Clack, "The Relation between Speech Intelligibility and the Electroacoustic Characteristics of Low Fidelity Circuitry," *J. Aud. Res.* **1**:357–381 (1961).

Hashimoto, K., and S. Saito, "Speech Quality of PCM Transmission System," *Elect Commun. Japan* **52**:20–27 (Aug. 1969).

Hawley, M. E., "Speech Communications in Noise: Some Equipment Problems," *J. Acoust. Soc. Am.* **28**:1256–1260 (1956).

Hawley, M. E., "Noise Shield for Microphones Used on Noisy Locations," *J. Acoust. Soc. Am.* **30**:188–190 (1958).

Hirsh, I. J., "Binaural Hearing Aids: A Review of Some Experiments," *J. Speech Hear. Disord.* **15**:114–123 (1950).

Hodgson, W. R., and C. Murdock, Jr., "Effects of the Earmold on Speech Intelligibility in Hearing Aid Use," *J. Speech Hear. Res.* **13**:290–297 (1970).

Hodgson, W. R., and R. J. Sung, "Comparative Performance of Hearing Aid Microphone and Induction Coil for a Sentence Intelligibility Test," *J. Aud. Res.* **12**:261–264 (1972).

Holywell, K., and G. Harvey, "Helium Speech," *J. Acoust. Soc. Am.* **36**:210–211 (1964).

Howell, K., and A. M. Martin, "An Investigation of the Effects of Hearing Protectors on Vocal Communication in Noise," *J. Sound Vib.* **41**:181–196 (1975).

Jerger, J. F., "Behavioral Correlates of Hearing Aid Performance," *Bull. Prosthetics Res.* **10-7**:62–75 (1967).

Jerger, J. F., R. Carhart, and D. Dirks, "Binaural Hearing Aids and Speech Intelligibility," *J. Speech Hear. Res.* **4**:137–148 (1961).

Jerger, J. F., C. Malmquist, and C. Speaks, "A Comparison of Some Speech Intelligibility Tests in the Evaluation of Hearing Aid Performance," *J. Speech Hear. Res.* **9**:253–259 (1966).

Jerger, J. F., and J. Thelin, "Effects of Electroacoustic Characteristics of Hearing Aids on Speech Understanding," *Bull. Prosthetics Res.* **10-10**:159–197 (1968).

Jirsa, R. W., and W. R. Hodgson, "Effect of Harmonic Distortion in Hearing Aids on Speech Intelligibility for Normals and Hypacousics," *J. Aud. Res.* **10**:213–217 (1970).

Kelly, J. C., and M. D. Steer, "The Retention of Improved Intelligibility in Voice Communication," *Q. J. Speech* **38**:167–170 (1952).

Klumpp, R. G., and J. C. Webster, "Acoustical Aspects of Speech Communication System Designed for Operation in High Level Ambient Noise," *J. Aud. Eng. Soc.* **6**:179–183 (July 1958).

Krüger, K., and W. Willms, "Versuche zur Verbesserung von Telephonieanlagen für geräuscherfüllte Räume," *Z. tech. Phys.* **16**:585–590 (1935).

Kryter, K. D., "Effects of Ear Protective Devices on the Intelligibility of Speech in Noise," *J. Acoust. Soc. Am.* **18**:413–417 (1946).

Kryter, K. D., "Speech Bandwidth Compression through Spectrum Selection," *J. Acoust. Soc. Am.* **32**:547–556 (1960).

Kryter, K. D., J. C. R. Licklider, and S. S. Stevens, "Premodulation Clipping in A-M Voice Communication," *J. Acoust. Soc. Am.* **19**:125–131 (1947).

Kryter, K. D., J. C. R. Licklider, J. C. Webster, and M. E. Hawley, "Speech Communication," in *Human Engineering Guide to Equipment Design*, C. T. Morgan et al., eds. McGraw-Hill, New York (1963).

Lindeman, H. E., "Possible Reduction of Speech Intelligibility When Wearing Ear Defenders," (A) *Int. Audiol.* **9**:358–359 (1970).

McClellan, M. E., "Aided Speech Discrimination in Noise with Vented and Unvented Earmolds," *J. Aud. Res.* **7**:93–99 (1967).

Makinson, W., "Electro-Acoustic Transducers and Intercommunication Systems for Aircraft," *J. Inst. Electr. Eng.* **94 III**:441–451 (1947).

Markman, F., "Assessment of Transmission Properties of Telephone Instruments Based on Articulation Tests," *Ericsson Tech.* **9**:3–50 (1953).

Meurman, O. H., "The Distortion of Hearing Aids and the Intelligibility of Speech," *Duodecim* (Helsinki) **75**:88–93 (1959). in Finnish, abstract in English.

Miller, G. A., and S. Mitchell, "Effects of Distortion on the Intelligibility of Speech at High Altitudes," *J. Acoust. Soc. Am.* **19**:120–125 (1947).

Miller, G. A., and F. M. Wiener, *Transmission and Reception of Sounds under Combat Conditions*, Columbia Univ. Press, New York (1948).

Morrow, C. T., "Reaction of Small Enclosures on the Human Voice, Part I: Specifications Required for Satisfactory Intelligibility," *J. Acoust. Soc. Am.* **19**:645–652 (1947).

Morrow, C. T., and A. J. Brouns, "Speech Communication in Diving Masks, I. Acoustics of Microphones and Mask Cavities," *J. Acoust. Soc. Am.* **50**:1–9 (1971).

Morrow, C. T., and A. J. Brouns, "Speech Communication in Diving Masks, II. Psychoacoustic and Supplementary Tests," *J. Acoust. Soc. Am.* **50**:10–22 (1971).

Nakatani, L. H., "Measuring the Ease of Comprehending Speech," *Proc.*

7th Int. Cong. Acoust., Akadémiai Kiadó, Budapest (1971), pp. 701–703.

Nakatsui, M., "Synthetic Study on the Perceptual Nature of Vowel Produced under High Ambient Pressure," *J. Acoust. Soc. Japan* **31**:221–227 (1975).

Naujoks, J., "Sprachübertragung mit dem Ohrmikrophon," *NTZ-Nachrichtentech. Z.* **12**:400–402 (1959).

Niederjohn, R. J., and J. H. Grotelueschen, "The Enhancement of Speech Intelligibility in High Noise Levels by High-Pass Filtering Followed by Rapid Amplitude Compression," *IEEE Trans. Acoust. Speech Sig. Proc.* **ASSP-24**:277–282 (1976).

Olsen, W. O., and R. Carhart, "Development of Test Procedures for Evaluation of Binaural Hearing Aids," *Bull. Prosthetics Res.* **10-7**:22–49 (1967).

Orchik, D. J., and H. J. Oyer, "A Modified Traditional Hearing Aid Evaluation Procedure," *J. Aud. Res.* **12**:8–13 (1972).

Oyer, H. J., "Relative Intelligibility of Speech Recorded Simultaneously at the Ear and Mouth," *J. Acoust. Soc. Am.* **27**:1207–1212 (1955).

Pestalozza, G., and A. Lazzaroni, "Le capacità discriminative dell'apparato uditivo nell'ascolto di messaggi parlanti contemporei," *Riv. Audiol. Prat.* (Milano) **7**:77–96 (July–Sept. 1957).

Pickett, J. M., and I. Pollack, "Intelligibility at High Voice Levels and the Use of a Megaphone," *J. Acoust. Soc. Am.* **30**:1100–1104 (1958).

Radley, W. G., "Speech Communication under Conditions of Deafness or Loud Noise," *J. Inst. Electr. Eng.* **95 I**:201–216 (1948), disc. **96 I**:312–313 (1949).

Revoile, S. G., "Speech Discrimination Ability with Ear Inserts," *Bull. Prosthetics Res.* **10-10**:198–205 (1968).

Richards, D. L., *Telecommunication by Speech,* Butterworths, London (1973).

Sheets, B. V., and L. D. Hedgecock, "Hearing Aid Amplification for Optimum Speech Reproduction," *J. Speech Hear. Disord.* **14**:373–379 (1949).

Shore, I., R. C. Bilger, and I. J. Hirsh, "Hearing Aid Evaluation: Reliability of Repeated Measurements," *J. Speech Hear. Disord.* **25**:152–170 (1960).

Snow, W. B., "Effects of Intentional Interference with Speech Intelligibility," *J. Aud. Eng. Soc.* **17**:42–48 (1969).

Spieth, W., J. F. Curtis, and J. C. Webster, "Responding to One of Two Simultaneous Messages," *J. Acoust. Soc. Am.* **26**:391–396 (1954).

Spieth, W., and J. C. Webster, "Listening to Differentially Filtered Competing Voice Measures," *J. Acoust. Soc. Am.* **27**:866–871 (1955).

Steel, R. W., and L. E. Cassel, "Effect of Transmission Errors on the Intelligibility of Vocoded Speech," *IEEE Trans. Commun. Syst.* **CS-11**:118–123 (1963).

Stover, W. R., "Technique for Correcting Helium Speech Distortion," *J. Acoust. Soc. Am.* **41**:70–74 (1967).

Subrahmanyam, D. L., and G. E. Peterson, "Time-Frequency Scanning in Narrow-Band Frequency Transmission," *IEEE Trans. Audio* **AU-7**:148–160 (1959).

Thomas, I. B., and F. E. Flavin, "The Intelligibility of Speech Transposed Downward in Frequency by One Octave," *J. Aud. Eng. Soc.* **18**:56–62 (1970).

Tillman, T. W., R. Carhart, and W. O. Olsen, "Hearing Aid Efficiency in a Competing Speech Situation," *J. Speech Hear. Res.* **13**:789–811 (1970).

Tillman, T. W., R. M. Johnson, and W. O. Olsen, "Earphone versus Soundfield Threshold Sound-Pressure Levels for Spondee Words," *J. Acoust. Soc. Am.* **39**:125–133 (1966).

Tobias, J. V., "Auditory Processing for Speech Intelligibility Improvement," *Aerosp. Med.* **41**:728–733 (1970).

Villchur, E., "Signal Processing to Improve Speech Intelligibility in Perceptive Deafness," *J. Acoust. Soc. Am.* **53**:1646–1657 (1973).

von Braunmühl, H. J., and W. Weber, "Beitrag zur Frage der Sprachübertragung aus geräuscherfüllten Räumen," *Electr. Nachrichtentech.* **13**:414–419 (1936).

Weber, M., "An Effective Bandwidth Reduction for Communication Use in a VHF/UHF Satellite Link," *IEEE Trans. Audio Electroacoust.* **AU-17**:222–224 (1969).

Webster, J. C., and L. N. Solomon, "Effects of Response Complexity upon Listening to Competing Messages," *J. Acoust. Soc. Am.* **27**:1199–1203 (1955).

Webster, J. C., and P. O. Thompson, "Responding to Both of Two Overlapping Messages," *J. Acoust. Soc. Am.* **26**:396–402 (1954).

Williams, C. E., J. A. Forstall, and J. W. Greene, "The Use of In-Flight Manikin Recordings for Evaluating the Communication Effectiveness of Flight Helmets," *IEEE Trans. Audio Electroacoust.* **AU-19**:97–102 (1971).

Yanagisawa, T., and K. Furihata, "Pickup of Speech Signal by Utilization of Vibration Transducer under High Ambient Noise," *J. Acoust. Soc. Japan* **31**:213–220 (1975). in Japanese, abstract and figures in English.

Yanick, P., Jr., "Improvement in Speech Discrimination with Compression vs. Linear Amplification," *J. Aud. Res.* **13**:333–338 (1973).

25

Reprinted from *IRE Proc.* 35(9):880–890 (1947)

The Design of Speech Communication Systems*

LEO L. BERANEK†, SENIOR MEMBER, I.R.E.

Summary—A method is presented for calculating the ability of a communication system to transmit speech intelligibly in the presence of noise. The total speech arriving at the ear of a listener is determined by adding the orthotelephonic gain of the system to the speech spectrum which would be produced by a talker at the eardrum of a listener at a distance of 1 meter. The total noise arriving at the ear is determined in terms of its spectrum level from measurements of the noise pickup of the microphone and the acoustic attenuation of the earphone cushions. The area lying between the spectrum level of the peaks of the speech and the spectrum level of the total noise arriving at the eardrum when plotted on a distorted frequency scale determines a quantity called articulation index which can be correlated with articulation scores. Methods for determining the maximum gain permissible in the system are discussed. The validity of the method is established by comparison of calculated with carefully measured articulation scores.

I. INTRODUCTION

VOICE COMMUNICATION using microphones, earphones, or telephone receivers has risen to a new level of importance as modern transport has increased in complexity and tempo. No longer is it adequate to communicate by radiotelegraph signals between aircraft and the ground or by messages handed from the engineer to the station master. These slow methods, by which only a minute quantity of information can be exchanged while the vehicle moves into sight and out again, have had to give way to the efficiency of the spoken word. Furthermore, as the number of vehicles has increased, and as the time allotted for an exchange of vital information has decreased, speech as we ordinarily know it has had to be replaced by a group of code words such as "angels" for "height in thousands of feet," "mattress" for "bottom of a cloud layer in thousands of feet," and "wilco" for "message received, understood, and will be acted on." As airplanes increase in speed and number, landing operations at air terminals may require the use of even more condensed language, each word of which would convey the meaning contained normally in a sentence or even a paragraph.

The more information that each word conveys, the more significant becomes the loss of a word, and the more nearly perfect the communication system must be. As a result, the radio engineer finds nimself called on today to design equipment which will transmit and receive the most difficult words and syllables in an atmosphere of noise so loud that two people are unable to hear each other even when shouting.

* Decimal classification: 621.385×534. Original manuscript received by the Institute, June 13, 1946; revised manuscript received, September 30, 1946. Presented, National Technical Meeting of the Acoustical Society of America, New York, N. Y., May, 1946.
  This research, begun under Contract No. OEMsr-658 between Harvard University and the Office of Scientific Research and Development, is continuing under contract with the U. S. Navy, Office of Naval Research.
  † Formerly, Harvard University, Cambridge, Massachusetts; now, Massachusetts Institute of Technology, Cambridge, Massachusetts.

Through the pioneering efforts of the Bell Telephone Laboratories, considerable data had been accumulated by 1941 on what constitutes an effective communication system for the transmission of speech over telephone circuits. Their data apply primarily to the design of systems for operation at low signal levels in reasonably quiet surroundings with the talker speaking in a normal tone of voice. Their findings were succinctly summarized by Fletcher[1] when he wrote in 1942 that "substantially complete fidelity for the transmission of speech is obtained by a system having a frequency range from 100 to 7000 cycles per second and a volume range of 40 decibels." This statement, although conclusive, gives the design engineer no guidance on how far it is safe to depart from these specifications.

More recently French and Steinberg have presented a method for calculating the performance of voice communication systems in environs in which the ambient noise is moderate.[2] Their findings, and data obtained at the Electro-Acoustic and Psycho-Acoustic Laboratories (Harvard) during the past five years, form the basis of the procedure for calculating the performance of voice communication systems in any environment of noise which is presented in this paper.

II. THE ARTICULATION TEST

The articulation test has been used[3,4] as a quantitative measure of the intelligibility of speech transmitted over communication systems. In performing the test, an announcer reads carefully prepared lists of syllables or words to a group of listeners, and the percentage of items correctly recorded by these listeners is called the articulation score. Differences in talkers, listeners, or word material profoundly affect the score, hence only those tests which are performed under identical conditions can be compared. In order to determine how a particular communication system is likely to perform it must be subjected, during the articulation test, to those stresses which it will encounter in use, such as interfering noise, reduced atmospheric pressure at altitude, method of holding or facing the mircophone, etc.

During the initial stages of design, articulation testing is costly and slow. Hence, the need arises for a method of calculating the effect on speech intelligibility brought about by changes in the physical characteristics of the system or the ambient noise in which it will oper-

[1] H. Fletcher, "Hearing, the determining factor for high-fidelity transmission," PROC. I.R.E., vol. 30, pp. 266–277; June, 1942.
[2] N. R. French and J. C. Steinberg, "Factors governing the intelligibility of speech sounds," *Jour. Acous. Soc. Amer.*, vol. 19, pp. 90–119; January, 1947.
[3] H. Fletcher and J. C. Steinberg, "Articulation testing methods," *Bell Sys. Tech. Jour.*, vol. 8, pp. 806–854; October, 1929.
[4] J. P. Egan and F. M. Wiener, "On the intelligibility of bands of speech in noise," *Jour. Acous Soc. Amer.*, vol. 18, pp. 435–441; October, 1946.

ate. It is not implied that the articulation test can be dispensed with, for in the final analysis it is the only way one can make certain that all possible variables have been taken into account.

III. The Character of Speech

The average spectrum of speech, produced at a distance of one meter by typical young male voices in an anechoic (echo-free) chamber[5] and measured by a microphone compensated to be flat over the frequency range indicated, is shown by the upper curve of Fig. 1.[6] Some

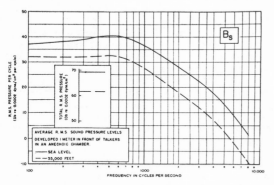

Fig. 1—Average spectrum level of speech measured in one-cycle band-widths in decibels versus frequency for young male voices talking at a level six decibels below the maximum they could sustain without straining their voices. Microphone placed one meter in front of talkers in an anechoic (echo-free) chamber. Upper curve taken at sea level; lower at 35,000 feet simulated altitude. One decibel has been added to remove the effect of pauses between words in the total spectrum level.

voices were considerably stronger than others; the maximum spread of the data obtained on seven subjects was of the order of ± 7 to ± 10 decibels. It is seen that the average total sound pressure level at one meter for half-effort is about 68 decibels.

Oscillographic records[6] showed that about 20 to 25 per cent of the total talking time was consumed by the space between words. Hence, approximately one decibel was added into the spectrum level of Fig. 1 to yield the average level of the speech itself. These curves, at sea level and 35,000 feet of altitude will be referred to as B_s versus frequency in later use.

Dunn and White published data showing the root-mean-square pressures developed by the voice in successive $\frac{1}{8}$-second intervals in fourteen contiguous frequency bands.[7] An extension of their findings, taken from footnote reference 2, is shown in Fig. 2. Inspection

[5] L. L. Beranek and H. P. Sleeper, Jr., "Design and construction of anechoic sound chambers," *Jour. Acous. Soc. Amer.*, vol. 18, pp. 140–150; July, 1946.

[6] H. W. Rudmose, K. C. Clark, F. D. Carlson, J. C. Eisenstein, and R. A. Walker, "The effects of high altitude on speech and hearing," Paper No. 31, 31st Meeting, Acoustical Society of America, New York, N. Y., May 11, 1946.

[7] H. K. Dunn and S. D. White, "Statistical measurements on conversational speech," *Jour. Acous. Soc. Amer.*, vol. 11, pp. 278–288; January, 1940.

of the frequency range between 500 and 4000 cycles per second shows that the contour lines are essentially parallel. Hence, taking the 1000- to 1400-cycle-per-second

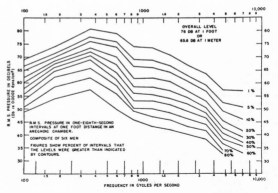

Fig. 2—Root-mean-square sound-pressure levels measured in successive $\frac{1}{8}$-second-long intervals at one-foot distance in an anechoic chamber (from French and Steinberg). Contours show percentage of intervals in which the level exceeded the values shown on the ordinate at different frequencies.

band as typical of all bands in this region, a plot was made of cumulative level distribution in the $\frac{1}{8}$-second intervals. (See Fig. 3.) The long time average sound pressure for that band was 62 decibels. Now as was just stated, about 20 per cent of the intervals of speech

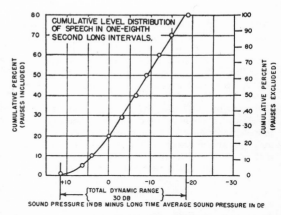

Fig. 3—Curve showing cumulative level distribution of speech in an octave band in $\frac{1}{8}$-second-long intervals versus the sound-pressure level in decibels minus long-time average sound-pressure level in decibels. The right-hand ordinate has been added to the original graph of French and Steinberg.

are consumed by pauses between words and breathing. If the right-hand side of the graph is observed the important conclusion is reached that, the *total dynamic range of speech is about 30 decibels in any one band.*

IV. The Nature of Hearing

Extensive data have been taken to determine the average threshold of hearing for the population of the United States. The threshold curve for young people most commonly published[8] and later found to hold for acute young ears[9] is shown in (a) of Fig. 4. Another type of threshold curve derived recently[10] by adding a correction curve to the American Standards Association curve for the difference between pressure in the free-field and at the eardrum is shown as (b) of Fig. 5. It gives the threshold levels in terms of the pressure produced at the eardrum.

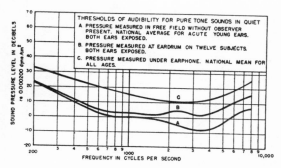

Fig. 4—Thresholds of audibility for pure tone sounds with subjects in quiet.

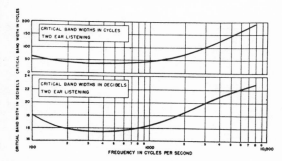

Fig. 5—Widths of critical masking bands plotted as a function of frequency. The upper curve gives the critical bandwidths in cycles per second and the lower curve is ten times the logarithm to the base ten of the upper.

At the other extreme we need to know the maximum intensity of a pure tone or speech which the ear can tolerate without discomfort or injury. Recent unpublished data obtained at the Central Institute for the Deaf, St. Louis, Missouri, have shown that three different upper thresholds for pure tones or speech will be

determined by a group of listeners depending upon how much exposure to intense noises they have had previously. These thresholds are essentially constant as a function of frequency and are known as thresholds of (a) discomfort, (b) tickle, and (c) pain; and for listeners who have not been exposed to high noise levels the values for pure tones are approximately 110, 132, and 140 decibels respectively, re 0.000200 dyne/cm². These three thresholds will be approximately 10 decibels higher for people who have been exposed to loud noises for several hours daily over a period of several days.

Of interest in communication at high altitudes is the variation of hearing acuity with decreasing atmospheric pressures. Data taken at the Electro-Acoustic Laboratory[8] indicate that there is no measurable change in the average threshold of hearing between sea level and 35,000 feet.

One needs only to turn to everyday experience to know that a sound which is faintly audible is "drowned out" or *masked* when even a moderately loud noise is produced nearby. By definition, the *masking* of a pure tone by noise is equal to the difference between the new and the old threshold levels of the tone, i.e., $M = T - T_0$ where M is the masking, T_0 is the threshold level of the pure tone in quiet, and T is the level of the pure tone when it is just audible with the noise present. All three values are expressed in decibels.

Of great importance in understanding the ability of the ear to interpret transmitted speech is the way in which various noises mask desired sounds. Extensive tests have shown that for noises with a continuous spectrum, it is the noise in the immediate frequency region of the masked tone which contributes to the masking.[11] For example, if a band of noise with a continuous spectrum is used to mask a tone of 800 cycles per second, it will be found that after the band (centered about 800 cycles per second) is made increasingly wider than 50 cycles per second, the same amount of masking will be obtained as was attained for a band exactly 50 cycles wide. For narrower bands the masking decreases in proportion to the logarithm of the bandwidth. The bandwidth at which the masking just reaches its stable value is known as a *"critical band."* Most noise produced in aircraft, locomotives, tanks, engine or boiler rooms, wind tunnels, and near spinning or weaving machines is of a continuous spectrum type although the spectrum may slope upward or downward. Bands of speech appear to be masked by continuous-spectra noises in much the same way as pure tones are masked by them. For this reason it is possible to divide the speech spectrum into narrow bands and study each band independently of the others.

Published data[11,12] indicate that the critical bandwidth is a function of frequency, and curves are shown in

[8] Acoustical Society of America—American Standard for Noise Measurements Z24.2–1942, *Jour. Acous. Soc. Amer.* vol. 14, pp. 102–110; July, 1942.

[9] J. C. Steinberg, H. C. Montgomery, and M. B. Gardner, "Results of the world's fair hearing tests," *Bell Sys. Tech. Jour.*, vol. 19, pp. 533–562; October, 1940.

[10] F. M. Wiener and D. A. Ross, "The pressure distribution in the auditory canal in a progressive sound field," *Jour. Acous. Soc. Amer.*, vol. 18, pp. 401–408; October, 1946.

[11] H. Fletcher, "Auditory patterns," *Rev. Mod. Phys.*, vol. 12, pp. 47–65; January, 1940.

[12] Psycho-Acoustic Laboratory, Harvard University, "The masking of signals by noise," O.S.R.D. Report No. 5387; October 1, 1945.

two ways in Fig. 5.[2] Observations indicate that when a critical band of frequencies is at a just-audible level the total energy in the band is the same as the energy of a just-audible pure tone located at the center of the band.

A relation between the masking of a pure tone whose frequency lies between 200 and 8000 cycles per second and the level of a masking noise of the continuous spectrum type is shown in Fig. 6.[12] This curve shows that the masking increases linearly with noise level.

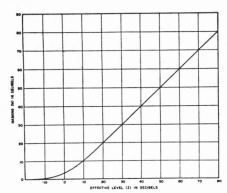

Fig. 6—Relation between masking and the effective level of a critical band width. M is the change in the threshold of a pure tone due to the noise. Z is the number of decibels that the total energy in a critical band is above its threshold level.

V. ORTHOTELEPHONIC GAIN

Before proceeding farther, a definition of a perfect communication system will be made. Although subject to proof by test, it is obvious that two intelligent people with normal hearing, speaking in loud, clear tones could understand each other nearly perfectly if placed in an absolutely quiet room, free from reflecting surfaces and facing each other at a distance apart of one meter. With this condition as a reference, a perfect communication system is defined as one which produces exactly the same sounds at the ear of a listener as would be produced in the above-described situation. The same talker would need to be used in both cases. Orthotelephonic gain[13] is now defined as

$$\text{Orthotelephonic Gain} = 20 \log_{10} (p_2/p_1) \qquad (1)$$

where p_1 is the pressure produced by the talker in a free sound field at a distance of one meter and p_2 is the pressure measured in a free sound field which produces with the listener present the same loudness in his ear as that produced by the communication system under test. These data must be taken in narrow frequency bands as a function of frequency. Alternatively, p_1 is the pressure produced by a talker at the eardrum of a listener seated facing a talker in an anechoic chamber at a distance of one meter, and p_2 is the pressure at the eardrum produced

by the communication system under test. That is to say, the orthotelephonic gain can be measured either *subjectively*, i.e., by the loudness produced, or *objectively*, by using a small probe microphone to determine the pressures at the eardrum. Actually these two measurements of orthotelephonic gain appear not to be equivalent. For reasons still obscure, it seems that to produce the same sensation of loudness about 6 or 7 decibels more sound pressure must be produced at the eardrum by an earphone than by a loudspeaker at a meter's distance.[14] Hence the orthotelephonic gain obtained using the loud-

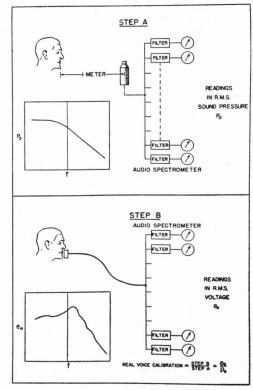

Fig. 7—Procedure for obtaining the real-voice calibration of a microphone. Upper step shows measurement of speech spectrum; lower shows measurement of voltage output of microphone.

ness-balance technique described later will be 6 or 7 decibels less than that determined by measuring pressures at the eardrum with a probe tube. The method of handling this difficulty will be described later.

[13] A. H. Inglis, "Transmission features of the new telephone sets," *Bell Sys. Tech. Jour.*, vol. 17, pp. 358–380; July, 1938.

[14] Recent data demonstrating this point were taken by F. M. Wiener at Harvard. Reference should also be made to L. J. Sivian and S. D. White, "On minimum audible sound fields," *Jour. Acous. Soc. Amer.*, vol. 4, pp. 288–321; April, 1933. (The difference between curves *B* and *C* may, in part, be due to this effect.)

From a physical standpoint, it is difficult to measure the orthotelephonic response in one step. It is customary, therefore, to perform the measurement in two steps, first by measuring the "real-voice" response of the microphone and secondly, by measuring the "real-ear" response of the earphone. Then the two are added together to yield the orthotelephonic response, taking into account the loss or gain of the interconnecting amplifier or transmission line.

The first step in the determination of the real-voice response of a microphone (see Fig. 7) is to measure the speech spectrum of the particular talker and word material used. A standard microphone is placed before the talker in an anechoic chamber at a distance of one meter. Then speaking at half-effort, the talker produces a voltage at the output of the microphone which is analyzed[15] by a group of parallel filters to yield the root-mean-square sound pressure p_0. The second step is to replace the standard microphone with the microphone under test and to repeat the measurement. The ratio of the root-mean-square voltage produced by the microphone under test across its load resistor e_0 to the root-mean-square pressure obtained in step A (p_0) for each of the frequency bands yields the real-voice calibration. If pressure at the eardrum is desired, a transfer curve from free field to eardrum is necessary. Such a curve for an average of twelve subjects is given as (A) in Fig. 16(f).[10]

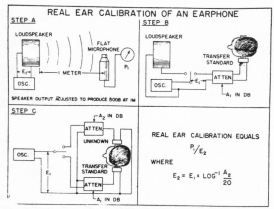

Fig. 8—Subjective procedure for measuring the real-ear calibration of an earphone by a loudness-balance method.

As stated before, the real-ear calibration of an earphone can be determined either objectively or subjectively. The procedure necessary for measuring the pressure directly at the eardrum involves the use of a very small probe tube attached to a capacitor microphone and is a delicate and physiologically dangerous measurement. Reference should now be made to Fig. 8, where

[15] H. W. Rudmose, K. C. Clark, F. D. Carlson, J. C. Eisenstein, and R. A. Walker, "An integrating audio-spectrometer," Paper No. 42, 31st Meeting, *Acoustical Society of America*, May 11, 1946.

the procedure for subjective calibration is given. In step A, a loudspeaker, located at a distance of one meter from a standard microphone, is energized by an oscillator whose output voltage is adjusted to a value of E_1 for which a convenient sound level is indicated by the microphone. Next, a high-fidelity earphone, known as the transfer standard, is placed over one ear of an observer whose head replaces the microphone. In step B the switch is thrown to connect the transfer standard to the output of the attenuators, and the voltage E_1 is reduced by an attenuation of A_1 until the earphone produces a sound which the listener judges to be as loud as that produced by the loudspeaker with a voltage E_1 across it. Then, in step C, the earphone under test is placed on the opposite ear and the attenuator A_2 is adjusted until the same loudness is produced by the unknown as is produced by the transfer standard. Automatic, frequent switching of the voltage E_1 between the two sources of sound being compared in each of the two cases leads to results which are repeatable to a satisfactory degree. For results typical of a population, a number of human subjects must be used and the data averaged at each frequency. The real-ear calibration then is expressed as being the voltage required to produce the same loudness at the ear as is produced by a sound field measured before the listener enters it.

The orthotelephonic gain is now found by either (2) or (3) below:

O.T. Gain (Subjective Method)
$$= 20 \log (e_0/p_0) + 20 \log (E_2/e_0) + 20 \log (P_1/E_2) \quad (2)$$

where P_1 is the free-field pressure necessary to produce the same loudness in the ear as was produced by the earphone with a voltage E_2 across it; E_2/e_0 is the voltage amplification of the amplifier; and e_0 is the voltage produced by the microphone across the input resistor of the amplifier by a voice which produces a pressure p_0 at a distance of one meter in a free field. Alternatively,

O.T. Gain (Objective Method)
$$= 20 \log (e_0/p_0) + 20 \log R + 20 \log (e_2/e_0)$$
$$+ 20 \log (p_e/e_2) \quad (3)$$

where R is the ratio of the pressure produced at the eardrum of a listener by a source of sound to the pressure which would be produced by the same source at the listener's head position if he were removed from the field (see Fig. 16 (f), curve A), p_e is the pressure produced at the eardrum of a listener by the earphone with a voltage e_2 across it, and the other quantities are the same as before.

VI. Microphone and Earphone Noise Pickup

To measure the noise-pickup characteristics of a microphone, a person holding the microphone in a normal manner is immersed in a diffuse noise field having a reasonably flat spectrum. The voltage e' produced by the microphone across its load resistor is determined by the audio spectrometer. Then the spectrum of the noise p' is measured by the spectrometer at the position where the person's head was located, using a standard microphone. The ratio e'/p' as a function of frequency as just measured is the noise pickup characteristic of the microphone.

The amount of ambient noise reaching the ear through the earphone cushion is dependent on the noise attenuation properties of the cushion. The cushion attenuation can be measured either subjectively or objectively. To measure the attenuation subjectively, a person is seated in a diffuse noise field having a continuous spectrum bandwidth of about 20 cycles per second. The level of the noise is adjusted by means of an attenuator in the noise amplifying circuit so that the noise sounds equally loud with the cushion on as it did before adjustment of the noise with the cushion off. The change of the setting of the attenuator in decibels is a measure of the cushion attenuation at that frequency. Alternatively, the cushion attenuation is measured objectively by determining the change in pressure at the eardrum when the cushion is placed on the ear with the person seated in a diffuse sound field from its value with the cushion off. Similar to the results obtained for determination of orthotelephonic gain, the cushion attenuation seems to be greater for the subjective than that for the objective type of measurement by about 6 or 7 decibels.

The important conclusion is now drawn that it is necessary, to avoid ambiguity of results, *always to pair objective orthotelephonic gain with objective cushion attenuation measurements and subjective orthotelephonic gain with subjective measurements in the method of calculation which follows.*

VII. CONCEPT OF ARTICULATION INDEX

The concept of *articulation index* advanced by French and Steinberg and the basis of both their calculation scheme and the one given in this paper was introduced by Harvey Fletcher many years ago. The articulation index A is defined as a number obtained from articulation tests using nonsense syllables under the assumption that any narrow band of speech frequencies of a given intensity in the absence of noise carries a contribution to the total index, which is independent of the other bands with which it is associated, and that the totals of all the bands is the sum of the contributions of the separate bands.[2] It is necessary to prove that there is an unique function relating syllable or word articulation to A for any given articulation crew and choice of word list. In determining an articulation index (A) under the conditions stated above, there are essentially two parameters of a linear communication system that can be varied: (a) the level of the speech above the threshold of hearing, and (b) the frequency response of the system. Linear systems free from noise are assumed.

The procedure necessary for determining the relationships between syllable articulation, articulation index

(A), gain and frequency response for a given articulation crew have been presented by French and Steinberg[2] and will not be repeated here. From those data they derived a curve of articulation index (A) versus cut-off frequency of a group of low pass filters (see Curve B of Fig. 9) under the special condition of optimal loudness

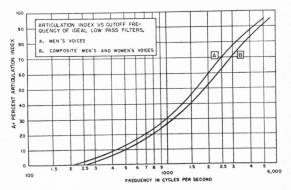

Fig. 9—Articulation index versus cutoff frequency of ideal low-pass filters as determined by French and Steinberg.

at the ear and negligibly low noise levels for combined men's and women's voices. Curve A of this graph, for men's voices alone, is based on an estimate, but will be used as the basis of discussion here. From Curve A, several things can be perceived:

1. Extending the frequency range of a communication system below 200 or above 6000 cycles per second contributes almost nothing to the intelligibility of speech.

2. Each of the following frequency bands makes a 5 per cent contribution to the articulation index (A), provided the orthotelephonic gain of the system is optimal (about +10 decibels) and there is no noise present. Male voices are assumed.

TABLE I
FREQUENCY BANDS OF EQUAL CONTRIBUTION TO ARTICULATION INDEX

No.	Limits	Mean	No.	Limits	Mean
1	200 to 330	270	11	1660 to 1830	1740
2	330 to 430	380	12	1830 to 2020	1920
3	430 to 560	490	13	2020 to 2240	2130
4	560 to 700	630	14	2240 to 2500	2370
5	700 to 840	770	15	2500 to 2820	2660
6	840 to 1000	920	16	2820 to 3200	3000
7	1000 to 1150	1070	17	3200 to 3650	3400
8	1150 to 1310	1230	18	3650 to 4250	3950
9	1310 to 1480	1400	19	4250 to 5050	4650
10	1480 to 1660	1570	20	5050 to 6100	5600

Throughout the following discussion a distorted frequency scale based on Table I and plotted as shown in Fig. 10 will be used. On this graph is shown the information of Section III of this paper, namely, the total dynamic range of speech in each of the bands (Fig. 3) plotted as 12 decibels above and 18 decibels below the average root-mean-square spectrum of speech of Fig. 1. If the ear is able to hear all the region represented by the shaded area, speech should be perfectly intelligible

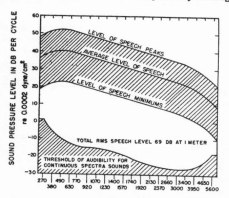

Fig. 10—Total speech spectrum and threshold of audibility for continuous spectrum sounds plotted versus frequency on distorted frequency scale.

and the per cent articulation index A should be equal to one hundred. The premises now made and to be proven are that *the articulation index A is (a) linearly related to the per cent of the shaded area of Fig. 10 which can be heard by the listeners, and is (b) uniquely related to articulation scores for any given syllable, word, or sentence list and crew of talkers and listeners used during the test.*

The following nomenclature will now be introduced:

$$A = \sum_n W_n \cdot (\Delta A)_{max} = \sum_n 0.05 W_n \qquad (4)$$

where

A = total articulation index = sum of contributions of all bands

(ΔA) = contribution of any one band

$(\Delta A)_{max}$ = maximum contribution of any one band = 0.05

W_n = per cent of maximum contribution contributed by any band.

Fletcher[1] states that studies at the Bell Telephone Laboratories show that the ear integrates such varying sounds as speech over about $\frac{1}{8}$-second intervals. For example, the integrated sound energy in a critical bandwidth over a $\frac{1}{8}$-second interval will sound as loud as a pure tone in the same frequency band which produces the same energy in each $\frac{1}{8}$-second interval. The $\frac{1}{8}$-second intervals of the data of Figs. 2 and 3 are short enough so that this statement applies to them. Hence, if a critical bandwidth of speech is expressed as root-mean-square sound pressure level (in decibels) in $\frac{1}{8}$-second intervals, the resulting 30-decibel spread in levels can be plotted as a function of frequency on the same graph along with a continuous spectrum masking noise, provided the

latter is expressed as sound pressure level in decibels *for critical bandwidths*. The difference between the upper side of the 30-decibel spread and the noise curve will be equal to the level by which the peak levels of speech exceed the masking level of the noise (by virtue of Fig. 6). Also, the threshold of hearing (A, Fig. 4) can be plotted on the same graph to show the level of the speech above the threshold level for the cases when no noise is present.

It is generally customary to express noises in terms of their *spectrum levels*, i.e., in terms of energy contained in one-cycle-wide bands. To convert levels in a critical bandwidth to levels in one-cycle-wide bandwidths, the lower curve of Fig. 5 should be subtracted from the speech, noise, and threshold curves just described. The curves of Fig. 10 are already plotted in this way. Noise, expressed in terms of its spectrum level, can be plotted directly on that graph and the difference between the upper edge of the shaded region and the spectrum level of the noise will be equal to the level of the speech peaks above the masking level of the noise.

If assumptions (a) and (b) stated in italics above are valid, W_n for each band of equal contribution to speech intelligibility can be written

$$W_n = \frac{(\text{level of speech peaks}) - (\text{level of noise})}{30}, \qquad (5)$$

where W_n is limited to unity as a maximum value.

VIII. Experimental Validation of the Concept of Articulation Index

To demonstrate that the concept of articulation index is useful it is necessary first to show that a given area

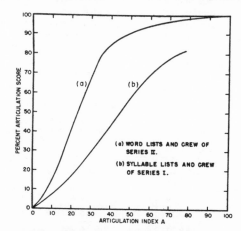

Fig. 11—Experimentally determined relations between word or syllable articulation and articulation index A.

of Fig. 10 is uniquely related to measured articulation scores, regardless of whether the area is spread over a wide frequency range with a small speech-noise difference in each band or over a narrow frequency range in any part of the graph with the W's near unity. Carefully taken articulation data from the Psycho-Acoustic and Electro-Acoustic Laboratories for twelve quite different interphone systems[4] operating with two different continuous spectra noises at the listeners' ears were examined by the author. This group of measurements will be referred to as Series I, and the widths of the frequency bands can be found from Figs. 12 and 13. For each of

With Noise B, where the noise spectrum had almost the same shape as the speech spectrum, less area was required to produce the same syllable intelligibility as for Noise A, which had an essentially flat spectrum. This is particularly true for the wide-band systems, numbers 1 and 2. The reason for this must be that the ear is more able psychologically to piece together fragmentary information from many bands into the complete syllable than it is if more information is given in fewer bands.

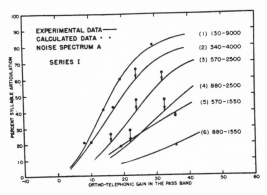

Fig. 12—Comparison of experimentally determined and calculated articulation scores for speech transmission systems numbers 1 to 6 in Noise Spectrum A.

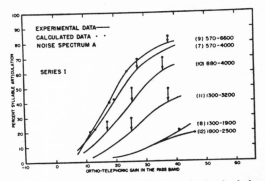

Fig. 13—Comparison of experimentally determined and calculated articulation scores for speech transmission systems numbers 7 to 12 in Noise Spectrum A.

those systems the articulation index was computed by plotting one of the two noise spectra on the same graph as the speech spectrum of Fig. 10 to which the ortho-telephonic gain of the system had been added. The results are shown in Table II. The gain settings of the amplifier assumed in the calculations were chosen from the articulation tests as those which yielded 20, 40, 60, and 80 per cent articulation. Examination of the top row of Table II, for example, shows that the average of the computed articulation indices for the twelve systems necessary to produce 20 per cent syllable articulation in the presence of Noise A is equal to 0.0249.

However, this effect is important only when the signal-to-noise ratio is small. The average articulation index for the two noises is shown in the extreme right-hand column of Table II and these values are plotted in Fig. 11 as curve (b). This curve shows the relation between articulation score and articulation index (A) for the syllable lists and crew used during these tests.

Using curve (b), the complete articulation curves for the twelve systems were computed and the results are shown in comparison with the measured scores in Figs. 12 and 13. The method has reliably rank-ordered all of the systems. Because the two types of noises are ex-

TABLE II
COMPUTED ARTICULATION INDEXES FOR SERIES I TESTS

Per cent Articulation		System Number												Average A	Average A for A and B
	Noise	1	2	3	4	5	6	7	8	9	10	11	12		
20	A	0.233	0.224	0.276	0.296	0.219	0.244	0.243	0.240	0.215	0.278	0.293	0.227	0.249	0.218
	B	0.101	0.143	0.212	0.237	0.191	0.242							0.218	
40	A	0.376	0.388	0.435	0.425	0.364		0.394		0.369	0.453	0.443		0.405	0.372
	B	0.252	0.304	0.319	0.363	0.342								0.340	
60	A	0.515	0.579	0.546				0.598		0.530	0.605			0.574	0.513
	B	0.411	0.462	0.491	0.451									0.453	
80	A	0.770								0.818				0.794	0.739
	B	0.651	0.720											0.685	

tremes of what are usually found in practice, the results will be generally better for practical situations.

Similar results are shown in Table III for a second series of tests performed on three types of aircraft interphones. The curve of articulation score versus A is shown as (a) in Fig. 11 and the calculated versus measured scores are shown in Fig. 14. Because words rather

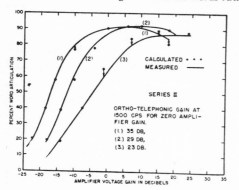

Fig. 14—Comparison of experimentally determined and calculated articulation scores for three types of interphone systems in an untreated bomber.

than syllables were used in the Series II tests, the relation between articulation score and A is different from that for Series I tests as would be expected.

TABLE III

COMPUTED ARTICULATION INDEXES FOR SERIES II TESTS

Per Cent Articulation	System Number			Average A
	1	2	3	
20	0.125	0.123	0.114	0.121
40	0.187	0.177	0.185	0.183
60	0.252	0.254	0.280	0.262
80	0.324	0.336	0.385	0.348

IX. MAXIMUM GAIN SETTINGS

Inspection of the data in Fig. 14 shows that, for the particular articulation crew used in Series II experiments, the scores reached a maximum and then turned down again as the gain was increased. It is believed that no estimates have been made before on what constitutes the maximum gain to which an audio system can be adjusted before no further contribution to speech intelligibility is obtained.

On the basis of the average articulation-index data versus per cent articulation of Table III and of additional datum points computed for the cases where the speech peak curves did not exceed 90 decibels, but where the word-articulation scores approached 90 per cent, a fairly well-defined relationship between A and the per cent word articulation was established (see (a) of Fig. 11). Then, for the three systems just described, articulation indices were computed for a number of points in the region where the gain curves had flattened off, or

started to bend downward, utilizing one of four assumptions successively: (a) setting no upper limit beyond which no contribution to A would be permitted; (b) setting the limit at 100 decibels; (c) at 95 decibels, and (d) at 90 decibels. The results are shown in Table IV in terms of the deviations of A from the value it should have to lie on the per cent word articulation versus A relationship of Fig. 10(a).

TABLE IV

DEVIATION OF COMPUTED ARTICULATION INDEXES FROM PER CENT WORD ARTICULATION VERSUS A RELATION OF FIG. 14.

System	Amplifier Gain	Ceiling Value			
		Unlimited	100	95	90
1	18	0.195	0.087	−0.009	−0.111
1	10	0.062	0.047	−0.001	−0.080
1	0	*	*	0.000	−0.017
2	22	0.177	0.084	−0.006	−0.102
2	18	0.108	0.071	0.010	−0.089
2	6	*	*	−0.004	−0.025
3	24	0.125	0.080	0.026	−0.087
3	15	*	0.168	0.052	0.010
Average Deviation		0.133	0.089	0.008	−0.063

* Speech peaks did not rise above level of following column.

A limiting value of 95 decibels yields values of A more nearly correct than for any one of the other three. It is concluded, then, that the region above 95 decibels per cycle should not be considered as contributing to A. A speech level of 95 decibels per cycle corresponds to an over-all speech level of about 125 decibels, which approximates the region of "tickle" in the ear. For this reason, if for no other, the speech peaks should not be amplified beyond this point.

A complete graph is shown in Fig. 15 for System 2 of Series II with an amplifier gain of +6 decibels. The

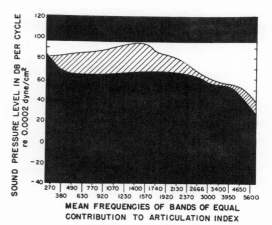

Fig. 15—Chart demonstrating the calculation of articulation index. Upper black region shows probable area of no contribution to articulation index. Lower black area shows masking effect of noise. Shaded region shows speech area presented to ear of a listener in the presence of the noise and is equal to the articulation index A.

lower black region is the total root-mean-square noise level arriving at the eardrum from the microphone and through the earphone cushions. The shaded region shows the area of speech which is not masked out by the interfering noise. The upper black area is the region of no contribution to A. The articulation index A is about 0.5 in this example.

X. Determination of Systems Performance

In order to calculate the articulation index of a voice communication system, data of the type described in Sections V and VI are needed. These data are often tedious to obtain. As an alternative, use of response data taken on artificial voices or ears (couplers) will sometimes permit the computation of approximate articulation indices.[16]

The articulation index for a particular interphone system will now be calculated to demonstrate the method in detail. Both the talker and the listener will be assumed to be in the same noise field. It is further assumed that the system is substantially free from nonlinear distortion, and hence, amenable to treatment by this procedure. Articulation scores have previously been obtained so that the accuracy of the results can be checked.

1. The *real-voice response of the carbon microphone* is shown in Fig. 16(a) as the root-mean-square voltage produced across a 100-ohm resistor by a human voice which, without the microphone to interfere, would produce a root-mean-square sound pressure level of 74 decibels at a distance of one meter in an anechoic chamber.

2. *An objectively measured real-ear response of an ANB-H-1A headset* in the doughnut-type cushions is shown in Fig. 16(b). The curves are plots of sound pressure in decibels re 0.000200 dyne per centimeter squared produced in the *outer* ear canal of an average listener as a function of frequency by the headset with one volt impressed across the terminals of the two earphones of the headset in series.

3. *The response characteristic of the amplifier* is assumed to be flat and the voltage gain at 1000 cycles per second is expressed as:

$$\text{Amplifier Gain} = 20 \log E_2/E_1$$

where

    $E_1 =$ voltage developed by the microphone across a 200-ohm load resistor

    $E_2 =$ voltage delivered by the amplifier across its load measured at 1000 cycles per second.

4. *The noise pickup characteristic of the microphone* is given in Fig. 16(c).

5. *The objectively measured noise-exclusion characteristics of the doughnut type of earphone cushions* are given in Fig. 16(d).

6. The *ambient noise spectrum* used for the articulation tests is shown in Fig. 16(e).

7. The real-ear and real-voice curves along with the response of the amplifier, are combined to yield the *orthotelephonic gain of the over-all system*. Two decibels were added to the microphone response to account for the difference between the 100-ohm test resistor used with the microphone and the amplifier input impedance of 200 ohms.

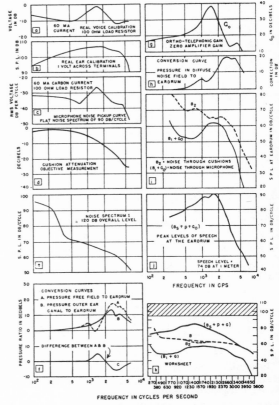

Fig. 16—Detailed steps in calculation of articulation index. The procedure is outlined in the text.

A correction must be added to the data of curves (a) and (b) above if they are to be used in the calculation of the orthotelephonic gain. The curve for converting free-field pressure to pressure at the eardrum is given as (a) in Fig. 16(f). This curve should be *subtracted* from Fig. 16(a) to convert the real-voice calibration curve of the microphone to give the voltage produced by the microphone for a constant sound pressure of 74 decibels at the eardrum of an average listener.

The curve for converting the pressure in the outer ear, under the cushion, over to the pressure at the eardrum is

---

[16] Specifications on acceptable artificial voices and ears are being drawn up by Sub-Committee Z-24-B of the American Standards Association at this time.

given as (b) in Fig. 16(f). This curve then should be *added* to those of Fig. 16(b) for the real-ear calibrations of the headsets to convert them to sound pressure produced at the eardrum for a constant voltage of 1 volt across the headset. Because the curves (b) and (a) are subtracted to yield the orthotelephonic gain, their difference given as the smoothed curve (c) can be used.

The orthotelephonic response of the system with a gain control setting of zero is given in Fig. 16(g) (see (3)) and will be designated as G in the remainder of this section. It was found by adding together curves (a), (b), and (c) of (f) minus a constant factor of 74 decibels.

8. *Three noises arrive at the ear*, (1) that entering at the microphone, (2) that entering through the cushion, and (3) that produced by amplifier. For this problem, the amplifier was adequately quiet.

To determine the noise entering at the ear via the microphone, curves (b), (c), and (e), the gain of the amplifier, and curve (b) of (f) are added together. If the gain control is adjusted during the experiment, the curve showing the noise arriving at the ear from the microphone must be adjusted upward or downward accordingly. The total noise arriving at the ear from the microphone will be designated as (B_1+G), to show that the values must be changed when the gain of the amplifier is changed.

The noise entering the system at the earphone through the cushion is designated as B_2 and is determined by adding together the curves of (d) and (e). These data must be corrected to produce the pressure at the eardrum. An approximate curve for this purpose is shown in (h). The values of (B_1+G_0) for zero gain control setting and B_2 for our illustrative problem are shown in (i).

9. The peaks of speech lie about 12 decibels above the average level and so the curve of Fig. 2 called B_s should be displaced upward by 12 decibels for our purposes. We shall call the new curve (B_s+p), where $p=12$ decibels. To get the spectrum level of the peaks of speech arriving at the ear, we need to add in the curve for the orthotelephonic gain and the correction curve A of (f), thereby yielding (B_s+p+G). For talking levels which measure different from 68 decibels at a distance of one meter, the value of B_s should be corrected accordingly. The values of (B_s+p+G) with zero gain control setting for our illustrative examples are shown in Fig. 16(j).

10. *To calculate the articulation index*, the first step in the process of determining the articulation index is to plot (B_s+p+G), B_2 and (B_1+G) on a graph with the distorted frequency scale of Fig. 10. The value of each of

these quantities at the mean frequency of the band is plotted in the center of the band as shown.

To determine the total noise produced at the ear, an energy summation of the noises (B_1+G) and B_2 must be made. This can be done easily on the graph by plotting a new curve B which lies 3 decibels above (B_1+G) and B_2 if the two have the same value, i.e., cross each other; 2 decibels above the larger if the larger lies 2 decibels above the lesser; 1 decibel above the larger if it lies 6 decibels above the lesser; and on the larger if it lies greater than 7 decibels above the lesser (see Fig. 16(k)). The useable area for contributing to intelligible speech lies between (B_s+p+G) and B and is similar to the shaded region of Fig. 15. In case B should lie so low that it crosses over the threshold of hearing at the bottom of the graph, an energy summation of B and the threshold curve should be made as though the threshold curve was determined by a noise having a continuous spectrum. The discovery of the identity of the threshold curve with a continuous spectrum noise is to be attributed to the Bell Telephone Laboratories. For each of the bands $(\Delta A)=0.05\ W_n$ (see (4) and (5)), and can easily be determined by using a small scale marked from 0 to 0.05 with each 0.01 division being equal in length to 6 decibels on the graph. The total articulation index equals the sum of the (ΔA) values for the twenty different bands. If the (B_s+p+G) and the B curves lie more than 30 decibels apart, a value of 0.05 should be assigned to that band as being its maximum contribution. If (B_s+p+G) lies above 95 decibels, only the contribution up to 95 should be counted. For this example, A is 0.495. The measured articulation score was 88 per cent using words.

In general, an entirely satisfactory system for a given ambient noise is one for which the articulation index is greater than 0.5, while an unsatisfactory system will have an A of less than 0.3. For values of A between 0.5 and 0.3, the system should be viewed with suspicion and subjected to an actual articulation test using the exact ambient noise spectrum if possible. Approximate values of word or syllable articulation scores can be obtained from Fig. 11, but it must be remembered that those relationships are valid only for a particular test crew and lists of speech material.

ACKNOWLEDGEMENT

The author wishes to express his appreciation to the Bell Telephone Laboratories and the Psycho-Acoustic and Electro-Acoustic Laboratories at Harvard for making available the foundation material for this study.

26

Reprinted from *Nature* **214**(5093):1164 (1967)

Speech Communication in Very Noisy Environments

COLIN CHERRY
ROGER WILEY

Imperial College of Science and Technology

WE have conducted experiments on speech communication in extremely noisy environments; one of our findings is particularly surprising, and may be of value to understanding situations in which intense noise is inherently present.

The speech signals used consisted of readings (male voice) from various forms of literature, including newspapers and technical matter, and the aim was to assess communication, rather than intelligibility of single words or sounds. The speech was recorded on tape and passed through a filter of bandwidth 350–800 cycles/sec. This provided a "control" signal which indicated, substantially, only the instants of the vowel sounds (together with some high-energy consonant elements). This narrow band signal was then used to gate the original speech signal. An amplitude-limiter was applied so that only those sounds of high energy were passed. The result then consisted of a staccato sequence of only the high energy voiced speech sounds, which have extremely low intelligibility, even with running speech.

If, however, white noise alone is added in the gaps of this signal and steadily increased, there comes a certain amplitude at which almost full intelligibility of the speech is restored. Nothing is added but white noise. We have found that the amplitude of noise necessary is fairly critical for any individual listener, but that it varies considerably (over 40 dB) between different listeners. All listeners were of the English culture. An average increase in the intelligibility would be, for example, from 20 per cent (no noise added) to at least 70 per cent (noise added).

This general result was expected on the hypothesis that speech consists essentially of accurate time patterning of sounds; it is essentially a rhythmic activity and the precision of timing is very important. The extent of the result, however, was quite unexpected. What remnants of speech have been held unchanged in this processed signal possess the most important factor of syllabic rhythm. The noise bursts, in themselves having no information content, are nevertheless positioned accurately in the rhythmic stream of speech sound elements, and the listener hears a human being speaking. This experiment stresses the vital importance of the temporal patterning of speech to perception. Our intention now is to investigate conversation in similar conditions.

Automatic Evaluation of Time-Varying Communication Systems

MICHAEL H. L. HECKER
GOTTFRIED VON BISMARCK
CARL E. WILLIAMS

INTRODUCTION

MOST SPEECH-communication systems can be regarded as having temporally stable transmission characteristics. Such systems may be evaluated subjectively with standard intelligibility test procedures employing speakers and listeners.[1],[3],[6] Except for analysis–synthesis systems (e.g., vocoders), these systems may also be evaluated objectively with electronic devices which are designed to compute the Articulation Index (AI).[8] Three such devices are presently available: the Voice Interference Analysis Set (VIAS),[4] the Speech Communication Index Meter (SCIM),[9] and the Predicted Speech Intelligibility Computer (PSI/COMP).[1] For systems with stable char-

acteristics, AI is a valid measure of system performance, because it can be uniquely related to speech intelligibility.

In other communication systems, such as HF radio systems and tropospheric-scatter systems,[5] the transmission characteristics vary with time. It is difficult to evaluate these systems subjectively; most intelligibility test procedures are applicable only to systems which have constant characteristics. The objective evaluation of time-varying systems appears to be more feasible, since electronic devices can measure the characteristics of a system in a short time interval, and compute scores in rapid succession. In the absence of comparable data from subjective evaluations, however, the validity of such machine scores is open to question. Considering the range over which system characteristics often vary and the rate of variation, the intelligibility of speech transmitted over time-varying systems may well be influenced by such factors as temporal masking,[2] attention, and fatigue.

To explore the validity of machine scores in a practical situation, an actual time-varying system was evaluated subjectively, using a special test procedure. The transmission characteristics of a typical tropo system were recorded on magnetic tape. Three 3-minute program tapes were prepared from this recording. Twenty-five 3-minute speech tapes, each containing a sequence of 60 test words, were also prepared. A given program tape was reproduced 25 times, each time together with a different speech tape, to provide 25 words for the calculation of each of 60 intelligibility scores. The program tape was also reproduced through one-third octave band filters to provide spectral information from which AI's could be computed at the same 60 points in time where intelligibility scores were obtained. These AI's, which represent scores that might be computed by an electronic device, were then converted to equivalent intelligibility scores. These latter scores were compared with the scores obtained from listeners to determine how closely the intelligibility of the tropo system could be predicted from machine scores.

[1] PSI/COMP is a commercial instrument developed by Bolt Beranek and Newman Inc., Cambridge, Mass. It is similar in concept to SCIM.[9]

Manuscript received September 28, 1967. This work was supported by the Electronic Systems Division, Air Force Systems Command, under Contract AF19(628)-5874. This paper was presented at the 1967 Conference on Speech Communication and Processing, Cambridge, Mass.

M. H. L. Hecker was with Bolt Beranek and Newman Inc., Cambridge, Mass. He is now with Stanford Research Institute, Menlo Park, Calif. 94025

G. von Bismarck and C. E. Williams are with Bolt Beranek and Newman Inc., Cambridge, Mass. 02138.

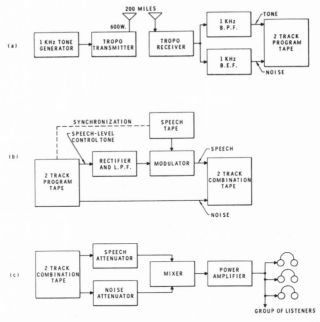

Fig. 1. Block diagrams of instrumentation used to (a) record program tape, (b) prepare combination tape, and (c) reproduce combination tape.

PREPARATION OF PROGRAM TAPES

A block diagram of the instrumentation used to record the program tapes is shown in Fig. 1(a). An experimental Air Force tropo system was used, which consisted of a transmitter and a receiver separated by 200 miles. Although the system could provide several modes of diversity operation, these were not employed. A constant-level 1-kHz tone was applied to one of the voice channels at the transmitter to represent the speech signal ordinarily transmitted over the system. The output of the receiver was processed by two filters. One filter was a sharp-skirted bandpass filter centered on the tone, and the other filter was a complementary sharp-skirted band-elimination filter. The output of the bandpass filter served to describe how the level of a received speech signal might vary as a function of time. The output of the band-elimination filter described how the level and spectrum of the received noise varied. The two filter outputs were recorded simultaneously with a two-channel tape recorder.

Recordings were made at various transmitter power settings. After listening to the recordings obtained and observing graphic level tracings of the time-varying noise, a 30-minute recording made at a power setting of 600 watts was selected. This recording was reduced to three 3-minute sections to furnish three program tapes. The editing was accomplished so that different types of interference patterns were included, and so that the test words (on the speech tapes) would occur in a variety of positions with respect to the interference. A short burst of white noise was inserted at the beginning of each program tape to facilitate accurate synchronization with the speech tapes.

PREPARATION OF SPEECH TAPES

It was considered desirable to obtain as many intelligibility scores as possible for each program tape. This and other considerations led to the selection of the Modified Rhyme Test (MRT).[6] Since MRT words can be readily presented and marked by listeners at the rate of 1 word every 3 seconds, 60 intelligibility scores could be obtained for each 3-minute program tape.

The speech material of the MRT consists of six 50-word lists, which are approximately equally difficult. Each list is composed of 25 words in which the initial consonant is tested, and 25 words in which the final consonant is tested. For the present application, a rearrangement of this material appeared to be necessary. If the standard 50-word lists were to be used, 50 speech tapes would be required. The effort of preparing and administrating this many speech tapes seemed unwarranted. Also, considering that 60 intelligibility scores were to be obtained for each program tape, it seemed desirable to use more than 6 basic lists. It was, there-

TABLE I
Word Contents of Twelve 25-Item Half Lists of the Modified Rhyme Test

	No.	A	B	C	D	E	F	G	H	I	J	K	L
							Half List						
Initial Consonant Variable	1	sold	fold	gold	told	hold	cold	bed	shed	red	led	fed	wed
	2	dig	wig	pig	rig	big	fig	kick	lick	sick	tick	wick	pick
	3	book	took	look	cook	hook	shook	hark	dark	mark	lark	park	bark
	4	gale	male	tale	bale	sale	pale	peel	reel	feel	heel	keel	eel
	5	will	hill	kill	till	fill	bill	foil	oil	coil	boil	soil	toil
	6	fame	same	came	name	game	tame	ten	pen	men	hen	then	den
	7	rang	fang	hang	bang	sang	gang	pin	sin	tin	win	din	fin
	8	sip	rip	tip	hip	dip	lip	sun	nun	gun	fun	run	bun
	9	feat	meat	heat	seat	beat	neat	tent	bent	dent	went	rent	sent
	10	hot	got	not	pot	lot	tot	raw	paw	law	jaw	thaw	saw
	11	dust	just	rust	must	gust	bust	kit	bit	fit	sit	wit	hit
	12	top	cop	pop	hop	shop	mop	nest	vest	west	test	hest	rest
Final Consonant Variable	13	dig	dip	dim	did	dill	din	may	way	say	gay	day	pay
	14	duck	dun	dung	dub	dug	dud	ban	bath	back	bass	bat	bad
	15	fizz	fig	fin	fill	fib	fit	bean	beach	beat	beam	bead	beak
	16	came	cape	cane	case	cave	cake	bun	bus	but	buff	buck	bug
	17	kick	king	kid	kit	kin	kill	heath	heap	heal	hear	heat	heave
	18	late	lay	lake	lace	lane	lame	cut	cub	cuff	cup	cud	cuss
	19	pale	pane	pace	pay	page	pave	map	mat	math	man	mass	mad
	20	pig	pick	pip	pin	pill	pit	pass	pack	pat	pad	path	pan
	21	pun	puff	pup	puck	pus	pub	peace	peas	peak	peal	peat	peach
	22	rave	rake	race	rate	raze	ray	sake	sale	save	sane	safe	same
	23	seep	seen	seethe	seem	seed	seek	sad	sag	sass	sat	sap	sack
	24	sub	sum	sud	sun	sup	sung	sit	sing	sin	sick	sip	sill
	25	teach	tear	tease	teal	team	teak	tab	tan	tam	tang	tack	tap

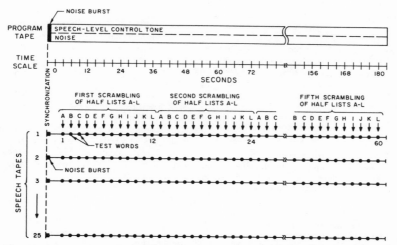

Fig. 2.　Diagram showing how a program tape was combined with 25 speech tapes to provide a 25-word half list at each of 60 points in time of program tape.

303

fore, decided to construct twelve 25-word lists. To provide lists that would be equally difficult, various data obtained with the MRT[7],[10] were examined in detail.

The twelve 25-word lists, referred to as Half Lists A-L, are given in Table I. The relative difficulty of these lists was checked experimentally.[11] Although some lists appeared to be slightly more difficult than others, the balance that was achieved was considered adequate.

Five randomizations of the 12 half lists were prepared to provide a half list at each of 60 points in time. The first word in each of the 60 randomized half lists was identified as a word to be included in Speech Tape 1. In the same manner, the remaining words in each half list were marked for inclusion in Speech Tapes 2 to 25. Each speech tape would thus consist of 60 words, but these words do not constitute any particular half list. The relation between the contents of a given program tape and the test words of the 25 speech tapes is illustrated in Fig. 2.

The 25 speech tapes were recorded by an adult male speaker, who had considerable experience in reading test materials. The recordings were made with high-quality equipment in a sound-treated studio. A flashing light signal controlled from a pulse generator was used during the recording to help the speaker maintain the required 3-second interval between words. Although the words were not embedded in a carrier phrase and no item numbers were recorded, the speaker tried to read all words for a given speech tape with the same vocal effort.

To check the accuracy of the timing of the words, graphic level tracings were made of each speech tape. These tracings were aligned with a time scale that indicated the exact positions where the words should occur. Corrections were calculated for those words which occurred more than 100 ms too early or too late, and these corrections were then used to edit the speech tapes. A short burst of white noise was inserted at the beginning of each speech tape to facilitate accurate synchronization with the program tapes.

PREPARATION AND ADMINISTRATION OF COMBINATION TAPES

To ensure accurate synchronization between the program tapes and the speech tapes, it was decided to combine the tapes prior to their presentation to listeners. A block diagram of the instrumentation used to prepare the combination tapes is shown in Fig. 1(b). Two tape recorders were coupled electrically so that the tapes could be started simultaneously. Visual markers on both sets of tapes, positioned just before the noise bursts, were used to accomplish the alignment. The 1-kHz tone reproduced from the program tape was rectified and lowpass filtered, and the resulting dc signal was applied to a modulator. This modulator was used to vary the level of the speech signal reproduced from the speech tape. The output of the modulator and the time-varying noise reproduced from the program tape were recorded

with a two-channel tape recorder. This arrangement allowed independent settings of the speech and noise levels during the administration of the combination tapes.

Since 3 program tapes had to be combined with 25 speech tapes, a total of 75 combination tapes were prepared. These combination tapes were ordered according to a test design and administered to a group of 10 listeners. The listeners were provided with special 60-item response forms, which were similar to the forms normally used with the MRT. A block diagram of the instrumentation used for administering the combination tapes is shown in Fig. 1(c). The speech attenuator was adjusted so that the maximum sound pressure level of the speech (corresponding to the highest level of the 1-kHz tone on the program tapes) was 71 dB under the earphones.[2] Similarly, the noise attenuator was adjusted so that the maximum sound pressure level of the noise was 78 dB.[2]

CALCULATION OF ARTICULATION INDEX

In order to calculate an AI at each point in time where an intelligibility score was obtained (referred to as a word location), it was first necessary to subject the program tapes to a detailed spectral analysis. The instrumentation used to obtain the required spectral data is shown in Fig. 3. A graphic level tracing was prepared of the 1-kHz tone to provide information regarding the speech level at each word location. This tracing was calibrated in terms of the maximum level at which the speech had been presented to the listeners. The time-varying noise was reproduced sequentially through 15 one-third-octave band filters. The center frequencies of these filters ranged from 200 Hz to 5 kHz. A graphic level tracing was prepared from the output of each filter; these tracings were calibrated in terms of the maximum overall level at which the noise had been presented.

By means of a time scale common to all tracings, the speech level and the noise spectrum at each word location could now be uniquely determined. The tracings were read at each word location and, from this information, AI's were calculated with the aid of a digital computer. The calculated AI's were then converted to equivalent MRT scores, using data obtained in a related study.[11]

The related study was concerned with the masking of speech by aircraft noise. Recordings of various aircraft flyovers were assembled into three 3-minute program tapes which were similar to the program tapes prepared in the present study. Both studies employed the same 25 speech tapes and the identical test procedure for obtaining intelligibility scores. In the aircraft study, AI's were also computed at the 60 word locations of each program tape. One important difference between the two studies was the rate at which the noise varied.

----

[2] With reference to the 0.0002 microbar.

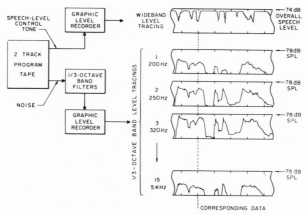

Fig. 3.   Block diagram of instrumentation used to measure overall speech level and noise spectrum for calculation of Articulation Index.

Whereas the overall noise level in the present study could change by as much as 25 dB within an interval of 400 ms (average duration of test words), the overall level of the aircraft noise never changed by more than 5 dB during the same interval. Another difference was the fact that, in the aircraft study, the speech tapes were presented to listeners at a uniform level. Considering these differences, it was assumed that a more reliable relation between AI and MRT scores could be obtained from the aircraft study than from the present study.

COMPARISON BETWEEN OBTAINED AND PREDICTED SCORES

For each word location of each program tape, the intelligibility score obtained from the listeners was compared with the score predicted from the AI calculation. Plots of the relation between these obtained and predicted scores were prepared for each program tape. The plot for Program Tape I is shown in Fig. 4. Each point in this plot represents a word location. Word locations where the obtained scores were predicted correctly can be identified by points that lie on an imaginary diagonal line. The horizontal displacement of points from such a line is a measure of how accurately the obtained scores were predicted.

To facilitate an analysis of the incorrect predictions, it was necessary to define a region, centered about the diagonal line, over which the obtained scores could be considered correctly predicted. This region, shown in Fig. 4 by two dashed lines, was adopted from the aircraft study mentioned above. When the data of the aircraft study were arranged in the same manner as the present data, the chosen region enclosed 156 of the 180 word locations (87 percent of all data). Assuming that the distribution of the aircraft data was only moderately skewed, the region corresponded to approximately 1.5

standard deviations, measured in one direction from the mean.

In an effort to determine why the obtained scores were predicted incorrectly at certain word locations, the graphic level tracings of the program tapes were carefully examined. This examination revealed that at the word locations of interest either the speech level, the noise level, or both levels varied considerably. As a consequence, different portions of a given word were subjected to different amounts of interference. Considering the nature of the MRT, those portions containing the initial and final consonants were probably more important in the determination of the obtained score than any other portions. The AI calculation, however, from which the predicted score was determined, only sampled the interference at one point in time. This point corresponded to the central portion of the word which contains the vowel.

All incorrectly predicted intelligibility scores could be explained in terms of this general finding: At the boundaries of the average word duration (approximately 400 ms) where the initial and final consonants occurred, the interference conditions were appreciably different from the conditions that prevailed in the center of the duration, where the AI was calculated. Consider, for example, Word Location I:41, where the predicted test score was too low (see Fig. 4). The level tracings for this word location are shown in Fig. 5. The temporal course of the speech level suggests that the initial and final consonants were barely attenuated. This was not taken into account by the AI calculation; the speech level used in the AI calculation was read too low on the tracing. To determine the amount by which the speech level was read too low, the AI calculation was repeated with various higher speech levels until the result approximated the AI value that corresponded to the ob-

305

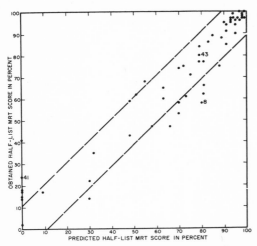

Fig. 4. Plot of predicted versus obtained half-list MRT scores (corrected for chance) for 60 points in time of Program Tape I.

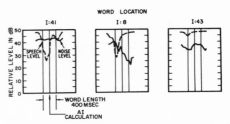

Fig. 5. Speech and overall noise level tracings for 3 word locations in Program Tape I.

tained score. For this word location, the correction factor was +5 dB.

The level tracings for several word locations showed an interesting trend. The speech and noise levels used in the corrected AI calculations tended to agree more with the levels existing at the position of the initial consonant than with those existing at the position of the final consonant. No satisfactory explanation could be found for this trend.

Now consider Word Location I:8, where the predicted test score was too high (see Fig. 4). The level tracings for this word location are shown in Fig. 5. The speech level used in the AI calculation did not take into account the extreme attenuation at the position of the initial consonant and was, therefore, read too high. It is also possible that the noise level was read too low, since the noise level used in the AI calculation was lower than the noise level which existed at the position of the initial consonant. While both of these factors undoubtedly contributed to a predicted test score that was too high, it is difficult to determine which factor was the dominant one.

At Word Location I:43, the predicted score was nearly the same as the obtained score (see Fig. 4). The level tracings for this word location are also shown in Fig. 5. The speech and noise levels are clearly more uniform over the word duration than the levels shown for Word Locations I:41 and I:8. The tracings do not exhibit any features which might have led to incorrect predictions.

CONCLUSIONS

Within the criterion of accuracy employed in this study, approximately 76 percent of the intelligibility scores obtained from listeners could be correctly pre-

dicted from the computed AI's. All incorrect predictions could be attributed to the fact that, whereas an intelligibility score was influenced by the system characteristics for about 400 ms, the AI was essentially computed for a single point in time. Contrary to theoretical expectations, the incorrect predictions could not be related to such factors as temporal masking, attention, or fatigue. The results of this study suggest that fewer incorrect predictions would have been made if the speech and noise level tracings had both been averaged over a 400-ms interval at each word location. Perhaps the number of incorrect predictions could have been reduced even further if, in obtaining average speech and noise levels for each AI calculation, the initial portion of the interval had been given more weight than the final portion.

The computed AI's were intended to represent scores which might be obtained with an electronic device. Despite their general validity, the AI's are clearly not representative in the sense that they are based on instantaneous measurements. All of the available devices employ circuits which integrate the system characteristics over an extended period of time before an AI is computed. If such a device were used to process the program tapes prepared in this study, and if the integration time and sampling rate of the device were properly adjusted, then the resulting AI's should accurately predict the obtained intelligibility scores. It is concluded, therefore, that the existing electronic devices are potentially suitable for the automatic evaluation of time-varying communication systems.

Although it is difficult to make specific recommendations for the possible modification of these devices, the results of this study suggest that the time intervals over which the devices presently integrate the received "speech" and noise signals are too long. In the SCIM,[9] for example, the "speech" is integrated over 1 second and the noise over 2 seconds. For the evaluation of time-varying systems, an integration time of approximately 500 ms for both "speech" and noise would appear to be more appropriate. This interval corresponds roughly to the duration of a syllable.

Since individual machine scores are difficult to interpret, it may be desirable to have the devices compute a large number of AI's before an average score is displayed. The average score could then be used to estimate the probability that a syllable will be correctly identified over the system, regardless of when the syllable is transmitted. It is clear that such scores must eventually be related to how well longer message units (e.g., phrases and sentences) can be understood. The ultimate measure of system performance is not the intelligibility of a series of independent test words, but the ease and reliability with which system users can transmit and receive operational messages.

REFERENCES

[1] J. P. Egan, "Articulation testing methods," *Laryngoscope*, vol. 58, pp. 955–991, 1948.
[2] L. L. Elliott, "Backward masking: Monotic and dichotic conditions," *J. Acoust. Soc. Am.*, vol. 34, pp. 1108–1115, 1962.
[3] G. Fairbanks, "Test of phonemic differentiation: The rhyme test," *J. Acoust. Soc. Am.*, vol. 30, pp. 596–600, 1958.
[4] R. E. Fitts, "Electronic evaluation of voice communications systems," Electromagnetic Lab., Rome Air Development Center, Air Force Systems Command, Rept. RADC-TDR-63-355, August 1963.
[5] F. A. Gunther, "Tropospheric scatter communications," *IEEE Spectrum*, vol. 3, pp. 79–100, September 1966.
[6] A. S. House, C. E. Williams, M. H. L. Hecker, and K. D. Kryter, "Articulation-testing methods: Consonantal differentiation with a closed-response set," *J. Acoust. Soc. Am.*, vol. 37, pp. 158–166, 1965.
[7] A. S. House, C. E. Williams, M. H. L. Hecker, and K. D. Kryter, "Psychoacoustic speech tests: A modified rhyme test," Decision Sciences Lab., Electronic Systems Div., Air Force Systems Command, Rept. ESD-TDR-63-403, June 1963.
[8] K. D. Kryter, "Methods for the calculation and use of the articulation index," *J. Acoust. Soc. Am.*, vol. 34, pp. 1689–1697, 1962.
[9] K. D. Kryter and J. H. Ball, "SCIM—A meter for measuring the performance of speech communication systems," Decision Sciences Lab., Electronic Systems Div., Air Force Systems Command, Rept. ESD-TDR-64-674, October 1964.
[10] C. E. Williams, M. H. L. Hecker, K. N. Stevens, and B. Woods, "Intelligibility test methods and procedures for the evaluation of speech communication systems," Decision Sciences Lab., Electronic Systems Div., Air Force Systems Command, Rept. ESD-TR-66-677, December 1966.
[11] C. E. Williams, K. N. Stevens, M. H. L. Hecker, and K. S. Pearsons, "The speech interference effects of aircraft noise," Federal Aviation Administration, Dept. of Transportation, Rept. FAA-DS-67-19, September, 1967

Reprinted from *Speech Monogr.* **27**:63–69 (1960)

THE USE OF FAST LIMITING TO IMPROVE THE INTELLIGIBILITY OF SPEECH IN NOISE

ELWOOD A. KRETSINGER and NORTON B. YOUNG

Comparisons were made between the conventional speech clipper and an experimentally fast speech limiter to determine which system produced the more intelligible speech in the presence of noise. It was found that fast limiting produced significantly higher intelligibility than clipping at both 10 db. and 20 db. of compression. It was assumed that the measured difference in harmonic and intermodulation distortion of the two systems was the causal factor.

S INCE the early days of electrical voice communication various schemes have been devised for altering the speech waveform in order to enhance the efficiency of its transmission and reception. During World War II it was learned that the intelligibility of discrete words could be improved by increasing the amplitude of the consonants relative to that of the vowels.[1] This was accomplished by electronically clipping the peaks of the waveform so that all sounds, consonants and vowels alike, were made equal in amplitude. For the consonants (normally about 12 db. weaker than vowels) this resulted in a considerable net gain. The development has been particularly beneficial in radio voice transmission where noise often masks the weak signal. The speech clipper, however, is non-linear and generates a high order of harmonic and intermodulation distortion. These distortion products, particularly those associated with intermodulation, tend to mask in-

telligibility after the fashion of ambient noise.[2] It would seem, therefore, that any system which could produce the same consonant-to-vowel ratio as the clipper without the latter's characteristic distortion would yield still more intelligible speech reception where noise is a masking factor.[3]

Any consideration of compression with low distortion must take into account the popular peak limiter. This circuit has relatively little distortion and is employed extensively in standard broadcasting stations to prevent over-modulation of the carrier. It is, however, "slow" in its operation. While the clipper acts instantaneously upon the individual sound, the limiter requires a finite period to attack the leading edge of the waveform and a much longer period to release the trailing edge. Release times for conventional limiter application will range from .2 to 1.5 seconds, and it is customary to favor the longer interval in order to avoid instability and distor-

Mr. Kretsinger is Associate Professor of Speech and Mr. Young Assistant Professor of Speech and Speech Therapist at the University of Oregon.

[1] K. D. Kryter, J. C. R. Licklider, and S. S. Stevens, "Premodulation Clipping in *AM* Voice Communication," *The Journal of the Acoustical Society of America*, No. 1 (January 1947), 125-131.

[2] Leo J. Beranek, *Acoustic Measurements* (New York, 1949), p. 689.

[3] The masking noise referred to here is that which is introduced *after* compression (channel noise and acoustic noise at the receiving location). Noise entering the system *prior* to compression (particularly circuit noise with amplitude similar to that of the weak consonants) will receive the same full amplification accorded the consonants. Thus, while the consonant-to-vowel ratio will be improved, the vowel-to-noise ratio will suffer. To prevent the latter condition from giving rise to a masking problem of its own, it is imperative that noise be minimized in the preamplifier. A noise level of —40 db. is usually acceptable in communications, so if it is planned to utilize 20 db. of compression, then a —60 db. noise level in the preamplifier is necessary. Acoustic background noise at the microphone site must likewise be controlled.

tion.[4] This means that a weak sound such as a consonant, following immediately after a strong sound such as a vowel, will be compressed or limited along with the stronger sound. The bias voltage developed by the vowel for the purpose of lowering the system gain (limiting action) is still present upon the arrival of the consonant. The limiter, therefore, while effective in its normal application of controlling the dynamic range of the general sound level, is too slow for improving the consonant-to-vowel ratio within discrete words.

There was recently announced a new limiter design which features a release time of 22 milliseconds.[5] This is almost ten times faster than the fastest conventional limiter. Considering the speed of this new circuit and the inherently lower distortion of limiters as opposed to clippers, the authors were prompted to compare the two systems in a word intelligibility test.

THE PROBLEM

The problem was phrased in the form of two specific questions:

1. What is the relative effectiveness, at moderate compression, of fast limiting and clipping in improving speech intelligibility in the presence of noise?

2. What is the relative effectiveness, at deep compression, of fast limiting and clipping in improving speech intelligibility in the presence of noise?

The term "moderate compression" was applied to a 10 db. increase of the input signal relative to the threshold of compression.[6] The term "deep compres-

sion" was applied to a 20 db. increase of the input signal relative to the threshold of compression.

PROCEDURE

A typical speech clipper was constructed and, in conformity with standard communications practice, a 300-3000 cycle band-pass filter was used to suppress unwanted harmonics.[7] The basic circuit is shown in Figure 1. Measurements revealed that 10 db. of clipping produced 16.8 per cent intermodulation distortion and 13 per cent harmonic distortion, while 20 db. of clipping produced 23 per cent and 18 per cent respectively.[8] One of the fast limiters, the Limpander, Model LE-2, was obtained from the Electronic Systems Engineering Company, Oklahoma City, and the basic circuit is shown in Figure 2. It was found that 10 db. of limiting produced 11.9 per cent intermodulation distortion and 2.1 per cent harmonic distortion, while 20 db. of limiting produced 12.4 per cent and 4.6 per cent respectively. Figure 3 shows the effect of the two methods of compression on the shape of a 1 KC sine wave. Figure 4 shows the frequency response of both systems.

Two hundred and fifty phonetically balanced words were employed in the following manner. Fifty words, C.I.D. Auditory Test W-22, List 4A, were recorded on tape using 10 db. of limiting. Another fifty words, List 3A, were recorded with 20 db. of limiting. The same

[4] Donald E. Maxwell, "Dynamic Performance of Peak-Limiting Amplifiers," *Proceedings of the I.R.E.*, XXXV (November 1947), 1350.

[5] Donald B. Daniel, "The Consonant Amplifier-Limiter," *Radio and Television News* (March 1957), 49-51.

[6] Threshold or 0 db. of compression was established as that preamplifier gain setting which would drive the clipper or fast limiter *just short* of the point where a sine wave out-

put (as viewed on an oscilloscope) no longer increased proportionally with the advance of the linear-tapered gain control.

[7] *The Radio Amateur's Handbook* (West Hartford, Conn., 1956), p. 248.

[8] Intermodulation distortion was measured with a Heathkit, Model IM-1 distortion meter employing test signals of 60 cycles and 3000 cycles at a ratio of four to one. Harmonic distortion was measured with a Hewlett Packard, Model 330B distortion meter employing a test signal of 1000 cycles.

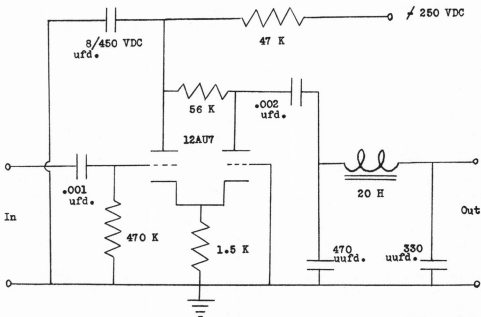

FIGURE 1. Speech clipper with low-pass filter. Positive and negative peaks of the waveform are clipped by driving the output section of the 12AU7 alternately to cut-off and to plate-current saturation.

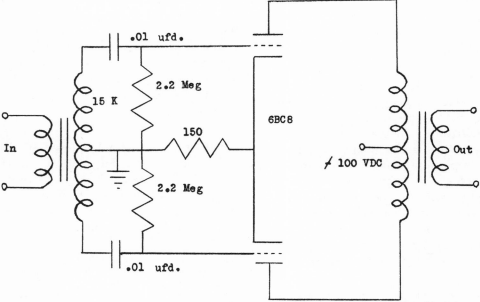

FIGURE 2. Simplified fast limiter diagram showing the essential push-pull grid bias features. Note the low-impedance driving source and the RC time constant of $2.2 \times .01 \times 10^{-6}$ or 22 milliseconds. The 6BC8 is a variable *mu* tube. When the input signal exceeds the cathode bias, the grids draw current and charge the coupling capacitors, thus creating an additional grid bias which reduces the *mu* or gain of the amplifier. Distortion produced by the non-linear operation is predominantly even-order harmonic and is largely phase cancelled in the push-pull configuration. In the actual circuit several stages are cascaded to provide the desired amount of limiting within acceptable distortion limits.

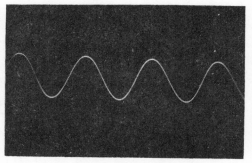

o db. Compression

FIGURE 3. Showing 1 KC oscilloscopic wave-forms taken at the output terminals of each system of compression.

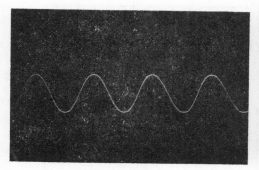

10 db. Fast Limiting

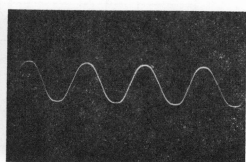

20 db. Fast Limiting

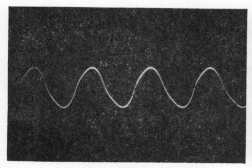

10 db. Clipping-Filtering

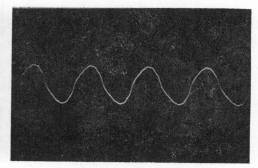

20 db. Clipping-Filtering

two word lists were then recorded using 10 db. and 20 db. of clipping. A fifth recording, List 2E, was made without compression as a condition of control. These two hundred and fifty recorded words were dubbed on to another tape along with white noise at 3 db. below the speech level. This operation was a mixing process involving no compression. The composite tape was then separated into five shorter tapes, each representing different methods and degrees of speech compression in the presence of noise, for random presentation in subsequent tests. Word presentation order within each tape remained the same.

Thirty speech students, twenty women and ten men, were screened for normal hearing and used as subjects in the study. Each subject listened to all the test words in a sound-treated studio over

311

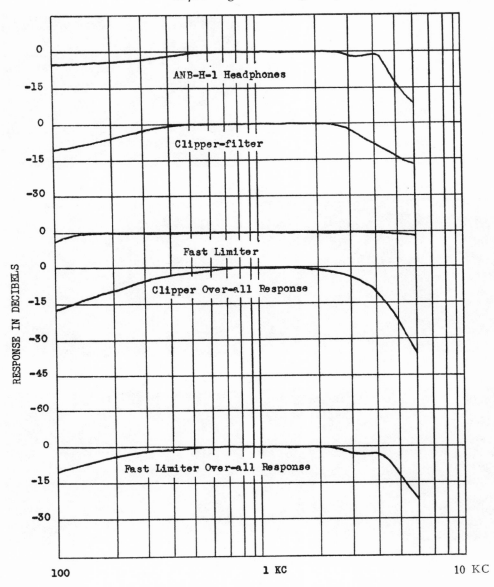

FIGURE 4. Frequency response of both systems of compression.

ANB-H-1 headphones at a level of 70 db. (re .0002 dyne/cm²). The subject tried to identify each word by repeating it over a studio microphone. This procedure was followed for each of the thirty subjects.

ANALYSIS OF DATA

Each error in identification subtracted 2 per cent from the subject's score for that particular condition of compression. The total data appear in Table I. Referring to Table II it will be noted

TABLE I

GROUP INTELLIGIBILITY SCORES ARRANGED AS TO
TYPE AND LEVEL OF COMPRESSION

Subjects	0 db	C-10 db	C-20 db	L-10 db	L-20 db
1	52	64	60	88	76
2	50	72	76	94	84
3	54	74	78	90	90
4	62	70	48	78	72
5	64	80	66	96	84
6	56	58	50	76	70
7	60	70	62	88	86
8	54	64	44	78	72
9	60	56	58	90	82
10	50	62	50	90	68
11	58	70	70	88	86
12	54	58	60	84	86
13	72	68	68	88	82
14	72	70	62	86	86
15	62	56	76	90	84
16	60	64	50	80	80
17	52	58	74	88	78
18	64	68	66	90	74
19	58	46	60	80	84
20	54	50	48	76	70
21	52	66	54	88	80
22	54	64	60	74	72
23	48	58	68	86	76
24	54	62	46	84	76
25	62	72	64	90	78
26	52	64	60	82	66
27	58	66	66	82	78
28	52	50	60	72	76
29	54	74	68	86	80
30	52	50	66	82	68
Mean	56.87	63.47	61.27	84.80	78.13
SD	5.90	8.06	9.10	5.87	6.50
SE	1.10	1.50	1.69	1.10	1.20

TABLE II

COMPARISON OF MEAN INTELLIGIBILITY SCORES

Larger Mean	Smaller Mean	D_m	t
C-10 db (63.47)	0 db (56.87)	6.60	3.54 (1%)
C-20 db (61.27)	0 db (56.87)	4.40	2.18 (5%)
L-10 db (84.80)	0 db (56.87)	27.93	18.01 (1%)
L-20 db (78.13)	0 db (56.87)	21.26	13.12 (1%)
L-10 db (84.80)	C-10 db (63.47)	21.33	11.46 (1%)
L-20 db (78.13)	C-20 db (61.27)	16.86	8.14 (1%)
L-10 db (84.80)	L-20 db (78.13)	6.67	4.11 (1%)
C-10 db (63.47)	C-20 db (61.27)	2.20	.97 (not sig)

that each of the four conditions of compressed speech resulted in significantly higher intelligibility scores than the control condition of no compression. Fast limiting produced significantly higher scores than the corresponding conditions of clipping. All t's were calculated on the basis of unrelated measures, i.e. no r was used to lower the standard error.

All findings involving both compression circuits were well beyond the 1 per cent level of confidence. Moderate compression produced significantly better results in the case of fast limiting than did deep compression. With clipping, on the other hand, the difference was not significant.

Summary and Conclusions

In an effort to test the hypothesis that fast limiting is superior to clipping as a technique for improving the intelligibility of speech in the presence of noise, the two methods of compression were employed in making tape recordings of phonetically balanced words. These recordings were then mixed with white noise and played back to thirty subjects who tried to identify the test words. The study sought to answer the following two questions:

1. What is the relative effectiveness, at moderate compression, of fast limiting and clipping in improving speech intelligibility in the presence of noise?

2. What is the relative effectiveness, at deep compression, of fast limiting and clipping in improving speech intelligibility in the presence of noise?

In answer to the first question, it was found that moderate fast limiting produced significantly higher intelligibility scores than moderate clipping. The difference in mean scores yielded a t of 11.46 (1 per cent). This was taken to mean that, as regards moderate compression, fast limiting is apparently more effective than clipping. In answer to the second question, it was found that fast limiting produced significantly higher intelligibility scores than clipping when both were at deep compression. The difference in mean scores yielded a t of 8.14 (1 per cent). This was taken to mean that, as regards deep compression, fast limiting is apparently more effective than clipping.

Implications for further investigation of the uses of fast limiting as an aid to intelligibility include the consideration of optimum operational parameters. Relationships, for example, between amounts of compression and various signal-to-noise ratios may afford fruitful areas for study.

Part VIII

APPLICATIONS TO RESEARCH ON
SPEECH AND HEARING

Editor's Comments
on Papers 29, 30, and 31

The research described in Parts II, III, and IV was primarily
research on intelligibility, although frequently it was valuable for
other fields as well. The investigations cited in this part have used
intelligibility testing primarily as an investigatory tool. The majority
of the papers concern speech perception. The experimenters are
interested in knowing when and why a stimulus is perceived as
speech and the relationships between the observed acoustical
characteristics and the perception as a particular speech sound or
class of sounds. The acoustical clues are pitch, duration, vocal
effort, level of speaking, formant structure, transitions, and general spectral distribution with time. Other factors observable are the
preceding and following sounds, the context of the whole speech
sample, and the language, age, sex, and other characteristics of
the talker. All of these have been investigated in the literature cited
here. The world's leading institution for research in this field is
Haskins Laboratory in New Haven, Connecticut, where, first under
Franklin S. Cooper and now under Alvin M. Liberman, programs of
very fundamental importance have been pursued by the small
resident staff and large numbers of distinguished visiting scholars.
Papers by researchers working there are cited throughout this
volume and are recommended to the serious reader. They show
rather conclusively that only a few speech sounds are discrete
entities which may be treated like a letter of type, independent of
other sounds. Most speech sounds differ acoustically whenever
they are in different contexts, although listeners identify them as
the same. There is no small or even finite number of these variations.

Two papers by Peterson (1966) are required reading for the student of the dynamics of speech production and of phonetic parameters. The papers of Mushnikov (1972, 1973, 1974) are also excellent. Lane (1965) explains how, according to the motor theory, the acoustic stimulus and the perception of speech are linked by the articulatory movements and their sensory feedback and also presents the shortcomings of the motor theory. Any simple interpretation of this idea is complicated by Kimura's (1968) finding that the right ear advantage is as strong for speech played backwards as for forward speech. (However, Kellogg, in the paper cited in Part I, stated that he was able to learn to understand backwards speech, and years later, when the editor knew him as a distinguished retired engineer, he still could speak backwards after a fashion in short sentences.) Pickett (1957, 1958, 1960 (2)) made important contributions to speech perception understanding; Solomon (1960) used a very different approach to defining the dimensions of perception; Delattre (1968) found the acoustic clues necessary and sufficient to synthesize French consonants and used them to isolate articulatory correlates; Chistovich (1962) explored the dynamics of identification decisions; Fain (1973) explored the differences among Russian consonants; and Wang (1973) used sequential analysis of the confusion matrices to support or deny the existence of natural perceptive features.

Speech intelligibility techniques have been used to investigate fields other than speech perception. Survey papers by Carre (1974) and by Fujimura (1966) describe the whole field of speech research in France and in Japan at the time they were written. Fry (1974, 1975) on ear advantages, Conrad (1962, 1964 (2)) on memory effects, and Cherry (1956) and Lochner (1961) on binaural summation all are recommended. Other applications cited are memory bridges, verbal transformations, and language differences.

All three papers here are classics in the field. Paper 29 by Peterson was the starting point for much later research because it established the principle that vowels can be defined in a three-dimensional space by means of the formant versus time patterns and used matching of speech sounds and words by listeners to show that these definitions are unique. Paper 30 by Miller and Nicely is most often cited as the first analysis of confusion matrices to determine the articulatory features. Readers should note that there is an error in the paper as reproduced. The last sentence on page 339 should read, "Row sums would give the frequencies that each syllable was spoken by the talkers. Column sums would give the frequencies that each syllable was written by the listeners."*

*J. Acoust. Soc. Am. **27**:(617) (1955).

Paper 31 by Rabbitt uses intelligibility testing as a means of investigating the memory capability of the human brain.

BIBLIOGRAPHY

Aaronson, D., N. Markowitz, and H. Shapiro, "Perception and Immediate Recall of Normal and 'Compressed' Auditory Sequences," *Percept. Psychophysiol.* **9**:338–344 (1971).

Ades, A. E., "Bilateral Component in Speech Perception?" *J. Acoust. Soc. Am.* **56**:610–616 (1974).

Agui, T., and T. Hosomura, "The Study on the Reversibility of Phoneme Dyads," *J. Acoust. Soc. Japan* **31**:521–528 (1975). in Japanese, abstract and figures in English.

Allen, G. D., "Acoustic Level and Vocal Effort as Cues for the Loudness of Speech," *J. Acoust. Soc. Am.* **49**:1831–1841 (1971).

Blumstien, S., and W. Cooper, "Identification versus Discrimination of Distinctive Features in Speech Perception," *Q. J. Exp. Psychol.* **24**:207–214 (1972).

Burgtorf, W., and H. K. Oehlschlägel, "Untersuchungen über die Richtungsabhängige Wahrnehmbarkeit verzögerter Schallsignale," *Acustica* **14**:254–266 (1964).

Bushnel, R. G., "L'intelligibilité et certaines données psychophysiologiques sous-estimées," in *Proc. 8th Int. Cong. Acoust.* R. W. B. Stevens, ed. (1975), pp. 123–148.

Byers, V. W., "Initial Consonant Intelligibility by Hearing-Impaired Children," *J. Speech Hear. Res.* **16**:48–55 (1973).

Carey, P. W., "Verbal Retention after Shadowing and after Listening," *Percept. Psychophysiol.* **9**:79–83 (1971).

Carré, R., "A Summary of Speech Research Activities in France," *IEEE Trans. Acoust. Speech Sig. Proc.* **ASSP-22**:268–272 (1974).

Cherry, C., "Two Ears—but One World," in *Sensory Communication*, W. A. Rosenblith, ed., M.I.T. Press, Cambridge, Mass. (1961).

Cherry, C., "On Listening with Both Ears," *Proc. 4th Int. Cong. Acoust.* Copenhagen (1962), **2** pp. 55–67.

Cherry, E. C., and B. M. Sayers, "Human 'Cross-Correlator'—A Technique for Measuring Certain Parameters of Speech Perception," *J. Acoust. Soc. Am.* **28**:889–895 (1956).

Chistovich, L. A., "Classification of Rapidly Repeated Speech Sounds," *Sov. Phys.—Acoust.* **6**:393–398 (1961).

Chistovich, L. A., "Temporal Course of Speech Sound Perception," H18 in *Proc. 4th Int. Cong. Acoust.* Copenhagen (1962).

Chistovich, L. A., and V. A. Kozhevnikov, *Speech*, Pavlov Inst. of Physiology, Leningrad (1965). in Russian.

Chistovich, L. A., V. A. Kozhevnikov, and V. I. Galunov, *Voprosy teorii i metodov issledovaniya vospriyatiya rechevykh signalov*, Leningrad (1969). trans. as *Theory and Methods of Research on Perception of Speech Signals*, Joint Publ. Res. Serv. no 50423, Washington (29 Apr. 1970).

Chomsky, N., and M. Halle, *The Sound Pattern of English*, Harper & Row, New York (1968).

Conrad, R., "An Association between Memory Errors and Errors Due to Acoustic Masking of Speech," *Nature* **193**:1314–1315 (1962).

Conrad, R., "Acoustic Confusions in Immediate Memory," *Brit. J. Psychol.* **55**:75–84 (1964).

Conrad, R., and A. J. Hull, "Information, Acoustic Confusion and Memory Span," *Brit. J. Psychol.* **55**:429–432 (1964).

Coston, G. N., and S. H. Ainsworth, "The Effects of Omissions and Substitutions of Selected Consonants on Intelligibility," *Brit. J. Disord. Commun.* **7**:184–188 (1972).

Dallett, K. M., "Intelligibility and Short-Term Memory in the Repetition of Digit Strings," *J. Speech Hear. Res.* **7**:362–368 (1964).

Danhauer, J. L., and S. Singh, *Multidimensional Speech Perception by the Hearing Impaired: A Treatise on Distinctive Features*, Univ. Park Press, Baltimore (1975).

Daniloff, R. G., T. H. Shriner, and W. R. Zemlin, "Intelligibility of Vowels Altered in Duration and Frequency," *J. Acoust. Soc. Am.* **44**:700–707 (1968).

Delattre, P., "From Acoustic Cues to Distinctive Features," *Phonetica* **18**:198–230 (1968).

Fant, G., *Speech Sounds and Features*, M.I.T. Press, Cambridge, Mass. (1973).

Fant, G., and M. A. A. Tatham, eds., *Auditory Analysis and Perception of Speech*, Academic Press, New York (1975).

Fry, D. B., "Right Ear Advantage for Speech Presented Monaurally," *Lang. and Speech* **17**:142–151 (1974).

Fry, D. B., "Ear Advantage for Speech in Groups of Right- and Left-Handed Subjects," *Lang. and Speech* **18**:264–269 (1975).

Fujimura, O., "Current Research Activities of Speech Groups in Japan," *J. Acoust. Soc. Am.* **39**:428–431 (1966).

Galunov, V. I., and L. A. Chistovich, "Relationship of Motor Theory to the General Problem of Speech Recognition," *Sov. Phys.—Acoust.* **11**:357–365 (1966).

Gershuni, G. V., *Fiziologicheskaia Akustika, Bibliograficheskii Ukazatel' Sovetskoi Literatury 1917–1950*, Academy of Science USSR, Moscow (1960).

Gilbert, J. H., ed., *Speech and Cortical Functioning*, Academic Press, New York (1972).

Gupta, J. P., and R. Ahmed, "Consonantal Context and Vowel Perception in Normal and Clipped Speech," *J. Inst. Telecommun. Eng.* **17**:477–480 (1971).

Hála, B., M. Romportl, and P. Janota, eds., *Proc. 6th Int. Cong. Phonetic Sci*, Prague, 7–13 Sept. 1967, Hueber, Munich (1970).

Hemeyer, T. F., and D. J. Sharf, "Effect of Speech-Sound Cue on Ear Asymmetry in Dichotic Listening," *Lang. and Speech* **17**:312–323 (1974).

Hirsh, I. J., "Acoustical Bases of Speech Perception," *J. Sound Vib.* **27**:111–122 (1973).

Jakobson, R., C. G. M. Fant, and M. Halle, *Preliminaries to Speech Analysis*, M.I.T. Press, Cambridge, Mass. (1963).

Kanamori, Y., and K. Kido, "Context Effect in Perception of Vowels in CVC Syllables," (L) *J. Acoust. Soc. Japan* **31**:269–270 (1975).

Kanamori, Y., and K. Kido, "Effect of Context on Vowel Perception," *J. Acoust. Soc. Japan* **32**:3–11 (1976).

Kimura, D., and S. Folb, "Neural Processing of Backwards Speech Sounds," *Science* **161**:395–396 (1968).

Klatt, D. H., "Linguistic Uses of Segmental Duration in English: Acoustical and Perceptual Evidence," *J. Acoust. Soc. Am.* **59**:1208–1221 (1976).

Lafon, J., "La reconnaissance phonétique et sa mesure," *Ann. Télécommun.* **15**:27–37 (1960).

Lane, H. L., "Motor Theory of Speech Perception: A Critical Review," *Psychol. Rev.* **72**:275–310 (1965).

Lane, H. L., A. C. Catania, and S. S. Stevens, "Voice Level: Autophonic Scale, Perceived Loudness, and Effects of Sidetone," *J. Acoust. Soc. Am.* **33**:160–167 (1961).

Lane, H. L., B. Tranel, and C. Sisson, "Regulation of Voice Communication by Sensory Dynamics," *J. Acoust. Soc. Am.* **47**:618–624 (1970).

Lass, N. J., K. J. Silvis, and S. A. Settle, "The Verbal Transformation Effect: Effect of Context on Subjects' Reported Verbal Transformations," *J. Aud. Res.* **14**:157–161 (1974).

Lass, N. J., M. G. Wellford, and D. L. Hall, "The Verbal Transformation Effect: A Comparative Study of Male and Female Listeners," *J. Aud. Res.* **14**:109–116 (1974).

Lehiste, I., and G. E. Peterson, "The Identification of Filtered Vowels," *Phonetica* **4**:161–177 (1959).

Liberman, A. M., "Some Results of Research on Speech Perception," *J. Acoust. Soc. Am.* **29**:117–123 (1957).

Liberman, A. M., F. S. Cooper, D. P. Shankweiler, and M. Studdert-Kennedy, "Perception of the Speech Code," *Psychol. Rev.* **74**:431–461 (1967).

Liberman, A. M., F. Ingemann, L. Lasker, P. Delattre, and F. S. Cooper, "Minimum Rules for Synthesizing Speech," *J. Acoust. Soc. Am.* **31**:1490–1499 (1953).

Lochner, J. P. A., and J. F. Burger, "The Subjective Masking of Short Time Delayed Echoes by Their Primary Sounds and Their Contribution to the Intelligibility of Speech," *Acustica* **8**:1–10 (1958).

Lochner, J. P. A., and J. F. Burger, "The Binaural Summation of Speech Signals," *Acustica* **11**:313–317 (1961).

Meyer-Eppler, W., "Reversed Speech and Repetition Systems as a Means of Phonetic Research," *J. Acoust. Soc. Am.* **22**:804–806 (1950).

Morgan, B. J. T., S. M. Chambers, and J. Morton, "Acoustic Confusion of Digits in Memory and Recognition," *Percept. Psychophysiol.* **14**:375–383 (1973).

Morrow, C. T., "Reaction of Small Enclosures on the Human Voice. Part II. Analyses of Vowels," *J. Acoust. Soc. Am.* **20**:487–497 (1948).

Mushnikov, V. N., and L. A. Chistovich, "Method for the Experimental Investigation of the Role of Component Loudnesses in the Recognition of a Vowel," *Sov. Phys.—Acoust.* **17**:339–344 (1972).

Mushnikov, V. N., and L. A. Chistovich, "Experimental Testing of the Band Hypothesis of Vowel Perception," *Sov. Phys.—Acoust.* **18**:250–254 (1973).

Mushnikov, V. N., and L. A. Chistovich, "Phoneme Boundary Fluctuations," *Sov. Phys.—Acoust.* **19**:362–366 (1974).

Newman, E. B., "The Pattern of Vowels and Consonants in Various Languages," *Am. J. Psychol.* **64**:369–379 (1951).

Oeken, F.-W., "Kritisches zur Formattheorie der Vokale," *Phonetica* **10**:22–33 (1963).

Ormestad, H., *An Acoustical Investigation of Observing Ability and Speech Articulation and the Intelligibility of Norwegian Speech Sounds*, Akademisk Forlag, Oslo (1955). in Norwegian, summary in English.

Palmer, R. D., "Cerebral Dominance and Auditory Assymetry," *J. Psychol.* **58**:157–167 (1964).

Paul, H., "Ratio of Correct to Incorrect Alternatives: A Test of the Frequency Hypothesis of Verbal Discrimination Learning," *J. Exp. Psychol.* **88**:285–286 (1971).

Peterson, G. E., and H. L. Barney, "Control Methods Used in a Study of Vowels," *J. Acoust. Soc. Am.* **24**:175–184 (1952).

Peterson, G. E., and J. E. Shoup, "The Elements of an Acoustic Phonetic Theory," *J. Speech Hear. Res.* **9**:68–99 (1966).

Peterson, G. E., and J. E. Shoup, "A Physiological Theory of Phonetics," *J. Speech Hear. Res.* **9**:5–67 (1966).

Pickett, J. M., "Perception of Vowels Heard in Noise of Various Spectra," *J. Acoust. Soc. Am.* **29**:613–620 (1957).

Pickett, J. M., "Perception of Compound Consonants," *Lang. and Speech* **1**:288–304 (1958).

Pickett, J. M., and L. R. Decker, "Time Factors in the Perception of a Double Consonant," *Lang. and Speech* **3**:11–17 (1960).

Pickett, J. M., and H. Rubenstein, "Perception of Consonant Voicing in Noise," *Lang and Speech* **3**:155–163 (1960).

Plummer, R. N., "High Frequency Deafness and Discrimination of 'High Frequency' Consonants," *J. Speech Disord.* **8**:373–381 (1943).

Postman, L., and M. R. Rosenzweig, "Perceptual Recognition of Words," *J. Speech Hear. Disord.* **22**:245–253 (1957).

Rabbitt, P., "Recognition: Memory of Words Correctly Heard in Noise," *Psychon. Sci.* **6**:383–384 (1966).

Richardson, E. G., and E. Meyer, eds., *Technical Aspects of Sound*, vol. 3, Elsevier, Amsterdam (1962).

Roeser, R. J., D. F. Johns, and L. L. Price, "Effects of Intensity on Dichotically Presented Digits," *J. Aud. Res.* **12**:184–186 (1972).

Savage, S., and N. J. Kanak, "The Effect of Frequency and Number of Pairs in a Verbal Discrimination Task," *Bull. Psychon. Soc.* **2**:278–280 (1973).

Scharfe, D. J., and H. Ostreicher, "Effect of Forward and Backward Coarticulation on the Identification of Speech Sounds," *Lang. and Speech* **16**:196–206 (1973).

Schindler, O., *Il materiale fonemico*, Omega, Turin (1973).

Schroeder, M. R., "Parameter Estimation in Speech: A Lesson in Unorthodoxy," *Proc. IEEE* **58**:707–712 (1970).

Solomon, L. N., J. C. Webster, and J. F. Curtis, "A Factorial Study of Speech Perception," *J. Speech Hear. Res.* **3**:101–107 (1960).

Stevens, K. N., and A. S. House, "An Acoustical Theory of Vowel Production and Some of Its Implications," *J. Speech Hear. Res.* **4**:303–320 (1961).

Stevens, K. N., and A. S. House, "Perturbation of Vowel Articulations by Consonantal Context: An Acoustical Study," *J. Speech Hear. Res.* **6**:111–128 (1963).

Tannahill, J. C., and L. V. McReynolds, "Consonant Discrimination as a Function of Distinctive Feature Differences," *J. Aud. Res.* **12**:101–108 (1972).

Thomas, I. B., P. B. Hill, F. S. Carroll, and B. Garcia, "Temporal Order in the Perception of Vowels," *J. Acoust. Soc. Am.* **48**:1010–1013 (1970).

Tobias, J. V., ed., *Foundations of Modern Auditory Theory*, 2 vols., Academic Press, New York (1972).

Treisman, A. M., and S. Fearnley, "Can Simultaneous Speech Stimuli Be Classified in Parallel?" *Percept. Psychophysiol.* **10**:1–7 (1971).

Tsunoda, T., "The Difference of the Cerebral Dominance of Vowel Sounds among Different Languages," *J. Aud. Res.* **11**:305–314 (1971).

Tsunoda, T., "Cerebral Dominancy Shift of Non-Verbal Sounds under Influencing of Speech," *J. Acoust. Soc. Japan* **31**:203–212 (1975).

Voegelin, C. F., and Z. S. Harris, "Methods of Determining Intelligibility among Dialects of Natural Languages," *Proc. Am. Phil. Soc.* **95**:322–329 (1951).

Wang, M. D., and R. C. Bilger, "Consonant Confusions In Noise: A Study of Perceptual Features," *J. Acoust. Soc. Am.* **54**:1248–1266 (1973).

29

Reprinted from *Acoust. Soc. Am. J.* **24**(6):629–637 (1952)

The Information-Bearing Elements of Speech

GORDON E. PETERSON

Bell Telephone Laboratories, Inc., Murray Hill, New Jersey

(Received August 11, 1952)

This study deals with those aspects of speech which are phonetically significant. A technique has been developed with which phonetically equivalent speech samples may be obtained in different phonetic contexts and from different speakers. Data on two front vowels by different types of speakers are presented. The technique has also been applied to the evaluation of words containing these two vowels.

INTRODUCTION

ONE of the fundamental linguistic processes is the transformation of speech to writing. It is generally recognized, of course, that certain information present in speech is lost in the written form. The fact that we are reasonably well satisfied with the orthographic representation of speech for a great many communications, however, is adequate evidence that much of the meaning present in speech is also to be found in its written counterpart.

Through the process of reading aloud, written material can be reconverted to speech, also. When the printed page is read aloud, however, the voice characteristics of the individual who initiated the communication normally are lost.

At the present time, these two linguistic processes, the transformation of speech to writing and the transformation of writing to speech, are possible only through human performance. There is considerable reason to believe, however, that they could be carried out by automatic systems. There are, of course, many applications which could be made of devices which could carry out these operations automatically.

Crude observations indicate that the orthographic representations of speech correspond most closely to certain positions and movements of the articulatory organs. These, of course, are reflected in certain spectrum-time patterns in the acoustical speech signal.[1] The phonetician has studied the relationship between speech formations and common orthography, and by the use of a modified writing he is able to set down a sequence of symbols which correspond to articulations more consistently than do the letters of ordinary orthography. In such phoentic writing somewhere between 50 and 100 characters are usually adequate for the representation of any one dialect.

It is of considerable practical interest that a very great saving in channel capacity could be realized if it were possible to transmit only the phonetic content of speech, rather than the full speech band. It is recognized, of course, that there are other aspects of speech which bear information and which are of considerable importance.[2] Examples are the fundamental pitch of the voice and the voice quality, such as breathy or harsh. These characteristics for the most part convey information about the speaker: who he is, the condition of his health, and his reactions to what he is saying.

The fact that a rather limited number of phonetic discriminations are required in interpreting speech, along with many other facts about speech, would suggest that a fairly limited number of parameters may actually be involved in the definition of the phonetic content of speech. The derivation of these parameters is probably the most fundamental step in the entire process of reducing speech to its phonetic content.[3]

It is the chief purpose of this paper to discuss those parameters which determine the phonetic value of vowel sounds as they occur in speech. One of the most direct approaches to the solution of this problem would be to obtain a large sample of phonetically equivalent vowel sounds produced by different speakers. Toward this objective, a method will be described which has been developed for the study of the various psychophysical characteristics of speech signals.

EXPERIMENTAL METHOD

In the data reported by Peterson and Barney, the language backgrounds of a group of listeners were used to obtain a distribution of phonetic judgments on vowel sounds.[4] Only certain pronunciations of the vowel within a word fell near the peak of the distribution and were judged alike by a large number of subjects. As shown by the data reported for the listening tests, however, the distributions of judgments were not equally sharp for all vowels. Also, in the study it was found that the problem of evaluating the energy spectrum of the vowel was confused by the change in spectrum as time progressed within the word.

The experimental method employed in the present study was developed for the purpose of studying simple speech patterns not easily referred to phonetically untrained subjects and to increase the flexibility of experimental design. Reference speech samples are played on a magnetic tape repeater to the experimenter and the subject in a sound treated room. The subject then attempts to imitate or match the reference in phonetic value. When the experimenter with the aid of

[1] G. A. Kopp and H. C. Green, J. Acoust. Soc. Am. 17, 74 (1946).
[2] G. E. Peterson, Language 27, 541 (1951).
[3] G. E. Peterson, J. Speech and Hearing Disorders 17, 175 (1952).
[4] G. E. Peterson and H. L. Barney, J. Acoust. Soc. Am. 24, 175 (1952).

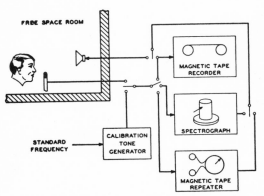

FIG. 1. Arrangement of equipment employed in the vowel matching experiments.

the subject judges that a successful match has been obtained, the sample is retained for analysis.

The schematic diagram shows the arrangement of equipment for the experiments to be reported here. The speech sounds were recorded through a condenser microphone from the free space room at the Murray Hill Laboratories. The reference sounds were first recorded onto the magnetic tape recorder. Suitable pronunciations were selected for use on the magnetic tape repeater.

The reference sounds were played to each subject through the loudspeaker in the free space room. Matches were recorded directly on the sound spectrograph[5]

which served as the second repeating mechanism, so that the two speech samples could be carefully compared aurally. When a match was judged adequate, a spectrographic analysis was made, and the match was then transferred to the magnetic tape recorder for permanent record, where it is available should other types of analysis be desired.

In present communication technology, the weak link in a system of this sort, of course, is the loudspeaker. Inadequacies at this step can be considerably reduced, however, by having the person who produced the reference samples serve as the experimenter. In one sense the loudspeaker then provides only a constant reference for the experimenter who can reproduce in live voice when desired the sample under study. Likewise, he hears the live voice pronunciations of the subject. In the present study, the various acoustic paths were never found in conflict, but served to supplement each other.

Calibrations of the equipment are shown in Fig. 2. The pulse tone calibration technique, as previously reported, was employed.[4] Figure 2(a) is for the spectrograph alone. Figure 2(b) represents a 100-cps calibration tone placed on the magnetic tape recorder, then reproduced over the magnetic tape repeater through the loudspeaker to the condenser microphone, and analyzed on the sound spectrograph. Figure 2(c) shows a narrow band spectrogram of a 500-cps calibrating tone; 2(d) gives the time scale, as obtained with a broad band analysis of a 100-cps pulse; and 2(e) shows a calibration of the amplitude scale.

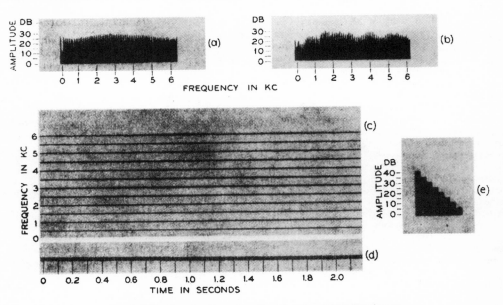

FIG. 2. Calibration of equipment employed in the matching experiments.

[5] Koenig, Dunn, and Lacy, J. Acoust. Soc. Am. 17, 19 (1946).

The main source of error in our control of frequency was found to lie in the sound spectrograph which we employed. Narrow band (50 cps) amplitude sections were used throughout the study.[6] This procedure is desirable, of course, in order to obtain the fundamental voice frequency. In order to locate zero frequency readily, a cam was placed in the spectrograph each time at a point where no signal was recorded. In order to check the frequency scale changes, calibrations were made periodically during the tests; these calibrations were usually made before and after each run with a particular subject. The spectrographic analyses were then corrected according to these calibration patterns.

Figure 3 shows the results of such calibrations during the period when the data were taken on the two sustained vowels reported in this paper. The values for Δf represent changes in 3000 cps.

In order to study the matching method, tests with the vowels [ɪ] and [æ] were carried out, and these data are reported here. The reference vowels were approximately one second in length and were derived from sustained vowels of a greater length. A gate circuit was employed to provide an artificial build-up and decay for the vowels of about 0.025 second. The spectral nature of the sustained vowels is shown in the series of amplitude sections in Fig. 4. In such vowel spectra the regions of energy concentration are known as formants. The sound shown here was produced by the speaker who pronounced the reference vowels. The sections are at 0.020-second intervals.

VOWEL MATCHES

A group of matched vowels was obtained for men, women and children. Previous work has shown the basic significance of the positions of the formants in frequency,[2,7,8] and Fig. 5 shows the frequency of the second formant *versus* the frequency of the first formant for the two vowels studied. Two amplitude sections, located at different points in time, were made for many of these vowels, and in these cases points for both measurements are plotted.

There are various methods which may be employed in the measurement of formant positions. One of the objectives of these studies with the matching technique is to derive a basic method of formant evaluation. This general problem will be treated in a subsequent paper reporting the analyses of several sets of matched vowels which have been obtained.

In the formant measurements represented in Fig. 5, a smooth envelope curve is drawn through the harmonics, and the frequencies of the peaks of the envelope curve are then derived. Actually the curve is sketched in by eye, and an attempt is made to maintain the largest

[6] L. G. Kersta, J. Acoust. Soc. Am. **20**, 796 (1948).
[7] P. Delattre, French Rev. **21**, 477 (1948).
[8] R. K. Potter and G. E. Peterson, J. Acoust. Soc. Am. **20**, 528 (1948).

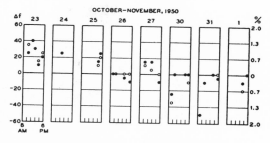

FIG. 3. Measured frequency variations in the analyzing equipment.

curvature possible without allowing the curve to become double valued.

Another method of formant measurement is shown in Fig. 6. In this figure the frequency of the highest harmonic within the second formant is plotted against the frequency of the highest harmonic within the first formant. The straight lines in both Fig. 5 and Fig. 6 pass thorugh the origin, so that they represent lines of constant formant ratio.

In these figures, as has been shown previously, the points for the men generally have the lower frequency values, those for the women are higher in frequency, and those for children are still higher.[8] The points shown with x in Fig. 5 are for the speaker whose data appear in the upper graphs of Figs. 11–18, showing plots of words.

The effect of formant amplitude is also treated in Fig.

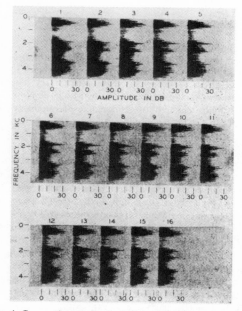

FIG. 4. Consecutive amplitude sections at 0.020-second intervals on a sustained vowel.

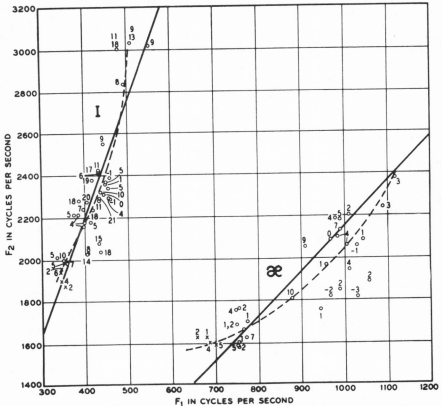

FIG. 5. The frequency of the second formant *versus* the frequency of the first formant for the two sets of matched vowels.

5. The numbers associated with the individual points show the amplitude of the first formant minus the amplitude of the second formant in decibels. It has been suggested that amplitude could enter into the evaluation of the frequency of a formant in the sense that there could be an interchange of frequency and amplitude. This possibility is suggested by the fact that data on the hearing of tones show a symmetrical distribution of stimulation, with greater activity above the position of the stimulus tone than below. Thus, points which lie below and to the right of the distributions might have small A_1-A_2, indicating a low A_1 to correct for a high F_1 or a high A_2 to correct for a low F_2. An examination of the amplitude values on Fig. 5, however, will show that there is no simple systematic effect of amplitude in the case of these two formants.

In Fig. 7 the values for the fundamental frequency of the vowel, F_0, have been associated with each point. The fundamental frequency is shown by the length of the line as a third dimension. The level of the F_2 *vs* F_1 plane is at 100 cps. A study of these data has also shown that there is no simple systematic manner in which F_0

could affect or correct F_1 *vs* F_2 to reduce the scatter in the plots.

It has been shown previously that two dimensions are inadequate for the determination of vowel value,

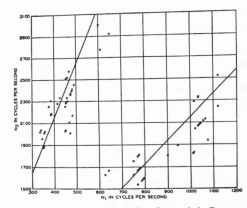

FIG. 6. The frequency of the highest harmonic in F_2 *versus* the frequency of the highest harmonic in F_1 for the data shown in Fig. 5.

particularly when a wide range of speakers is considered.[2] For example, the distribution for [y] will overlap the distribution for [i], and that for [œ] will overlap that for [ɛ]. This results from the increase in formant frequency which is observed for speakers with smaller cavities. This difficulty can only be resolved by at least one additional dimension, and for any given vowel the values of this dimension should vary according to the position of the vowel within the F_2 vs F_1 plane.

In Fig. 5 arbitrary curves were drawn through the distributions of points. The distance along the curve for each point was then determined by drawing a perpendicular from the point to the respective curve. The distances along the curve at which the perpendiculars intercepted the curve are represented by the abscissa s in Fig. 8 and Fig. 9.

In Fig. 8 the fundamental frequency of the vowel, F_0, is shown plotted against s. In Fig. 9 the frequency of the third formant, F_3, is shown plotted against s. The numbers associated with each point are for the amplitude of the first formant minus the amplitude of the third formant in decibels. The first formant serves as a good reference since it almost always had the highest amplitude value for these vowels. As in the case of $A_1 - A_2$, it is seen in Fig. 9 that $A_1 - A_3$ appears to have little significance in the identification of a particular vowel.

The values for F_3 are sufficiently well correlated with s to serve as a discriminating parameter while F_0 appears to have little significance as such a parameter. It should be noted, of course, that these results represent the front vowels only. It is probable that a different situation regarding F_3 and F_0 obtains for the back vowels.

The general conclusion is that front vowels could be rather readily identified by observing the positions in frequency of the peaks of the first three formants.

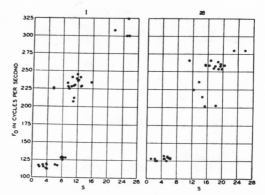

FIG. 8. The relation of fundamental frequency to position along a curve representing the distribution in F_2 versus F_1.

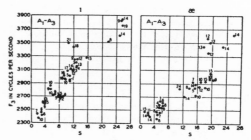

FIG. 9. The relation of the frequency of the third formant to position along a curve representing the distribution in F_2 versus F_1.

These values must then be referred to a measured distribution. It would seem, however, that fundamental phonetic parameters should have the same value when the vowel value is the same, regardless of the type of speaker. No simple principle, however, has as yet been found for obtaining the same parameter values when the same vowel value is pronounced by different types of speakers.

A group of amplitude sections from various matches to the vowel [ɪ] are shown in Fig. 10. These vowels are included in the plots of Figs. 5–9; the formant peak positions follow the pattern shown in Fig. 5. The marked variation in aspects other than the formant peak positions, such as the depth of the regions between the formants, indicates that such other factors probably are not fundamental in determining vowel value. The first spike at the beginning of each spectrum pattern is zero frequency marked by the spectrograph carrier oscillator. The frequency scale is only approximate, of course, since each amplitude section must be corrected to its own calibration pattern.

WORDS

Of very great interest is the identification of vowels as they occur within words. A basic problem here is

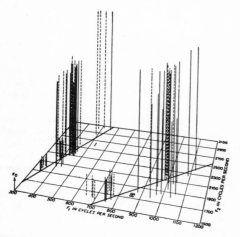

FIG. 7. Graph of F_2 versus F_1 with fundamental frequency shown as the third dimension.

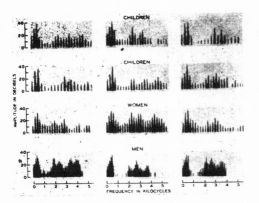

Fig. 10. Amplitude sections from matches to the vowel [ɪ].

that of the quantization of speech as occurs routinely in the phonetic transcription of speech. Such identification of the vowels and consonants is a fundamental step in analysis in the transmission of the phonetic content of speech and in the design of voice operated devices.

In order to study vowels as they occur in words, two subjects recorded groups of words containing the vowels [ɪ] and [æ]. The matching method was then employed in the study of these words. Each word was reproduced on the magnetic tape repeater, and the subject who originally pronounced the word was asked to match a vowel to it. This matching procedure proved to be entirely practical from the point of view of subject performance and was carried out with approximately the same facility as that for sustained vowel matches.

The data for [ɪ] are shown in Figs. 11–14, and the data for [æ] are shown in Figs. 15–18. The points in

these plots were all obtained from narrow band amplitude sections.[6] These sections represent an integrating time of approximately 0.020 second. It should perhaps be mentioned that the minimum integrating time on the amplitude sectioner of the sound spectrograph is controlled not only by the filter build-up time, but also by the operate time across the cam which controls the condenser charge circuit.

At the left in the figures for the words are shown formant positions *versus* time. The sampling interval was 0.040 second, which is considerably longer than would be desired. Extreme positions reached by the formants at initial and terminal consonant junctures usually would be missed at times with this sampling interval. The importance of the influence has been described in the identification of consonants,[1] and the extreme formant positions are of interest in consonant identification. In the present study of vowel identification these extreme positions are believed irrelevant.

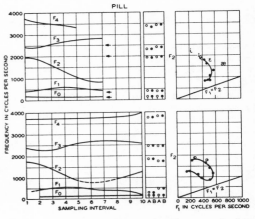

Fig. 12. Formant patterns, the F_2 *versus* F_1 trace, and points for the vowel matches for the word "pill."

The two upper graphs in each figure are for one subject, and the two lower graphs are for the other. The arrows on the graph in the upper left are representative formant values selected from a number of independent speakings of the vowel. The phonetic symbols in the graph in the upper right of the figures give such representative values for F_2 *versus* F_1 for the four front unrounded vowels by this speaker. Similar data are not available for the other subject. The points in the F_1 *vs* F_2 traces are those at the sampling intervals shown on the left, and the arrow shows the direction of the trace in time.

The vowel matches to these words are shown in the center of the figures and by the circles on the righthand plots. Two matches were made to each word, and two amplitude sections were made of each match.

It will be noted that the matches fall very near the

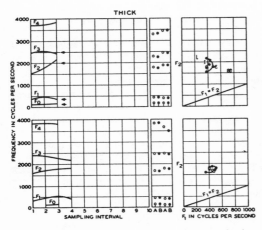

Fig. 11. Formant patterns, the F_2 *versus* F_1 trace, and points for the vowel matches for the word "thick."

traces; the deviations appear to be within the range of variation inherent in the method, and the measurement procedures as indicated by the vowel matches shown in Fig. 5. As indicated previously, the points shown with x on Fig. 5 are for the subject whose data are shown in the upper graphs of Figs. 11–18.

The matches to the words as shown at the right are rather consistently placed where the points are spaced close together. Unfortunately, the sampling interval was so great that this observation cannot be checked accurately in some cases. In the cases where there was sufficient sampling, however, it is clear that the evaluation of the moving formant patterns is made where the formants are changing most slowly in frequency as a function of time.

It has been shown previously that at least three formants are required for front vowel identification. Three-dimensional plots of some of these words and

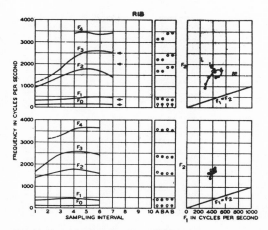

FIG. 14. Formant patterns, the F_2 *versus* F_1 trace, and points for the vowel matches for the word "rib."

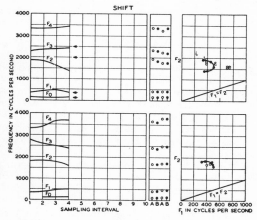

FIG. 13. Formant patterns, the F_2 *versus* F_1 trace, and points for the vowel matches for the word "shift."

their matches have shown that the principles evident in the two-dimensional graphs also apply in the three-dimensional case.

The words shown here were selected because they involved various types of fairly marked influence patterns. It is possible that the influences associated with a particular vowel within a syllable have some effect upon the vowel evaluation. It is hoped that a more extensive set of data on the evaluation of vowels within words can be obtained in order to examine this possibility.

PHONETIC THEORY

These experiments are in accord with the concept of the phone as a class of speech elements which, under given psychophysical conditions, have the same phonetic value.[3] The phonetic value of a speech sound, of course, is independent of language and meaning.

In selecting sounds which are phonetically equivalent, human judgment is required. The basis for this judgment is a major research interest in experimental phonetics. It has been known for a long time that phonetic equivalence is in part related to articulatory formation. The present data show that in the case of the front vowels the judgment of phonetic equivalence is closely related to the frequency positions of the formants, which, of course, are controlled by physiological positions in the vocal mechanism.

It is possible that the precision of vowel identification represented by the formant measurements presented here has actually approached the degree of accuracy with which one can discriminate vowel sounds produced by the human vocal mechanism. A fundamental study of this problem is much needed.

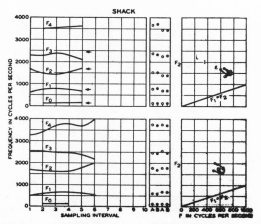

FIG. 15. Formant patterns, the F_2 *versus* F_1 trace, and points for the vowel matches for the word "shack."

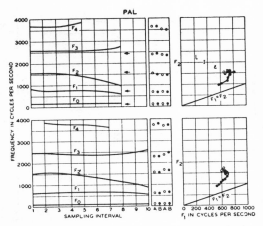

FIG. 16. Formant patterns, the F_2 versus F_1 trace, and points for the vowel matches for the word "pal."

Since speech is produced under the control of audition, we would not expect to find a greater accuracy in the phonetically significant characteristics of the acoustical wave than could be perceived by the ear. Thus a certain variability is to be expected in acoustical wave forms which are judged phonetically equivalent even under highly controlled experimental procedures. It is entirely possible, however, that the accuracy with which a given characteristic of the acoustical wave can be measured may be much greater than the accuracy with which the wave can be evaluated phonetically.

Since the definition of the phone involves discrimination by an auditor, an operational definition of the phone requires that we specify some specific or some typical listener. Consider a large group of speech samples and a single reference speech sample. We may now instruct our specified auditor to compare in phonetic

value each sample within the group with the reference. He will find that some few samples completely match the reference phonetically. Other samples may match only one time portion of the reference. The smallest time portions of the speech samples which phonetically match a portion of the reference are members of the same phone. The determination of a phonetic match, of course, requires a series of judgments comparing the speech samples with the reference, with some specified degree of consistency.

The assignment of groups of phones to a more general class is largely arbitrary. The division may be made in terms of a particular dialect within a language. In this case the phones are grouped into phonemes. For the purpose of phonetic transcription, as in the case of phonetic transmission or phonetic typewriting, the boundaries would probably best be established by a group of phoneticians. Such a group should be sufficiently familiar with the constraints within the vocal mechanism and with the phonemic divisions within the various languages that a practical division could be made.

CONCLUSIONS

The data which have been presented here indicate the general analytical procedures which should be followed in the identification of front vowels within a consonant-vowel-consonant syllable. First we must set up a three-dimensional coordinate system for the first three formants. Volumes within this space must then be defined, with boundaries chosen arbitrarily to suit whatever system of phone allocation may be found most practical.

In order to identify the vowel within a given word, a formant trace of the word must next be constructed within the three-dimensional coordinate system. A suitable sampling time interval would be about 0.010 second. The position along the trace at which the time

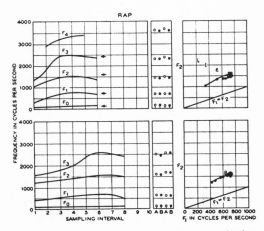

FIG. 17. Formant patterns, the F_2 versus F_1 trace, and points for the vowel matches for the word "rap."

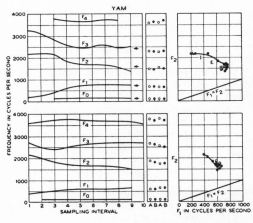

FIG. 18. Formant patterns, the F_2 versus F_1 trace, and points for the vowel matches for the word "yam."

samples are spaced most closely should next be observed. Finally, the vowel is identified by noting the particular vowel volume in which this portion of the trace lies.

The observations in this study are in terms of acoustical data. To those familiar with the intricacies of articulatory formations, however, the conclusions are probably what one would expect. In fact, a close scruting of the spectrograms in the book *Visible Speech* seems sufficient to show that these are the principles at work.[9]

[9] Potter, Kopp, and Green, *Visible Speech* (D. Van Nostrand Company, Inc., New York, 1947).

Several members of the Bell Laboratories have been of great assistance to the author in carrying out this study. I am indebted to E. E. David, H. K. Dunn, R. K. Kraichnan, and J. C. Steinberg for valuable suggestions about the method and for discussions of the general problem. I should particularly like to thank Mr. A. J. Prestigiacomo, who constructed the magnetic tape repeater and who set up and calibrated the remaining equipment employed in the study. While the author served as experimenter in the free space room, Mr. Prestigiacomo operated the recording and sound analyzing equipment throughout the experiment.

THE JOURNAL OF THE ACOUSTICAL SOCIETY OF AMERICA   VOLUME 27, NUMBER 2   MARCH, 1955

An Analysis of Perceptual Confusions Among Some English Consonants

GEORGE A. MILLER AND PATRICIA E. NICELY

Lincoln Laboratory, Massachusetts Institute of Technology, Cambridge, Massachusetts

(Received December 1, 1954)

Sixteen English consonants were spoken over voice communication systems with frequency distortion and with random masking noise. The listeners were forced to guess at every sound and a count was made of all the different errors that resulted when one sound was confused with another. With noise or low-pass filtering the confusions fall into consistent patterns, but with high-pass filtering the errors are scattered quite randomly. An articulatory analysis of these 16 consonants provides a system of five articulatory features or "dimensions" that serve to characterize and distinguish the different phonemes: voicing, nasality, affrication, duration, and place of articulation. The data indicate that voicing and nasality are little affected and that place is severely affected by low-pass and noisy systems. The indications are that the perception of any one of these five features is relatively independent of the perception of the others, so that it is as if five separate, simple channels were involved rather than a single complex channel.

THE over-all effects of noise and of frequency distortion upon the average intelligibility of human speech are by now rather well understood. One limitation of the existing studies, however, is that results are given almost exclusively in terms of the articulation score, the percentage of the spoken words that the listener hears correctly. By implication, therefore, all of the listener's errors are treated as equivalent and no knowledge of the perceptual confusions is available. The fact is, however, that mistakes are often far from random. A closer look at the problem suggests that we might learn something about speech perception and might even improve communication if we knew what kinds of errors occur and how to avoid the most frequent ones. Such was the reasoning that led to the present study.

Perhaps the major reason that confusion data are not already available is the cost of collecting them. Every phoneme must have a chance to be confused with every other phoneme and that large number of potential confusions must be tested repeatedly until statistically reliable estimates of all the probabilities are obtained. Such data are obtained from testing programs far more extensive than would be required to evaluate some specific system.

In order to reduce the magnitude of the problem to more manageable size, we decided to study a smaller set of phonemes and to explore the potential value of such data within that smaller universe. Since the consonants are notoriously confusable and are quite important for intelligibility, we decided to begin with a comparison of 16 consonants: $|p|$, $|t|$, $|k|$, $|f|$, $|\theta|$, $|s|$, $|\int|$, $|b|$, $|d|$, $|g|$, $|v|$, $|\eth|$, $|z|$, $|\mathbf{3}|$, $|m|$, and $|n|$. These 16 make up almost three quarters of the consonants we utter in normal speech and about 40 percent of all phonemes, vowels included. It was our suspicion that when errors begin to occur in articulation tests, the culprits would usually be found among this set of 16 phonemes. A further reason for being interested in consonants is that the information-bearing aspects of these sounds are less well understood than is the case for vowels; we hoped to pick up some clues as to what the important features of these phonemes might be.

The major portion of the work to be reported here was done with the aforementioned 16 consonants. However, a number of other, even smaller, experiments were conducted with subsets of those 16. In general, the results of the smaller studies agree with and support the conclusions of the larger study. These results will be introduced into the discussion where appropriate, but the major emphasis will be placed on the 16-consonant data.

EXPERIMENTAL PROCEDURES

Five female subjects served as talkers and listening crew; when one talked, the other four listened. Since the tests lasted several months, some of the original crew members departed and were replaced; care was taken to train new members adequately before their data were used. The subjects were, with one Canadian exception, citizens of the United States. None had defects of speech or hearing and all were able to pronounce the 16 nonsense syllables without any noticeable dialect. Since rhythm, intonation, and vowel differences were not involved, we have assumed that regional differences in speech habits were not a significant source of variability in the data.

The 16 consonants were spoken initially before the vowel |a| (father). The list of 200 nonsense syllables spoken by the talker was prepared in advance so that the probability of each syllable was 1 in 16 and so that their order was quite random within the list and from one list to the next. The syllables were spoken at an average rate of one every 2.1 seconds and the listeners were forced to respond—to guess, if necessary—for every syllable. When the speech was near the threshold of hearing, the listeners were kept in synchrony with the talker by a tone that was turned on at fixed intervals. Otherwise, a 2.1-second pause was inserted after every block of five syllables. With four listeners, there were 800 syllable-response events per talker for which confusions could be studied. Pooling the five talkers gives us 4000 observations at each condition tested.

At the completion of each test of 200 syllables, the talker went from the control room back to the test room and the crew proceeded to tabulate their responses. Each listener had a table showing what syllable was spoken and what syllable she had written in response; each cell of the table represented one of the $16 \times 16 = 256$ possible syllable-response pairs, and the number entered in that cell was the frequency with which that syllable-response pair occurred. We shall refer to such tables as "confusion matrices."

A headrest on the talker's chair insured that the distance to the WE-633A microphone was constant at 15 inches. The speech 15 inches from the talker's lips was about 60 db re 0.0002 dyne/cm². The speech voltage was amplified, then filtered (if frequency distortion was to be used), then mixed with noise, then amplified again and presented to the listeners by PDR-8 earphones. In all tests the noise voltage was fixed at -32 db below one volt across the earphones and the signal-to-noise ratio was varied by changing the gain in the speech channel. A separate amplifier was used to drive a monitoring VU-meter with the output of the microphone. The gain to the VU-meter was fixed so that the talker could maintain her speech level at a constant value. The talkers did succeed rather we a constant level; several hundred sample peak deflections gave an average of $+0.18$ standard deviation of 1.04. However, it shou that with this system, the signal-to-noise ratios are set by the peak deflection of the VU needle and that peak occurs during the vowel. The consonants, which are consistently weaker than the vowel, were actually presented at much less favorable signal-to-noise ratios than such a vowel-to-noise ratio would seem to indicate. It was, therefore, especially important to keep the same speech level for all tests since otherwise the vowel-to-consonant ratio might have changed significantly and the data would not be comparable.

The frequency response of the system was essentially that of the earphones, which are reasonably uniform between 200 and 6500 cps. A low-pass filter at 7000 cps in the random noise generator insured that noise voltages could be converted directly to sound pressure levels according to the earphone calibration. A Krohn-Hite 310-A variable band-pass filter was used to introduce frequency distortion into the speech channel; the skirts dropped off at a rate of 24 db per octave and the cutoff frequency was taken as the frequency 3 db below the peak in the pass band.

RESULTS

The results of these tests are confusion matrices. Since these matrices represent a considerable investment and since other workers may wish to apply summary statistics differing from those which we have chosen, the complete confusion matrices are presented in Tables I–XVII. Data for all listeners and all talkers have been pooled so that 4000 observations are summarized in each matrix; on the average, each syllable was judged 250 times under every test condition.

Tables I–VI summarize the data obtained when the speech-to-noise ratio was -18, -12, -6, 0, $+6$, and $+12$ db and the band width was 200–6500 cps. Tables VII–XII summarize the data when the high-pass cutoff was fixed at 200 cps and the low-pass cutoff was 300, 400, 600, 1200, 2500, and 5000 cps with a speech-to-noise ratio corresponding to $+12$ db for unfiltered speech. Tables XII–XVII summarize the data when the low-pass cutoff was fixed at 5000 cps and the high-pass cutoff was 200, 1000, 2000, 2500, 3000, and 4500 cps with a speech-to-noise ratio that would have been $+12$ db if the speech had not been filtered.

In these tables the syllables that were spoken are indicated by the consonants listed vertically in the first column on the left. The syllables that were written by the listener are indicated horizontally across the top of the table. The number in each cell is the frequency that each stimulus-response pair was observed. The number of correct responses can be obtained by totalling the frequencies along the main diagonal. Row sums would give the frequencies that each syllable was written by the listeners.

A GENERALIZATION OF THE ARTICULATION SCORE

The standard articulation score is obtained from Tables I–XVII by summing the frequencies along the main diagonal and dividing the total by n, the number of observations. Although this score is useful, it tells us nothing about the distribution of errors among the off-diagonal cells. If we wanted to reconstruct an adequate picture of the confusion matrix, we would need other scores to supplement the usual articulation score.

In order to generalize the articulation score, we can combine stimuli (and their corresponding responses) into groups in such a way that confusions within groups are more likely than confusions between groups. Combining stimuli creates a smaller confusion matrix that shows the confusions between groups, and the sum along the diagonal gives a new articulation score for this new, smaller matrix. The new score will be greater than the original score, since all the responses that were originally correct remain so and in addition all the confusions within each group are now considered to be "correct" in the new score. If the original score, A, is supplemented with such an additional score, A', we would reconstruct the data matrix by spreading the fraction A along the main diagonal. Then $A'-A$ would go off the diagonal but within groups, and $1-A'$ would be distributed off the diagonal between groups. This general strategy can be repeated quite simply if the several groupings used form a monotonic increasing sequence of sets: $A \leq A' \leq A''$, etc.

A simple example will illustrate this technique. A test was conducted at $S/N = -12$ db over a 200–6500-cps channel using six stop consonants in front of the vowel $|a|$. The confusion matrix for 2000 observations

TABLE I. Confusion matrix for $S/N = -18$ db and frequency response of 200–6500 cps.

	p	t	k	f	θ	s	ʃ	b	d	g	v	ð	z	ʒ	m	n
p	14	27	22	23	25	22	14	15	16	7	17	11	12	11	16	12
t	16	26	21	15	15	18	14	7	10	6	17	9	13	11	9	13
k	20	22	24	15	14	29	12	4	11	9	12	10	16	11	17	14
f	27	22	27	23	13	12	10	19	20	14	16	16	15	3	13	18
θ	17	18	18	13	15	21	12	14	20	14	23	6	14	9	12	14
s	18	17	23	11	18	21	17	11	24	15	15	16	11	13	17	5
ʃ	16	20	27	17	13	37	14	10	21	7	20	18	9	8	16	15
b	12	11	24	15	19	15	12	24	20	19	24	12	15	11	18	17
d	16	24	18	13	15	15	14	22	25	21	25	17	18	13	15	25
g	11	20	29	9	18	18	15	26	30	14	18	14	16	20	24	22
v	9	17	18	11	7	12	9	25	14	13	15	15	19	11	12	17
ð	16	11	10	7	6	14	10	20	17	18	15	7	17	12	18	18
z	18	18	15	9	13	19	7	22	14	9	21	12	23	10	22	12
ʒ	8	16	17	14	12	15	7	22	18	8	15	11	15	11	18	13
m	19	24	15	14	14	14	8	14	15	12	13	8	11	6	25	28
n	11	18	20	6	9	18	9	14	14	13	9	8	10	12	33	32

TABLE II. Confusion matrix for $S/N = -12$ db and frequency response 200–6500 cps.

	p	t	k	f	θ	s	ʃ	b	d	g	v	ð	z	ʒ	m	n
p	51	53	65	22	19	6	11	2		2	3	3	1	5	8	5
t	64	57	74	20	24	22	14	2	3	1	1	2	1	1	5	1
k	50	42	62	22	18	16	11	4	1	1	1	2			4	2
f	31	22	28	85	34	15	11	3	5		8	8	3		3	
θ	26	22	25	63	45	27	12	6	9	3	11	9	3	2	7	2
s	16	15	16	33	24	53	48	3	5	6	3	1	6	2		1
ʃ	23	32	20	14	27	25	115	1	4	5	3		6	3	4	2
b	4	2	2	18	7	7	1	60	18	18	44	25	14	6	20	10
d	3		1	4	7	4	11	18	48	35	16	24	26	14	9	12
g	3	1	1	1	4	5	7	20	38	29	16	29	29	38	10	9
v		1	1	12	5	4	5	37	20	23	71	16	14	4	14	9
ð		1	4	17	2	3	2	53	31	25	50	33	23	5	13	6
z	6	1	2	2	6	14	8	23	29	27	24	19	40	26	3	6
ʒ	3	2	2	1		6	7	7	30	23	9	7	39	77	5	14
m		1			1	1		11	3	6	8	11		1	109	60
n	1			1		1		2	2	6	7	1	1	9	84	145

334

TABLE III. Confusion matrix for $S/N = -6$ db and frequency response of 200–6500 cps.

	p	t	k	f	θ	s	ʃ	b	d	g	v	ð	z	ʒ	m	n
p	80	43	64	17	14	6	2	1	1		1	1			2	
t	71	84	55	5	9	3	8	1			1		2		2	3
k	66	76	107	12	8	9	4					1	1		2	
f	18	12	9	175	48	11	1	7	2	1	2	2				
θ	19	17	16	104	64	32	7	5	4	5	6	4	5			
s	8	5	4	23	39	107	45	4	2	3	1	1	3	2		
ʃ	1	6	3	4	6	29	195			3					2	1
b	1			5	4	4		136	10	9	47	16	6	1	5	4
d							8	5	80	45	11	20	20	26	1	
g					2			3	63	66	3	19	37	56		3
v				2		2		48	5	5	145	45	12		4	
ð					6			31	6	17	86	58	21	5	6	
z					1		1	7	20	27	16	28	94	44		4
ʒ					1			1	26	18	3	8	45	129		1
m	1							4			4	1	3		177	46
n				4				1		5	2		7	1	6	47	163

TABLE IV. Confusion matrix for $S/N = 0$ db and frequency response of 200–6500 cps.

	p	t	k	f	θ	s	ʃ	b	d	g	v	ð	z	ʒ	m	n
p	150	38	88	7	13											
t	30	193	28	1												
k	86	45	138	4	1		1									1
f	4	3	5	199	46	4		1				1			1	
θ	11	6	4	85	114	10					2					
s		2	1	5	38	170	10						2			
ʃ		3	3			3	267									
b				7	4			235	4		34	27	1			
d									189	48		4	8	11		
g									74	161		4	8	25		
v				3	1			19			177	29	4	1		
ð								7		10	64	105	18			
z									17	23	4	22	132	26		
ʒ								2	3		1	1	9	191		1
m								1							201	6
n												3		1	8	240

TABLE V. Confusion matrix for $S/N = +6$ db and frequency response of 200–6500 cps.

	p	t	k	f	θ	s	ʃ	b	d	g	v	ð	z	ʒ	m	n
p	162	10	55	5	3							1				
t	8	270	14													
k	38	6	171	1												
f	5	1	2	207	57			3			1					
θ	5	1	2	71	142	3					2	2				
s			1	1	7	232	2					1				
ʃ						1	239									
b				1	2			214			31	12				
d									206	14		9	1	2		
g								11	64	194		4	2	1		
v				1	1			14	2		205	39	5		2	1
ð								2	4		55	179	22	2		
z								3	10		2	20	198	3		
ʒ								3	4				2	215		
m															217	3
n								1							2	285

TABLE VI. Confusion matrix for $S/N = +12$ db and frequency response of 200–6500 cps.

	p	t	k	f	θ	s	ʃ	b	d	g	v	ð	z	ʒ	m	n
p	240		41	2	1											
t	1	252	1	1						1						
k	18	3	219													
f				225	24			5			2					
θ	9		1	69	185			3				1				
s						232										
ʃ							236									
b				1				242			24	12	1			
d									213	22				1		
g				1					33	203		3				
v								6			171	30			1	
ð				1				1		3	22	208	4			1
z									2	4	1	7	238			
ʒ														244		
m												1			274	1
n																252

TABLE VII. Confusion matrix for $S/N = +12$ db and frequency response of 200–300 cps.

	p	t	k	f	θ	s	ʃ	b	d	g	v	ð	z	ʒ	m	n
p	47	61	68	15	11	17	9	3	3	1		1	2	2	3	1
t	59	63	64	19	15	14	13	3	4	1		5	2	2	2	2
k	37	47	56	10	13	15	10	1	2	1		2		1		1
f	21	29	21	38	37	47	19	2	2	1		2	2	3	3	1
θ	13	23	25	23	39	54	39	2	2	1	4	5	1	1	4	5
s	16	25	10	29	52	65	34	1	4	2		5	1	1	1	2
ʃ	15	33	23	18	28	70	41	1	1			7	3	1	1	2
b		1	1	8	8	5	3	98	28	17	38	19	9	2	8	7
d	1		1	11	7	12	5	70	84	33	12	10	24	9	1	
g	4	1	2	7	5	13	8	56	74	33	13	15	21	13	6	1
v		2	1	1	2	1	1	44	34	18	77	34	36	14	2	1
ð	1				3		1	22	16	19	45	46	23	11	11	8
z	2	3	2	2	4	3	2	15	15	20	46	35	64	21	2	
ʒ	1	1		1	2		1	11	15	24	54	42	70	39	2	5
m			1	1	2	2		1	3	3	4	5	1	4	161	60
n	1	3	2	1	1	1	2	1	3	2	2	4	2	2	133	108

TABLE VIII. Confusion matrix for $S/N = +12$ db and frequency response of 200–400 cps.

	p	t	k	f	θ	s	ʃ	b	d	g	v	ð	z	ʒ	m	n
p	72	68	90	20	15	4	1	2	4	1		1				2
t	73	72	74	20	8	6	3	1	2	2		2		1		
k	63	74	127	9	7	5	2			1		1	1	1		1
f	7	7	10	63	69	41	8	3	1	1	1	3		1	1	
θ	5	8	11	60	85	45	14	2	4	2	6	5	1			
s	1	6	5	19	49	125	60	5	2	1	2	9	4			
ʃ	2	6	8	8	22	69	89	2	4	1		3	5	1		
b		1	1	19	14	5		134	20	13	14	11	4	1	2	1
d			2		1	6	4	19	120	23	2	3	11	3		2
g			2	1		5	1	11	116	59	8	7	11	4	1	2
v		1		1	1	2		25	4	8	111	55	18	2	2	2
ð		1	1	6	5	1		43	16	15	75	66	23	11	1	4
z	2		2	1	5	5	2	21	20	17	18	33	91	25	1	1
ʒ				4			2	1	27	29	11	16	83	78	1	
m								12	3	1	1				219	57
n					1	1		12	3	1	1	2			99	120

TABLE IX. Confusion matrix for $S/N = +12$ db and frequency response of 200–600 cps.

	p	t	k	f	θ	s	ʃ	b	d	g	v	ð	z	ʒ	m	n
p	115	43	70	10	3	2						1				
t	69	63	71	4	4							1				
k	59	49	134	4	1					1						
f	2	3	2	126	89	11	1	2			1	8	1		1	1
θ	2	1	1	103	97	35	7	2	1		5	1				1
s	3	3		34	88	93	26	4	1			7		1		
ʃ	3	6	12	7	31	98	87	1	2	1	2	1	1			
b			1	10	5	1		201	13		13	4				
d		1		1	1	6	1	29	169	39	3	3	6	5		
g				1		7		12	99	97		4	8	11		1
v				5	2			14	1	2	141	57	9	4	1	
ð								10	6	10	109	90	31	7	1	
z						1	2	3	15	30	17	42	116	22		1
ʒ			1				1		10	21	8	17	110	116		
m					1							1			215	39
n				1											119	120

TABLE X. Confusion matrix for $S/N = +12$ db and frequency response of 200–1200 cps.

	p	t	k	f	θ	s	ʃ	b	d	g	v	ð	z	ʒ	m	n
p	165	46	31	3	1			1				1				
t	91	83	68	4	1	2		1				2				
k	48	55	147	2	3							1				
f	16	4	3	146	60	3	2	11			1	2				
θ	4	3		109	76	17	2	12	1			2	1	1		
s	2	1	1	43	83	83	11	3		1	1	7				
ʃ	1	6	2	12	41	86	90		6	4		4				
b				14	5			223	4		5	1				
d	1			1		3	4	4	173	37		2	1	2		
g	1					1			102	107		2	7	7		
v	2	2		2	1			23	1	2	163	62	14	3	1	
ð				1		3	2	27	6	32	87	107	36	7		
z	1							4	12	48	10	15	114	39		1
ʒ						1	2	3		35	1	16	60	134	2	
m	1									1					229	9
n															5	247

TABLE XI. Confusion matrix for $S/N = +12$ db and frequency response of 200–2500 cps.

	p	t	k	f	θ	s	ʃ	b	d	g	v	ð	z	ʒ	m	n
p	215	29	26	5	1											
t	74	91	47													
k	15	16	201													
f	6		1	186	31	2		3				7				
θ	1	5	1	93	81	25	1	1		2	2	4				
s	1	3	1	31	78	142	9	1		1		5				
ʃ			1		23	210				1						
b				11	6	1		206	4		11	1				
d							1	1	217	30			1	6		
g				2		1	1	1	54	169		1		3		
v				1	2	1		36		1	178	39	9		1	
ð				3	6	2		14		17	58	146	45	1		
z						2			17	40	7	24	122	20		
ʒ				1			5		5	9			11	265		
m															242	18
n															2	242

TABLE XII. Confusion matrix for $S/N = +12$ db and frequency response of 200–5000 cps.

	p	t	k	f	θ	s	ʃ	b	d	g	v	ð	z	ʒ	m	n
p	228	7	7	1			1									
t		236	8													
k	26	5	213													
f	6	1	1	194	35			3			1	3				
θ		2	2	96	146	2		2	1		1	8				
s		2		1	31	204	1	1	9	4		7				
ʃ						1	243									
b				13	12			207	2	3	19	8				3
d									240	9			2			1
g								1	41	199			2			1
v				3	3			20		2	182	47	2			1
ð					7			10	3	22	49	170	19	3		
z			1					3	8	24	2	22	145	3		
ʒ							1	2					13	264		
m															213	11
n																248

TABLE XIII. Confusion matrix for $S/N = +12$ db and frequency response of 1000–5000 cps.

	p	t	k	f	θ	s	ʃ	b	d	g	v	ð	z	ʒ	m	n
p	179	9	44	6	3					2	1					
t		272	3					1	1							1
k	15	1	227					1	1		2					1
f	12	1		162	28	3	1	34			6		1		4	
θ	8	2	7	39	125	13	2	6	2	1	4	19	3	1	1	1
s				3	28	200	1	2	1	1	4	6	9	2		
ʃ						1	221									
b	2			9	10	1		130		6	74	24	2	8	16	
d		2					1		195	35	6	2	2	8		5
g				2					48	151		3	4	5		11
v	1			28	8			48	1	3	145	33	3		17	1
ð	1			1	14			8	11	12	31	116	26	5	21	6
z			1	2		24	2	1	19	7	3	31	163	4	2	1
ʒ				1		20		2		2				207		
m	3		2	5	4	1		10			6		1	1	224	1
n			1	1	1			1	8	4	2	1	1	1	1	207

TABLE XIV. Confusion matrix for $S/N = +12$ db and frequency response of 2000–5000 cps.

	p	t	k	f	θ	s	ʃ	b	d	g	v	ð	z	ʒ	m	n
p	94	32	26	15	6	3	1	10	4	4	13	12	1	5	3	3
t	7	223	3	3	1		3		7	1	1	1		5	1	
k	24	25	126	4	7		2	3	6	15	1	3	1	2	7	2
f	38	7	19	72	24	5	2	24	3	12	28	11	4	3	12	4
θ	22	7	11	20	63	27		19	8	13	22	26	16		12	10
s	2	9	1	5	23	148		1			3	4	44	6		8
ʃ	1	1					208	1					1	28		
b	15	5	5	37	12	2		72	7	8	40	30	4		40	7
d	2	6	7		2			4	192	19	4	6	3	2	2	23
g	2	1	3	1	8	4	1	8	44	122	10	6	6	1	3	20
v	17	1	12	13	7		1	39	5	14	42	23	2	4	32	12
ð	5		6	9	20	5		17	16	19	17	64	20	1	36	25
z	3	2	2	5	8	44		5	22	7	1	13	99		7	9
ʒ							37			4				199		
m	10	4	3	8	7	2	1	9	5	10	10	16	2		113	26
n	2		2		3	2		1	20	11	3	7	6	3	4	192

TABLE XV. Confusion matrix for $S/N = +12$ db and frequency response of 2500–5000 cps.

	p	t	k	f	θ	s	ʃ	b	d	g	v	ð	z	ʒ	m	n
p	69	30	37	26	16	4	4	21	9	18	13	12	9	3	7	10
t	4	164	9	2	2	2		1	4	4	1	2	2		3	
k	20	35	76	9	11	5	6	3	5	25	5	3	15	11	7	4
f	27	8	7	24	28	7	8	15	8	14	34	14	6	2	11	11
θ	15	19	7	20	49	10	8	12	16	16	13	20	10	5	16	16
s	6	8	2	1	19	160	4		16	10	8	11	27	2	7	11
ʃ	1	1	2	1	5	1	204	1				1	2	44		1
b	23	4	10	13	17		2	48	17	17	34	28	10	1	28	12
d	1	7	6	5	4	2	1	1	128	16	8	6	5	13	5	16
g	6	3	16	5	6	5	2	17	39	85	11	13	6	7	6	13
v	22	6	6	26	18	3	3	33	12	9	32	28	7	2	18	7
ð	21	11	9	16	28	4	2	35	14	22	20	44	10	2	24	22
z	4	5	1	2	9	60	5	1	27	21		12	86	6	2	3
ʒ	2	4	2			3	49	1	7	1	2	1	5	167		
m	18	3	7	11	16	8	2	13	16	12	16	21	3	1	68	37
n	8	4	12	7	9	2		10	22	17	13	8	5	4	16	119

TABLE XVI. Confusion matrix for $S/N = +12$ db and frequency response of 3000–5000 cps.

	p	t	k	f	θ	s	ʃ	b	d	g	v	ð	z	ʒ	m	n
p	31	15	15	15	14	11	6	19	11	8	15	15	5	9	12	19
t	11	184	16	6	5	5	5	8	9	3	4	2	5	3	6	4
k	15	35	50	7	16	7	2	14	14	24	7	9	8	9	8	7
f	19	12	12	15	19	8	2	25	16	25	15	12	6	2	17	11
θ	15	14	13	13	30	15	3	15	24	12	14	17	10	3	14	20
s	4	4	8	11	8	140	4	7	8	6	6	11	35	7	2	7
ʃ		6	2	3	1	4	177	1	2	2	1	6	1	23	7	
b	17	13	11	25	23	8	1	27	13	19	25	13	5	6	17	13
d	14	23	15	11	11	4	3	15	63	25	14	10	13	6	19	14
g	14	15	17	17	12	8	1	23	39	45	14	10	13	7	17	16
v	19	19	22	18	20	8	10	35	18	16	19	21	7		28	16
ð	19	13	12	12	24	8	6	22	24	15	24	21	10	5	33	16
z	9	21	9	7	17	59	6	6	11	13	10	15	41	4	10	14
ʒ	4	6	1	5	1	11	51	3	3	7	1	10	9	128	7	5
m	16	7	14	11	19	5	4	31	16	17	17	10	10	6	58	19
n	16	7	12	6	16	7	6	14	29	16	13	22	7	4	19	58

TABLE XVII. Confusion matrix for $S/N = +12$ db and frequency response of 4500–5000 cps.

	p	t	k	f	θ	s	ʃ	b	d	g	v	ð	z	ʒ	m	n
p	26	21	23	16	24	20	4	15	16	14	20	9	10	9	16	9
t	10	141	12	3	4	4	3	5	11	5	7	11	4	5	8	3
k	16	34	25	14	11	13	8	20	20	8	18	13	20	10	12	22
f	9	9	22	18	18	6	6	18	17	9	17	19	9	3	27	13
θ	16	21	25	5	20	10	2	29	23	24	27	28	11	5	16	10
s	8	5	15	7	11	138	7	6	4	11	13	7	34	5	6	7
ʃ	3	3	7	1	1	12	190	1	4	2	2	4	6	26	6	4
b	12	8	23	11	18	13	9	26	14	18	21	14	11	6	16	16
d	24	26	28	16	19	8	4	19	18	19	13	11	6	3	16	14
g	12	16	17	14	21	11	10	12	17	21	18	19	7	10	22	13
v	21	11	17	15	24	12	8	19	15	14	33	23	6	3	23	16
ð	18	19	15	16	20	7	5	24	16	16	22	28	9	11	24	10
z	8	12	8	8	7	64	5	12	10	9	12	17	51	11	6	8
ʒ	5	18	10	8	9	11	57	5	4	5	9	11	15	85	9	7
m	8	13	20	13	15	14	7	18	8	16	16	17	12	2	15	18
n	20	15	15	18	15	7	6	19	20	12	17	15	12	4	21	16

TABLE XVIII. Confusion matrix at $S/N = -12$ db with a 200–6500-cps channel.

	p	t	k	b	d	g	Sum
p	117	58	115	14	10	2	316
t	74	101	103	8	4	6	296
k	105	109	153	5	8	4	384
b	13	9	10	217	45	26	320
d	3	4	5	47	200	117	376
g	3	11	8	45	147	94	308
							2000

is given in Table XVIII. There are 882 entries on the main diagonal, so $A = 0.441$. If we group the consonants $|pk|$, $|t|$, $|b|$, and $|dg|$, there are 1366 correct responses, so $A' = 0.683$. If we again group $|ptk|$ and $|bdg|$, there are 1873 correct responses, so $A'' = 0.9365$. Now if we wish to reconstruct the matrix from these three articulation scores, we would first divide the 882 correct responses equally among the six diagonal cells, which gives 147 observations per cell. When we add the four cells for $|pk|$ and $|dg|$ to the diagonal cells, the count increases from 882 to 1366, so the additional 484 observations must be divided equally among the four additional cells, which gives 121 per cell for $|pk|$ and $|dg|$ confusions. When we add the eight remaining cells for the $|ptk|$ and $|bdg|$ groups, the count increases from 1366 to 1873, so the additional 507 observations must be divided evenly among those eight cells, which gives 63.4 per cell. The remaining 127 observations are then divided equally among the 18 cells remaining in the lower left and upper right quadrants, which gives 7.1 per cell. In this way the generalized, three-valued articulation score gives a reasonably clear picture of the distribution of errors.

The procedure just described can lead to serious errors if the stimulus frequencies are quite disparate. For example, if one stimulus is presented much more often than any other, it will contribute more to the total number of correct responses and then the equipartition of correct responses among the diagonal cells will be in error. In such cases the original data matrix should first be corrected to the frequencies that would presumably have been obtained if the stimuli had been equally frequent. This correction is made by multiplying the entries in each row by n/kn_i, where n_i is the frequency of occurrence of the ith stimulus ($i = 1, 2, \cdots, k$) in a sample of n observations. Then the "articulation scores corrected for stimulus frequencies" are calculated for the revised matrix. To reconstruct the data matrix, the corrected frequencies should be partitioned as before and then each row multiplied by kn_i/n in order to remove the correction and regain the original stimulus frequencies. Whenever an experimenter employs some unusual (nonuniform) distribution of stimulus frequencies, this fact should be stated explicitly in order to avoid misinterpretations of the articulation scores so obtained.

Some such generalization of the articulation score seems essential in order to preserve the data on clustering of errors. In our own analysis of the data, however, we have preferred a somewhat more elaborate statistical analysis. We have presented this simpler technique for the reader who feels that the information measures we have employed are too abstract or do not permit a simple reconstruction of the original matrix. Having pointed out this simpler technique, however, we shall make little use of it in the following discussion.

LINGUISTIC FEATURES

For many years linguists and phoneticians have classified phonemes according to features of the articulation process used to generate the sounds. These features of speech production are reflected in certain acoustic characteristics which are presumably discriminated by the listener. When we begin to look for reasonable ways to group the stimuli in order to summarize the pattern of confusions, it is natural to turn first to these articulatory features for guidance. In order to describe the 16 consonants used in this study we adopted the following set of features as a basis for classification.

(1) *Voicing.* In articulatory terms, the vocal cords do not vibrate when the consonants $|ptkf\theta s\int|$ are produced, and they do vibrate for $|bdgv\eth z\mathfrak{z}mn|$. Acoustically, this means that the voiceless consonants are aperiodic or noisy in character, whereas a periodic or line-spectrum component is superimposed on the noise for voiced consonants. In addition, in English the voiceless consonants seem to be more intense and the voiceless stops have considerable aspiration, a sort of breathy noise between the release of pressure and the beginning of the following vowels, and may be somewhat briefer than the voiced stops. Thus the articulatory difference is reflected in a variety of acoustic differences.

(2) *Nasality.* To articulate $|m|$ and $|n|$ the lips are closed and the pressure is released through the nose by lowering the soft palate at the back of the mouth. The nasal resonance introduced in this way provides an acoustic difference. In addition, $|mn|$ seem slightly longer in duration than their stop or fricative counterparts and somewhat more intense. Also, the two nasals are the only consonants in this study lacking the aperiodic component of noisiness.

(3) *Affrication.* If the articulators close completely, the consonant may be a stop or a nasal, but if they are brought close together and air is forced between them, the result is a kind of turbulence or friction noise that distinguishes $|f\theta s\int v\eth z\mathfrak{z}|$ from $|ptkbdgmn|$. The acoustic turbulence is in contrast to the silence followed by a pop that characterizes the stops and to the periodic, almost vowel-like resonance of the nasals.

(4) *Duration.* This is the name we have arbitrarily adopted to designate the difference between $|s\int z\mathfrak{z}|$ and the other 12 consonants. These four consonants are

long, intense, high-frequency noises, but in our opinion it is their extra duration that is most effective in setting them apart.

(5) *Place of Articulation.* This feature has to do with where in the mouth the major constriction of the vocal passage occurs. Usually three positions, front, middle, and back, are distinguished, so that we have grouped $|pbfvm|$ as front, $|td\theta s\eth zn|$ as middle, and $|kg\int\!\!3|$ as back consonants. Although these three positions are easy to recognize in the production of these sounds, the acoustic consequences of differences in place are most complex. Of the various accounts of the positional feature that have been given, the work done by the Haskins Laboratory[1,2] seems to provide the best basis for an interpretation of our data. For the voiced stops $|bdg|$ the most important acoustic clue to position seems to be in the initial portion of the second formant

TABLE XIX. Classification of consonants used to analyze confusions.

Consonant	Voicing	Nasality	Affrication	Duration	Place
p	0	0	0	0	0
t	0	0	0	0	1
k	0	0	0	0	2
f	0	0	1	0	0
θ	0	0	1	0	1
s	0	0	1	1	1
$\int$	0	0	1	1	2
b	1	0	0	0	0
d	1	0	0	0	1
g	1	0	0	0	2
v	1	0	1	0	0
$\eth$	1	0	1	0	1
z	1	0	1	1	1
3	1	0	1	1	2
m	1	1	0	0	0
n	1	1	0	0	1

of the vowel $|a|$ that follows; if this formant frequency rises initially, it is a $|b|$, but if it falls it is $|d|$ or $|g|$. Since the vowel formant is relatively audible, the front $|b|$ is easily distinguished from the middle $|d|$ and the back $|g|$. The latter two positions are much harder to distinguish and probably cannot be differentiated until their aperiodic, noisy components become sufficiently audible so that high-frequency noise can be assigned to middle $|d|$ and low-frequency noise to back $|g|$. For the voiceless stops $|ptk|$, however, the story is different because the transitional portion of the second formant occurs during the period of aspiration, before vocalization has begun, and is correspondingly much harder to hear. The plosive part of the voiceless stops is relatively intense, however, so that the high-fre-

[1] Liberman, Delattre, and Cooper, Am. J. Psychol. **65**, 497–516 (1952).

[2] Liberman, Delattre, Cooper, and Gerstman, Psychol. Monographs **68**, No. 8, 1–13 (1954).

quency noise of middle $|t|$ distinguishes it from the low-frequency noise of front $|p|$ and back $|k|$. The distinction between $|p|$ and $|k|$ is slightly harder to hear because it seems to depend upon hearing the aspirated transition into the second vowel resonance. What acoustic representation there is for place of articulation of the fricative sounds is even more obscure. Probably the middle $|sz|$ are distinguished from the back $|\int\!\!3|$ on the basis of the high-frequency energy in $|sz|$. The distinction between front $|fv|$ and middle $|\theta\eth|$, however is uncertainly attributable to slight differences in the transition to the following vowel. The distinctions between $|f|$ and $|\theta|$ and between $|v|$ and $|\eth|$ are among the most difficult for listeners to hear and it seems likely that in most natural situations the differentiation depends more on verbal context and on visual observation of the talker's lips than it does on the acoustic difference. In any event, when we summarily assign these consonants into three classes on the basis of "articulatory position," we are thereby concealing a host of difficult problems. The positional feature is by all odds the most superficial and unsatisfactory of the five features we have employed.

In Table XIX a digital notation is used to summarize the classification of these 16 consonants on the basis of these five features. From Table XIX it is easy to see in what ways any two of the consonants differ.

Now if we apply the groupings given in Table XIX to the data matrices in Tables I–XVII, we can obtain a set of articulation scores, one score for each feature. For example, we can group the voiceless consonants together *versus* the voiced consonants and so estimate the probability that the voicing feature will be perceived correctly—the articulation score for voicing. The necessary summations for each feature for every table have been made and are given in Table XX.

A COVARIANCE MEASURE OF INTELLIGIBILITY

The recent development of a mathematical theory of communication has made considerable use of a measure

TABLE XX. Frequencies of correct responses in Tables I–XVII.

Condition	S/N	Band	All	Voice	Nasal	Frict	Durat	Place
1	−18	200–6500	313	2286	3200	2032	2600	1439
2	−12	200–6500	1080	3586	3742	2610	3095	1842
3	−6	200–6500	1860	3877	3921	3202	3429	2386
4	0	200–6500	2862	3977	3992	3706	3780	3099
5	6	200–6500	3336	3985	3998	3861	3910	3472
6	12	200–6500	3634	3985	3997	3916	3980	3691
7	12	200–300	1059	3725	3864	2922	2905	1717
8	12	200–400	1631	3801	3939	3402	3388	2088
9	12	200–600	1980	3903	3991	3696	3475	2341
10	12	200–1200	2287	3891	3994	3641	3526	2616
11	12	200–2500	2913	3927	3999	3778	3673	3224
12	12	200–5000	3332	3920	3999	3811	3853	3522
13	12	1000–5000	2924	3735	3861	3566	3801	3476
14	12	2000–5000	2029	3208	3573	3087	3689	2992
15	12	2500–5000	1523	2857	3472	2871	3552	2587
16	12	3000–5000	1087	2527	3283	2601	3390	2227
17	12	4500–5000	851	2283	3267	2463	3260	1927
Random guessing			250	2031	3125	2000	2500	1406

of covariance between input and output. This measure has been defined in terms of the mean logarithmic probability (MLP). If the input variable is x, which can assume the discrete values $i=1,2,\cdots,k$ with probability p_i, then the measure of the input is

$$\mathrm{MLP}(x)=E(-\log p_i)=-\sum_i p_i \log p_i.$$

If the logarithm is taken to the base 2, then the measure can be called the number of binary decisions needed on the average to specify the input, or the number of bits of information per stimulus. A similar expression holds for the output variable y, which can assume the values $j=1,2,\cdots,m$. Similarly, the number of decisions needed to specify the particular stimulus-response pair is $\mathrm{MLP}(xy)$, where p_{ij} is the probability of the joint occurrence of input i and output j. A measure of covariance of input with output is given by

$$T(x;y)=\mathrm{MLP}(x)+\mathrm{MLP}(y)-\mathrm{MLP}(xy)$$

$$=-\sum_{i,j} p_{ij} \log \frac{p_i p_j}{p_{ij}}.$$

$T(x;y)$ is often referred to as the transmission from x to y in bits per stimulus. The relative transmission is given by

$$T_{\mathrm{rel}}(x;y)=T(x;y)/H(x).$$

Since $H(x)\geq T(x;y)\geq 0$, the ratio varies from 0 to 1; if the transmission is poor and the response is not closely correlated to the stimulus, then $T_{\mathrm{rel}}(x;y)$ will be near zero, but if the response can be predicted with considerable accuracy from the stimulus, then $T_{\mathrm{rel}}(x;y)$ will be near unity.

In practice the true probabilities are not known and must be estimated from the relative frequencies

obtained in a finite sample taken during the experiment. The maximum likelihood estimate of $T(x;y)$ is obtained by using n_i/n, n_j/n, and n_{ij}/n in place of p_i, p_j, and p_{ij}, respectively, where n_i is the frequency of stimulus i, n_j is the frequency of response j, and n_{ij} is the frequency of the joint occurrence of stimulus i and response j in a sample of n observations. In Tables I–XVII the cell entries are the n_{ij}, row sums give n_i, column sums give n_j, and n is 4000. Like most maximum likelihood estimates, this estimate will be biased to overestimate $T(x;y)$ for small samples; in the present case, however, the sample is large enough that the bias can safely be ignored.

The covariance measure of intelligibility can be applied to the several linguistic features separately in just the same way that the articulation score for each feature was obtained for Table XX. For example, we can construct a fourfold confusion matrix by grouping the voiceless sounds together as one stimulus and the voiced sounds as the other and then tabulating the frequency of voiceless responses to voiceless stimuli, of voiced responses to voiceless stimuli, of voiceless responses to voiced stimuli, and of voiced responses to voiced stimuli. For this 2 by 2 confusion matrix we can calculate the covariance of response with stimulus in the same way as described above and so measure the transmission of information about voicing. Similar measures can be calculated for nasality, affrication, duration, and position.

This breakdown of the confusion matrix into five smaller matrices and the measurement of transmission for each one of these five separately is equivalent to considering that we are actually testing five different communication channels simultaneously.[3] Of course, the five channels will probably not be independent. Some interaction or "cross talk" is to be expected, in the sense that knowing one feature may make some other feature easier to hear. However, the impressive thing to us was that this cross talk was so small and that the features were perceived almost independently of one another.

At first thought one might expect that if all five channels were independent, then the sum of the information transmitted by the separate channels should equal approximately the transmission calculated for all five taken together in the whole 16 by 16 matrix. This first thought would be true except for one fact; the inputs to the five channels are not independent and, therefore, even if the channels themselves are independent, the amounts transmitted through each channel will be related.

In Table XXI the average amounts of information in bits per stimulus that the listeners received are presented for the composite channel and for the five subchannels individually for all 17 conditions of masking and filtering. The last row in the table gives the amounts

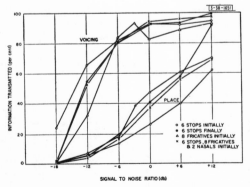

FIG. 1. The relative information transmitted about voicing (top four curves), and place (bottom four curves) is plotted as a function of signal-to-noise ratio in decibels. The four curves for each feature were obtained from four independent experiments using different test vocabularies. Voicing information is transmitted at signal-to-noise levels 18 db below those needed for place information.

[3] W. J. McGill, Psychometrika 19, 97–116 (1954).

TABLE XXI. Amounts of information transmitted in bits per stimulus in Tables I–XVII for composite channel and for each feature separately.

Condition	S/N	Band	All	Voice	Nasal	Frict	Durat	Place
1	−18	200–6500	0.061	0.021	0.008	0.000	0.001	0.001
2	−12	200–6500	0.959	0.516	0.264	0.069	0.087	0.058
3	−6	200–6500	1.834	0.797	0.397	0.279	0.249	0.249
4	0	200–6500	2.797	0.944	0.495	0.620	0.483	0.578
5	6	200–6500	3.226	0.951	0.543	0.782	0.636	0.856
6	12	200–6500	3.546	0.956	0.555	0.853	0.751	1.090
7	12	200–300	1.155	0.623	0.371	0.159	0.042	0.025
8	12	200–400	1.686	0.709	0.457	0.393	0.218	0.125
9	12	200–600	2.159	0.821	0.520	0.614	0.272	0.231
10	12	200–1200	2.379	0.805	0.523	0.583	0.281	0.359
11	12	200–2500	2.828	0.852	0.544	0.702	0.419	0.721
12	12	200–5000	3.185	0.847	0.521	0.730	0.581	0.936
13	12	1000–5000	2.643	0.638	0.350	0.506	0.520	0.872
14	12	2000–5000	1.582	0.273	0.160	0.229	0.426	0.499
15	12	2500–5000	1.053	0.130	0.083	0.143	0.348	0.296
16	12	3000–5000	0.624	0.048	0.023	0.067	0.235	0.143
17	12	4500–5000	0.455	0.014	0.002	0.045	0.193	0.068
Maximum possible			4.000	0.989	0.544	1.000	0.811	1.546

that would be transmitted if no mistakes at all occurred (on the assumption that all 16 syllables occurred equally often). The degree of redundancy in the input is indicated by the fact that the sum of the transmissions for the five channels is 4.890 bits, whereas the composite channel can transmit only 4 bits. This difference means that some of the input information is going through more than one channel. However, for the conditions and phonemes tested, the sum for the five channels can be used to give a rough approximation for the composite channel if the sum is corrected by the factor 4/4.89. If all of the features were transmitted equally well, this correction factor would be exact, but in most cases it is only an approximation.

The fact that the measures for the separate channels can be summed in a simple manner to give an approximate value for the total transmission is of considerable practical significance. This perceptual independence of the several features implies that all we need to know about a system is how well it transmits the necessary clues for each feature; measurements for the individual features can be made much more quickly and easily than can a measurement for the composite channel, and the correction factor for the input redundancy depends entirely on the input vocabulary and not upon an experimental test.

In the following we shall discuss the relative transmission measures. The relative measure is computed from Table XXI by dividing each entry in that table by the maximum value given at the bottom of each column. The advantage of the relative measure is that it permits an easy comparison of one channel with another. Differences in transmission due simply to the fact that the input to one channel was greater than the input to another channel are removed when we examine the relative efficiency of the two channels. We ask simply, what fraction of its input did each channel transmit? The ratio of transmitted to input information provides us with a normalized measure of stimulus-response covariation.

DISCUSSION

In Fig. 1 the normalized covariance measure—relative transmission in percent—is plotted as a function of the signal-to-noise ratio for two linguistic features, voicing and place of articulation, for the data presented in Tables I–VI. In Fig. 2 a similar plot is shown for the features of nasality, affrication, and duration. In addition to the data in Tables I–VI, the results of three smaller studies are also plotted on the same graph. In one of these smaller studies only the six stop consonants $|p|$, $|t|$, $|k|$, $|b|$, $|d|$, and $|g|$, were used initially before the vowel $|a|$. In a second study these same six stop consonants occurred finally after the phonemes $|ta|$. And in the third study only the eight fricative consonants $|f|$, $|\theta|$, $|s|$, $|\int|$, $|v|$, $|\delta|$, $|z|$, and $|3|$ were used initially before the vowel $|a|$. Both voicing and place of articulation are involved in these three smaller test vocabularies, so the relative transmission for these two features can be compared in Fig. 1 with the results obtained from the complete set of 16 consonants. Duration was also tested with fricative sounds and this function is added in Fig. 2. The comparisons show a gratifying degree of agreement from one study to the next.

The glaringly obvious statement that must be made about Figs. 1 and 2 is that voicing and nasality are much less affected by a random masking noise than are the other features. Affrication and duration, which are so similar that a single function could represent them both, are somewhat superior to place but far inferior to voicing and nasality. Voicing and nasality are discriminable at signal-to-noise ratios as poor as −12 db whereas the place of articulation is hard to distinguish at ratios less than 6 db, a difference of some 18 db in efficiency.

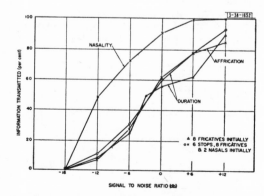

FIG. 2. The relative information transmitted about nasality, affrication, and duration is plotted as a function of signal-to-noise ratio in decibels. The two curves for duration were obtained from independent experiments using different test vocabularies. Nasality and voicing are equally discriminable.

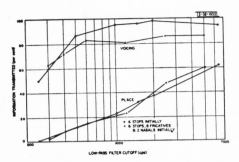

FIG. 3. The relative information transmitted about voicing and place is plotted as a function of the cutoff frequency of the low-pass filter. The two curves for each feature were obtained from independent experiments. The relation between voicing and place is the same for low-pass filtering as for masking with random noise (see Fig. 1).

In Figs. 3 and 4 similar functions are drawn for the results given in Tables VII–XII for low-pass filters. An additional small study with just the six stop consonants is also represented in Fig. 3. Figure 3 looks much like Fig. 1; voicing is greatly superior to place of articulation. Figure 4 is similar to Fig. 2, except that the results for affrication and duration are now somewhat different. These comparisons show that there is a considerable correspondence between masking by random noise and filtering by low-pass filters. This correspondence seems reasonable if we think of the high-frequency components of speech as relatively weak and therefore most susceptible to masking by the uniform spectrum of the noise. That is to say, the uniform noise spectrum should mask high frequencies more than low, so it is in effect a kind of low-pass system.

Whereas low-pass filtering and noise have much the same effect on speech perception, high-pass filtering presents a totally different picture. In Fig. 5 the relative transmissions calculated from Tables XII–XVII are plotted for all five features as a function of the filter cutoff frequency. With a minor exception for duration, all features deteriorate in about the same way as the low frequencies are removed. Duration holds up some-

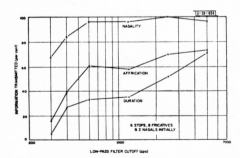

FIG. 4. The relative information transmitted about nasality, affrication, and duration is plotted as a function of the cutoff frequency of the low-pass filter. Nasality is somewhat more discriminable than voicing.

what better, probably because $|s|$, $|\int|$, $|z|$, and $|3|$ are characterized in part by considerable high-frequency energy. This homogeneity reflects a fact that can be seen from visual inspection of Tables XIII–XVII; the errors do not cluster or fall into obvious patterns in the confusion matrix, but seem to distribute almost randomly over the matrix. When an error occurs with high-pass filtering, there is little chance of predicting what the error will be. Thus we find an important difference between high- and low-pass filtering; low-pass filters affect the several linguistic features differentially, leaving the phonemes audible but similar in predictable ways, whereas high-pass filters remove most of the acoustic power in the consonants, leaving them inaudible and, consequently, producing quite random confusions. Of course, this difference must be tempered by the fact that a random noise was used along with the filters, so that the noise acted "with" the low-pass filter to eliminate high frequencies but "against" the high-pass filter in such a way as to produce a narrow band-pass system. However, casual observations made since these tests were completed convince us that the difference cannot be explained entirely in this way and that, even without noise, audibility is the problem for high-pass systems and confusibility is the problem for low-pass systems.

An important application of data on filtered speech has been to divide the frequency scale into segments making equal contributions to intelligibility. The high-pass and low-pass functions are plotted on the same graph and the frequency at which the two functions cross is said to divide the frequency scale into two equivalent parts; the frequencies above the crossover are exactly as important as the frequencies below the crossover frequency. We have observed this traditional method of analysis in Fig. 6 where the solid functions are the articulation scores and they are seen to cross at about 1550 cps. This frequency is somewhat lower than one would expect for female talkers, but the test vocabulary used here may not permit valid comparisons with other research.

We would like to argue that the meaning of these crossover points is apt to be a bit tricky. In the first place, the point depends crucially upon the test materials, in the sense that we can obtain very different crossover points for the different linguistic features: 450 cps for nasality, 500 cps for voicing, 750 cps for affrication, 1900 cps for place of articulation, and 2200 cps for duration. What crossover point we get depends on how we load the test vocabulary with these different features. In the second place, high- and low-pass filters do different things to speech perception, as we pointed out previously. If we plot the relative amount of information transmitted, instead of the articulation score, we obtain the dashed functions shown in Fig. 6. The crossover point for the information measure is about 1250 cps, a good 300 cps lower than for the articulation score.

By the same argument as before, there is as much information above 1250 cps as there is below. Why do these two measures give different divisions of the frequency scale? The answer lies in the fact that low-pass errors are more predictable and so carry some information, whereas high-pass errors are more random and contain no hint about what the true message might have been. Relative to the articulation scores, therefore, the high-pass information is smaller and the low-pass information is greater; the relative shifts move the crossover point downward in frequency. Which of these two crossover points is the more meaningful? Here the answer depends upon what use is to be made of the voice communication system. If isolated words, numerals, station call letters, etc. are the only messages, then a miss is as good as a mile; there is no redundancy in the message to enable the listener to correct an error, so the percentage of messages correctly received is what we want to know. On the other hand, if connected discourse in all its notorious redundancy is sent over the system, a listener can detect perceptual errors on the basis of context and can correct them more easily if they are consistent and predictable; then the transmission measure is what we want to know. However, if we arrive at a position where we must weight the frequency scale one way for isolated words and another way for conversational speech, the beautiful simplicity that makes the traditional crossover argument so attractive seems spurious. Our own intuitions would lead us to search for a different line of attack on the problem.

It may be possible to evaluate voice communication systems more adequately if we explore the implications of the multiple-channel argument used to analyze our data. It is not obvious that things will be any simpler if we must replace a single complicated channel with a dozen simpler channels in our theoretical model of speech perception. However, transmission of the separate features may be easier to relate to the system parameters. Even if a completely automatic computational procedure cannot be developed along multiple-channel lines, a short series of relatively simple articulation tests may suffice to determine the necessary parameters. In any event, the development and standardization of tests for the individual features would seem to have considerable value for the diagnosis both of inefficient equipments and of hard-of-hearing people.

One advantage of a multichannel approach to speech perception is that the message, as well as the equipment, is included in the analysis. Given any specific vocabulary of speech signals, we can calculate the relative importance of each feature for distinguishing the alternative signals and so derive a weighting factor for each channel. If the messages are coded properly into those channels or features that the system handles well, considerable advantage may be gained. For ex-

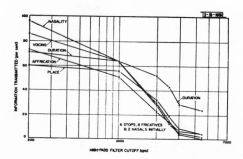

FIG. 5. The relative information transmitted about all five features is plotted as a function of the cutoff frequency of the high-pass filter. The effect of eliminating the low frequencies is the same on all features except duration.

ample, a low-pass system would perform best for speech signals that were distinguishable on the basis of voicing and nasality.

A set of rules for developing an optimally distinguishable vocabulary for a given communication system would be rather complex and involved. There is, however, a very simple procedure for testing any given vocabulary. If the relative efficiencies of the system for the several features are known, we may know that some features will not be transmitted and cannot be used to distinguish two signals. Any two phonemes that differ only with respect to such missing features can be regarded as equivalent stimuli for the listener. Now suppose that we take any one of such a set of equivalent stimuli and use it wherever any of the set occurs; for example, if $|p|$, $|t|$, and $|k|$ are indistinguishable, we might use $|t|$ for all three. When all the speech signals are rewritten with $|t|$ wherever $|p|$, $|t|$, or $|k|$ occurred before and similar substitutions are made for all other sets of equivalent stimuli, the rewritten signals will approximate what the listener will hear. If we now alphabetize the rewritten signals, we will probably find some that are identical. These are the signals that will be confused and we can then take steps to eliminate such confusions.

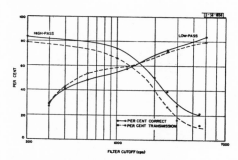

FIG. 6. Both the articulation score and relative information transmitted are plotted as a function of the frequency cutoff for both high-pass and low-pass filters. The crossover points are different for the two measures.

For example, if we look at Figs. 3 and 4 to see what happens when frequencies above 1000 cps are filtered out of the speech, we find that the features of place and duration are effectively absent and that voicing, nasality, and affrication are doing all the work. In other words, the filter has effectively deleted the last two columns in Table XIX. With those two columns gone there are really just five distinguishable phonemes left: $|ptk|$, $|f\theta s\int|$, $|bdg|$, $|v\eth z\math022|$, and $|mn|$. Replace these by, say, $|t|$, $|s|$, $|d|$, $|z|$, and $|n|$, respectively. Now when we rewrite the vocabulary of speech signals with just these five consonants instead of the original 16, we will discover which signals are transformed into indistinguishable forms by the filter. Insofar as possible, no two signals should be the same in their rewritten versions. The basic idea behind this procedure is that redundancy in the input signals will be most effective in reducing errors if we insure that frequent confusions do not transform one permissable signal into another permissable signal.

We have explored the validity of this substitution scheme for just those conditions described in the preceding example. Sentences and longer texts were rewritten with the indicated substitution of five for 16 phonemes. Such rewritten passages are appropriately called "elliptic" English, the ellipsis referring to the omission of two features, place and duration. With a little practice it was possible to speak the elliptic passages at normal rates and with normal intonation. Over a high quality communication system the elliptic speech was intelligible but sounded a little as though the talker had a marked dialect or speech defect. Then the low-pass filters were introduced. When all the frequencies above 1000 cps were removed (the conditions for which the substitutions were designed), the ellipsis could no longer be detected. Elliptic speech sounded just the same as normal speech under these conditions of distortion. A similar result was obtained with a masking noise at signal-to-noise ratios of about 0 db. The illusion is quite compelling and this demonstration that we could duplicate the effects of noise or distortion by deleting certain features of the speech increased our confidence in a multichannel model of speech perception.

An interesting sidelight on elliptic speech is provided by the art of ventriloquism. A ventriloquist talks without moving his lips. The consonants $|p|$, $|f|$, $|b|$, $|v|$, $|m|$, and $|w|$ are normally produced with lip movements and so pose a problem. A variety of solutions are possible; these sounds are avoided or omitted or produced out of the side of the mouth, or made in alternative ways (especially $|f|$ and $|v|$). In most of the older books on ventriloquism, however, a system of substitutions is proposed; $|k|$ for $|p|$, $|g|$ for $|b|$, and $|n|$ for $|m|$ are common suggestions. These substitutions should be especially satisfactory for the "voice in a box" trick, where the high frequencies should be attenuated in passing through the walls of the box and the confusion of sounds would be expected to occur naturally.

The place of articulation, which was hardest to hear correctly in our tests, is the easiest of the features to see on a talker's lips. The other features are hard to see but easy to hear. Lip reading, therefore, is a valuable skill for listeners who are partially deafened because it provides just the information that the noise or deafness removes.

31

Reprinted from Q. J. Exp. Psychol. **20**, Pt. 3:241–248 (Aug. 1968)

CHANNEL-CAPACITY, INTELLIGIBILITY AND IMMEDIATE MEMORY

PATRICK M. A. RABBITT*

From the Medical Research Council Applied Psychology Research Unit, Cambridge

When subjects try to remember lists of digits played to them through pulse-modulated white noise the number of errors they make is greater than would be expected if digit-recognition errors and immediate memory errors were independent (Exp. 1).

A second experiment compared recall of digits in early list positions, when digits in subsequent list positions were presented through noise, and in clear. Digits in early positions were less well remembered when digits in later list positions had to be discriminated through noise.

In a third experiment prose passages were played to subjects who subsequently answered questions about their factual content. Judged by this technique recall of the first half of a prose passage is less accurate if the second half must be heard through noise than if the entire passage is heard through a good fidelity system. These results together are interpreted as demonstrations that increased difficulty of recognition of speech through noise may interfere with other activities, (conveniently termed "rehearsal") which may be necessary to efficiently retain data in memory.

INTRODUCTION

Words transmitted through communications links, such as telephones, may be distorted by the characteristics of the system or partially masked by noise. It has been shown that there are at least two different ways in which noise or distortion can reduce the efficiency with which speakers can communicate with each other.

(1) The noise may make it impossible, or very difficult, to recognize all the words presented. This fact is obvious, and extremely well attested (Kryter, 1960). It is now possible to specify which bands of the frequency-intensity spectra convey the different kinds of information necessary in various semantic and syntactic contexts— and consequently to judge the extent to which the perception of the cues which are used to recognise words are modified by various kinds of masking or distortion (Webster and Klumpp, 1965).

(2) When masking or distortion is not sufficient to produce errors of recognition a listener may nevertheless have to make more effort to distinguish what is said to him. This may imply that a listener who can correctly report words presented over a degraded circuit may be less competent if he is required to simultaneously perform other unrelated tasks (Broadbent, 1958). In an information-theory framework we may suppose that in order to recognize degraded speech listeners have to use "spare channel capacity" which they could otherwise distribute between two tasks so as to maintain efficiency on both (Poulton, 1958; Brown, 1964).

Many experiments have shown that two unrelated tasks may compete to pre-empt a single channel of limited capacity (Poulton, 1958; Brown, 1964). It is less clear how such a model would operate in a case where one of two simultaneous tasks requires the subject to recognize words presented to him through noise, while the "secondary task" consists in remembering the words which are recognized, or in performing some conceptual transformations upon them. Such a task emphasises

*Now at Institute of Experimental Psychology, 1 South Parks Road, Oxford.

the logical difficulties in defining what a subject has achieved when he is said to have "recognized" a sequence of words.   Does he recognize the sense of the words in that he can supply synonyms for them?   Can he remember the words in the order in which they were presented?   Or can he simply mimic the sounds which he heard? If we assume that some, or all, of these may be empirically separable processes (Chistovitch, 1965) we can also enquire whether they compete for channel capacity in the same way as two or more simultaneously conducted perceptual-motor tasks.

Recent experiments (Posner and Rossman, 1965) suggest that items are maintained in immediate memory by some activity, conveniently termed "rehearsal," which requires part of the subject's channel-capacity.   Any activity intervening between the presentation of items to the subject and his subsequent reproduction of them is assumed to occupy channel capacity, inhibiting rehearsal and reducing the probability that items will be correctly recalled.   Posner and Rossman (1965) showed that interpolated secondary tasks of high information-load produced greater decrement in recall than low information-load tasks.   Variations in the information-load of signals may be expressed in terms of their mutual discriminability (Crossman, 1955; Laming, 1968).   The question therefore arises whether recognizing some words may not be regarded as a secondary task pre-empting channel-capacity required for the retention of other words—with the corollary that when recognition is made more difficult by noise, interference with rehearsal may be correspondingly greater.

Two experiments were made to determine whether items which are difficult to recognize are also less easy to remember.   Experiment 1 is a direct test for an interaction between reduced discriminability of presented items and the probability that they will be correctly recalled.   It was made to discover whether levels of noise which have little or no effect on performance when lists of digits have to be recognized and transcribed nevertheless significantly reduce the efficiency with which they can be stored and recalled.

EXPERIMENT I

Method

Forty lists of eight digits in random order without repeats were recorded by an experienced male speaker at the rate of 1 digit/sec. with 10 sec. pauses between successive lists.   In the experimental design these were considered as four successive groups of ten lists (A_1, A_2, B_1 and B_2).   The original tape was re-recorded through a simulated G.P.O. telephone-link incorporating a Modulated Noise Reference Unit (M.N.R.U.).   This latter device enables noise in the band 0 to 3.5 kc/s. to be added to the speech signal in such a manner that the intensity of the added noise is directly proportional to the instantaneous speech amplitudes.   The noise intensity therefore varies with the speech-signal, maintaining a constant signal-to-noise ratio.

The master list was re-recorded through this link four times to give the following paradigms where (N) indicates that digits were recorded with the M.N.R.U. set to give a 0dB. signal to noise ratio and (C) indicates that the M.N.R.U. was switched out of the link and that the list was recorded with the maximum fidelity which the system allowed.

(1) $A_1(N)$ $A_2(C)$ $B_1(N)$ $B_2(C)$;

(2) $A_1(N)$ $A_2(C)$ $B_1(C)$ $B_2(N)$;

(3) $A_1(C)$ $A_2(N)$ $B_1(N)$ $B_2(C)$;

(4) $A_1(C)$ $A_2(N)$ $B_1(C)$ $B_2(N)$;

Each of these tapes was played to two separate groups of 10 subjects.   One of these groups transcribed the A lists and remembered and reproduced the B lists while the other reversed the order of conditions.   The tape-recorder was stopped after every 10 lists, when the subjects were told whether the next 10 lists were to be read through noise or in clear.

348

Subjects

Subjects were 36 men and 44 women volunteers from the A.P.R.U. civilian panel. They were aged from 26 to 68 years (Mean = 47.2 years).

Results

Lists were scored correct only if all digits presented were reported in the correct order. The mean number of lists correctly reproduced in each Condition is set out in Table I.

TABLE I

MEAN NUMBER OF LISTS OF EIGHT DIGITS CORRECTLY REPRODUCED
EXPERIMENT I.

	Digits presented in clear	Digits presented in with OdB. signal to noise ratio
Transcription	10·00 ($\sigma = 0$)	9·64 ($\sigma = 0·48$)
Memory	4·02 ($\sigma = 3·9$)	2·84 ($\sigma = 4·2$)

Analysis of variance gave significant terms for Order ($p<0·01$) for differences between subjects ($p<0·01$) Transcription vs. Memory ($p<0·001$) and for Noise ($p<0·001$). The interaction term for Noise vs. Memory was significant ($p<0·01$).

Discussion

Lists of eight digits are less likely to be correctly recalled when they are presented through noise than when they are presented in clear. The significant Memory/Noise interaction discounts the simple hypothesis that the recall-errors for degraded digits represent the simple sum of the (estimated) recognition errors and of the recall errors when digits are presented in clear.

Two different explanations are possible. Lists of items are less well-remembered if they are acoustically confusable with each other than if they are acoustically distinct (Conrad, 1962, 1964; Wickelgren, 1965). (Digits presented through noise are acoustically less discriminable from each other than digits presented in clear—and may be less well-recalled for this reason alone.) The alternative hypothesis is the one which we wish to test. The process of recognizing digits through noise may pre-empt channel capacity necessary for their efficient retention in immediate memory storage.

The second hypothesis would be confirmed if the probability of recall of digits presented in clear were reduced when other digits, in the same list, were presented through noise. Such an effect could be either proactive or retroactive. Experiment 2 was therefore designed to test for both these possibilities.

EXPERIMENT 2

Method

Fifty-six lists, each containing eight different digits, were made up by selection from random number tables. Each list was recorded by a male speaker as two groups of four digits read at 1 digit/sec. with a 2 sec. pause between groups and a 10 sec. pause between lists. Subjects were instructed to listen to and to remember both groups of digits, but were only required to repeat one group. The group to be recalled was post-cued by the instruction "Group 1" or "Group 2" recorded 1·5 sec. after the end of each list.

The set of 56 lists was then re-recorded through the simulated G.P.O. telephone line and M.N.R.U. described for Experiment 1. The M.N.R.U. was either switched in (Noise) or out of link (Clear). Half-lists were recorded either through noise or in clear to give equal numbers (i.e. 14) with each of the four possible compositions Noise/Noise; Noise/Clear; Clear/Noise and Clear/Clear. Post-cuing instructions were so allocated that the subject was required to recall Group 1 and Group 2 seven times under each of these four conditions of list-composition. Eight conditions of presentation and recall could thus be compared. The order in which subjects experienced list-composition and cueing instructions was subjectively random. All subjects experienced the sequence of lists in the same order.

The set of 56 lists was presented to (89) subjects tested in groups of 11 to 21 people. Conditions were as described for Experiment 1.

Subjects

Subjects were 89 members of the A.P.R.U. civilian panel aged from 25 to 69 years (Mean = 45·3 years).

Results

Half-lists were scored correct if the four digits requested were reported in their correct order. The mean number of half-lists correctly reported in each of the eight presentation and recall conditions are set out in Table II.

TABLE II

Mean Number of Half-Lists of Digits Correctly Reproduced under Eight Conditions of Presentation and Recall

Experiment 2

	Recall of first group				Recall of second group			
	C/C	C/N	N/N	N/C	C/C	C/N	N/N	N/C
Mean No. of groups correctly recalled	4·53	4·14	3·54	4·44	6·10	5·67	5·91	6·31
σ	3·46	3·8	3·01	2·97	1·66	2·76	2·18	0·13

Analysis of variance gave significant terms for comparisons between presentations in Noise and in Clear ($p < 0.001$) and for recall of second half-lists as against first half-lists ($p < 0.001$). The term for differences between subjects was also significant ($p < 0.01$).

The interesting question was whether the recall of digits in one part of the list was affected if digits elsewhere in the list were presented through noise. This was examined by calculating S^2 from the residual term for the An.o.Va. in order to obtain a rank-order of significant differences for half-lists in each condition of presentation and recall. It appeared that first half-lists (whether presented in noise or in clear) were better recalled when the subsequent half-list was presented in clear than when it was presented in noise ($p < 0.01$). The opposite effect was not obtained, that is, recall of a second half-list was no better when the first half-list was presented in clear than when it was presented through noise.

Discussion

The first group of digits was better recalled if the second group was presented in Clear than if it was presented through Noise. There was no evidence that presentation of the first group through Noise affected recognition or retention of the second group. These results cannot be explained on the hypothesis that noise makes digits harder to remember only because it renders them acoustically less discriminable from each other. Consistent with these results is the hypothesis that rehearsal of the first group of digits is inhibited if the channel is pre-empted by the task of recognizing a second group through noise. There are theoretical (Crossman, 1955; Laming, 1968) and empirical (Rabbitt, 1963) reasons for supposing that human channel capacity can be defined (interchangeably) in terms of the number of items between which subjects may have to discriminate (information load) and the mutual discriminability of the items with which subjects are concerned. This result is therefore consistent with Posner and Rossman's (1965) evidence that the maintenance of items in immediate memory requires channel-capacity which may be pre-empted by secondary tasks in proportion to their information load. It further appears that the recognition of digits through noise constitutes such a "secondary" task, interfering with the retention of digits previously heard. Items presented through noise may be poorly remembered (Exp. 1) not only because they are incorrectly recognized, but because the difficulty of recognizing some items interferes with the retention of others (Exp. 2).

It is rare that the act of "communication" for which a speech-link is used simply involves an exchange of lists of words (Rabbitt, 1966) or of groups of digits (Exp. 1 and 2). The slow tempo of conversation and the considerable redundancy of language make it possible that under everyday circumstances the burden on a listener's information processing system would be low enough to allow him sufficient time (and so, implicitly, sufficient channel-capacity) to both understand and remember the content of continuous speech transmitted to him through low levels of noise. A more naturalistic experiment, therefore, would test whether recall of the content of connected discourse presented in clear is affected when, before recalling it, a listener is subsequently required to try to understand and remember speech presented to him through noise. An experiment was made to test this point.

EXPERIMENT 3

Apparatus and procedure

Two prose passages, 682 and 712 words long, were made up from the text of articles in back numbers of "Scientific American." These were then recorded on magnetic tape by a male speaker at approximately 120 words/min. The durations of the passages, as read, were 5 min. 8 sec. (Passage A) 5 min. 23 sec. (Passage B).

The master tape on which these passages were recorded was then re-recorded through a simulated G.P.O. telephone link and G.P.O. Modulated Noise Reference Unit (M.N.R.U.).

Each of the two passages was re-recorded once with the M.N.R.U. switched out of the circuit (No Noise Condition) and once with the M.N.R.U. switched out for the first half of the passage, and switched in for the second half at a setting which maintained the noise intensity 5 dB. below the intensity of the speech signal (Clear/Noise Condition). The halves of the passage were defined with respect to the sentence-ending nearest to the mid-point located by a word-count.

For each passage a list of 10 questions was made up to test the listener's recall of the material read to him. The first five questions could be answered only by reference to information presented in the first half of the passage. No information relevant to these questions was repeated in the second half of the passage. The second five questions similarly required information presented only in the second half of each passage.

Separate groups of 11 to 22 subjects each heard one of these passages recorded under one of these conditions (i.e. No Noise, or Clear/Noise). Passages were played to subjects on a "Ferrograph" 5A tape-recorder through a Phillips ZA 29431 external speaker system.

The Clear/Noise condition, when used, was described to the subjects in advance. The passage was then played. After the passage had ended subjects removed appropriate question sheets from envelopes and wrote down their answers to the questions. In this way 36 subjects heard passage A in the No Noise Condition and 36 heard passage A in the Clear/Noise Condition. Similarly two groups of 26 subjects each heard passage B under one of these conditions.

Subjects

The subjects were 124 members of the A.P.R.U. civilian subject panel.   Thirty-eight of these people were men and 86 were women.   Their ages ranged from 22 to 68 years (Mean = 42·6 years).   Fifty-two of these subjects had previously participated in experiments investigating long- and short-term memory.

Results

Questions were framed so that answers would be unambiguously correct or wrong; i.e. a single name, figure or binary (Yes/No) choice was required by each.   The scorer awarded 1 point for each correct answer, and 0 points for any other answer.   The mean scores made by subjects on the first and second halves of each passage in each condition are given in Table III below.

TABLE III

MEAN NUMBERS OF QUESTIONS CORRECTLY ANSWERED

EXPERIMENT 3

	N	*First half of passage*	*Second half of passage*
Passage A			
No Noise	36	2·1 ($\sigma = 1·7$)	3·2 ($\sigma = 1·9$)
Clear/Noise	36	1·7 ($\sigma = 1·4$)	2·5 ($\sigma = 1·6$)
Passage B			
No Noise..	26	1·8 ($\sigma = 1·6$)	2·6 ($\sigma = 1·5$)
Clear/Noise	26	1·2 ($\sigma = 1·1$)	2·4 ($\sigma = 1·8$)

Separate groups of subjects heard each of two passages under two conditions.   Scores represent the mean number of questions relating to first and second halves of passages correctly answered (max. possible 5 in each case).

For each passage scores on the first five questions obtained by the No Noise group were compared by a Mann-Whitney U-test against equivalent scores obtained by the Clear/Noise group.   For both passages, scores obtained by the No Noise group were significantly higher (Passage A, $p<0·05$ two-tailed and Passage B, $p<0·025$ two-tailed).   Recall scores for the second halves of the passages were also significantly higher for the No Noise groups than for the Clear/Noise groups ($p<0·01$. two-tailed, in each case).   These latter differences do not concern the present argument, since we cannot tell whether they mean that subjects did not correctly hear, or whether they could not remember the material presented to them.   There was no interaction between the success with which individual questions were answered, and the effects of noise.

Discussion

This experiment suggests a complex picture of the activity of a subject who attempts to remember a prose passage which is read aloud to him.   Attention to a continuous flow of new data reduces the opportunity for rehearsal of material already in store and renders its recall more uncertain.   A skilled listener must therefore, presumably, learn to divide his attention between the analysis of new information and the rehearsal of information in store.   In doing this he will be considerably aided by redundancy (either in stored material or in current input).   It is well known that the recall of prose passages has the character of a précis, in which certain salient details are related to each other in terms of the system of causal relationships which are most probable (and so redundant) in the context of the subject's life-experience (Bartlett, 1932). It is tempting, therefore, to say that the subject recognizes redundancy in prose passages, and does not tax his limited capacity by attempting to store redundant material verbatim, since he can reconstruct redundant connecting links from data in long-term memory storage ("schemata").

This usage conceals an assumption about the mechanism necessary to recognize and use redundancy. It may not be evident to a listener which details are "salient" and which "redundant" until much of a passage has been heard. Evidently a listener would operate most efficiently if he did not rehearse all the material presented to him, as it were by rote, but rather attempted selective rehearsal, editing material in storage both in terms of the new information which he continuously receives and in terms of other information which he may hold in long-term memory. Thus the "salient" and "redundant" features of a passage may be progressively distinguished and selectively rehearsed or forgotten as the episode progresses.

Such a process would evidently require an highly complex and carefully-timed selective shifting of attention between material currently being presented and material held in storage. It would be consistent with this model that any increase in the complexity of one of these interlocking and competing processes would reduce the efficiency with which the others can be carried on. In this context it is again evident that under conditions approximating to those encountered in everyday life levels of noise on speech-communications links which do not prevent listeners from hearing what is said to them may nevertheless prevent them from efficiently using the information which they receive.

Apart from these theoretical considerations the present results raise a clear practical issue. Intelligibility tests are again shown to provide very crude indices of the extent to which noise on speech communications links may limit the efficiency of the people who use them (Broadbent, 1958; Rabbitt, 1966). Communications links, such as telephones, are not simply used to transmit lists of words or phonemes but often to conduct complex transactions. Because such transactions make demands on memory storage and retrieval, any attenuation of these functions may represent a serious liability. In assessing the efficiency and comfort with which systems may be used it is evidently necessary to bear in mind that the effects of noise cannot be disregarded until a point is reached at which recognition errors occur. The present results suggest that even levels of noise which do not have measurable effects on intelligibility may nevertheless cause measurable decrements in the ability of listeners to carry out the transactions for which communications systems may be required.

REFERENCES

BARTLETT, F. C. (1932). *Remembering.* London: Cambridge University Press.

BROADBENT, D. E. (1958). *Perception and Communication.* London: Pergamon. Pp. 73–80.

BROWN, I. D. (1964). The measurement of perceptual load and reserve capacity. *Trans. Ass. industr, med. Offrs.* **14**, 44–9.

CHISTOVITCH, L. A. (1965). In CHISTOVITCH, L. A. and KOZHEVNIKOV, V. A. (Eds.). *Rech 'Artikulatsia i Vospriatie.* Moscow.

CONRAD, R. (1962). An association between memory errors and errors due to acoustic masking of speech. *Nature,* **193**, 1314–5.

CONRAD, R. (1964). Acoustic confusions in immediate memory. *Brit. J. Psychol.,* **55**, 75–84.

CROSSMAN, E. R. F. W. (1955). The measurement of discriminability. *Quart. J. exp. Psychol.,* **7**, 176–95.

KRYTER, K. D. (1960).   Human engineering principles for the design of speech communications systems.   *Operations Applications Office, Air Force Command and Control Development Centre, A.F.C.C.D.D. Tech. Report* 60.   27.

LAMING, D. R. J. (1968).   *Information Theory of Choice-Reaction Times*.   London: Academic Press.

POSNER, M. I., and ROSSMAN, E. (1965).   Effect of size and location of informational transforms upon short-term retention.   *J. exp. Psychol.*, **70**, 496–505.

POULTON, E. C. (1958).   Measuring the order of difficulty of visual-motor tasks.   *Ergonomics*, **1**, 234–9.

RABBITT, P. M. A. (1963).   Information load and discriminability.   *Nature*. **197**, 726.

RABBITT, P. M. A. (1966).   Recognition: memory for words correctly heard in noise.   *Psychon. Sci.*, **6**, 383–4.

WICKELGREN, W. A. (1965).   Acoustic similarity and intrusion errors in short-term memory.   *J. exp. Psychol.*, **70**, 102–8.

WEBSTER, J. C., and KLUMPP, R. C. (1965).   Speech interference aspects of Navy noises.   *Res. Develop. Rep. NEL/REP.* 1314.   *U.S. Navy Electronics Lab., San Diego, California.*

Part IX

APPLICATIONS TO SPEECH SYNTHESIS
AND ANALYSIS

Editor's Comments
on Papers 32, 33, and 34

32 CARPENTER and LAVINGTON
The Influence of Human Factors on the Performance of a Real-Time Speech Recognition System

33 OLSON, BELAR, and de SOBRINO
Demonstration of a Speech Processing System Consisting of a Speech Analyzer, Translator, Typer, and Synthesizer

34 VOIERS
Diagnostic Evaluation of Speech Intelligibility

To build devices that will speak and that will recognize speech long has been a goal of dreamers, magicians, and scientists. (These are not mutually exclusive categories.) The best way to test how well such devices produce intelligible sounds or discriminate among words and talkers is by intelligibility tests using the machine as the talker or the listener. This part concerns such uses of intelligibility tests. A companion Benchmark volume* is devoted to synthesis and synthesizers, so this part concentrates on the analyzers. The companion volume contains reproductions of several papers that otherwise would be candidates for reproduction in this part, and the bibliography for this part includes papers (indicated by ¶) that have been reproduced there. The reader is urged to consult Flanagan and Rabiner, for it is very complete and has been edited by two of the foremost authorities in the field.

Speech recognition devices can be categorized in several ways. The most primitive ones do not recognize words at all, but merely distinguish between speech and other kinds of signals such as noise and music. Intelligibility tests are not applied to them. Other devices recognize a few words, usually the ten digits, but "open sesame" is an earlier example. If they recognize this limited vocabulary from several talkers, they are quite accomplished indeed. Recognition of a medium sized vocabulary from a single speaker is about equally difficult, and recognition of such a vocabulary from a variety of speakers, male, female, and childish, is beyond the capability of present devices. Of course, word recogni-

* Flanagan, J. L., and L. R. Rabiner, *Speech Synthesis*, Dowden, Hutchinson & Ross, Stroudsburg, Pa. (1973).

tion implies somé sort of accuracy, and the acceptable accuracy depends on the application. Emerson's compensatory principle operates, because the smallest vocabularies—the digits or *up, down, right, left*—are used for applications which require the highest accuracy. Such instructions are already codes devised to expedite communications and are not tolerant of errors.

Most of the papers that report the greatest advances in recognizing speech are not the outstanding papers in the evaluation of the systems. The papers that have been chosen for reproduction here are outstanding in different ways. Paper 32 by Carpenter and Lavington is the only one to report quantitatively the relationships between the talkers' utterances and their knowledge of the machine's success in recognizing those utterances. The results the experimenters obtained may be familiar to travellers who find that repetition regularly reduces intelligibility in a foreign language whether the traveller is the talker or the listener. Paper 33 by Olson, Belar, and de Sobrino is unique because it describes a system that was intended to recognize a small vocabulary of business words in four languages, and for some of these words, to do all the functions commonly wanted in an ideal device, i.e., translation, transmission, typing, and reproduction as speech. The performance of the system was evaluated using speakers with different native languages. Paper 34 has been prepared especially for this volume to describe the features of an intelligibility test that has proved to be particularly useful in evaluating vocoders (Voiers, 1968) and other synthesis-analysis equipment.

The editor could not hope to summarize the progress in speech analysis and recognition or even the literature on speech synthesis that has appeared since the publication of Flanagan and Rabiner. The bibliography does list most of the more important papers in archival journals. Lindgren (1965), Marill (1961), and Simmons (1961) are all good summaries up to their dates of publication, but much has been learned since then. The reader is urged to consult the papers of Atal (1970), Bezdel (1969, 1970), De Mori (1970, 1971), Denes (1960), Dixon (1968), Dudley (1958), Fant (1959), Gudonavichyus (1974), Haton [1972 (2)], Hill (1972), Itahashi (1973), Miller (1970), Pierce (1969), Pols (1971), Ruske (1971), Sakai (1960, 1963), Teacher (1967), Velichko (1970), and the special issue of the *IEEE Transactions on Acoustics, Speech, and Signal Processing* in 1975.

BIBLIOGRAPHY

Anke, D., and P. Hoeschelle, "Einfache Erkennungsgeräte für die gesprochenen Zahlen Null bis Neun," *Kybernetik* **4**:228–234 (1968).

¶ Atal, B. S., and S. L. Hanauer, "Speech Analysis and Synthesis by Linear Prediction of the Speech Wave," *J. Acoust. Soc. Am.* **50**:637–655 (1971).

Atal, B. S., and L. R. Rabiner, "A Pattern Recognition Approach to Voiced-Unvoiced-Silence Classification with Applications to Speech Recognition," *IEEE Trans. Acoust. Speech Sig. Proc.* **ASSP-24**:201–212 (1976).

Atal, B. S., and M. R. Schroeder, "Adaptive Predictive Coding of Speech Signals," *Bell Syst. Tech. J.* **49**:1973–1986 (1970).

Backhausen, W. J., "Automatische Spracherkennung als Dekodierung der phonetischen Information?" *Phonetica* **25**:27–52 (1952).

Baker, J. K., "The DRAGON System—An Overview," *IEEE Trans. Acoust. Speech Sig. Proc.* **ASSP-23**:24–29 (1975).

Barik, H. C., "Some Innovations in a Computer Approach to the Analysis of Speech Patterns," *Lang. and Speech* **15**:196–207 (1972).

Becker, R. W., and F. Poza, "Acoustic Phonetic Research in Speech Understanding," *IEEE Trans. Acoust. Speech Sig. Proc.* **ASSP-23**:416–426 (1975).

Berger-Vachon, C., and G. Mesnard, "Les méthode sequentielles de décision appliquées à la reconnaissance de la parole," *Automatisme* **19**:96–100 (1974).

Bezdel, W., "Some Problems in Man-Machine Communication Using Speech," *Int. J. Man-Mach. Stud.* **2**:157–168 (1970).

Bezdel, W., and J. S. Bridle, "Speech Recognition Using Zero-Crossing Measurements and Sequence Information," *Proc. Inst. Electr. Eng.* **116**:617–623 (1969).

Bezdel, W., and B. A. Chandler, "Results of an Analysis and Recognition of Vowels by Computer Using Zero-Crossing Data, *Proc. Inst. Electr. Eng.* **112**:2060–2066 (1965).

Broad, D. J., "Basic Directions in Automatic Speech Recognition," *Int. J. Man-Mach. Stud.* **4**:105–118 (1972).

Burghardt, H., and H. Hess, "Statistische Untersuchungen der Null-durchgangs—und Extremwert Intervalle zur Unterscheidung von Vokalen," *NTZ-Nachrichtentech. Z.* **24**:389–393 (1971).

Buron, R., "Le traitement de la parole et les ordinateurs," *Rev. Acoust.* **1**:187–190 (1968).

Calavrytinos, P., and M. R. Schroeder, "Sprecherunabhängige Worterkennung ohne Segmentierung," *Acustica* **36**:184–191 (1976).

Cherry, C., *On Human Communication: A Review, a Survey, and a Criticism,* 2nd ed., M.I.T., Cambridge, Mass. (1966).

Christiansen, H. M., L. Schweizer, A. Séthy, and F. Hoffenreich, "New Correlation Vocoder," *J. Acoust. Soc. Am.* **40**:614–620 (1966).

¶ Cooper, F. S., P. C. Delattre, A. M. Liberman, J. M. Borst, and L. J. Gerstman, "Some Experiments on the Perception of Synthetic Speech Sounds," *J. Acoust. Soc. Am.* **24**:597–606 (1952).

Cooper, W. E., "Adaption of Phonetic Feature Analyzers for Place of Articulation," *J. Acoust. Soc. Am.* **56**:617–627 (1974).

David, E. E., Jr., "Artificial Auditory Recognition in Telephony," *IBM J. Res. Dev.* **2**:294–309 (Oct. 1958).

Davis, K. H., R. Biddulph, and S. Balashek, "Automatic Recognition of Spoken Digits," *J. Acoust. Soc. Am.* **24**:637–642 (1952).

De Mori, R., "Speech Analysis and Recognition by Computer Using Zero-Crossing Information," *Acustica* **25**:269–279 (1971).

De Mori, R., "Experiments in the Automatic Segmentation of Continuous Speech," *Acustica* **34**:158–166 (1976).

De Mori, R., L. Gilli, and A. R. Meo, "A Flexible Real-Time Recognizer of Spoken Words for Man-Machine Communication," *Int. J. Man-Mach. Stud.* **2**:317–326 (1970).

Denes, P., "The Design and Operation of the Mechanical Speech Recognizer at University College, London," *J. Brit. Inst. Radio Eng.* **19**:219–230 (1959).

Denes, P., "Theoretical Aspects of Mechanical Speech Recognition," *J. Brit. Inst. Radio Eng.* **19**:211–218 (1959).

Denes, P., and M. V. Mathews, "Spoken Digit Recognition Using Time-Frequency Pattern Matching," *J. Acoust. Soc. Am.* **32**:1450–1455 (1960).

Dixon, N. R., and H. D. Maxey, "Terminal Analog Synthesis of Continuous Speech Using the Diphone Method of Segment Assembly," *IEEE Trans. Audio Electroacoust.* **AU-16**:40–50 (1968).

Dolyatovskii, V. A., "Organization and Simulation of an Acoustic Analyzer," trans. from *Modelirovaniye v Biologii i Meditsine* **2**:72–84 (1966) as Joint Publ. Res. Serv. No. 46275 (23 Aug. 1968).

Dudley, H., "Phonetic Pattern Recognition Vocoder for Narrow-Band Speech Transmission," *J. Acoust. Soc. Am.* **30**:733–739 (1958).

Dudley, H., and S. Balashek, "Automatic Recognition of Phonetic Patterns in Speech," *J. Acoust. Soc. Am.* **30**:721–732 (1958).

¶ Dudley, H., R. R. Riesz, and S. S. A. Watkins, "A Synthetic Speaker," *J. Franklin Ins.* **227**:739–764 (1939).

¶ Dunn, H. K., "The Calculation of Vowel Resonances and an Electrical Vocal Tract," *J. Acoust. Soc. Am.* **22**:740–753 (1950).

Dunn, H. K., and H. L. Barney, "Artificial Speech in Phonetics and Communications," *J. Speech Hear. Res.* **1**:23–39 (1958).

Erman, L. D., and D. R. Reddy, "Implications of Telephone Input for Automatic Speech Recognition," in *Proc. 7th Int. Cong. Acoust.*, Akadémiai Kiadó, Budapest (1971), **3**, pp. 85–88.

Fant, G., "Acoustic Analysis and Synthesis of Speech with Applications to Swedish," *Ericsson Tech.* **15**:3–108 (1959).

Fatehchand, R., "Machine Recognition of Spoken Words," in *Advances in Computers*, F. L. Alt, ed., Academic Press, New York (1960), vol. 1, pp. 193–229.

Favella, L. F., M. Reineri, and G. U. Righini, "On a Mathematical Procedure for Detecting Significant Parameters in the Classification of a Statistical Ensemble of Phonemes and Its Applications," *Kybernetik* **5**:187–194 (1969).

Fievet, F., A. Maissis, and P. Walrave, "La reconnaissance en temps réel de la parole," *Automatisme* **15**:3–11, 70–77 (1970).

Fischer-Jørgensen, E., "The Phonetic Basis for Identification of Phonemic Elements," *J. Acoust. Soc. Am.* **24**:611–617 (1952).

Flanagan, J. L., "Band Width and Channel Capacity Necessary to Transmit the Formant Information of Speech," *J. Acoust. Soc. Am.* **28**:592–596 (1956).

Flanagan, J. L., *Speech Analysis, Synthesis, and Perception*, 2nd ed., Springer-Verlag, Heidelberg (1972).

¶ Flanagan, J. L., C. H. Coker, L. R. Rabiner, R. W. Schafer, and N. Umeda, "Synthetic Voices for Computers," *IEEE Spectrum* **7**:22–45 (Oct. 1970).

Flanagan, J. L., and A. S. House, "Development and Testing of a Formant-Coding Speech Compression System," *J. Acoust. Soc. Am.* **28**:1099–1106 (1956).

Flanagan, J. L., and L. R. Rabiner, *Speech Synthesis*, Dowden, Hutchinson & Ross, Stroudsburg, Pa. (1973).

Forgie, J. W., and C. D. Forgie, "Results Obtained from a Vowel Recognition Computer Program," *J. Acoust. Soc. Am.* **31**:1480–1489 (1959).

Fry, D. B., "Theoretical Aspects of Mechanical Speech Recognition," *J. Brit. Inst. Radio Eng.* **19**:211–218 (1959).

Fry, D. B., and P. Denes, "Experiments in Mechanical Speech Recognition," in *Information Theory, 3rd London Symposium*, C. Cherry, ed., Butterworths, London (1956), pp. 206–212.

Fry, D. B., and P. B. Denes, "The Solution of Some Fundamental Problems in Mechanical Speech Recognition," *Lang. and Speech* **1**:35–58 (1958).

Fujimura, O., "Syllable as a Unit of Speech Recognition," *IEEE Trans. Acoust. Speech Sig. Proc.* **ASSP-23**:82–87 (1975).

Fujisaki, H., et al., "Automatic Recognition of Connected Vowels Using a Functional Model of the Coarticulatory Process," (L) *J. Acoust. Soc. Japan* **29**:636–638 (1973).

Fujisaki, H., and O. Kunisaki, "Analysis and Recognition of Voiceless Fricative Consonants in Japanese, (L) *J. Acoust. Soc. Japan* **31**:741–742 (1975).

Fujisaki, H., N. Nakamura, and K. Yoshimune, "Analysis, Nominalization, and Recognition of Sustained Japanese Vowels," (L) *J. Acoust. Soc. Japan* **26**:152–154 (1970).

Fujisaki, H., Y. Sato, Y. Noguchi, and T. Yamakura, "Automatic Recognition of Semivowels in Spoken Words," (L) *J. Acoust. Soc. Japan* **31**:696–697 (1975).

Furui, S., F. Itakura, and S. Saito, "Talker Recognition by Longtime Averaged Speech Spectrum," *Electron. Commun. Jap.* **55**:54–61 (Oct. 1972).

Gilli, L., and A. R. Meo, "Sequential System for Recognizing Spoken Digits in Real Time," *Acustica* **19**:38–48 (1967–1968).

Gudonavichyus, R. V., A. M. Zaezdnyi, and A. B. Chitavichyus, "Automatic Recognition of Words in a Finite Set by Their Structural Connections with Implicit Time," *Sov. Phys.—Acoust.* **19**:529–532 (1974).

Guelke, R. W., "Transmission of Information by Means of Speech," *Proc. Inst. Radio Electron. Eng. Aust.* **26**:192–197 (1965).

Halle, M., and K. N. Stevens, "Speech Recognition: A Model and a Program for Research," *IRE Trans. Inf. Theory* **IT-8**:155–159 (1962).

Halsey, R. J., and J. Swaffield, "Analysis-Synthesis Telephony, with Special Reference to the Vocoder," *J. Inst. Electr. Eng.* **95 III**:391–406, disc. 406–411 (1948).

Harris, C. M., "A Speech Synthesizer," *J. Acoust. Soc. Am.* **25**:970–975 (1953).

¶ Harris, C. M., "A Study of the Building Blocks in Speech," *J. Acoust. Soc. Am.* **25**:962–969 (1953).

Haton, J. -P., "Reconnaissance de la parole, bilan de vingt années de recherches et tendances actuelles," *Ann. Télécommun.* **27**:77–88 (1972).

Haton, J. -P., "A Practical Application of A Real-Time Isolated-Word Recognition System Using Syntactic Constraints," *IEEE Trans. Acoust. Speech Sig. Proc.* **ASSP-22**:416–419 (1974).

Haton, J. -P., and M. Lamotte, "Extraction de paramètres et compression de l'information: application à la reconnaissance de la parole," *C.R. Acad. Sci. Paris* **A273**:415–418 (1971).

Haton, J. -P., and M. Lamotte, "Prétraitement et reconnaissance de la parole. Simulation et réalisations practiques," *Automatisme* **17**:63–64 (1972).

Hess, W. J., "A Pitch-Synchronous Digital Feature Extraction System for Phonemic Recognition of Speech," *IEEE Trans. Acoust. Speech Sig. Proc.* **ASSP-24**:14–25 (1976).

Hill, D. R., "Man-Machine Interaction Using Speech," in *Advances in Computers*, F. L. Alt and M. Rubinoff, eds., Academic Press, New York (1971) vol. 11, pp. 166–230.

Hill, D. R., "An Abbreviated Guide to Planning for Speech Interaction with Machines: The State of the Art," *Int. J. Man-Mach. Stud.* **4**:383–410 (1972).

Hillix, W. A., "Use of Two Nonacoustic Measures in Computer Recognition of Spoken Digits," *J. Acoust. Soc. Am.* **35**:1978–1984 (1963).

Hillix, W. A., M. N. Fry, and R. L. Hershman, "Computer Recognition of Spoken Digits Based on Six Nonacoustic Measures," *J. Acoust. Soc. Am.* **38**:790–796 (1965).

Hinrichs, O., and J. Gonschorek, "Ein Spracherkennungsgerät mit selbsttätiger Anpassung an Sprechgeschwindigkeit," *NTZ-Nachrichtentech. Z.* **24**:177–182 (1971).

Hiramatsu, K., "Zero-Crossing Information of S.S.B. Speech Signal," *J. Acoust. Soc. Japan* **18**:301–309 (1962), in Japanese, abstract in English.

Hiramatsu, K., and Y. Kumakawa, "Speech Band Compression System Using S.S.B.-Clipping-Formac," *J. Acoust. Soc. Japan* **18**:310–319 (1962). in Japanese, abstract in English.

¶ Holmes, J. N., I. G. Mattingly, and J. N. Shearme, "Speech Synthesis by Rule," *Lang. and Speech* **7**:127–143 (1964).

Howard, C. R., H. J. Manley, and J. C. Stoddard, "A Comparison of Two Types of Digitalized Autocorrelation Vocoders," *J. Aud. Eng. Soc.* **15**:404–406 (1967).

Hyde, S. R., "Recognition of Speech by Machine," *Post Office Electr. Eng. J.* **62**:100–104 (1969).

Ichikawa, A., Y. Nakano, and K. Nakata, "Evaluation of Various Parameter Sets in Spoken Digits Recognition," *IEEE Trans. Audo Electroacoust.* **AU-21**:202–209 (1973).

Ichikawa, A., Y. Nakano, and K. Nakata, "Improvement of Spoken Digit Recognition Using Partial Autocorrelation Functions," *J. Acoust. Soc. Japan* **29**:410–417 (1973). in Japanese, abstract in English.

Itahashi, S., and K. Kido, "Speech Recognition—Spoken Word Recognition Using Dictionary and Phonological Rule," *J. Acoust. Soc. Japan* **27**:473–482 (1971). in Japanese, abstract in English.

Itahashi, S., S. Makino, and K. Kido, "Discrete-Word Recognition Using a Word Dictionary and Phonological Rules," *IEEE Trans. Audio Electroacoust.* **AU-21**:239–248 (1973).

Itahashi, S., H. Suzuki, and K. Kido, "Discrimination of Some Consonants in Words with the Aid of a Dictionary," *Electron. Commun. Japan* **54**:107–114 (Jan. 1971).

Itakura, F., and S. Saito, "Speech Information Compression Based on the Maximum Likelihood Spectral Estimation," *J. Acoust. Soc. Japan* **27**:463–472 (1971). in Japanese, abstract in English.

Jassem, W., ed., *Speech Analysis and Synthesis*, Pánstwowe Wydawn Naukowe, Warsaw (1968).

Jelinek, F., "Continuous Speech Recognition by Statistical Methods," *Proc. IEEE* **64**:532–556 (1976).

Kanamori, Y., Y. Shigeno, and K. Kido, "Psychological Auditory Description of Formant Frequency and Vowel Recognition," (L) *J. Acoust. Soc. Japan* **31**:96–97 (1975).

Keller, T. G. von, "Die Kennzeichnung von Sprachlauten durch Spektrum, Autokorrelationfunktion und Nulldurchgangsabstände," *NTZ-Nachrichtentech. Z.* **20**:287–295 (1967).

Keller, T. G. von, "An On-Line Recognition System for Spoken Digits," *J. Acoust. Soc. Am.* **49**:1288–1296 (1971).

King, J. H., Jr., and C. J. Tunis, "Some Experiments in Spoken Word Recognition," *IBM J. Res. Dev.* **10**:65–79 (1966).

Kirillov, N., and L. Fatkin, "Experiments in the Recognition of Speech Sounds by Machines," *Vopr. Psikhol.* **3**:45–56 (1962). in Russian.

Klatt, D. H., and K. N. Stevens, "On the Automatic Recognition of Continuous Speech: Implications from a Spectrogram-Reading Experiment," *IEEE Trans. Audio Electroacoust.* **AU-21**:210–216 (1973).

Koenig, W., H. K. Dunn, and L. Y. Lacy, "The Sound Spectrograph," *J. Acoust. Soc. Am.* **18**:19–49 (1946).

Kozhevnikov, V., and L. Chistovich, eds., *Rech', Artikulyatsiya i Vospriyatiye*, Izdatel'stvo Nauka, Moskow (1965), trans. as *Speech: Articulation and Perception*, Joint Publ. Res. Ser. No. 30543, Washington (10 June 1965).

Kulya, V. I., "Influence on Speech Perception of Phase Relations in Its Spectrum," *Tellecommun. Radio Eng.* **24**:46–52 (July 1970).

Kusch, H., "Automatic Recognition of Spoken Numbers (Digits)," *NTZ-Commun. J.* **4**:201–206 (1965).

Lavington, S. H., "Computer Simulation of a Speech-Recognition System," *Inst. Electr. Eng. Proc.* **116**:1053–1059 (1969).

Lavington, S. H., and L. E. Rosenthal, "Some Facilities for Speech Processing by Computer," *Comput. J.* **9**:330–339 (1967).

Lea, W. A., "Towards Versatile Speech Communication with Computers," *Int. J. Man-Mach. Stud.* **2**:107–155 (1970).

Lesser, V. R., et al., "Organization of Hearsay II Speech Understanding System," *IEEE Trans. Acoust. Speech Sig. Proc.* **ASSP-23**:11–24 (1975).

Lindgren, N., "Automatic Speech Recognition," *IEEE Spectrum* **2**:114–136 (Mar. 1965) and 44–59 (Apr. 1965).

Makhoul, J., "Speaker Adaption in a Limited Speech Recognition System," *IEEE Trans. Comput.* **C-20**:1057–1063 (1971).

Mangold, H., "Untersuchungen zur automatische Erkennung isolierter Befehlwörter in erhöhtem Störpegel," *NTZ-Nachrichtentech. Z.* **27**:105–108 (1974).

Marrill, T., "Automatic Recognition of Speech," *IEEE Trans. Hum. Factors Electron.* **HFE-2**:34–38 (1961).

Martin, T. B., "Practical Applications of Voice Input to Machines," *Proc. IEEE* **64**:487–501 (1976).

Meinhardt, J., "Beitrag zur Frage der Redundanzausnüzung bei der automatischen Spracherkennung," *Ilmenau. Tech. Hochsch. Wiss. Z.* **13**:135–138 (1967).

Meo, A. R., and G. Righini, "Riconoscitore instantaneo di suoni vocalici," *Alta Freq.* **34**:256–263 (1965).

Mercier, G., "Approximation stochastique et reconnaissance acoustique d'un vocabulaire limité," *Ann. Télécommun.* **25**:207–216 (1970).

Mercier, G., "Segmentation de la parole et reconnaissance des syllables à l'intérieur des mots," *Automatisme* **17**:69–75 (1972).

Miller, J. C., P. W. Ross, and C. M. Wine, "An Adaptive Speech Recognition System Operating in a Remote Time-Sharing Computer Environment," *IEEE Trans. Audio Electroacoust.* **AU-18**:26–32 (1970).

Myasnikova, E. N., *Ob'yektivnoye Raspoznavaniye Zvukov Rechi*, Energiya, Leningrad (1967), trans. as *Objective Recognition of Speech Sounds*, Joint Publ. Res. Serv. No. 43926, Washington (9 Jan. 1968).

Nagata, K., Y. Kato, and S. Chiba, "Spoken Digit Recognizer for the Japanese Language," *J. Aud. Eng. Soc.* **12**:336–342 (1964).

Nakata, K. "Automatic Recognition of Speech," *Electron. Commun. Japan* **46**:148–157 (Nov. 1963).

Neely, R. B., and D. R. Reddy, "Speech Recognition in the Presence of Noise," in *Proc. 7th Int. Cong. Acoust.* Akadémiai Kiadó, Budapest (1971), **3**, pp. 177–180.

Newell, A., et al., *Speech Understanding Systems: Final Report of a Study Group*, North Holland, Amsterdam (1973).

Olive, J. P., "Fundamental Frequency Rules for the Synthesis of Simple Declarative Sentences," *J. Acoust. Soc. Am.* **57**:476–482 (1975).

Olson, H. F., and H. Belar, "Phonetic Typewriter," *J. Acoust. Soc. Am.* **28**:1072–1081 (1956).

Olson, H. F., and H. Belar, "Phonetic Typewriter III," *J. Acoust. Soc. Am.* **33**:1610–1615 (1961).

Olson, H. F., H. Belar, and E. S. Rogers, "Speech Processing Techniques and Applications," *IEEE Trans. Audio Electroacoust.* **AU-15**:120–126 (1967).

Otten, K. W., "Approaches to the Machine Recognition of Conversational Speech," in *Advances in Computers*, F. L. Alt and M. Rubinoff, eds., Academic Press, New York (1971), vol. 11, pp. 127–165.

Pierce, J. R., "Whither Speech Recognition?" (L) *J. Acoust. Soc. Am.* **46**:1049–1051 (1969).

Pols, L. C. W., "Real-Time Recognition of Spoken Words," *IEEE Trans. Comput.* **C-20**:972–978 ' (1971).

Rabiner, L. R., and M. R. Sambur, "Some Preliminary Experiments in the Recognition of Connected Digits," *IEEE Trans. Acoust. Speech Sig. Proc.* **ASSP-24**:170–182 (1976).

¶ Rabiner, L. R., R. W. Schafer, and J. L. Flanagan, "Computer Synthesis of Speech by Concatenation and Format-Coded Words," *Bell Syst. Tech. J.* **50**:1541–1558 (1971).

Reddy, D. R., "Phoneme Grouping for Speech Recognition," *J. Acoust. Soc. Am.* **41**:1295–1300 (1967).

Reddy, D. R., "Speech Recognition by Machine: A Review," *Proc. IEEE* **64**:501–531 (1976).

Ross, P. W., "A Limited-Vocabulary Adaptive Speech-Recognition System," *J. Aud. Eng. Soc.* **15**:414–419 (1967).

Rothauser, E., "Automatische Spracherkennung," *NTZ-Nachrichtentech. Z.* **20**:381–384 (1967).

Ruske, G., E. Paulus, R. Schrag, and T. Schotolo, "Die Wirksamkeit spektraler Merkmale bei der automatischen Erkennung gesprochener deutscher Konsonanten," *Acustica* **25**:220–232 (1971).

Sakai, T., and S. Doshita, "The Automatic Speech Recognition System for Conversational Sound," *IEEE Trans. Electron. Comput.* **12**:835–846 (1963).

Sakai, T., S. Doshita, Y. Niimi, and K. Tabata, "Fundamental Studies of Speech Analysis and Synthesis," *Amer. Ann. Deaf* **113**:156–167 (1968).

Sakai, T., and S. Inoue, "New Instruments and Methods for Speech Analysis," *J. Acoust. Soc. Am.* **32**:441–450 (1960).

Sakoe, H., and S. Chiba, "A Dynamic Programming Approach to Continuous Speech Recognition," in *Proc. 7th Int. Cong. Acoust.* Akadémiai Kiadó, Budapest (1971), **3**, pp. 65–68.

Scarr, R. W. A., "Normalization and Adaption of Speech Data for Automatic Speech Recognition," *Int. J. Man-Mach. Stud.* **2**:41–59 (1970).

Scarr, R. W. A., "Word Recognition Machine," *Proc. Inst. Electr. Eng.* **117**:203–212 (1970).

Scholes, R. J., "Phonemic Categorization of Synthetic Vocalic Stimuli by Speakers of Japanese, Spanish, Persian, and American English, *Lang. and Speech* **10**:46–68 (1967).

Schroeder, M., "Vocoders: Analysis and Synthesis,of Speech," *Proc. IEEE* **54**:720–734 (1966).

Shearme, J. N., and P. F. Leach, "Some Experiments with a Simple Word Recognition System," *IEEE Trans. Audio Electroacoust.* **AU-16**:256–261 (1968).

Shigenaga, M., and H. Ariizumi, "Automatic Recognition of Spoken Consonants," *J. Acoust. Soc. Japan* **21**:263–271 (1965). in Japanese, abstract in English.

Sholtz, P. N., and R. Bakis, "Spoken Digit Recognition Using Vowel-Consonant Segmentation," *J. Acoust. Soc. Am.* **34**:1–5 (1962).

Simmons, P. L., "Automation of Speech, Speech Synthesis and Synthetic Speech, a Bibliographical Survey from 1950–1960," *IRE Trans. Audio* **AU-9**:191–196 (1961).

Spogen, L. R., H. N. Shaver, D. E. Baker, and B. V. Blom, "Speech Processing by the Selective Amplitude Sampling System," *J. Acoust. Soc. Am.* **32**:1621–1625 (1960).

Spreen, O., J. Borkowski, and A. Benton, "Auditory Word Recognition as a Function of Meaningfulness, Abstractness, and Phonetic Structure," *J. Verbal Learn. Verbal Behav.* **6**:101–104 (1967).

Steinberg, J. C., and N. R. French, "The Portrayal of Visible Speech," *J. Acoust. Soc. Am.* **18**:4–18 (1946).

Steinbuch, K., "Automatische Spracherkennung," *NTZ-Nachrichtentech. Z.* **11**:446–454 (1958).

¶ Stevens, K. N., and A. S. House, "Development of a Quantitative Description of Vowel Articulation," *J. Acoust. Soc. Am.* **27**:484–493 (1955).

¶ Stevens, K. N., S. Kasowski, and C. G. M. Fant, "An Electrical Analogue of the Vocal Tract," *J. Acoust. Soc. Am.* **25**:734–742 (1953).

Suzuki, J., and M. Nakatsui, "Preliminaries to the Recognition of Japanese Conversational Speech," *J. Radio Res. Lab.* **12**:15–38 (Jan. 1965).

Teacher, C. F., H. G. Kellett, and L. R. Focht, "Experimental, Limited Vocabulary, Speech Recognizer," *IEEE Trans. Audio Electroacoust.* **AU-15**:127–130 (1967).

Terhardt, E., "Beitrag zur automatische Erkennung gesprochener Zahlen," *Kybernetik* **3**:136–143 (1966).

Tillman, H. G., "Automatische Identifikation von Sprechern. I u.II Teil," *NTZ-Nachrichtentech. Z.* **20**:706–708, 709–713 (1967).

Twaddell, W. F., "Phonemes and Allophones in Speech Analysis," *J. Acoust. Soc. Am.* **24**:607–611 (1952).

Velichko, V. M., and N. G. Zagoruyko, "Automatic Recognition of 200 Words," *Int. J. Man-Mach. Stud.* **2**:223–234 (1970).

Voiers, W. D., "The Present State of Digital Vocoding Technique: A Diagnostic Evaluation," *IEEE Trans. Audio Electroacoust.* **AU-16**:275–279 (1968).

Walker, D. E., "The SRI Speech Understanding System," *IEEE Trans. Acoust. Speech Sig. Proc.* **ASSP-23**:397–416 (1975).

Warns, O., "Die Verständlichkeit synthetischer Sprache," *Frequenz* **11**:169–175 (June 1957).

Washizawa, S., et al., "A Spoken-Digit Recognition Scheme and Its Computer Simulation," in *Rep. of 6th Int. Cong. Acoust.*, Y. Kohasi, ed., Maruzen, Tokyo (1968), pp. B135–B138.

White, G. M., and R. B. Neely, "Speech Recognition Experiments with Linear Prediction, Bandpass Filtering, and Dynamic Programming," *IEEE Trans. Acoust. Speech Sig. Proc.* **ASSP-24**:183–188 (1976).

Winckel, F., "Analyse and Synthese der Sprachlaute," *Funk und Ton* **8**:50–54, 99–102 (1954).

Woods, W. A., "Motivation and Overview of SPEECHLIS: An Experimental Sig. Proc. **ASSP-23**:2–10 (1975).

Zagoruyko, N. G., and G. Y. Voloshina, "Auditory Pattern Recognition," in *Raspoznavaniye Slukhouykh Obrazov*, N. G. Zagoruyko and G. Y. Voloshina, eds., Nauka, Novosibirsk (1969), trans. in Joint Publ. Res. Serv. No. 53606, Washington (15 July 1971).

Zwicker, E., W. Hess, and E. Terhardt, "Erkennung gesprochener Zahlworte mit Funktionsmodell und elektronischer Rechenanlage," *Kybernetic* **3**:267–272 (1967).

32

Reprinted from *Acoust. Soc. Am. J.* **53**(1):42–45 (1973)

The influence of human factors on the performance of a real-time speech recognition system

B. E. CARPENTER AND S. H. LAVINGTON

Department of Computer Science, The University, Manchester M13 9PL, England

(Received 20 January 1971; revised 24 August 1971)

The performance of real-time speech recognition systems is observed to depend upon the environments in which they are used. Human factors, caused for example by operator frustration, significantly affect success rates. A set of experiments with a word recognition system is described which quantifies this change, whilst the system is being used to control the movement of a displayed cross on a screen.
SUBJECT CLASSIFICATION: 9.10.

INTRODUCTION

Although some recent word recognition devices have demonstrated high success rates while giving real-time operation,[1,2] no systems are known which can maintain their performance in a practical application. This is due in part to their inability to make allowance for human factors, which become noticeable in live situations such as voice-control environments. There is a need to quantify the performance degradation due to these human factors. In order to collect relevant data, a real-time word recognition system is required which operates in an on-line control situation, with some kind of feedback to the operator. A means is needed for recording comprehensive measurements throughout an experimental run extending to several tens of words, and it would be advantageous if the speech recognition strategy were capable of easy modification to facilitate the testing of hypotheses.

An experimental system which approximates the above requirements has been set up using a PDP-8 computer, in conjunction with some speech-processing hardware. The hardware extracts three simple parameters from the speech waveform, namely, envelope amplitude, rate of zero-axis crossings, and rate of occurrence of points of zero time derivative. All parameters are measured over 10-msec intervals. Their relation to acoustic features has been discussed elsewhere.[3,4] These three simple parameters permit good word segmentation to be achieved, but sound classification is sometimes unreliable. Thus, a 12-word vocabulary yields recognition scores of typically 83%. However, the system is simple enough to permit comprehensive analysis of its performance and, in addition, is easily modifiable. The fact that recognition scores are less than ideal is not necessarily disadvanta-geous, since the *relative* influence of human factors is being studied, and also since operator frustration is itself one of the effects of interest. An assessment of recognition strategy is not the main theme of this report; further discussion may be found in Ref. 4.

I. EXPERIMENT METHOD

For experiments on human factors, the above word recognition system was used with a five-word command vocabulary consisting of "up," "down," "left," "right," "stop." Recognition of a word was made to cause movement of a small cross displayed on a cathode-ray tube attached to the PDP-8 computer. "Right" and "left" cause horizontal movement at a steady speed, and "up" and "down" produce vertical movement. Diagonals may be traced by combining horizontal and vertical movements. Thus, a speaker may control the position of the cross by voice, and there is rapid visual feedback of the recognition program's response to each utterance. During an experimental run, the recognition program was made to preserve on a 32K disk backing store a record of each spoken word, consisting of (a) its time of occurrence relative to the start of the run; (b) the decision reached by the recognition program; (c) a list of constituent segments, each with its duration and parameter values. This information, together with a simultaneous audio tape recording, is sufficient to study a speaker's behavior whilst controlling the displayed cross.

As speakers, two subjects of each sex were used, with accents as indicated in Table I. The "inexperienced" speakers were normal adults who had had no previous contact with the system. Only one speaker (F8) had contributed to the system's training data. Initially, each subject was requested to read out a list of 32 words, consisting of the vocabulary "right," "left," "up," "down," and "stop" in random order with the cathode-ray tube switched off. This therefore constituted a dummy run for experimental control purposes. The words were spoken one at a time into a microphone. The cue for each word was given by a light on the front panel of the speech hardware as soon as processing of the previous word was complete. Subjects were requested to speak "normally." Although the experiments were conducted in a large general laboratory, no abnormal distractions were permitted to occur. An audio tape recording and a record on the disk store was made for subsequent analysis of the subjects' behavior while reading the random list.

Approximately a minute after reaching the end of the random list, a live run was commenced. The subject was shown the cross displayed in the center of the cathode-ray tube screen and told that he could control its movement by use of the words in the vocabulary used in the random list. Speaker M2 was told to continue until the program stopped, but the other speakers were told to continue only as long as they wished. All subjects succeeded in exerting a degree of control over the movement of the cross, as is indicated in more detail in the next section. The four speakers, in common with many others in previous informal experiments, tended to trace out closed figures. Each controlled the display for between 4 and 11 min, uttering on average 23 words per minute.

After the live run just described, each subject was required to read out a further random list of the five command words as a final dummy control run, with the cathode-ray tube display switched off. The information stored on the disk during all three phases of the experiment was then printed out by a special program. Following comparison with the audio tape recording, there was available a continuous record of what words each speaker said and of the machine's responses, together with numerical information describing each utterance. The analysis of this record for the four subjects is now described.

II. RESULTS

A. Overall Success Rates

A general view of the results may be obtained from Table II. This gives the average recognition success rates for the experienced and the inexperienced ("naive") speakers, during the various phases of the experiment. In calculating the averages, each word in the vocabulary was given equal weighting. Note that in Table II, the results for the live runs have been divided into two sections to emphasize any change in success as the run progressed. The figures for each row in Table II refer to groups of between 60 and 200 utterances, and their standard deviations are all in the range 3% to 6%. Thus, all the observed differences

TABLE I. Speakers.

Subject No.	Sex	Experience	Accent
M2	M	Accustomed to system, but not a training speaker	R. P. Southern English
F8	F	Accustomed to system, and also a training speaker	Slight Northern English
M31	M	Inexperienced	Slight Midland English
F12	F	Inexperienced	General American (Pennsylvania)

between success rates in the various conditions are statistically significant.

For the naive speakers, there is clear evidence that the subjects adapt to the machine's requirements during the fedback live run, and that this adaptation has some continuing effect during the reading of the final random list. It is of interest to note also that the speaking rate of the naive subjects increased from 32 words per minute to 40 words per minute between the initial and final random lists.

For the experienced speakers, there is also evidence of adaptation during the live run, and it is seen that the final success rate during the live run (70%) is not significantly different from that for the naive speakers (71%). The better performance on the first random list and the worse one on the final random list are evidence of long-term effects of the subject's degree of previous experience with the system, although the mechanisms involved are obscure.

Since the word recognition system is fixed, the changes in recognition success rates must represent changes in articulation due to human factors. It is of interest to investigate the nature of these changes in more depth. To commence this investigation, certain correlation coefficients between data recorded on the disk in various phases of the experiments were computed. For measurements made on segments chosen at random from all five words, correlation coefficients were calculated as follows: (a) between data from the initial and the final random lists; (b) between data from the first and the second half of live run; and (c) between data from both random lists and the whole live run.

TABLE II. Overall experimental results.

Phase of experiment	Success rate (experienced speakers)	Success rate (naive speakers)
Initial random list	64%	55%
First half of live run	50%	66%
Second half of live run	70%	71%
Final random list	50%	71%

TABLE III. Conditional success rates—Live runs.

Speaker	Success (percent) First attempt	Success (percent) Repeats
M2	61%	51%
F8	54%	34%
M31	75%	73%
F12	71%	56%

For all speakers, all these coefficients were approximately equal to 0.85, which is significant at the 0.1% level $(n \geq 60)$. In other words, there is no overall statistical difference between speech data generated in the various phases of the experiment. Thus the changes in the data, which lead to significant changes in the recognizability of the speech, must be sought on a detailed word-by-word basis.

B. Detailed Examination of Data

An idea of the variation in pronunciation from word to word during the live runs can be gained by studying the conditional success rates given in Table III. For each speaker, this table lists the success rates for first attempts at a particular word and for subsequent repetitions if the first attempt fails. In some cases consecutive attempts are separated by an utterance of "stop," which has been ignored in the calculations. It can be seen that, in general, the chance of success is lower for a repetition. A more detailed analysis showed that speaker M31 was exceptional in having a relatively high chance of successful repetition, and for speaker M2 it was noted that for one particular word, "right," the repetition success rate was 85%, compared to 60% for first attempts. However, the general trend is towards lower success for repetitions, as is seen in Table III.

From these observations, it may be deduced that substantial changes in the speech data occur on a very short-term basis (i.e., between an utterance and its repetition) in response to erroneous actions by the word recognizer. In most cases, the changes result in an even worse mistake, although in isolated instances the change is beneficial.

In order to establish whether these changes were systematic or not, a detailed graphical examination was carried out for particular features of particular words. For example, changes in the nature of the vowel segment for the word "right" were examined for each speaker as the live run progressed, and also during the dummy runs (random lists). The results of these examinations were generally inconclusive, although there was a tendency for periods of largely successful utterances in the live runs to be characterized by steady parameter values, and for areas of error to contain parameter changes of as much as 75%, between successive occurrences of an utterance. This may be interpreted as the subject's "hunting" for the correct pronunciation. There was no evidence that this hunting

process was other than random, though the condensed nature of the analysis record may have masked some subtle effects. In general, it must be concluded that there was little *systematic* adaptation on the part of the speaker.

In passing, it should be noted that there is a limit to the degree of control a speaker can exercise over his own articulation. Thus, Potter and Steinberg[5] observed a 10% variation when a trained phonetician attempted to repeat certain vowel sounds on different occasions. Such a lack of articulatory precision could tend to render ineffective a subjectively systematic hunting strategy. In a supplementary experiment to investigate this point, a detailed analysis was performed for speaker M2 as he attempted to repeat exactly certain words. The repetitions were judged to be identical by trained listeners, but it was typically found that when the data was analyzed using digital techniques,[6] vowel duration, vowel pitch, and the frequency of the major spectral resonances all remained within about 5% for repetitions, and the three simple parameters used for recognition remained within about 25%.[4] This degree of imprecision is smaller than the changes of up to 75% noted above during hunting.

To return to the results of the five-word command vocabulary live runs, it may be assumed that if a subject consciously adapts his pronunciation, he does so because he intends to move closer to some subjective ideal for that word. The fact that his changes do not in general make the repeated utterances more recognizable by the PDP-8 program suggests that the speaker's subjective ideal pronunciation differs from the target pronunciation required by the program. This is despite the facts that the word recognition system treats speech structurally in a way not dissimilar to conventional phonetics, and that it was trained using data generated by speakers instructed to speak "normally." Thus it might be concluded that the differing situations in which speakers were placed during the training and during the experiments described in this paper lead to differing subjective norms of pronunciation—though no statistical *overall* difference in the speech data was detected between dummy and live runs. Another difficulty is that the speaker's efforts to adapt may be hindered in the present recognition system by the existence of more than one version of each word in the training data. Thus, in attempts to find the correct target pronunciation, the speaker may encounter more than one target. This inevitably confuses the speaker's adaptation process, which is in any case subjective. Some evidence that such confusion occurred during the live runs was found during the graphical analysis of results.

A supplementary experiment was therefore carried out to discover whether the speaker's efforts to adapt are aided by a reduction in the number of targets for each word. A reduced training data paper-tape was

TABLE IV. Overall success rates for Speaker M2 with reduced training data.

Phase of experiment	Success rate
Initial random list	57%
First half of live run	46%
Second half of live run	49%
Final random list	31%

compiled for the PDP-8 program by including in it only the most frequently encountered versions of each word. This tape contained approximately 17% of the training data used by the original word recognition system employed in the previous experiments. A recognition system incorporating the reduced training data was used to conduct an experimental run with speaker M2, using the same procedure as that described in Sec. I. The overall success rates obtained are given in Table IV. Comparison with Table II shows that the principal effect of the reduction in the training data is a reduction in all success rates. Furthermore, the increase in success rate during the feedback live run in Table IV is too small to be significant; also, the success rate for repeats was found to be very much worse than in Table III. To verify that speaker M2 had not merely lost his skill, a repeat run was performed with the original full training data, and success rates similar to those in Table II were again obtained. It may be concluded, therefore, that the speaker's adaptation process was hindered in this system, rather than helped, by the reduction in the number of targets for each word. It is not clear whether these conclusions would apply even if very high success rates could be obtained with one target per word, since frustration must have had a considerable effect for success rates in Table IV as low as 46%.

III. CONCLUSIONS

It has been shown that the performance of a real-time word recognition system is significantly affected by the environment in which the system is used. Relative changes of 25% in the success rate have been noted for environmental changes which may appear subjectively to be more modest. During on-line control situations (the live runs of Tables II and IV), human factors can produce dramatic changes ($\pm 75\%$) in the detected speech parameters over a short time interval. These changes, which occur at times of operator frustration, are not generally systematic. The experiments highlight the importance of taking all relevant human factors into account during the training phase of a word recognition device. A possible way of furthering this aim would be to make the training phase indistinguishable from the live run—e.g., tracing out known geometrical figures on the cathode-ray tube with the present recognition system. In view of the large possible variation in speech parameters, the adaptation strategy for the recognition device during this training phase is not a simple one.

ACKNOWLEDGMENT

The authors wish to thank Professor T. Kilburn of the Department of Computer Science at the University of Manchester for providing the experimental facilities.

[1] R. W. A. Scarr, "Word Recognition Machine," Proc. IEE 117, 203–212 (1970).
[2] J. C. Miller, P. W. Ross, and C. M. Wine, "An Adaptive Speech Recognition System Operating in a Remote Time-Sharing Computer Environment," Trans. IEEE AU-18, 26–32 (1970).
[3] B. E. Carpenter, "Some Experiments in Automatic Speech-Recognition," Ph.D. thesis, Univ. Manchester (1970).
[4] S. H. Lavington, "Computer Simulation of a Speech Recognition System," Proc. IEE 116, 1053–1058 (1969).
[5] R. K. Potter and J. C. Steinberg, "Towards the Specification of Speech," J. Acoust. Soc. Amer. 22, 807–820 (1950).
[6] S. H. Lavington and L. E. Rosenthal, "Some Facilities for Speech Processing by Computer," Computer J. 9, 330–339 (1967).

Demonstration of a Speech Processing System Consisting of a Speech Analyzer, Translator, Typer, and Synthesizer

HARRY F. OLSON, HERBERT BELAR, AND RICARDO DE SOBRINO

RCA Laboratories, Princeton, New Jersey

(Received June 29, 1962)

A public demonstration of a rudimentary speech-processing system consisting of a speech analyzer, language translator, type decoder, and speech synthesizer was given at the Meeting of the Acoustical Society of America in New York, May 23–26, 1962. Each word spoken into the microphone was analyzed, converted to a syllable code, transmitted as a syllable code, synthesized to speech, or converted to the typed page either in the same language or other languages. The two language inputs were English and French, the synthesized speech outputs were English, French, and Spanish and the typed outputs were English, French, German, and Spanish.

INTRODUCTION

A PUBLIC demonstration of a rudimentary speech-processing system consisting of a speech analyzer, language translator, type decoder, and speech synthesizer was given at the Sixty-Third Meeting of the Acoustical Society of America on May 24, 25, and 26, 1962, in the Hotel New Yorker, New York. This paper describes the elements of the speech-processing system, the complete speech-transmission system, and the demonstrations.

SPEECH ANALYZER

A schematic block diagram of the speech analyzer and syllable encoder is shown in Fig. 1.

The first element is the microphone, which has been specially designed and built for this application. The input to the microphone is speech consisting of syllables or monosyllabic words, spoken one at a time. The resultant audio signals from the microphone are amplified, compressed, limited, and suppressed in the normalizing input system. The suppressor is in the form of an expander with a preset gain. When the signal is below a threshold value, the gain can be considerably decreased.

When the signal level is above that value, the suppressor gain remains constant over a certain preset amplitude range of the signal; but for further increases in signal level above this range, the compressor limiter begins to reduce the gain. The amplitude-normalizing system has the advantage of allowing a larger amount of compression to be used without difficulties with acoustic feedback, and of reducing the effect of low-level noises.

The amplitude-processed audio signal is divided and fed through eight bandpass filters. The signal in each band of frequencies is again amplified and rectified and the dc voltages obtained are proportional to the envelope in both positive and negative directions. Amplitude and amplitude-sensing circuits are provided for different setups. The output of each channel may be quantized directly by operating a relay above a predetermined threshold. In addition, the comparison circuit can be connected so that a relay will operate whenever the level in that channel is greater than the level in the channel of next lower frequency. This type of amplitude-comparison circuit provides information on the first derivative of the frequency spectrum con-

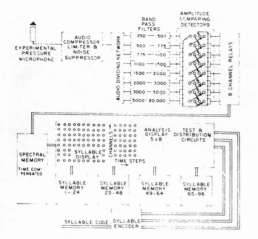

FIG. 1. Speech analyzer which converts speech input to the microphone into the corresponding syllable code.

sidered as a curve. If the amplitude-comparison network for a channel is connected to both adjacent channels, as indicated in the schematic diagram of Fig. 1, then a relay will operate when the signal level in the channel is greater by a predetermined amount than the average of the channels. This state of affairs, in effect, corresponds to specifying the second derivative of the curve representing the contour of the frequency spectrum at any one time. As a result, the output of the analyzers is in the form of quantized spectral information varying with time as the syllable is spoken.

The spectral memory is time compensated for the speed of talking. The time compensation consists of 70 relays, which set up the first column in the frequency-spectrum display and then transfers the spectrum information derived from the analyzer system in the form of an eight-bit code to the next column. There the system rests until there is a change. A significant change causes the second-column display to lock and the input is stepped over to the third column and so on. After the fifth column has been set up, the next and last change disconnects the input and the entire spectrum time display is held. A readout command is formed by operating a relay in the proper sequence followed by

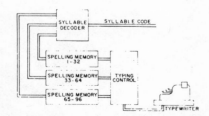

FIG. 2. Coded typer which converts the syllable-code input to the corresponding typed word.

cancellation of the display and resetting to the initial position. The display having an eight-bit spectrum and five time steps provides a matrix of 40 fields.

The syllable display, namely, the sequence of quantized frequency-spectrum information, is a 40-bit matrix; so every display corresponding to each individual voicing can be looked upon as a pattern, or simpler still, a binary number of 40 digits. This number corresponding to the syllable display is fed to the syllable memories after the completion of each voicing. The syllable memories recognize the syllable display and produce a code identifying the syllable.

The output of the syllable memory is connected to syllable encoder which converts the syllables to a code for transmission of the syllable code.

TYPE DECODER

A schematic block diagram of the type decoder consisting of the syllable decoder, spelling memory, typing control, and typewriter is shown in Fig. 2. The syllable decoder converts the coded input to the appropriate syllable of the spelling memory. The spelling memory of the typing console has one spelling relay for each word.

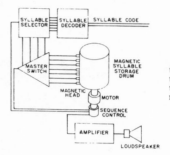

FIG. 3. Speech synthesizer which converts the syllable-code input to the corresponding reproduced word.

A particular relay corresponding to a syllable is operated by completing the circuit for that relay in the syllable memory to which it is connected. The spelling relays in the typing control are wired to bus wires representing the different keys of the typewriter through separate sets of relay springs corresponding to the spelling desired. A set of sequence bus wires is connected to every one of the relays. To prevent jamming of the typewriter, only one spelling relay can be operated at a time. Operation of the typewriter feeds back a signal to the typing-control unit which causes a stepping switch to transfer to the readout portion of the second sequence bus. This action operates the typewriter again by connection to the desired spelling wired into the second set of contacts of that relay. A total of seven functions can be set up for each relay. The resetting of the spelling memory is automatic. The preceding discussion indicates that the syllable code input is converted to the typed syllable on paper.

SPEECH SYNTHESIZER

A schematic block diagram of the speech synthesizer consisting of the syllable decoder, syllable selector, syllable storage, amplifier, and loudspeaker is shown in Fig. 3. In this synthesizer the syllable code input is converted to reproduced speech from the loudspeaker. The syllable code is fed to the syllable decoder. The syllable decoder converts the coded input to the appropriate syllable of the syllable selector. The syllable selector operates the master switch which connects the appropriate magnetic head to the amplifier through the sequence control. The syllables are recorded on the magnetic drum. The stored syllables are reproduced by means of the magnetic heads. The sequence control completes the connection between the master switch and the amplifier in the appropriate interval. The loudspeaker converts the speech signal output from the amplifier into speech sounds.

LANGUAGE TRANSLATOR

The language translation is carried out on a word-for-word basis. This of course means that meaningful translation can occur only for phrases and sentences

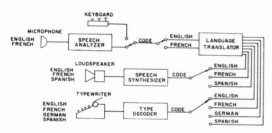

FIG. 4. A schematic block diagram of the speech-processing-demonstration equipment depicting the elements, and the input and output functions.

which are amenable to such procedures. However, simple commands, directions, and explanations can be carried out with this type of translation.

The translator used for converting the syllable code in one language to the syllable code in another language is a switching system that converts the syllable code in one language to the syllable code in another language for operating the speech synthesizer or code typer.

DEMONSTRATION SYSTEM

A block diagram depicting the elements and the input and output functions of the speech transmission demonstration equipment is shown in Fig. 4. Photographs of the demonstration equipment with labels indicating the elements and a group of spectators witnessing a demonstration are shown in Figs. 5 and 6.

When the system of Fig. 4 operates as a speech-transmission system, speech is converted to a syllable

FIG. 5. A photograph depicting the elements of the speech-transmission equipment.

code by means of the speech analyzer of Fig. 1, then transmitted as a syllable code and synthesized from the syllable code to speech by means of the speech synthesizer of Fig. 3. In this way each word spoken into the microphone is reproduced as the same word in the same language or translated and reproduced as the corresponding word in another language. The advantage of the system is the extremely small bandwidth required to transmit speech. Only 23 bits per second are required to transmit speech at normal rates of talking.

When the system of Fig. 4 operates as a speech-to-printed-page transmission system, speech is converted to a syllable code by means of the speech analyzer of Fig. 1, then transmitted as a syllable code and converted to the typed page from the syllable code by means of the type decoder of Fig. 2. In this way each word spoken into the microphone is converted into the same typed word on paper or translated and converted into the corresponding typed word on paper in another language.

When the system of Fig. 4 operates as a coded-speech reproducer, the syllable code is manually produced by means of the keyboard, transmitted as a syllable code, and reproduced by means of the speech synthesizer of Fig. 3.

FIG. 6. A photograph of the speech-processing demonstration.

TABLE I. Translated words.

Voice input		Print output				Voice output		
English	French	English	French	German	Spanish	English	French	Spanish
Stop		Stop	Halte	Halt	Alto	Stop	Halte	Alto
I		I	je	Ich	yo	I	je	yo
see		see	vois	sehe	veo	see	vois	veo
six		six	six			six		
tanks		tanks	tanques	panzer	carros	tanks	tanques	carros
	oui	yes	oui			yes		
	je	I	je	ich	yo	I	je	yo
	vois	see	vois	sehe	veo	see	vois	veo
	six	six	six			six		
	tanques	tanks	tanques	panzer	carros	tanks	tanques	carros
	halte	stop	halte	halt	alto	stop	halte	alto

DEMONSTRATIONS

Demonstrations of the system depicted in Fig. 4 involve the following words and capacities:

English words which can be processed, transmitted, typed, and reproduced as speech.

a	is	sells	speak
ah	it	sends	spell
are	left	shall	stop
burns	new	she	sure
by	no	shells	tanks
can	oil	shore	thanks
come	please	should	the
Dear	read	Sir	you
Earl	school	six	york
I	see	space	yours

French words which can be processed, transmitted, typed, and reproduced as speech.

Halte	oui	tanques
je	six	vois

English words which can be processed, transmitted and typed.

Gen.	Mr.
Sar	Ol
noff	son

Translated words.

Additional words by translation are provided as depicted in Table I.

Demonstrations of the system depicted in Fig. 4 provide the following capacities:

System can understand 52 words in two languages.

46 English words
6 French words

Print output from speech input 62 words in four languages.

48 English words
6 French words

4 German words
4 Spanish words

Speech output from speech input 50 words in three languages.

42 English words
4 French words
4 Spanish words

Maximum transmission rates.

Speech input to print output 60 syllables per minute.
Speech input to speech output 30.5 syllables per minute.

Performance

The accuracy of the machine is another important consideration. If an average of 200 voicings of a syllable or word are made to establish the code the accuracy will be 98%. The code of each syllable or word used in the demonstration was set up from more than 200 voicings by H. B. in which case under normal operation conditions 98% accuracy of the system was obtained. With the code thus set up for H. B., the score obtained by R. d. S., of a different national origin than H. B., was 98% for 20 words. For the remainder of the words there was a decreasing reliability ranging from 96% to almost zero. With the code set up for H. B., the score obtained by G. S., of a different national origin than either H. B., or R. d. S., was 98% for 17 words. For the remainder of the words there was a decreasing reliability ranging from 96% to almost zero. In view of the three different national origins, the high scores for R. d. S. and G. S. for a code set up for H. B. are quite remarkable. Of course, when the code was established for R. d. S. from 200 voicings the accuracy obtained was 98% for him and similar results were obtained by G. S. when the code was established for him.

The results today for others than the one for whom the code was established is far superior than for the systems used three years ago when the code was for all practical purposes almost a personal one.

34

This article was written expressly for this Benchmark volume

DIAGNOSTIC EVALUATION OF SPEECH INTELLIGIBILITY

William D. Voiers

*Dynastat Inc.,
Austin, Texas 78705*

INTRODUCTION

It is generally acknowledged that a listener's apprehension of speaker's linguistic intent is a dual process. One aspect of the process, the perceptual aspect, involves discrimination of the immediate acoustical manifestations of the speaker's intent with regard to the identity of a phoneme. The other, apperceptual aspect involves inferences from contextual features, i.e., from sources other than the phonemic information-bearing features of the speech signal. Thus, the listener's uncertainty with regard to the identity of a phoneme may be reduced by his knowledge of (1) the structure of the language involved (Howes, 1957), (2) explicit or implicit situational constraints on his response options (Miller, Lichten, and Heise, 1951), (3) the circumstances occasioning the communication (Bruce, 1958), (4) the dialectal and idiolectal characteristics of the speaker (Peters, 1955), and (5) the immediately prior history of the speech signal itself (Miller, Heise, and Lichten, 1951).

Both aspects of speech apprehension are of scientific interest, but the dual character of the process complicates the task of evaluating speech intelligibility under all circumstances where the basis of evaluation is the degree of correlation between a speaker's intent and a listener's response. To the extent that the influence of contextual constraints on the listener's responses is unknown, test results based on such responses are of questionable validity. Since the effects of contextual constraints on test results are ultimately determined by the listener's conception of such constraints, the validity of the test results depends not only on its intrinsic structure, but also on the listener's knowledge of that structure, of the test materials, of the nature of his response options, etc. Cognizance of this problem is evident in the designs of most intelligibility tests in use today, but altogether satisfactory solutions have proved difficult to achieve.

In the case of the Harvard PB lists (Egan, 1948), for example, the recommended procedure for controlling the effects of the listener's familiarity involves an extensive regimen of training, terminated when it appears that his level of performance has reached an asymptote. Such training serves most obviously to alter the difficulty level of the listener's task and to obscure the relationship between gross test scores and intelligibility in the "real world." A more serious matter is the possibility that familiarity with the PB lists effects qualitative changes in the listener's task and, ultimately, in the implications of his performance. As Miller and Nicely (1955) have shown, the discriminations required for phonemic recognition differ greatly in terms of intrinsic difficulty. In view of this phenomenon, it would seem to be an extremely tenuous assumption that the facilitative effects of familiarity are exerted equally on all aspects of the speech discrimination task. Hence, it is quite conceivable that familiarization training serves to desensitize free-response word-recognition tests to specific deficiencies of the transmission channel, speaker, or listener being evaluated. In any case, such tests are subject to other extraneous contextual influences. For, one thing, interphonemic constraints inherent in the language result in hopeless confounding of the contextual and stimulus determinants of the listener's response. The situation is further complicated by the fact that, given no explicit restrictions, listeners tend to favor those test words which are most frequently used in normal conversation and print (Howes, 1957).

Testing procedures in which stimulus uncertainty is limited to a single phoneme, as in the Fairbanks Rhyme Test (Fairbanks, 1958), provide improved control of the effects of interphonemic constraints, but do not effectively control other contextual factors. When, however, this approach is combined with explicit restriction of response options—as in the Modified Rhyme Test (House, Williams, Hecker, and Kryter, 1965), the Phonemically Balanced Rhyme Test (Clarke, 1965), and the Consonant Recognition Test (Preusse, 1959)—improved control of other contextual factors is achieved. Pollack, Rubenstein, and Decker (1959) have demonstrated the efficacy of explicitly restricted response options for controlling the effects of a priori expectations based on the listener's familiarity with the language in general and the test materials in particular. Whatever its advantages, however, explicit restriction of the listener's options also entails some hazards.

To restrict the listener's options in an arbitrary or unsystematic manner may be simply to substitute one set of unknown contextual constraints for another. Depending on the available response options, the listener may be forced, on one hand, to give responses which are misleading as to his perceptions of other features. On the other hand, he may be deprived of the opportunity to reveal specific deficiencies of the channel or other entity being evaluated if the appropriate options are not available to him. Additionally, the task of diagnostic interpretation of erroneous responses can become extremely difficult where care has not been exercised in designing restricted-response or multiple-choice test items.

The hazards of explicit response restriction can be minimized by means of test items in which all response options are a priori, equally attractive and, when chosen, of unambiguous significance. For example, in the response set:

bee pea vee dee me,

each erroneous option differs from the correct response, "bee," in terms of a single elementary attribute or "distinctive feature." Tests composed of such items may be quite useful in circumstances where the listener does not experience repeated exposure to the test materials. For repeated use with the same listener, however, it is generally desirable to have different randomizations of the materials, i.e., to vary the response option used as the stimulus for a given item. If for example, "pea," were the stimulus word in the above case, the differences between the stimulus and the various response options would no longer be unidimensional. Only "bee" differs from "pea" by a single feature, *voicing*. All other options differ by two or more features.

Clearly, the multiple-choice approach to intelligibility testing has limitations as well as advantages, but the more serious of these limitations can be minimized by the use of two-choice tests items. With a two-choice testing scheme, erroneous responses can, but for the effects of chance, be unequivocally attributed to the characteristics of the transmission system or other entity being tested. Moreover, ambiguity as to the specific cause of an erroneous response can be eliminated by the use of minimally contrasting response options.

A means to the end of developing a two-choice, "minimal contrasts" test is provided by a phonemic taxonomy derived from the distinctive feature systems of Miller and Nicely (1955) and of Jakobson, Fant, and Halle (1952). This taxonomy served as a basis for the design of the Diagnostic Rhyme Test.

THE DIAGNOSTIC RHYME TEST

The Diagnostic Rhyme Test (DRT), first described in 1965 (Voiers, Cohen, and Mickunas), was designed to implement the principles discussed above. It has undergone a succession of minor refinements, but its formal structure is unchanged. In this test, each item involves two rhyming words, the initial consonants of which differ by a single distinctive feature. The listener's task is simply to judge which of two words has been spoken, implicitly indicating whether or not he has apprehended the speaker's implicit intent with respect to the critical feature.

The phonemic taxonomy on which the DRT is based is shown in Table I. The labels given the seven features are drawn from various sources. *Voicing* and *nasality* are represented in virtually every system for the classification of consonant phonemes. *Sustention* corresponds to the *continuant-interrupted* feature-opposition of Jakobson, Fant, and Halle (JFH) and to the *affriction* feature of Miller and Nicely (MN). *Sibilation* corresponds to the *strident-mellow* opposition of JFH and to the *duration* feature of MN. *Graveness* and *compactness* are subsumed by the *place* feature of MN and are taken directly from the JFH system. *Vowel-likeness* is used here to distinguish the glides from the true consonants. The articulatory antecedents and acoustical correlates of these features are described extensively in the literature. Discussions of them can be found in Miller and Nicely (1955), Jakobson, Fant, and Halle (1952), Delattre (1968), and elsewhere.

In accordance with the principle that consonants carry the bulk of the linguistic information in English, and that they are more vulnerable to signal impoverishment, the DRT, like the Fairbanks Rhyme Test, is concerned with the apprehensibility of consonants only. Also like the Fairbanks Rhyme Test, the DRT deals with consonant apprehensibility only in the initial position. Although there is some evidence that not all consonants are equally apprehensible in the initial, intervocalic, and final positions, their feature structures do not change.

The Diagnostic Rhyme Test (DRT) is more properly described in terms of a set of principles for item construction and selection than in terms of a specific corpus of test materials. Thus, the ninety-six rhyming word pairs shown in Table II represent only one realization of these principles. In the table, the positive state (e.g., voiced) of each feature is represented in the left member of each pair; the negative state (e.g., unvoiced) is represented in the right member of each pair.

The apprehensibility of every attribute is tested in each of eight vowel contexts, as represented by two vowels from each quadrant of the vowel-articulation space. There are two grossly equivalent items (e.g., meat-beat and need-deed) in each vowel context, which redundancy permits tests of the reliability of listener performance over the course of a testing session. Either member of each pair may be chosen as the stimulus word in a given instance without changing the function of the item. Choice of stimulus word from each item affects only the state (positive or negative), not the identity, of the feature involved.

There are some minor exceptions to the rule of "unidimensional difference" between members of the word pairs in Table II. This results from the fact that all compact phonemes are classified indifferently with respect to *graveness*. However, the results of Miller and Nicely's research on phonemic confusions, and of research with the DRT itself, suggest that this solution conforms most nearly with the facts of phonemic perception.

In recognition of evidence that the state of a feature may not be equally apprenhensible in every manifestation, various constraints were observed in assembling the corpus of test words:

1. For half of the items designed to test for the apprehensibility of *voicing*, both critical phonemes involve friction (i.e., are affricates or affricatives); for half, the critical phonemes are stops.
2. Half of the *nasality* items in each vowel context involve a grave phoneme-pair (i.e., /m-b/; half involve an acute pair (i.e., /n-d/).

Table I Consonant Taxonomy Used in the Construction of the DRT

	/m	n	v	∂	z	3	3̂	b	d	g	w
Voicing	+	+	+	+	+	+	+	+	+	+	+
Nasality	+	+	−	−	−	−	−	−	−	−	−
Sustention	−	−	+	+	+	+	−	−	−	−	+
Sibilation	−	−	−	−	+	+	+	−	−	−	−
Graveness	+	−	+	−	−	0	0	+	−	0	+
Compactness	−	−	−	−	−	+	+	−	−	+	−
Vowel-like*	−	−	−	−	−	−	−	−	−	−	+

	r	l	j	f	θ	s	∫	∫̂	p	t	k	h/
Voicing	+	+	+	−	−	−	−	−	−	−	−	−
Nasality	−	−	−	−	−	−	−	−	−	−	−	−
Sustention	+	+	+	+	+	+	+	−	−	−	−	+
Sibilation	−	−	−	−	−	+	+	+	−	−	−	−
Graveness	−	0	0	+	−	−	0	0	+	−	0	0
Compactness	−	0	+	−	−	−	+	+	−	−	+	+
Vowel-like*	+	+	+	−	−	−	−	−	−	−	−	−

* The DRT does not test for the apprehensibility of the opposition, vowel-like—nonvowel-like. However, test words are chosen so as not to confound this attribute with the six attributes for which discriminability is tested.

3. Half of the items designed to test for the apprehensibility of *sustention* involve a voiced phoneme-pair; half, an unvoiced pair.
4. Half of the items concerned with *sibilation* involve voiced phonemes; half, unvoiced phonemes.
5. In the case of *graveness*, items were constructed such that, for each vowel context, one item lies in the voiced "plane," one in the unvoiced; one lies in the sustained "plane," one in the interrupted.
6. *Compactness* items were constructed such that both states of *vowel-likeness*, *sibilation*, *voicing*, and *sustention* were given equal representation in the test, though not in all vowel contexts.

Various other symmetries are embodied in the design of the DRT, though the criterion of symmetry is less rigorous in some cases than in others.

Administering the DRT

The manner in which the DRT is administered depends on the purpose for which it is being used, but some general guidelines can be provided.

It is usually most convenient to order the test words such that the apprenhensibility of each feature is tested every seven items and such

Table II Stimulus Words Used in the DRT

VOICING	NASALITY	SUSTENTION
VEAL-FEEL	MEAT-BEAT	VEE-BEE
BEAN-PEEN	NEED-DEED	SHEET-CHEAT
GIN-CHIN	MITT-BIT	VILL-BILL
DINT-TINT	NIP-DIP	THICK-TICK
ZOO-SUE	MOOT-BOOT	FOO-POOH
DUNE-TUNE	NEWS-DUES	SHOES-CHOOSE
VOLE-FOAL	MOAN-BONE	THOSE-DOZE
GOAT-COAT	NOTE-DOTE	THOUGH-DOUGH
ZED-SAID	MEND-BEND	THIN-DEN
DENSE-TENSE	NECK-DECK	FENCE-PENCE
VAST-FAST	MAD-BAD	THAN-DAN
GAFF-CALF	NAB-DAB	SHAD-CHAD
VAULT-FAULT	MOSS-BOSS	THONG-TONG
DAUNT-TAUNT	GNAW-DAW	SHAW-CHAW
JOCK-CHOCK	MOM-BOMB	VON-BON
BOND-POND	KNOCK-DOCK	VOX-BOX

SIBILATION	GRAVENESS	COMPACTNESS
ZEE-THEE	WEED-REED	YIELD-WIELD
CHEEP-KEEP	PEAK-TEAK	KEY-TEA
JILT-GILT	BID-DID	HIT-FIT
SING-THING	FIN-THIN	GILL-DILL
JUICE-GOOSE	MOON-NOON	COOP-POOP
CHEW-COO	POOL-TOOL	YOU-RUE
JOE-GO	BOWL-DOLE	GHOST-BOAST
SOLE-THOLE	FORE-THOR	SHOW-SO
JEST-GUEST	MET-NET	KEG-PEG
CHAIR-CARE	PENT-TENT	YEN-WREN
JAB-GAB	BANK-DANK	GAT-BAT
SANK-THANK	FAD-THAD	SHAG-SAG
JAWS-GAUZE	FOUGHT-THOUGHT	YAWL-WALL
SAW-THAW	BONG-DONG	CAUGHT-THOUGHT
JOT-GOT	WAD-ROD	HOP-FOP
CHOP-COP	POT-TOT	GOT-DOT

that the vowel context varies over an eight-item cycle. This permits every seventh item to be a filler or experimental item, but other counterbalanced arrangements of test materials can be employed.

When the DRT is used for purposes of evaluating speech communications equipment, it is generally desirable to use recordings of the test materials by more than one speaker and to use crews of eight to ten listeners. For this purpose the optimal rate of word presentation is one word per 1.4 seconds (Cohen, 1965), but other rates may be used in special cases. The listener's task is simply to strike out the member of the word pair he judges to have been uttered. Multiple randomizations (with certain constraints) of the test materials, and of the arrangement of response options on the listener's response form, can be employed without altering the structure of the test.

Scoring the DRT

DRT data can be scored in a number of ways, depending on the interests of the investigator. Generally, primary interest will attach to the six major diagnostic scores. However, separate scores for the apprehensibility of each state of each feature are often of interest, since many experimental conditions affect the apprehensibility of each of the states of the various features in an asymmetrical manner.

The resulting discrepancy between scores for the two states of an attribute is termed *bias*. It is also possible to fractionate the above scores in other ways, e.g., into separate scores for the apprehensibility of *sustention* in voiced and unvoiced phonemes; separate scores for *voicing* in frictional and nonfrictional phonemes, and so on.

Finally, a total score, representing the average of the six major diagnostic scores, is of interest in most circumstances. All DRT scores are adjusted by means of the familiar correction for guessing:

$$S = \frac{100(R - W)}{T} ,$$

where S is the "true" percent-correct responses, R is the observed number of correct responses, W is the observed number of incorrect responses, and T is the total number of items involved.

Validity of the DRT

Obviously, the usefulness of the DRT would be quite limited if it failed to yield qualitatively different results, i.e., different patterns of diagnostic scores, for different types of deficiencies in the channel, speaker, or listener being tested. In fact it has proved to be quite sensitive in this respect. Voiers, Sharpley, and Hehmsoth (1973) found that differences among normal speakers and normal listeners are reliably reflected in diagnostic score patterns. Different forms of signal distortion, including those associated with different speech-processing and communication systems, yield characteristic patterns (Voiers, Cohen, and Mickunas, 1965).

Although it is not feasible, here, to examine the validity of the DRT in all of its various applications, some representative cases can be described.

Effects of Noise on Diagnostic Rhyme Tests Scores

Since noise is without question the most ubiquitous deterrent to human speech communication, its effects on DRT scores have obvious implications with regard to the validity and usefulness of the test. The major results of one investigation (Voiers, 1973a) are presented in Figure 1. For purposes of this investigation, recordings of the DRT materials by six male speakers were presented diotically over headphones to a crew of eight listeners at a level of approximately 72 dB SPL. Continuous, bandlimited Gaussian noise was mixed with the speech in an 8-

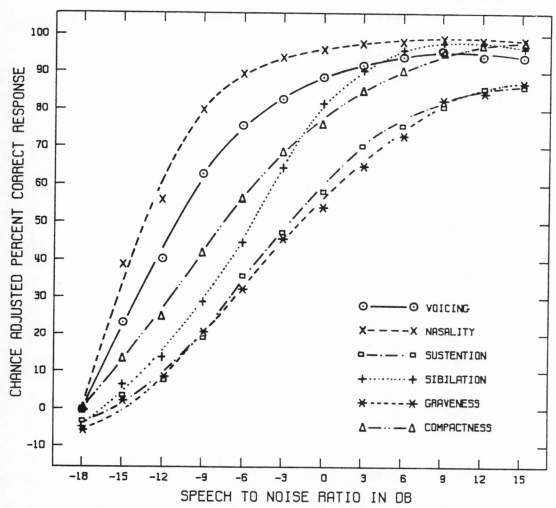

Figure 1. Effect of Noise on Individual Diagnostic Scores (after Voiers, 1973a)

kHz band. Each data point in the figure represents an average for four administrations of the test materials by six speakers to a crew of eight listeners.

The results in Figure 1 are consistent with the findings of other investigators, e.g., Miller and Nicely (1955). *Voicing* and *nasality* are least vulnerable to noise masking. One of the "place features," *graveness*, is extremely vulnerable, but the other, *compactness*, is relatively immune. *Sibilation* (Miller and Nicely's *duration*) appears, here, to be relatively less susceptible than Miller and Nicely's results indicate. A possible explanation is that the DRT sibilation scale includes a number of items in which the affricates /ʃ/ and /ʒ/ are opposed to the stops /k/ and /g/, respectively, whereas Miller and Nicely did not include the affricates in their test materials.

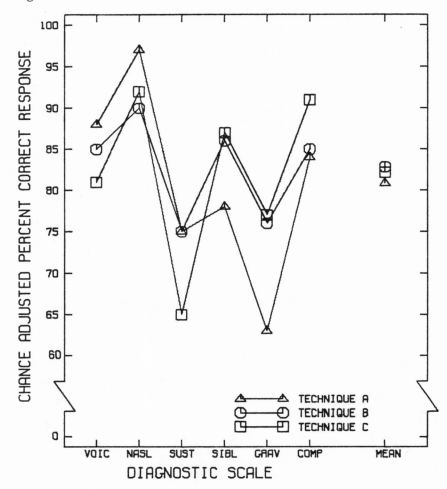

Figure 2. Diagnostic Profiles for Three Digital Speech Processing Techniques

Other minor discrepancies between these results and those of Miller and Nicely are easily atttributable to differences between the two investigations in terms of the sex of the speakers, the vowel contexts involved, and the experimental and analytical procedures used.

In any case, the patterns of scores shown here is quite consistent with the known facts of acoustic phonemics and attests effectively to the validity of the DRT in this application.

Evaluation of Communication Equipment

The DRT has been extensively used for purposes of overall diagnostic evaluation of communication systems and devices (e.g., Smith, 1969; Voiers, 1968). This use is illustrated in Figure 2, where diagnostic profiles are compared for three digital speech-processing techniques (selected for comparability of overall intelligibility). Common to these

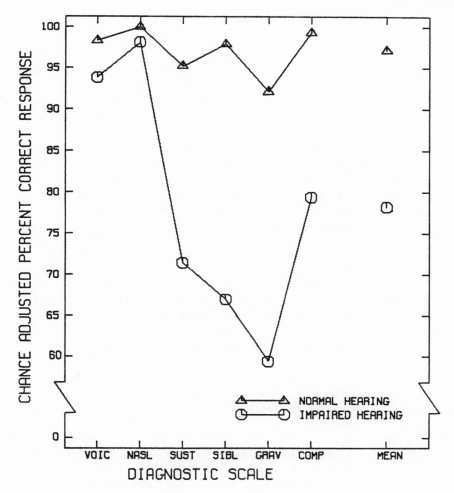

Figure 3. Diagnostic Profiles (averages) for Normal-Hearing and Sensorineural Hearing-impaired Listeners (after Olroyd, 1972)

cases and to a diversity of other forms of speech-signal impoverishment are the depressed scores on the sustention and graveness scales. However, the diagnostic patterns defined by the relationships of scores on these scales to each other, and to the remaining scales, serves effectively to distinguish among various speech-processing and coding techniques. The DRT yields a characteristic pattern of scores for each of the major classes of speech-encoding techniques, but is also capable of distinguishing between minor variations of a given technique. For example, the degree of bias observed on the sustention scale has proved to be particularly useful in evaluating the gain-control devices employed with channel vocoders. Bias on the voicing scale has served to pinpoint deficiencies of voicing-detection circuits in pitch-extracting speech-processing systems.

Clinical Use of the DRT

Thus far, the DRT has been used in clinical contexts on only few occasions (Olroyd, 1972; Stewart, Strong, and Palmer, 1976). Additional
research will be required to determine its full potential for purposes of
speech audiometry and diagnosis, but the results of an investigation by
Olroyd give some indication of the extent of this potential. Shown in
Figure 3 are diagnostic profiles based on average scores for samples of
normal-hearing and sensorineural hearing-impaired subjects. Differences are evident, but the pattern for the hearing-impaired group is
similar to that obtained with normal-hearing subjects under conditions
of severe high-frequency attenuation. Individuals with impaired hearing for high frequencies, such as those represented here, apprehend
voicing and *nasality* quite well, but have considerable difficulty with
the remaining features (Voiers, 1967).

Miller and Nicely, among others, have remarked upon the complementary relationship that exists between the phonemic information
structure of the audible speech signal and the visible speech signal
(i.e., what an observer sees as he looks at the face of a speaker). There
is a large body of experimental and anecdotal evidence which suggests
that the visible manifestations of voicing and nasality are virtually non-
existent, whereas the visible manifestations of other features vary from
moderately to highly conspicuous. The DRT has been used to provide
some clarification of this issue.

In an investigation by Voiers (1973), normal hearing subjects observed the faces of speakers who were seated behind the window of a
double-walled acoustic chamber as they uttered the DRT words. For
one part of the experiment, the subjects were required to respond on
the basis of visible cues alone. For the second part, the visible speech
signal was supplemented by an audible speech signal, low-passed at
400 Hz and presented to the subjects over a loudspeaker located in
their observation room. Since research by Miller and Nicely (1955) and
by Voiers (1967) had shown that *voicing* and *nasality* are uniquely resis-
tant to such drastic impoverishment of the speech signal, it was of interest to know whether the subjects could effectively utilize complementary items of information from two sense modalities. The results in
Figure 4 indicate that they could. Given a supplementary acoustic signal, the subjects apprehended *voicing* and *nasality* with little difficulty,
while assimilating information with respect to the others features from
the visible speech signal.

The results of this experiment resolved several issues with regard to
the information structure of the visible speech signal and confirmed
previous indications that the lower range of the speech spectrum contains much of the information lacking in the visible signal—a fortunate
happenstance for individuals who suffer from the most common form
of hearing impairment. Further details of these results are described
elsewhere (Voiers, 1973), but those presented here serve at least to further demonstrate the adaptability of the DRT.

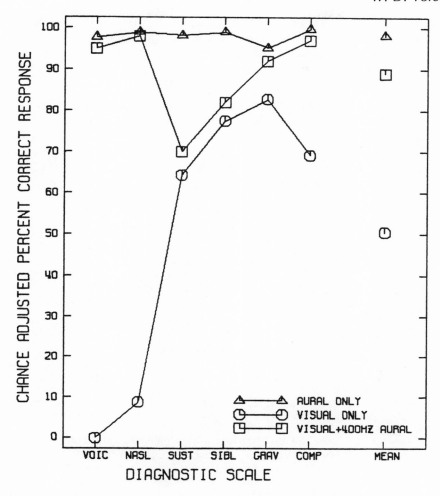

Figure 4. Diagnostic Profiles for Three Modes of Speech Presentation (after Voiers, 1973b)

OVERVIEW

In this brief presentation an attempt has been made to demonstrate the usefulness of the diagnostic approach to the evaluation of speech intelligibility. For the various applications discussed here, the advantages of a two-choice test with minimally-contrasting response options are evident, particularly where the parameters of the test exhibit a high degree of correspondence with common types of deficiencies in the performances of speech processing systems, speakers, and listeners.

The DRT has undergone extensive development and refinement during the past twelve years. Its sensitivity and reliability have been amply demonstrated. The important issue, however, is not the DRT, *per se*, but rather the principles it embodies. The development of a French adaptation of the DRT (Peckels and Rossi, 1971) represents but one testament to the robustness of these principles. It is hoped that other investigators will find occasion to take further advantage of them.

ACKNOWLEDGMENTS

Marion Cohen and Alan Sharpley have made many significant contributions to the refinement of the Diagnostic Rhyme Test. Caldwell Smith was among the first members of the engineering community to recognize the need for such a test. His advice and encouragement during the past twelve years are gratefully acknowledged. Dennis McFadden provided valuable advice and criticism during the preparation of the manuscript.

REFERENCES

1. Bruce, D. J., "The Effect of Listener's Anticipations on the Intelligibility of Heard Speech," *Lang. and Speech* **1**:79–97 (1958).
2. Clarke, F. R., "Technique for Evaluation of Speech Systems," Final Report, Contract No. DA28-043-AMC-00227 (E) USAEL (1965).
3. Cohen, M. F., "Effects of Stimulus Presentation Rate upon Intelligibility-Test Scores," *J. Acoust. Soc. Am.* **37**:1206 (A) (1965).
4. Delattre, P., "From Acoustic Cues to Distinctive Features," *Phonetica* **18**:198–230 (1968).
5. Egan, J. P., "Articulation Testing Methods," *Laryngoscope* **58**:955–991 (1948).
6. Fairbanks, G., "Test of Phonemic Differentiation: The Rhyme Test," *J. Acoust. Soc. Am.* **30**:596–600 (1958).
7. House, A. S., C. E. Williams, H. L. Hecker, and K. D. Kryter, "Articulation Testing Methods: Consonantal Differentiation with a Closed Response Set," *J. Acoust. Soc. Am.* **37**:158–166 (1965).
8. Howes, D., "On the Relation between the Intelligibility and Frequency of Occurrence of English Words," *J. Acoust. Soc. Am.* **29**:296–305 (1957).
9. Jakobson, R., C. G. M. Fant, and M. Halle. "Preliminaries to Speech Analysis: The Distinctive Features and Their Correlates," Tech. Rep. No. 13, Acoustics Laboratory, MIT (1952).
10. Miller, G. A., G. A. Heise, and W. Lichten, "The Intelligibility of Speech as a Function of the Context of the Test Materials," *J. Exp. Psychol.* **41**:329–335 (1951).
11. Miller, G. A., and P. Nicely, "An Analysis of Perceptual Confusions among Some English Consonants," *J. Acoust. Soc. Am.* **27**:338–352 (1955).
12. Olroyd, M. H., "Employment of the Diagnostic Rhyme Test (DRT) with Normal-hearing and Sensori-neural Hearing-impaired Listeners," Unpublished dissertation, Louisiana State University (1972).
13. Peckels, J. P., and M. Rossi, "Le test de diagnostic par paires minimales, adaptation au français du diagnostic rhyme test de W. D. Voiers," *Journees d'Etudes sur la Parole, Groupment des Acousticiens de Langue Française* (Apr. 1971).
14. Peters, R. W., "The Effect of Length of Exposure to Speaker's Voice on Listener Reception," Joint Project Report No. 44, The Ohio State University Research Foundation and U.S. Naval School of Aviation Medicine (1955).
15. Pollack, I., H. Rubenstein, and C. Decker, "Intelligibility of Known and Unknown Message Sets," *J. Acoust. Soc. Am.* **31**:273–279 (1959).
16. Preusse, J. W., "The Consonant Recognition Test," U.S. Army Electronics Command, ECOM Rep. No. ECOM-3207 (1959).

17. Smith, C. P., "Perception of Vocoder Speech Processed by Pattern Matching," *J. Acoust. Soc. Am.* **46**:1562–1571 (1969).
18. Stewart, S. E., W. J. Strong, and E. P. Palmer, "Experiments on the Intelligibility of Speech Codes for the Severely Hearing Impaired," Paper presented at the 92nd Meeting of the Acoustical Society of America, (Nov. 1976).
19. Voiers, W. D., "Performance Evaluation of Speech Processing Devices, III. Diagnostic Evaluation of Speech Intelligibility," Final Report, Contract No. AF19(628)4987, AFCRL (1967).
20. Voiers, W. D., "The Present State of Digital Vocoding Technique: A Diagnostic Evaluation," *IEEE Trans. Audio Electroacoust.* **AU-16**(2):275–279 (1968).
21. Voiers, W. D., "More on the Effects of Noise on the Apprehensibility of Consonant Attributes," *J. Acoust. Soc. Am.* **54**:299–300(A) (1973a).
22. Voiers, W. D., "Experimental Investigation of the Consonant Information Structure of the Visible Speech Signal," *Proceedings of the Symposium: Intelligibilite de la Parole—Speech Intelligibility*, 325–334, Liege (1973b).
23. Voiers, W. D., M. F. Cohen, and J. Mickunas, "Evaluation of Speech Processing Devices, I. Intelligibility, Quality, Speaker Recognizability," Final Report, Contract No. AF19(628)4195, OAS (1965).
24. Voiers, W. D., A. D. Sharpley, and C. J. Hehmsoth, "Research on Diagnostic Evaluation of Speech Intelligibility," Final Report, Contract No. AF19628-70-C-0182, AFSC (1973).

Part X

SPEECH QUALITY AND SPEAKER RECOGNITION

Editor's Comments
on Papers 35 Through 40

This part concerns subjects closely related to speech intelligibility, i.e., measures of speech quality, recognition of the talker from the sound of his voice, and identification of the talker by sound spectrograms. The subject of quality of transmitted speech has been investigated more thoroughly and over a longer period than the other two subjects. Two of the characteristics of a system that listeners judge to have high quality are intelligibility and identifiability of the speaker. Frequently these are dimensions on which quality judgements are made implicitly or explicitly, but several studies have shown that either attribute is possible without the other. Freedom from noise, distortions, and irregularities in the frequency response curves is a characteristic that distinguishes high quality, even though, in small amounts, these defects do not interfere with intelligibility or identification. Most experimenters [e.g., Olson (1947)] have concluded that listeners prefer wide frequency ranges and full dynamic ranges, but Chinn (1945) found that restricted frequency ranges and rather low peak intensities were preferred by a majority of listeners regardless of age, sex, education, musical training, or their habit of listening to AM or FM radio. Kirk (1956) reported somewhat similar conclusions for college students.

Paper 35 by Rothaus, Urbanek, and Pachl reviews and compares the methods regularly used to measure speech quality. Rothauser was also chairman of the committee which prepared the IEEE standard, which is the only one adopted in the United States for these measurements. Paper 36 by Sapozhkov is an unusually good example of the category judgement method applied to individual speech sounds in various contexts. Munson (1962) used modifications of paired comparison testing to get a single scale; Richards (1958) discusses measures of performance of communications links and systems and developed measures using effort, naturalness, and time required to communicate; Swaffield (1959) reviews measures for international telephone quality. Papers by Eisler (1966), McDermott (1969), and McGee (1964) report application of the recently developed statistical techniques of factor analysis and dimensional scaling to extract scales and measures from psychological data. They are recommended reading.

The application of statistics to intelligibility testing was mentioned in Part IV and, although the earlier investigators were not much concerned with more than the analysis of variance of the results, some experimenters encouraged the use of the full battery of analytical techniques in the design and analysis of the tests. In talker recognition experiments, the applications are such that the investigators are concerned as much about mistaken identifications as with correct ones. The whole field of statistical decision theory as it was developed for radar and sonar detections and false alarms is applicable to speech recognition. Thus the percentages of correct and incorrect identifications are equally important, and, whether the identification is by human or by machine, the recognition criteria can be adjusted so that either percentage is favored at the expense of the other.

The ability to recognize the talker's voice is a characteristic much prized in speech communications. In addition to the comfort and assurance that a listener receives when the talker's voice seems natural to him, part of speech communication consists of receiving rhythms, accents, changes of pitch, and nonspeech sounds from a familiar and recognizable voice. Paper 37 by

391

Compton is one of the few analyses of the factors that affect recognition; there are few good papers on this subject in the literature.

Quite another use of talker recognition is to exercise privilege. Voice recognition may become an acceptable alternative to personal recognizance, photograph, or signature as a means of establishing identity in some cases for admittance to restricted areas, cashing checks, using credit cards, borrowing books or tools, voting, and similar activities. Some systems were operational on this principle in early 1976. Paper 38 by Pruzansky is an excellent early example of research on automatic recognition techniques. The bibliography of Holmgren (1966) may be of assistance to readers, but most of the literature on recognition has appeared since 1966.

The sound spectrograph was developed at Bell Labs in the 1930s for use as a research instrument. For a sample of speech a little more than two seconds long it shows intensity as a grey scale on a plot of frequency versus time. In the 1940s a book [Potter (1947)] and the first six papers in volume 18 of *JASA* were published describing the spectrograph and some of its uses, and a commercial instrument became available. Many laboratories used it in a wide range of research applications, but it was not very successful in clinical, educational, or engineering applications. Improvements and refinements were added, one of which drew lines through the points of equal intensity. The patterns look like topographic contours or isobars. Kersta noted indications that the spectrograms of a person's voice were highly characteristic of him and might be used to distinguish him from others, so he called the patterns voiceprints. In Paper 39 Kersta presented his position. In 1969 a group of eminent acoustical scientists expressed their reservations and disagreement in a paper published both in *Science* and, with the addition of appendices, in *JASA* [Bolt (1969)]. It is a landmark paper, but it has not been reproduced here because it is in two widely available journals and has been reproduced in David (1972). Instead, a later paper by the same group of authors is reproduced here as Paper 40. Readers should also read Hecker (1971) for a thorough discussion with a large bibliography. The bibliography for this section includes papers in law journals on the subject of identification in criminal cases by voiceprints.

In the editor's opinion voiceprints are unfortunately named. The contour spectrograms seems to have more in common with handwriting samples than with fingerprints insofar as immutability, dependence upon the environment and material on which they are recorded, permanence, and susceptibility to influence by emotion, stress, and deception are concerned. It seems that the introduction of evidence regarding recognition of the identity of talkers from recordings of their voices, whether the recognition is aural or visual, or both, is likely to be and should be decided on a case-by-case basis made under established rules of evidence that need to be extended for the case of visual recognition. Expert testimony is likely to be requested by prosecution and defense. Until now the testimony that has been admitted has been by individuals who have by themselves determined the identity or lack thereof. The technical papers in the scientific journals have supported the ability of groups of people to make correct identifications only while acting as a group. None of the papers cited states the reliability of any individual or any subgroup in making identifications. In November 1976 the National Academy of Sciences began an investigation of the use of sound spectrograms to supply evidence in courts. The results will be examined with great interest by students of speech.

BIBLIOGRAPHY

Anonymous, "Voiceprint Identification," *Georgetown Law. J.* **61**:703–745 (1973).

Arkhipova, A. D., and M. A. Sapozhkov, "The Quality of Vocoder Speech," *Sov. Phys.—Acoust.* **16**:292–298 (1971).

Atal, B. S., "Automatic Speaker Recognition Based on Pitch Contours," *J. Acoust, Soc. Am.* **52**:1687–1697 (1972).

Atal, B. S., "Effectiveness of Linear Prediction Characteristics of the Speech Wave for Automatic Speaker Identification and Verification," *J. Acoust. Soc. Am.* **55**:1304–1312 (1974).

Atal, B. S., "Automatic Recognition of Speakers from Their Voices," *Proc. IEEE* **64**:460–473 (1976).

Black, J. W., W. Lashbrook, E. Nash, H. J. Oyer, C. Pedrey, O. I. Tosi, and H. Truby, "Reply to 'Speaker Identification by Speech Spectrograms: Some Further Observations'," *J. Acoust. Soc. Am.* (L) **54**:535–537 (1973).

Bolt, R. H., F. S. Cooper, E. E. David, Jr., P. B. Denes, J. M. Pickett, and K. N. Stevens, "Identification of a Speaker by Speech Spectrograms," *Science* **166**:338–343 (1969) and, with appendices, as "Speaker Identification by Speech Spectrograms: A Scientist's View of Its Reliability for Legal Purposes," *J. Acoust. Soc. Am.* **47**:597–612 (1970).

Bordone-Sacerdote, C., and G. G. Sacerdote, "Some Spectral Properties of Individual Voices," *Acustica* **21**:199–210 (1969).

Bornemann, H., "Die Bewertung der Übertragungsgüte von Fernsprechersystem," *Eur. Fernsprechdienst* 32–38 (1939).

Braun, K., "Die Bedeutung und Bestimmung der Übertragungsgüte in Fernsprechverkehr," *Telegr. u. Fernspr. Tech.* , **29**:147–151 (1940).

Bricker, P. D., R. Gnanadesikan, M. V. Mathews, S. Pruzansky, P. A. Tukey, K. W. Wachter, and J. L. Warner, "Statistical Techniques for Talker Identification," *Bell Syst. Tech. J.* **50**:1427–1454 (1971).

Brown, B. L., W. J. Strong, and A. C. Rencher, "Perceptions of Personality from Speech: Effects of Manipulations of Acoustical Parameters," *J. Acoust. Soc. Am.* **54**:29–35 (1973).

Brown, B. L., W. J. Strong, and A. C. Rencher, "Fifty-four Voices from Two: The Effect of Simultaneous Manipulations of Rate, Mean Fundamental Frequency, and Variance of Fundamental Frequency on the Ratings of Personality from Speech," *J. Acoust. Soc. Am.* **55**:313–318 (1974).

Carré, R., "Identification des locuteurs: exploitation des données relative aux frequences des formants," in *Proc. 7th Int. Cong. Acoust.*, Akadémiai Kiadó, Budapest (1971), **3**, pp. 29–32.

Chinn, H. A., and P. Eisenberg, "Tonal Range and Sound-Intensity Preferences of Broadcast Listeners," *Proc. IRE* **33**:571–581 (1945).

Clarke, F. R., and R. W. Becker, "Comparison of Techniques for Discriminating among Talkers," *J. Speech Hear. Res.* **12**:747–761 (1969).

Das, S. K., and W. S. Mohn, "A Scheme for Speech Processing in Automatic Speaker Verification," *IEEE Trans. Audio Electroacoust.* **AU-19**:32–43 (1971).

David, E. E., Jr., and P. B. Denes, eds., *Human Communication: A Unified View*, McGraw-Hill, New York (1972).

Diehl, C. F., and E. T. McDonald, "Effect of Voice Quality on Communication," *J. Speech Hear. Disord.* **21**:233–237 (1956).

Eckersley, P. P., "To What Extent Does Distortion Really Matter in the Transmission of Speech and Music?" *J. Inst. Electr. Eng.* **95**:471–474 (1948).

Eisler, H., "Measurement of Perceived Acoustic Quality of Sound-Reproducing Systems by Means of Factor Analysis," *J. Acoust. Soc. Am.* **39**:484–492 (1966).

Endres, W., W. Bambach, and G. Flösser, "Voice Spectrograms as a Function of Age, Voice Disguise, and Voice Imitation," *J. Acoust. Soc. Am.* **49**:1842–1848 (1971).

Flohrer, W., "Die Beeinträchtigung der Natürlichkeit von Sprache durch Löcher in Übertragungsfrequenzband," *Frequenz* **22**:175–178 (1968).

Friedhoff, A. J., M. Alpert, and R. L. Kurtzberg, "An Electro-Acoustic Analysis of the Effects of Stress on Voice," *J. Neuropsychiatr.* **5**:266–272 (1964).

Garvin, P. L., and P. Ladefoged, "Speaker Identification and Message Identification in Speech Recognition," *Phonetica* **9**:193–199 (1963).

Glenn, J. W., and N. Kleiner, "Speaker Identification Based on Nasal Phonation," *J. Acoust. Soc. Am.* **43**:368–372 (1968).

Goodman, D. J., B. J. McDermott, and L. H. Nakatani, "Subjective Evaluation of PCM Coded Speech," *Bell Syst. Tech. J.* **55**:1087–1109 (1976).

Gosewinkel, M., "Messung der Eigenschaften von Fernsprechern," *Arch. tech. Messen* **307**:171–174 (1961), **308**:199–202 (1962).

Gubrynowicz, R., "Méthode d'analyse statistique du spectre de la parole: application à la reconnaissance automatique du locuteur," in *Proc. 7th Int. Cong. Acoust.*, Akadémiai Kiadó, Budapest (1971), **3**, pp. 25–28.

Hakala, E., and H. Savolainen, "Messprobleme bei der Analyse von Sonogrammen," *Phonetica* **14**:91–96 (1966).

Hargreaves, W. A., and J. A. Starkweather, "Recognition of Speaker Identity," *Lang. and Speech* **6**:63–67 (1963).

Hecker, M. H. L., *Speaker Recognition: An Interpretive Survey of the Literature*, American Speech and Hearing Association Monograph No. 16, Washington (1971).

Hecker, M. H. L., and C. E. Williams, "On Interrelations among Speech Quality, Intelligibility and Speaker Identifiability," A15 in *Proc. 5th Int. Cong. Acoust.* Liege (1965).

Hecker, M. H. L., and C. E. Williams, "Choice of Reference Conditions for Speech Preference Tests," *J. Acoust. Soc. Am.* **39**:946–952 (1966).

Helder, G., "Customer Evaluation of Telephone Circuits with Delay," *Bell Syst. Tech. J.* **45**:1157–1191 (1966).

Hennessey, J. J., and C. H. A. Romig, "A Review of Experiments Involving Voiceprint Identification," *J. Forensic Sci.* **16**:183–198 (1971).

Hollien, H., "Peculiar Case of 'Voiceprints'," (L) *J. Acoustic. Soc. Am.* **56**:210–213 (1974).

Holmgren, G. L., "Speaker Recognition, Speech Characteristics, Speech Evaluation and Modification of the Speech Signal—a Selected Bibliography," *IEEE Trans. Audio and Electroacoust.* **AU-14**:32–39 (1966).

Jones, W., "Evidence vel non. The *Non* Sense of Voiceprint Identification," *Kentucky Law Rev.* **62**:301–326 (1974).

Josephson, R. L., "Mr. Kersta's Magic Box: The Admissibility of Voiceprint Evidence in Criminal Cases," *Houston Law Rev.* **10**:85–100 (1972).

Kamine, B. S., "The Voiceprint Technique: Its Structure and Reliability," *San Diego Law Rev.* **6**:213–241 (1969).

Kersta, L. G., "Speaker Identification by Spectrographic Voiceprints of Voiceprint Laboratories," in *Rep. of 6th Int. Cong. Acoust.*, Y. Kohasi, ed., Maruzen, Tokyo (1968). pp. B147–B150.

Kersta, L. G., "Voiceprint Identification and Application," *Fingerprint and Identification*, **51**:3–8, 22 (May 1970).

Kirk, R. E., "Learning, a Major Factor in Influencing Preferences for High-Fidelity Reproducing Systems," *IRE Trans. Audio* **AU-4**:133–136 (1956).

Kitamura, O., S. Namba, and R. Matsumato, "Factor Analytical Research of Tone Colour," in *Rep. of 6th Int. Cong. Acoust.*, Y. Kohasi, ed., Maruzen, Tokyo (1968), pp. A117–A120.

Kramer, E., "Judgement of Personal Characteristics and Emotions from Nonverbal Properties of Speech," *Psychol. Bull.* **60**:408–420 (1963).

Law, H. B., and R. A. Seymour, "A Reference Distortion System Using Modulated Noise," *Proc. Inst. Electr. Eng.* **109B**:484–487 (1962).

Lehiste, I., and D. Meltzer, "Vowel and Speaker Identification in Natural and Synthetic Speech," *Lang. and Speech* **16**:356–364 (1973).

Li, K.-P., J. E. Dammann, and W. D. Chapman, "Experimental Studies in Speaker Verification, Using an Adaptive System," *J. Acoust. Soc. Am.* **40**:966–978 (1966).

Liberman, A. M., F. S. Cooper, D. P. Shankweiler, and M. Studdert-Kennedy, "Why Are Speech Spectrograms Hard to Read?" *Am. Ann. Deaf* **113**:127–133 (1968).

Luck, J. E., "Automatic Speaker Verification Using Cepstral Measurements," *J. Acoust. Soc. Am.* **46**:1026–1032 (1969).

Lummis, R. C., "Speaker Verification by Computer Using Speech Intensity for Temporal Registration," *IEEE Trans. Audio Electroacoust.* **AU-21**:165–173 (1973).

McDermott, B. J., "Multidimensional Analyses of Circuit Quality Judgements," *J. Acoust. Soc. Am.* **45**:774–781 (1969).

McGee, V. E., "Semantic Components of the Quality of Processed Speech," *J. Speech Hear. Res.* **7**:310–323 (1964).

McGehee, F., "The Reliability of the Identification of Human Voice," *J. Gen. Psychol.* **17**:249–271 (1937).

McGehee, F., "An Experimental Study in Voice Recognition," *J. Gen. Psychol.* **31**:53–65 (1944).

Mafune, Y., and T. Yoshida, "Distribution of Subjective Evaluations in Five Auditoriums and Discussion," in *Rep. of 6th Int. Cong. Acoust.*, Y. Kohasi, ed., Maruzen, Tokyo (1968), pp. E73–E76.

Mamoux, J.-P., "Identification de la voix humaine," *Médecine Legale & Dommage Corporel* **4**:35–38 (1971).

Modena, G., "Evaluation de la réduction de la qualité d'une transmission téléphonique par la méthode des opinions et des isopréference," *Acustica* **23**:229–232 (1970).

Mohn, A. S., Jr., "Two Statistical Feature Evaluation Techniques Applied to Speaker Identification," *IEEE Trans. Comput.* **C-20**:979–987 (1971).

Munson, W. A., and J. E. Karlin, "Isopreference Method for Evaluating Speech Transmission Circuits," *J. Acoust. Soc. Am.* **34**:762–774 (1962).

Nakatani, L. H., and K. D. Dukes, "A Sensitive Test of Speech Communication Quality," *J. Acoust. Soc. Am.* **53**:1083–1092 (1973).

Nash, E., and O. I. Tosi, "Identification of Suspects by the Voiceprint Technique," *Police Chief* **38**:49–51 (Dec. 1971).

Nickson, A. F. B., R. W. Muncey, and P. Dubout, "The Acceptability of Artificial Echoes with Reverberant Speech and Music," *Acustica* **4**:447–450 (1954).

Nishinomiya, G., "Improvement of Acoustic Feedback Stability of Public Address System by Warbling," in *Rep. of 6th Int. Cong. Acoust.*, Y. Kohasi, ed., Maruzen, Tokyo (1968), pp. E93–E96.

Ochiai, Y., "Einige Beiträge zur Stimmkunde vom Standpunkt der Vokalklangfarbequalitäten," *Acustica* **14**:303–312 (1964).

Ochiai, Y., and T. Fukumura, "Sur les qualités essentielles des vocales," *Ann. Télécommun.* **15**:277–291 (1960).

Olson, H. F., "Frequency Range Preference for Speech and Music," *J. Acoust. Soc. Am.* **19**:549–555 (1947).

Pachl, W. P., G. E. Urbanek, and E. H. Rothauser, "Preference Evaluation of a Large Set of Vocoded Speech Signals," *IEEE Trans. Audio Electroacoust.* **AU-19**:216–224 (1971).

Pollack, I., J. M. Pickett, and W. H. Sumby, "On the Identification of Speakers by Voice," *J. Acoust. Soc. Am.* **26**:403–406 (1954).

Potter, R. K., "Visible Patterns of Sound," *Science* **102**:463–470 (1945).

Potter, R. K., G. A. Kopp, and H. C. Green, *Visible Speech*, D. Van Nostrand, New York (1947).

Reich, A. R., K. L. Moll, and J. F. Curtis, "Effects of Selected Vocal Disguises upon Spectrographic Speaker Identification," *J. Acoust. Soc. Am.* **60**:919–925 (1976).

Richards, D. L., and J. Swaffield, "Assessment of Speech Communication Links," *Proc. Inst. Electr. Eng.* **106 B**:77–92 (1958).

Reisz, R. R., and E. T. Klemmer, "Subjective Evaluation of Delay and Echo Suppressors in Telephone Communications," *Bell Syst. Tech. J.* **42**:2919–2941 (1963).

Rosenberg, A. E., "Automatic Speaker Verification: A Review," *Proc. IEEE* **64**:475–487 (1976).

Rosenberg, A. E., "Evaluation of an Automatic Speaker Verification System over Telephone Lines," *Bell Syst. Tech. J.* **55**:723–744 (1976).

Rothauser, E. H., et al., "IEEE Recommended Practice for Speech Quality Measurements," *IEEE Trans. Audio Electroacoust.* **AU-17**:227–246 (1969).

Rothauser, E. H., G. E. Urbank, and W. P. Pachl, "Isopreference Methods for Speech Evaluation," *J. Acoust. Soc. Am.* **44**:408–418 (1968).

Sambur, M. R., "Speaker Recognition Using Orthogonal Linear Prediction," *IEEE Trans. Acoust. Speech Sig. Proc.* **ASSP-24**:283–289 (1976).

Schiaffino P., "Influenza dell'effetto locale sulla qualitá di transmissione," *Alta Freq.* **30**:767–770, trans. as "Influence of Sidetone on Quality of Transmission," 834–836 (1961).

Schjonneberg, K., and F. Olson, "Listening Test Methods and Evaluation," *J. Aud. Eng. Soc.* **9**:29–36 (1961).

Sessler, G. M., and J. E. West, "Influence of Bandwidth and Reverberation Time on Preference Evaluation of Speech," in *Rep. of 6th Int. Cong. Acoust.*, Y. Kohasi, ed., Maruzen, Tokyo (1968), pp. C29–C32.

Sessler, G. M., and J. E. West, "Subjective Importance of Low and High Frequency Components of Speech," *Proc. 7th Int. Cong. Acoust.*, Akadémiai Kaidó, Budapest (1971), **3**, pp. 257–260.

Shearme, J. N., and J. N. Holmes, "An Experiment Concerning the Recognition of Voices," *Lang. and Speech* **2**:123–131 (1959).

Stevens, K. N., C. E. Williams, J. R. Carbonell, and B. Woods, "Speaker Authentication and Identification: A Comparison of Spectrographic and Auditory Presentations of Speech Material," *J. Acoust. Soc. Am.* **44**:1596–1607 (1968).

Su, L.-S., K.-P. Li, and K. S. Fu, "Identification of Speakers by Use of Nasal Coarticulation," *J. Acoust. Soc. Am.* **56**:1876–1882 (1974).

Swaffield, J., and D. L. Richards, "Rating of Speech Links and Performance of Telephone Networks," *Proc. Inst. Electr. Eng.* **106B**: 65–76 (1959).

Tedford, W. H., Jr., and T. V. Frazier, "Further Study of the Isopreference Method of Circuit Evaluation," *J. Acoust. Soc. Am.* **39**:645–649 (1966).

Tosi, O. I., "The Problem of Speaker Identification and Elimination," in *Measurement Procedures in Speech, Hearing, and Language*, S. Singh, ed., Univ. Park Press, Baltimore (1975), pp. 399–431.

Tosi, O., H. Oyer, W. Lashbrook, C. Pedrey, J. Nichol, and E. Nash. "Experiment on Voice Identification," *J. Acoust. Soc. Am.* **51**:2030–2043 (1972).

Ungeheuer, G., "Ein enfaches Verfahren zur akustischen Klassifikation von Sprechern," A17 in *Proc. 5th Int. Cong. Acoust.* Liège (1965).

Voiers, W. D., "Perceptual Bases for Speaker Identity," *J. Acoust. Soc. Am.* **36**:1065–1073 (1964).

Voiers, W. D., "The Present State of Digital Vocoding Technique: A Diagnostic Evaluation," *IEEE Trans. Audio Electroacoust.* **AU-16**:275–279 (1968).

Welch, E. J., Jr., "Voiceprint Identification: A Reliable Index?" *Trial Magazine* **9**:45–47 (Jan.–Feb. 1973).

West, W., "Telephone Transmission Testing by Subjective Methods," *Post Office Electr. Eng. J.* **31**:286–292 (1939).

Williams, C. E., "Aural Speaker Recognition and Speech Communication System Evaluation," in *Proc. 7th Int. Cong. Acoust.*, Akadémiai Kaidó, Budapest (1971), **3**, pp. 89–92.

Wilson, P., "A Repeatable Technique for Listening Tests," *J. Aud. Eng. Soc.* **15**:73–75 (1967).

Witter, H. L., and D. P. Goldstein, "Quality Judgements of Hearing Aid Transduced Speech," *J. Speech Hear. Res.* **14**:312–322 (1971).

Wolf, J. J., "Efficient Acoustic Parameters for Speaker Recognition," *J. Acoust. Soc. Am.* **51**:2044–2056 (1972).

Yanagisawa, T., and T. Nimura, "Experiments on Subjective Tonal Evaluation in Artificial Composite Sound Field in Anechoic Room," *J. Acoust. Soc. Japan* **26**:67–77 (1970). in Japanese, abstract and figures in English.

Young, M., and R. Campbell, "Effects of Context on Talker Identification," *J. Acoust. Soc. Am.* **42**:1250–1254 (1967).

Zalewski, J., W. Majewski, and H. Hollien, "Cross Correlation of Long-Term Speech Spectra as a Speaker Identification Technique," *Acustica* **34**:20–24 (1975).

Reprinted from *Acoust. Soc. Am. J.* **49**(4), Pt. 2:1297–1308 (1971)

A Comparison of Preference Measurement Methods

E. H. ROTHAUSER

IBM Zurich Research Laboratory, 8803 Rüschlikon, Switzerland

G. E. URBANEK* AND W. P. PACHL†

Institute for Telecommunications, University of Technology, Vienna, Austria

The present paper compares four methods for measuring the speech-quality parameter preference. The scales of the isopreference method, the category judgment method, the relative preference method, and the absolute preference judgment method (a proposed modification of the category judgment method) are related to a "preference unit" scale. Capabilities and performance of the methods are discussed and illustrated by evaluating a set of test signals with different types of degradation containing a subset of clearly discriminable signals. The paper tries to show how far preference results gained with one method allow prediction of corresponding results in terms of another method. Because of the quantitative limitations of subjective tests and especially since the four methods use different approaches and have different application ranges, it is not unexpected that the preference unit scale has been found to be more of scientific rather than of practical engineering interest. Listeners have been found capable of discriminating reliably, even without reference or anchor signals, more than the five quality steps provided by the category judgment method, and somehow also by the relative preference method. The proposed absolute preference judgment method recognizes this finding and, therefore, yields much better agreement with the isopreference method than the two other methods, which are apparently too strongly quantized.

INTRODUCTION

In a previous paper[1] we have outlined a utilitarian concept of speech quality. The parameter preference has been described as one component of speech quality, and a specific method for the evaluation of preference has been proposed. The present paper has been devoted to a more detailed study of the parameter preference by comparing several measurement methods. While three of the four measurement methods considered are well known,[1–3] the fourth method seems to be an interesting variation of the category judgment method. Stimulated by an idea of Munson and Karlin,[4] but now based on a study of the above four methods, a preference unit scale is derived which will turn out to be a useful tool for the comparison of these methods.

I. PREFERENCE MEASUREMENT METHODS

A. General

Preference answers the question: "How well does an average listener like a particular speech test signal as a source of information?" Thus, preference describes the average attitude of a listener towards a test signal alone, or while comparing it consecutively with a speech reference signal with reproducible characteristics. It is an expression for the degree to which one speech signal is preferred to another one regardless of the particular reasons of a listener for his decision.

Such qualitative definitions are insufficient for quantitative evaluations of the different preference measurement methods. We shall need definitions which allow construction and use of a rating scale and which consider differences in the reactions of single listeners, groups, and populations in the statistical sense.

Qualitative definitions are the following: If two speech signals A and B are compared with each other, the speech signal preferred by the majority of the listeners will have the higher preference. Two signals are equal in preference, i.e., they are isopreferent, when half of the listeners favor one signal. These definitions allow the establishment of preference scales.

The direct comparison of two speech signals is the most basic method for making a preference decision and forms the basis of all relative methods. Although it is the most direct approach to answer the question: "Which one of two signals A and B is qualitatively better?" the method does not yield a single absolute preference value. For this reason it will not be considered as one of the measurement methods to be discussed in the following.

For the time being, it seems to be appropriate to consider several different measurement methods. It seems impossible now to standardize only one method, because none of the known methods combines simplicity, accuracy, reproducibility, and applicability to all conceivable practical problems. In view of the different scales and preference results obtained by the various methods, a detailed comparison of these methods is needed. An important problem in this context is that a score measured for one signal with one particular method does not allow for conclusive comparisons with the scores of a second signal evaluated by means of another measurement procedure.

The methods have been separated into two groups and are described in the following sections. In the first group, the relative methods, listeners have to express their preference always for one signal out of a pair of presented signals, the test signal and some reference signal. In the second group, the absolute methods, the listeners are requested to make preference judgments on isolated signals in terms of some absolute value system.

B. Relative Methods

1. Isopreference Method

In this method,[5-7] preference is expressed in terms of a reference signal, the quality of which is continuously and reproducibly adjustable. The quality of the reference signal is degraded by adding a certain amount of a degradation signal to a high-fidelity speech signal. Now the isopreference level of a test signal is defined by the specific signal-to-noise (S/N) ratio of the reference signal where 50% of all the listeners favor the reference signal, i.e., when both signals are isopreferent.

Two types of reference signals have been employed in the isopreference tests, both of them utilizing shaped random noise for the generation of their respective degradation signals. These reference signals, ADD (high-fidelity speech degraded by additive noise) and DIG (high-fidelity speech degraded by multiplicative noise), are fundamentally different, not only with regard to the generation principle, but also with regard to their auditory impression. The reference signals should be adjustable over an S/N range of about 60 dB to cover the "total" quality range. The test results are given by isopreference levels.

2. Relative Preference Method

In this method,[3,6] the quality of the test signal is measured relative to the qualities of a special set of

five fixed reference signals that represent fundamentally different types of speech distortion. Test signal A is presented together with each signal B_i out of the set of reference signals in repeated signal pairs AB_iAB_i. Comparisons are performed in a random sequence with all the pairs of speech signals possible in both the forward and the reverse order of presentation. All the possible combinations of the different reference signals are also presented in this procedure. In our studies of the relative preference method, we have selected the following five reference signals: (1) high-fidelity speech; (2) low-passed speech (limiting frequency 800 Hz); (3) one-way rectified speech; (4) clipped speech (30 dB); and (5) full-wave rectified speech. The requirement that the signals be consistently preferred by the listeners in the order given above has been proved by isopreference tests as well as by direct comparison of all the possible pairs among these five signals. The test results are expressed as preference rating numbers (PRN) between 0 and 10 on a dimensionless preference rating scale.

C. Absolute Methods

1. Absolute Preference Judgment

The main advantage of the category judgment method, its capability to describe preference in terms of a very small number of categories, can be construed to be also its main disadvantage. At first, the listeners sometimes find it annoying to describe their complex impressions of speech quality in terms of only five categories. Often the listeners would prefer to get a chance to describe their impressions with higher accuracy. Secondly, a quantization of judgments to a small number of categories does not offer any advantage if the final goal of the absolute rating is a mean score, which is normally given as an unquantized decimal number.

The absolute preference judgment method avoids the above disadvantages of the category judgment method. Here the listeners are requested to evaluate the test signals in terms of numbers from 0 to 10, where zero is the worst signal and 10 corresponds to the best signal. The listeners may use decimal fractions between integers if they think they can improve the accuracy of their judgments thereby. Obviously, no quantization of these listener responses is useful or necessary if the goal of the test is an evaluation in terms of a mean score.

2. Category Judgment Method

In the category judgment method,[2,6,8,9] the quality impression of a speech test signal is described by the listeners in terms of five response categories: excellent (5), good (4), fair (3), poor (2), and unsatisfactory (1). The test starts with a familarization period during which the test signals are introduced to the listeners, and one or two reference signals are presented, of which the "correct" category evaluation is identified to the listeners. In the evaluation phase the test signals are presented in a random order and the listeners are asked to mark the one category which corresponds to their quality impression of the presented speech signal. From the listeners' responses a mean opinion score (MCJ) or cumulative preferences can now be calculated.

II. A PREFERENCE UNIT SCALE

A. Desired Properties

There are several ways to compare the different preference evaluation scales. The most primitive approach would be to compare each of the four scales with any other scale, resulting in at least six correspondence diagrams. A much better approach to the comparison problem would be to "standardize" the most accurate evaluation scale. Following this idea, we should select the isopreference method as our standard method and express all the other evaluation scales in terms of the S/N ratio of the reference signals ADD or DIG. This solution is indeed feasible, and in Sec. II-C we shall make use also of this approach which, in spite of its simplicity, does not satisfy all expectations. It has already been shown[1,4] that there are indications that the relation between preference and the S/N ratio of the reference signals is a nonlinear one. A certain difference in decibels corresponds to a much smaller preference variation for high speech quality than for very low speech quality. A similar argument holds for the reliability of isopreference judgments as a function of speech quality. The standard deviations for high speech quality are much larger than those for low speech quality as measured in decibels. Another very desirable property of a standard preference scale would be that differences on this scale would allow prediction of the percentage of listeners preferring the signal with the higher preference number PU. A mathematical formulation of this property could be

$$p(X_2 > X_1) = \phi[k(PU_{X_2} - PU_{X_1})], \qquad (1)$$

where $p(X_2 > X_1)$ denotes the percentage of a listener population who prefer signal X_2 to signal X_1, and ϕ stands for the cumulative normal distribution. In Sec. II-B a scale with this desired property will be constructed. It will be called preference unit (PU) scale. At first one might suspect that any one of the four methods discussed might serve as a starting point for the construction of the PU scale. However, it can easily be seen that the two quantized methods, i.e., the relative preference method and the category judgment method are not very ideal for this purpose. We shall find that the PU scales constructed on the basis of the isopreference method and the absolute preference judgment method are practically identical. This very satisfying result establishes preference as a unidimen-

sional measure of speech quality which can be evaluated by several completely different methods. While the PU scale is an apparently ideal tool for comparisons between the different measurement methods, the fact should not be disregarded that the variability of listeners and the possibility of correlation effects (Sec. IV) in the judgment of speech signals limits for practical purposes the significance of a statement like: "This signal A has the preference value PU$_A$."

B. Construction Based on Analog Methods

1. Proposed Scale Structure

Following ideas of Munson and Karlin,[4] we can describe the PU rating of a certain speech signal which has been measured in terms of the "individual preference units (IPU)" of one of the above methods by

$$(PU)_x = K \int_{IPU=a}^{IPU=x} \frac{1}{\sigma} d(IPU),$$

with

$$K = 100 \Big/ \int_a^b \frac{1}{\sigma} d(IPU). \qquad (2)$$

Here a and b denote the lower and upper limits of the quality range considered, and K is computed to give a PU scale which has 100 units from a to b. In the following, we shall extract the function σ from the large body of test evidence which we have accumulated in testing with the isopreference method and the absolute preference judgment method. As can be seen from the above equations, the desired PU scale is invariant to constant factors of σ. It will be shown later that this property allows for the scale construction to utilize all the test evidence available on the σ of single listeners, that of groups, and that of a population. Based on such σ evaluations and properly defined limits a and b, separate PU scales for ADD and DIG, as well as for the absolute preference judgment method, will be constructed.

2. Isopreference Method

a. Determination of σ

Single listener: In the isopreference method, the quality of the speech test signal A is described in terms of the "isopreferent" setting of a continuously variable parameter x of the reference signal B. The decision probability of a single listener to prefer B in the setting x will be called

$$p(x) = p(B \mid A, Bx),$$

which becomes, for variable x, the psychometric function of the listener. A useful approximation for this is the shape of a cumulative normal distribution

$$p(x) = \Phi\left(\frac{x - \mu_i}{\sigma}\right) = \frac{1}{(2\pi)^{\frac{1}{2}} \cdot \sigma} \cdot \int_{-\infty}^{x} \exp\left[-\frac{(\xi - \mu_i)^2}{2\sigma^2} d\xi\right]. \qquad (3)$$

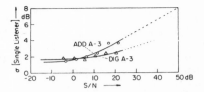

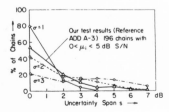

FIG. 1. Definition of the uncertainty span s for AB decisions at settings of the reference signal at x_i.

This approximation curve has the desired properties: $p(x)=0.5$ for $x=\mu_i$, i.e., for isopreference, where μ_i denotes the isopreference level of the individual listener; $p(x) \to 0$ for $x \to -\infty$, i.e., for A better than Bx; and $p(x) \to 1$ for $x \to \infty$, i.e., for Bx better than A. The standard deviation σ is a measure for the size of the uncertainty range in which the listeners somehow give random decisions.

The result of an isopreference test run, where the reference signal is available in our test setup only in quantized steps of 1 dB may be a sequence of A and B decisions as shown in Fig. 1. An estimate for the standard deviation σ of the psychometric function can be derived from investigations of the uncertainty spans s in a large number of such test runs. A chain of ordered decisions from a test run starts for increasing quality of the reference signals with a number of "certain" A decisions and ends with a number of "certain" B decisions. Between these regions there is an uncertainty range, where decisions may be random. This uncertainty range may include not only the uncertainty span s denoted, but also the decisions at x_3 or x_8 of Fig. 1. As we have no test evidence for this latter assumption, we have to get along with the easily observable uncertainty span. In terms of Fig. 1, the uncertainty span is defined to reach from $\frac{1}{2}(x_3+x_4)$ to $\frac{1}{2}(x_7+x_8)$, thus yielding $s=\frac{1}{2}(x_7+x_8-x_3-x_4)=x_8-x_3-1$, or in more general words, s is defined as the difference, minus 1 dB, between the ends of the closed A and B decision chains.

Given a large number of listener responses from various isopreference tests, we can try to estimate the value of σ of the psychometric function assumed to be underlying all those listener responses. If statistical independence of single decisions is assumed, the probability of a certain sequence of A's and B's can be calculated as the product of the respective probabilities. The distribution of the size of uncertainty spans in listener responses will be a function of σ. With Eq. 3 we have computed this distribution for some values of σ and incremental steps of 1 dB for the reference signal as used in our tests. The results are plotted in Fig. 2 together with a distribution gained empirically. This empirical distribution is based on the evaluation

of 196 AB chains from different listeners and different isopreference tests utilizing the additive reference signal. As σ will be shown to depend on speech quality, the 196 chains have been selected to belong only to the evaluation of test signals found to have an isopreference level between 0 and 5 dB. Comparison of the computed distribution with our empirical distribution allows for an estimate of the σ of the psychometric function to be $\sigma \approx 1.5$ dB. This estimate for the σ of the single listener is valid only in the above-mentioned quality range.

Now we shall construct a dependence of σ on speech quality for the two reference signals ADD and DIG. While Fig. 2 describes the full distribution of the uncertainty span s, we shall simplify our further considerations by utilizing as a basis for the computation, of σ, only the percentage of closed chains in our test data, i.e., chains which have an uncertainty span of zero. Figure 2 illustrates that the percentage of the closed chains ($s=0$) does indeed provide a good measure for σ. Using this approach, we have constructed Fig. 3, which gives an estimate for the value of σ for the interesting quality range of ADD and DIG.

Listener group and population: Figures 4 and 5 show the mean-square deviation S_G in test repetitions with four

FIG. 3. Estimate of σ for ADD A-3 and DIG A-3 over the total quality range considered.

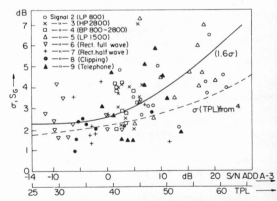

FIG. 2. Estimation of the value of σ of the psychometric function for the quality range $0 \div 5$ dB (ADD A-3). Our test results (triangles) are compared to computed distributions (circles) for $\sigma=1,2,$ and 3 dB.

FIG. 4. Measured mean-square deviations S_G of trained listener groups for different speech test signals with the reference signal ADD A-3. The solid line shows the σ (ADD A-3) from Fig. 3 multiplied by a factor of 1.6 chosen to indicate that a linear relation between σ and an approximation curve of the S_G distribution is conceivable. The dashed curve σ(TPL) taken from the literature is shown to allow for a comparison of test experience.

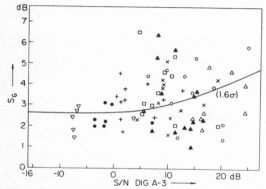

FIG. 5. Measured mean-square deviations S_G of trained listener groups for the different speech test signals of Fig. 4, but with the reference signal DIG A-3. The solid line shows the σ (DIG A-3) from Fig. 3 with the same intention as in Fig. 4.

trained listener groups (8–10 listeners each) for eight different speech test signals as a function of our two reference signals ADD and DIG. The approximation curves in these two figures are not derived from the plotted test data, but are taken from Fig. 3 by multiplying the σ given there by a factor of 1.6, which is of no further significance in agreement with Sec. II-B-1. As the approximation curve constructed in this manner is not contradicted by the experimental data, we feel encouraged to maintain our hypothesis of a linear relation between the σ of a single listener, that of groups, and that of a population. The large number of different groups and different test signals in the last two figures gives widely scattered data. Considering the large number of people involved in these tests we feel entitled to call them a population. If we pool all the listener decisions separately for each test signal, we get mean-square deviations for the population as given in Figs. 6 and 7. The approximation curve, which is again derived from Fig. 3, indicates how much larger the deviations for the population are compared to those of a single listener, but shows clearly that our assumption of a linear relation between the σ of a single listener and that of a population is indeed reasonable.

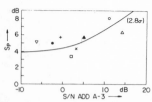

FIG. 6. Computed mean-square deviations S_P for the test evidence of Fig. 4 broken down by the different test signals. The solid line again indicates a possible linear relation between σ, and an approximation curve of the S_P distribution for this "population" of trained listeners (see Ref. 1).

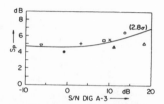

FIG. 7. Computed mean-square deviations S_P for the test evidence of Fig. 5 broken down by the different test signals. The solid line again indicates a possible linear relation between σ, and an approximation curve of the S_P distribution for this "population" of trained listeners.

b. Scale Construction

The construction of a preference unit scale based on Eq. 2 requires established knowledge of σ as a function of the individual preference scale and of determining appropriate values for a and b. In the above subsection, σ has been described as a function of the reference signals ADD and DIG. The lower integration boundary can be set with good accuracy to $a_{ADD} = -14$ dB (S/N−ADD), given by the complete masking of the speech signal by the degradation noise. The reference signal DIG does not exhibit such a clear masking threshold. Therefore the isopreferent level to a_{ADD} has been chosen with $a_{DIG} = -16$ dB (S/N −DIO). The upper boundary of the PU scale depends on the quality of the test setup and is given by the detection threshold of the degradation signal. We have decided that we can consider test signals up to an upper quality boundary of $b_{ADD} = 50$ dB (S/N−ADD), which is equivalent to $b_{DIG} = 40$ dB (S/N−DIG). Further evidence supporting these assumptions can be found in Figs. 12 and 13. In order to establish a point of reference, an S/N ratio of 0 dB means in this context equal subjective loudness of the speech signal and of the added degradation signal. It is now possible to construct two separate PU scales, PU$_1$ and PU$_2$, considering the experimental evidence for the reference signals ADD and DIG. These relations are given in Fig. 8. This figure also contains the TPU scale of Munson and Karlin,[4] which has been drawn to have the same lower

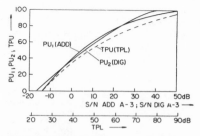

FIG. 8. The individual preference unit scales PU$_1$ based upon ADD A-3, and PU$_2$ based upon DIG A-3 are compared to the TPU scale from the literature.

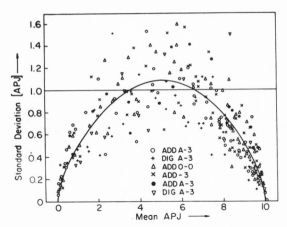

FIG. 9. Measured standard deviations for two listening groups evaluating with the absolute preference judgment method different settings of variations of our reference signals ADD and DIG. An approximation curve has been fitted empirically to the distribution.

limits as our reference signal ADD. The difference at the upper preference limit is easily explained by the fact that their TPU scale has been constructed to reach up to the quality of a real-life speaker.

3. Absolute Preference Judgment Method

The APJ method is basically different from the isopreference method in so far as it obviously does not know the "uncertainty span" of a single listener when he judges a particular test signal. Hence, the function σ of preference has to be determined directly from judgments of whole listening groups. Figure 9 describes the standard deviations as a function of mean APJ's found during the evaluation of different settings of several versions of our reference signals ADD and DIG with two listening groups, each consisting of ten listeners. Although the values are widely scattered, a smooth curve was drawn through the data points. The figure shows very clearly a result which to some extent could have been predicted beforehand. The standard deviations are largest in the middle of the quality range and decrease continuously to zero towards the lower (APJ=0) and upper (APJ=10) limit of the APJ scale. The unexpected result in this figure is that the mean

standard deviation is typically smaller than one preference mark.

From the approximation curve of Fig. 9 and the obvious integration limits $a_{APJ}=0$ and $b_{APJ}=10$, we can construct by using Eq. 2 the desired PU scale PU_3 based upon the APJ method. This relation is shown in Fig. 10.

C. Comparison of Preference Scales

1. Equivalence of the Three PU Scales

The desire to establish one unidimensional rating scale for the speech quality parameter preference requires the equivalence of the three preference unit scales PU_1, PU_2, and PU_3. These scales have been individually derived for each measurement method. Equivalence in the requested sense shall mean that for any test signal X the three methods yield numerically the same PU value on their respective PU scales. For the present purpose of scale comparison, we shall use only DIG and ADD as test signals, and we have averaged over a large number of test results to come as close as possible to the opinion of a population. In Sec. III we shall study how well the general results derived here will hold for isolated evaluation of some signals by one of our listener groups.

The equivalence of three PU scales will be shown indirectly. We shall tentatively assume that $PU_1 = PU_2 = PU_3$, and then we shall try to show that the constructed relations between any two of the three individual preference scales in terms of ADD, DIG, and APJ can be verified by direct measurements. The degree of conformity between constructed relations and relations found experimentally can be taken as a measure of transitivity, the existence of which is a prerequisite for a unidimensional preference rating scale.

a. PU_1 Equal to PU_2

The relation between the two reference signals ADD and DIG found by repeated direct bivariate isopreference testing has been given in a previous paper,[1] and is repeated in Fig. 11 together with its uncertainty

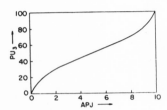

FIG. 10. The individual preference unit scale PU_3 for the APJ method constructed from Fig. 9.

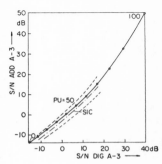

FIG. 11. A correspondence (solid line) between the two reference scales ADD A-3 and DIG A-3 is constructed from Fig. 8 by postulating $(PU_1) = (PU_2) = (PU)$. This correspondence is shown to lie within the uncertainty range (dashed curves) of the Standard isopreference curve SIC described in our previous paper.

range. In addition, this figure shows the constructed PU scale based on interpolated distributions of different σ's and plotted in the same fashion as the standard isopreference curve (SIC) against ADD and DIG. The desired condition seems to be satisfactorily fulfilled. The constructed curve for the PU values can really be said to coincide with the SIC. Figure 11 also serves a second purpose. It allows the SIC between ADD and DIG to be graded in terms of PU values.

b. PU_1 and PU_2 equal to PU_3

After showing that $PU_1 = PU_2$ holds, the relation $PU_2 = PU_3$ would obviously be satisfied by verifying $PU_1 = PU_3$ only, but both of the two remaining relations will be displayed individually. The result of this comparison procedure is given in Figs. 12 and 13, which show as solid curves the constructed relations between APJ's and the two reference signals ADD and DIG. Similarly as in Fig. 11, the two curves have been found by combining Figs. 8 and 10. In both Figs. 12 and 13 the direct measurement data from evaluating the two reference signals ADD and DIG by means of absolute preference judgments are given additionally.

As the constructed curves can be said to be really a good approximation to the test data, the assumption of the equivalence of the three PU scales seems to be justified within the accuracy limits of our subjective measurements. Starting from this unified PU scale, we can try to establish relations to the preference scales of the two quantized methods.

2. Relations to the Quantized Scales

a. Category Judgment Method

The quantized methods require a different approach for describing their scales in terms of PU values. The relation between MCJ and PU values will be found by measuring different settings of the reference signals ADD and DIG with the category judgment method. The corresponding scores of a listener group are shown in Figs. 14 and 15, where the data points are directly

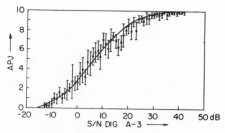

FIG. 13. This figure corresponds to Fig. 12, but for the reference signal DIG A-3.

approximated by a smooth curve. Together with Fig. 8 and the approximation curves, we can now construct the relation between MCJ's and PU values. These relations for ADD and DIG are given in Fig. 16 together with the mean of the two curves, which will be taken as the desired MCJ/PU relation. The mean curve starts at a PU value of about 12 instead of starting at PU = 0. This is an effect of the strong quantization of the category judgment method, because the listeners will assign the worst category "unsatisfactory (1)" to all those ADD and DIG signals which do not yet qualify for the category "poor (2)." Consequently, some speech signals in this quality range are judged worse than they would have been rated if the listeners had been able to make finer distinctions. A corresponding effect can be observed at the upper end of the speech-quality range.

b. Relative Preference Method

In order to derive the relation between a relative preference scale and the PU scale, the same approach can be taken as in Sec. II-C-2-a for the category judgment method. In this sense, Figs. 17, 18, and 19 show for one particular case the evaluation of our well-known variable signals ADD and DIG as test signals in terms of the relative preference method and constructed from these data the desired relation between PRN and PU values.

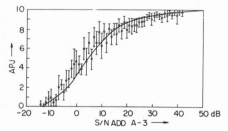

FIG. 12. Two different evaluations of our reference signal ADD A-3 by the APJ method are shown. For the direct approach, means and standard deviations for a group of 10 listeners are given. The solid curve has been constructed from Figs. 8 and 10 by assuming $(PU_1) = (PU_3) = (PU)$.

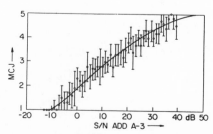

FIG. 14. The reference signal ADD A-3 is evaluated with the MCJ method. Means and standard deviations for a group of 10 listeners are given together with a direct approximation curve for these test data.

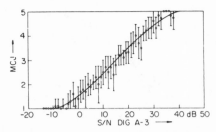

FIG. 15. This figure corresponds to Fig. 14, but for the reference signal DIG A-3.

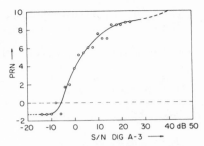

FIG. 17. The reference signal ADD A-3 is evaluated with the relative preference method using the set of reference signals from Table I. The mean results are directly approximated (solid curve).

In contrast to the other comparisons of scales in this paper, the relation of Fig. 19 is not "absolute," but depends strongly on the selection of the five reference signals necessary for relative preference measurements. Our relation here has been derived utilizing the set of reference signals described in Sec. I-C-2. The freedom of the experimenter to select an appropriate set of reference signals can occasionally lead to somehow unexpected test results. If the test signal lies outside the quality range covered by the reference signals, its PRN rating may, in accordance with the formula[3]

$$PRN = 1.25(n-1), \qquad (4)$$

have values from -1.15 up to 11.25 instead of an expected range of 0–10, because it may then happen that the number of decisions n for the test signal becomes 0 or 10 out of a possible maximum of 10.

Another basic problem connected with the derivation of the desired PRN/PU relation is the following: Assuming that the set of reference signals has been chosen to cover a relatively large quality range, the PRN scale for the single listener will practically be a staircase function, because the listener will rarely be forced to make ambiguous decisions. To support this fact we can point out that, within a total quality range of about 50 dB, there lie only three reference signals, giving rise to uncertainties determined by the psychometric functions with σ's of about 1.5 dB. The other two of the five reference signals serve only to limit the quality range considered. Usually the quantized character of the responses of a single listener remains un-

noticed when the responses of a listener group are considered. While for the single listener according to Eq. 4 only 10 different test results are possible in terms of PRN, only the utilization of a larger group allows characterization of test signals in less quantized form. A practical case in which even the utilization of a group of 10 listeners does not completely mask the staircase character of the PRN scale seems to be observable in Fig. 17 for the PRN rating of 8.75. Summarizing, it might be interesting to note that the relative preference method shows a very strong quantization for the single listener and an apparently better discrimination for the group, while for the isopreference method the opposite is true. There the possible accuracy as a function of σ is better for a single listener (Fig. 3) than that for a group (Figs. 4 and 5).

III. EVALUATION OF A SET OF TEST SIGNALS

A. Comparative Presentation of Test Results

In Sec. II relations between individual scales and the PU scale have been established by using as a link the signals ADD and DIG either as test or reference signals. In this section we shall try to illustrate the validity of the above relations by using them for the evaluation of a set of test signals with fundamentally different types of degradation. A description of the test signals

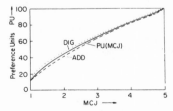

FIG. 16. A relation between the PU scale and the MCJ scale is constructed from Figs. 8, 14, and 15. The small differences between the relations for ADD A-3 and DIG A-3 justify the assumption of a mean correspondence curve (solid line).

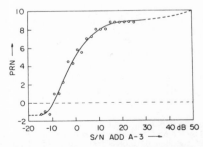

FIG. 18. This figure corresponds to Fig. 17, but for the reference signal DIG A-3.

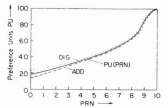

FIG. 19. A relation between the PU scale and the PRN scale is constructed from Figs. 8, 17, and 18. The solid line constitutes the mean between the ADD and DIG relations.

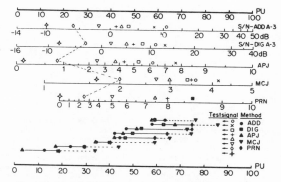

FIG. 20. The individual preference scales are plotted against the PU scale. The test signals of Table I illustrate the validity of the scale relations presented. In the upper part of the figure, the test signal evaluations appear directly along the individual scales. In the lower part, the same results are rearranged to show signal evaluations broken down by test methods.

chosen, some of which have very similar preference values, is given in Table I.

The results of our test case are summarized in Fig. 20. In the upper part of this figure, the scales of the different methods have been drawn in relation to the PU scale. These relations have been taken from Figs. 8, 10, 16, and 19. The test results for the signals given in Table I have been plotted along the respective scales. The results for a particular test signal are connected by thin lines. Intersections of these thin lines indicate differences in rank ordering of the test signals by the different methods. The lower part of Fig. 20 presents the same information as the upper part, but in a different form. Here the results are broken down by test signals rather than by measurement methods. Thus, in the upper part of the figure, test result markers denote test signals, while in the lower part of the figure the solid markers denote measurement methods.

B. Interpretation of Test Results

Correct rank ordering of the set of test signals chosen might be viewed in the first instance as a good measure for the compatibility of the different evaluation methods. Unfortunately, in principle it is not possible to determine the true rank order within a set of dissimilar test signals. We can only expect—and Fig. 20 supports this expectation—that rank ordering of signals is largely independent of the evaluation method. This expectation is based on the tacit assumption that the

TABLE I. Test signals employed.

Signal No.	Description	Marker in Fig. 20
0	Low-passed speech; cutoff frequency 800 Hz; attenuation rate 40 dB/oct	○
1	Low-passed speech; cutoff frequency 1500 Hz; attenuation rate 40 dB/oct	×
2	Bandpassed speech; 800–2800 Hz; attenuation rate 40 dB/oct	□
3	Local telephone connection	+
4	High-passed speech; cutoff frequency 28 kHz; attenuation rate 40 dB/oct	△
5	Half-wave rectified speech	▽
6	Peak-clipped speech; approx 30 dB	◇
7	Full-wave rectified speech	(open star)

test signals have clearly different qualities, a condition which has been met by the majority of the test signals chosen. A detailed explanation of the few rank order variations in Fig. 20 seems to be impossible. According to our test experience, any combination of the following reasons may occur: The test signals may be too similar with regard to preference, either absolutely or in terms of a particular measurement method; listeners may belong to classes of a population which are biased for or against certain test signals, a bias which may be influenced by training, by previous unintentional exposures to other speech signals, and other effects.

The comparative performance of the different methods seems to be illustrated best by the lower part of Fig. 20. Inspection shows that the two isopreference evaluations are in rather good agreement with the APJ ratings, while the two quantized methods yield widely differing results. The category judgment method gives results with a strong positive offset. We suspect—but had no time to prove our assumption—that this biasing could be overcome by appropriate anchoring signals. The relation between the MCJ scale and the PU scale was established by presenting to the listeners the full quality range of our signals ADD or DIG in one test run. This procedure made an anchor unnecessary. In the present test case only the test signals were presented to the listeners. The missing upper and lower quality bounds as anchors may have led to the observable confusion. In judging the performance of the relative preference method it should be pointed out that only signals 1, 2, 3, and 4 were really used as test signals, while the other signals 7, 6, 5, 0, and high-fidelity speech were assigned the *a priori* ratings 0, 2.5, 5, 7.5, and 10, in agreement with the isopreference evaluation of these signals described in Sec. II-C-2. Another disadvantage of the quantized methods becomes evident in our test example, at least for the relative preference

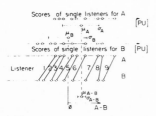

FIG. 21. A hypothetical test situation is described showing the influence of correlation effects. The upper part shows for a group of nine listeners individual decisions, mean scores, and standard deviations for the two test signals A and B. The middle part shows that strong positive correlation exists between the decisions of individual listeners. Considering this correlation, the lower part of the figure shows the resulting high discriminability of the test signals A and B.

method. Here we find in two cases the same ratings for two different test signals which are clearly discriminable by the continuous methods.

IV. DISCRIMINABILITY OF TEST SIGNALS AND THE PU-SCALE CONCEPT

In order to draw final conclusions from the test case of Sec. III, it will be necessary to consider the size of typical uncertainty ranges which accompany subjective measurements of this type. In the following, some aspects of this problem will be discussed. The discriminability of test signals is not simply describable by the difference of their respective PU values, but depends also very strongly on the "similarity" of the two test signals and on the methods used to measure these PU values.

It seems to be obvious that much finer discriminations in quality are possible between nearly identical test signals than if the inherent degradations of the signals are of a completely different nature. A definition of "similarity" is very difficult in this context if it should allow the prediction in all cases that two test signals will turn out to be "similar." It is *a priori* clear that test signals with the same type of degradation will be identified to be similar if the degree of degradation is only slightly different. Examples for such signals are different settings of our reference signals ADD or DIG. Our test experience calls for a much wider definition of similarity. This extended definition is illustrated in Fig. 21. It shows the result of a hypothetical test with nine listeners. Test signals A and B have been measured separately by some test method, e.g., the isopreference method. While the mean scores μ_A and μ_B are different, the size of the standard deviations σ_A and σ_B do not leave much hope for a clear-cut discriminability between the two signals A and B. Inspection of the individual scores shows, however, that all listeners had a definite preference for signal A, a fact that gets lost in the usual averaging procedure. If this correlation of the decisions on signals A and B by the individual listeners

is considered, it becomes possible to compute new values μ_{AB} and σ_{AB} for the discriminability for A and B. The middle part of Fig. 21 shows the same scores of the single listeners as the upper part, but identifies by whom the decisions were made. The lowest part of the figure shows the computed distribution for the discriminability. The strong positive correlation leads to a much better discriminability of A against B than we could expect of the original σ values. In the computation of σ_{AB} here and in our practical studies,[10,11] we have been using the t test, which is a well-known statistical method.[12,13]

The best possible discriminability should occur if the signals to be compared are nearly identical, as postulated above. Figure 22 shows test results for two situations which come as close as possible to this case. In a chain of isopreference tests with the reference signal ADD, different settings of ADD served as test signals. An equivalent procedure was repeated with the reference signal DIG evaluating different settings of DIG. Figure 22 shows for both cases the standard deviation σ observed in these tests and the proportional difference limen (DL). Roughly, we may say that the DL is relatively independent of speech quality and is smaller than 1 dB in terms of the S/N ratio of the two reference signals. The small values of DL and σ in Fig. 22 are in sharp contrast to the σ distributions for dissimilar signals shown in Figs. 4 and 5; σ values there are about three times as large.

When Munson and Karlin presented their PU scale, which they called TPU-scale,[4] they assumed that such a scale could not only be used to describe the quality of a test signal with sufficient accuracy, but also that the distances between two test signals on this scale could serve as a measure of discriminability between the two test signals. The existence of pronounced correlation effects in listener decisions on "similar" test signals renders hopeless the idea that any PU scale can be directly a general measure of discriminability, unless these correlation effects are properly considered. In addition to the correlation problem, also the first part of the original PU scale ideas needs some qualifications. While it is fairly easy to construct a one-to-one relation between one measurement method and a PU scale, new difficulties are entailed if the results of several measurement methods are to be compared on one PU scale. The relations between the individual scales and the PU scale as they were established in Sec. IV are quite flexible links, e.g., the interpolation of σ distributions or the projection of test signal evaluations from one scale to another. It is extremely difficult to estimate the errors that must be expected if two test signals which have been evaluated by different methods are compared. All these difficulties call for a cautious interpretation of Fig. 20. The result of this interpretation may be positive or negative, depending on the concepts that should be proved or disproved.

V. SUMMARY AND CONCLUSIONS

In a utilitarian definition, speech quality can be said to be describable in terms of four parameters: intelligibility, preference, loudness, and speaker recognizability. The relative importance of these four parameters depends heavily on the application of the system, the speech quality of which is to be evaluated.

The present paper tries to make a comparison between four preference measurement methods. Three of them, the isopreference method,[1] the relative preference method,[3] and the category judgment method,[2] have been previously described in the literature. The absolute preference judgment method is proposed in this paper. It improves the category judgment method by replacing the five categories by a decimal description of preference in numbers from 0–10. This change allows acceptance of all the information a listener may want to give, and hereby achieves a more accurate quality description than the old method. A detailed comparison between the four measurement methods is given later in this section.

A preference unit scale has been used as a vehicle for comparing the measurement methods. Its concept was originally introduced by Munson and Karlin in conjunction with their version of the isopreference method. The concept has been extended here to define a preference unit (PU) scale with relations to all four methods considered. While the continuous methods could be directly related to the PU scale, the quantized methods were only indirectly linked to the PU scale; i.e., the scales were related to each other by the evaluation of some test signals. The original hope that the establishment of such a PU scale would allow for a descriptive evaluation of test signals independent of the measurement method did not fully materialize. An evaluation of the PU scale concept has to contain the following three statements:

(1) The identical rank ordering of a set of test signals should be a logical consequence of the facts: (a) preference is by definition a unidimensional subjective measure, and (b) all transformations of the individual evaluation scales to the PU scale are monotonous. Inspection of Fig. 20 shows that for a set of clearly discriminable signals the above requirement is met (e.g., the reference signals for the relative preference method given in Sec. I-B-2). Figure 20 also shows, however, that rank order violations may occur for signals with smaller differences in preference.

(2) The PU scale is constructed in such a way that two just discriminable signals have the same distance between them on the scale regardless of the quality range in which they lie. It is shown in this paper that this distance is not one constant value, but depends strongly on the measurement method used and also on correlation effects which may occur in the comparison of "similar" signals.

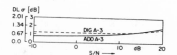

FIG. 22. The two curves give the difference limen DL for our reference signals ADD A-3 and DIG A-3. These relations were established in isopreference tests.

(3) Comparisons between signal evaluations gained by different methods are of limited value and can only be endorsed under special circumstances. This is not surprising if the sensitivity of the individual methods to changes of the test situation is considered.

Recommendation of a single method as a result of the present study is not possible. Selection of a method will depend strongly on the purpose of the test and the costs and time that can be spent on it. The following points should be considered for the selection of one out of the four test methods:

(1) The continuous methods give more comparable results among themselves than the quantized methods do with any other method. Our test experience with the absolute preference judgment method shows that listeners can make better evaluations using this relatively simple method than the two quantized methods make allowances for on their respective scales. This fact leads us to believe that the two quantized methods should be modified to allow for finer discriminations. In this sense, replacement of the category judgment method by the absolute preference judgment method should be considered; the relative preference method should either be extended to use more than five reference signals, which may make it cumbersome to handle, or the quality range to be evaluated by this method should be reduced to fit the requirements of specific test situations.

(2) The desirability of an accommodation of the listeners to the test signals may form an important cue. The absolute methods are neutral in this respect. The isopreference method leads, at least during a test run, to a familiarization of the listener with the test signals, which helps to get consistent results. The relative preference method intentionally tries to make it difficult for the listeners even to recognize the test signal within the set of signal pairs presented.

(3) It is often assumed that the test effort required—and especially the total costs of an evaluation by the different methods—will determine the method to be chosen. This may be true for engineering evaluations during the design and development of some new system. The final acceptance of this system by users can only be determined in tests as close as possible to real-life conditions. In a case which calls for full accommodation of the listeners to the system and for testing of the listeners' responses during actual use of the system, differences between the costs of the preference measurement methods may become insignificant.

(4) The preference of operator and listeners for a certain measurement method may influence its choice. Again, the absolute methods are, owing to their simplicity, preferred by both parties to the relative methods. From the latter, the operator finds it much easier to run an isopreference test than to provide a tape for a relative preference test. The listeners are of the opposite opinion, as relative preference tests consist, from their viewpoint, almost completely of trivial decisions, while isopreference tests are purposely designed to present only signal pairs which require nontrivial decisions from at least some small fraction of the listening group.

The present paper concentrates on a comparison of preference measurement methods by means of the preference unit scale. The test evidence used for the discussion consisted largely of clearly discriminable signals which allowed for a more or less consistent rank ordering. In practical cases, one may be faced with a set of test signals which are by no means clearly discriminable. Problems of this nature have to be discussed if the capabilities and the performance of preference test methods are to be understood fully. In this direction, we shall report our findings from a completed study in a final paper on preference measurement techniques.

ACKNOWLEDGMENTS

The authors are grateful to Professor G. Kraus for helpful discussions and the support of his institute, also to IBM for supporting this work.

The research reported in this document has been sponsored in part by the U. S. Government under contract.

* Now with RCA Ltd., Vienna Branch Office, Vienna, Austria.

† Now with IBM Laboratory, Vienna, Austria.

[1] E. H. Rothauser, G. E. Urbanek, and W. P. Pachl, "Isopreference Method for Speech Evaluation," J. Acoust. Soc. Amer. **44**, 408–418 (1968).

[2] D. L. Richards and J. Swaffield, "Assessment of Speech Communication Links," Proc. IEE **106**, 77 (1959).

[3] M. H. L. Hecker and C. E. Williams, "Choice of Reference Conditions for Speech Preference Tests," J. Acoust. Soc. Amer. **39**, 946 (1966).

[4] W. A. Munson and J. E. Karlin, "Isopreference Method for Evaluating Speech-Transmission Circuits," J. Acoust Soc. Amer. **34**, 762 (1962).

[5] E. H. Rothauser, "Modified Isopreference Method for Audio-Quality Measurements," J. Acoust. Soc. Amer. **35**, 1899(A) (1963).

[6] IEEE Standards Publication No. 297, "IEEE Recommended Practice for Speech Quality Measurements" (June 1969).

[7] E. H. Rothauser and G. E. Urbanek, "Speech Quality Measurements," Annual Report AF 61(052)-856 (1965).

[8] J. Swaffield and D. L. Richards, "Rating of Speech Links and Performance of Telephone Networks," Proc. IEE **106**, 65 (1959).

[9] D. A. Lewinski, "A New Objective for Message Circuit Noise," Bell System Tech. J. **48**, 719 (1964).

[10] E. H. Rothauser, G. E. Urbanek, and W. P. Pachl, "Speech Quality Measurements," Final Sci. Rep. AF 61(052)-856 (1967).

[11] E. H. Rothauser, G. E. Urbanek, and W. P. Pachl, "A Comparison of Preference Measurement Methods," 1967 Conference on Speech Communication and Processing, Boston (6–8 Nov. 1967).

[12] M. Fisz, *Probability Theory and Mathematical Statistics* (Wiley, New York, 1963).

[13] J. P. Guilford, *Psychometric Methods* (McGraw–Hill, New York, 1954).

36

Reprinted from *Soc. Phys.—Acoust.* **18**(1):80–83 (1972)

METHOD OF INVESTIGATING AND RATING SPEECH-TRANSMISSION EQUIPMENT

M. A. Sapozhkov

Moscow Communications Electrical Engineering Institute
Translated from Akusticheskii Zhurnal, Vol. 18, No. 1,
pp. 101–105, January–March, 1972
Original article submitted July 10, 1970

A method of rating and investigating speech-transmission systems is discussed; it is based on the audition of specially compiled syllable tables and the rating of each speech sound on a five-point scale. This approach makes it possible not only to assess intelligibility, but also to evaluate the overall speech quality on the basis of individual speech sounds.

Considerable attention has been directed in the last 40 years to the problems of speech intelligibility and, most particularly, to its measurement. It is reasonable to presume that this problem has now been solved. More difficult to solve is the problem of assessing the quality and naturalness of speech intonation and, accordingly, of relating the assessment of speech tone quality to the characteristics of speech-transmission equipment. So far the assessment of speech quality for the purpose of rating the quality of equipment has been conducted by the group audition of a series of transmissions. This is an extremely laborious technique and is often impracticable, even for laboratory conditions. Similarly, it permits only an integral assessment to be obtained for the naturalness of speech, without explaining which speech elements are distorted or what are the causes of the distortions incurred by the speech-transmission equipment.

In connection with the need for obtaining a quantitative rating of the naturalness of speech a new method has been proposed and approved for testing the fidelity of the output of speech-transmission equipment.[1] The method is basically a variant of the audition method [2], but it can be used to obtain, in addition to an over-all rating of the system, a differential rating as well in terms of the fidelity of reproduction of each of the speech sounds. This makes it possible to determine the causes of any speech distortions in the equipment and to develop measures for their elimination.

Essentially the method entails the recording of tape of specially selected test syllables uttered by a talker (or talkers). The recording is made both directly and through the system being tested. First the undistorted syllable is recorded, and then (for example, three times) the same syllable is recorded after transmission through the tested system. Different syllables are separated by brief pauses for noting down the observations. These records are audited and evaluated by experimental auditors (listeners). The naturalness rating criterion has been borrowed from teachers of foreign languages, who use a similar procedure for evaluating the correct pronounciation of their pupils. The naturalness of each sound included in the syllable is rated on a five-point scale according to the same criteria by which the pupil pronunciation is rated. A rating of excellent is assigned when the reproduced sound is absolutely faithful to the undistorted version. If the reproduced sound differs slightly from the undistorted sound but the deviations do not perceptibly diminish the naturalness, a good rating is assigned. A satisfactory rating is assigned when the reproduced sound differs appreciably from the undistorted sound but still retains all of the fundamental characteristics of the original sound. An unsatisfactory rating is given for reproduced sounds that are recognizable only by corollary criteria. A rating of very poor is

[1]The method was approval-tested by L. P. Blokhina, R. K. Potapova, A. K. Lidikh, A. D. Arkhipova, and P. S. Kornilov. The pertinent data and results have been published in [1].

TABLE 1. Results of Auditor Analysis

Auditor No.		1	2	3	4	5	6	7	8	Sum
Combinations and sounds										
БУЩ	Б	Д	normal	normal	normal	normal	normal	normal	normal	normal
	У	О	normal	normal	Э	normal	normal	О	normal	normal
	Щ	normal	normal	normal	normal	normal	III	III	normal	normal
ГЕФ	Г	normal	unclear	normal	Д	Д	normal	normal	normal	normal
	Е	А	normal	normal	normal	normal	normal	normal	normal	normal
	Ф	С	С	С	С	С	С	С	С	weak
ГУТЬ	Г	normal	normal	normal	normal	normal	normal	normal	normal	normal
	У	normal	normal	normal	normal	normal	normal	normal	normal	normal
	ТЬ	Ц	normal	normal	ЧЬ	normal	Т	sibil.	ТЬЦ	weak
ТЫШ	Т	normal	normal	normal	normal	normal	normal	normal	normal	normal
	Ы	normal	normal	normal	normal	sibil.	sibil.	Щ	normal	satis.
	Ш	sibil.	normal	Щ	normal	normal	normal	normal	normal	normal
ДИП	Д	normal	unclear	normal	normal	normal	unclear	unclear	normal	normal
	И	Ы	normal	Ы	Ы	Э		normal	Е	weak
	П	Т	unclear	Т	П	Т		Т	П	weak
ПЮМ	П	Т	normal	Т	Т	Т	Т	Т	normal	weak
	Ю	normal	normal	Ю^У	normal	normal	normal	И^е	normal	normal
	М	Н	normal	normal	normal	normal	normal	normal	Н	normal

Note: The table gives the verbal ratings as stated by the auditors; however, numerical ratings are better suited to processing and will be used hereinafter.

assigned to sounds that are distorted beyond recognition. The overall rating is defined as the average, rounded off to the nearest integer.[2]

The method was tested on a special instrument. The test syllables were taken from the VKAS (All-Union Committee on Articulation Standards) articulation tables, their number and composition being chosen so as to reflect all initial combinations of the type consonant-vowel (C-V) and consonance (multiple consonant)-vowel (CC-V) and almost all final combinations of the type vowel-consonant (V-C) and vowel-consonance (V-CC) included in the tables. More than 300 of these closed syllables were obtained.[3] The syllables were grouped into six tables according to the type of initial consonants and consonances: single plosives; initial plosives in consonances; single fricatives; initial fricatives in consonances; sonorants; and affricates. The predilection for initial sounds was dictated by the decision to investigate primarily the transmission of initial sounds through the system. Since final consonants and consonances, as well as vowels, are included in the tables in roughly equal measure, they are rated for only one of the tables. For a complete investigation, of course, tables should be included with groupings according to final consonants and consonances.

A portion of a table with the auditor rating responses is given in Table 1.[4] Each auditor responded with the rating "normal" or his interpretation of the given sound (for example, the entry "D" signifies that the sound of P was perceived as D). Only three gradations of naturalness are given in the "sum" column: normal (excellent and good), satisfactory (if the majority was rated "normal"), and weak (poor and very poor). These gradations were subsequently assigned numerical values of 4, 3, and 2. The replacement of 5 by 4 and of 1 by 2 in this case[5] did not tend to lower the average ratings appreciably, because scarcely more excellent ratings than ratings of "very poor" were obtained.

[2]The practicality of rounding off (or not rounding off) can be argued after the method has been subjected to long-range tests.

[3]The composition of the syllables could probably have been chosen to be more representative of the phonemic content of the Russian language, but this was not particularly necessary for the present study.

[4]Cyrillic letters are transliterated in the text, but are retained intact in the tables so as to preserve phonetic accuracy. The approximate sounds of the letters may be obtained by consulting the transliteration scheme found at the end of this article. Note especially the following peculiarities of Russian: "a" as in "father"; hard "g"; "e" as in "diet"; "zh" = French "j"; "i" = $\overline{ee}$; short "i"; "o" as in "gone"; Italianate trilled "r"; "u" = $\overline{oo}$; "kh" = energetically aspirated "h"; hard sign " (obstruent effect); "y" approximately like "i" in "rid"; soft sign ' (palatalization); "é" as in "get." – Publisher.

[5]This was done because only one system was tested. The five-point system is better suited to the testing of systems having diverse characteristics.

TABLE 2. Naturalness Rating of Synthesized Speech Sounds

Syllable table I	i	f	Syllable table II	i	Syllable table III	i	Syllable table IV	i	Syllable table V	i	Syllable table VI	i
бут	3	4	пляс	4	сось	4	скол	3	рях	4	пай	4
няп	3	4	прюх	3	хачь	4	штоф	3	ляш	3	щем	3
дюрь	3	4	грах	4	сичь	3	стяс	3	нул	3	чорь	3
дум	3	4	трят	3	шеть	4	фсях	3	лысь	4	чеп	4
дыс	3	4	трух	3	шись	4	свох	2	рюсь	2	чащ	4
бер	2	3	грун	2	жоф	2	скет	2	муй	3	чет	4
гум	2	4	трен	2	фек	3	фсёп	2	мяс	3	пот	3
геф	4	2	прыл	3	вех	2	свам	3	няк	3	печь	4
бап	3	3	кром	4	сул	3	скип	4	рём	3	чир	3
дян	3	4	длес	4	вунь	3	стачь	3	мяй	4	чул	4
деп	2	3	крыс	2	хял	3	фсат	3	роп	3	цей	4
пюрь	2	3	тряпь	3	воль	4	стям	2	ноп	3	щос	4
геф	4	2	прят	3	сель	3	фсел	3	рель	3	щум	3
кась	4	3	глес	2	хуф	2	штяк	4	мес	3	щеп	3
дуч	4	4	прас	3	фыл	3	стул	3	нёпь	3	пырь	4
порь	2	3	длян	3	жась	2	штар	3	лёчь	4	поп	2
пяф	2	3	дреть	4	сых	3	птысь	4	нин	4	пял	4
гуть	4	4	траф	3	жеп	2	фсот	3	люп	3	неф	3
пып	4	3	крюп	2	жоль	3	стек	3	ных	4	пол	4
бяс'	3	4	плюх	3	сёй	3	фсяп	2	нент	3	пем	2
кеп	3	4	плык	2	фай	3	стях	3	лет	3	чещь	4
лес	3	4	дват	3	самь	3	скуф	2	нюф	3	чят	4
тущ	2	4	трюль	3	зах	2	свел	3	мял	3	чтыш	4
гипь	3	2	трёп	2	жик	3	штом	3	лофь	3	чтусь	4
тас	4	4	глон	4	зичь	3	скаф	3	мёл	4	чтар	4
дас	4	4	прень	2	шарь	3	сяяс	3	рар	3	чтим	3
пел	4	4	трок	3	жен	2	свым	3	лиль	3	чтет	3
тёщ	3	4	двяй	3	холь	3	фсуй	2	рян	3	чтип	4
лёч	3	3	драк	3	сёф	3	свинь	3	луть	4	чтуф	4
тап	4	4	крус	3	хет	2	стонь	4	нать	3	чтюсь	4
пыст	3	4	длем	3	вуф	3	снем	2	рычь	3	чтяс	3
пуч	4	4	плип	3	зырь	2	свуп	2	руш	3	чтён	4
бяй	4	4	прош	3	сяг	2	стяр	3	меп	3		
гом	3	4	крац	3	фок	3	фсек	2	меи	3		
боть	3	3	дван	3	шусь	3	фсук	2	люр	3		
бюп	3	4	прчш	3	фип	3	стех	2	лем	3		
быр	3	2	дветь	3	вюр	2	стёт	3	рыр	3		
тян	4	4	плут	3	жус	3	стом	3	нял	4		
бём	3	4	прё	3	вачь	3	стын	3	мыл	4		
тяк	4	3	двят	3	сем	2	фсын	3	рет	2		
тып	4	4	трят	3	веш	2			мыр	2		
лип	3	2	крет	3	сюй	3			нян	3		
бяп	4	4	длос	4	фусь	3			мил	3		
тиль	4	4	прай	3	зёк	3			мос	2		
лянт	4	4	криф	3	вёк	2			рел	2		
бал	3	4	кроц	4	высь	3			лёк	4		
кусть	3	3	плёк	3	вял	2			лан	3		
тюн	3	4	длёс	4	хем	2			мон	3		
доп	3	3	плуй	3	шок	3			лор	2		
теш	3	3	трук	3	воп	2			люй	3		
тям	3	4	крёл	3	шуп	3			лыс	4		
пюм	3	4	глаф	3	фем	2			рещь	3		
дён	3	3	грямь	4	сазнь	2						
кип	3	4	глин	3	вёй	3						
пюзнь	3	4	крян	3	вель	3						
пяс	3	4	дряш	3	вяф	2						
панъ	3	4	дрюн	3								
коть	3	3	глям	2								
пёф	2	2	плёф	2								
точ	2	2	дрот	3								
бурь	2	3										
дюр	3	2										
гел	4	4										
пёть	3	2										
кис	3	4										
дель	3	4										
гял	4	4										
Sums	**207**	**232**		**180**		**149**		**118**		**162**		**113**

Note: For key, refer to the Appendix.

The system chosen for the tests was a formant vocoder [3]. Eight well-trained auditors (teachers) participated in the rating. The repeatability of the results was established by threefold audition of certain tables. Very good agreement was obtained. All the rating results for each syllable were tested for variance (within the limits of the double standard).

Sample ratings of the speech sounds are given in Table 2, in which "i" denotes initial sounds and "f" denotes final sounds. The data for the groups of initial and final sounds, as well as for vowels are given in summary form in Table 3.

An analysis of these data shows that, not too surprisingly, the affricates are synthesized the best of all the initial sounds in the formant vocoder; they obtained 60% excellent and good ratings, whereas for all the other groups approximately 20% received excellent and good ratings (from 10% for the single fricatives to 23 or 24% for the single plosives and sonorants). The largest number of poor and very poor gratings was obtained for single fricatives (43%), and the smallest number for the affricates and sonorants (9 and 11%). Of the initial sounds, the worst synthesized were the single fricatives. Finals were generally better synthesized than initials, and of the final sounds the best synthesized were the sonorants, while the worst were the plo-

TABLE 3. Numerical Ratings by Sound Groups

Sound group	Sum of ratings	No. of syllables	Average rating
Initial:			
single plosives	207	67	3.1
plosives in consonances	180	60	3.0
single fricatives	149	56	2.7
fricatives in consonances	118	40	3.0
sonorants	162	52	3.1
affricates	113	32	3.5
Average for initials	929	307	3.0
Finals	232	67	3.5
Vowels	270	67	4.0
Grand average			3.5

sives. The synthesized vowels generally received a good rating. In the majority of cases the errors were due to the perception of U as O and of O as U.

It was readily established that the inadequate synthesis of initial fricatives was determined mainly by the low upper limit of the frequency range of the analyzer (3500 Hz). Thus, when the frequency range of the analyzer was expanded upward to 5000 Hz, the naturalness of the fricatives was greatly improved. Also, the replacement of the RC ladders at the parameter outputs (in the analyzer) by a low-frequency filter with LC elements yielded a significant improvement in the naturalness of the plosive sounds and the trilled R.

It was found that the distortion of the vowels U and O was determined by the steep decline of the analyzer frequency characteristic on the low-frequency side (below 500 Hz). The correction of this characteristic significantly enhanced the naturalness of the vowel sounds, increasing their rating almost to excellent.

APPENDIX

Transliteration System

RUSSIAN		ENGLISH
А	а	a
Б	б	b
В	в	v
Г	г	g
Д	д	d
Е	е	e
Ж	ж	zh
З	з	z
И	и	i
Я	я	ï
К	к	k
Л	л	l
М	м	m
Н	н	n
О	о	o
П	п	p
Р	р	r
С	с	s
Т	т	t
У	у	u
Ф	ф	f
Х	х	kh
Ц	ц	ts
Ч	ч	ch
Ш	ш	sh
Щ	щ	shch
Ъ	ъ	"
Ы	ы	y
Ь	ь	'
Э	э	é
Ю	ю	yu
Я	я	ya

LITERATURE CITED

1. L. P. Blikhina, R. K. Potapova, A. D. Arkhipova, A. K. Lidikh, P. S. Kornilov, and M. A. Sapozhkov, "Naturalness of synthesized speech with reference to the formant vocoder," Paper at the Conference Dedicated to A. S. Popov [in Russian], Moscow (1969).
2. "IEEE recommended practice for speech quality measurements," IEEE Trans. Audio and Electroacoustics, AU-17, 3, 225-246 (1969).
3. A. D. Arkhipova and M. A. Sapozhkov, "The quality of vocoder speech," Akust. Zh., 16, 3, 345-353 (1970) [Sov. Phys. — Acoust., 16, 292 (1971)].

37

38

Copyright © 1963 by the Acoustical Society of America

Reprinted from *Acoust. Soc. Am. J.* **35**(11):1748–1752 (1963)

Effects of Filtering and Vocal Duration upon the Identification of Speakers, Aurally*

Arthur J. Compton

Department of Speech, The Ohio State University, Columbus, Ohio
(Received 19 November 1962)

The purposes of this study were to investigate (1) the effect of various conditions of high-pass and low-pass filtering of the voice upon the identification of speakers; (2) the effect of various durations of recorded segments of the voice upon the identification of speakers; and (3) the relationship of fundamental frequency to misidentification of speakers. Fifteen recorded segments of the vowel [i] for each of 9 speakers were presented to listeners. All listeners were familiar with the speakers' voices through daily contact. The 15 segments of the vowel differed only in duration. The samples of the speakers' voices were heard under 7 conditions of high-pass and low-pass filtering. The task of the listeners was to identify the speakers by writing the name of one of 9 speakers after the presentation of each vowel stimulus. The results of the investigation indicate that (1) durations of 1/40 of a second are sufficient for identifying speakers; (2) the greater the severity of filtering, the greater the duration of the sample of voice required for identification of speakers; (3) attenuation of frequencies of the voice below 1020 cps does not affect the ability of listeners to identify speakers; (4) attenuation of frequencies of the voice above 1020 cps substantially reduces the ability of listeners to identify speakers; and (5) there is an inverse relationship between the relative degree to which speakers' voices are confused and the range, in cps, between the fundamental frequencies of the speakers' voices.

INTRODUCTION

IDENTIFICATION of speakers by their voices is a common experience. Most listeners have little difficulty in identifying the voices of familiar speakers over the telephone or on the radio. Recognition of the voices of familiar speakers in the darkness or when the speaker is out of sight of the listener is also a common occurrence. Moreover, the ability to recognize speakers' voices is a "skill" that is particularly helpful to the blind. In most instances, such as the ones just cited, immediate recognition of speakers saves the time of both the speaker and the listener, but it is not essential.

Under certain circumstances, immediate identification of speakers' voices may be highly important to efficient communication. For example, in communication systems in which a listener must attend to a number of voices, immediate recognition of speakers conserves channel time. Attending to a number of voices is frequently an integral part of the work of such persons as policemen in radio cruisers, taxicab drivers, radio operators in aircraft-control stations, those who use "intercom" systems in large organizations, and switchboard operators. In some instances in which listeners operate in the presence of a number of voices, rapid and accurate identification may even assume a role of importance comparable to the intelligibility of the message itself.

Of primary interest in this investigation is the timbre or quality of the voice, which purportedly conveys the identity of the speaker. Thus, an attempt was made to avoid additional cues peculiar to the speech of individual speakers by using only a sustained vowel as the basis for identification. The variables under investigation were (1) the duration of the sample of voice and (2) the degree to which the voice is filtered. A related study conducted by Pollack, Pickett, and Sumby[1] was also concerned with the effect of the duration of the sample of speech and the severity of filtering of the voice upon the identification of speakers. In this study, however, the listeners heard various durations of recorded contextual material. The investigators

---

* Part of this study derives directly from a master's thesis by Arthur J. Compton under the direction of John W. Black, The Ohio State University, 1961.

[1] L. Pollack, J. M. Pickett, and W. H. Sumby, J. Acoust. Soc. Am. **26**, 403 (1954).

attempted to minimize additional speaking cues, apart from vocal quality, by selecting speakers who were "reasonably homogeneous in rate and manner of speaking"; the speakers read "equivalent or identical texts." They concluded that (1) identification of speakers increases as the duration of the sample of voice increases and (2) identification decreases as the severity of filtering increases. The purposes of this study, then, were to investigate further (1) the effect of various durations of recorded segments of the voice upon the ability of listeners to identify speakers; (2) the effect of various conditions of high-pass and low-pass filtering of the voice upon the ability of listeners to identify speakers; and (3) the relationship of fundamental frequency to misidentification of speakers.

PROCEDURES

Fifteen recorded segments of the vowel [i] for each of 9 speakers, or a total of 135 stimuli, were randomly presented to 15 listeners; all listeners were familiar with the speakers' voices through daily contact. The 15 segments of the vowel differed only in duration and ranged from 25 to 1500 msec. The samples of the speakers' vowels were heard under 7 conditions of high-pass and low-pass filtering. All stimuli were presented at suprathreshold levels through sets of binaural earphones. The task of the listeners was to identify the speakers by writing the name of 1 of the 9 speakers after the presentation of each stimulus. A training period was given prior to the experiment to insure that all of the listeners could recognize the speakers' voices and to acquaint the judges with the nature of the task.

The 9 male speakers used in this study were selected because their voices were familiar, through daily contact, to the members of the listening panel. All speakers had normal voices and were either members of the staff or graduate students in the Department of Speech at The Ohio State University.

The recorded samples of voice were obtained by instructing each speaker to practice sustaining the vowel [i] at his normal level of voice until he could monitor his voice at a steady-intensity level as indicated by a VU meter. After the practice period, each speaker was instructed to (1) state his name, (2) count to three, and (3) sustain the [i] of *three*. The purpose of counting was to obtain a recorded vowel that approximated the "habitual" pitch of the speakers. All recordings were made in a sound-treated room. The microphone (Altec 21-D condenser type) was suspended at a distance of approximately 6 in. from the mouth. All recordings were made at a predetermined intensity level on a Magnecorder tape recorder (model PT 6V).

The 15 durations of the vowel used in this study were 25, 50, 75, 100, 150, 200, 250, 300, 350, 400, 500, 750, 1000, 1250, and 1500 msec. The method of recording the various durations was developed by using a three-channel tape recorder (Ampex model 353R) and a series of pulse generators (Tektronix 163). The speakers' sustained vowels were duplicated on the first channel of a magnetic-tape recording. A 3-sec steady-state sample of each speaker's vowel was then recorded on the second channel; a short pulse corresponding to the same point in time as the onset of each 3-sec sample was simultaneously recorded on channel three. This three-channel tape recording provided the method for recording the various durations of the samples of voice used in the investigation. By regulating the intervals between the two pulses emitted by two pulse generators, and using the recorded pulses on the third channel of the tape to activate a waveform generator, any length segment up to 3 sec could be recorded from the 3-sec vowels on the second channel. This method also insured that the samples of voice were always taken not only from the same segment of a vowel, but that the initial recording point of the samples remained constant. The accuracy of the timing mechanism was validated by comparing the interval between the pulses emitted by the pulse generators with a calibrated reference sweeptone of a dual-beam oscilloscope (Tektronix 502). The schematic diagram of the instrumentation for recording the various durations of the speakers' voices and validating the accuracy of the timing mechanism is shown in Fig. 1.

The 7 conditions of filtering required 7 duplications and randomizations of the recorded samples of the speakers' voices. A number identifying order of presentation of each stimulus item preceded each sample, and a 10-sec interval separated each item. The recorded samples of the speakers' voices were played from a Magnecorder (model PT 6V) into a variable high-pass and low-pass filter set (Allison model 2 AR, with an attenuation of 35 dB per octave beyond cutoff frequency) and duplicated with an Ampex recorder (model 601). The 7 conditions of filtering were:

No filter	1020 cps low pass
255 cps high pass	510 cps low pass
510 cps high pass	255 cps low pass
1020 cps high pass	

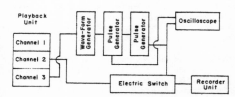

FIG. 1. Schematic diagram of instrumentation for recording the various durations of the speakers' voices and validating the accuracy of the timing mechanism.

TABLE I. Mean percentages of correct identification of 9 speakers' voices for each of 15 durations of the vowel [i] under 7 conditions of filtering.[a]

Condition of filtering	Duration of the vowel in milliseconds														
	25	50	75	100	150	200	250	300	350	400	500	750	1000	1250	1500
No filter	36	43	50	51	53	47	56	55	62	51	63	65	52	59	57
255 high pass	36	35	41	56	51	58	62	55	61	56	64	63	59	61	67
510 high pass	25	36	46	53	46	43	53	56	56	52	59	49	54	65	58
1020 high pass	27	37	40	53	56	60	66	58	56	64	61	60	65	62	60
1020 low pass	12	26	29	30	30	29	30	30	36	33	36	35	37	35	37
510 low pass	10	23	21	30	31	30	27	33	32	39	28	33	31	33	35
255 low pass	8	10	12	18	17	20	20	20	24	22	28	24	27	22	26

[a] At least 28% correct identification is required for identification of the speakers' voices to be significantly greater than chance at the 5% level of confidence.

ANALYSIS AND RESULTS

I. Effect of the Duration of Short Samples of Voice Heard at Fifteen Different Durations upon the Identification of Speakers

In the experimental conditions, the listeners were to identify each stimulus item as the voice of 1 of 9 speakers. Consequently, 11% of the listeners' responses were expected to be "correct" by chance. The critical difference (c.d.) between chance identification of the speakers and identification required for significance at the 5% level of confidence was determined by the formula[2] c.d. $= 100 \ (t_{.05})(pq/N)^{\frac{1}{2}} = 100 \ (2.145)[(.11) \times (.89)/15]^{\frac{1}{2}} = 17.31$; thus, an obtained value of at least 28% correct identification of the speakers' voices (17.3%+11%) is required for significance at the 5% level of confidence. The mean percentage values in Table I for the nonfiltered condition indicate that the listeners were able to identify the speakers when samples of voice were heard at the shortest duration of 25 msec.

Under the least severe high-pass filtering condition of 255 cps, the 25-msec sample was also sufficient for identification of the speakers while a 50-msec sample was required for the two more-severe high-pass conditions. When the speakers' voices were heard under low-pass filtering, a 75-msec segment was required for the

TABLE II. Mean percentages of correct identification of 9 speakers' voices under 7 conditions of filtering (values of 15 durations of Table I, pooled).

Condition of filtering	Mean percent correct
No filter	54
255 high pass	55
510 high pass	55
1020 high pass	55
1020 low pass	31
510 low pass	29
255 low pass	20

[2] In this formula, as applied to the present study, p is the proportion of responses expected to occur from chance selection, q is a proportion complementary to p ($q = 1 - p$). N is the number of listeners, and $t_{.05}$ equals a ratio of a deviation to a standard error at the 5% level of confidence for N-1 degrees of freedom. Since a proportion is 1/100 of a percentage, the value obtained in the formula can be expressed as a percentage by multiplying it by 100.

1020-cps condition and a 100-msec for the 510-cps condition. For the most severe low-pass condition of 255 cps, however, the listeners could not identify the speakers even at the longest duration of 1500 msec. These results, then, indicate that the greater the severity of filtering, the greater the duration of the sample of voice required for identification of speakers.

II. Effect of Various Conditions of Filtering of the Voice upon the Identification of Speakers

The mean percentages of correct identification of the speakers' voices for the 7 conditions of filtering are summarized in Table II. Thus, the value of 54 in the upper right-hand column of the table indicates that the mean identification of the 9 speakers' voices was 54% when their voices were heard by the listeners under the nonfiltered condition. This value might be computed from Table I as the mean value of row one. A comparison of the mean value for the nonfiltered condition with the mean value for the high-pass conditions of filtering indicates that the high-pass conditions did not affect the listeners' ability to identify the speakers' voices; i.e., the mean percentages of correct identification of the speakers' voices under the three high-pass conditions are essentially the same as that of the nonfiltered condition. Consequently, the most severe high-pass condition, in which frequencies of the speakers' voices were attenuated below 1020 cps, produced no change in identification when compared with the unfiltered voices.

Conversely, the mean values in Table II for the low-pass conditions of filtering indicate a decrease in identification of from 23% to 34% when compared with the mean value for the nonfiltered condition. Thus, even the least severe low-pass condition, in which frequencies of the speakers' voices were attenuated above 1020 cps, substantially reduced the listeners' ability to identify the speakers.

III. Relationship of Fundamental Frequency to Misidentification of the Speakers' Voices

In tabulating the data of this investigation, it was observed that the order in which the speakers' voices

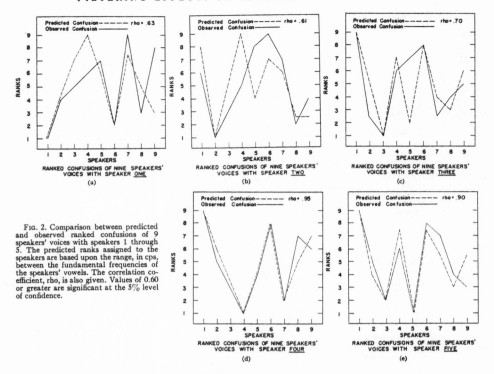

FIG. 2. Comparison between predicted and observed ranked confusions of 9 speakers' voices with speakers 1 through 5. The predicted ranks assigned to the speakers are based upon the range, in cps, between the fundamental frequencies of the speakers' vowels. The correlation coefficient, rho, is also given. Values of 0.60 or greater are significant at the 5% level of confidence.

were confused with a particular speaker was approximately the same under the various conditions of filtering. This would seem to suggest that confusion of speakers' voices is related to one or more characteristics of the voice that are either (1) not significantly affected by the conditions of filtering, or (2) altered in proportionate degrees. One characteristic of the speakers' voices that might be expected to remain relatively unaffected by filtering is pitch. The purpose of this analysis, then, is to explore the possibility of a relationship between fundamental frequency and misidentification of speakers' voices.

The various speakers were assigned ranks according to the order in which they would be expected to be confused with each other had pitch been the cause of misidentification. Thus, 9 sets of ranks were assigned to the speakers, and each set was, in effect, the predicted order in which the listeners would confuse the 9 speakers with one of the speakers. The criterion for assigning ranks was the range, in cps, between fundamental frequencies of the speakers' vowels used in this study. A rank of 9 thus indicated the greatest range between fundamentals, and consequently, minimum

confusion.[3] Since no two speakers had identical fundamentals, a rank of 1 indicated that the listeners would most often "confuse" a speaker with himself.

A comparison between the predicted and observed ranked confusions of the 9 speakers' voices with speakers 1 through 9 is presented in Figs. 2 and 3. The similarity between the predicted order in which the speakers were expected to be confused with each speaker and the observed order of confusion, was tested by means of Spearman's rank correlation coefficient, rho. In this instance, a high correlation would indicate that the predicted order of confusion of the speakers is similar to the order in which they were confused in the experimental conditions. The correlations of observed and predicted order of confusions with each of the 9 speakers were, respectively, 0.63, 0.61, 0.70, 0.95, 0.90, 0.68, 0.93, 0.70, 0.90. All of these values are significantly greater than zero beyond the 5% level of confidence. Consequently, the range, in cps, would seem to have

---

[3] For purposes of the present analysis, the correct identifications of speakers' voices were also treated as confusions, since some ot the speakers were misidentified more frequently than they were recognized under certain conditions of filtering.

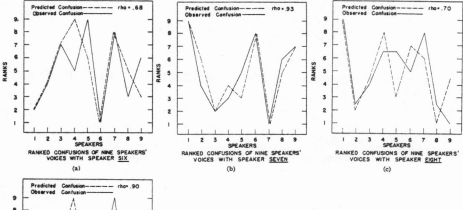

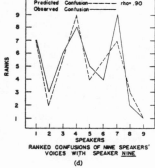

FIG. 3. Comparison between predicted and observed ranked confusions of 9 speakers' voices with speakers 6 through 9. The predicted ranks assigned to the speakers are based upon the range, in cps, between the fundamental frequencies of the speakers' vowels. The correlation coefficient, rho, is also given. Values of 0.60 or greater are significant at the 5% level of confidence.

provided a reliable method of predicting the degree to which the speakers' voices were actually confused.

CONCLUSIONS

Within the limitations of the procedures of this investigation, particularly the use of only the vowel [i], the following conclusions were drawn from the results of the investigation:

1. Durations of 1/40 sec are sufficient for identifying speakers.

2. The greater the severity of filtering, the greater the duration of the sample of voice required for identification of speakers.

3. Filtering of frequencies of the voice below 1020 cps does not affect the ability of listeners to identify speakers.

4. Filtering of frequencies of the voice above 1020 cps substantially reduces the ability of listeners to identify speakers.

5. There is an inverse relationship between the relative degree to which speakers' voices are confused and the range, in cps, between the fundamental frequencies of the speakers' voices.

Reprinted from *Acoust. Soc. Am. J.* **35**(11):354–358 (1963)

Pattern-Matching Procedure for Automatic Talker Recognition

Sandra Pruzansky

Bell Telephone Laboratories, Inc., Murray Hill, New Jersey
(Received 18 December 1962)

A pattern-matching procedure for automatic recognition of talkers was used to study the effects of variations in patterns upon recognition performance. Several utterances of common words, excerpted from context, were spoken by ten talkers and converted to time-frequency-energy patterns. Some of each talker's utterances were used to form reference patterns and the remaining utterances served as test patterns. The recognition procedure consisted of cross-correlating the test patterns with the reference patterns and selecting the talker corresponding to the reference pattern with the highest correlation as the talker of the test utterance. The same recognition procedure was used with patterns reduced to two dimensions. The recognition score for three-dimensional patterns was 89%. Reducing the original patterns to time-energy patterns resulted in a lower recognition score; however, when only spectral information was retained, recognition results were the same as those for three-dimensional patterns. No errors were made in recognition based on a small sample of patterns consisting of pooled spectra of several different voiced sounds.

INTRODUCTION

RECOGNITION of talkers by human observers has been studied from several different points of view. Meeker and Nelson,[1] in evaluating transmission systems, found that trained listeners were able to identify talkers from an ensemble of five, with a high degree of accuracy. Pollack, Pickett, and Sumby,[2] studying the effect of each of several variables upon identification performance, showed that the speech wave conveyed considerable information about talker identification if the listener heard a long enough speech sample. Kersta,[3] using a visual display of acoustic features, showed that a group of trained observers was able to identify talkers by spectrogram matching. All of these studies indicate that talkers can be identified primarily on the basis of acoustic cues. The present study is concerned with ways in which a computer can be programmed to recognize talkers solely on the basis of acoustic information.

Several studies have demonstrated the feasibility of automatic recognition of speech sounds based only on acoustic information, provided the sample of words to be recognized is limited. A report of one such study by

Denes and Mathews[4] described a spectral-pattern correlation procedure for the automatic recognition of spoken digits. They reported that no errors occurred when reference patterns and patterns to be recognized were based on utterances of the same talker, but the error rate was high when one-talker reference patterns were used to recognize utterances by different talkers. These results suggested that characteristic inter-talker differences might exist in the spectral patterns of talkers uttering the same text. Accordingly, a pilot experiment was undertaken to assess the feasibility of automatic talker recognition by spectral pattern matching. The basic program used in the Denes–Mathews study was altered to perform talker recognition rather than word recognition and applied to the spectral patterns from the same study. This technique proved quite successful with the materials of limited vocabulary and small sample of talkers. (See Appendix for a brief description of this experiment and discussion of results.) Therefore, the study was expanded, using a larger and less restricted set of materials to examine the effects of certain stimulus parameters upon recognition performance.

The experiment reported here begins with a pattern-matching procedure using three-dimensional patterns; the same recognition scheme is then used for patterns reduced to two dimensions. Most of the recognition

[1] W. F. Meeker and A. L. Nelson, "Vocoder Evaluation Studies," Radio Corporation of America, AFCRL 547 (30 June 1962).
[2] I. Pollack, J. M. Pickett, and W. H. Sumby, J. Acoust. Soc. Am. 26, 403–406 (1954).
[3] "Voice Spectrograms for Unique Personal Identifications," Bell Labs Record 40, 214–215 (1962).
[4] P. B. Denes and M. V. Mathews, J. Acoust. Soc. Am. 32, 1450–1455 (1960).

results are based on individual words with identity of the word provided; however, some work done with patterns consisting of the pooled spectra of several different voiced sounds is also discussed.

PREPARATION OF MATERIALS

Five sentences were specially constructed to include words commonly occurring in telephone conversations. Ten talkers (7 male and 3 female) read each sentence several times. The speech signal was led from the sound-treated recording booth over a Western Electric 633 microphone and Bogen RP2 preamplifier to an Ampex 300 tape recorder.

After the recordings were made, the ten key words, spoken several times by each talker, were excerpted from context in the following manner. A sentence was recorded on a continuous tape loop. The loop output was split, one lead going directly to one track of a two-track Ampex tape recorder, the other to one channel of a Grason–Stadler electronic switch, which was used for monitoring purposes. A 1000-cps tone, gated by the second channel of the electronic switch, was recorded on the other track of the tape recorder at a time coincident with the desired word. This was accomplished by listening to the output of the monitor channel and adjusting the timers, which controlled the gate width, until just the desired word was located. A block diagram of the apparatus is shown in Fig. 1.

Digital representation of the spoken words in the form of spectral patterns was obtained by spectral analysis, quantization, and digital recording. Spectral analysis was accomplished by playing back the recordings through a 16-channel filter bank and a special 17th channel which bandpassed 4000–7000 cps. The center frequencies of the other bandpass filters were arranged at approximately equal intervals along the Koenig scale and covered the range 200–4000 cps. The cross-over point between adjacent filters occurred at the 6-dB point. The output of the filter bank was sampled sequentially by a multiplexer at a rate of 100 samples per second. The samples were quantized into 10-bit binary numbers which were recorded on digital tape; analogue-digital conversion and digital recording equipment have been described elsewhere.[5] The 1000-cps tone was used to control the starting and stopping operation of the digital recording equipment; thus, only the key words were recorded on digital tape. A special code marking the beginning of each word was included on the tape. This tape was used as the input to an IBM 7090 computer.

RECOGNITION PROCEDURE

Pattern matching, in general, consists of comparing an unknown pattern with standard patterns that serve

[5] E. E. David, Jr., M. V. Mathews, and H. S. McDonald, "Description and Results of Experiments with Speech Using Digital Computer Simulation," 1958 IRE Wescon Convention Record, Part 7.

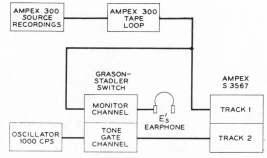

FIG. 1. A block diagram of apparatus for excerpting words from context.

as references. The present procedure involved comparing individual array points of the unknown with corresponding array points of the reference patterns. Since the patterns were allowed to vary in length, alignment was critical.

The method of aligning the beginnings of utterances, as used for the digits, was unsatisfactory for excerpted words, so a different alignment scheme was developed. The new procedure involved locating the maximum of the energy-vs-time function of each word and lining up these points. Specifically, the point selected was the midpoint of the longest run of time sections during which the energy exceeded 75% of the maximum.

Reference patterns were formed by adding together corresponding array points of three utterances of the same word by the same talker, making ten different reference patterns (one for each talker) for each word. The procedure used for recognition of talkers consisted of cross-correlating the array of the remaining single utterances of each word with each of the ten reference arrays for that word using the product-moment coefficient of correlation. This measure is defined by[6]

$$r = \Sigma xy / N\sigma_x\sigma_y.$$

In the present application x and y, deviation measures of corresponding array points from the respective means of the test and reference arrays, are summed over time and frequency (or one of these dimensions, depending on the type of pattern under test); N is the number of cross products, and the sigmas are the standard deviations of the two arrays. This measure renders the cross products independent of the means and variances of the two arrays. The talker corresponding to the reference pattern with the highest correlation was recognized as the talker of the test utterance.

RESULTS

The recognition results for patterns of energy in the time-frequency plane $(e\text{-}t\text{-}f)$ are shown in Fig. 2(a) in the form of a confusion matrix; the asterisks indicate

[6] Q. McNemar, *Psychological Statistics* (John Wiley & Sons, Inc., New York, 1949).

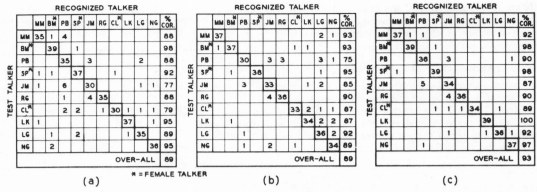

FIG. 2. Inter-talker confusions for: (a) time-frequency-energy patterns, (b) frequency-energy patterns, and (c) combined results.

female talkers. Talkers were correctly recognized for 89% of the 393 utterances tested. Results for individual talkers, shown in the right column of Fig. 2(a), ranged from 77% correct to 98% correct. The distribution of errors among words is shown in Fig. 3(a); it can be seen that the errors were not uniformly distributed over all of the words.

The correlation procedure was used to examine recognition performance with two-dimensional patterns, eliminating temporal information. The original e-t-f patterns were reduced to energy-frequency arrays (e-f) containing 17 array points—each point being simply the sum of energy from each of the time sections for that frequency band. A confusion matrix for these patterns is shown in Fig. 2(b). With the time dimension eliminated, talkers were still correctly recognized for 89% of the 393 utterances tested; the percentage of correct recognition for each talker is shown in the right-hand column of Fig. 2(b). However, the distribution of errors differs from that of the e-t-f patterns. There is also a difference in the error rate for individual words as shown in the graph of Fig. 3(b).

The effect on recognition success of eliminating spectral information was also observed. Two-dimensional patterns, consisting of the total energy in each time section, were formed by summing the energy in the 17 frequency bands at each time section. The patterns were aligned by the same method used for the three-dimensional patterns. Only 47% of the unknowns were correctly recognized. Although recognition success for individual talkers ranged from 30 to 81%, only two talkers had more than 45% of approximately 40 utterances correctly recognized.

Since the distributions of errors for the two- and three-dimensional patterns were quite different, it is possible that an increase in recognition success might be achieved by combining the results from the two best pattern types. An examination of agreement and error for e-f and e-t-f patterns showed that of the 321 cases in which the two patterns agreed on the answer, only 4

of these answers were wrong, and of the 72 cases in which they disagreed, they were both wrong in only 9 cases. A simple linear combination of the e-f and e-t-f correlations, equally weighted, resulted in correct resolution of 50 of the disagreements. Inter-talker confusions and distribution of errors among words are shown in Fig. 2(c) and Fig. 3(c), respectively. Over-all correct recognition was 93%. This is a slight improvement over the results with either pattern type alone.

Pooled Spectra

Since the talkers apparently were able to be distinguished on the basis of frequency spectra alone, it was speculated that distinctiveness might be retained in the long-time frequency spectra of these voices. Once again the original patterns were reduced to two dimensions (e-f), this time modified to represent an approximation to the long-time spectra of voiced speech. First, the voiced portions of speech were detected in a manner similar to that described by Lochbaum.[7] Then a reference pattern for each talker was formed by summing the energy of the voiced speech across approximately 30 different utterances (3 sets of 10 different words). Each test pattern consisted of different utterances of single sets of the same text. This reduced the number of patterns to be recognized from almost 400 to only 40. Using the same recognition procedure as was used with single words, all 40 patterns were correctly recognized.

A perfect score on a given sample provides little information about the capability of a recognition scheme, except that it has not been adequately tested. Consequently, the possibility of extrapolation to a larger sample of talkers was explored. Examination of correlation coefficients indicated that a model similar to that of Green and Birdsall[8] seemed applicable to the

[7] C. C. Lochbaum, J. Acoust. Soc. Am. **32**, 914 (A) (1960).
[8] D. M. Green and T. G. Birdsall, "The Effect of Vocabulary Size on Articulation Score," University of Michigan, AFCRC TR 57–58, AD 146, 759 (January 1958).

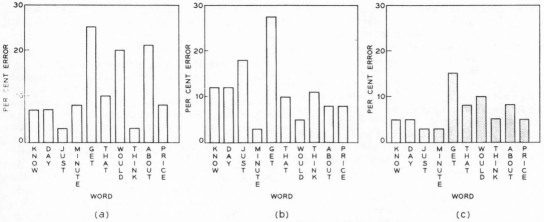

FIG. 3. Error-rate variation among words: (a) time-frequency-energy patterns, (b) frequency-energy patterns, and (c) combined results.

problem of predicting the percentage of correct recognition as a function of the number of talkers to be recognized. First, the distribution of correlation coefficients for the same-talker reference and test patterns (correct distribution) was examined. Transforming these data to z scores,[6] where

$$z = \tfrac{1}{2}\log_e(1+r) - \tfrac{1}{2}\log_e(1-r),$$

rendered this distribution normal. The calculated standard deviation was very close to the theoretical value $[\sigma_z = 1/(N-3)^{\frac{1}{2}}]$ and the within-subject variance larger than the between-subject variance. This is further evidence that the z scores are samples from a single normal population. A chi-square test of the distribution of all of the different-talker reference and test patterns indicated that the z transforms of these values were normally distributed about a mean that was considerably smaller than that of the correct-answer distribution; the standard deviation was almost the same.

The model expresses the percentage of correct recognition for n talkers as the probability (P_a) that a sample from the population of correct-answer z scores (H_1) is greater than n samples from the population of wrong-answer z scores (H_0), where

$$P_a = \int_{-\infty}^{+\infty} \left(\int_{-\infty}^{z} f(y/H_0)dy \right)^n f(x/H_1)dx.$$

In this application it appears that H_0 and H_1 are normally distributed with essentially the same standard deviation; so we may let

$$f(y/H_0) = \frac{1}{\sigma(2\pi)^{\frac{1}{2}}} \exp\left[\frac{-(y-m_0)^2}{2\sigma^2} \right],$$

and

$$f(x/H_1) = \frac{1}{\sigma(2\pi)^{\frac{1}{2}}} \exp\left[\frac{-(x-m_1)^2}{2\sigma^2} \right].$$

It is seen that P_a, for a given n, depends solely upon the difference between means of the two populations. Assuming the sample means are the best estimate of the population means, this model predicts 99% correct recognition for 100 talkers; assuming that the true population means are each $2\sigma_m$ (standard error of the mean) closer to each other, a pessimistic estimate, P_a is 0.90 for an n of 100.

DISCUSSION

The present experiments demonstrate the success of one particular automatic talker-recognition procedure for a limited sample of talkers uttering words excerpted from a sentence context. Of 393 utterances 89% were correctly recognized when recognition was based on patterns of energy in the time-frequency plane. Recognition remained high, 89% correct, for two-dimensional patterns of energy and frequency. Combining data from both of the patterns resulted in 93% correct recognition. This is not the first report of a successful automatic-recognition technique; however, most of the previous studies, dealing with the problem of automatic recognition of speech sounds, have required the abstraction of distinctive features either by expert judgment or by statistical decision processes. The present results indicate that a relatively simple pattern-matching procedure, which involves no abstraction of features, might be quite useful in automatic recognition of talkers.

No attempt has been made to determine the number of parameters necessary to identify a talker. However, recognition performance did remain high with considerable reduction of information. When only spectral information was retained, reducing the number of cross products to 17 per correlation, results were as good as when the correlation procedure used about 50 times as many cross products. This indicates that voices might be able to be specified by relatively few parameters.

Not all reduced patterns yielded high recognition scores; recognition based on temporal patterns of energy was quite poor. However, in most cases there were very high correlations between the unknown pattern and each of the reference patterns (above 0.90) and very small differences between the pattern selected and the other nine. Either the distribution of energy in time for a given word was quite similar between talkers in this sample, or the procedure used to line up the time sections (matching the portions of peak energy) tended to make the patterns more similar. If the former alternative be true, and words differ in their energy-time patterns, such patterns might be useful in word recognition, where representations of words invariant with talkers are desirable.

Although this experiment provides some information about physical specification of talkers for a limited number of persons, little can be learned from the present data about what *people* use as cues to talker identity. However, these results can be compared with recognition performance by human observers if a task comparable to that given the computer can be developed. If there is any similarity between man and machine performance, the present pattern-matching scheme might serve as a tool for exploring factors important to human recognition of talkers.

The results with pooled spectra have perhaps the most interesting implications for talker recognition and speech recognition. Their reliability and generality are limited because the sample was small and the test and reference patterns included voiced portions of exactly the same text words; therefore, they represent "idealized" long-time spectra, and not true random samples of voiced speech of equivalent duration. Within these limitations, however, the results suggest that spectral distinctiveness of talkers is retained in long-time spectra. The implications of this distinctiveness are that: (1) spectral procedures for recognition of vowels, say, will be plagued by these differences between talkers, and (2) if the differences are reliable, a finite sample of standard text might be used to adjust speech recognizers to a particular talker.

APPENDIX

The Denes–Mathews materials consisted of digitalized patterns of utterances of the digits zero through nine spoken in isolation by five male talkers. Each utterance was recorded on digital tape as a separate block of data. Each block consisted of the first 60 sweeps of a multiplexer (sampling 70 times per second) across 17 filter channels, making 1020 array points per pattern. Patterns were aligned so that the beginning of the utterances they represented would coincide. The beginning was located as the time section that first exceeded 10% of the peak energy. Reference patterns consisted of three utterances of the same digit by a talker. There were five reference arrays for each digit and a total of 100 test utterances, two utterances of each digit by each talker.

Recognition by cross correlation of reference and test patterns resulted in correct recognition of talkers for 94% of the utterances tested. Converting the patterns to a standard duration by changing the time scale did not change recognition scores; however, the distribution of errors differed. When recognition was based on two-dimensional patterns in the time-energy plane, considerably more errors were made; the talkers were correctly recognized for only 78% of the utterances tested. However, using two-dimensional patterns of frequency and energy resulted in 98% correct recognition. No consistent error pattern emerged for the different digits; the errors were spread over all the digits regardless of pattern alteration.

ACKNOWLEDGMENTS

The author is indebted to Mr. P. D. Bricker and Mr. M. V. Mathews for help in planning this experiment, for much needed statistical advice, and for their valuable guidance throughout the course of the study.

Reprinted from *Nature* **196**(4861):1253–1257 (1962)

VOICEPRINT IDENTIFICATION

By L. G. KERSTA

Bell Telephone Laboratories, Inc., Murray Hill, New Jersey

VOICEPRINT identification is a method by which people can be identified from a spectrographic examination of their voice. Closely analogous to fingerprint identification, which uses the unique features found in people's fingerprints, voiceprint identification uses the unique features found in their utterances. Fingerprinting uses the inked impressions of the ten fingers; voiceprinting uses the spectrographic impressions of the utterances of ten words frequently used in telephone conversations. Thus, when the source material is contextual, the voiceprints for specific cue words are extracted and compared with previously recorded voiceprints of the same cue words.

Fig. 1 illustrates two types of voiceprints of the word 'you' uttered by the same male voice. The voiceprint shown on the left is a conventional bar spectrogram, showing time proceeding from left to right and frequency increasing from bottom to top. The amplitude, or loudness, is indicated by the density of

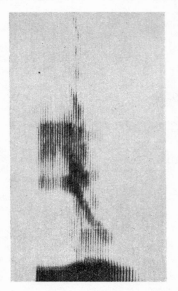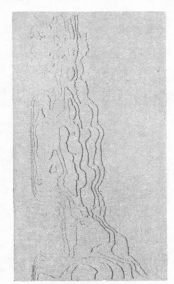

Fig. 1. Male voice uttering 'you'. Bar voiceprint on the left; contour voiceprint on the right

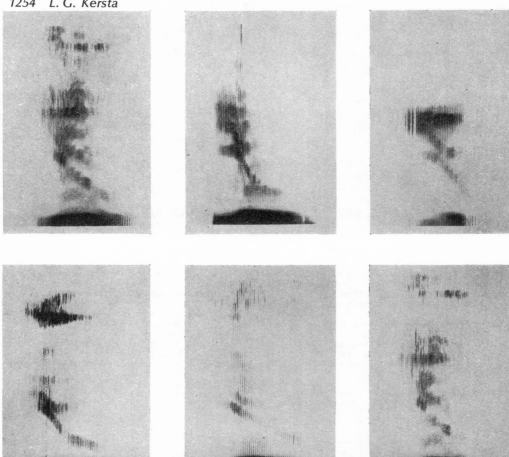

Fig. 2.   Bar voiceprints of five male speakers uttering 'you'.   One of the speakers uttered 'you' twice.
Upper left and lower right were spoken by the same person

the marking. The range of loudness detectable this way is only a little better than 2 to 1 because of the limits imposed by the spectrogram paper characteristics. The contour spectrogram (voiceprint) shown on the right has the same time and frequency dimensions as the bar spectrogram. The amplitude, however, is shown by seven quantized or contour steps. The term 'contour' seemed applicable because the amplitude contours on this type voiceprint are like the altitude contours on a topographical map. With contour portrayals, amplitude doubles with each inward progression from one contour to the next, and we arrive at amplitude peaks as one arrives at altitude peaks on a topographical map.

Subjective experiments were conducted to learn how well subjects could match voiceprints when presented in random matrices, and secondly, how well individual unknown prints could be identified with the correct speaker in a population of previously uttered and filed prints. These results will be presented and discussed later in this article.

Fig. 2 shows a sample array of bar voiceprints of the word 'you'. There are six utterances by five male speakers. Can you detect the two bar prints which were uttered by the same persons ? Similarly, Fig. 3 shows contour voiceprints of the word 'you' uttered by the same speakers, but the order has been changed. Can you detect the two contour prints uttered by the same person ?

You probably had no difficulty in selecting the matching prints, so let us now explore the speech mechanism and see why each person's voice is unique. Fig. 4 illustrates the human vocal mechanism.   The parts which principally determine voiceprint uniqueness are the vocal cavities and the articulators.   The vocal cavities are resonators which, much like organ pipes, cause energy to be reinforced in specific spectrum areas, dependent on their sizes. The major cavities affecting speech are the throat, nasal and two oral cavities formed in the mouth by the setting of the tongue. The contribution of the vocal cavities to voice uniqueness lies in their size and the manner in

426

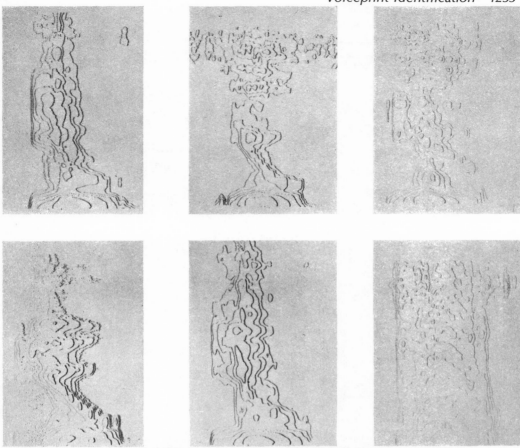

Fig. 3. Contour voiceprints of five male speakers uttering 'you'. One of the speakers uttered 'you' twice.
Upper left and lower middle were spoken by the same person

which they are coupled. The likelihood of two people having all vocal cavities the same size and coupled identically seems remote. A still greater factor in determining voice uniqueness is the manner in which the articulators are manipulated during speech. The articulators include the lips, teeth, tongue, soft palate, and jaw muscles, the controlled dynamic interplay of which results in intelligible speech. We well know that intelligible speech is not spontaneously acquired by infants. It is a studied process of the imitation of those around him who are successfully communicating. The desire to communicate causes the infant to accomplish intelligible speech by successive steps of trial and error. Success requires that he learn a dynamic complex manipulation of interrelated muscles controlling the movement of several articulators. Again, the chance that two individuals would have the same dynamic use-patterns for their articulators would be remote. My claim to voice pattern uniqueness then rests on the improbability that two speakers would have vocal cavity dimensions and articulator use-patterns identical enough to confound voiceprint identification methods. Final proof of identification uniqueness depends on

a sufficiently large population sample to support the present claims. Recently, when fingerprint identification experts were asked if fingerprinting afforded unique and infallible identification, they replied: "We do not surely know, because we have information for only 93 million people so far".

Let us now consider the identification successes for several subjective experiments. The subjects used in these identification experiments were female high school students 16–17 years old. They were each given about one week of training in voiceprint reading and detection of unique clues in voiceprints. In all, eight girls were used for various periods during the past year. They worked in panels of two because it was found that success scores were markedly better when two panellists were able to consult each other about their identification selections.

Data from an experiment in voiceprint matching are shown in Fig. 5. The voiceprints used here were four different discrete utterances by 5, 9 and 12 male speakers. The words used were 10 frequently used words in English conversation, namely: *the, to, and, me, on, is, you, I, it,* and *a*. The subjects were given a random matrix of voiceprints for the 5, 9 or 12

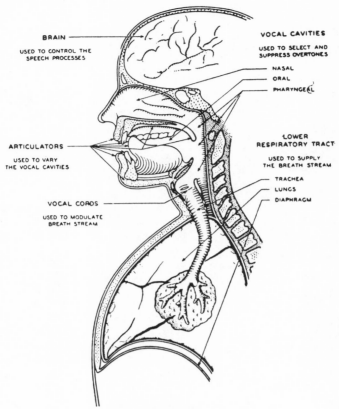

Fig. 4.   Diagram of the vocal tract

'talker' groups. Each matrix included four different utterances for each word used. The resultant random matrices included 20, 36 and 48 voiceprints respectively. The experiments were conducted for both bar and contour type voiceprints. As can be seen the lumped errors for all cue words ranged from 0·35 to 1·0 per cent for bar prints, and from 0·37 to 1·5 per cent for contour prints. The number of data for each point is shown in the legend and in all cases was more than 800. Errors recorded for individual words ranged from 1·8 per cent for the word *to* to no errors for the word *a*.

Data in Fig. 6 illustrates the success of voiceprint matching when the cue words were extracted from contextual material. These results show that the lumped error for all cue words is approximately 1·0 per cent. It will be remembered that comparable data (Fig. 5) for discretely spoken words showed a lumped error of 0·8 per cent. The error for these results as shown (Fig. 6) range from 2·0 per cent for the word *is* to no errors for the word *you*.

In the following experiments an identification game was played. It was presumed that one had on file a number of voiceprints identified with a group of people. It was further presumed that there were some unidentified voiceprints for some of the same population. The object of the game was to identify

the unknown prints with one of the group of file prints. The file population with which the unknown had to be identified varied between 9 and 15. The results of one such experiment are shown in Fig. 7. These data indicate that in 2,000 identification attempts, the lumped error of misidentifications when using all cue words was 1·0 per cent. I would like to make it clear that the errors shown are for identifications made with single cue words. This is analogous to attempting fingerprint identification with the print of only one finger. In practice, a voiceprint identification would generally be made using several cue words. The identification error in such a case would be the product of the errors for each word. The resultant percentage error would, of course, be very small. It will be noted that the cue words are shown on the abscissa and the error index for each word on the ordinate. The range is from 3·0 per cent for the word *is* to no errors recorded for words *I*, *on* and *it*.

As one may suspect, some voices are more difficult to identify than others. Fortunately, no voices used so far can be classed as difficult to identify. Results in Fig. 8 show the subjective errors committed in identifying a group of 11 male talkers. The identification errors range from 2·4 per cent for two talkers to no errors for three talkers. Each datum point indicated contains at least 163 identification attempts.

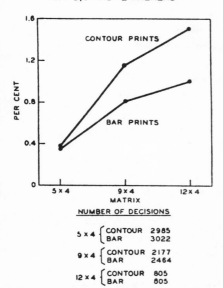

VOICE PRINT IDENTIFICATION
PRINT MATCHING EXPERIMENT
FOR MATRIXES OF 4 UTTERANCES
FOR 5,9 AND 12 TALKERS

NUMBER OF DECISIONS

5 × 4 { CONTOUR 2985
BAR 3022

9 × 4 { CONTOUR 2177
BAR 2464

12 × 4 { CONTOUR 805
BAR 805

Fig. 5. Lumped data errors for voiceprint matching experiments with random matrices

VOICE PRINT IDENTIFICATION
PRINT MATCHING EXPERIMENT WITH
WORDS EXCERPTED FROM CUE SENTENCES
9 SPEAKER × 4 UTTERANCE MATRIX

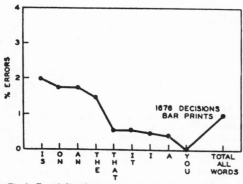

Fig. 6. Error indices for cue words in print matching experiment

The talkers, incidentally, were chosen as normal male voices with no marked dialectal influences.

Experiments similar to those described previously were also conducted for female voices. There was no evidence of complicating difficulties and the data are comparable with those shown for male voices.

A sampling of data has been presented here which was limited in scope because of space restrictions for this article. Other experimental data encourage me to believe that unique identifications from voiceprints can be made.

VOICE PRINT IDENTIFICATION
IDENTIFICATION PROBLEMS USING WORDS
EXCERPTED FROM CUE SENTENCES
9 TALKERS 2 REFERENCE PRINTS

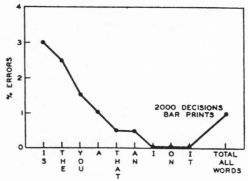

Fig. 7. Identification problem errors for each cue word

VOICE PRINT IDENTIFICATION
IDENTIFICATION PROBLEM ERRORS
COMMITTED FOR EACH TALKER

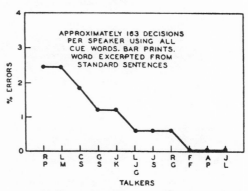

Fig. 8. Identification errors committed for each talker

Work continues, there being questions to answer and problems to solve. Among these are: (1) Is the voice unique enough to afford infallible identifications? This requires sampling the voices of a much larger section of the population. (2) Does the voice of an adult change significantly with time? If so, how? (3) How will attempts to disguise the voice succeed? (4) How successful in disguise are voice mimics? All these questions must be answered by substantiating experimental evidence. It is my opinion, however, that identifiable uniqueness does exist in each voice, and that masking, disguising, or distorting the voice will not defeat identification if the speech is intelligible.

Work is in progress to devise a classification and indexing system for filing voiceprints. The system must afford compactness, rapid access, and reduce the population of filed prints needed for subjective identification to a relatively small number. Several ideas for automation are being examined and seem to hold promise in meeting the foregoing requirements.

40

Reprinted from *Acoust. Soc. Am. J.* **54**(2):531–534 (1974)

Speaker identification by speech spectrograms: some further observations*

Richard H. Bolt

Bolt Beranek and Newman Incorporated, 50 Moulton Street, Cambridge, Massachusetts 02138

Franklin S. Cooper

Haskins Laboratories, 270 Crown Street, New Haven, Connecticut 06510

Edward E. David, Jr.

Gould Incorporated, 8550 West Bryn Mawr Avenue, Chicago, Illinois 60631

Peter B. Denes

Bell Laboratories, Murray Hill, New Jersey 07974

James M. Pickett

Gallaudet College, Washington, D. C. 20002

Kenneth N. Stevens

Research Laboratory of Electronics, Massachusetts Institute of Technology, Cambridge, Massachusetts 02139
(Received 5 February 1973)

This letter reviews recent research on speaker identification by means of comparisons of speech spectrograms by human observers. Various factors affecting the reliability of identification are discussed, particularly those that would be present in practical forensic situations. Our interpretations of the new data lead us to reiterate our previous conclusion: that the degree of reliability of identification under practical conditions has not been scientifically established.

Subject Classification: 9.1, 9.9.

In 1969 and 1970 we reviewed the scientific basis of speaker identification through the use of speech spectrograms in connection with legal proceedings.[1,2] We cited experimental results that showed, for example, error rates ranging from 6% to 63% false identifications under various conditions that could be encountered in forensic situations. We concluded that the scientific information available at that time was not adequate to provide valid estimates of the degree of reliability of voice identification by examination of spectrograms.

In our papers we suggested and described some experiments required to establish this technique on a scientifically solid basis. The key question to be answered is of the form: What are the odds? What are the probabilities of correct identification, of incorrect identification, or of missed identification, of a person through examination of speech spectrograms representing his voice and the voices of other persons? What are the probabilities under the particular set of conditions involved in the forensic situation? Relevant conditions include the selection and number of persons represented by the spectrograms examined, the methods by which the voice samples were recorded, the time and circumstances when the recordings were made,

and the confidence criteria of the examiner in making his decisions.

We concern ourselves only with these scientific questions about the determination of probabilities. Whether any particular value of these probabilities would qualify speech spectrograms as admissible for evidence in court is a legal question about which we offer no judgment.

The present paper updates our review of this subject. We now take into account new information which appeared in 1971 and 1972.

A project on voice identification through acoustic spectrography has been completed by Dr. O. Tosi and his co-workers at Michigan State University; the results have appeared in two laboratory reports[3,4] and in a paper in this JOURNAL.[5] This project simulated in the laboratory some of the conditions present in practice and these are our primary concern. Other workers have investigated the acoustic characteristics that bear on speaker identification[6–8] and the effects of the speech context.[9,10] Hecker has reviewed the basic problems.[11]

Tosi's experiments and similar experiments by others[12] employ the following procedure. Some number of observers participate in the experiment by examining spectrograms and making judgments about them. An observer receives a set of "known" spectrograms and one or more "unknown" spectrograms, which respectively represent a set of "known" persons and a single, "unknown" person whose identity is not divulged to the observer. By examining the spectrograms, the observer judges whether the "unknown" person is the same as one of the "known" persons and, if so, which one. Preliminary training may be provided for the observers; in Tosi's study one month of training was given.

Tosi's experiments involved the effects of five variables: (1) The number of speakers in the known set; (2) open versus closed tests—in open tests the observer was not told whether the unknown speaker was represented in the known set, but in closed tests he was told that the unknown was represented in the set; (3) the context of the speech materials—test words were spoken either in isolation or in sentences; (4) certain characteristics of the speech transmission system; and (5) contemporary versus noncontemporary voice samples—the voice samples to be compared were recorded either on the same occasion (contemporary) or on different occasions (noncontemporary).

Identification errors are of two types: (1) Errors of *false identification*: The observer selects from the known set a speaker who is not the person represented in the unknown spectrograms, and (2) errors of *false rejection* or missed identification: in open tests the observer wrongly decides that the unknown speaker is not represented in the known set.

In the forensic situation, false identification could erroneously single out a particular individual as one of the "suspected" persons. Such errors take on special significance in that they relate to the possible conviction of an innocent person. Errors of false rejection on the other hand, are important in investigative work because they may lead to the elimination of a guilty person from consideration as a suspect.

A wide range of results was obtained in Tosi's study, depending on how the experimental variables were combined.[13] At one extreme, error scores were below one percent for closed tests with words spoken in isolation and with contemporary voice samples. Other results more relevant to forensic applications were found for noncontemporary voice samples (in this case recorded one month later), open rather than

closed tests, and words spoken in various sentence contexts rather than in isolation. Several of the results for these forensically relevant conditions provide insight into the problem of speaker identification by spectrograms. When the unknown spectrogram actually represented one of the speakers in the known set, the observers failed to recognize the speaker about 29% of the time.[14] They either identified the unknown as the wrong speaker (5%), or, more frequently, they decided that the unknown speaker was not one of the known speakers (24%).

The results for trials in which the unknown speaker was *not* represented in the known set are given in Table I. For tests in which all unknown spectrograms were *contemporary* the rate of false identifications ranged from 2.0% to 4.5%, depending on the number of voices in the known set. On the other hand, when the unknown spectrograms were *noncontemporary*, this error rate more than doubled to the range of 4.9% to 9.8%.

Why was the percent of false identification higher for noncontemporary voice samples? Speakers' voices might be expected to change from one recording occasion to another, but if the observers used the same average criterion for a match the percent of false identification should not change unless there were differences in similarity between the voices included in the several test sets. Was there some aspect of the experimental design that would account for the result? Was there a change, between the two kinds of tests, in the criterion used by the observers for accepting a match? The reports offer no explanation of this result.

Another result of Tosi's experiments that has substantial consequences for the forensic situation is an increase in the error rate when the context of the test words is changed from words in isolation (an average error rate of 7% for noncontemporary spectrograms) to words embedded in random sentence contexts (16%). Different sentence contexts are known to modify the acoustic characteristics of words. These findings, coupled with the above mentioned increases in error rates for noncontemporary as opposed to contemporary unknown spectrograms, suggest that any experimental condition that is likely to cause a change in the acoustic characteristics of an utterance will lead to an increased probability of error. This increase occurs both for errors of false identification and errors of false rejection.

Not examined in Tosi's study are some other factors that can change the sounds a speaker produces, factors that can increase the intraspeaker variability—these in turn can increase the probability of error. For example it is well known that changes in the psychological state of a talker, induced through emotions or other types of stress, can cause substantial changes in the characteristics of his speech sounds.[15] In a forensic situation additional emotional factors of this kind tend to be present. Other factors that can potentially modify the

TABLE I. Percent errors of false identification reported in the study of Tosi *et al.*, for open tests, words in random context, and trials in which the unknown speaker was not represented in the set of known speakers. Data taken from Appendix B of Ref. 3, rounded off to the nearest 0.1%.

Number of individuals in known set of voices	Contemporary spectrograms	Noncontemporary spectrograms
10	2.0%	4.9%
20	4.0%	8.3%
40	4.5%	9.8%

characteristics of a speaker's voice are the noise level surrounding him, attempts at mimicking or disguise,[7] room acoustics, and recording conditions. Further research is needed to determine the influence of these factors on the reliability of speaker identification.

Because of these sources of increased intraspeaker variability, we regard the 5% to 10% false-identification rates seen in Table I as artificial minima which are likely to increase when conditions depart from the laboratory situation in which the voice samples were recorded. This evaluation of the projection that can safely be made from Tosi's experimental findings differs sharply from his own interpretation[16] and from that expressed in a letter[17] written and circulated by Dr. Peter Ladefoged; further, we question the basis on which claims[18] have been made that the dominant view of the scientific community is now in agreement with those interpretations.

In our previous papers we compared voice identification with fingerprint identification (See Ref. 2, pp. 606–608). We drew a contrast between the stable, anatomical nature of the finger ridge patterns and the changeable patterns of a person's speech. Tosi's results provide direct evidence of the detrimental effect of intraspeaker variability on voice identification and its inherent dissimilarity to fingerprint identification.

The experiments of Hazen[9,10] indicate high identification errors for words from conversation. His first experiment involved closed tests, spectrograms of test words spoken in isolation, and 50 speakers in the known set. In a second experiment with the same observers and speakers, the same test words were taken from conversation, and both closed and open tests were carried out. The closed tests resulted in 3% error with the words spoken in isolation[19] compared with 20% for words taken from conversation.[20] On the open tests with words from conversation[21] the false identifications were 17% and the false rejections were 67%.

The present level of knowledge about personal voice characteristics, their recognition, and how they change under different conditions is still rudimentary. The recent work on speaker identification from spectrograms does not provide any new understanding as to which spectrographic features correlate most clearly or efficiently with the speaker's identity. Research on this question is in progress,[6,8] but results have not yet been applied to the problems of speaker identification from spectrograms. At the present time, therefore, the spectrographic identification of a voice by a trained observer appears to rely on a broad assessment of loosely defined points of similarity rather than on a carefully specified set of objectively defined spectrographic attributes. The Tosi experiments, in fact, show considerable disagreement among different panels of observers as to what constitutes a match when they are given the same matching task. For example, in situations where an incorrect identification is made by one

panel, other panels are by no means in agreement with this assessment. In fact, the percent of time that an error of false identification is made by at least one panel (out of nine used in the study) is several times higher than the values given in Table I, which are average data over all panels.

The decision criterion of the observer is of critical importance in personal identification. The Tosi study required the observers to rate their subjective certainty for each decision. A detailed breakdown of decision errors was not given as a function of level of certainty except to say that about 60% of the errors were committed on decisions rated by the observers as uncertain. Further studies are needed to provide a better understanding of the decision process. For example, no explanation is now possible as to why, in open tests, an observer who is uncertain cannot simply reject the unknown spectrogram as not being similar enough to any of the known spectrograms.

Table I illustrates the influence of another variable not fully analyzed in the Tosi reports: the effect of the size of the known set. Increasing the number of persons in the known set from 10 to 40 at least doubled the probability of making a false identification. This result suggests that the use of still larger population sizes would further increase the probability of false identification.

The Tosi reports refer to a field study of voice identifications by the Michigan Department of State Police which employed both spectrographic and auditory comparison of voices in actual police cases.[22] It was found that no positive identification was contradicted by other police evidence. However, we do not consider this type of evidence a reliable criterion of the correctness of identification. The only true criterion of correctness of identification is sure knowledge of the identity of the speaker.

In discussing the forensic application, Tosi and his colleagues say that the error rates may in fact be lower than the values found in their experiments. They reason that a prudent practitioner can exercise caution and can listen to the voice samples as well as view the spectrograms. However, the Tosi reports give no scientific data that define the practitioner's error rate, or show how the rate might vary with his degree of caution, or indicate what improvement can be had by listening.

The Tosi study has improved our understanding of some of the problems of voice identification from spectrograms by indicating the influence of several important variables on the accuracy of identification. In uncovering factors that tend to increase identification errors, however, the study has not given us a definitive answer to the question: "How reliably can a person be identified by examining the spectrographic patterns of his speech sounds?" Under certain laboratory conditions and for some selected sample of the population, the probability of making an error in identification can be stated. But for the less-than-ideal conditions encountered in forensic situations, the indications are that the probability of error will increase substantially. Further studies are needed, with particular attention to the examiner's decision criteria, the selection of speaker population, the time lapse between voice samples, background-noise conditions, and the psychological condition of the speaker.

As scientists rather than lawyers, we offer no judgment as to whether or to what extent speech spectrograms should be used for identification in the courts. We wish only to point out that present methods for such use lack an adequate scientific basis for estimating reliability in many practical situations and that laboratory evaluations of these methods show increasing errors as the conditions for evaluation move toward real-life situations. We hope that our explanations of some of the factors that affect speaker identification will provide the legal profession with helpful information on which to base its own judgments concerning the admissibility of the spectrographic method.[23]

*The views given here are those of the authors as individuals. Additional background about this report will be found in J. Acoust. Soc. Am. **46**, 867–868 (1969).

[1]R. H. Bolt, F. S. Cooper, E. E. David, Jr., P. B. Denes, J. M. Pickett, and K. N. Stevens, "Identification of a Speaker by Speech Spectrograms," Science **166**, 338–343 (1969).

[2]R. H. Bolt, F. S. Cooper, E. E. David, Jr., P. B. Denes, J. M. Pickett, and K. N. Stevens, "Speaker Identification by Speech Spectrograms: A Scientists' View of its Reliability for Legal Purposes," J. Acoust. Soc. Am. **47**, 597–612 (1970).

[3]O. Tosi, H. J. Oyer, W. Lashbrook, C. Pedry, and J. Nichol, "Voice Identification through Acoustic Spectrography," Report SHSLR 171, Department of Audiology and Speech Sciences, Michigan State University, East Lansing, Michigan (Feb. 1971).

[4]O. Tosi, H. J. Oyer, W. Lashbrook, C. Pedry, J. Nichol, and E. Nash, "An Experiment on Voice Identification: Excerpts from Report SHSLR 171," Department of Audiology and Speech Sciences, Michigan State University, East Lansing, Michigan (July 1971).

[5]O. Tosi, H. Oyer, W. Lashbrook, C. Pedrey, J. Nichol, and E. Nash, "Experiment on Voice Identification," J. Acoust. Soc. Am. **51**, 2030–2043 (1972).

[6]J. J. Wolf, "Efficient Acoustic Parameters for Speaker Recognition," J. Acoust. Soc. Am. **51**, 2044–2056 (1972).

[7]W. Endres, W. Bambach, and G. Flosser, "Voice Spectrograms as a Function of Age, Voice Disguise, and Voice Imitation," J. Acoust. Soc. Am. **49**, 1824–1848 (1971).

[8]M. R. Sambur, "Speaker Recognition and Verification Using Linear Prediction Analysis," J. Acoust. Soc. Am. **53**, 354(A) (1973).

[9]B. M. Hazen, "Speaker Identification Using Spectrograms Made on Different Spectrographs," M.S. Thesis, State University of New York at Buffalo (1972).

[10]B. M. Hazen, "The Effects of Changing Phonetic Context on the Voiceprint Identification Technique," Ph.D. Thesis, State University of New York at Buffalo (1972).

[11]M. Hecker, *Speaker Recognition: An Interpretative Survey of the Literature* (American Speech and Hearing Association, Washington, D. C., 1971), ASHA Monograph No. 16.

[12]See, for example, L. G. Kersta, Nature (Lond.) **196**, 1253 (1962); K. N. Stevens, C. E. Williams, J. P. Carbonell, and B. Woods, J. Acoust. Soc. Am. **44**, 1596 (1968).

[13]See Ref. 3, Table 3, p. 34.

[14]See Ref. 3, p. 37.

[15]M. H. L. Hecker, K. N. Stevens, G. von Bismarck, and C. E. Williams, "Manifestations of Task-Induced Stress in the Acoustic Speech Signal," J. Acoust. Soc. Am. **44**, 993–1001 (1968). C. Williams, and K. Stevens, "Emotion and Speech: Some Acoustical Correlates," J. Acoust. Soc. Am. **52**, 1238–1250 (1972).

[16]See Ref. 5, pp. 2041–2042.

[17]P. Ladefoged, "An Opinion on "Voiceprints," *Working Papers in Phonetics* (U.C.L.A. Phonetics Laboratory, University of California at Los Angeles, California, 1971), No. 19, p. 84–87.

[18]See, for example, testimony on December 15, 1971, in the case of U.S. versus Raymond, U.S. District Court, District of Columbia, Case #Cr 800-71.

[19]See Ref. 9, Table 4, p. 21.

[20]See Ref. 10, Table 12, p. 41.

[21]See Ref. 10, Table 9, p. 34.

[22]Department of Michigan State Police, *Voice Identification Research, PR 72-1 ,* (U.S. Department of Justice, Superintendent of Documents, U.S. G.P.O., Washington, D.C., 1972), No. 2700-0144, pp. 77–78.

[23]For a review of the legal questions see J. Crim. Law, Criminol. Police Sci. 63, 343–355 (1972); and Georgetown Law J. **61**, 703–745 (1973).

AUTHOR CITATION INDEX

Meo, A. R., 359, 360, 363
Mercier, G., 363
Mesnard, G., 358
Meurman, O. H., 286
Meyer, A., 67
Meyer, E., 163, 321
Meyer-Eppler, W., 320
Miasnikova, E. N., 67
Michaels, S. B., 71
Michéa, R., 106
Mickunas, J., 387
Mier, M., 113
Mikeska, E. E., 228
Mikhailov, V. G., 126
Miller, G. A., 10, 67, 81, 90, 95, 126, 155,
    172, 187, 194, 210, 224, 269, 286,
    386
Miller, I., 172
Miller, J., 71, 176, 187, 191, 194
Miller, J. C., 363, 369
Miller, J. D., 67, 72
Millin, J. P., 172
Miller, J. R., 169
Miller, L. N., 228
Miller, R. L., 88
Milner, P., 173
Miron, M. S., 64, 209
Mishkin, M., 113
Mitchell, S., 81, 286
Mohn, A. S., Jr., 396
Mohn, W. S., 394
Modena, G., 396
Mol, H., 163
Moles, A., 222
Moll, K. L., 397
Moncur, J. P., 67
Monro, S., 213
Montani, A., 94
Montgomery, H. C., 291
Mood, A. M., 212
Moore, W. E., 169
Moray, N., 67
Morgan, B. J. T., 320
Morrical, K. C., 171, 269
Morris, R. M., 124
Morrow, C. T., 67, 286, 320
Morton, J., 320
Moser, H. M., 67, 68
Mosteller, F., 106
Mulac, A., 64
Mullins, C. J., 244

Muncey, R. W., 163, 396
Munson, W. A., 15, 130, 135, 136, 163,
    396, 410
Murdock, C., Jr., 285
Murphy, R. L., 67
Mushnikov, V. N., 320
Myasnikov, L. L., 67
Myasnikova, E. N., 363

Nábělek, A. K., 67
Nachchon, I., 67
Nagata, K., 363
Nakamura, N., 360
Nakano, Y., 361
Nakata, K., 361, 363
Nakatani, L. H., 286, 394, 396
Nakatsui, M., 68, 287, 365
Namba, S., 395
Nash, E., 393, 396, 398, 433
Naujoks, J., 287
Neely, K. K., 68, 70, 245
Neely, R. B., 363, 365
Neil, J. H., 245
Nelson, A. L., 420
Nelson, D. A., 173
Newell, A., 363
Newman, E. B., 320
Nicely, P. E., 210, 386
Nichol, J., 398, 433
Nichols, R. H., Jr., 241
Nickson, A. F. B., 163, 396
Niederjohn, R. J., 71, 287
Niese, H., 222
Niimi, Y., 364
Nimura, T., 63, 398
Nishinomiya, G., 396
Nixon, J. C., 169, 172
Nixon, C. W., 68
Noble, C. E., 107
Noble, W. G., 245
Noguchi, Y., 360
Nordlund, B., 68, 222
North, C., 239
Nowicki, J., 68

Obata, J., 16
Ochiai, Y., 396
Oehlschlägel, H. K., 318
Oeken, F.-W., 68, 321
Ohta, F., 68
Okada, A., 72

SUBJECT INDEX

About the Editor

MONES E. HAWLEY is Vice President of Professional Services International Corporation and a management consultant. Until recently he was Director of Research for Planning Research Corporation, which he joined in 1962; prior to that he was Manager of Plans and Requirements at RCA. He received his degrees in physics from the University of Rochester and specialized in acoustics before becoming a planner and director of consultants in operations research, economics, and management.